E. Nader, A. Würzner

Englisches Lesebuch für höhere Lehranstalten

E. Nader, A. Würzner

Englisches Lesebuch für höhere Lehranstalten

ISBN/EAN: 9783742891051

Manufactured in Europe, USA, Canada, Australia, Japa

Cover: Foto ©Andreas Hilbeck / pixelio.de

Manufactured and distributed by brebook publishing software (www.brebook.com)

E. Nader, A. Würzner

Englisches Lesebuch für höhere Lehranstalten

ENGLISCHES LESEBUCH

FÜR

HÖHERE LEHRANSTALTEN.

MIT
LITTERARHISTORISCHEN UND ERLÄUTERNDEN
ANMERKUNGEN, EINER KARTE DER BRITISCHEN INSELN
UND
EINEM PLAN VON LONDON.

HERAUSGEGEBEN

VON

DR. E. NADER, UND DR. A. WÜRZNER,
PROF. A. D. K. K. STAATS-OBERREALSCHULE   PROF. A. D. K. K. STAATS-OBERREALSCHULE
IN I. BEZIRK   IM III. BEZIRK

IN WIEN.

DRITTE, UNVERÄNDERTE AUFLAGE.

AUSGABE FÜR DEUTSCHLAND.

WIEN.   1895.   LEIPZIG.
ALFRED HÖLDER.   G. E. SCHULZE.

Verzeichnis der Lesestücke.

A. Prosaische Lesestücke.

I. Erzählungen.

Seite
1. Geschichten von König Alfred.
   I. Wie König Alfred lesen lernte 1
   II. König Alfred und die Bäuerin 1
2. Knud's Verweis 2
3. Dr. Johnson und Mrs. Thrale . . . 2
4. Bacon's Tod 2
5. Wilhelm der Rote . 3
6. General Wolfe 3
7. Aus Newton's Jugend 4
8. Die Bekehrung der Engländer . . 4
9. Prinz und Richter 5
10. Das weifse Schiff 6
11. Entdeckung der Dampfkraft . . . 8
12. Der grofse Brand von London . . 9
13. Vertreibung der Acadier 10
14. Der kleine Schornsteinfeger . . . 10
15. James Watt 12
16. Der Alchemist, von Seymour (nach Chaucer) . . . 14
17. Aus "Robinson Crusoe," von D. Defoe.
   I. Robinson's Schiffbruch 17
   II. Robinson rettet Freitag . . . 20
18. Aus "Gulliver's Reisen," von J. Swift.
   I. Im Lande der Riesen 23
   II. Die Akademie 30
19. Mr. Bramble und Lord Oxmington, von T. Smollett 33
20. Korporal Trim erzählt eine Geschichte, von L. Sterne 36
21. Geschichte eines philosophischen Vagabunden, von O. Goldsmith . . 41
22. Eine Audienz bei der Königin Elisabeth, von W. Scott 51
23. Die Pickwickier auf der Jagd, von Ch. Dickens 55

Seite
24. Dobbin's und Cuff's Kampf, von W. M. Thackeray 61
25. Der Tod Warwick's des "Königmachers," von E. L. Bulwer . . . 67
26. König Lear, von Ch. Lamb . . . 71

II. Beschreibungen und Schilderungen.

1. Raleigh's zwei Pflanzen, aus Royal Readers 83
2. Eine Sturmnacht auf dem Meere, von Ch. Dickens 84
3. London und seine Nahrung, aus Royal Readers 85
4. Altenglisches Leben, aus Royal Readers.
   I. Zur Zeit der Sachsen 88
   II. Zur Zeit der Normannen . . 94
5. England zur Zeit Shakespeare's, von E. Goadby 98
6. Das englische Theater im 16. Jahrhundert, von E. Dowden 100
7. Englisches Leben im 18. Jahrhundert, von Lord Stanhope . . 102
8. Englands schwarze Diamanten, aus Household Words 107
9. Die Entwicklung Londons, aus Household Words 108
10. Aus "The Sketch-book," von W. Irving.
    I. Landleben in England . . . 112
    II. Ein Weihnachtsabend . . . 118
    III. John Bull 122
11. Hyde Park, aus Household Words 127
12. Eine Cricketpartie, v. Th. Hughes 128
13. Englische Bedienung, von Ch. Dickens 134

14. Großbritannien und seine Bevölkerung, von J. R. Green 136
15. Englische Verfassung, aus Royal Readers 139

III. Geschichte und Schrifttum.

1. Die Römer in Britannien, von H. Mackenzie 142
2. Charakterbilder aus der englischen Geschichte, von D. Hume.
   I. Alfred, König von England . 145
   II. Wilhelm der Eroberer . . . 146
3. Die Schlacht bei Hastings, von F. Palgrave 146
4. Verschmelzung der Engländer und Normannen, von Th. B. Macaulay 150
5. Richard Löwenherz in Palästina, von E. Gibbon 152
6. Magna Charta, von D. Hume . . 155
7. Königin Elisabeth, von D. Hume 156
8. Maria, Königin der Schotten, von W. Robertson 157
9. Die Armada, von J. R. Green . . 159
10. Die Pulververschwörung, von R. Gardiner 162
11. Cromwell, von E. Hyde, Earl of Clarendon 164
12. Cromwell und Napoleon, von Th. B. Macaulay 167
13. Cromwell's äußere Erscheinung, von Th. Carlyle 171
14. Schlacht bei Culloden, v. T. Smollett 171
15. Der Prozess gegen Warren Hastings, von Th. B. Macaulay 174
16. Über den nordamerikanischen Freiheitskrieg, von G. Bancroft . . . 177
17. Nelson's Tod, von R. Southey . 179
18. Beowulf, von H. Sweet 184
19. Chaucer, von Warton-Hazlitt . . 185
20. Ursachen des Aufschwunges der engl. Litteratur im Zeitalter der Königin Elisabeth, von W. Hazlitt 188
21. Bacon, von H. Hallam 191
22. William Shakespeare, von W. F. Collier 193
23. Milton's Paradise Lost, von S. Johnson 196
24. Über die Litteratur zur Zeit der Königin Anna, von F. Jeffrey . . 200
25. Oliver Goldsmith, von W. M. Thackeray 203
26. Byron, von Th. Moore 209

IV. Abhandlungen und Betrachtungen.

1. Über das Studium, von F. Bacon 214
2. Genauigkeit im sprachlichen Ausdruck, von Th. Hobbes 215
3. Über das Lesen, von J. Locke . . 216
4. Über die Unzufriedenheit, von J. Addison 218
5. Über den Handel Englands, von J. Addison 222
6. Der Schwätzer, von R. Steele . . 225
7. Die Liebe zum Leben, von O. Goldsmith 227
8. Das Wunderbare in der Dichtkunst, von H. Fielding 229
9. Einseitige Gelehrsamkeit, von S. Johnson 233
10. Wahl des Berufes, von H. Blair . 235
11. Roman und Drama, von W. Scott 238
12. Dichtkunst und Civilisation, von Th. B. Macaulay 240
13. Charakter der Cordelia, von A. Jameson 243

V. Briefe.

1. Raleigh's letzter Brief 246
2. Locke an Mr. Molyneux . . . 247
3. Richardson an Aaron Hill . . . 248
4. Chesterfield an seinen Sohn . . 250
5. Johnson an Chesterfield 252
6. Lady Montagu an Pope 253
7. Burke an Richard Shackleton . . 255
8. Robert Burns an Moore 257
9. Byron an seine Mutter 257
10. Byron an Walter Scott 259
11. Dickens an Thomas Mitton . . . 260

VI. Reden.

1. Abgeordnete und Wähler, von E. Burke 262
2. Gegen Warren Hastings, von E. Burke 264

	Seite		Seite
3. Über den Krieg mit Amerika, von W. Pitt d. Ä.	266	7. Über das englische Unterrichtswesen, von Th. B. Macaulay	280
4. Über die Abschaffung des Sklavenhandels, von W. Pitt d. J.	271	8. Über die irischen Verhältnisse, von Th. B. Macaulay	292
5. Über die Friedensvorschläge von Seite des ersten Consuls, von Ch. Fox	274	9. Über die englische Litteratur, von Th. B. Macaulay	293
6. Über die Parlamentsreform, von Lord Brougham	277	10. Gegen den Materialismus, von W. E. Gladstone	298

B. Dichtungen.

I. Lyrische und kürzere epische Gedichte.

	Seite
1. Englische Volkshymne	303
2. "Herrsche, Britannia," von J. Thomson	303
3. Die letzte Rose, von Th. Moore	304
4. Vergänglichkeit, von Th. Moore	305
5. Abendglocken, von Th. Moore	305
6. Sehnsucht nach der Heimat, von Th. Moore	305
7. Hans Gerstenkorn, von R. Burns	306
8. Abschied vom Hochland, von R. Burns	307
9. Frühlingslied, von W. Wordsworth	308
10. "Unser sind sieben," von W. Wordsworth	308
11. An Milton, von W. Wordsworth	309
12. Englands Heimstätten, von F. Hemans	310
13. Ein Lebenspsalm, von H. W. Longfellow	311
14. Der Dorfschmied, von H. W. Longfellow	312
15. Des Sklaven Traum, von H. W. Longfellow	313
16. Das Glück von Edenhall, von H. W. Longfellow	315
17. Beowulf's Fahrt zu den Dänen, von H. W. Longfellow	316
18. Belsazar, von Lord Byron	318
19. Der Untergang des Heeres Sennacherib's, von Lord Byron	318
20. Zeit und Ewigkeit, v. P. B. Shelley	319
21. An die Nacht, von P. B. Shelley	319
22. Weltwanderer, von P. B. Shelley	320
23. Klagen der Armen, von R. Southey	321
24. Vergangenheit, von R. Southey	321
25. Der Brunnen von St. Keyne, von R. Southey	322
26. Des Kriegers Traum, von Th. Campbell	324
27. Englands Matrosen, von Th. Campbell	324
28. Wilhelm der Eroberer, von Ch. Mackay	325
29. Wiegenlied, von S. W. Scott	326
30. Lady Clare, von A. Tennyson	327
31. Neujahrsnacht, von A. Tennyson	329
32. Alexander Selkirk, von W. Cowper	330
33. Vor Sonnenaufgang im Thale von Chamouni, von S. T. Coleridge	332
34. Am letzten Tage, von E. Young	334
35. Alexander's Fest, von J. Dryden	335
36. London, von J. Dryden	338
37. London nach dem Feuer, von J. Dryden	339
38. Allgemeines Gebet, von A. Pope	340
39. Windsor Forest zur Zeit Wilhelm's des Rothen, von A. Pope	341
40. König Lear und seine drei Töchter, aus Percy's Reliques	342

II. Epische und dramatische Dichtungen (Fragmente).

1. Aus "Das verlorene Paradies," von J. Milton.
   I. Satan und die gefallenen Engel in der Hölle 347
   II. Der Gottessohn im Kampfe . 352

	Seite
2. Aus "Der Sang des letzten Minstrel," von W. Scott	355
3. Aus "Ritter Harold's Pilgerfahrt," von Lord Byron.	
I. Abschied vom Vaterlande	365
II. Die Schlacht von Waterloo	367
III. An das Meer	370
4. Die Lotosesser, von A. Tennyson	371
5. Aus "König Lear," von W. Shakespeare	376
6. Aus "Der Kritiker," von R. B. Sheridan	392
7. Aus "Die Gesellschaft," von T. W. Robertson	397

	Seite
Litterarhistorische Anmerkungen	404
Erläuternde Anmerkungen	451
Kurzes Register zu den wichtigsten sachlichen Anmerkungen	517
Tabelle I. Englisches Geld	519
Tabelle II. Englisches Mafs	519
Tabelle III. Englisches Gewicht	520
Tabelle IV. Englische Könige	520
Tabelle V. Die Grafschaften der britischen Inseln	521
Karte der britischen Inseln.	
Plan von London.	

Verzeichnis der Schriftsteller.

Mit Angabe der Seiten der Musterstücke (in gewöhnlichem Druck), der litterarhistorischen Lesestücke (in runden Klammern) und der Anmerkungen (fettgedruckt).

Addison 218. 222. **413.**
Bacon 214. (2. 191.) **410.**
Bancroft 177. **449.**
[Beowulf] 316. (184.) **404.**
Blair 235. **430.**
Brougham 277. **448.**
Burke 255. 262. 264. **432.**
Bulwer 67. **448.**
Burns 257. 306. 307. **435.**
Byron 257. 259. 318. 365. 367. 370. (209.) **440.**
Campbell 322. 324. **435.**
Carlyle 171. **449.**
Chatham (Pitt) 266. **432.**
Chaucer 14. (185.) **406.**
Chesterfield (Stanhope) 250. (252.) **420.**
Clarendon (Hyde) 164. **412.**
Coleridge 332. **437.**
Collier 193.
Cowper 330. **436.**
Defoe 17. 20. **416.**
Dickens 55. 84. [107. 108. 127. H. W.] 134. 260. **447.**
Dowden 100.
Dryden 335. 338. 339. **412.**
Fielding 229. (238.) **423.**
Fox 274. **434.**
Gardiner 162.
Gibbon 152. **431.**
Gladstone 298. **450.**
Goadby 98.
Goldsmith 41. 227. (203.) **425.**
Green 136. 159.
Hallam 191.
Hazlitt 185. 188. **409.**
Hemans 310. **444.**
Hobbes 215. **411.**
Hughes 128.
Hume 145. 146. 155. **430.**
Irving 112. 118. 122. **444.**

Jameson 243. **409.**
Jeffrey 200, vgl. **440. 449.**
Johnson 196. 233. 252. (2.) **427.**
Lamb 71. **409.**
Locke 216. 247. **413.**
Longfellow 10. (Nr. 13.) 311. 312. 313. 315. 316. **444.**
Macaulay 150. 167. 174. 240. 280. 292. 293. **445.**
Mackay 325. **450.**
Mackenzie 142.
Milton 347. 352. (196.) **411.**
Montagu 253. **420.**
Moore 209. 304. 305. (257.) **443.**
Palgrave 146. **446.**
Percy 342. **429.**
Pitt der Jüngere 271. **434.**
Pitt der Ältere s. Chatham.
Pope 340. 341. (253.) **415.**
Raleigh 246. (83.) **409.**
Richardson 248. **422.**
Robertson (Dr. W.) 157. **431.**
Robertson (T. W.) 397.
Scott 51. 238. 326. 355. (259.) **439.**
Shakespeare 376. (98. 100. 188. 193. 243.) **407.** vgl. **415. 429.**
Shelley 319. 320. **442.**
Sheridan 392. (238.) **434.**
Smollett 33. 171. **424.**
Stanhope (Mahon) 102. **449.**
Steele 225. **414.**
Sterne 36. **425.**
Southey 179. 321. 322. **438.**
Sweet 184.
Swift 23. 30. **418.**
Tennyson 327. 329. 371. **450.**
Thackeray 61. 203. **446.**
Thomson 303. **421.**
Wordsworth 308. **436.**
Young 334. **421.**

A. PROSE.

I. NARRATIVE PIECES.

1. STORIES ABOUT KING ALFRED.

1. How King Alfred Learned to Read.

Up to the age of twelve years Alfred was fond of hunting and other sports, but he had not been taught any sort of learning, not so much as to read his own tongue. But he loved the Old-English songs; and one day his mother had a beautiful book of songs with richly painted pictures and initial letters, such as you may often see in ancient books. And she said to her children, "I will give this beautiful book to the one of you who shall first be able to read it." And Alfred said, "Mother, will you really give me the book when I have learned to read it?" And Queen Osburh said, "Yea, my son." So Alfred went and found a master, and soon learned to read. Then he came to his mother, and read the songs in the beautiful book and she gave it to him.

II. King Alfred and the Cakes.

About the year 878 England was quite overrun by the Danes, the English army was scattered and King Alfred obliged to disguise himself as a peasant. Thus he went and stayed in the hut of a cowherd or swineherd who knew who he was, though his wife did not know him. One day the woman set some cakes to bake, and bade the king, who was sitting by the fire mending his bow and arrows, to watch them. Alfred thought more of his bow and arrows than he did of the cakes, and let them burn. Then the woman ran in, and cried out: "Why do you not turn the cakes? You're glad enough to eat them, when they are done."

2. Canute's Reproof.

Canute, King of Denmark and Norway as well as of England, was often very much flattered by his courtiers. Some of his flatterers went one day so far in their flattery as to say that nothing was impossible for him. The King, who disliked flattery very much, ordered his chair to be set on the sea-shore, while the tide was rising. When the water approached, he commanded it to retire, and to obey the voice of him, who was lord of the ocean. The water, however, came nearer and nearer, till at last the waves washed his feet. He now turned to his courtiers and said: "Look, how powerful I am." From that time forward his courtiers stopped their flattery.

3. Dr. Johnson and Mrs. Thrale.

Dr. Johnson, one of the most learned Englishmen that ever lived, paid very little attention to outward appearances. The first time he was in company with Mrs. Thrale, with whom he afterwards became very intimate, that lady was quite shocked at his manners. Among other things, when he found that his tea was not sweet enough, he dipped his fingers into the sugar-basin and helped himself without ceremony. Every well-bred person in the room blushed with shame, but Mrs. Thrale was so angry that she ordered the servant to take the sugar-basin from the table immediately, as if it had been dirtied by the doctor's fingers. The doctor took no notice of it, but quietly swallowed his dozen cups of tea as usual. When he had done, instead of putting his cup and saucer upon the table, he calmly threw them both under the grate. The whole tea-table was thrown into confusion. Mrs. Thrale screamed out: "Why, doctor, what have you done? You have spoiled the handsomest set of china I have in the world!" "I am very sorry for it, Ma'am," answered Dr. Johnson, "but I assure you, I did it out of good breeding. You sent away the sugar-basin before, because I had put my fingers into it, and so I supposed that you would never touch anything again which I had once soiled with my hands."

4. The Death of Francis Bacon.

Francis Bacon, the great apostle of experimental philosophy, was destined to be its martyr. It had occurred to him that snow might be used with advantage for the purpose of preventing animal substances from putrefying. On a very cold day, early in the spring of the year 1626, he alighted from his coach near Highgate, in order to try the experiment. He went into a cottage, bought a fowl, and with his own hands stuffed it with snow. While thus engaged he felt a sudden chill, and was soon so much indisposed that it was impossible for him to return to Gray's Inn. The Earl of Arundel, with whom he was well acquainted, had a house at Highgate. To that house Bacon was carried. The Earl was absent; but the servants who were in charge of the place showed great respect and attention to the illustrious guest. Here, after an illness of about a week, he expired early on the morning of Easterday, 1626. His mind appears to have retained its strength and liveliness to the end. He did not forget the fowl which had caused his death. In the last letter that he ever wrote, with fingers which, as he said, could not steadily hold a pen, he did not omit to mention that the experiment of the snow had succeeded "excellently well."

5. William Rufus.

William Rufus, or the Red, who was so named from the colour of his hair, was very fond of hunting. Upon a day in August he was chasing a deer in the New Forest in Hampshire, accompanied only by Sir Walter Tyrrel, who was a famous sportsman. This was the last time, that the King was ever seen alive. It was almost night, when a poor charcoal burner, passing through the Forest with his cart came upon the solitary body of a dead man, shot with an arrow in the breast, and still bleeding; it was the body of the King. He got it into his cart. It was driven in the cart by the charcoal burner next day to Winchester Cathedral, where it was buried. Sir Walter Tyrrel, who was fearful of being suspected as the King's murderer, had instantly set spurs to his horse and fled to the sea-shore. He escaped to Normandy, and claimed the protection of the King of France. In France he swore that King William was suddenly shot dead by an arrow from an unseen hand, while they were hunting together.

6. General Wolfe.

You have heard of the death of general Wolfe. This happened in America (1759). The young general, who was only thirty-five, was carrying on a most desperate attack against the town of Quebec; and, after having overcome many dreadful difficulties, he received a shot in the wrist. He did not, however, leave his post, but wrapped his hand in his handkerchief, and went on giving his orders as if nothing had happened; and, whilst leading forward his grenadiers with their bayonets fixed, another shot came and entered his breast. He fell, and struggling in the agonies of death, and just expiring, he heard a voice cry, "They run!" upon which he seemed, for a moment, to revive, and, asking "who run?" was informed, "the French;" he then sank on the breast of the soldier who supported him; and his last words were, "I die happy:" words expressive of the deep interest which a good soldier feels, as to the success of his endeavours to benefit his country.

7. Newton as a Boy.

Men of great learning and talent, whom all people admire and praise, are often found to be more modest than persons of inferior qualities. Sir Isaac Newton, the eminent philosopher, was one of those great, and at the same time modest men.

When a little boy at school, he surprised every body by the curious little machines which he made with his own hands. He had a number of saws, hatchets, hammers, and other tools, which he used very cleverly. A windmill being put up near the place where he lived, he frequently went to look at it, and pried into every part of it, till he became thoroughly acquainted with it, and the way in which it moved. He then began with his knife, and saw, and hammer, and made a small windmill, exactly like the large one: it was a very neat and curious piece of workmanship. He sometimes set it upon the house-top, that the wind might turn it round. He also contrived to cause a mouse to turn his mill. This little animal being put inside a hollow wheel, its endeavours to get forward turned the wheel, and set the machinery in motion. There was also some corn placed above the wheel, and when the mouse tried to get at the corn, it made the mill go round.

Having got an old box from a friend, he made it into a water-clock, that is, a clock driven by a small fall of water. It was very like our common clocks, but much smaller, being only about four feet high. There was a dial-plate at the top, with the figures of the hours. The hour-hand was turned by a piece of wood, which either fell or rose by water dropping upon it. This stood in the room where he lay, and he took care, every morning, to supply it with plenty of water. It pointed out the hours so well, that the people in the house would go to see what was the hour by it. It was kept in the house as a curiosity long after Isaac went to college. The room in which Isaac lodged was full of drawings of birds, beasts, men, ships, and mathematical figures, all neatly made upon the wall with charcoal.

8. Conversion of the English.

About a hundred years after the coming of the Saxons, some little Angle children were stolen from their parents, and carried to Rome to be sold for slaves. As they stood in the market-place, a good priest, named Gregory, passed by, and as their fair skins, light hair, and blue eyes, made them remarkable among the dark Italian faces around them, he stopped to look at them, and asked to what nation they belonged. He was told that they were Angles: on which he exclaimed "Angles! yes, they have angels' faces, and ought to be heirs with the angels in heaven."

He asked many questions about their country, and when he heard that it was still in the darkness of heathenism, he conceived a great desire to bring about its conversion to Christianity. A few years afterwards he was made Pope, or Bishop of Rome, and immediately sent a number of clergy to preach the Gospel in England, with a priest named Augustine at their head.

This was in the year 596, just after Ethelbert, King of Kent and Lord of Britain, had been married to Bertha, daughter of the King of Paris. She was a Christian, and persuaded her husband to listen to the teaching of St. Augustine. After a time he was baptized in the little old British Church of St. Martin. at Canterbury; and many of his subjects having followed his example, St. Augustine was consecrated to be their bishop. His successors — the archbishops of Canterbury — have ever since been the primates, or chief bishops, of all England.

9. The Prince and the Judge.

Henry V. was as brave a King as ever sat on the English throne, and gained one of the greatest victories ever won by English soldiers. But when he was Prince of Wales, he was a very wild and riotous youth. He mixed with low companions, who led him to do many base and foolish acts, quite unworthy of a Prince. On one occasion, one of his friends was tried for some offence before the Lord Chief Justice. He was found guilty, and was ordered to be sent to prison. When the Prince, who was in the court, heard the sentence, he fell into a great rage. He spoke very rudely to the Judge, and commanded him to let his friend off.

"Prison," he said, "is no place for a Prince's friend. I am Prince of Wales, and I forbid you to send this man to prison, like a common thief." "Prince or no Prince," replied the Judge, "you have no right to speak thus to the King's Judge. I have sworn to do justice; and justice I shall do." The Prince, getting more enraged, then tried to set the prisoner free himself. But the Judge told him it was none of his business, and ordered him to cease from such riot in court. The calmness with which the Judge spoke made the Prince still more angry; and he rushed up to the bench, and struck the Judge a severe blow on the face!

For this, the Judge ordered the officers of the court to seize the Prince, and take him to prison with his friend. "I do this," he said,

"not because he has done me harm, but because he has insulted the honour of the law." Turning again to the Prince, he added, "Young man, you will one day be King. How can you expect your subjects to obey you then, if you yourself thus disobey the King's laws now?"
5 On hearing this, the Prince was very much ashamed of himself. He had not a word to say; but, laying down his sword, he bowed to the Judge, and walked quietly off to prison.
When the King (Henry IV.) heard of this incident, he said, "Happy is the King that has a Judge who so fearlessly enforces the
10 laws, and a son who knows how to submit to them."—
Shortly after this Prince had been crowned King, many of his people came to pay their respects to him. Some of those who knew how wild he had been as a young man, were anxious to know how he would act as King. Among the rest came some of his former
15 riotous companions, expecting, no doubt, to be made at once the King's chief favourites. But they were mistaken. The King told them that he had given up his foolish ways, and advised them to do the same. Nor would he let them come about his person, until they had shown that they had learned better manners. The Judge also came,
20 not knowing how he would be received. He feared that he might lose his office; but he did not care, as he had only done his duty. He also was mistaken. The King received him very kindly, and thanked him for the sharp lesson he had given him. He told him still to keep the office which he had so worthily filled. "If ever," said the King,
25 "I have a son who shall behave as I did to you, may I have a Judge as bold and faithful as you to correct him!"

10. The White Ship.

Henry the First went over to Normandy with his son Prince William and a great retinue, to have the Prince acknowledged as his
30 successor by the Norman nobles, and to contract the promised marriage between him and the daughter of the Count of Anjou. Both these things were triumphantly done, with great show and rejoicing: and on the twenty-fifth of November, in the year one thousand one hundred and twenty, the whole retinue prepared to embark at the Port of
35 Barfleur, for the voyage home.
On that day, and at that place, there came to the King, Fitz-Stephen, a sea-captain, and said, "My liege, my father served your father all his life, upon the sea. He steered the ship with the golden boy upon the prow, in which your father sailed to conquer England.
40 I beseech you to grant me the same office. I have a fair vessel in the harbour here, called the White Ship, manned by fifty sailors of

renown. I pray you, Sire, to let your servant have the honour of
steering you in the White Ship to England!" "I am sorry, friend,"
replied the King, "that my vessel is already chosen, and that I cannot,
therefore, sail with the son of the man who served my father. But
the Prince and all his company shall go along with you, in the fair 5
White Ship, manned by the fifty sailors of renown."

An hour or two afterwards, the King set sail in the vessel he
had chosen, accompanied by other vessels, and, sailing all night with
a fair and gentle wind, arrived upon the coast of England in the
morning. While it was yet night, the people in some of those ships 10
heard a faint wild cry come over the sea, and wondered what it was.

Now, the Prince was a dissolute, debauched young man of
eighteen, who bore no love to the English, and had declared that
when he came to the throne he would yoke them to the plough like
oxen. He went aboard the White Ship, with one hundred and forty 15
youthful nobles like himself, among whom were eighteen noble ladies
of the highest rank. All this gay company, with their servants and
the fifty sailors, made three hundred souls aboard the fair White Ship.

"Give three casks of wine, Fitz-Stephen," said the Prince, "to
the fifty sailors of renown! My father the King has sailed out of the 20
harbour. What time is there to make merry here, and yet reach
England with the rest?" "Prince," said Fitz-Stephen, "before morning
my fifty and the White Ship shall overtake the swiftest vessel in
attendance on your father the King, if we sail at midnight!" Then
the Prince commanded to make merry; and the sailors drank out the 25
three casks of wine; and the Prince and all the noble company danced
in the moonlight on the deck of the White Ship.

When, at last, she shot out of the harbour of Barfleur, there
was not a sober seaman on board. But the sails were all set, and
the oars all going merrily. Fitz-Stephen had the helm. The gay young 30
nobles and the beautiful ladies, wrapped in mantles of various bright
colours to protect them from the cold, talked, laughed, and sang. The
Prince encouraged the fifty sailors to row harder yet, for the honour
of the White Ship. Crash! A terrific cry broke from three hundred
hearts. It was the cry the people in the distant vessels of the King 35
heard faintly on the water. The White Ship had struck upon a rock —
was filling — going down!

Fitz-Stephen hurried the Prince into a boat, with some few
nobles. "Push off," he whispered; "and row to the land. It is not
far, and the sea is smooth. The rest of us must die." But, as they 40
rowed away, fast, from the sinking ship, the Prince heard the voice
of his sister Mary, the Countess of Perche, calling for help. He never

in his life had been so good as he was then. He cried, in an agony. "Row back at any risk! I cannot bear to leave her!" They rowed back. As the Prince held out his arms to catch his sister, such numbers leaped in that the boat was overset. And in the same
5 instant the White Ship went down.

Only two men floated. They both clung to the main yard of the ship, which had broken from the mast, and now supported them. One asked the other who he was? He said, "I am a nobleman, Godfrey by name, the son of Gilbert de L'Aigle. And you?" said he. "I am
10 Berold, a poor butcher of Rouen," was the answer. Then, they said together, "Lord be merciful to us both!" and tried to encourage one another, as they drifted in the cold benumbing sea on that unfortunate November night.

By-and-by, another man came swimming towards them, whom
15 they knew, when he pushed aside his long wet hair, to be Fitz-Stephen. "Where is the Prince?" said he. "Gone! Gone!" the two cried together. "Neither he, nor his brother, nor his sister, nor the King's niece, nor her brother, nor any one of all the brave three hundred, noble or commoner, except we three, has risen above the
20 water!" Fitz-Stephen, with a ghastly face, cried, "Woe! woe to me!" and sank to the bottom.

The other two clung to the yard for some hours. At length the young noble said faintly, "I am exhausted, and chilled with the cold, and can hold no longer. Farewell, good friend! God preserve
25 you!" So, he dropped and sank; and of all the brilliant crowd, the poor butcher of Rouen alone was saved. In the morning, some fishermen saw him floating in his sheepskin coat, and got him into their boat — the sole relater of the dismal tale.

For three days, no one dared to carry the intelligence to the
30 King. At length, they sent into his presence a little boy, who, weeping bitterly, and kneeling at his feet, told him that the White Ship was lost with all on board. The King fell to the ground like a dead man, and never, never afterwards, was seen to smile.

II. The Power of Steam.

35 About two hundred years ago, a man bearing the title of the Marquess of Worcester, was sitting, on a cold night, in a small, mean room before a blazing fire. This was in Ireland; and the man was a prisoner. A kettle of boiling water was on the fire, and he sat watching the steam, as it lifted the lid of the kettle and rushed
40 out of the nose.

He thought of the power of the steam, and wondered what would
be the effect if he were to fasten down the lid, and stop up the nose.
He concluded that the effect would be to burst the kettle. "How
much power, then," thought he, "there must be in steam!" As soon
as he was let out of prison, he tried an experiment. "I have taken,"
he writes, "a cannon, and filled it three-quarters full of water, stopping
firmly up both the vent of it and the mouth; and having made a
good fire under it, within twenty-four hours it burst, and made a
great noise." After this, the marquess contrived a rude machine, which,
by the power of steam, drove up water to the height of forty feet.

About one hundred years after this, a little boy, whose name
was James Watt, and who lived in Scotland, sat one day looking at
a kettle of boiling water, and holding a spoon before the steam that
rushed out of the nose. His aunt thought he was idle, and said, "Is
it not a shame for you to waste your time so?" But James was not
idle. He was thinking of the power of the steam in moving the spoon.

James grew to be a good and great man, and contrived those
wonderful improvements in the steam-engine which have made it so
useful in our day.

12. The Great Fire of London.

On the third of September, 1666, a great fire broke out at a
baker's shop near London Bridge, on the spot on which the Monument
now stands as a remembrance of those raging flames. It spread
and spread, and burned and burned, for three days. The nights were
lighter than the days: in the day-time there was an immense cloud
of smoke, and in the night-time there was a great tower of fire
mounting up into the sky, which lighted the whole country landscape for ten miles round. Showers of hot ashes rose into the air
and fell on distant places; flying sparks carried the conflagration
to great distances, and kindled it in twenty new spots at a time;
church steeples fell down with tremendous crashes; houses crumbled
into cinders by the hundred and the thousand. The summer had
been intensely hot and dry, the streets were very narrow, and the
houses mostly built of wood and plaster. Nothing could stop the
tremendous fire but the want of more houses to burn; nor did it
stop until the whole way from the Tower to Temple Bar was a
desert, composed of the ashes of thirteen thousand houses and eighty-
nine churches.

This was a terrible visitation at the time, and occasioned great
loss and suffering to the two hundred thousand burnt-out people,
who were obliged to lie in the fields under the open night sky, or in

hastily-made huts of mud and straw, while the lanes and roads were rendered impassable by carts which had broken down as they tried to save their goods. But the Fire was a great blessing to the City afterwards, for it arose from its ruins very much improved — built more regularly, more widely, more cleanly and carefully, and therefore much more healthily.

The Catholics were accused of having wilfully set London in flames: one poor Frenchman, who had been mad for years, even accused himself of having with his own hand fired the first house. There is no reasonable doubt, however, that the fire was accidental.

13. The Acadians.

In the year 1713, Acadia, or, as it is now named, Nova Scotia, was ceded to Great Britain by the French. The wishes of the inhabitants seem to have been little consulted in the change, and they with great difficulty were induced to take the oaths of allegiance to the British Government. Some time after this, war having again broken out between the French and British in Canada, the Acadians were accused of having assisted the French, from whom they were descended, and connected by many ties of friendship, with provisions and ammunition, at the siege of Beau Séjour. Whether the accusation was founded on fact or not, has not been satisfactorily ascertained; the result, however, was most disastrous to the primitive, simple-minded Acadians. The British Government ordered them to be removed from their homes, and dispersed throughout the other colonies, at a distance from their much beloved land. This resolution was not communicated to the inhabitants till measures had been matured to carry it into immediate effect; when the Governor of the colony, having issued a summons calling the whole people to a meeting, informed them that their lands, tenements, and cattle of all kinds were forfeited to the British crown, that he had orders to remove them in vessels to distant colonies, and they must remain in custody till their embarkation.

14. The Little Chimney-Sweep.

There was formerly in London, on the first of May, a great feast given to the chimney-sweepers of the metropolis. It was given at Montague-House, the town-residence of the Montague family, in remembrance of the following circumstance:

When Lady Montague was at her country-seat in summer, she used to send her little boy Edward to walk every day with the footman, who had strict orders never to lose sight of him. One day, however, the servant met an old acquaintance, and went into an alehouse with him, to drink a glass of ale; meanwhile he left the little boy running about by himself. The servant stopped at the ale-house for some time, and when he came out to look for the child to take him home to dinner, he could not find him. He wandered about till night, inquired at every cottage and at every house, but in vain: no Edward could be found.

The poor mother, as may well be imagined, was in the greatest anxiety about the absence of her dear boy; but it would be impossible to describe her grief and despair, when the footman returned and told her he did not know what had become of him. People were sent to seek him in all directions; advertisements were put in all the newspapers; bills were stuck up in London and in most of the great towns of England, offering a considerable reward to any person who would bring him or give any news of him. But all endeavours were in vain, and it was concluded that the poor boy had fallen into some pond, or that he had been stolen by gipsies, who would not bring him back, because they were afraid of punishment.

Lady Montague passed two long years in this miserable uncertainty. She did not return to London, as usual, in the winter, but passed her time in grief alone in the country. At length, one of her sisters married, and, after many refusals, Lady Montague consented to give a ball and supper on the occasion at her town-house. She went to town, to overlook the preparations, and while the supper was cooking, the whole house was alarmed by a cry of: Fire! One of the cooks had overturned a saucepan, and set fire to the chimney. The chimney-sweepers were sent for, and a little boy was sent up; but the smoke nearly suffocated him, and he fell into the fire-place. Lady Montague came herself with some vinegar and a smelling-bottle. She bathed his temples and his neck, when suddenly she screamed out: "Oh, Edward!" — and fell senseless on the floor. She soon recovered, and took the little sweep in her arms, pressed him to her bosom and cried: "It is my dear Edward; it is my lost boy!" Lady Montague had recognised her son by a mark on his neck.

When the master chimney-sweeper was asked, where he had obtained the child, he said he had bought him about a year before of a gipsy-woman, who said he was her son. All that the boy could remember was that some people had given him fruit and told him they would take him home to his mamma. But that they took him a long way upon a donkey, and after keeping him for a long while, they told him he must go and live with the chimney-sweep, who was his father. That they had beaten him so much, whenever he spoke of his mamma and his fine house, that he was almost afraid to think of it. But he said, his master, the chimney-sweeper, had treated him very well.

Lady Montague rewarded the man handsomely, and from that time she gave a feast to all the chimney-sweepers of the metropolis on the 1st of May, the birthday of little Edward.

15. James Watt.

Inventors have set in motion some of the greatest industries of the world. To them society owes many of its chief necessaries, comforts, and luxuries; and by their genius and labour daily life has been rendered in all respects more easy as well as enjoyable. Our food, our clothing, the furniture of our homes, the glass which admits the light to our dwellings at the same time that it excludes the cold, the gas which illuminates our streets, our means of locomotion by land and by sea, the tools by which our various articles of necessity and luxury are fabricated, have been the result of the labour and ingenuity of many men and many minds. Mankind at large are all the happier for such inventions, and are every day reaping the benefit of them in an increase of individual well-being as well as of public enjoyment.

Though the invention of the working steam-engine — the king of machines — belongs, comparatively speaking, to our own epoch, the idea of it was born many centuries ago. Like other contrivances and discoveries, it was effected step by step — one man transmitting the result of his labours, at the time apparently useless, to his successors, who took it up and carried it forward another stage, — the prosecution of the inquiry extending over many generations. Thus the idea promulgated by Hero of Alexandria was never altogether lost; but, like the grain of wheat hid in the hand of the Egyptian mummy, it sprouted and again grew vigorously when brought into the full light of modern science. The steam-engine was nothing, however, until it emerged from the state of theory, and was taken in hand by practical mechanics; and what a noble story of patient, laborious investigation, of difficulties encountered and overcome by heroic industry, does not that marvellous machine tell of! It is indeed, in itself, a monument of the power of self-help in man. Grouped around it we find Savary, the military engineer; Newcomen, the Dartmouth blacksmith; Cawley, the glazier; Potter, the engine-boy; Smeaton, the civil engineer; and, towering above all, the laborious, patient, never-tiring James Watt, the mathematical-instrument maker.

Watt was one of the most industrious of men; and the story of his life proves, what all experience confirms, that it is not the man of the greatest natural vigour and capacity who achieves the highest results, but he who employs his powers with the greatest industry and the most carefully disciplined skill — the skill that comes by labour, application, and experience. Many men in his time knew far more than Watt, but none laboured so assiduously as he did to turn all 5 that he did know to useful practical purposes. He was, above all things, most persevering in the pursuit of facts. He cultivated carefully that habit of active attention on which all the higher working qualities of the mind mainly depend.

Even when a boy, Watt found science in his toys. The quadrants 10 lying about his father's carpenter's shop led him to the study of optics and astronomy; his ill health induced him to pry into the secrets of physiology; and his solitary walks through the country attracted him to the study of botany and history. While carrying on the business of a mathematical-instrument maker, he received an 15 order to build an organ; and, though without an ear for music, he undertook the study of harmonics, and successfully constructed the instrument. And, in like manner, when the little model of Newcomen's steam-engine, belonging to the University of Glasgow, was placed in his hands to repair, he forthwith set himself to learn all that was then 20 known about heat, evaporation, and condensation, — at the same time plodding his way in mechanics and the science of construction, the results of which he at length embodied in his condensing steam-engine.

For ten years he went on contriving and inventing — with little hope to cheer him, and with few friends to encourage him. He 25 went on, meanwhile, earning bread for his family by making and selling quadrants, making and mending fiddles, flutes, and musical instruments; measuring mason-work, surveying roads, superintending the construction of canals, or doing anything that turned up, and offered a prospect of honest gain. At length, Watt found a fit partner 30 in another eminent leader of industry — Matthew Boulton, of Birmingham: a skilful, energetic, and far-seeing man, who vigorously undertook the enterprise of introducing the condensing-engine into general use as a working power; and the success of both is now matter of history. 35

Many skilful inventors have from time to time added new power to the steam-engine; and, by numerous modifications, rendered it capable of being applied to nearly all the purposes of manufacture — driving machinery, impelling ships, grinding corn, printing books, stamping money, hammering, planing, and turning iron; in short, of 40 performing every description of machinal labour where power is required. One of the most useful modifications in the engine was that devised by Trevithick, and eventually perfected by George Stephenson and his son, in the form of the railway locomotive, by which social changes of immense importance have been brought about, of even greater consequence, considered in their results on human progress and civilization, than the condensing-engine of Watt.

16. The Alchemist.

There was once an astrologer whose iniquities would have been sufficient to infect the largest city, even were it as vast as Niniveh, Rome, Alexandria, or Troy. If I were to live for a thousand years, I should not have come to the end of all the abominable things he did; and his manner was so cunning and smooth that he easily persuaded men to believe him, until by longer acquaintance they had lost all trust in his word. Let me, however, beg that none of this company take offence because I speak of the evils worked by this astrologer, for none knows better than I that there are also good astrologers. Besides, in every calling there must be some unworthy ones, just as among the apostles of Christ there was a traitor, though that did not prevent the rest from being wise and holy men.

At the time of which I tell there lived in London a surgeon. Full many years had he dwelt in that part, and had the good word of all who knew him. In the house where he lodged he made himself so pleasant, and withal so serviceable, that he was not suffered to pay for either food or clothing.

To his chamber there came one day the wicked astrologer already mentioned, begging the loan of some gold, which should without fail be returned to him in a few days. "Let me have it only for three days," he said; "and if at the expiration of that time I do not return it, I give you permission to have me hanged by the neck."

The surgeon did what he was entreated; and, with many expressions of gratitude and renewed promises of punctuality in returning the loan, the astrologer went his way. Surely enough, upon the third morning he brought back the money.

"I can never say nay to a man who is so true to his word," remarked the surgeon. But the astrologer seemed more offended than pleased, for such a speech seemed (to his mind) to imply that there had been previous doubt of his truth. So he began to say that it would indeed be a new thing were *he* not to be believed, for never, thank God! had he returned evil in place of gold or silver which had been lent him. Then he added, "Since you have rendered me this service, I also will return you one. My friend, you shall learn my philosophy."

"Will you really instruct me in that?" cried the delighted surgeon. "Sir, I do indeed thank you heartily." "Let your servant bring in two or three ounces of quicksilver," said the astrologer, "and when he returns I will promise that you shall see something wonderful." The surgeon immediately dispatched his servant with proper directions; and when he came back with the quicksilver, the astrologer bade them heap coals on the fire, and then, taking a crucible from his bosom, displayed it to his friend.

"Take this instrument into your own hand," he said; "put into it one ounce of the quicksilver, and so begin without further delay to be a philosopher. There are few men, I can assure you, to whom I would attempt to teach so wonderful a science; but as you have done me a favour, I do not object to render you one in return. First of all, then, you shall perceive that I can make this quicksilver as good and as fine as the silver in either of our purses. I possess a powder which will effect this marvel; but before I begin, you must dismiss this man, for you and I should be alone to work our philosophy."

The servant was accordingly dismissed from the chamber, and to work went the two friends, the surgeon having to blow the fire while the astrologer cast into the crucible a powder, made of chalk or glass, or some other such matter, "not worth a flie."

"Now, because I have so sincere an affection for you," said he, "your own hands shall accomplish this business."

This promise greatly delighted the credulous surgeon, as you may suppose, and he began with busy haste to arrange the coals in the manner he was directed. While he was thus occupied, the false astrologer took cautiously from his pocket a coal made of beech, in which a hole had been already drilled. This hole was filled with silver filings, and was then stopped up with wax, which of course, would melt easily when exposed to heat.

This he held concealed in his hand, while he exclaimed, "Friend, friend! you are doing amiss. Let me see to the fire myself, and do you meanwhile wipe the perspiration from your brow, for I perceive that being unaccustomed to the work you suffer greatly."

The surgeon willingly relinquished his post, and while he wiped his streaming face, the deceiver laid his coal over the very middle of the crucible, and blew away well, so that the flames instantly began to rise.

"Now we may sit down for a moment's rest, and drink something to support us," he said; and all this time the beechen coal was burning away, while the silver filings escaped out of the hole, and flowing down into the crucible, completely covered it contents.

"Now," said the astrologer, "I feel pretty well convinced that you have not an ingot in the house, so come with me and let us search for a chalk stone, which I will endeavour to shape like to one. We must also have a bowl or pan of water."

They went out together from the chamber, carefully locking the door behind them; but they soon returned, and the astrologer began shaping the chalk stone into the fashion of an ingot. While he did so, however, he managed secretly to draw from his sleeve a thin plate of silver, which weighed an ounce, and he shaped the ingot in length and breadth of this plate of silver, so slyly that the surgeon never saw what he was doing; he then concealed it again in his sleeve.

Taking the crucible from the fire he poured the melted silver filings into the ingot, cast it into the pan of water, and bade his dupe look in. Can I picture his delight when he put in his hand and drew forth an unmistakable piece of silver? nor can I tell you how he entreated that this marvellously subtle craft should be made clear to him.

"I would wish you to try a second time," returned the other, "so that you may become so expert that there can be no danger of failure when I am not by to assist you."

The surgeon was very willing, so they took a second ounce of quicksilver, and set to work. This time the crafty man stirred up the powder in the crucible with a stick he carried, and which was hollowed out and filled with silver filings, just after the fashion of the beechen coal, and as the wax which stopped the end melted, these filings fell down into the crucible.

Again, then, was the surgeon beguiled, and more earnestly than ever he begged for instruction in so strange a science.

"Have you any copper here?" said the astrologer. This the surgeon did happen to possess, and when it was brought, the astrologer took an ounce of it, and put it into the crucible. When it was melted he poured it into the ingot, which he cast into the pan of water. This time he put his own hand in, and taking slyly the plate of silver from his sleeve he left it at the bottom of the pan, while he took up the piece of copper and hid it. He then bade the surgeon put in his hand and pick up the silver.

"Now let us take these three pieces of silver to a goldsmith, and get him to prove them," said the pretended instructor. This they did then; and of course nothing could be said against the metal, for it was just as pure as it could be.

Never was bird in springtime blither than this surgeon; never did nightingale in May sing more joyously. "Pray, friend," he cried, "tell me the cost of this recipe; it must be very valuable, as by it such marvels are worked."

"Ah! there you are right," was the answer. "It is indeed most precious, and therefore very costly. Throughout the length and breadth of all England only one friar knows the secret besides myself."

"For Heaven's sake tell me the price of possessing it," cried the surgeon. "If I can, I will pay, however large it may be."

"Well, for friendship's sake, I will put it as low as I possibly can. You have done me a service for which I wish to prove my gratitude, so you shall possess the secret for a payment of forty pounds."

The surgeon, without a moment's hesitation, took from his coffer forty nobles, and placed them in the astrologer's hand, little supposing that he was paying for a fraudulent and worthless recipe. He was then bidden keep the secret, because the envy of other men, if they knew he had it, would be so bitter that his life would scarcely be safe. The surgeon promised that, so far as he was concerned, nothing should ever transpire; and with mutual expressions of good-will, the two parted, nor ever saw each other more.

It is needless that I should tell you that at his very first essay the much-deceived man found that his costly recipe was a lie, and that his forty pounds had been expended for nought. Perhaps he would also learn to take heed lest he too anxiously desired to increase his money, for in so doing it was possible to be robbed of what he already had; and also, that if there be such a thing, as the much-talked-of philosopher's stone, it is evidently God's will that men remain in ignorance of it.

M. SEYMOUR, CHAUCER'S STORIES.

17. ROBINSON CRUSOE.
I. Robinson is Shipwrecked.

Nothing can describe the confusion of thought which I felt, when I sank into the water; for though I swam very well, yet I could not deliver myself from the waves so as to draw breath, till that wave having driven me, or rather carried me, a vast way on towards the shore, and having spent itself, went back, and left me upon the land almost dry, but half dead with the water I took in. I had so much presence of mind, as well as breath left, that seeing myself nearer the main land than I expected, I got upon my feet, and endeavoured to make on towards the land as fast as I could, before another wave should return and take me up again: but I soon found it was impossible to avoid it, for I saw the sea come after me as high as a great hill, and as furious as an enemy, which I had no means or strength to contend with; my business was to hold my breath, and raise myself upon the water, if I could: and so, by swimming, to preserve my breathing, and pilot myself towards the shore, if possible; my greatest concern now being, that the sea, as it would carry me a great way towards the shore when it came on, might not carry me back again with it when it gave back towards the sea.

The wave that came upon me again, buried me at once twenty or thirty feet deep in its own body, and I could feel myself carried with a mighty force and swiftness towards the shore a very great way; but I held my breath, and assisted myself to swim still forward with all my might. I was ready to burst with holding my breath, when, as I felt myself rising up, to my immediate relief, I found my head and hands shoot out above the surface of the water; and though it was not two seconds of time that I could keep myself so, yet it relieved me greatly, gave me breath, and new courage. I was covered again with water a good while, but not so long but I held it out; and finding the water had spent itself, and began to return, I struck forward against the return of the waves, and felt ground again with my feet. I stood still a few moments, to recover breath, and till the waters went from me, and then took to my heels, and ran, with what strength I had, farther towards the shore. But neither would this deliver me from the fury of the sea, which came pouring in after me again; and twice more I was lifted up by the waves and carried forward as before, the shore being very flat.

The last time of these two had well nigh been fatal to me: for the sea having hurried me along, as before, landed me, or rather dashed me, against a piece of a rock, and that with such force, as it left me senseless, and indeed helpless, as to my own deliverance: for the blow taking my side and breast, beat the breath, as it were, quite out of my body; and had it returned again immediately, I must have been strangled in the water: but I recovered a little before the return of the waves, and seeing I should be covered again with the water, I resolved to hold fast by a piece of the rock, and so to hold my breath, if possible, till the wave went back. Now as the waves were not so high as at first, being nearer land, I held my hold till the wave abated, and then fetched another run, which brought me so near the shore, that the next wave, though it went over me, yet did not so swallow me up as to carry me away; and the next run I took, I got to the main land; where, to my great comfort, I clambered up the cliffs of the shore, and sat down upon the grass, free from danger, and quite out of the reach of the water.

I was now landed, and safe on shore, and began to look up and
thank God that my life was saved, in a case wherein there was, some
minutes before, scarce any room to hope. I believe it is impossible
to express, to the life, what the ecstacies and transports of the soul
are, when it is so saved, as I may say, out of the very grave: and I
do not wonder now at the custom, viz. that when a malefactor, who
has the halter about his neck, is tied up, and just going to be turned
off, and has a reprieve brought to him; I say, I do not wonder that
they bring a surgeon with it, to let him blood that very moment they
tell him of it, that the surprise may not drive the animal spirits from
the heart, and overwhelm him.

I walked about on the shore, lifting up my hands, and my whole
being, as I may say, wrapt up in the contemplation of my deliverance;
making a thousand gestures and motions, which I cannot describe;
reflecting upon all my comrades that were drowned, and that there
should not be one soul saved but myself; for, as for them, I never saw
them afterwards, or any sign of them, except three of their hats, one
cap, and two shoes that were not fellows.

I cast my eyes to the stranded vessel, when the breach and froth
of the sea being so big I could hardly see it, it lay so far off, and
considered, Lord! how was it possible I could get on shore?

After I had solaced my mind with the comfortable part of my
condition, I began to look round me, to see what kind of place I was
in, and what was next to be done; and I soon found my comforts
abate, and that, in a word, I had a dreadful deliverance: for I was
wet, had no clothes to shift me, nor any thing either to eat or drink,
to comfort me; neither did I see any prospect before me, but that
of perishing with hunger, or being devoured by wild beasts: and that
which was particularly afflicting to me was, that I had no weapon,
either to hunt and kill any creature for my sustenance, or to defend
myself against any other creature that might desire to kill me for
theirs. In a word, I had nothing about me but a knife, a tobacco-
pipe, and a little tobacco in a box. This was all my provision; and
this threw me into terrible agonies of mind, that, for a while, I ran
about like a madman. Night coming upon me, I began, with a heavy
heart, to consider what would be my lot if there were any ravenous
beasts in that country, seeing at night they always come abroad for
their prey.

All the remedy that offered to my thoughts at that time, was, to
get up into a thick bushy tree, like a fir, but thorny, which grew
near me, and where I resolved to sit all night, and consider the next
day what death I should die, for as yet I saw no prospect of life. I

walked about a furlong from the shore, to see if I could find any fresh
water to drink, which I did, to my great joy; and having drunk, and
put a little tobacco in my mouth to prevent hunger, I went to the tree,
and getting up into it, endeavoured to place myself so, that if I
should sleep, I might not fall; and having cut me a short stick, like
a truncheon, for my defence, I took up my lodging: and having been
excessively fatigued, I fell fast asleep, and slept as comfortably as, I
believe, few could have done in my condition: and found myself the
most refreshed with it that I think I ever was on such an occasion.

II. Robinson Rescues Friday.

I was surprised, one morning early, with seeing no less than
five canoes all on shore together on my side the island, and the
people who belonged to them all landed, and out of my sight. The
number of them broke all my measures; for seeing so many, and
knowing that they always came four, or six, or sometimes more, in
a boat, I could not tell what to think of it, or how to take my
measures, to attack twenty or thirty men single-handed; so I lay
still in my castle, perplexed and discomforted: however, I put myself
into all the same postures for an attack that I had formerly provided,
and was just ready for action, if anything had presented. Having
waited a good while, listening to hear if they made any noise, at
length, being very impatient, I set my guns at the foot of my ladder,
and clambered up to the top of the hill, by my two stages, as usual;
standing so, however, that my head did not appear above the hill, so
that they could not perceive me by any means. Here I observed, by
the help of my perspective-glass, that they were no less than thirty in
number, that they had a fire kindled, and that they had had meat
dressed. How they had cooked it that I knew not, or what it was;
but they were all dancing, in I know not how many barbarous
gestures and figures, their own way, round the fire.

While I was thus looking on them, I perceived, by my perspective, two miserable wretches dragged from the boats, where, it
seems, they were laid by, and were now brought out for the slaughter.
I perceived one of them immediately fell, being knocked down, I
suppose, with a club or wooden sword, for that was their way, and
two or three others were at work immediately cutting him open for
their cookery, while the other victim was left standing by himself,
till they should be ready for him. In that very moment, this poor
wretch seeing himself a little at liberty, nature inspired him with
hopes of life, and he started away from them, and ran with incredible
swiftness along the sands, directly towards me. I mean towards that

part of the coast where my habitation was. I was dreadfully frightened, that I must acknowledge, when I perceived him to run my way, and especially when, as I thought, I saw him pursued by the whole body, and now I expected that part of my dream was coming to pass, and that he would certainly take shelter in my grove; but I could not depend, by any means, upon my dream for the rest of it, viz., that the other savages would not pursue him thither, and find him there. However, I kept my station, and my spirits began to recover, when I found that there was not above three men that followed him; and still more was I encouraged when I found that he outstripped them exceedingly in running, and gained ground of them; so that if he could but hold it for half an hour, I saw easily he would fairly get away from them all.

There was between them and my castle the creek, which I mentioned often at the first part of my story, where I landed my cargoes out of the ship; and this I saw plainly he must necessarily swim over, or the poor wretch would be taken there: but when the savage escaping came thither, he made nothing of it, though the tide was then up; but plunging in, swam through in about thirty strokes, or thereabout, landed, and ran on with exceeding strength and swiftness. When the three persons came to the creek, I found that two of them could swim, but the third could not, and that, standing on the other side, he looked at the others, but went no farther, and soon after went softly back again; which as it happened, was very well for him in the main. I observed that the two who swam were yet more than twice as long swimming over the creek as the fellow was that fled from them. It came now very warmly upon my thoughts, and indeed irresistibly, that now was my time to get me a servant and perhaps a companion or assistant; and that I was called plainly by Providence to save this poor creature's life. I immediately got down the ladders with all possible expedition, fetched my two guns, for they were both but at the foot of the ladders, as I observed above, and getting up again, with the same haste, to the top of the hill, I crossed towards the sea, and having a very short cut, and all down hill, clapped myself in the way between the pursuers and the pursued, hallooing aloud to him that fled, who, looking back, was at first, perhaps, as much frightened at me as at them; but I beckoned with my hand to him to come back; and, in the meantime, I slowly advanced towards the two that followed; then rushing at once upon the foremost, I knocked him down with the stock of my piece. I was loath to fire, because I would not have the rest hear; though, at that distance, it would not have been easily heard, and being out of sight of the smoke too, they would not have easily known what to make of it. Having knocked this fellow down, the other who pursued with him stopped, as if he had been frightened, and I advanced apace towards him: but as I came nearer, I perceived presently he had a bow and arrow, and was fitting it to shoot at me: so I was then necessitated to shoot at him first, which I did, and killed him at the first shot.

The poor savage who fled, but had stopped, though he saw both his enemies fallen and killed, as he thought, yet was so frightened with the fire and noise of my piece, that he stood stock-still, and neither came forward nor went backward, though he seemed rather inclined to fly still, than to come on. I hallooed again to him, and made signs to come forward, which he easily understood, and came a little way; then stopped again, and then a little farther, and stopped again; and I could then perceive that he stood trembling, as if he had been taken prisoner, and had just been to be killed, as his two enemies were. I beckoned to him again to come to me, and gave him all the signs of encouragement that I could think of; and he came nearer and nearer, kneeling down every ten or twelve steps, in token of acknowledgment for my saving his life. I smiled at him, and looked pleasantly, and beckoned to him to come still nearer; at length he came close to me, and then he kneeled down again, kissed the ground, and laid his head upon the ground, and taking me by the foot, set my foot upon his head: this, it seems, was in token of swearing to be my slave for ever. I took him up, and made much of him, and encouraged him all I could. But there was more work to do yet: for I perceived the savage whom I knocked down was not killed, but stunned with the blow, and began to come to himself; so I pointed to him, and showing him the savage, that he was not dead; upon this he spoke some words to me, and though I could not understand them, yet I thought they were pleasant to hear; for they were the first sound of a man's voice that I had heard, my own excepted, for above twenty-five years.

But there was no time for such reflections now: the savage who was knocked down recovered himself so far as to sit up upon the ground, and I perceived that my savage began to be afraid: but when I saw that, I presented my other piece at the man, as if I would shoot him; upon this my savage, for so I call him now, made a motion to me to lend him my sword, which hung naked in a belt by my side: so I did. He no sooner had it, but he runs to his enemy, and, at one blow, cut off his head as cleverly, no executioner in Germany could have done it sooner or better: which I thought very strange for one who, I had reason to believe, never saw a sword in his life before, except their own wooden swords: however, it seems, as I learned afterwards, they make their wooden swords so sharp, so heavy, and the wood is so hard, that they will cut off heads even with them, aye, and arms, and that at one blow too. When he had done this, he comes laughing to me, in sign of triumph, and brought me the sword again, and with abundance of gestures, which I did not understand, laid it down, with the head of the savage that he had killed, just before me. But that which astonished him most, was to know how I had killed the other Indian so far off: so pointing to him, he made signs to me to let him go to him; so I bade him go, as well as I could. When he came to him, he stood like one amazed, looking at him, turned him first on one side, then on the other, looked at the wound the bullet had made, which, it seems, was just in his breast, where it had made a hole, and no great quantity of blood had followed; but he had bled inwardly, for he was quite dead.

He took up his bow and arrows, and came back; so I turned to go away, and beckoned to him to follow me, making signs to him that more might come after them. Upon this he signed to me that he should bury them with sand, that they might not be seen by the rest, if they followed; and so I made signs again to him to do so. He fell to work, and, in an instant, he had scraped a hole in the sand with his hands, big enough to bury the first in, and then dragged him into it, and covered him; and did so by the other also: I believe he had buried them both in a quarter of an hour. Then calling him away, I carried him, not to my castle, but quite away to my cave, on the farther part of the island: so I did not let my dream come to pass in that part, viz. that he came into my grove for shelter. Here I gave him bread and a bunch of raisins to eat, and a draught of water, which I found he was indeed in great distress for, by his running; and having refreshed him, I made signs for him to go and lie down to sleep, and pointing to a place where I had laid a great parcel of rice-straw, and a blanket upon it, which I used to sleep upon myself sometimes; so the poor creature lay down, and went to sleep. DANIEL DEFOE.

18. GULLIVER'S TRAVELS.
I. In the Country of the Giants.

Having been condemned by nature and fortune to an active and restless life, in two months after my return I again left my native country, and took shipping in the Downs, on the 20th day of June 1702, in the Adventure, Capt. John Nicholas a Cornishman commander, bound for Surat. We had a very prosperous gale till we arrived at

the Cape of Good Hope, where we landed for fresh water, but discovering a leak, we unshipped our goods, and wintered there; for, the captain falling sick of an ague, we could not leave the Cape till the end of March. We then set sail, and had a good voyage till we
5 passed the Straits of Madagascar: but having got northward of that island, and to about five degrees south latitude, the winds (which in those seas are observed to blow a constant equal gale between the north and west, from the beginning of December to the beginning of May) on the 19th of April began with much greater violence, and
10 more westerly than usual, continuing so for twenty days together, during which time we were driven a little to the east of the Molucca Islands, and about three degrees northward of the line, as our captain found by an observation he took the 2nd of May, at which time the wind ceased, and it was a perfect calm, whereat I was not a little
15 rejoiced. But he, being a man well experienced in the navigation of those seas, bid us all prepare against a storm, which accordingly happened the day following; for a southern wind, called the southern monsoon, began to set in.

It was a very fierce storm; the sea broke strange and dangerous.
20 During this storm, which was followed by a strong wind west-southwest, we were carried by my computation about five hundred leagues to the east, so that the oldest sailor on board could not tell in what part of the world we were. Our provisions held out well, our ship was staunch, and our crew all in good health; but we lay in the
25 utmost distress for water. We thought it best to hold on the same course, rather than turn more northerly, which might have brought us to the north-west parts of great Tartary, and into the frozen sea.

On the 16th of June, 1703, a boy on the top-mast discovered land. On the 17th, we came in full view of a great island or continent
30 (for we knew not whether) on the south side whereof was a small neck of land jutting out into the sea, and a creek too shallow to hold a ship of above one hundred tuns. We cast anchor within a league of this creek, and our captain sent a dozen of his men well armed in the long boat, with vessels for water, if any would be found.
35 I desired his leave to go with them, that I might see the country, and make what discoveries I could. When we came to land, we saw no river nor spring, nor any signs of inhabitants. Our men therefore wandered on the shore to find out some fresh water near the sea, and I walked alone about a mile on the other side, where I observed
40 the country all barren and rocky. I now began to be weary, and seeing nothing to entertain my curiosity, I returned gently down towards the creek; and the sea being full in my view, I saw our men

already got into the boat, and rowing for life to the ship. I was going to halloo after them, although it had been to little purpose, when I observed a huge creature walking after them in the sea, as fast as he could: he waded not much deeper than his knees, and took prodigious strides; but our men had the start of him half a league, and, the sea thereabouts being full of sharp-pointed rocks, the monster was not able to overtake the boat. This I was afterwards told, for I durst not stay to see the issue of the adventure, but ran as fast as I could the way I first went, and then climbed up a steep hill, which gave me some prospect of the country. I found it fully cultivated: but that which first surprised me was the length of the grass, which, in those grounds that seemed to be kept for hay, was about twenty feet high.

I fell into a high-road, for so I took it to be, though it served to the inhabitants only as a foot-path through a field of barley. Here I walked on for some time, but could see little on either side: it being now near harvest, and the corn rising at least forty feet. I was an hour walking to the end of this field, which was fenced in with a hedge of at least one hundred and twenty feet high, and the trees so lofty that I could make no computation of their altitude. There was a stile to pass from this field into the next. It had four steps, and a stone to cross over when you came to the uppermost. It was impossible for me to climb this stile, because every step was six feet high, and the upper stone above twenty. I was endeavouring to find some gap in the hedge, when I discovered one of the inhabitants in the next field advancing towards the stile, of the same size with him whom I saw in the sea pursuing our boat. He appeared as tall as an ordinary spire-steeple, and took about ten yards at every stride, as near as I could guess. I was struck with the utmost fear and astonishment, and ran to hide myself in the corn, from whence I saw him at the top of the stile looking back into the next field on the right hand, and heard him call in a voice many degrees louder than a speaking trumpet: but the noise was so high in the air, that at first I certainly thought it was thunder. Whereupon seven monsters, like himself, came towards him with reaping-hooks in their hands, each hook about the largeness of six scythes. These people were not so well clad as the first, whose servants or labourers they seemed to be: for, upon some words he spoke, they went to reap the corn in the field where I lay. I kept from them at as great a distance as I could, but was forced to move with extreme difficulty, for the stalks of the corn were sometimes not above a foot distant, so that I could hardly squeeze my body betwixt them. However I made a shift to go forward, till I came to a part of the field where the corn had been laid

by the rain and wind. Here it was impossible for me to advance a
step: for the stalks were so interwoven that I could not creep through,
and the beards of the fallen ears so strong and pointed, that they
pierced through my clothes into my flesh. At the same time I heard
5 the reapers not above a hundred yards behind me. Being quite
dispirited with toil, and wholly overcome by grief and despair, I lay
down between two ridges, and heartily wished I might there end
my days. I bemoaned my desolate widow, and fatherless children.
I lamented my own folly and wilfulness in attempting a second voyage
10 against the advice of all my friends and relations. In this terrible
agitation of mind I could not forbear thinking of Lilliput, whose inhabitants looked upon me as the greatest prodigy that ever appeared
in the world; where I was able to draw an imperial fleet in my hand,
and perform those other actions which will be recorded for ever in
15 the chronicles of that empire, while posterity shall hardly believe them,
although attested by millions. I reflected what a mortification it must
prove to me to appear as inconsiderable in this nation, as one single
Lilliputian would be among us. But this I conceived was to be the
least of my misfortunes: for, as human creatures are observed to be
20 more savage and cruel in proportion to their bulk, what could I expect but to be a morsel in the mouth of the first among these enormous barbarians, that should happen to seize me? Undoubtedly philosophers are in the right when they tell us that nothing is great
or little otherwise than by comparison. It might have pleased fortune
25 to have let the Lilliputians find some nation, where the people were
as diminutive with respect to them, as they were to me. And who
knows but that even this prodigious race of mortals might be equally
overmatched in some distant part of the world, whereof we have yet
no discovery.
30 Scared and confounded as I was, I could not forbear going on
with these reflections, when one of the reapers, approaching within
ten yards of the ridge where I lay, made me apprehend that with
the next step I should be squashed to death under his foot, or cut
in two with his reaping-hook. And therefore, when he was again about
35 to move, I screamed as loud as fear could make me. Whereupon
the huge creature trod short, and, looking round about under him
for some time, at last espied me as I lay on the ground. He considered a while with the caution of one who endeavours to lay hold
on a small dangerous animal, in such a manner that it shall not be
40 able either to scratch or bite him, as I myself have sometimes done
with a weasel in England. At length he ventured to take me up
behind by the middle between his forefinger and thumb, and brought

me within three yards of his eyes, that he might behold my shape
more perfectly. I guessed his meaning, and my good fortune gave
me so much presence of mind, that I resolved not to struggle in the
least as he held me in the air above sixty feet from the ground, although he grievously pinched my sides, for fear I should slip through
his fingers. All I ventured was to raise my eyes towards the sun,
and place my hands together in a supplicating posture, and to speak
some words in a humble melancholy tone, suitable to the condition
I then was in. For I apprehended every moment that he would dash
me against the ground, as we usually do any little hateful animal,
which we have a mind to destroy. But my good star would have it,
that he appeared pleased with my voice and gestures, and began to
look upon me as a curiosity, much wondering to hear me pronounce
articulate words, although he could not understand them. In the mean
time I was not able to forbear groaning and shedding tears, and
turning my head towards my sides; letting him know, as well as I
could, how cruelly I was hurt by the pressure of his thumb and
finger. He seemed to apprehend my meaning; for lifting up the lappet
of his coat, he put me gently into it, and immediately ran along
with me to his master, who was a substantial farmer, and the same
person I had first seen in the field.

The farmer having (as I suppose by their talk) received such
an account of me as his servant could give him, took a piece of small
straw, about the size of a walking staff, and therewith lifted up the
lappets of my coat, which it seems he had thought to be some kind
of covering that nature had given me. He blew my hairs aside to
take a better view of my face. He called his hinds about him, and
asked them (as I afterwards learned) whether they had ever seen in
the fields any little creature that resembled me: he then placed me
softly on the ground upon all four, but I got immediately up, and
walked slowly backwards and forwards to let those people see I had
no intent to run away. They all sat down in a circle about me, the
better to observe my motions. I pulled off my hat, and made a low
bow towards the farmer. I fell on my knees, and lifted up my hands
and eyes, and spoke several words as loud as I could. I took a purse
of gold out of my pocket, and humbly presented it to him. He received it on the palm of his hand, then applied it close to his eye
to see what it was, and afterwards turned it several times with the
point of a pin (which he took out of his sleeve) but could make nothing of it. Whereupon I made a sign that he should place his hand
on the ground. I then took the purse, and opening it, poured all the
gold into his palm. There were six Spanish pieces of four pistoles each,

besides twenty or thirty smaller coins. I saw him wet the tip of his little finger upon his tongue, and take up one of my largest pieces, and then another, but he seemed to be wholly ignorant what they were. He made me a sign to put them again into my pocket, which, after offering it to him several times, I thought it best to do.

The farmer by this time was convinced I must be a rational creature. He spoke often to me, but the sound of his voice pierced my ears like that of a water-mill, yet his words were articulate enough. I answered as loud as I could in several languages, and he often laid his ear within two yards of me; but all in vain, for we were wholly unintelligible to each other. He then sent his servants to their work, and, taking his handkerchief out of his pocket, he doubled and spread it on his left hand, which he placed flat on the ground with the palm upwards, making me a sign to step into it, as I could easily do, for it was not above a foot in thickness. I thought it my part to obey, and, for fear of falling, laid myself at full length upon the handkerchief, with the remainder of which he lapped me up to the head for farther security, and in this manner carried me home to his house. There he called his wife, and showed me to her; but she screamed and ran back, as women in England do at the sight of a toad or a spider. However, when she had a while seen my behaviour, and how well I observed the signs her husband made, she was soon reconciled, and by degrees grew extremely tender of me.

It was about twelve at noon, and a servant brought in dinner. It was only one substantial dish of meat (fit for the plain condition of a husbandman) in a dish of about four and twenty feet diameter. The company were the farmer and his wife; three children and an old grandmother. When they sat down, the farmer placed me at some distance from him on the table, which was thirty feet high from the floor. I was in a terrible fright, and kept as far as I could from the edge for fear of falling. The wife minced a bit of meat, then crumbled some bread on a trencher, and placed it before me. I made her a low bow, took out my knife and fork, and fell to eat, which gave them exceeding delight. The mistress sent her maid for a small dram-cup, which held about two gallons, and filled it with drink; I took up the vessel with much difficulty in both hands, and in a most respectful manner drank to her ladyship's health, expressing the words as loud as I could in English, which made the company laugh so heartily, that I was almost deafened with the noise. This liquor tasted like a small cider, and was not unpleasant. Then the master made me a sign to come to his trencher-side; but as I walked on the table, being in great surprise all the time, as the indulgent reader will easily conceive and excuse, I happened to stumble against a crust, and fell flat on my face, but received no hurt. I got up immediately, and observing the good people to be in much concern, I took my hat (which I held under my arm out of good manners) and, waving it over my head, made three huzzas, to show I had got no mischief by my fall. But advancing forward towards my master (as I shall henceforth call him) his youngest son who sat next him, an arch boy of about ten years old, took me up by the legs, and held me so high in the air, that I trembled every limb: but his father snatched me from him, and at the same time gave him such a box on the left ear, as would have felled a European troop of horse to the earth, ordering him to be taken from the table. But being afraid the boy might owe me a spite, and well remembering how mischievous all children among us naturally are to sparrows, rabbits, young kittens, and puppy-dogs, I fell on my knees, and pointing to the boy made my master to understand, as well as I could, that I desired his son might be pardoned. The father complied, and the lad took his seat again; whereupon I went to him, and kissed his hand, which my master took, and made him stroke me gently with it.

In the midst of dinner, my mistress's favourite cat leapt into her lap. I heard a noise behind me like that of a dozen stocking-weavers at work; and, turning my head, I found it proceeded from the purring of that animal, who seemed to be three times larger than an ox, as I computed by the view of her head, and one of her paws, while her mistress was feeding and stroking her. The fierceness of this creature's countenance altogether discomposed me; though I stood at the further end of the table, above fifty feet off; and although my mistress held her fast, for fear she might give a spring, and seize me in her talons. But it happened there was no danger; for the cat took not the least notice of me, when my master placed me within three yards of her. And as I have been always told, and found true by experience in my travels, that flying or discovering fear before a fierce animal is a certain way to make it pursue or attack you, so I resolved in this dangerous juncture to show no manner of concern. I walked with intrepidity five or six times before the very head of the cat, and came within half a yard of her; whereupon she drew herself back, as if she were more afraid of me: I had less apprehension concerning the dogs, whereof three or four came into the room, as it is usual in farmers' houses; one of which was a mastiff equal in bulk to four elephants, and a greyhound somewhat taller than the mastiff, but not so large.

When dinner was almost done, the nurse came in with a child of a year old in her arms, who immediately spied me, and began a squall that you might have heard from London Bridge to Chelsea, after the usual oratory of infants to get me for a play-thing. The mother out
5 of pure indulgence took me up, and put me towards the child, who presently seized me by the middle, and got my head into his mouth, where I roared so loud that the urchin was frightened, and let me drop, and I should infallibly have broken my neck, if the mother had not held her apron under me. The nurse to quiet her babe made use of
10 a rattle, which was a kind of hollow vessel filled with great stones, and fastened by a cable to the child's waist.

When dinner was done, my master went out to his labourers, and, as I could discover by his voice and gesture, gave his wife a strict charge to take care of me. I was very much tired, and disposed
15 to sleep, which my mistress perceiving, she put me on her own bed, and covered me with a clean white handkerchief but larger and coarser than the main-sail of a man of war.

II. The Academy.

The first professor I saw was in a very large room, with forty
20 pupils about him. After salutation observing me to look earnestly upon a frame, which took up the greatest part of both the length and breadth of the room, he said perhaps I might wonder to see him employed in a project for improving speculative knowledge by practical and mechanical operations. But the world would soon be sensible of
25 its usefulness; and he flattered himself that a more noble exalted thought never sprang in any other man's head. Every one knew how laborious the usual method is of attaining to arts and sciences; whereas by his contrivance the most ignorant person at a reasonable charge and with a little bodily labour might write books in philosophy, poetry,
30 politics, law, mathematics, and theology, without the least assistance from genius or study. He then led me to the frame, about the sides whereof all his pupils stood in ranks. It was twenty feet square, placed in the middle of the room. The superficies was composed of several bits of wood about the bigness of a dye, but some larger than
35 others. They were all linked together by slender wires. These bits of wood were covered on every square with paper pasted on them; and on these papers were written all the words of their language in their several moods, tenses, and declensions; but without any order. The professor then desired me to observe; for he was going to set
40 his engine at work. The pupils at his command took each of them hold of an iron handle, whereof there were forty fixed round the

edges of the frame; and giving them a sudden turn the whole disposition of the words was entirely changed. He then commanded six and thirty of the lads to read the several lines softly, as they appeared upon the frame; and where they found three or four words together, that might make part of a sentence, they dictated to the four remaining boys, who were scribes. This work was repeated three or four times, and at every turn, the engine was so contrived, that the words shifted into new places, as the square bits of wood moved upside down.

Six hours a day the young students were employed in this labour, and the professor showed me several volumes in large folio already collected of broken sentences, which he intended to piece together, and out of those rich materials to give the world a complete body of all arts and sciences: which, however, might be still improved and much expedited, if the public would raise a fund for making and employing five hundred such frames in Lagado, and oblige the managers to contribute in common their several collections.

He assured me that this invention had employed all his thoughts from his youth; that he had emptied the whole vocabulary into his frame, and made the strictest computation of the general proportion there is in books between the numbers of particles, nouns, and verbs, and other parts of speech.

I made my humblest acknowledgment to this illustrious person for his great communicativeness; and promised, if ever I had the good fortune to return to my native country, that I would do him justice, as the sole inventor of this wonderful machine; the form and contrivance of which I desired leave to delineate upon paper. I told him, although it were the custom of our learned in Europe to steal inventions from each other, who had thereby at least this advantage, that it became a controversy which was the right owner; yet I would take such caution, that he should have the honour entire, without a rival.

We went next to the school of languages, where three professors sat in consultation upon improving that of their own country.

The first project was to shorten discourse by cutting polysyllables into one, and leaving out verbs and participles; because in reality all things imaginable are but nouns.

The other project was a scheme of entirely abolishing all words whatsoever; and this was urged as a great advantage in point of health, as well as brevity. For it is plain, that every word we speak, is in some degree a diminution of our lungs by corrosion; and consequently contributes to the shortening of our lives. An expedient was therefore offered, that since words are only names for things, it would be more convenient for all men to carry about them such things as were necessary to express the particular business they are to discourse on. And this invention would certainly have taken place, to the great ease as well as health of the subject, if the women, in conjunction with the vulgar and illiterate, had not threatened to raise a rebellion, unless they might be allowed the liberty to speak with their tongues after the manner of their forefathers, such constant irreconcileable enemies to science are the common people. However, many of the most learned and wise adhere to the new scheme of expressing themselves by things; which has only this inconvenience attending it, that if a man's business be very great, and of various kinds, he must be obliged in proportion to carry a greater bundle of things upon his back, unless he can afford one or two strong servants to attend him. I have often beheld two of those sages almost sinking under the weight of their packs, like pedlars among us: who, when they met in the streets, would lay down their loads, open their sacks, and hold conversation for an hour together; then put up their implements, help each other to resume their burthens, and take their leave.

But for short conversations a man may carry implements in his pockets and under his arms enough to supply him: and in his house he cannot be at a loss. Therefore the room, where company meet who practise this art, is full of all things ready at hand, requisite to furnish matter for this kind of artificial converse.

Another great advantage proposed by this invention was, that it would serve as an universal language to be understood in all civilized nations, whose goods and utensils are generally of the same kind, or nearly resembling, so that their uses might easily be comprehended. And thus ambassadors would be qualified to treat with foreign princes, or ministers of state, to whose tongues they were utter strangers. —

I was at the mathematical school, where the master taught his pupils after a method scarce imaginable to us in Europe. The proposition and demonstration were fairly written on a thin wafer with ink composed of a cephalic tincture. This the student was to swallow upon a fasting stomach, and for three days following eat nothing but bread and water. As the wafer digested, the tincture mounted to his brain, bearing the proposition along with it. But the success has not hitherto been answerable, partly by some error in the quantum or composition, and partly by the perverseness of lads, to whom this bolus is so nauseous, that they generally steal aside and discharge it upwards, before it can operate; neither have they been yet persuaded to use so long an abstinence as the prescription requires.

JONATHAN SWIFT.

19. Mr. Bramble and Lord Oxmington.

A few days ago, my uncle and I, going to visit a relation, met with Lord Oxmington at his house, who asked us to dine with him next day, and we accepted the invitation. Accordingly, leaving our women under the care of Captain Lismahago, at the inn where we had lodged the preceding night, in a little town, about a mile from his lordship's dwelling, we went at the hour appointed, and had a fashionable meal served up with much ostentation, to a company of about a dozen persons, none of whom we had ever seen before. His lordship is much more remarkable for his pride and caprice, than for his hospitality and understanding; and, indeed, it appeared that he considered his guests merely as objects to shine upon, so as to reflect the lustre of his own magnificence. There was much state, but no courtesy; and a great deal of compliment, without any conversation.

Before the dessert was removed, our noble entertainer proposed three general toasts: then calling for a glass of wine, and bowing all round wished us a good afternoon. This was the signal for the company to break up, and they obeyed it immediately, all except our squire, who was greatly shocked at the manner of this dismission. He changed countenance, bit his lip in silence, but still kept his seat; so that his lordship found himself obliged to give us another hint, by saying, he should be glad to see us another time. "There is no time like the present time," cried Mr. Bramble: "your lordship has not yet drunk a bumper to 'the best in Christendom'." — "I'll drink no more bumpers to-day," answered our landlord; "and I am sorry to see you have drunk too many. — Order the gentleman's carriage to the gate." So saying, he rose and retired abruptly; our squire starting up at the same time, laying his hand upon his sword, and eying him with a most ferocious aspect. The master having vanished in this manner, our uncle bade one of the servants to see what was to pay; and the fellow answering, — "This is no inn:" — "I cry you mercy," cried the other; "I perceive it is not: if it were, the landlord would be more civil. There is a guinea, however; take it; and tell your lord that I shall not leave the country till I have had an opportunity to thank him in person for his politeness and hospitality."

We then walked down stairs through a double range of lackeys, and getting into the chaise, proceeded homewards. Perceiving the squire much ruffled, I ventured to disapprove of his resentment: observing that, as Lord Oxmington was well known to have his brain very ill-timbered, a sensible man should rather laugh, than be angry, at his ridiculous want of breeding. Mr. Bramble took umbrage at my presuming to be wiser than he upon this occasion: and told me that, as he had always thought for himself in every occurrence in life, he would still use the same privilege, with my good leave.

When we returned to our inn, he closeted Lismahago: and having explained his grievance, desired that gentleman to go and demand satisfaction of Lord Oxmington in his name. The lieutenant charged himself with this commission, and immediately set out a-horseback for his lordship's house, attended, at his own request, by my man Archy Macalpine, who had been used to military service; and truly, if Macalpine had been mounted upon an ass, this couple might have passed for the knight of La Mancha and his squire Panza. It was not till after some demur, that Lismahago obtained a private audience, at which he formally defied his lordship to single combat, in the name of Mr. Bramble, and desired him to appoint the time and place. Lord Oxmington was so confounded at this unexpected message, that he could not, for some time, make any articulate reply, but stood staring at the lieutenant with evident marks of perturbation. At length, ringing a bell with great vehemence, he exclaimed, — "What! a commoner send a challenge to a peer of the realm! Privilege! privilege! Here is a person brings me a challenge from the Welshman that dined at my table. An impudent fellow! My wine is not yet out of his head."

The whole house was immediately in commotion. Macalpine made a soldierly retreat with the two horses; but the captain was suddenly surrounded and disarmed by the footmen, whom a French valet-de-chambre headed in this exploit: and his person was passed through the horsepond. In this plight he returned to the inn, half mad with his disgrace. So violent was the rage of his indignation, that he mistook its object. He wanted to quarrel with Mr. Bramble: he said, he had been dishonoured on his account, and he looked for reparation at his hands. My uncle's back was up in a moment; and he desired him to explain his pretensions. "Either compel Lord Oxmington to give me satisfaction," cried he, "or give it me in your own person." "The latter part of the alternative is the most easy and expeditious," replied the squire, starting up: "if you are disposed for a walk, I'll attend you this moment."

Here they were interrupted by Mrs. Tabby, who had overheard all that passed. She now burst into the room, and running betwixt them, in great agitation — "Is this your regard for me," said she to the lieutenant, "to seek the life of my brother?" Lismahago, who seemed to grow cool as my uncle grew hot, assured her he had a

very great respect for Mr. Bramble. but he had still more for his own
honour, which had suffered pollution; but if that could be once puri-
fied. he should have no farther cause of dissatisfaction. The squire
said he should have thought it incumbent upon him to vindicate the
lieutenant's honour; but, as he had now carved for himself, he might
swallow and digest it as well as he could. In a word, what betwixt
the mediation of Mrs. Tabitha, the recollection of the captain, who
perceived he had gone too far, and the remonstrances of your humble
servant, who joined them at this juncture, those two originals were
perfectly reconciled: and then we proceeded to deliberate upon the
means of taking vengeance for the insults they had received from the
petulant peer; for, until that aim should be accomplished, Mr. Bramble
swore, with great emphasis, that he would not leave the inn where
we now lodged, even if he should pass his Christmas on the spot.

In consequence of our deliberations, we next day, in the fore-
noon, proceeded in a body to his lordship's house, all of us, with
our servants, including the coachman, mounted a-horseback, with our
pistols loaded and ready primed. Thus prepared for action, we
paraded solemnly and slowly before his lordship's gate, which we
passed three times in such a manner, that he could not but see us,
and suspect the cause of our appearance. After dinner we returned,
and performed the same cavalcade, which was again repeated the
morning following: but we had no occasion to persist in these
manœuvres. About noon we were visited by the gentleman at whose
house we had first seen Lord Oxmington. He now came to make
apologies in the name of his lordship, who declared he had no intention to give offence to my uncle, in practising what had been always
the custom of his house: and that as for the indignities which had
been put upon the officer, they were offered without his lordship's
knowledge. at the instigation of his valet-de-chambre. "If that be
the case," said my uncle, in a peremptory tone, "I shall be contented
with Lord Oxmington's personal excuses; and I hope my friend will
be satisfied with his lordship's turning that insolent rascal out of
his service." "Sir," cried Lismahago. "I must insist upon taking personal vengeance for the personal injuries I have sustained."

After some debate, the affair was adjusted in this manner. His
lordship, meeting us at our friend's house, declared he was sorry for
what had happened; and that he had no intention to give umbrage.
The valet-de-chambre asked pardon of the lieutenant upon his knees,
when Lismahago, to the astonishment of all present, gave him a
violent kick on the face, which laid him on his back, exclaiming in
a furious tone. "*Oui, je te pardonne.*"

Such was the fortunate issue of this perilous adventure, which threatened abundance of vexation to our family; for the squire is one of those who will sacrifice both life and fortune, rather than leave what they conceive to be the least speck or blemish upon their honour and reputation. His lordship had no sooner pronounced his apology, with a very bad grace, than he went away in some disorder; and, I dare say, he will never invite another Welshman to his table. TOBIAS SMOLLETT.

20. The Story of the King of Bohemia and His Seven Castles.

There was a certain King of Bo—he—

As the Corporal was entering the confines of Bohemia, my uncle Toby obliged him to halt for a single moment. He had set out bare-headed; having, since he pulled off his Montero-cap in the latter end of the last chapter, left it lying beside him on the ground.

— The eye of goodness espieth all things; — so that before the Corporal had well got through the first five words of his story, had my uncle Toby twice touched his Montero-cap with the end of his cane, interrogatively; — as much as to say, Why don't you put it on, Trim? — Trim took it up with the most respectful slowness, and casting a glance of humiliation, as he did it, upon the embroidery of the fore-part, which being dismally tarnished and frayed, moreover, in some of the principal leaves and boldest parts of the pattern, he laid it down again between his two feet, in order to moralize upon the subject.

— 'Tis every word of it but too true, cried my uncle Toby, that thou art about to observe: Nothing in this world, Trim, is made to last for ever.

— But when tokens of love and remembrance wear out, said Trim, what shall we say?

— There is no occasion, Trim, quoth my uncle Toby, to say anything else: and was a man to puzzle his brains till Doomsday, I believe, Trim, it would be impossible.

The Corporal perceiving my uncle Toby was in the right, and that it would be in vain for the wit of man to think of extracting a purer moral from his cap, without further attempting it, he put it on; and passing his hand across his forehead to rub out a pensive wrinkle, which the text and the doctrine between them had engendered, he returned, with the same look and tone of voice, to his story of the King of Bohemia and his seven castles.

The story of the King of Bohemia and his seven castles, continued.

There was a certain King of Bohemia: but in whose reign, except his own, I am not able to inform your honour. —

I do not desire it of thee, Trim, by any means, cried my uncle Toby.

— It was a little before the time, an' please your honour, when giants were beginning to leave off breeding, — but in what year of our Lord that was —

— I would not give a halfpenny to know, said my uncle Toby.

— Only, an' please your honour, it makes a story look the better in the face. —

— 'Tis thy own, Trim, so ornament it after thy own fashion; and take any date, continued my uncle Toby, looking pleasantly upon him; — take any date in the whole world thou choosest, and put it to, — thou art heartily welcome. —

The Corporal bowed; for of every century, and of every year of that century, from the first creation of the world down to Noah's flood: and from Noah's flood to the birth of Abraham; through all the pilgrimages of the patriarchs, to the departure of the Israelites out of Egypt: — and throughout all the Dynasties, Olympiads, Urbeconditas, and other memorable epochas of the different nations of the world, down to the coming of Christ, and from thence to the very moment in which the Corporal was telling his story, — had my uncle Toby subjected this vast empire of time, and all its abysses, at his feet. But as Modesty scarce touches with a finger what Liberality offers her with both hands open, — the Corporal contented himself with the very worst year of the whole bunch; which, to prevent your honours of the majority and minority from tearing the very flesh off your bones in contestation, I tell you plainly it was — the year next him; — which being the year of our Lord seventeen hundred and twelve, when the Duke of Ormond was playing the devil in Flanders, — the Corporal took it, and set out with it afresh on his expedition to Bohemia.

The story of the King of Bohemia and his seven castles, continued.

In the year of our Lord one thousand seven hundred and twelve, there was, an' please your honour, —

— To tell thee truly, Trim, quoth my uncle Toby, any other date would have pleased me much better, not only on account of the sad stain upon our history that year, in marching off our troops, and refusing to cover the siege of Quesnoi, though Fagel was carrying on the works with such incredible vigour, but likewise on the score,

Trim, of thy own story; because if there are, — and which, from what thou hast dropped, I partly suspect to be the fact, — if there are giants in it. —

— There is but one, an' please your honour.

— 'Tis as bad as twenty, replied my uncle Toby: — thou shouldst have carried him back some seven or eight hundred years out of harm's way, both of critics and other people, and therefore I would advise thee, if ever thou tellest it again, —

— If I live, an' please your honour, but once to get through it, I will never tell it again, quoth Trim, either to man, woman, or child. — Poo — poo! said my uncle Toby; — but with accents of such sweet encouragement did he utter it, that the Corporal went on with his story with more alacrity than ever.

The story of the King of Bohemia and his seven castles, continued.

There was, an' please your honour, said the Corporal, raising his voice and rubbing the palms of his two hands cheerly together as he began, a certain King of Bohemia, —

— Leave out the date entirely, Trim, quoth my uncle Toby, leaning forwards, and laying his hand gently upon the Corporal's shoulder to temper the interruption, — leave it out entirely, Trim; a story passes very well without these niceties; unless one is pretty sure of 'em. — Sure of 'em! said the Corporal, shaking his head.

— Right, answered my uncle Toby: it is not easy, Trim, for one, bred up as thou and I have been to arms, who seldom looks further forward than to the end of his musket, or backwards beyond his knapsack, to know much about this matter. — God bless your honour! said the Corporal, won by the manner of my uncle Toby's reasoning, as much as by the reasoning itself, he has something else to do: if not in action, or on a march, or upon duty in his garrison, — he has his firelock, an' please your honour, to furbish, — his accoutrements to take care of, — his regimentals to mend, — himself to shave and keep clean, so as to appear always like what he is upon the parade: what business, added the Corporal, triumphantly, has a soldier, an' please your honour, to know any thing at all of geography?

— Thou wouldst have said chronology, Trim, said my uncle Toby; for, as for geography, 'tis of absolute use to him: he must be acquainted intimately with every country and its boundaries where his profession carries him; he should know every town and city, and village and hamlet, with the canals, the roads, and hollow-ways which lead up to them. There is not a river or a rivulet he passes, Trim, but he should be able, at first sight, to tell thee what is its name, — in what mountains it takes its rise, — what is its course, — how far it is navigable, — where fordable, — where not; — he should know the fertility of every valley, as well as the hind who ploughs it, and be able to discribe, or, if it is required, to give thee an exact map of all the plains and defiles, the forts, the acclivities, the woods and morasses, through and by which his army is to march; — he should know their produce, their plants, their minerals, their waters, their animals, their seasons, their climates, their heat and cold, their inhabitants, their customs, their language, their policy, and even their religion.

Is it else to be conceived, Corporal, continued my uncle Toby, rising up in his sentry-box as he began to warm in this part of his discourse, — how Marlborough could have marched his army from the banks of the Maese to the plains of Blenheim and Hochstet? — Great as he was, Corporal, he could not have advanced a step, or made one single day's march, without the aids of geography. — As for chronology, I own, Trim, continued my uncle Toby, sitting down again coolly in his sentry-box, that, of all others, it seems a science which the soldier might best spare, was it not for the lights which that science must one day give him, in determining the invention of powder; the furious execution of which, renversing every thing like thunder before it, has become a new era to us of military improvements, changing so totally the nature of attacks and defences, both by sea and land and awakening so much art and skill in doing it, that the world cannot be too exact in ascertaining the precise time of its discovery, or too inquisitive in knowing what great man was the discoverer, and what occasions gave birth to it.

I am far from controverting, continued my uncle Toby, what historians agree in, that in the year of our Lord 1380, under the reign of Wencelaus, son of Charles the Fourth, — a certain priest, whose name was Schwartz, showed the use of powder to the Venetians in their wars against the Genoese; but 'tis certain he was not the first; because — if we are to believe Don Pedro, the bishop of Leon in his chronicle of King Alphonsus, who reduced Toledo, — in the year 1343, which was full thirty-seven years before that time, the secret of powder was well known, and employed with success, both by Moors and Christians, not only in their sea-combats, at that period, but in many of their most memorable sieges in Spain and Barbary: — and all the world knows that Friar Bacon had written expressly about it, and had generously given the world a receipt to make it by, above a hundred and fifty years before even Schwartz was born: —

and that the Chinese, added my uncle Toby, embarrass us, and all accounts of it, still more, by boasting of the invention some hundreds of years even before him. —

They are a pack of liars I believe, cried Trim. —

They are somehow or other deceived, said my uncle Toby, in this matter, as is plain to me from the present miserable state of military architecture amongst them; which consists of nothing more than a *fossé*, with a brick wall, without flanks; — and for what they gave us as a bastion at each angle of it, 'tis so barbarously constructed, that it looks for all the world, — Like one of my seven castles, an' please your honour, quoth Trim. —

My uncle Toby, though in' the utmost distress for a comparison, most courteously refused Trim's offer, — till Trim telling him he had half a dozen more in Bohemia, which he knew not how to get off his hands, — my uncle Toby was so touched with the pleasantry of heart of the Corporal, — that he discontinued his dissertation upon gunpowder, — and begged the Corporal forthwith to go on with his story of the King of Bohemia and his seven castles.

The story of the King of Bohemia and his seven castles, continued.

This unfortunate King of Bohemia, said Trim, — Was he unfortunate, then? cried my uncle Toby; for he had been so wrapped up in his dissertation upon gunpowder, and other military affairs, that though he had desired the Corporal to go on, yet the many interruptions he had given, dwelt not so strong upon his fancy as to account for the epithet. — Was he unfortunate, then, Trim? said my uncle Toby, pathetically. — The Corporal, wishing first the word and all its synonymas at the devil, forthwith began to run back in his mind the principal events in the King of Bohemia's story; from every one of which, it appearing that he was the most fortunate man that ever existed in the world, — it put the Corporal to a stand; for not caring to retract his epithet, — and less to explain it, — and, least of all, to twist his tale (like men of lore) to serve a system, — he looked up in my uncle Toby's face for assistance; — but seeing it was the very thing my uncle Toby sat in expectation of himself, — after a hum and a haw, he went on. —

The King of Bohemia, an' please your honour, replied the Corporal, was unfortunate, as thus: — that taking great pleasure and delight in navigation, and all sort of sea-affairs; — and there happening throughout the whole kingdom of Bohemia to be no sea-port town whatever. —

How the deuce should there, Trim? cried my uncle Toby: for Bohemia being totally inland, and having Silesia and Moravia to the east; Lusatia and Upper Saxony to the north; Franconia to the west; and Bavaria to the south, — Bohemia could not have been propelled to the sea without ceasing to be Bohemia; nor could the sea, on the other hand, have come up to Bohemia, without overflowing a great part of Germany, and destroying millions of unfortunate inhabitants, who could make no defence against it.

The Corporal made the bow of unfeigned conviction and went on. —

Now the King of Bohemia, with his Queen and courtiers, happening one fine summer's evening to walk out, — Aye, there the word happening is right, Trim, cried my uncle Toby; for the King of Bohemia and his Queen might have walked out or let it alone: — 'twas a matter of contingency, which might happen or not, just as chance ordered it. —

King William was of opinion, an' please your honour, quoth Trim, that every thing was predestined for us in this world: insomuch, that he would often say to his soldiers, that "every ball had its billet." — He was a great man, said my uncle Toby. — And I believe, continued Trim, to this day, that the shot which disabled me at the battle of Landen, was pointed at my knee, for no other purpose but to take me out of his service, and place me in your honour's, where I should be taken so much better care of in my old age. — It shall never, Trim, be construed otherwise, said my uncle Toby. —

The heart, both of the master and the man, were alike subject to sudden overflowings: a short silence ensued.

LAWRENCE STERNE.

21. The History of a Philosophic Vagabond.

Upon my arrival in town, my first care was to deliver your letter of recommendation to our cousin, who was himself in little better circumstances than I. My first scheme you know, Sir, was to be usher at an academy, and I asked his advice on the affair. Our cousin received the proposal with a true sardonic grin. Aye, cried he, this is indeed a very pretty career, that has been chalked out for you. I have been an usher at a boarding school myself; and may I die by an anodyne necklace, but I had rather be an under-turnkey in Newgate. I was up early and late: I was brow-beat by the master, hated for my ugly face by the mistress, worried by the boys within, and never permitted to stir out to meet civility abroad. But are you sure you are fit for a school? Let me examine you a little. Have you

been bred apprentice to the business? No. Then you won't do for a school. Can you dress the boys' hair? No. Then you won't do for a school. Have you had the small-pox? No. Then you won't do for a school. Have you got a good stomach? Yes. Then you will by no
5 means do for a school. No, Sir, if you are for a genteel easy profession, bind yourself seven years as an apprentice to turn a cutler's wheel; but avoid a school by any means. Yet come, continued he, I see you are a lad of spirit and some learning, what do you think of commencing author, like me? You have read in books, no doubt,
10 of men of genius starving at the trade: at present I'll show you forty very dull fellows about town that live by it in opulence. All honest jog-trot men, who go on smoothly and dully, and write history and politics, and are praised: men, Sir, who, had they been bred cobblers, would all their lives have only mended shoes, but never
15 made them.

Finding that there was no great degree of gentility affixed to the character of an usher, I resolved to accept his proposal: and having the highest respect for literature, hailed the *antiqua mater* of Grub-street with reverence. I thought it my glory to pursue a
20 track which Dryden and Otway trod before me. I considered the goddess of this region as the parent of excellence; and however an intercourse with the world might give us good sense, the poverty she entailed I supposed to be the nurse of genius. Big with these reflections, I sat down, and finding that the best things remained to
25 be said on the wrong side, I resolved to write a book that should be wholly new. I therefore dressed up three paradoxes with ingenuity. They were false, indeed, but they were new. The jewels of truth have been so often imported by others, that nothing was left for me to import, but some splendid things that, at a distance, looked every
30 bit as well. Witness, you powers, what fancied importance sat perched upon my quill while I was writing! The whole learned world, I made no doubt, would rise to oppose my systems; but then I was prepared to oppose the whole learned world. Like the porcupine I sat self-collected, with a quill pointed against every opposer.
35 "Well said, my boy," cried I, "and what subject did you treat upon? But I interrupt, go on; you published your paradoxes; well, and what did the learned world say to your paradoxes?"

Sir, replied my son, the learned world said nothing to my paradoxes: nothing at all, Sir. Every man of them was employed in
40 praising his friends and himself, or condemning his enemies; and unfortunately, as I had neither, I suffered the cruellest mortification, neglect.

As I was meditating one day in a coffee-house on the fate of my paradoxes, a little man happening to enter the room, placed himself in the box before me, and after some preliminary discourse, finding me to be a scholar, drew out a bundle of proposals, begging me to subscribe to a new edition he was going to give to the world of Propertius, with notes. This demand necessarily produced a reply that I had no money: and that concession led him to inquire into the nature of my expectations. Finding that my expectations were just as great as my purse, "I see," cried he, "you are unacquainted with the town; I'll teach you a part of it. Look at these proposals; upon these very proposals I have subsisted very comfortable for twelve years. The moment a nobleman returns from his travels, a Creolian arrives from Jamaica, or a dowager from her country-seat, I strike for a subscription. I first besiege their hearts with flattery, and then pour in my proposals at the breach. If they subscribe readily the first time, I renew my request to beg a dedication fee. If they let me have that, I smite them once more for engraving their coat of arms at the top. Thus continued he, I live by vanity and laugh at it. But between ourselves. I am now too well known, I should be glad to borrow your face a bit: a nobleman of distinction has just returned from Italy; my face is familiar to his porter: but if you bring this copy of verses, my life for it you succeed, and we divide the spoil."

"Bless us, George," cried I. "and is this the employment of poets now! Do men of their exalted talents thus stoop to beggary! Can they so far disgrace their calling, as to make a vile traffic of praise for bread?"

O no, Sir, returned he, a true poet can never be so base; for wherever there is genius there is pride. The creatures I now describe are only beggars in rhyme. The real poet, as he braves every hardship for fame, so he is equally a coward to contempt, and none but those who are unworthy protection condescend to solicit it.

Having a mind too proud to stoop to such indignities, and yet a fortune too humble to hazard a second attempt for fame I was now obliged to take a middle course, and write for bread. But I was unqualified for a profession where mere industry alone was to ensure success. I could not suppress my lurking passion for applause; but usually consumed that time in efforts after excellence which takes up but little room, when it should have been more advantageously employed in the diffusive productions of fruitful mediocrity. My little piece would therefore come forth in the midst of periodical publications, unnoticed and unknown. The public were more importantly employed, than to observe the easy simplicity of my style, or the harmony of my periods. Sheet after sheet was thrown off to oblivion. My essays were buried among the essays upon liberty, eastern tales, and cures for the bite of a mad dog; while Philautos, Philalethes, Philelutheros, and Philanthropos all wrote better, because they wrote faster, than I.

Now, therefore, I began to associate with none but disappointed authors, like myself, who praised, deplored, and despised each other. The satisfaction we found in every celebrated writer's attempts, was inversely as their merits. I found that no genius in another could please me. My unfortunate paradoxes had entirely dried up that source of comfort. I could neither read nor write with satisfaction; for excellence in another was my aversion, and writing was my trade.

In the midst of these gloomy reflections, as I was one day sitting on a bench in St. James's park, a young gentleman of distinction, who had been my intimate acquaintance at the university, approached me. We saluted each other with some hesitation; he almost ashamed of being known to one who made so shabby an appearance, and I afraid of a repulse. But my suspicions soon vanished; for Ned Thornhill was at the bottom a very good-natured fellow.

My friend's first care was to alter my appearance by a fine suit of his own clothes, and then I was admitted to his table upon the footing of half-friend, half-underling. My business was to attend him at auctions, to put him in spirits when he sat for his picture, and to take the left hand in his chariot when not filled by another. Besides this, I had twenty other little employments in the family. I was to do many small things without bidding; to carry the corkscrew; to stand godfather to all the butler's children; to sing when I was bid; to be never out of humour; always to be humble, and, if I could, to be very happy.

In this honourable post, however, I was not without a rival. A captain of marines, who was formed for the place by nature, opposed me in my patron's affections.

As this gentleman made it the study of his life to be acquainted with lords, though he was dismissed from several for his stupidity, yet he found many of them who were as dull as himself, that permitted his assiduities. As flattery was his trade, he practised it with the easiest address imaginable; but it came awkward and stiff from me; and as every day my patron's desire of flattery increased, so every hour being better acquainted with his defects, I became more unwilling to give it. Thus I was once more fairly going to give up the field to the captain, when my friend found occasion for my assistance. This was nothing less than to fight a duel for him.

I undertook the affair, disarmed my antagonist, and soon after had the pleasure of finding that the fellow was only a sharper. This piece of service was repaid with the warmest professions of gratitude; but as my friend was to leave town in a few days, he knew no other method of serving me, but by recommending me to his uncle Sir William Thornhill, and another nobleman of great distinction, who enjoyed a post under the government. When he was gone, my first care was to carry his recommendatory letter to his uncle, a man whose character for every virtue was universal, yet just. I was received by his servants with the most hospitable smiles; for the looks of the domestics ever transmit their master's benevolence. Being shown into a grand apartment, where Sir William soon came to me, I delivered my message and letter, which he read, and after pausing some minutes, "Pray, Sir," cried he, "inform me what you have done for my kinsman, to deserve this warm recommendation? But I suppose, Sir, I guess your merits, you have fought for him: and so you would expect a reward from me for being the instrument of his vices. I wish, sincerely wish, that my present refusal may be some punishment for your guilt; but still more, that it may be some inducement to your repentance." — The severity of this rebuke I bore patiently, because I knew it was just.

My whole expectations now, therefore, lay in my letter to the great man. As the doors of the nobility are almost ever beset with beggars, all ready to thrust in some sly petition, I found it no easy matter to gain admittance. However, after bribing the servants with half my worldly fortune, I was at last shown into a spacious apartment, my letter being previously sent up for his lordship's inspection. During this anxious interval I had full time to look round me. Every thing was grand and of happy contrivance: the paintings, the furniture, the gildings petrified me with awe, and raised my idea of the owner. Ah, thought I to myself, how very great must the possessor of all these things be, who carries in his head the business of the state, and whose house displays half the wealth of a kingdom; sure his genius must be unfathomable! During these awful reflections I heard a step come heavily forward. Ah, this is the great man himself! No, it was only a chambermaid. Another foot was heard soon after. This must be he! No, it was only the great man's valet-de-chambre. At last his lordship actually made his appearance. "Are you," cried he, "the bearer of this here letter?" I answered with a bow. "I learn by this," continued he, "as how that" — But just at that instant a servant delivered him a card, and without taking farther notice, he went out of the room, and left me to digest my own happiness at leisure. I saw no more of him, till told by a footman that his lordship was going to his coach at the door. Down I immediately followed, and joined my voice to that of three or four more, who came, like me, to petition for favours. His lordship, however, went too fast for us, and was gaining his chariot-door with large strides, when I hallooed out to know if I was to have any reply. He was by this time got in, and muttered an answer, half of which I only heard, the other half was lost in the rattling of his chariot-wheels. I stood for some time with my neck stretched out, in the posture of one that was listening to catch the glorious sounds, till looking round me, I found myself alone at his lordship's gate.

My patience, continued my son, was now quite exhausted: stung with the thousand indignities I had met with, I was willing to cast myself away, and only wanted the gulf to receive me. I regarded myself as one of those vile things that nature designed should be thrown by into her lumber-room, there to perish in obscurity. I had still, however, half a guinea left, and of that I thought fortune herself should not deprive me: but in order to be sure of this, I was resolved to go instantly and spend it while I had it, and then trust to occurrences for the rest. As I was going along with this resolution, it happened that Mr. Crispe's office seemed invitingly open to give me a welcome reception. In this office Mr. Crispe kindly offers all his majesty's subjects a generous promise of £30 a year, for which promise all they give in return is their liberty for life, and permission to let him transport them to America as slaves. I was happy at finding a place where I could lose my fears in desperation, and entered this cell, for it had the appearance of one, with the devotion of a monastic. Here I found a number of poor creatures, all in circumstances like myself, expecting the arrival of Mr. Crispe, presenting a true epitome of English impatience. Each untractable soul at variance with fortune, wreaked her injuries on their own hearts: but Mr. Crispe at last came down, and all our murmurs were hushed. He deigned to regard me with an air of peculiar approbation, and indeed he was the first man who for a month past talked to me with smiles. After a few questions, he found I was fit for every thing in the world. He paused a while upon the properest means of providing for me, and slapping his forehead as if he had found it, assured me, that there was at that time an embassy talked of from the synod of Pensylvania to the Chickasaw Indians, and that he would use his interest to get me made secretary. I knew in my own heart that the fellow lied, and yet his promise gave me pleasure, there was something so magnificent in the sound. I fairly, therefore, divided my half guinea, one half of which went to be added to his thirty thousand pounds, and with the other half I resolved to go to the next tavern to be there more happy than he.

As I was going out with that resolution, I was met at the door by the captain of a ship, with whom I had formerly some little acquaintance, and he agreed to be my companion over a bowl of punch. As I never chose to make a secret of my circumstances, he assured me that I was upon the very point of ruin in listening to the office-keeper's promises: for that he only designed to sell me to the plantations. But, continued he, I fancy you might by a much shorter voyage, be very easily put into a genteel way of bread. Take my advice. My ship sails to-morrow for Amsterdam. What if you go in her as a passenger? The moment you land all you have to do is to teach the Dutchmen English, and I'll warrant you'll get pupils and money enough. I suppose you understand English, added he, by this time, or the deuce is in it. I confidently assured him of that: but expressed a doubt whether the Dutch would be willing to learn English. He affirmed with an oath that they were fond of it to distraction: and upon that affirmation I agreed with his proposal, and embarked the next day to teach the Dutch English in Holland. The wind was fair, our voyage short, and after having paid my passage with half my moveables, I found myself as fallen from the skies a stranger in one of the principal streets of Amsterdam. In this situation I was unwilling to let any time pass unemployed in teaching. I addressed myself, therefore, to two or three of those I met, whose appearance seemed most promising, but it was impossible to make ourselves mutually understood. It was not till this very moment I recollected, that in order to teach the Dutchmen English, it was necessary that they should first teach me Dutch. How I came to overlook so obvious an objection is to me amazing; but certain it is I overlooked it.

This scheme thus blown up, I had some thoughts of fairly shipping back to England again: but falling into company with an Irish student who was returning from Louvain, our conversation turning upon topics of literature (for by the way it may be observed that I always forgot the meanness of my circumstances when I could converse upon such subjects), from him I learned that there were not two men in his whole university who understood Greek. This amazed me. I instantly resolved to travel to Louvain, and there live by teaching Greek; and in this design I was heartened by my brother student, who threw out some hints that a fortune might be got by it.

I set boldly forward the next morning. Every day lessened the burthen of my moveables, like Aesop and his basket of bread: for I paid them for my lodgings to the Dutch as I travelled on. When I came to Louvain, I was resolved not to go sneaking to the lower professors, but openly tendered my talents to the principal himself. I went, had admittance, and offered him my service as a master of the Greek language, which I had been told was a desideratum in his university. The principal seemed at first to doubt of my abilities: but of these I offered to convince him, by turning a part of any Greek author he should fix upon into Latin. Finding me perfectly earnest in my proposal, he adressed me thus. You see me, young man, I never learned Greek, and I don't find that I have ever missed it. I have had a doctor's cap and gown without Greek; I have ten thousand florins a year without Greek: I eat heartily without Greek; and in short, continued he, as I don't know Greek, I do not believe there is any good in it.

It was now too far from home to think of returning: so I resolved to go forward. I had some knowledge of music, with a tolerable voice, and now turned what was my amusement into a present means of subsistence. I passed among the harmless peasants of Flanders, and among such of the French as were poor enough to be very merry; for I ever found them sprigthly in proportion to their wants. Whenever I approached a peasant's house towards night-fall, I played one of my most merry tunes, and that procured me not only a lodging but subsistence for the next day. I once or twice attempted to play for people of fashion: but they always thought my performance odious, and never rewarded me even with a trifle. This was to me the more extraordinary, as whenever I used in better days to play for company, when playing was my amusement, my music never failed to throw them into raptures, and the ladies especially: but as it was now my only means, it was received with contempt: a proof how ready the world is to underrate those talents by which a man is supported.

In this manner I proceeded to Paris with no design but just to look about me, and then to go forward. The people of Paris are much fonder of strangers that have money than of those that have wit. As I could not boast much of either, I was no great favourite. After walking about the town four or five days, and seeing the outsides of the best houses, I was preparing to leave this retreat of venal hospitality, when passing through one of the principal streets, whom should I meet but our cousin to whom you first recommended me. This meeting was very agreeable to me, and I believe not displeasing to him. He inquired into the nature of my journey to Paris,

and informed me of his own business there, which was to collect
pictures, medals, intaglios, and antiques of all kinds, for a gentleman
in London, who had just stept into taste and a large fortune. I was
the more surprised at seeing our cousin pitched upon for this office,
as he himself had often assured me he knew nothing of the matter. 5
Upon asking how he had been taught the art of a cognoscente so
very suddenly, he assured me that nothing was more easy. The
whole secret consisted in a strict adherence to two rules: the one
always to observe, the picture might have been better if the painter
had taken more pains; and the other, to praise the works of Pietro 10
Perugino. But, says he, as I once taught you how to be an author
in London, I'll now undertake to instruct you in the art of picture-
buying at Paris.

With this proposal I very readily closed, as it was living, and
now all my ambition was to live. I went therefore to his lodgings, 15
improved my dress by his assistance, and after some time accompanied him to auctions of pictures, where the English gentry were
expected to be purchasers. I was not a little surprised at his inti-
macy with people of the best fashion, who referred themselves to his
judgment upon every picture or medal, as to an unerring standard of 20
taste. He made very good use of my assistance upon these occasions:
for when asked his opinion, he would gravely take me aside and ask
mine, shrug, look wise, return, and assure the company that he could
give no opinion upon an affair of so much importance. Yet there was
sometimes an occasion for a more supported assurance. I remember 25
to have seen him after giving his opinion that the colouring of a
picture was not mellow enough, very deliberately take a brush with
brown varnish, that was accidentally lying by, and rub it over the
piece with great composure before all the company, and then ask if
he had not improved the tints. 30

When he had finished his commission in Paris, he left me
strongly recommended to several men of distinction, as a person very
proper for a travelling tutor; and after some time I was employed
in that capacity by a gentleman who brought his ward to Paris, in
order to set him forward on his tour through Europe. I was to be 35
the young gentleman's governor, but with a proviso, that he should
always be permitted to govern himself. My pupil in fact understood
the art of guiding in money concerns much better than I. He was
heir to a fortune of about two hundred thousand pounds, left him by
an uncle in the West Indies; and his guardians, to qualify him for 40
the management of it, had bound him apprentice to an attorney. Thus
avarice was his prevailing passion: all his questions on the road were

how money might be saved; which was the least expensive course
of travelling; whether any thing could be bought that would turn to
account when disposed of again in London. Such curiosities on the
way as could be seen for nothing he was ready enough to look at;
but if the sight of them was to be paid for, he usually asserted that
he had been told they were not worth seeing. He never paid a bill
that he would not observe how amazingly expensive travelling was,
and all this though he was not yet twenty-one. When arrived at
Leghorn, as we took a walk to look at the port and shipping, he inquired the expense of the passage by sea home to England. This he
was informed was but a trifle compared to his returning by land, he
was therefore unable to withstand the temptation: so paying me the
small part of my salary that was due, he took leave, and embarked
with only one attendant for London.

  I now therefore was left once more upon the world at large;
but then it was a thing I was used to. However, my skill in music
could avail me nothing in a country, where every peasant was a better
musician than I: but by this time I had acquired another talent which
answered my purpose as well, and this was a skill in disputation. In
all the foreign universities and convents there are upon certain days
philosophical theses maintained against every adventitious disputant;
for which, if the champion opposes with any dexterity, he can claim
a gratuity in money, a dinner, and a bed for one night. In this
manner therefore I fought my way towards England, walked along
from city to city, examined mankind more nearly, and, if I may so
express it, saw both sides of the picture. My remarks, however, are
but few: I found that monarchy was the best government for the poor
to live in, and commonwealths for the rich. I found that riches in
general were in every country another name for freedom; and that
no man is so fond of liberty himself as not to be desirous of subjecting
the will of some individuals in society to his own.

  Upon my arrival in England, I resolved to pay my respects first
to you, and then to enlist as a volunteer in the first expedition that
was going forward; but on my journey down my resolutions were
changed, by meeting an old acquaintance, who I found belonged to
a company of comedians that were going to make a summer campaign
in the country. The company seemed not much to disapprove of me
for an associate. They all, however, apprized me of the importance
of the task at which I aimed; that the public was a many-headed
monster, and that only such as had very good heads could please it:
that acting was not to be learnt in a day, and that without some
traditional shrugs which had been, on the stage, and only on the stage,

these hundred years. I could never pretend to please. The next difficulty was in fitting me with parts, as almost every character was in keeping. I was driven for some time from one character to another, till at last Horatio was fixed upon, which the presence of the present company has happily hindered me from acting. OLIVER GOLDSMITH.

22. A Meeting in the Queen's Presence.

While the rival statesmen were anxiously preparing for their approaching meeting in the Queen's presence, even Elizabeth herself was not without apprehension of what might chance from the collision of two such fiery spirits, each backed by a strong and numerous body of followers, and dividing betwixt them, either openly or in secret, the hopes and wishes of most of her court. The band of Gentlemen Pensioners were all under arms, and a reinforcement of the yeomen of the guard was brought down the Thames from London. A royal proclamation was sent forth, strictly prohibiting nobles, of whatever degree, to approach the Palace with retainers or followers, armed with short, or with long weapons; and it was even whispered, that the High Sheriff of Kent had secret instructions to have a part of the array of the county ready on the shortest notice.

The eventful hour, thus anxiously prepared for on all sides, at length approached, and, each followed by his long and glittering train of friends and followers, the rival Earls entered the palace-yard of Greenwich at noon precisely.

As if by previous arrangement, or perhaps by intimation that such was the Queen's pleasure, Sussex and his retinue came to the Palace from Deptford by water, while Leicester arrived by land; and thus they entered the court-yard from opposite sides. This trifling circumstance gave Leicester a certain ascendency in the opinion of the vulgar, the appearance of his cavalcade of mounted followers showing more numerous and more imposing than those of Sussex's party, who were necessarily upon foot. No show or sign of greeting passed between the Earls, though each looked full at the other, both expecting perhaps an exchange of courtesies, which neither was willing to commence. Almost in the minute of their arrival the castle-bell tolled, the gates of the Palace were opened, and the Earls entered, each numerously attended by such gentlemen of their train whose rank gave them that privilege. The yeomen and inferior attendants remained in the court-yard, where the opposite parties eyed each other with looks of eager hatred and scorn, as if waiting with impatience for some cause of tumult, or some apology for mutual aggression. But they were restrained by the strict commands of their leaders, and overawed, perhaps, by the presence of an armed guard of unusual strength.

In the meanwhile, the more distinguished persons of each train followed their patrons into the lofty halls and antechambers of the royal Palace, flowing on in the same current, like two streams which are compelled into the same channel, yet shun to mix their waters. The parties arranged themselves, as it were instinctively, on the different sides of the lofty apartment, and seemed eager to escape from the transient union which the narrowness of the crowded entrance had for an instant compelled them to submit to. The folding doors at the upper end of the long gallery were immediately afterwards opened, and it was announced in a whisper that the Queen was in her presence-chamber, to which these gave access. Both Earls moved slowly and stately towards the entrance; Sussex followed by Tressilian, Blount, and Raleigh; and Leicester by Varney. The pride of Leicester was obliged to give way to court-forms, and with a grave and formal inclination of the head, he paused until his rival, a peer of older creation than his own, passed before him. Sussex returned the reverence with the same formal civility, and entered the presence-room. Tressilian and Blount offered to follow him, but were not permitted, the Usher of the Black Rod alleging in excuse, that he had precise orders to look to all admissions that day. To Raleigh, who stood back on the repulse of his companions, he said, "You, Sir, may enter," and he entered accordingly.

"Follow me close, Varney," said the Earl of Leicester, who had stood aloof for a moment to mark the reception of Sussex; and, advancing to the entrance, he was about to pass on, when Varney, who was close behind him, dressed out in the utmost bravery of the day, was stopped by the usher, as Tressilian and Blount had been before him. "How is this, Master Bowyer?" said the Earl of Leicester. "Know you who I am, and that this is my friend and follower?"

"Your Lordship will pardon me," replied Bowyer, stoutly; "my orders are precise, and limit me to a strict discharge of my duty."

"Thou art a partial knave," said Leicester, the blood mounting to his face, "to do me this dishonour, when you but now admitted a follower of my Lord of Sussex."

"My lord," said Bowyer. "Master Raleigh is newly admitted a sworn servant of her Grace, and to him my orders did not apply."

"Thou art a knave — an ungrateful knave," said Leicester; "but he that hath done, can undo — thou shalt not prank thee in thy authority long!"

This threat he uttered aloud, with less than his usual policy
and discretion, and having done so, he entered the presence-chamber,
and made his reverence to the Queen, who attired with even more
than her usual splendour, and surrounded by those nobles and statesmen
whose courage and wisdom have rendered her reign immortal, stood
ready to receive the homage of her subjects. She graciously returned
the obeisance of the favourite Earl, and looked alternately at him and
at Sussex, as if about to speak, when Bowyer, a man whose spirit
could not brook the insult he had so openly received from Leicester,
in the discharge of his office, advanced with his black rod in his
hand, and knelt down before her.

"Why, how now, Bowyer;" said Elizabeth, "thy courtesy seems
strangely timed!"

"My Liege Sovereign," he said, while every courtier around
trembled at his audacity. "I come but to ask, whether, in the discharge of mine office, I am to obey your Highness' commands, or
those of the Earl of Leicester, who has publicly menaced me with
his displeasure, and treated me with disparaging terms, because I
denied entry to one of his followers, in obedience to your Grace's
precise orders?"

The spirit of Henry VIII. was instantly aroused in the bosom
of his daughter, and she turned on Leicester with a severity which
appalled him, as well as all his followers.

"God's death! my lord," such was her emphatic phrase, "what
means this? We have thought well of you, and brought you near to
our person; but it was not that you might hide the sun from our
other faithful subjects. Who gave you license to contradict our orders,
or control our officers? I will have in this court, ay, and in this
realm, but one mistress, and no master. Look to it that master Bowyer
sustains no harm for his duty to me faithfully discharged; for, as I
am a Christian woman and crowned Queen, I will hold you dearly answerable. — Go, Bowyer, you have done the part of an honest man
and a true subject. We will brook no mayor of the palace here."

Bowyer kissed the hand which she extended towards him, and
withdrew to his post, astonished at the success of his own audacity.
A smile of triumph pervaded the faction of Sussex; that of Leicester
seemed proportionally dismayed, and the favourite himself, assuming
an aspect of the deepest humility, did not even attempt a word in
his own exculpation.

He acted wisely; for it was the policy of Elizabeth to humble
not to disgrace him, and it was prudent to suffer her, without opposition or reply, to glory in the exertion of her authority. The dignity

of the Queen was gratified, and the woman began soon to feel for the mortification which she had imposed on her favourite. Her keen eye also observed the secret looks of congratulation exchanged amongst those who favoured Sussex, and it was no part of her policy to give either party a decisive triumph.

"What I say to my Lord of Leicester," she said, after a moment's pause, "I say also to you, my Lord of Sussex. You also must needs ruffle in the court of England, at the head of a faction of your own?"

"My followers, gracious Princess," said Sussex, "have indeed ruffled in your cause, in Ireland, in Scotland, and against yonder rebellious Earls in the north. I am ignorant that —"

"Do you bandy looks and words with me, my lord?" said the Queen, interrupting him; "methinks you might learn of my Lord of Leicester the modesty to be silent, at least, under our censure. I say, my lord, that my grandfather and father, in their wisdom, debarred the nobles of this civilized land from travelling with such disorderly retinues; and think you that because I wear a coif, their sceptre has in my hand been changed into a distaff? I tell you, no king in Christendom will less brook his court to be cumbered, his people oppressed, and his kingdom's peace disturbed by the arrogance of overgrown power, than she who now speaks with you. — My Lord of Leicester, and you, my Lord of Sussex, I command you both to be friends with each other: or by the crown I wear, you shall find an enemy who will be too strong for both of you!"

"Madam," said the Earl of Leicester, "you who are yourself the fountain of honour, know best what is due to mine. I place it at your disposal, and only say, that the terms on which I have stood with my Lord of Sussex have not been of my seeking; nor had he cause to think me his enemy, until he had done me gross wrong."

"For me, Madam," said the Earl of Sussex, "I cannot appeal from your sovereign pleasure: but I were well content my Lord of Leicester should say in what I have, as he terms it, wronged him, since my tongue never spoke the word that I would not willingly justify either on foot or horseback."

"And for me," said Leicester, "always under my gracious Sovereign's pleasure, my hand shall be as ready to make good my words as that of any man who ever wrote himself Ratcliffe."

"My lords," said the Queen, "these are no terms for this presence; and if you cannot keep your temper we will find means to keep both that and you close enough. Let me see you join hands, my lords, and forget your idle animosities."

The two rivals looked at each other with reluctant eyes, each unwilling to make the first advance to execute the Queen's will.

"Sussex," said Elizabeth, "I entreat — Leicester, I command you."

Yet, so were her words accented, that the entreaty sounded like command, and the command like entreaty. They remained still and stubborn, until she raised her voice to a height which argued at once impatience and absolute command.

"Sir Henry Lee," she said, to an officer in attendance, "have a guard in present readiness, and man a barge instantly. — My Lords of Sussex and Leicester, I bid you once more to join hands — and, God's death! he that refuses shall taste of our Tower fare ere he see our face again. I will lower your proud hearts ere we part, and that I promise, on the word of a Queen!"

"The prison," said Leicester, "might be borne, but to lose your Grace's presence, were to lose light and life at once. — Here, Sussex, is my hand."

"And here," said Sussex, "is mine in truth and honesty; but —"

"Nay, under favour, you shall add no more," said the Queen. "Why, this is as it should be," she added, looking on them more favourably, "and when you, the shepherds of the people, unite to protect them, it shall be well with the flock we rule over."

WALTER SCOTT.

23. The Pickwickians Shooting Partridges.

It was a fine morning — so fine that you would scarcely have believed that the few months of an English summer had yet flown by. Hedges, fields, and trees, hill and moorland, presented to the eye their ever-varying shades of deep rich green; scarce a leaf had fallen, scarce a sprinkle of yellow mingled with the hues of summer, warned you that autumn had begun. The sky was cloudless; the sun shone out bright and warm; the songs of birds, and hum of myriads of summer insects, filled the air; and the cottage gardens, crowded with flowers of every rich and beautiful tint, sparkled in the heavy dew, like beds of glittering jewels. Everything bore the stamp of summer, and none of its beautiful colours had yet faded from the die.

Such was the morning, when an open carriage, in which were three Pickwickians (Mr. Snodgrass having preferred to remain at home), Mr. Wardle, and Mr. Trundle, with Sam Weller on the box beside the driver, pulled up by a gate at the road-side, before which stood a tall, raw-boned gamekeeper, and a half-booted, leather-leggined boy; each bearing a bag of capacious dimensions, and accompanied by a brace of pointers.

"I say," whispered Mr. Winkle to Wardle, as the man let down the steps. "they don't suppose we're going to kill game enough to fill those bags, do they?"

"Fill them!" exclaimed old Wardle. "Bless you, yes! You shall fill one, and I the other; and when we've done with them, the pockets of our shooting-jackets will hold as much more."

Mr. Winkle dismounted without saying anything in reply to this observation; but he thought within himself, that if the party remained in the open air, till he had filled one of the bags, they stood a considerable chance of catching tolerable colds in the head.

The tall gamekeeper looked with some surprise from Mr. Winkle, who was holding his gun as if he wished his coat-pocket to save him the trouble of pulling the trigger, to Mr. Tupman, who was holding his, as if he were afraid of it — as there is no earthly reason to doubt that he really was.

"My friends are not much in the way of this sort of thing yet, Martin," said Wardle, noticing the look. "Live and learn, you know. They'll be good shots one of these days. I beg my friend Winkle's pardon, though; he has had some practice."

Mr. Winkle smiled feebly over his blue neckerchief in acknowledgment of the compliment, and got himself so mysteriously entangled with his gun, in his modest confusion, that if the piece had been loaded, he must inevitably have shot himself dead upon the spot.

"You mustn't handle your piece in that ere way, when you come to have the charge in it, Sir," said the tall gamekeeper gruffly, "or I'm damned if you won't make cold meat of some on us."

Mr. Winkle, thus admonished, abruptly altered its position, and in so doing, contrived to bring the barrel into pretty smart contact with Mr. Weller's head.

"Hallo!" said Sam, picking up his hat, which had been knocked off, and rubbing his temple. "Hallo, Sir! if you comes it this vay, you'll fill one o' them bags, and something to spare, at one fire."

Here the leather-leggined boy laughed very heartily, and then tried to look as if it was somebody else, whereat Mr. Winkle frowned majestically.

"Well," said old Wardle. "The sooner we're off the better. Will you join us at twelve, then, Pickwick?"

Mr. Pickwick was particularly desirous to view the sport, the more especially as he was rather anxious in respect of Mr. Winkle's life and limbs. On so inviting a morning, too, it was very tantalizing to turn back, and leave his friends to enjoy themselves. It was, therefore, with a very rueful air that he replied, —

"Why, I suppose I must."

"Ain't the gentleman a shot, Sir?" inquired the long gamekeeper.

"No," replied Wardle; "and he's lame besides."

"I should very much like to go," said Mr. Pickwick — "very much."

There was a short pause of commiseration.

"There's a barrow t'other side the hedge," said the boy. "If the gentleman's servant would wheel along the paths, he could keep nigh us, and we could lift it over the stiles and that."

"The wery thing," said Mr. Weller, who was a party interested, inasmuch as he ardently longed to see the sport. "The wery thing. Well said, Small-check; I'll have it out, in a minute."

But here a difficulty arose. The long gamekeeper resolutely protested against the introduction into a shooting-party, of a gentleman in a barrow, as a gross violation of all established rules and precedents.

It was a great objection, but not an insurmountable one. The gamekeeper having been coaxed and feed, and having, moreover, eased his mind by "punching" the head of the inventive youth who had first suggested the use of the machine, Mr. Pickwick was placed in it, and off the party set; Wardle and the long gamekeeper leading the way, and Mr. Pickwick in the barrow, propelled by Sam, bringing up the rear.

"Stop, Sam," said Mr. Pickwick when they had got half across the first field.

"What's the matter now?" said Wardle.

"I won't suffer this barrow to be moved another step," said Mr. Pickwick, resolutely, "unless Winkle carries that gun of his, in a different manner."

"How am I to carry it?" said the wretched Winkle.

"Carry it with the muzzle to the ground," replied Mr. Pickwick.

"It's so unsportsman-like," reasoned Winkle.

"I don't care whether it's unsportman-like or not," replied Mr. Pickwick, "I am not going to be shot in a wheelbarrow, for the sake of appearances, to please anybody."

"I know the gentleman'll put that ere charge into somebody afore he's done," growled the long man.

"Well, well — I don't mind", said poor Mr. Winkle, turning his gun stock uppermost; — "there."

"Anythin' for a quiet life," said Mr. Weller; and on they went again.

"Stop," said Mr. Pickwick, after they had gone a few yards further.

"What now?" said Wardle.

"That gun of Tupman's is not safe: I know it isn't," said Mr. Pickwick.

"Eh? What! not safe!" said Mr. Tupman, in a tone of great alarm.

"Not as you are carrying it," said Mr. Pickwick. "I am very sorry to make any further objection, but I cannot consent to go on, unless you carry it, as Winkle does his."

"I think you had better, Sir," said the long gamekeeper, "or you're quite as likely to lodge the charge in your own vestcoat as in anybody else's."

Mr. Tupman, with the most obliging haste, placed his piece in the position required, and the party moved on again; the two amateurs marching with reserved arms, like a couple of privates at a royal funeral.

The dogs suddenly came to a dead stop, and the party advancing stealthily a single pace, stopped too.

"What's the matter with the dogs' legs?" whispered Mr. Winkle. "How queer they're standing!"

"Hush, can't you?" replied Wardle, softly. "Don't you see, they're making a point?"

"Making a point!" said Mr. Winkle, staring about him, as if he expected to discover some particular beauty in the landscape, which the sagacious animals were calling special attention to. "Making a point! What are they pointing at?"

"Keep your eyes open," said Wardle, not heeding the question in the excitement of the moment. "Now then."

There was a sharp whirring noise, that made Mr. Winkle start back as if he had been shot himself. Bang, bang, went a couple of guns; — the smoke swept quickly away over the field, and curled into the air.

"Where are they?" said Mr. Winkle, in a state of the highest excitement, turning round and round in all directions. "Where are they? Tell me when to fire. Where are they — where are they?"

"Where are they!" said Wardle, taking up a brace of birds which the dogs had deposited at his feet. "Where are they! Why here they are."

"No, no; I mean the others," said the bewildered Winkle.

"Far enough off, by this time," replied Wardle, coolly reloading his gun.

"We shall very likely be up with another covey in five minutes," said the long gamekeeper. "If the gentleman begins to fire now, perhaps he'll just get the shot out of the barrel by the time they rise."

"Ha! ha! ha!" roared Mr. Weller.

"Sam," said Mr. Pickwick, compassionating his follower's confusion and embarrassment.

"Sir."

"Don't laugh."

"Certainly not, Sir." So, by way of indemnification, Mr. Weller contorted his features from behind the wheelbarrow, for the exclusive amusement of the boy with the leggings, who thereupon burst into a boisterous laugh, and was summarily cuffed by the long gamekeeper, who wanted a pretext to hide his own merriment.

"Bravo, old fellow!" said Wardle to Mr. Tupman; "you fired that time, at all events."

"Oh yes," replied Mr. Tupman, with conscious pride. "I let it off."

"Well done. You'll hit something next time, if you look sharp. Very easy, ain't it?"

"Yes, it's very easy," said Mr. Tupman. "How it hurts one's shoulder, though. It nearly knocked me backwards. I had no idea these small fire-arms kicked so."

"Ah," said the old gentleman, smiling: "you'll get used to it, in time. Now then — all ready — all right with the barrow there?"

"All right, Sir." replied Mr. Weller.

"Come along then."

"Hold hard, Sir," said Sam, raising the barrow.

"Aye, aye," replied Mr. Pickwick; and on they went, as briskly as need be.

"Keep that barrow back now," cried Wardle, when it had been hoisted over a stile into another field, and Mr. Pickwick had been deposited in it once more.

"All right, Sir." replied Mr. Weller, pausing.

"Now, Winkle," said the old gentleman, "follow me softly, and don't be too late this time."

"Never fear," said Mr. Winkle. "Are they pointing?"

"No, no: not now. Quietly now, quietly." On they crept, and very quietly they would have advanced, if Mr. Winkle, in the performance of some very intricate evolutions with his gun, had not accidentally fired, at the most critical moment, over the boy's head, exactly in the very spot where the tall man's brain would have been, had he been there instead.

"Why, what on earth did you do that for?" said old Wardle, as the birds flew unharmed away.

"I never saw such a gun in my life," replied poor Winkle, looking at the lock, as if that would do any good. "It goes off, of its own accord. It will do it."

"Will do it!" echoed Wardle, with something of irritation in his manner. "I wish it would kill something of its own accord."

"It'll do that afore long, Sir," observed the tall man, in a low, prophetic voice.

"What do you mean by that observation, Sir?" inquired Mr. Winkle, angrily.

"Never mind, Sir — never mind," replied the long gamekeeper: — "I've no family myself, Sir; and this here boy's mother will get something handsome from Sir Geoffrey, if he's killed on his land. Load again, Sir — load again."

"Take away his gun," cried Mr. Pickwick from the barrow, horror-stricken at the long man's dark insinuations. "Take away his gun, do you hear, somebody?"

Nobody, however, volunteered to obey the command; and Mr. Winkle, after darting a rebellious glance at Mr. Pickwick, reloaded his gun, and proceeded onwards with the rest.

We are bound, on the authority of Mr. Pickwick, to state, that Mr. Tupman's mode of proceeding evinced far more of prudence and deliberation, than that adopted by Mr. Winkle. Still, this by no means detracts from the great authority of the latter gentleman, on all matters connected with the field: because, as Mr. Pickwick beautifully observes, it has somehow or other happened, from time immemorial, that many of the best and ablest philosophers, who have been perfect lights of science in matters of theory, have been wholly unable to reduce them to practice.

Mr. Tupman's process, like many of our most sublime discoveries, was extremely simple. With the quickness and penetration of a man of genius, he had at once observed that the two great points to be attained were — first, to discharge his piece without injury to himself, and, secondly, to do so, without danger to the by-standers; — obviously, the best thing to do, after surmounting the difficulty of firing at all, was to shut his eyes firmly, and fire into the air.

On one occasion, after performing this feat, Mr. Tupman, on opening his eyes, beheld a plump partridge in the very act of falling wounded to the ground. He was just on the point of congratulating Wardle on his invariable success, when that gentleman advanced towards him, and grasped him warmly by the hand.

"Tupman," said the old gentleman, "you singled out that particular bird?"

"No," said Mr. Tupman — "no."

"You did," said Wardle. "I saw you do it — I observed you pick him out — I noticed you as you raised your piece to take aim; and I will say this, that the best shot in existence could not have done it more beautifully. You are an older hand at this, than I thought you, Tupman; — you have been out before."

It was in vain for Mr. Tupman to protest, with a smile of self-denial, that he never had. The very smile was taken as evidence to the contrary; and from that time forth, his reputation was established. It is not the only reputation that has been acquired as easily, nor are such fortunate circumstances confined to partridge-shooting.

Meanwhile, Mr. Winkle flashed, and blazed, and smoked away, without producing any material results worthy of being noted down; sometimes expending his charge in mid-air, and at others sending it skimming along so near the surface of the ground, as to place the lives of the two dogs on a rather uncertain and precarious tenure. As a display of fancy-shooting, it was extremely varied and curious; as an exhibition of firing with any precise object, it was, upon the whole, perhaps a failure. It is an established axiom, that "every bullet has its billet." If it apply in an equal degree to shots, those of Mr. Winkle were unfortunate foundlings, deprived of their natural rights, cast loose upon the world, and billeted nowhere.

"Well," said Wardle, walking up to the side of the barrow, and wiping the streams of perspiration from his jolly red face: "smoking day, isn't it?"

"It is indeed," replied Mr. Pickwick. "The sun is tremendously hot, even to me. I don't know how you must feel it."

"Why," said the old gentleman, "pretty hot. It's past twelve, though. You see that green hill there?"

"Certainly."

"That's the place where we are to lunch; and, by Jove, there's the boy with the basket, punctual as clock-work."

CHARLES DICKENS.

24. Cuff's Fight with Dobbin.

Cuff's fight with Dobbin, and the unexpected issue of that contest, will long be remembered by every man who was educated at Dr. Swishtail's famous school. The latter youth (who used to be called Heigh-ho Dobbin, Gee-ho Dobbin, and by many other names indicative of puerile contempt) was the quietest, the clumsiest, and

as it seemed, the dullest of all Dr. Swishtail's young gentlemen.
His parent was a grocer in the city: and it was bruited abroad that
he was admitted into Dr. Swishtail's academy upon what are called
"mutual principles" — that is to say, the expenses of his board and
schooling were defrayed by his father, in goods not money; and he
stood there — almost at the bottom of the school — in his scraggy
corduroys and jacket, through the seams of which his great big bones
were bursting — as the representative of so many pounds of tea,
candles, sugar, mottled-soap, plums (of which a very mild proportion
was supplied for the puddings of the establishment), and other commodities. A dreadful day it was for young Dobbin when one of the
youngsters of the school, having run into the town upon a poaching
excursion for hardbake and polonies, espied the cart of Dobbin
& Rudge, Grocers and Oilmen, Thames Street, London, at the Doctor's
door, discharging a cargo of the wares in which the firm dealt.

Young Dobbin had no peace after that. The jokes were frightful,
and merciless against him. "Hullo, Dobbin," one wag would say,
"here's good news in the paper. Sugar is rising, my boy." Another
would set a sum — "If a pound of mutton-candles cost sevenpence-
halfpenny, how much must Dobbin cost?" and a roar would follow
from all the circle of young knaves, usher and all, who rightly
considered that the selling of goods by retail is a shameful and
infamous practice, meriting the contempt and scorn of all real
gentlemen.

"Your father's only a merchant, Osborne," Dobbin said in private to the little boy who had brought down the storm upon him.
At which the latter replied haughtily, "My father's a gentleman, and
keeps his carriage;" and Mr. William Dobbin, retreated to a remote
outhouse in the play-ground, where he passed a half-holiday, in the
bitterest sadness and woe. Who amongst us is there that does not
recollect similar hours of bitter, bitter childish grief? Who feels injustice; who shrinks before a slight; who has a sense of wrong so
acute, and so glowing a gratitude for kindness, as a generous boy?

Now, William Dobbin, from an incapacity to acquire the rudiments of Latin was compelled to remain among the very last of
Doctor Swishtail's scholars, and was "taken down" continually by
little fellows with pink faces and pinafores when he marched up with
the lower form, a giant amongst them, with his downcast, stupefied
look, his dog's-eared primer, and his tight corduroys. High and low,
all made fun of him. They sewed up those corduroys, tight as they
were. They cut his bed-strings. They upset buckets and benches, so
that he might break his shins over them, which he never failed to

do. They sent him parcels, which, when opened, were found to contain the paternal soap and candles. There was no little fellow but had his jeer and joke at Dobbin: and he bore everything quite patiently, and was entirely dumb and miserable.

Cuff, on the contrary, was the great chief and dandy of the Swishtail Seminary. He smuggled wine in. He fought the town-boys. Ponies used to come for him to ride home on Saturdays. He had his top-boots in his room, in which he used to hunt in the holidays. He had a gold repeater, and took snuff like the Doctor. He had been to the Opera, and knew the merits of the principal actors, preferring Mr. Kean to Mr. Kemble. He could knock you off forty Latin verses in an hour. He could make French poetry. What else didn't he know, or couldn't he do? They said even the Doctor himself was afraid of him.

Cuff, the unquestioned king of the school, ruled over his subjects, and bullied them, with splendid superiority. This one blacked his shoes, that toasted his bread, others would fag out, and give him balls at cricket during whole summer afternoons. 'Figs' was the fellow whom he despised most, and with whom, though always abusing him, and sneering at him, he scarcely ever condescended to hold personal communication.

One day in private, the two young gentlemen had had a difference. Figs, alone, in the school-room, was blundering over a home letter: when Cuff, entering, bade him go upon some message, of which tarts were probably the subject.

"I can't," says Dobbin: "I want to finish my letter."

"You *can't*," says Mr. Cuff, laying hold of that document (in which many words were scratched out, many were misspelt, on which had been spent I don't know how much thought, and labour, and tears; for the poor fellow was writing to his mother, who was fond of him, although she was a grocer's wife, and lived in a back parlour in Thames-street), "You *can't?*" says Mr. Cuff: "I should like to know why, pray? Can't you write to old Mother Figs to-morrow?"

"Don't call names", Dobbin said, getting off the bench, very nervous.

"Well, Sir, will you go?" crowed the cock of the school.

"Put down the letter," Dobbin replied: "no gentleman readth letterth."

"Well, *now* will you go?" says the other.

"No, I won't. Don't strike, or I'll *th*mash you," roars out Dobbin, springing to a leaden inkstand, and looking so wicked, that Mr. Cuff paused, turned down his coat sleeves again, put his hands into his pockets, and walked away with a sneer. But he never meddled personally with the grocer's boy after that; though we must do him the justice to say he always spoke of Mr. Dobbin with contempt behind his back.

Some time after this interview, it happened that Mr. Cuff, on a sunshiny afternoon, was in the neighbourhood of poor William Dobbin, who was lying under a tree in the play-ground, spelling over a favourite copy of the Arabian Nights which he had — apart from the rest of the school, who were pursuing their various sports — quite lonely, and almost happy.

Well, William Dobbin had for once forgotten the world, and was away with Sindbad the Sailor in the Valley of Diamonds, or with Prince Whatdyecallem and the Fairy Peribanou in that delightful cavern where the Prince found her, and whither we should all like to make a tour; when shrill cries, as of a little fellow weeping, woke up his pleasant reverie; and, looking up, he saw Cuff before him, belabouring a little boy.

It was the lad who had peached upon him about the grocer's cart; but he bore little malice, not at least towards the young and small. "How dare you, Sir, break the bottle?" says Cuff to the little urchin, swinging a yellow cricket-stump over him.

The boy had been instructed to get over the play-ground wall (at a selected spot where the broken glass had been removed from the top, and niches made convenient in the brick); to run a quarter of a mile; to purchase a pint of rum-shrub on credit; to brave all the Doctor's outlying spies, and to clamber back into the play-ground again: during the performance of which feat, his foot had slipt, and the bottle was broken, and the shrub had been spilt, and his pantaloons had been damaged, and he appeared before his employer a perfectly guilty and trembling, though harmless, wretch.

"How dare you, Sir, break it?" says Cuff; "you blundering little thief. You drank the shrub, and now you pretend to have broken the bottle. Hold out your hand, Sir."

Down came the stump with a great heavy thump on the child's hand. A moan followed. Dobbin looked up. The Prince Peribanou had fled into the inmost cavern with Prince Ahmed: the Roc had whisked away Sindbad the Sailor out of the Valley of Diamonds, out of sight, far into the clouds: and there was every-day life before honest William; and a big boy beating a little one without cause.

"Hold out your other hand, Sir," roars Cuff to his little schoolfellow, whose face was distorted with pain. Dobbin quivered, and gathered himself up in his narrow old clothes.

"Take that, you little devil!" cried Mr. Cuff, and down came the wicket again on the child's hand. — Don't be horrified, ladies, every boy at a public school has done it. Your children will so do and be done by, in all probability. Down came the wicket again; and Dobbin started up.

I can't tell what his motive was. Torture in a public school is as much licensed as the knout in Russia. It would be ungentlemanlike (in a manner) to resist it. Perhaps Dobbin's foolish soul revolted against that exercise of tyranny: or perhaps he had a hankering feeling of revenge in his mind, and longed to measure himself against that splendid bully and tyrant, who had all the glory, pride, pomp, circumstance, banners flying, drums beating, guards saluting, in the place. Whatever may have been his incentive, however, up he sprang, and screamed out, "Hold off, Cuff; don't bully that child any more; or I'll —"

"Or you'll what?" Cuff asked in amazement at this interruption. "Hold out your hand, you little beast."

"I'll give you the worst thrashing you ever had in your life," Dobbin said, in reply to the first part of Cuff's sentence; and little Osborne, gasping and in tears, looked up with wonder and incredulity at seeing this amazing champion put up suddenly to defend him while Cuff's astonishment was scarcely less; fancy brazen Goliah when little David stepped forward and claimed a meeting! and you have the feelings of Mr. Reginald Cuff when this rencontre was proposed to him.

"After school," says he, of course: after a pause and a look, as much as to say, 'Make your will, and communicate your best wishes to your friends between this time and that.'

"As you please," Dobbin said. "You must be my bottle-holder, Osborne."

"Well, if you like," little Osborne replied; for you see his papa kept a carriage, and he was rather ashamed of his champion.

Yes, when the hour of battle came, he was almost ashamed to say, "Go it, Figs;" and not a single other boy in the place uttered that cry for the first two or three rounds of this famous combat; at the commencement of which the scientific Cuff, with a contemptuous smile on his face, and as light and as gay as if he was at a ball, planted his blows upon his adversary, and floored that unlucky champion three times running. At each fall there was a cheer; and everybody was anxious to have the honour of offering the conqueror a knee.

"What a licking I shall get when it's over," young Osborne thought, picking up his man. "You'd best give in," he said to

Dobbin; "it's only a thrashing, Figs, and you know I'm used to it." But Figs, all whose limbs were in a quiver, and whose nostrils were breathing rage, put his little bottle-holder aside, and went in for a fourth time.

As he did not in the least know how to parry the blows that were aimed at himself, and Cuff had begun the attack on the three preceding occasions, without ever allowing his enemy to strike, Figs now determined that he would commence the engagement by a charge on his own part; and accordingly, being a left-handed man, brought that arm into action, and hit out a couple of times with all his might — once at Mr. Cuff's left eye, and once on his beautiful Roman nose.

Cuff went down this time, to the astonishment of the assembly. "Well hit, by Jove," says little Osborne, with the air of a connoisseur, clapping his man on the back. "Give it him with the left, Figs, my boy."

Figs' left made terrific play during all the rest of the combat. Cuff went down every time. At the sixth round, there were almost as many fellows shouting out, "Go it, Figs," as there were youths exclaiming, "Go it, Cuff." At the twelfth round the latter champion was all abroad, as the saying is, and had lost all presence of mind and power of attack or defence. Figs, on the contrary, was as calm as a quaker. His face being quite pale, his eyes shining open, and a great cut on his under lip bleeding profusely gave this young fellow a fierce and ghastly air, which perhaps struck terror into many spectators. Nevertheless, his intrepid adversary prepared to close for the thirteenth time.

If I had the pen of a Napier, or a Bell's Life, I should like to describe this combat properly. It was the last charge of the Guard — (that is, *it would* have been, only Waterloo had not yet taken place) — it was Ney's column breasting the hill of La Haye Sainte, bristling with ten thousand bayonets, and crowned with twenty eagles — it was the shout of the beef-eating British, as leaping down the hill they rushed to hug the enemy in the savage arms of battle — in other words, Cuff coming up full of pluck, but quite reeling and groggy, the Fig-merchant put in his left as usual on his adversary's nose, and sent him down for the last time.

"I think *that* will do for him," Figs said, as his opponent dropped as neatly on the green as I have seen Jack Spot's ball plump into the pocket at billiards; and the fact is, when time was called, Mr. Reginald Cuff was not able, or did not choose, to stand up again.

And now all the boys set up such a shout for Figs as would
make you think he had been their darling champion through the
whole battle; and as absolutely brought Dr. Swishtail out of his study,
curious to know the cause of the uproar. He threatened to flog Figs
violently, of course; but Cuff, who had come to himself by this time,
and was washing his wounds, stood up and said, "It's my fault, Sir,
— not Figs' — not Dobbin's. I was bullying a little boy; and he
served me right." By which magnanimous speech he not only saved
his conqueror a whipping, but got back all his ascendancy over the
boys which his defeat had nearly cost him.   W. M. THACKERAY.

25. The Death of Warwick, "The Kingmaker".

A few minutes afterwards, Warwick and his men saw two parties of horse leave the main body — one for the right hand, one for the
left — followed by long detachments of pikes, which they protected;
and then the central array marched slowly and steadily on towards
the scanty foe. The design was obvious — to surround on all sides
the enemy, driven to its last desperate bay. But Montagu and his
brother had not been idle in the breathing pause; they had planted
the greater portion of the archers skilfully among the trees. They
had placed their pikemen on the verge of the barricades, made by
sharp stakes and fallen timber, and where their rampart was un-
guarded by the pass which had been left free for the horsemen,
Hilyard and his stoutest fellows took their post, filling the gap with
breasts of iron. And now, as with horns and clarions — with a sea
of plumes, and spears, and pennons, the multitudinous deathsmen
came on, Warwick, towering in the front, not one feather on his eagle
crest despoiled or shorn, stood, dismounted, his visor still raised, by
his renowned steed. Some of the men had by Warwick's order removed the mail from the destrier's breast; and the noble animal,
relieved from the weight, seemed as unexhausted as its rider; save
where the champed foam had bespecked his glossy hide, not a hair
was turned; and the on-guard of the Yorkists heard his fiery snort,
as they moved slowly on. This figure of horse and horseman stood
prominently forth, amidst the little band. And Lovel, riding by
Ratcliffe's side, whispered, — "Beshrew me, I would rather King
Edward had asked for mine own head, than that gallant Earl's!"
"Tush, youth," said the inexorable Ratcliffe — "I care not of what
steps the ladder of mine ambition may be made!"

While they were thus speaking, Warwick, turning to Montagu
and his knights, said, — "Our sole hope is in the courage of our men.

And, as at Touton, when I gave the throne to yon false man, I slew, with my own hand, my noble Malech, to show that on that spot I would win or die, and by that sacrifice so fired the soldiers, that we turned the day — so now — o gentlemen, in another hour ye would jeer me, for my hand fails; this hand that the poor beast hath so often fed from! — Saladin, last of thy race, serve me now in death as in life. Not for my sake, o noblest steed that ever bore a knight — not for mine this offering!" He kissed the destrier on his frontal, and Saladin, as if conscious of the coming blow, bent his proud crest humbly, and licked his lord's steel-clad hand. So associated together had been horse and horseman, that had it been a human sacrifice, the bystanders could not have been more moved. And when, covering the charger's eyes with one hand, the Earl's dagger descended, bright and rapid — a groan went through the ranks. But the effect was unspeakable! The men knew at once, that to them, and them alone, their lord entrusted his fortunes and his life — they were nerved to more than mortal daring. No escape for Warwick — why, then, in Warwick's person they lived and died! Upon foe as upon friend, the sacrifice produced all that could tend to strengthen the last refuge of despair. Even Edward, where he rode in the van, beheld and knew the meaning of the deed. Victorious Touton rushed back upon his memory with a thrill of strange terror and remorse. "He will die as he has lived," said Gloucester, with admiration. "If I live for such a field, God grant me such a death!"

As the words left the Duke's lips, and Warwick, one foot on his dumb friend's corpse, gave the mandate, a murderous discharge from the archers in the covert, rattled against the line of the Yorkists, and the foe still advancing stepped over a hundred corpses to the conflict. Despite the vast preponderance of numbers, the skill of Warwick's archers, the strength of his position, the obstacle to the cavalry made by the barricades, rendered the attack perilous in the extreme. But the orders of Edward were prompt and vigorous. He cared not for the waste of life, and as one rank fell, another rushed on. High before the barricades, stood Montagu, Warwick, and the rest of that indomitable chivalry, the flower of the ancient Norman heroism. As idly beat the waves upon a rock as the ranks of Edward upon that serried front of steel. The sun still shone in heaven, and still Edward's conquest was unassured. Nay, if Marmaduke could yet bring back, upon the rear of the foe, the troops of Somerset, Montagu and the Earl felt that the victory might be for them. And often the Earl paused, to hearken for the cry of "Somerset" on the gale, and often Montagu raised his visor to look for the banners and the spears of the Lancastrian Duke.

And ever, as the Earl listened and Montagu scanned the field, larger and larger seemed to spread the armament of Edward. The regiment which boasted the stubborn energy of Alwyn was now in movement, and, encouraged by the young Saxon's hardihood, the Londoners marched on, unawed by the massacre of their predecessors. But Alwyn, avoiding the quarter defended by the knights, defiled a little towards the left, where his quick eye, inured to the northern fogs, had detected the weakness of the barricade in the spot where Hilyard was stationed; and this pass Alwyn (discarding the bow) resolved to attempt at the point of the pike — the weapon answering to our modern bayonet. The first rush which he headed, was so impetuous as to effect an entry. The weight of the numbers behind urged on the foremost, and Hilyard had not sufficient space for the sweep of the two-handed sword which had done good work that day. On pressed the Yorkists through the pass forced by Alwyn. "Yield, thee, stout fellow," said the bold trader to Hilyard, whose dogged energy, resembling his own, moved his admiration, and in whom, by the accent in which Robin called his men he recognised a north countryman; — "Yield, and I will see that thou goest safe in life and limb — look round — ye are beaten." "Fool," answered Hilyard, setting his teeth — "the People are never beaten!" And as the words left his lips, the shot from the re-charged bombard shattered him piecemeal. "On for London, and the Crown!" cried Alwyn — "the Citizens are the people!"

At this time, through the general crowd of the Yorkists, Ratcliffe and Lovel, at the head of their appointed knights, galloped forward to accomplish their crowning mission. Behind the column which still commemorates "the great battle" of that day, stretches now a trilateral patch of pasture land, which faces a small house. At that time this space was rough forest ground, and where now, in the hedge, rise two small trees, types of the diminutive offspring of our niggard and ignoble civilization, rose then two huge oaks, coeval with the warriors of the Norman conquest. They grew close together, yet, though their roots interlaced — though their branches mingled, one had not taken nourishment from the other. They stood, equal in height and grandeur, the twin giants of the wood. Before these trees, whose ample trunks protected them from the falchions in the rear, Warwick and Montagu took their last post. In front rose, literally, mounds of the slain, whether of foe or friend; for round them to the last had gathered the brunt of war, and they towered now, almost solitary in Valour's sublime despair, amidst the wrecks of battle, and against the irresistible march of Fate. As side by side they had gained this spot, and the vulgar assailants drew back leaving the bodies of the Dead their last defence from Death, they turned their visors to each other, as for one latest farewell on earth. "Forgive me, Richard!" said Montagu — "forgive me thy death; had I not so blindly believed in Clarence's fatal order, the savage Edward had never passed alive through the pass of Pontefract." "Blame not thyself," replied Warwick. "We are but the instruments of a wiser Will. God assoil thee, brother mine. We leave this world to tyranny and vice. Christ receive our souls!" For a moment their hands clasped, and then all was grim silence.

Wide and far, behind and before in the gleam of the sun, stretched the victorious armament, and that breathing pause sufficed to show the grandeur of their resistance — the defiance of brave hearts to the brute force of the Many. Where they stood they were visible to thousands, but not a man stirred against them. The memory of Warwick's past achievements — the consciousness of his feats that day — all the splendour of his fortunes and his name, made the mean fear to strike, and the brave ashamed to murder. The gallant D'Eyncourt sprang from his steed, and advanced to the spot. His followers did the same. "Yield, my lords — yield! Ye have done all that men could do." "Yield, Montagu," whispered Warwick. "Edward can harm not thee. Life has sweets; so they say, at least." "Not with power and glory gone. We yield not, Sir Knight," answered the Marquis, in a calm tone. "Then die! and make room for the new men whom ye so have scorned!" exclaimed a fierce voice; and Ratcliffe, who had neared the spot, dismounted, and hallooed on his blood hounds.

Numbers rushed on numbers, as the fury of conflict urged on the lukewarm; Montagu was beaten to his knee — Warwick covered him with his body — a hundred axes resounded on the Earl's stooping casque — a hundred blades gleamed round the joints of his harness: — a simultaneous cry was heard; — over the mounds of the slain, through the press into the shadow of the oaks dashed Gloucester's charger. The conflict had ceased — the executioners stood mute in a half-circle. Side by side, axe and sword still griped in their iron hands, lay Montagu and Warwick. The young Duke, his visor raised, contemplated the fallen foes in silence. Then dismounting, he unbraced with his own hand the Earl's helmet. Revived for a moment by the air, the hero's eyes unclosed, his lips moved, he raised, with a feeble effort, the gory battle axe, and the armed crowd recoiled in terror. But the Earl's soul dimly conscious, and about to part, had escaped from that scene of strife - its later thoughts of wrath and vengeance — to more gentle memories, to such memories as fade the last from true and manly hearts! "Wife! — child!" murmured the Earl, indistinctly.

"Anne — Anne! — Dear ones, God comfort you!" And with these words the breath went — the head fell heavily on its mother earth — the face set, calm and undistorted, as the face of a soldier should be, when a brave death has been worthy of a brave life.

"So," muttered the dark and musing Prince, unconscious of the throng, "so perishes the Race of Iron! Low lies the last Baron who could control the throne and command the people. The Age of Force expires with knighthood and deeds of arms. And over this dead great man I see the New Cycle dawn. Happy, henceforth he who can plot, and scheme, and fawn, and smile!" Waking with a start, from his reverie, the splendid dissimulator said, as in sad reproof, — "Ye have been overhasty, knights and gentlemen. The House of York is mighty enough to have spared such noble foes. Sound trumpets! Fall in file! Way, there — way! King Edward comes! Long live the King!"

E. L. BULWER.

26. King Lear.

Lear, king of Britain, had three daughters: Gonerill, wife to the duke of Albany; Regan, wife to the duke of Cornwall; and Cordelia, a young maid, for whose love the king of France and duke of Burgundy were joint suitors, and were at this time making stay for that purpose in the court of Lear.

The old king, worn out with age and the fatigues of government, he being more than fourscore years old, determined to take no further part in state affairs, but to leave the management to younger strengths, that he might have time to prepare for death, which must at no long period ensue. With this intent he called his three daughters to him, to know from their own lips which of them loved him best, that he might part his kingdom among them in such proportions as their affection for him should seem to deserve.

Gonerill, the eldest, declared that she loved her father more than words could give out, that he was dearer to her than the light of her own eyes, dearer than life and liberty, with a deal of such professing stuff, which is easy to counterfeit where there is no real love, only a few fine words delivered with confidence being wanted in that case. The king, delighted to hear from her own mouth this assurance of her love, and thinking truly that her heart went with it, in a fit of fatherly fondness bestowed upon her and her husband one third of his ample kingdom.

Then calling to him his second daughter, he demanded what she had to say. Regan, who was made of the same hollow metal as her sister, was not a whit behind in her professions, but rather declared that what her sister had spoken came short of the love which she professed to bear for his highness; insomuch that she found all other joys dead, in comparison with the pleasure which she took in the love of her dear king and father.

Lear blessed himself in having such loving children, as he thought; and could do no less, after the handsome assurances which Regan had made, than bestow a third of his kingdom upon her and her husband, equal in size to that which he had already given away to Gonerill.

Then turning to his youngest daughter Cordelia, whom he called his joy, he asked what she had to say, thinking no doubt that she would glad his ears with the same loving speeches which her sisters had uttered, or rather that her expressions would be so much stronger than theirs, as she had always been his darling, and favoured by him above either of them. But Cordelia, disgusted with the flattery of her sisters, whose hearts she knew were far from their lips, and seeing that all their coaxing speeches were only intended to wheedle the old king out of his dominions, that they and their husbands might reign in his lifetime, made no other reply but this, — that she loved his majesty according to her duty, neither more nor less.

The king, shocked with this appearance of ingratitude in his favourite child, desired her to consider her words, and to mend her speech, lest it should mar her fortunes.

Cordelia then told her father, that he was her father, that he had given her breeding, and loved her; that she returned those duties back as was most fit, and did obey him, love him, and most honour him. But that she could not frame her mouth to such large speeches as her sisters had done, or promise to love nothing else in the world. Why had her sisters husbands, if (as they said) they had no love for anything but their father? If she should ever wed, she was sure the lord to whom she gave her hand would want half her love, half of her care and duty; she should never marry like her sisters, to love her father all.

Cordelia, who in earnest loved her old father even almost as extravagantly as her sisters pretended to do, would have plainly told him so at any other time, in more daughter-like and loving terms, and without these qualifications, which did indeed sound a little ungracious; but after the crafty flattering speeches of her sisters, which she had seen draw such extravagant rewards, she thought the handsomest thing she could do was to love and be silent. This put her affection out of suspicion of mercenary ends, and showed that she loved, but not for gain; and that her professions, the less ostentatious they were, had so much the more of truth and sincerity than her sisters'.

This plainness of speech, which Lear called pride, so enraged the old monarch — who in his best of times always showed much of spleen and rashness, and in whom the dotage incident to old age had so clouded over his reason, that he could not discern truth from flattery, nor a gay painted speech from words that came from the heart — that in a fury of resentment he retracted the third part of his kingdom which yet remained, and which he had reserved for Cordelia, and gave it away from her, sharing it equally between her two sisters and their husbands, the dukes of Albany and Cornwall, whom he now called to him, and in presence of all his courtiers bestowing a coronet between them, invested them jointly with all the power, revenue, and execution of government, only retaining to himself the name of king; all the rest of royalty he resigned; with this reservation, that himself, with a hundred knights for his attendants was to be maintained by monthly course in each of his daughters' palaces in turn.

So preposterous a disposal of his kingdom, so little guided by reason and so much by passion, filled all his courtiers with astonishment and sorrow; but none of them had the courage to interpose between this incensed king and his wrath, except the earl of Kent, who was beginning to speak a good word for Cordelia, when the passionate Lear on pain of death commanded him to desist; but the good Kent was not so to be repelled. He had been ever loyal to Lear, whom he had honoured as a king, loved as a father, followed as a master; and he had never esteemed his life further than as a pawn to wage against his royal master's enemies, nor feared to lose it when Lear's safety was the motive; nor now that Lear was most his own enemy, did this faithful servant of the king forget his old principles, but manfully opposed Lear, to do Lear good; and was unmannerly only because Lear was mad. He had been a most faithful counsellor in times past to the king, and he besought him now, that he would see with his eyes (as he had done in many weighty matters), and go by his advice still: and in his best consideration recall this hideous rashness: for he would answer with his life his judgment, that Lear's youngest daughter did not love him least, nor were those empty-hearted whose low sounds gave no token of hollowness. When power bowed to flattery, honour was bound to plainness. For Lear's threats, what could he do to him, whose life was already at his service? That should not hinder duty from speaking.

The honest freedom of this good earl of Kent only stirred up the king's wrath the more, and like a frantic patient who kills his physician, and loves his mortal disease, he banished this true servant, and allotted him but five days to make his preparations for departure, but if on the sixth his hated person was found within the realm of Britain, that moment was to be his death. And Kent bade farewell to the king, and said, that since he chose to show himself in such fashion, it was but banishment to stay there; and before he went, he recommended Cordelia to the protection of the gods, the maid who had so rightly thought, and so discreetly spoken; and only wished that her sisters' large speeches might be answered with deeds of love; and then he went as he said, to shape his old course to a new country.

The king of France and duke of Burgundy were now called in to hear the determination of Lear about his youngest daughter, and to know whether they would persist in their courtship to Cordelia, now that she was under her father's displeasure, and had no fortune but her own person to recommend her; and the duke of Burgundy declined the match, and would not take her to wife upon such conditions; but the king of France understanding what the nature of the fault had been which had lost her the love of her father, that it was only a tardiness of speech, and the not being able to frame her tongue to flattery like her sisters, took this young maid by the hand, and saying that her virtues were a dowry above a kingdom, bade Cordelia to take farewell of her sisters, and of her father, though he had been unkind, and she should go with him, and be queen of him and of fair France, and reign over fairer possessions than her sisters': and he called the duke of Burgundy in contempt a waterish duke, because his love for this young maid had in a moment run all away like water.

Then Cordelia with weeping eyes took leave of her sisters, and besought them to love their father well, and make good their professions: and they sullenly told her not to prescribe to them, for they knew their duty; but to strive to content her husband, who had taken her (as they tauntingly expressed it) at Fortune's alms. And Cordelia, with a heavy heart departed, for she knew the cunning of her sisters, and she wished her father in better hands than she was about to leave him in.

Cordelia was no sooner gone, than the devilish dispositions of her sisters began to show themselves in their true colours. Even before the expiration of the first month, which Lear was to spend by agreement with his eldest daughter Gonerill, the old king began to find out the difference between promises and performances. This wretch having got from her father all that he had to bestow, even to the giving away of the crown from off his head, began to grudge even those small remnants of royalty which the old man had reserved to himself, to please his fancy with the idea of being still a king. She could not bear to see him and his hundred knights. Every time she met her father, she put on a frowning countenance; and when the old man wanted to speak with her, she would feign sickness, or anything to be rid of the sight of him; for it was plain that she esteemed his old age a useless burden, and his attendants an unnecessary expense: not only she herself slackened in her expressions of duty to the king, but by her example, and (it is to be feared) not without her private instructions, her very servants affected to treat him with neglect, and would either refuse to obey his orders, or still more contemptuously pretend not to hear them. Lear could not but perceive this alteration in the behaviour of his daughter, but he shut his eyes against it as long as he could, as people commonly are unwilling to believe the unpleasant consequences which their own mistakes and obstinacy have brought upon them.

True love and fidelity are no more to be estranged by ill, than falsehood and hollow-heartedness can be conciliated by good usage. This eminently appears in the instance of the good earl of Kent, who, though banished by Lear, and his life made forfeit if he were found in Britain, chose to stay and abide all consequences, as long as there was a chance of his being useful to the king his master. See to what mean shifts and disguises poor loyalty is forced to submit sometimes; yet it counts nothing base or unworthy, so as it can but do service where it owes an obligation! In the disguise of a serving man, all his greatness and pomp laid aside, this good earl proffered his services to the king, who not knowing him to be Kent in that disguise, but pleased with a certain plainness, or rather bluntness in his answers, which the earl put on (so different from that smooth oily flattery which he had so much reason to be sick of, having found the effects not answerable in his daughter), a bargain was quickly struck, and Lear took Kent into his service by the name of Caius as he called himself, never suspecting him to be his once great favourite, the high and mighty earl of Kent.

This Caius quickly found means to show his fidelity and love to his royal master; for Gonerill's steward that same day behaving in a disrespectful manner to Lear, and giving him saucy looks and language, as no doubt he was secretly encouraged to do by his mistress, Caius, not enduring to hear so open an affront put upon his majesty, made no more ado but presently tripped up his heels, and laid the unmannerly slave in the kennel; for which friendly service Lear became more and more attached to him.

Nor was Kent the only friend Lear had. In his degree, and as far as so insignificant a personage could show his love, the poor fool, or jester, that had been of his palace while Lear had a palace, as it was the custom of kings and great personages at that time to keep a fool (as he was called) to make them sport after serious business: this poor fool clung to Lear after he had given away his crown, and by his witty sayings would keep up his good humour, though he could not refrain sometimes from jeering at his master for his imprudence in uncrowning himself, and giving all away to his daughters; at which time, as he rhymingly expressed it, these daughters

> For sudden joy did weep,
> And he for sorrow sung,
> That such a king should play bo-peep,
> And go the fools among.

And in such wild sayings, and scraps of songs, of which he had plenty, this pleasant honest fool poured out his heart even in the presence of Gonerill herself, in many a bitter taunt and jest which cut to the quick; such as comparing the king to the hedge-sparrow, who feeds the young of the cuckoo till they grow old enough, and then has its head bit off for its pains: and saying, that an ass may know when the cart draws the horse (meaning that Lear's daughters, that ought to go behind, now ranked before their father); and that Lear was no longer Lear, but the shadow of Lear: for which free speeches he was once or twice threatened to be whipped.

The coolness and falling off of respect which Lear had begun to perceive, were not all which this foolish fond father was to suffer from his unworthy daughter: she now plainly told him that his staying in her palace was inconvenient so long as he insisted upon keeping up an establishment of a hundred knights, that this establishment was useless and expensive, and only served to fill her court with riot and feasting; and she prayed him that he would lessen their number, and keep none but old men about him, such as himself, and fitting his age.

Lear at first could not believe his eyes or ears, nor that it was his daughter who spoke so unkindly. He could not believe that she who had received a crown from him could seek to cut off his train, and grudge him the respect due to his old age. But she persisting in her undutiful demand, the old man's rage was so excited, that he called her a detested kite, and said that she spoke an untruth; and so indeed she did, for the hundred knights were all men of choice behaviour and sobriety of manners, skilled in all particulars of duty, and not given to rioting or feasting, as she said. And he bid his horses to be prepared, for he would go to his other daughter, Regan, he and his hundred knights: and he spoke of ingratitude, and said it was a marble-hearted devil, and showed more hideous in a child than the sea-monster. And he cursed his eldest daughter Gonerill so as was terrible to hear: praying that she might never have a child, or if she had, that it might live to return that scorn and contempt upon her which she had shown to him: that she might feel how sharper than a serpent's tooth it was to have a thankless child. And Gonerill's husband, the duke of Albany, beginning to excuse himself for any share which Lear might suppose he had in the unkindness, Lear would not hear him out, but in a rage ordered his horses to be saddled, and set out with his followers for the abode of Regan, his other daughter. And Lear thought to himself how small the fault of Cordelia (if it was a fault) now appeared, in comparison with her sister's and he wept: and then he was ashamed that such a creature as Gonerill should have so much power over his manhood as to make him weep.

Regan and her husband were keeping their court in great pomp and state at their palace; and Lear dispatched his servant Caius with letters to his daughter, that she might be prepared for his reception, while he and his train followed after. But it seems that Gonerill had been beforehand with him, sending letters also to Regan, accusing her father of waywardness and ill humours, and advising her not to receive so great a train as he was bringing with him. This messenger arrived at the same time with Caius, and Caius and he met: and who should it be but Caius's old enemy the steward, whom he had formerly tripped up by the heels for his saucy behaviour to Lear. Caius not liking the fellow's look, and suspecting what he came for, began to revile him, and challenged him to fight, which the fellow refusing, Caius, in a fit of honest passion, beat him soundly, as such a mischief-maker and carrier of wicked messages deserved: which coming to the ears of Regan and her husband, they ordered Caius to be put in the stocks, though he was a messenger from the king her father, and in that character demanded the highest respect: so that the first thing the king saw when he entered the castle, was his faithful servant Caius sitting in that disgraceful situation.

This was but a bad omen of the reception which he was to expect; but a worse followed, when upon inquiry for his daughter and her husband, he was told they were weary with travelling all night, and could not see him; and when lastly, upon his insisting in a positive and angry manner to see them, they came to greet him, whom should he see in their company but the hated Gonerill, who had come to tell her own story, and set her sister against the king her father!

5   This sight much moved the old man, and still more to see Regan take her by the hand: and he asked Gonerill if she was not ashamed to look upon his old white beard. And Regan advised him to go home again with Gonerill, and live with her peaceably, dismissing half of his attendants, and to ask her forgiveness; for he
10 was old and wanted discretion, and must be ruled and led by persons that had more discretion than himself. And Lear showed how preposterous that would sound, if he were to go down on his knees, and beg of his own daughter for food and raiment, and he argued against such an unnatural dependence, declaring his resolution never to re-
15 turn with her, but to stay where he was with Regan, he and his hundred knights; for he said that she had not forgot the half of the kingdom which he had endowed her with, and that her eyes were not fierce like Gonerill's, but mild and kind. And he said that rather than return to Gonerill, with half his train cut off, he would go over
20 to France, and beg a wretched pension of the king there, who had married his youngest daughter without a portion.

    But he was mistaken in expecting kinder treatment of Regan than he had experienced from her sister Gonerill. As if willing to outdo her sister in unfilial behaviour, she declared that she thought
25 fifty knights too many to wait upon him: that five and-twenty were enough. Then Lear, nigh heart-broken, turned to Gonerill, and said that he would go back with her, for her fifty doubled five-and-twenty, and so her love was twice as much as Regan's. But Gonerill excused herself, and said, What need of so many as five-and-twenty? or even
30 ten? or five? when he might be waited upon by her servants, or her sister's servants? So these two wicked daughters, as if they strove to exceed each other in cruelty to their old father who had been so good to them, by little and little would have abated him of all his train, all respect (little enough for him that once commanded a king-
35 dom), which was left him to show that he had once been a king! Not that a splendid train is essential to happiness, but from a king to a beggar is a hard change, from commanding millions to be without one attendant: and it was the ingratitude in his daughters' denying it, more than what he would suffer by the want of it, which
40 pierced this poor king to the heart; insomuch, that with this double ill-usage, and vexation for having so foolishly given away a kingdom, his wits began to be unsettled, and while he said he knew not what,

he vowed revenge against those unnatural hags, and to make examples of them that should be a terror to the earth!

While he was thus idly threatening what his weak arm could never execute, night came on, and a loud storm of thunder and lightning with rain; and his daughters still persisting in their resolution not to admit his followers, he called for his horses, and chose rather to encounter the utmost fury of the storm abroad, than stay under the same roof with these ungrateful daughters: and they, saying that the injuries which wilful men procure to themselves are their just punishment, suffered him to go in that condition, and shut their doors upon him.

The winds were high, and the rain and storm increased, when the old man sallied forth to combat with the elements, less sharp than his daughters' unkindess. For many miles about there was scarce a bush: and there upon a heath, exposed to the fury of the storm in a dark night, did king Lear wander out, and defy the winds and the thunder: and he bid the winds to blow the earth into the sea, or swell the waves of the sea till they drowned the earth, that no token might remain of any such ungrateful animal as man. The old king was now left with no other companion than the poor fool, who still abided with him, with his merry conceits striving to outjest misfortune, saying, it was but a naughty night to swim in, and truly the king had better go in and ask his daughters' blessing.

Thus poorly accompanied, this once great monarch was found by his ever-faithful servant the good earl of Kent, now transformed to Caius, who ever followed close at his side though the king did not know him to be the earl: and he said, "Alas! sir, are you here? creatures that love night, love not such nights as these. This dreadful storm has driven the beasts to their hiding places. Man's nature cannot endure the affliction or the fear." And Lear rebuked him and said, these lesser evils were not felt, where a greater malady was fixed. When the mind is at ease, the body has leisure to be delicate; but the tempest in his mind did take all feeling else from his senses, but of that which beat at his heart. And he spoke of filial ingratitude, and said it was all one as if the mouth should tear the hand for lifting food to it; for parents were hands and food and everything to children.

But the good Caius still persisting in his entreaties that the king would not stay out in the open air, at last persuaded him to enter a little wretched hovel which stood upon the heath, where the fool first entering, suddenly ran back terrified, saying that he had seen a spirit. But upon examination this spirit proved to be nothing more than a poor Bedlam beggar, who had crept into this deserted hovel for shelter, and with his talk about devils frightened the fool, one of those poor lunatics who are either mad, or feign to be so, the better to extort charity from the compassionate country people, who go about the country, calling themselves poor Tom and poor Turlygood, saying "Who gives anything to poor Tom?" sticking pins and nails and sprigs of rosemary into their arms to make them bleed; and with such horrible actions, partly by prayers, and partly with lunatic curses, they move or terrify the ignorant country-folks into giving them alms. This poor fellow was such a one; and the king seeing him in so wretched a plight, with nothing but a blanket about his loins, could not be persuaded but that the fellow was some father who had given all away to his daughters, and brought himself to that pass: for nothing he thought could bring a man to such wretchedness but the having unkind daughters.

And from this and many such wild speeches which he uttered, the good Caius plainly perceived that he was not in his perfect mind, but his daughters' ill-usage had really made him go mad. And now the loyalty of this worthy earl of Kent showed itself in more essential services than he had hitherto found opportunity to perform. For with the assistance of some of the king's attendants who remained loyal, he had the person of his royal master removed at daybreak to the castle of Dover, where his own friends and influence, as earl of Kent, chiefly lay; and himself embarking for France, hastened to the court of Cordelia, and did there in such moving terms represent the pitiful condition of her royal father, and set out in such lively colours the inhumanity of her sisters, that this good and loving child with many tears besought the king her husband, that he would give her leave to embark for England, with a sufficient power to subdue these cruel daughters and their husbands, and restore the old king her father to his throne; which being granted, she set forth, and with a royal army landed at Dover.

Lear having by some chance escaped from the guardians whom the good earl of Kent put over him to take care of him in his lunacy, was found by some of Cordelia's train, wandering about the fields near Dover, in a pitiable condition, stark mad, and singing aloud to himself, with a crown upon his head which he had made of straw, and nettles, and other wild weeds that he had picked up in the cornfields. By the advice of the physicians, Cordelia, though earnestly desirous of seeing her father, was prevailed upon to put off the meeting, till by sleep and the operation of herbs which they gave him, he should be restored to greater composure. By the aid of these skilful physicians, to whom Cordelia promised all her gold and jewels for the recovery of the old king. Lear was soon in a condition to see his daughter.

A tender sight it was to see the meeting between this father and daughter; to see the struggles between the joy of this poor old king at beholding again his once darling child, and the shame at receiving such filial kindness from her whom he had cast off for so small a fault in his displeasure: both these passions struggling with the remains of his malady, which in his half-crazed brain sometimes made him that he scarce remembered where he was, or who it was that so kindly kissed him and spoke to him: and then he would beg the standers-by not to laugh at him, if he were mistaken in thinking this lady to be his daughter Cordelia! And then to see him fall on his knees to beg pardon of his child: and she, good lady, kneeling all the while to ask a blessing of him, and telling him that it did not become him to kneel, but it was her duty, for she was his child, his true and very child Cordelia! and she kissed him (as she said) to kiss away all her sisters' unkindness, and said that they might be ashamed of themselves, to turn their old kind father with his white beard out into the cold air, when her enemy's dog, though it had bit her (as she prettily expressed it), should have stayed by her fire such a night as that, and warmed himself. And she told her father how she had come from France with purpose to bring him assistance; and he said that she must forget and forgive, for he was old and foolish, and did not know what he did: but that to be sure she had great cause not to love him, but her sisters had none. And Cordelia said that she had no cause, no more than they had.

So we will leave this old king in the protection of this dutiful and loving child, where, by the help of sleep and medicine, she and her physicians at length succeeded in winding up the untuned and jarring senses which the cruelty of his other daughters had so violently shaken. Let us return to say a word or two about those cruel daughters.

These monsters of ingratitude, who had been so false to their old father, could not be expected to prove more faithful to their own husbands. They soon grew tired of paying even the appearance of duty and affection, and in an open way showed they had fixed their loves upon another. It happened that the object of their guilty loves was the same. It was Edmund, a natural son of the late earl of Gloucester, who by his treacheries had succeeded in disinheriting his brother Edgar, the lawful heir, from his earldom, and by his wicked practices was now earl himself; a wicked man, and a fit object for the love of such wicked creatures as Goneril and Regan. It falling out about this time that the duke of Cornwall, Regan's husband, died. Regan immediately declared her intention of wedding this earl of Gloucester, which rousing the jealousy of her sister, to whom as well as to Regan this wicked earl had at sundry times professed love, Gonerill found means to make away with her sister by poison; but being detected in her practices, and imprisoned by her husband the duke of Albany for this deed, and for her guilty passion for the earl which had come to his ears, she, in a fit of disappointed love and rage, shortly put an end to her own life. Thus the justice of Heaven at last overtook these wicked daughters.

While the eyes of all men were upon this event, admiring the justice displayed in their deserved deaths, the same eyes were suddenly taken off from this sight to admire the mysterious ways of the same power in the melancholy fate of the young and virtuous daughter, the lady Cordelia, whose good deeds did seem to deserve a more fortunate conclusion: but it is an awful truth, that innocence and piety are not always successful in this world. The forces which Gonerill and Regan had sent out under the command of the bad earl of Gloucester were victorious, and Cordelia, by the practices of this wicked earl, who did not like that any should stand between him and the throne, ended her life in prison. Thus, Heaven took this innocent lady to itself in her young years, after showing her to the world an illustrious example of filial duty. Lear did not long survive this kind child.

Before he died, the good earl of Kent, who had still attended his old master's steps from the first of his daughters' ill-usage to this sad period of his decay, tried to make him understand that it was he who had followed him under the name of Caius: but Lear's care-crazed brain at that time could not comprehend how that could be, or how Kent and Caius could be the same person: so Kent thought it needless to trouble him with explanations at such a time; and Lear soon after expiring, this faithful servant to the king, between age and grief for his old master's vexations, soon followed him to the grave.

How the judgment of Heaven overtook the bad earl of Gloucester, whose treasons were discovered, and himself slain in single combat with his brother, the lawful earl; and how Gonerill's husband, the duke of Albany, who was innocent of the death of Cordelia, and had never encouraged his lady in her wicked proceedings against her father, ascended the throne of Britain after the death of Lear, is needless here to narrate: Lear and his Three Daughters being dead, whose adventures alone concern our story.   CHARLES LAMB.

II. DESCRIPTIVE PIECES.
1. Raleigh's Two Plants.

In the reign of Queen Elizabeth, two plants were brought to England, for the first time, by Sir Walter Raleigh, both of which are now very much used — the tobacco-plant and the potato. Sir Walter had sailed across the seas to America, in search of new lands; and he brought back both these plants with him.

When he was in America, he had seen the Indians smoke, and before long he acquired the habit himself. He became extremely fond of smoking, and frequently indulged in the practice.

When he returned to England, he was sitting by the fire one day, and began to smoke. When his servant saw the smoke coming from his master's mouth, he thought that he was on fire!

But very soon the old servant got used to seeing people with smoke coming out of their mouths; and all the young nobles of the court began to smoke because Sir Walter did so.

At first, people did not like the potato at all; nobody would eat it. Yet Sir Walter told them how useful it would be. The potato, he said, could be made to grow in England. He told them that, when the corn-harvest failed — which it often used to do — people need not starve if they had plenty of potatoes.

Queen Elizabeth, who was a very clever woman, listened to what Sir Walter said, and had potatoes served up at her own table. There the grand people who dined with her majesty were obliged to eat them. But they spread a report that the potato was poisonous, because it belongs to the same order as the deadly nightshade and many other poisonous plants. So, in spite of all that the Queen could do, no one would eat potatoes, and they were left for the pigs.

The people did not find out their mistake till many years afterwards. The poor potato was despised and forgotten till the reign of the French king Louis XVI., when there lived a Frenchman who had made a study of growing plants for food. He felt sure that he could make the potato a great blessing to the country; and he began at once to try.

After a great deal of trouble he succeeded. People laughed at him at first, and would not take any notice of what he said. But he went on growing the potato till he brought it to perfection. Even then no one would have eaten it, if its part had not been taken by the king. He had large pieces of ground planted with potatoes, and went about with the flower of the potato in his button-hole.

No one dared to laugh at the king; and when he said that potatoes were to be eaten, people began to find out how good and wholesome they were. By degrees the potato was more and more liked; and now there is hardly any vegetable that is more highly esteemed. ROYAL READERS.

2. A Dreary Night at Sea.

A dark and dreary night; the people nestling in their beds or circling late about the fire; Want, colder than Charity, shivering at the street corners; church-towers humming with the faint vibration of their own tongues, but newly resting from the ghostly preachment, 'One!' The earth covered with a sable pall as for the burial of yesterday: the clumps of dark trees, its giant plumes of funeral feathers, waving sadly to and fro; all hushed, all noiseless, and in deep repose, save the swift clouds that skim across the moon, and the cautious wind, as, creeping after them upon the ground, it stops to listen, and goes rustling on, and stops again, and follows like a savage on the trail. Whither go the clouds and wind so eagerly? If like guilty spirits they repair to some dread conference with powers like themselves, in what wild region do the elements hold council, or where unbend in terrible disport? Here! Free from that cramped prison called the earth, and out upon the waste of waters. Here, roaring, raging, shrieking, howling, all night long.

Hither come the sounding voices from the caverns of the coast of that small island sleeping a thousand miles away so quietly in the midst of angry waves; and hither, to meet them, rush the blasts from unknown desert places of the world. Here, in the fury of their unchecked liberty, they storm and buffet with each other, until the sea, lashed into passion like their own, leaps up in ravings mightier than theirs, and the scene is whirling madness. On, on, on, over the countless miles of angry space, roll the long heaving billows. Mountains and caves, are here, and yet are not; for what is now the one, is now the other; then all is but a boiling heap of rushing water. Pursuit, and flight, and mad return of wave on wave, and savage struggle, ending in a spouting up of foam that whitens the black night; incessant change of place, and form, and hue; constancy in nothing but eternal strife: on, on, on, they roll, and darker grows the night, and louder howl the winds, and more clamorous and fierce become the million voices in the sea, when the wild cry goes forth upon the storm, 'A ship!'

Onward she comes, in gallant combat with the elements, her tall masts trembling, and her timbers starting on the strain; onward she comes, now high upon the curling billows, now low down in the hollows of the sea, as hiding for the moment from its fury; and every storm-voice in the air and water cries more loudly yet, 'A ship!' Still she comes striving on; and at her boldness and the spreading cry, the angry waves rise up against each other's hoary heads to look; and round about the vessel, as far as the mariners on her deck can pierce into the gloom, they press upon her, forcing each other down, and starting up, and rushing forward from afar, in dreadful curiosity. High over her they break; and round her surge and roar; and giving place to others, moaningly depart, and dash themselves to fragments in their baffled anger; still she comes onward bravely. And though the eager multitude crowd thick and fast upon her all the night, and dawn of day discovers the untiring train yet bearing down upon the ship in an eternity of troubled water, onward she comes, with dim lights burning in her hull, and people there, asleep: as if no deadly element were peering in at every seam and chink, and no drowned seaman's grave, with but a plank to cover it, were yawning in the unfathomable depths below. CHARLES DICKENS.

3. London and its Food.

If, early on a summer morning, before the smoke of countless fires had narrowed the horizon of the metropolis, a spectator were to ascend to the top of St. Paul's, and take his stand upon the balcony that with gilded rail flashes like a fringe of fire on the summit of the dome, he would see sleeping beneath his feet the greatest camp of men upon which the sun has ever risen. As far as he could distinguish by the morning light, he would behold stretched before him the mighty map of the metropolis; and could he ascend still higher, he would note the stream of life overflowing the brim of hills which enclose the basin in which it stands.

In the space swept by his vision would lie the congregated habitations of two and three-quarter millions of his species, — but how vain are figures to convey an idea of so vast a multitude! If Norway, stretching from the Frozen Ocean down to its southern extremity in the North Sea, were to summon all its people to one vast conclave, they would number little more than half the souls within the London bills of mortality! Switzerland, in her thousand valleys, could not muster such an army: and even busy Holland, within her mast-thronged harbours, humming cities, and populous plains, could barely overmatch the close-packed millions within sound of the great bell at his feet.

As the spectator gazed upon this extraordinary prospect, the first stir of the awakening city would gradually steal upon his ear. The rumbling of wheels, the clang of hammers, the clear call of the human voice, all deepening by degrees into a confused hum, would proclaim that the mighty city was once more rousing to the labour of the day; and the blue columns of smoke climbing up to heaven would intimate that the morning meal was at hand.

At such a moment the thought would naturally arise in his mind, — In what manner is such an assemblage victualled? By what complicated wheels does all the machinery move by which two and three-quarter millions of human beings sit down to their meals day by day, as regularly and quietly as though they only formed a snug little party at Lovegrove's on a summer afternoon?

As thus he mused respecting the means by which the supply and demand of so vast a multitude are brought to agree, so that every one is enabled to procure exactly what he wants, at the exact time, without loss to himself or injury to the community, thin lines of steam, sharply marked for the moment, as they advanced one after another from the horizon and converged towards him, would indicate the arrival of the great commissariat trains, stored with produce from all parts of these isles and from the adjacent continent. Could his eye distinguish in addition the fine thread of that far-spreading web which makes London the most sensitive spot on the Earth, he would be enabled to take in at a glance the two agents — Steam and Electricity — which keep the balance true between the wants and the supply of London.

The inadequacy of figures to convey a clear impression to the mind of the series of units of which the sums are composed, renders it impossible to give more than a faint idea of the enormous supplies of food required to victual the capital for a single year. But the conception may be somewhat assisted by varying the process. Country journals now and then astonish their readers by calculations to show how many times the steel pens manufactured in England would form a chain around their own little town, or how many thousand miles the matches of their local factory would extend if laid in a straight line from the centre of their market-place. Let us try our hand on the same sort of picture, and endeavour to fill the eye with a prospect that would satisfy the appetite of the far-famed Dragon of Wantley himself.

If we fix upon Hyde Park as our exhibition-ground, and pile together all the barrels of beer consumed in London in a single year, they would form a thousand columns not far short of a mile in perpendicular height.

Let us imagine ourselves on the top of this tower, and we shall have a look-out worthy of the feast we are about to summon to our feet.

Herefrom we discover the Great Northern Road, stretching far away into the length and breadth of the land. Lo! as we look, a mighty herd of oxen, with loud bellowing, is beheld approaching from the north. For miles and miles the mass of horns is conspicuous winding along the road, ten abreast; and even thus, the last animal of the herd would be seventy-two miles away, and the drover goading his shrinking flank considerably beyond Peterborough.

On the other side of the park, as the clouds of dust clear away we see the Great Western Road, as far as the eye can reach, thronged with a bleating mass of wool; and the shepherd at the end of the flock (ten abreast), and the dog that is worrying the last sheep, are just leaving the environs of Bristol, one hundred and twenty-one miles from our beer-built tower.

Along Piccadilly, Regent Street, the Strand, Fleet Street, Cheapside, and the eastward Mile End Road line, for seven and a half miles, street and causeway are thronged with calves (still ten abreast); and in the great parallel thorough-fares of Bayswater Road, Oxford Street, and Holborn, we see nothing for nine long miles but a slow-pacing, deep-grunting herd of swine.

As we watch this moving mass approaching from all points of the horizon, the air suddenly becomes dark — a black pall seems drawn over the sky — it is the great flock of birds (game, poultry, and wild-fowl) that are come up to be killed. As they fly wing to wing, and tail to beak, they form a square whose superficies is not much less than the whole enclosed portion of St. James's Park, or fifty-one acres.

No sooner does this huge flight clear away than we behold the park at our feet covered with hares and rabbits. Feeding two thousand abreast, they extend from the marble arch to the round pond in Kensington Gardens — at least a mile.

Let us now pile up all the half-quartern loaves consumed in the metropolis in the year, and we shall find they form a pyramid which measures two hundred square feet at its base, and rises into the air a height of one thousand two hundred and ninety-three feet, or nearly three times that of St. Paul's.

Turning now toward the sound of rushing waters, we find that the seven companies are filling the mains for the day. If they were allowed to flow into the area of the adjacent St. James's Park, they would in the course of the twenty-four hours flood its entire space with a depth of thirty inches of water, and the whole annual supply would be quite sufficient to submerge the City part of London (one mile square) ninety feet.

Of the fish we confess we are able to say nothing: when numbers mount to billions, the calculations become too trying to our patience. We have little doubt, however, that they would be quite sufficient to make the Serpentine one solid mass.

Of ham and bacon, again, preserved meats, and all the countless comestibles, we have taken no account; and, in truth, they are little more to the great mass than the ducks and geese were to Sancho Panza's celebrated mess — "the skimmings of the pot".

The railways having poured this enormous amount of food into the metropolis, as the main arteries feed the human body, it is distributed by the various dealers into every quarter of the town: first into the wholesale markets, or great centres; then into the sub-centres, or retail-shops; and lastly into the moving centres, or barrows of the hawkers.

By this means nourishment is poured into every corner of the town, and the community at large is supplied as effectually as are the countless tissues of the human body by the infinitely divided net-work of capillary vessels. These food distributors amount to about 100,000. Among them are no less than 7000 grocers, nearly 10,000 bakers, and 7000 butchers.   ROYAL READERS.

4. OLD ENGLISH LIFE.
I. Life in Saxon England.

When the sun rose on Old England, its faint red light stirred every sleeper from the sack of straw, which formed the only bed of the age. Springing from this rustling couch, and casting off the coarse sheeting and coverlets of skin, the subjects of King Alfred donned the day's dress. Men wore linen or woollen tunics, which reached to the knee; and, over these, long fur-lined cloaks, fastened with a brooch of ivory or gold. Strips of cloth or leather, bandaged crosswise from the ankle to the knee over red and blue stockings; and black, pointed shoes, slit along the instep almost to the toes, and fastened with two thongs, completed the costume of an Anglo-Saxon gentleman. The ladies, wrapping a veil of silk or linen upon their delicate curls, laced a loose-flowing gown over a tight-sleeved bodice, and pinned the graceful folds of their mantles with golden butterflies and other tasteful trinkets.

The breakfast hour in Old England was nine o'clock. This meal consisted probably of bread, meat, and ale, but was a lighter repast than that taken when the hurry of the day lay behind. It was eaten often in the bower. Between breakfast and noon-meat at three lay the most active period of the day. Let me picture a few scenes in Old English life, as displayed in the chief occupations of the time.

Leaving the ladies of his household to linger among the roses and lilies of their gardens, or to ply their embroidering needles in some cool recess of the orchard, festooned with broad vine leaves and scented with the smell of apples, the earl or thane went out to the porch of his dwelling, and, sitting there upon a fixed throne, gave alms to a horde of beggars, or presided over the assembly of the local court.

Autumn brought delightful days to the royal and noble sportsmen of Old England. Galloping down from his home, perched, as were all great English houses, on the crest of a commanding hill, the earl, with all care or thought of work flung aside, dashed with his couples of deep-chested Welsh hounds into the glades of a neighbouring forest, already touched with the red and gold of September.

Gaily through the shadowy avenues rang the music of the horns, startling red deer and wild boars from their coverts in the brushwood. Away after the dogs, maddened by a fresh scent, goes the gallant hunt — past swine-herds with their goads, driving vast herds of pigs into the dales, where beech-mast and acorns lie thick upon the ground — past wood-cutters, hewing fuel for the castle fire, or munching their scanty meal of oaten bread about noon; nor is bridle drawn until the game, antlered or tusked, has rushed into the strong nets spread by attendants at some pass among the trees.

Hawking long held the place of our modern shooting. Even the grave and business-like Alfred devoted his pen to this enticing subject. And we can well understand the high spirits and merry talk of a hawking party, cantering over rustling leaves, all white and crisp with an October frost, on their way to the reedy mere, where they made sure of abundant game. On each rider's wrist sat a hooded falcon, caught young, perhaps in a dark pine-wood of Norway, and carefully trained by the falconer, who was no unimportant official in an Old English establishment.

Arrived at the water, the party broke into sets; and as the blue heron rose on his heavy wing, or a noisy splashing flight of ducks sprang from their watery rest, the hood was removed, and the game shown to the sharp-eyed bird, which, soaring loose into the air from the up-flung wrist, cleft his way in pursuit with rapid pinion, rose above the doomed quarry, and descending with a sudden swoop, struck fatal talons and yet more fatal beak into its back and head, and bore it dead to the ground. A sharp gallop over the broken surface had meantime brought the sportsman up in time to save the game, and restore the red-beaked victor to his hood and perch.

But hunting and hawking were the pastimes of the rich. While fat deer fell under the hunter's dart, and blue feathers strewed the banks of lake and river, the smith hammered red iron on his ringing anvil — the carpenter cut planks for the mead-bench or the bower-wall, or shaped cart-wheels and plough-handles for the labours of the farm — the shoemaker, who also tanned leather and fashioned harness, plied his busy knife and needle — the furrier prepared skins for the lining of stately robes — and in every cloister monks, deep in the mysteries of the furnace, the graving-tool, the paint-brush, and a score of similar instruments, manufactured the best bells, crucifixes, jewelry, and stained glass then to be found in the land.

The Old English farmers were rather graziers than tillers of the soil. Sheep for their wool, swine for their flesh, kine for their beef and hides, dotted the pastures and grubbed in the forests near every steading. But there was agriculture too. A picture of an Old English farm-house would present, though of course in ruder form, many features of its modern English successor. Amid fields, often bought for four sheep an acre, and scantily manured with marl after the old British fashion, stood a timbered house, flanked by a farm-yard full of ox-stalls and stocked with geese and fowl. A few bee-hives — the islands of the sugar-cane not being yet discovered — suggested a mead-cask always well filled, and a good supply of sweetmeats for the board; while an orchard, thick with laden boughs, supplied pears and apples, nuts and almonds, and in some districts figs and grapes.

From the illustrations of an Old English manuscript we know something of the year's farm-work. January saw the wheel of the iron plough drawn down the brown furrows by its four oxen, harnessed with twisted willow ropes or thongs of thick whale-skin. They dug their vineyards in February, their gardens in March. In April, when seed-time was past, they took their ease over horns of ale. May prepared for the shearing of the wool. June saw the sickles in the wheat; July heard the axe among the trees. In August barley was mown with scythes. In September and October hounds and hawks engrossed every day of good weather. Round November fires farming implements were mended or renewed; and the whirling flail, beating the grain from its husk, beat also December chills from the swiftly-running blood. We find in the threshing scene a steward, who stands keeping count, by notches on a stick, of the full baskets of winnowed grain which are pouring into the granary.

Ships came from the Continent to Old England, laden with furs and silks, gems and gold, rich dresses, wine, oil, and ivory: bearing back, most probably, blood-horses, wool for the looms of Flanders, and in earlier times English slaves for the markets of Aix-la-Chapelle and Rome. The backward condition of trade may be judged from a law which enacted that no bargain should be made except in open court, in presence of the sheriff, the mass-priest, or the lord of the manor.

Merchants, travelling in bands for safety, and carrying their own tents, passed round the different country towns at certain times, when holiday was kept and village sports filled the green with noisy mirth. The wives and daughters of Old English cottages loved bright ribbons and showy trinkets, after the fashion of their sex. So while Gurth was wrestling on the grass, or grinning at the antics of the dancing bear, Githa was investing her long-hoarded silver pennies in some strings of coloured beads or an ivory comb.

Close to the merchant or pedler (if we give him the name which best expresses to modern ears the habit of his life) stood an attendant with a pair of scales, ready to weigh the money in case of any considerable sale. Slaves and cattle formed, in early times in England, a common medium of exchange. Whenever gold shone in the merchant's sack, it was chiefly the Byzantine gold solidus, shortly called Byzant, worth something more than nine of our shillings. Silver Byzants, worth two shillings, also passed current; and in earlier times Roman money, stamped with the heads of emperors, found its way into English purses.

By the English in olden times a journey was never undertaken for mere pleasure, for many perils beset the way. The rich went short journeys in heavy waggons, longer journeys on horseback — the ladies riding on side-saddles as at present. But most travelling was performed afoot. Horsemen carried spears, for defence against robbers or wild beasts; pedestrians held a stout oak staff, which did double work in aiding and in defending the traveller. The stirrup was of an odd triangular shape, the spur a simple spike. A cover wrapped the head, and a mantle the body of the traveller. That they sometimes carried umbrellas we know; but these were probably very rare, being confined, like gloves, to the very highest class.

Ale-houses, in which too much time was spent, abounded in the towns; but in country districts inns were scarce. There were indeed places, like an Eastern caravansary, where travellers, carrying their own provisions, found a refuge from wind and rain by night within bare stone walls: the patched-up ruins, perhaps, of an old Roman villa or barrack, which afforded a cheerless shelter to the weary, dripping band. But the hospitality of the Old English folk, implanted both by custom and by law — not after the narrow modern fashion of entertaining friends, who give parties in return, but the welcoming to bed and board of all comers, known and unknown — caused the lack of inns to be scarcely felt, except in the wilder districts of the land.

No sooner did a stranger show his face at the iron-banded door of an Old English dwelling than water was brought to wash his hands and feet: and when he had deposited his arms with the keeper of the door, he took his place at the board among the family and friends of the host. For two nights no question pried into his business or his name: after that time the host became responsible for his character. There were few solitary wayfarers; for the very fact of being alone excited suspicion, and exposed the traveller to the risk of being arrested, or perhaps slain, as a thief.

The central picture in Old English life — the great event of the day — was Noon-meat, or dinner in the great hall. A little before three, the chief and all his household, with any stray guests who might have dropped in, met in the hall, which stood in the centre of its encircling bowers — the principal apartment of every Old English house. Clouds of wood-smoke, rolling up from a fire which blazed in the middle of the floor, blackened the carved and gilded rafters of the arched roof before it found its way out of the hole above, which did duty as a chimney.

Tapestries of purple dye, or glowing with variegated pictures of saints and heroes, hung, or, if the day was stormy, flapped upon the chinky walls. In palaces and in earls' mansions coloured tiles, wrought like Roman tesserae into a mosaic, formed a clean and pretty pavement: but the common flooring of the time was of clay, baked dry with the heat of winter evenings and summer noons. The only articles of furniture always in the hall were wooden benches: some of which, especially the high settle or seat of the chieftain, boasted cushions, or at least a rug.

While the hungry crowd, fresh from woodland and furrow, were lounging near the fire or hanging up their weapons on the pegs and hooks that jutted from the wall, a number of slaves, dragging in a long, flat, heavy board, placed it on movable legs, and spread on its upper half a handsome cloth. Then were arranged with other utensils for the meal some flattish dishes, baskets of ash-wood for holding bread, a scanty sprinkling of steel knives shaped like our modern razors, platters of wood, and bowls for the universal broth.

The ceremony of "laying the board", as the Old English phrased it, being completed, the work of demolition began. Great round cakes of bread — huge junks of boiled bacon — vast rolls of broiled eel — cups of milk — horns of ale — wedges of cheese — lumps of salt butter — and smoking piles of cabbages and beans, melted like magic from the board under the united attack of greasy fingers and grinding jaws. Kneeling slaves offered to the lord and his honoured guests long skewers or spits, on which steaks of beef or venison smoked and sputtered, ready for the hacking blade.

Poultry, too, and game of every variety, filled the spaces of the upper board; but, except naked bones, the crowd of loaf-eaters, as Old English domestics were suggestively called, saw little of these daintier kinds of food. Nor did they much care, if to their innumerable hunches of bread they could add enough pig to appease their hunger. Hounds, sitting eager-eyed by their masters, snapped with sudden jaws at scraps of fat flung to them, or retired into private life below the board with some sweet bone that fortune sent them.

With the washing of hands, performed for the honoured occupants of the high settle by officious slaves, the solid part of the banquet ended. The board was then dragged out of the hall: the loaf-eaters slunk away to have a nap in the byre, or sat drowsily in corners of the hall: and the drinking began. During the progress of the meal, Welsh ale had flowed freely in horns or vessels of twisted glass. Mead, and in very grand houses wine, now began to circle in goblets of gold and silver, or of wood inlaid with those precious metals.

Most of the Old English drinking-glasses had rounded bottoms, like our soda-water bottles, so that they could not stand upon the table — a little thing, which then as in later times suggested hard drinking and unceasing rounds. Two attendants, one to pour out the liquor, and the other to hand the cups, waited on the carousers, from whose company the ladies of the household soon withdrew. The clinking of cups together, certain words of pledge, and a kiss, opened the revel.

In humbler houses, story-telling and songs, sung to the music of the harp by each guest in turn, formed the principal amusement of the drinking-bout. But in great halls, the music of the harp — which, under the poetic name of "glee-wood", was the national instrument — of fiddles played with bow or finger, of trumpets, pipes, flutes, and horns, filled the hot and smoky air with a clamour of

sweet sounds. The solo of the ancient *scóp* or maker, who struck his
five stringed harp in praise of old Teutonic heroes, was exchanged
in later days for the performances of the glee-man, who played on
many instruments, danced with violent and often comical gestures,
5 tossed knives and balls into the air, and did other wondrous feats of
jugglery.

Meantime the music and the mead did their work upon maddened brains: the revelry grew louder; riddles, which had flown thick
around the board at first, gave place to banter, taunts, and fierce
10 boasts of prowess; angry eyes gleamed defiance ; and it was well if
in the morning the household slaves had not to wash blood-stains
from the pavement of the hall, or in the still night, when the drunken
brawlers lay stupid on the floor, to drag a dead man from the red
plash in which he lay.

15 From the reek and riot of the hall the ladies escaped to the
bower, where they reigned supreme. There, in the earlier part of the
day, they had arrayed themselves in their bright-coloured robes,
plying tweezers and crisping-irons on their yellow hair, and often
heightening the blush that Nature gave them with a shade of rouge.
20 There, too, they used to scold and beat their female slaves, with a
violence which said more for their strength of lung and muscle than
for the gentleness of their womanhood.

When their needles were fairly set agoing upon those pieces of
delicate embroidery, known and prized over all Europe as "English
25 work", some gentlemen dropped in, perhaps harp in hand, to chat
and play for their amusement, or to engage in games of hazard and
skill, which seem to have resembled modern dice and chess. When
in later days supper came into fashion, the round table of the bower
was usually spread for *Evening-food*, as this meal was called. And
30 not long afterwards, those bags of straw, from which they sprang at
sunrise, received for another night their human burden, worn out with
the labours and the revels of the day.

II. Life in Norman England.

The tall frowning keep and solid walls of the great stone
35 castles, in which the Norman barons lived, betokened an age of
violence and suspicion. Beauty gave way to the needs of safety.
Girdled with its green and slimy ditch, round the inner edge of
which ran a parapeted wall pierced along the top with shot-holes,
stood the buildings, spreading often over many acres.

40 If an enemy managed to cross the moat and force the gateway,
in spite of a portcullis crashing from above, and melted lead pouring

in burning streams from the perforated top of the rounded arch, but little of his work was yet done; for the keep lifted its huge angular block of masonry within the inner bailey or court-yard, and from the narrow chinks in its ten-foot wall rained a sharp incessant shower of arrows, sweeping all approaches to the high and narrow stair, by which alone access could be had to its interior.

These loop-holes were the only windows, except in the topmost story, where the chieftain, like a vulture in his rocky nest, watched all the surrounding country. The day of splendid oriels had not yet come in castle architecture.

Thus a baron in his keep could defy, and often did defy, the king upon his throne. Under his roof, eating daily at his board, lived a throng of armed retainers; and around his castle lay farms tilled by martial franklins, who at his call laid aside their implements of husbandry, took up the sword and spear, which they could wield with equal skill, and marched beneath his banner to the war.

With robe ungirt and head uncovered each tenant had done homage and sworn an oath of fealty, placing his joined hands between those of the sitting baron, and humbly saying as he knelt, "I become your man from this day forward, of life and limb and of earthly worship; and unto you I shall be true and faithful, and bear to you faith for the tenements that I claim to hold of you, saving the faith that I owe unto our sovereign lord the king." A kiss from the baron completed the ceremony.

The furniture of a Norman keep was not unlike that of an English house. There was richer ornament — more elaborate carving. A faldstool, the original of our arm-chair, spread its drapery and cushions for the chieftain in his lounging moods. His bed now boasted curtains and a roof, although, like the English lord, he still lay only upon straw. Chimneys tunnelled the thick walls, and the cupboards glittered with glass and silver. Horn lanterns and the old spiked candlesticks lit up his evening hours, when the chess-board arrayed its clumsy men, carved out of walrus-tusk, then commonly called whale's-bone. But the baron had an unpleasant trick of breaking the chess-board on his opponent's head, when he found himself checkmated; which somewhat marred said opponent's enjoyment of the game. Dice of horn and bone emptied many a purse in Norman England. Tables and draughts were also sometimes played.

Dances and music whiled away the long winter nights; and on summer evenings the castle court-yards resounded with the noise of foot-ball, kayles (a sort of ninepins), wrestling, boxing, leaping, and the fierce joys of the bull-bait. But out of doors, when no fighting was on hand, the hound, the hawk, and the lance attracted the best energies and skill of the Norman gentleman.

Rousing the forest-game with dogs, they shot at it with barbed and feathered arrows. A field of ripening corn never turned the chase aside: it was one privilege of a feudal baron to ride as he pleased over his tenants' crops, and another to quarter his insolent hunting-train in the farm-houses which pleased him best! The elaborate details of woodcraft became an important part of a noble boy's education; for the numerous bugle calls and the scientific dissection of a dead stag took many seasons to learn.

After the Conquest, to kill a deer or own a hawk came more than ever to be regarded as the special privilege of the aristocracy. The hawk, daintily dressed as befitted the companion of nobility, with his head wrapped in an embroidered hood, and a peal of silver bells tinkling from his rough legs, sat in state, bound with leathern jesses to the wrist, which was protected by a thick glove. The ladies and the clergy loved him. By many a mere the abbots ambled on their ponies over the swampy soil, and sweet shrill voices cheered the long-winged hawk, as he darted off in pursuit of the soaring quarry.

The author of "Ivanhoe", and kindred pens, have made the tournament a picture familiar to all readers of romance. It therefore needs no long description here. It was held in honour of some great event — a coronation, wedding, or victory. Having practised well during squirehood at the *quintain*, the knight, clad in full armour, with visor barred and the colours of his lady on crest and scarf, rode into the lists, for which some level green was chosen and surrounded with a palisade.

For days before, his shield had been hanging in a neighbouring church, as a sign of his intention to compete in this great game of chivalry. If any stain lay on his knighthood, a lady, by touching the suspended shield with a wand, could debar him from a share in the jousting. And if, when he had entered the lists, he was rude to a lady, or broke in any way the etiquette of the tilt-yard, he was beaten from the lists with the ashwood lances of the knights.

The simple joust was the shock of two knights, who galloped with levelled spears at each other, aiming at breast or head, with the object either of unhorsing the antagonist, or, if he sat his charger well, of splintering the lance upon his helmet or his shield. The mellay hurled together, at the dropping of the prince's baton, two parties of knights, who hacked away at each other with axe and mace and sword, often gashing limbs and breaking bones in the wild excitement

of the fray. Bright eyes glanced from the surrounding galleries upon
the brutal sport; and when the victor, with broken plume, and dusty,
battered, red-splashed armour, dragged his weary or wounded limbs
to the footstool of the beauty who presided as Queen over the festival,
her white hands decorated him with the meed of his achievements.

The Normans probably dined at nine in the morning. When
they rose they took a light meal; and ate something also after their
day's work, immediately before going to bed. Goose and garlic formed
a favourite dish. Their cookery was more elaborate, and, in comparison, more delicate, than the preparations for an English feed;
but the character for temperance, which they brought with them from
the Continent, soon vanished.

The poorer classes hardly ever ate flesh, living principally on
bread, butter, and cheese; — a social fact which seems to underlie
that usage of our tongue by which the living animals in field or stall
bore English names — ox, sheep, calf, pig, deer; while their flesh,
promoted to Norman dishes, rejoiced in names of French origin —
beef, mutton, veal, pork, venison. Round cakes, piously marked with
a cross, piled the tables, on which pastry of various kinds also
appeared. In good houses cups of glass held the wine, which was borne
from the cellar below in jugs.

Squatted around the door or on the stair leading to the Norman
dining-hall, which was often on an upper floor, was a crowd of
beggars or lickers, who grew so insolent in the days of Rufus, that
ushers, armed with rods, were posted outside to beat back the noisy
throng, who thought little of snatching the dishes as the cooks carried them to table.

The juggler, who under the Normans filled the place of the
English glee-man, tumbled, sang, and balanced knives in the hall; or
out in the bailey of an afternoon displayed the acquirements of his
trained monkey or bear. The fool, too, clad in coloured patch-work,
cracked his ribald jokes and shook his cap and bells at the elbow
of roaring barons, when the board was spread and the circles of
the wine began.

While knights hunted in the greenwood or tilted in the lists,
and jugglers tumbled in the noisy hall, the monk in the quiet Scriptorium compiled chronicles of passing events, copied valuable manuscripts, and painted rich borders and brilliant initials on every page.
These illuminations form a valuable set of materials for our pictures
of life in the Middle Ages.

Monasteries served many useful purposes at the time of which
I write. Besides their manifest value as centres of study and literary

work, they gave alms to the poor, a supper and a bed to travellers; their tenants were better off and better treated than the tenants of the nobles; the monks could store grain, grow apples, and cultivate their flower-beds with little risk of injury, from war, because they had spiritual thunders at their call, which awed even the most reckless of the soldiery into a respect for sacred property.

Splendid structures those monasteries generally were, since that vivid taste for architecture which the Norman possessed in a high degree, and which could not find room for its display in the naked strength of the solid keep, lavished its entire energy and grace upon buildings lying in the safe shadow of the Cross. Nor was architectural taste the only reason for their magnificence. Since they were nearly all erected as offerings to Heaven, the religion of the age impelled the pious builders to spare no cost in decorating the exterior with fret-work and sculpture of Caen stone, the interior with gilded cornices and windows of painted glass.

As schools, too, the monasteries did no trifling service to society in the Middle Ages. In addition to their influence as great centres of learning, English law had enjoined every mass-priest to keep a school in his parish church, where all the young committed to his care might be instructed. This custom continued long after the Norman Conquest. In the Trinity College Psalter we have a picture of a Norman school, where the pupils sit in a circular row around the master as he lectures to them from a long roll of manuscript. Two writers sit by the desk, busy with copies resembling that which the teacher holds.

The youth of the middle classes, destined for the cloister or the merchant's stall, chiefly thronged these schools. The aristocracy cared little for book-learning. Very few indeed of the barons could read or write. But all could ride, fence, tilt, play, and carve extremely well; for to these accomplishments many years of pagehood and squirehood were given.

The only Norman coin we have is the silver penny. Round half-pence and farthings were probably issued. As in Old English days, the gold was foreign. In the reign of the Conqueror, and for some time afterwards, tax-collectors and merchants reckoned money after the English fashion.   ROYAL READERS.

5. The England of Shakespeare.

The England of Shakespeare would have sorely puzzled the modern statistician. The facts of the Elizabethan age which can be expressed in tables of figures are very mean and paltry. Omitting

Ireland and Scotland, the population of the country was not greater than the present population of London. The land was fertile, but it was imperfectly cultivated. There were no very large towns to act as reservoirs of national feeling, to warn an erring monarch, and to sustain a vacillating government. London and Bristol, Norwich and York, Plymouth and Coventry were separated by long reaches of wild land and bad roads. They were practically as far apart as Paris and Madrid, Berlin and Vienna, Rome and Athens are at the present day. The construction of one of our monster ironclads would have absorbed the annual national revenue of those times.

The nobles were still rich and powerful, the middle classes were rising into prominence, the common people were scattered and poor. The army, when called into existence, was a medley of military survivals. Billmen and archers, pikemen and harquebusiers, some in armour and others in stuff tunics, shouldered each other in the national array. The navy was scanty and ill-manned: the vessels hardly equal to our medium-sized coasters; the sailors armed, for the most part, with bows and arrows; the cannon of primitive construction and of short range. The fame of the country had suffered in the contraction of its Continental power. Its enemies were numerous. The Pope was threatening. France doubtful, Spain hostile. Ireland always in rebellion, the Scotch troublesome and intriguing. The country was divided by religious faction, trade languished. The destinies of the nation were in the hands of a woman who had many whims, many wooers, and more personal favourites than were good for her peace of mind or the contentment of her people.

The something statistics could not completely show, even if they tabulated the men of mark in politics, literature, and science, was the character of the people. "Walled towns, stored arsenals and armouries, goodly races of horses, elephants, ordnance, artillery, and the like — all this," said Lord Bacon, "is but a sheep in a lion's skin except the breed and disposition of the people be stout and warlike." The Elizabethan Englishmen were noted for their personal stoutness and hardihood. Their pluck was undoubted. "As fierce as an Englishman" was a French proverb. The Dutch thought them lazy and given to spectacle; they were "fond of great ear-filling noises, such as cannon-firing, drum-beating, and bellringing." "Handsome and well-shaped," according to Paul Hentzner, the German, they were also "stout-hearted, vehement, eager, cruel in war, zealous in attack, little fearing death; not revengeful, but fickle, presumptuous, rash, boastful, deceitful; very suspicious, especially of strangers." Evidently a people capable of great things, but not yet appraised at their true value, or shaped with the lineaments of a settled and solid character. They had yet to show "the mettle of their pasture," in battle and adventure, on sea and land, in literature and the arts.

But how the time and the land ever came to produce William Shakespeare will always be somewhat of a marvel. Shakespeare's father was a yeoman, and anything but a man of marked culture. Splendid opportunities, rare teachers, enthusiastic companions will sometimes kindle the flame that flashes into genius. Until he had become known as a poet, and his character was set, Shakespeare had none of these. A great man will sometimes be the receptive pupil of another, who may be too infirm, too roughly-nurtured, to convey his message to the world. Shakespeare had no such advantage. He lived amongst men whose fame was already half established, and yet thrust himself easily over their heads and shoulders. Other men have left behind them diaries, letters, memoirs. Shakespeare lives in his works. His age is there; his secret is there.

Sometimes the man makes the age, and at others the age creates the man. No one has yet contended that Shakespeare made his age, but perhaps we do not understand as clearly as we might the part played by the age in limning and moulding him. He was not its creature, and yet the features of the age have left their impress on everything he wrote. His dramas and comedies seem to have been written in the street and the public tavern rather than in the closet, so rich are they in contemporary references, in slang expressions, sly hits, snatches of ballads, descriptions of living characters, and all the wit and humour of the time. A description of his age is therefore an essential part of any estimate of the man. To know the surroundings of a man is to come so much nearer to the man himself, to see things with his eyes, and almost to touch that untold life which throbs within and behind his works, like the inner brightness that seems ever glowing from beneath the surface of the purest marble.

It is not enough to chat about his birth and marriage, the dates of his works and the number of his rhymed lines. Nor is it very helpful to narrate the full story of the age, as it is found in histories and Court biographies. We may understand all that touched Queen Elizabeth, or King James, and yet be as far off as ever from living in their England, from striking hands with Shakespeare and looking into his serene brown eyes. E. GOADBY.

6. Performance of a Play in the 16th Century.

Within the theatre a miscellaneous crowd assembled. Most commonly the performance began at three o'clock and lasted from two

to three hours. In the public theatres the centre of the building was
open to the sky and without seats, only the stage and the gallery
being roofed, and admission to the open space, or "yard," cost from
one penny or twopence to sixpence, while as much as a shilling, two
shillings, or half-a-crown was given to obtain a place in the best
parts of the house. The private theatres were fully roofed, and during
a performance the interior was lit with torches. Upon the rush strewn
stage sat young gallants, who drank and smoked and joked while
they waited for the appearance of the black-robed Prologue. Below,
apprentices, tradesmen, sailors, and low women crushed and swayed,
cracked nuts, and fought for bitten apples. If ladies appeared in the
"rooms," or boxes, it was considered correct that they should conceal
their faces behind masks. In due time a flourish of trumpets announced that the play was to begin, and a flag was hung out from
the top of the building. Upon the trumpet's third sounding the prologue
was delivered, the curtain divided and drew back, and the actors
were discovered. They appeared in costumes which were often costly,
but which made slight pretension to historical propriety. The female
parts were played by boys or young men. Of movable scenery there
was none. The stage was hung with arras, and overhead a blue canopy represented "the heavens." Sometimes when a tragedy was to
be enacted the stage-hangings were black. At the back of the stage
was a balcony which served for many purposes: it was inner room,
upper room, window, balcony, battlements, hill-side, Mount Olympus,
any place in fact which was supposed to be separated from and above
the scene of the main action. Here Juliet appeared to Romeo, and
probably here the play-king and play-queen in Hamlet enacted their
parts. A change of scene was indicated by some suggestive piece o
stage furniture — a bed to signify a bed-chamber: a table with
pens upon it to signify a counting-house; or, more simply, a board
bearing in large letters the name of the place intended was brough
upon the stage. While the play was going forward the clown would
amuse the occupants of the yard — the "groundlings," as they were
called — with extempore joking, not set down by the poet. Between
the acts there was dancing and singing, and at the end of the play
the clown put the audience into good humour before they separated,
with a jig, that is, a farcical song accompanied by dancing and the
music of his pipe or tabor. Sometimes a short epilogue was delivered.
Finally the actors knelt and offered up a prayer for the Queen.

EDWARD DOWDEN.

7. English Life in the 18th Century.

Besides the slowness, the risk, and the cost of travelling, which might tend to diminish the journeys to London in that age, the country gentlemen were also in some measure kept away by their estrangement from the two first princes of the House of Hanover. Not a few who had been loyal subjects of Queen Anne disliked the reign of her German cousins, and began to cast a wistful look towards her nearer kindred beyond the sea. Without partaking, or desiring to partake, the Jacobite designs, they would at least, while giving in due form "the King," as their first toast after dinner, make a motion with the glass to pass it on the other side of the water-decanter which stood before them, and imply or speak the words, "over the water." They would revile all adherents of the Court as "a parcel of Roundheads and Hanover Rats." Roundhead, as is well known, was the by-word first applied to the Calvinistic preachers in the Civil Wars, from the close-cropped hair which they affected as distinguished from the flowing curls of the Cavaliers. The second phrase was of far more recent origin. It so chanced that not long after the accession of the House of Hanover, some of the brown, that is the German or Norway rats, were first brought over to this country (in some timber as is said); and being much stronger than the black, or till then the common rats, they in many places quite extirpated the latter. The word (both the noun and the verb to rat) was first as we have seen, levelled at the converts to the government of George the First, but has by degrees obtained a wider meaning and come to be applied to any sudden and mercenary change in politics.

While we may reject in all the more essential features such gross caricatures as those of Squire Western and Parson Trulliber, we yet cannot deny that many both of the country gentlemen and clergy in that age showed signs of a much neglected education. For this both our Universities, but Oxford principally, must be blamed. "I have heard," says Dr. Swift, "more than one or two persons of high rank declare they could learn nothing more at Oxford and Cambridge than to drink ale and smoke tobacco; wherein I firmly believed them, and could have added some hundred examples from my own observations in one of these Universities," — meaning that of Oxford. At Cambridge such men as Professor Saunderson had kept up the flame, worthily maintaining her high mathematical renown. But even there it is plain, from the letters of Gray, how little taste for poetry and literature lingered in her ancient halls. Oxford, on the other hand, so justly famed both before that age and after it, had then sunk down to the lowest pitch of dullness and neglect. Gibbon tells us of his tutor at Magdalen College, that this gentleman well remembered he had a salary to receive, and only forgot he had a duty to perform. The future historian was never once summoned to attend even the ceremony of a lecture, and in the course of one winter might make unreproved, in the midst of term, a tour to Bath, a visit into Buckinghamshire, and a few excursions to London. We may incline to suspect the testimony of the sceptic against any place of Christian education, but we shall find it confirmed in its full extent by so excellent and so eminent a member of our Church as Dr. Johnson. Here is his own account of his outset at Pembroke College. "The first day after I came I waited on my tutor Mr. Jordan, and then stayed away four. On the sixth Mr. Jordan asked me why I had not attended. I answered, I had been sliding in Christ Church meadow." This apology appears to have been given without the least compunction, and received without the least reproof.

It is painful to read such charges against a University so rich in her foundations, so historic in her fame, and standing once more high in the respect of those who have been trained within her walls. But the case is even worse, if possible, when we come to her system of Degrees. In granting these, the Laudian Statutes still in name and theory prevailed. But in practice there appeared a degree of laxity which, were the subject less important, would be wholly ludicrous. Lord Eldon, then Mr. John Scott of University College, and who passed the Schools in February, 1770, gave the following account of them: "An examination for a Degree at Oxford was in my time a farce. I was examined in Hebrew, and in History. 'What is the Hebrew for the place of a skull?' I replied, 'Golgatha.' 'Who founded University College?' I stated (though, by the way, the point is sometimes doubted), that King Alfred founded it. 'Very well, Sir', said the Examiner, 'you are competent for your Degree!'" Similar to this is the description in 1780 by the Rev. Vicesimus Knox: "The Masters take a most solemn oath that they will examine properly and impartially. Dreadful as all this appears, there is always found to be more of appearance in it than reality, for the greatest dunce usually gets his Testimonium signed with as much ease and credit as the finest genius. . . . . The Statutes require that he should translate familiar English phrases into Latin. And now is the time when the Masters show their wit and jocularity. I have known the questions on this occasion to consist of an inquiry into the pedigree of a racehorse!" The Commissioners of 1850, who quote these testimonies, add that at the time in question the Examiners were chosen by the candidate himself from among his friends, and that he was expected to provide a dinner for them after the examination was over. Oaths upon this subject, as upon most others, proved to be no safeguard. Oaths at Oxford were habitually taken because the law required them, and habitually disregarded, because their fulfilment had become impossible in some cases, and inconvenient in many more.

From this ignominious state the studies of the University were not rescued till the commencement of the present century. In 1800 a new Statute was passed, chiefly, it is said, at the instance of Dr. Eveleigh, Provost of Oriel, which reformed the whole system of Examination and awarded honours to the ablest candidates. By another Statute, in 1807, a further great improvement was effected. A division then was made between the Classical and the Mathematical Schools, and the first who attained the highest rank in each was a future Prime Minister, — Sir Robert Peel.

The remissness of the tutors at Oxford and at Cambridge led, of course, to other neglects of duty in those whom they had failed to teach. Such neglects were only too apparent in the Church of England of that age.

Among the laity, as might have been expected, a corresponding neglect of Church ordinances was too often found. Bishop Newton cites it as a most signal and unusual instance of religious duty, that Mr. George Grenville "regularly attended the service of the Church every Sunday morning, even while he was in the highest offices." Not only was Sunday the common day for Cabinet Councils and Cabinet dinners, but the very hours of its morning service were frequently appointed for political interviews and conferences. It is gratifying to reflect, how clear and constant since that time has been the improvement on such points. The Lord Lieutenant, and for very many former years the representative, of one of the Midland shires, has told me that when he came of age there were only two landed gentlemen in his county who had family prayers, whilst at present, as he believes, there are scarcely two that have not.

The Dissenters of that age, or some of them, might have more zeal, but had even less of learning. In some cases we find their deficiencies acknowledged by themselves. Here is one entry from the Minutes of the Methodist Conference, in May 1765. "Do not our people in general talk too much, and read too little? They do."

Besides such ill practices as drinking and gaming, we may further ascribe to that age not merely a more frequent breach of moral obligations, but also, even where no fault of conduct is imputed, a want of moral refinement.

Although in the last century the common level of female education was undoubtedly less high than now, there seems some ground to conjecture that then a greater number of ladies studied the dead languages.

We may picture to ourselves, as an instance, Lady Mary Wortley Montagu in her girlhood, seated in "the little parlour" which she has described at Thoresby, and with the old oaks of the forest full in view, but relinquishing a summer stroll beneath them to con over the Latin version of Epictetus, and to render it in English, while Bishop Burnet, by her side, smiled on her young endeavours, and directed them.

Yet her learning never caused Lady Mary to contemn the pursuits more especially allotted to her sex; on the contrary, we find her say, in one of her later letters, while treating of her granddaughter's education, "I think it as scandalous for a woman not to know how to use a needle, as for a man not to know how to use a sword."

It may be worthy of note, that in the earlier part of the last century, a young lady whose education was completed was addressed in the same form as if already married. As she was a "spinster" by law, so was she a "mistress" by courtesy. Thus, for example, Lady Mary Wortley Montagu directs her letters for the maiden sister of her husband, to Mrs., instead of Miss, Wortley. This peculiarity is the more remarkable, since, at a shortly previous period, the very opposite, at least among certain classes, prevailed in France. As an instance, we may observe, in the "Impromptu de Versailles", that the wife of the greatest genius for comedy of modern times, bore the title, not of Madame, but of Mademoiselle, Molière.

A greater contrast can scarcely be conceived than between the dresses of the present day and those in vogue a hundred or a hundred and fifty years ago. Even with the aid of Kneller's pictures we can scarcely bring to our mind's eye our grandmothers in their hoops and hair-powder, or our grandfathers with their huge periwigs and their clumsy shoes, with buckles at their feet and at their knees, with rich velvet for their morning attire, and always with a sword at their side. A gold snuff-box took the present place of a cigar-case, and a gold-headed cane the present place of a switch. So high were the heels then commonly worn, that Governor Pitt was enabled, in travelling, to conceal in a cavity which he had formed in one of them the great diamond which he had brought from the East Indies. Towards the time of the American War the ladies adopted a new and strange head-dress, building up their hair into a most lofty tower or pinnacle, until the head, with its adjuncts, came to be almost a fourth of the whole figure. Several varieties of this extravagant fashion may be traced in the engravings of that day. "I have just had my hair dressed," writes Miss Burney's Evelina. "You cannot think how oddly my head feels; full of powder and black pins, and a great cushion on the top of it!" Towards the time, however, of the Peace of 1783, there began to spread among both sexes a taste for greater plainess and simplicity of attire. This taste, like most others on this subject, appears to have come from France, and to have proceeded, in some degree, from the precept and example of Rousseau. But America also, it is said, gave an impulse in the same direction. Wraxall — for his authority, though slight, may suffice for such matters as these — complains, towards the year 1781, that Mr. Fox, who in early youth paid great attention to his dress, had grown wholly to neglect it. "He constantly, or at least usually, wore in the House of Commons, a blue frock coat and a buff waistcoat, neither of which seemed, in general, new, and both sometimes appeared to be thread-bare. Nor ought it to be forgotten that these colours then constituted the distinguishing badge or uniform of Washington and the American insurgents." Yet here I cannot but suspect some misrepresentation of the motive. It is hard to believe, even of the most vehement days of party-spirit, that any Englishman could avowedly assume, in the House of Commons, the colours of those who, even though on the most righteous grounds, bore arms against England; and I should be willing to take in preference any other explanation that can be plausibly alleged.

By the influence, then, in some measure perhaps of both America and France, velvet coats and embroidered stomachers were, by degrees, relinquished. Swords were no longer invariably worn by every one who claimed to be of gentle birth or breeding. They were first reserved for evening suits, and finally consigned as at present to Court dresses. Nevertheless, several years were needed ere this change was fully wrought. In Guy Mannering, where the author refers to the end of the American War, he observes of morning suits that "though the custom of wearing swords by persons out of uniform had been gradually becoming obsolete, it was not yet so totally forgotten as to occasion any particular remark towards those who chose to adhere to it." Thus it may be difficult to fix the precise period of this change. But no one, on reflection, will deny its real importance. To wear a sword had been, until then, the distinguishing mark of a gentleman or officer. It formed a line of demarcation between these classes and the rest of the community, it implied some-

thing of deference in the last, and something of "knightliness", as
Spenser terms it, in the former. Immediately after the cessation of
this ancient usage, we find Burke lamenting that the age of chivalry
was gone. Yet, although there was, or in theory at least there might
be, some advantage in this outward sign of the feelings and the duties comprehended in the name of Gentleman, we must own that it
was balanced by other evils, and especially by the greater frequency
of duels it produced. Where both parties wore their swords, there
was a constant temptation to draw and use them in any sudden
quarrel. I may allege as a fair example the case, in 1765, of
Mr. Chaworth and his country neighbour, Lord Byron, the grand-uncle
and predecessor of the poet. These gentlemen had been dining together at the Nottinghamshire Club, which was held once a month
at a tavern in Pall Mall. A discussion arose as to the comparative
merits of their manors in point of game, and Mr. Chaworth was at
length provoked into declaring that if it were not for Sir Charles
Sedley's care and his own, Lord Byron would not have a hare on his
estate. Upon this they withdrew to another room lighted by a single
tallow-candle, where they drew their swords and fought, and where
Mr. Chaworth was killed. Lord Byron was brought to trial before
his Peers, and found guilty of Manslaughter only.

LORD STANHOPE.

8. The Black Diamonds of England.

The history and adventures of the "great diamonds" of Eastern,
Northern, Southern, and Western potentates, have been often chro-
nicled: their several values have been estimated at hundreds of
thousands, and at millions: but not a syllable has ever been breathed of
their utility. The reason is obvious: these magnificent diamonds are
of no practical use at all, being purely ornamental luxuries. Now,
it has occurred to us that the diamonds indigenous to England, are
the converse of these brilliant usurpers of the chief fame of the
nether earth (to say nothing of the vainglories on the upper surface)
being black, instead of prismatic white; opaque, instead of trans-
picuous: and in place of deriving a fictitious and fluctuating value
from scarcity and ornamental beauty, deriving their value from the
realities of their surpassing utility and great abundance. They certainly make no very striking figure in the ball-room dress of prince
or princess: but it is their destiny and office to carry comfort to the
poor man's home, as well as to the mansion of the rich; they are
not to be looked upon as treasures of beauty, they are to be shovelled
out and burnt; they are not the bright emblems of no change and

no activity, but like heralds, sent from the depths of night, where Nature works her secret wonders, to advance those sciences and industrial arts which are equally the consequence and the re-acting cause of the progress of humanity.

The use of coals has now extended, not only over the civilised world, but in its potent form of steam has reached most of the remoter regions. From Suez to Singapore are steam vessels in course of passage, and the line is carried to Australia. The American locomotives have made their way to the shores of the Pacific, their vessels carry onward the traffic to China and the Indian Islands from the east: "and thus," as writes a learned critic, discoursing of the virtues of steam coal, "complete the circuit of the globe." Whereby, "a steam voyage round the world is so practicable, that the merchant and tourist may make the circuit within a year, and yet have time enough to see and learn much at many of the principal stations on his way."

All rightful honour, then, to these priceless Diamonds — whether they be black spirits, or furnace-white, flame-red spirits, or ashy-grey — whether cannel coal and caking coal — cherry coal and stone-coal — whether any of the forty kinds of Newcastle coal, or any of the seventy species of the great family, from the highest class of the bituminous, down to the one degree above old coke.

HOUSEHOLD WORDS.

9. The Development of London.

Londoners of to-day, and more than Londoners, are easily amused by recollections of the Town as it was once. In the time of the Black Prince, for example, when its west end was formed by Holborn Bars and the Temple gate, that gate was not the Temple Bar as we now see it: but consisted of two rough pillars of stone supporting iron chains; which at sunset were stretched accross the roadway to keep out intruders. The Strand on one side of the City, and Whitechapel on the other, were country highroads, with pretty hedgerows, and trees. London Bridge was thickly studded with wooden tenements on either side, beetling over the coping and peeping into the dark muddy stream below. The Lord Mayor lived in the middle house upon the bridge; and a terrible gate at the Southwark end bristled with iron spikes intended for the accommodation of the heads of traitors.

It certainly is not easy to imagine city boys going out birdnesting between Temple Bar and Charing Cross — a country village then, half-way to the remote hamlet of Westminster; nor can one readily picture London damsels gathering primroses or violets on the site of Exeter Hall, or sitting to rest on the green sward where Drury Lane Theatre now stands. Marylebone was then a famous hunting-ground, whither ambassadors and foreigners of distinction were taken to enjoy the finest sport that Middlesex afforded.

In those days a few noblemen's mansions alone stood in solitary grandeur westward of Temple Bar, dotted along the banks of the Thames. The City was the whole of London. It seems strange in these later days to read with how much magnificence a Spanish ambassador dwelt in a fine mansion in Petticoat Lane; but Petticoat Lane had sweeter environs at that time than it has now.

When, shortly after the battle of Poitiers, great festivities took place within the City, amongst other brave doings, was the entertainment given by one Picard, a wealthy citizen, to four monarchs, the kings of England, Cyprus, France, and Scotland; the two latter being prisoners. The dinner hour of the nobility was then nine in the morning; supper being served at five, and the bedtime not later than nine or ten. The captive monarchs had not a great distance to journey to that City feast: only from the Savoy Palace, formerly the residence of John of Gaunt, "time-honoured Lancaster," to Cheapside; whilst the British sovereign, sojourning within the Tower, had a still shorter ride. The royal wardrobe was then kept in a house from which the present Wardrobe Street derived its name, and the Exchequer was situated at the west end of Poultry.

The inhabitants of London did not amount to a hundred thousand at the time of the Reformation, and there was neither any necessity nor desire to pass beyond the City limits, until the reign of Elizabeth. Of the domestic architecture previous to that time there is scarcely any specimen existing now in London. Bricks were introduced in the middle of the fifteenth century; but it was not until after the great fire that the use of them became general. The nobility and gentry were content to dwell in houses of the rudest form and the commonest materials, and trod earthen floors scattered over with green rushes. Queen Elizabeth herself dwelt in a house of timber, lath, and plaster. Yet monarchs and citizens enjoyed themselves after their own way. We read of rare festivities, for example, at the castle or palace of the Earl of Warwick the king-maker, now covered by Warwick Lane, that adjoins Newgate Market. Baynard's Castle too, was the scene of not a little gaiety; and, if all be true that we find told in musty chronicles, its regal and ducal tenants were not always in bed by nine. This once royal residence stood where one now finds the City Flour Mills at the base of Dowgate Hill.

The first great causes of the westward growth of the metropolis, which began in Elizabeth's time, were the increasing population, and the growing value of ground within the City walls. Noblemen not only found themselves being built in by warehouses and shops, but perceived that the spacious grounds by which their mansions were surrounded, would fetch high prices if sold in building lots. Fine sites for new dwellings were to be had westward of Temple Bar. The city palaces, therefore, being made over to wealthy citizens, the aristocracy began to move in the direction of the Strand, Lincoln's Inn Fields, then Whetstone Park, Westminster, and St. Martin's. Sir Francis Walsingham and the Earl of Essex bade adieu to their lordly mansions in Seething Lane, Tower Street; the Earl of Essex going to the Strand. From princely dwellings on the site of the present East India House in Leadenhall Street a whole covey of the nobility had taken flight towards the western suburbs. Amongst them were the Cravens, the Nevills, the Burleighs, the Zouches, and other aristocratic families of note. His grace of Suffolk became sick of the city during the reign of Edward the Sixth, and bade adieu for ever to his palace in the Minories. This neighbourhood, however, boasted of some noble denizens even as late as in the reign of Charles the First, when we find Earl Rivers resident in Savage Gardens, bringing the fashionable world to his stately saloons east of Grace-church Street.

In Elizabeth's reign the migration to the suburbs began, as we have already said, but her majesty and her ministers, when they beheld mansions and shops rising in rapid succession to the westward of Temple Bar, feared it would not only be difficult to govern and preserve order in so large a metropolis as they seemed likely to have, but actually impossible to provide all the inhabitants with a sufficiency of food and fuel! Accordingly a proclamation was issued, prohibiting any further extension of the City, under pain of imprisonment for two years. This edict was null. The growth was natural, and was not to be stopped. King James in like manner, would have stopped the progress of house-building; but he found himself unable to do more than issue useless proclamations.

The first house erected in Piccadilly was the mansion built by Lord Burlington, then in the midst of fields and lanes. It is said that when the king asked the owner why he preferred living so far from London, he replied that he wished for solitude and repose; and felt certain that he had found a place where no one could build near him. But if the aristocracy and some trades-people showed so strong a desire to quit the City, too much of the outward pressure must not be ascribed to the want of building space within the City walls;

for we know that, not long before the time when Burlington House
was built, there were gardens and fields between Shoe Lane and
Chancery Lane. One objection made against the City was the smoke.
Both before and after the time of the Commonwealth, there were
many and loud complaints against the intolerable smoke of the City,
which is described by the writers of the day as driving out the
aristocracy. What our forefathers would have thought of the cloud
under which we now are living, may be judged from the fact that
at the time when "the sulphur fumes of the new fuel, called coal,"
first aroused their fears for their own health, London contained no more
than a hundred and thirty thousand people.

By the end of the reign of Charles the Second, nearly all the
nobility had left the City, and had taken up their abode along the
banks of the Thames, between Temple Bar and Westminster, in the
then rising neighbourhood of St. James's, or in some of the new and
fashionable squares of Lincoln's Inn, Covent Garden, Leicester, or
Soho. The first square known in this country was that of Covent
Garden, built by Inigo Jones: a church and two piazzas forming
three sides, whilst the fourth was the wall of the Duke of Bedford's
garden, situated between Covent Garden and the Strand. One or two
others followed: and after many years, Bloomsbury Square was
visited by strangers, as one of the wonders of the day.

Before the Fire of London, Paternoster Row, instead of being
a great publishers' mart, was the Regent Street of the fashionable
world; there the most costly embroidery, the most delicate lace-work
and the richest silks were to be purchased; and so thronged was
this favoured spot with the carriages and chairs of the nobility, that
it was often found a difficult matter to force a way through the gay
crowd. The tradesmen of course followed the nobility in their migration westward; and we find the great silkmen, mercers, and lacemen
of the day, soon afterwards established in Ludgate Street, and in
Henrietta Street, and Bedford Street adjoining Covent Garden.

After the aristocracy of rank was gone westward, there was an
aristocracy of wealth which still clung to the City. The bankers,
merchants, manufacturers, and tradesmen of the east had it all to
themselves within the City walls, and how they were lodged, and how
they fared, may be gathered by a peep at the stately red brick edi-
fices, with massive fronts, and capacious warm interiors which still
abound within the city. One has but to look into one or two of these
noble dwellings long since converted to commercial uses, to understand how grandly our City ancestors of the eighteenth century maintained their state whilst yet Clapham and Tulse Hill were not;

when Regent's Park existed but as an extensive dairy farm; and Tyburn was a village known best as Jack Ketch's place of business.

The reign of George the Third, extended over half a century, may be named as a distinct era in the great movement westward. Oppressed by the growing population of the City many of the upper rank of merchants betook themselves to the spots chosen by the aristocracy. The noblemen of Soho Square or Bloomsbury — finding themselves cheek by jowl with bankers, brewers, and African merchants — took alarm, and began to move still farther westward.

Then arose Portland Place, and Portman Square, and indeed most of the streets and places to the westward of Hanover Square as far as Hyde Park. The nobles of the City rapidly filled up the vacant ground in Russel and Bloomsbury Squares, and similar localities. At this period the custom began of affixing name plates to house-doors, and the names of streets to corners. These were improvements; but streets were wretchedly paved with footways scarcely above the road: the lighting was very bad: and, in some of the best squares, which now are adorned with gardens, there stood heaps of filth and rubbish. The connexions between the heart of London and the suburbs were of the worst kind, and the roads to Hoxton and Clerkenwell were impassable after dusk — dangerous even in the daytime — on account of the highwaymen by which they were infested. HOUSEHOLD WORDS.

10. FROM "THE SKETCH-BOOK".
1. Rural Life in England.

Oh! friendly to the best pursuits of man,
Friendly to thought, to virtue, and to peace,
Domestic life in rural pleasure passed. *Cowper.*

The stranger who would form a correct opinion of the English character, must not confine his observations to the metropolis. He must go forth into the country; he must sojourn in villages and hamlets; he must visit castles, farm-houses, cottages; he must wander through parks and gardens; along hedges and green lanes; he must loiter about country churches; attend wakes and fairs, and other rural festivals; and cope with the people in all their conditions, and all their habits and humours.

In some countries the large cities absorb the wealth and fashion of the nation; they are the only fixed abodes of elegant and intelligent society, and the country is inhabited almost entirely by boorish peasantry. In England, on the contrary, the metropolis is a mere gathering place, or general rendezvous, of the polite classes, where

they devote a small portion of the year to a hurry of gaiety and
dissipation, and having indulged this carnival, return again to the
apparently more congenial habits of rural life. The various orders of
society are therefore diffused over the whole surface of the kingdom,
and the most retired neighbourhoods afford specimens of the different ranks.

The English, in fact, are strongly gifted with the rural feeling.
They possess a quick sensibility to the beauties of nature, and a
keen relish for the pleasures and employments of the country. This
passion seems inherent in them. Even the inhabitants of cities, born
and brought up among brick walls and bustling streets, enter with
facility into rural habits, and evince a turn for rural occupation. The
merchant has his snug retreat in the vicinity of the metropolis,
where he often displays as much pride and zeal in the cultivation of
his flower-garden, and the maturing of his fruits, as he does in the
conduct of his business, and the success of his commercial enterprises. Even those less fortunate individuals, who are doomed to pass
their lives in the midst of din and traffic, contrive to have something
that shall remind them of the green aspect of nature. In the most
dark and dingy quarters of the city, the drawing-room window resembles frequently a bank of flowers; every spot capable of vegetation has its grass-plot and flower-bed; and every square its mimic
park, laid out with picturesque taste, and gleaming with refreshing
verdure.

Those who see the Englishman only in town, are apt to form
an unfavourable opinion of his social character. He is either absorbed
in business, or distracted by the thousand engagements that dissipate time, thought, and feeling, in this huge metropolis. He has,
therefore, too commonly a look of hurry and abstraction. Wherever
he happens to be, he is on the point of going somewhere else; at
the moment he is talking on one subject, his mind is wandering to
another; and while paying a friendly visit, he is calculating how he
shall economize time so as to pay the other visits allotted to the
morning. An immense metropolis like London is calculated to make
men selfish and uninteresting. In their casual and transient meetings,
they can but deal briefly in commonplaces. They present but the cold
superficies of character — its rich and genial qualities have no time
to be warmed into a flow.

It is in the country that the Englishman gives scope to his
natural feelings. He breaks loose gladly from the cold formalities and
negative civilities of town; throws off his habits of shy reserve, and
becomes joyous and free-hearted. He manages to collect round him

all the conveniences and elegancies of polite life, and to banish its restraints. His country-seat abounds with every requisite, either for studious retirement, tasteful gratification, or rural exercise. Books, paintings, music, horses, dogs, and sporting implements of all kinds, are at hand. He puts no constraint, either upon his guests or himself, but in the true spirit of hospitality provides the means of enjoyment, and leaves every one to partake according to his inclination.

The taste of the English in the cultivation of land, and in what is called landscape gardening, is unrivalled. They have studied nature intently, and discover an exquisite sense of her beautiful forms and harmonious combinations. Those charms, which in other countries she lavishes in wild solitudes, are here assembled round the haunts of domestic life. They seem to have caught her coy and furtive graces, and spread them, like witchery, about their rural abodes.

Nothing can be more imposing than the magnificence of English park scenery. Vast lawns that extend like sheets of vivid green, with here and there clumps of gigantic trees, heaping up rich piles of foliage. The solemn pomp of groves and woodland glades, with the deer trooping in silent herds across them; the hare, bounding away to the covert; or the pheasant, suddenly bursting upon the wing. The brook, taught to wind in the most natural meanderings, or expand into a glassy lake — the sequestered pool, reflecting the quivering trees, with the yellow leaf sleeping on its bosom, and the trout roaming fearlessly about its limpid waters; while some rustic temple or sylvan statue, grown green and dank with age, gives an air of classic sanctity to the seclusion.

These are but a few of the features of park scenery; but what most delights me, is the creative talent with which the English decorate the unostentatious abodes of middle life. The rudest habitation, the most unpromising and scanty portion of land, in the hands of an Englishman of taste, becomes a little paradise. With a nicely discriminating eye, he seizes at once upon its capabilities, and pictures in his mind the future landscape. The sterile spot grows into loveliness under his hand; and yet the operations of art which produce the effect are scarcely to be perceived. The cherishing and training of some trees; the cautious pruning of others; the nice distribution of flowers and plants of tender and graceful foliage; the introduction of a green slope of a velvet turf; the partial opening to a peep of blue distance, or silver gleam of water: all these are managed with a delicate tact, a pervading, yet quiet assiduity, like the magic touching with which a painter finishes up a favourite picture.

The residence of people of fortune and refinement in the country has diffused a degree of taste and elegance in rural economy, that descends to the lowest class. The very labourer, with his thatched cottage and narrow slip of ground, attends to their embellishment. The trim hedge, the grass-plot before the door, the little flower-bed bordered with snug box, the woodbine trained up against the wall and hanging its blossoms about the lattice, the pot of flowers in the window, the holly providentially planted about the house, to cheat winter of its dreariness, and throw in a semblance of green summer to cheer the fireside; all these bespeak the influence of taste, flowing down from high sources, and pervading the lowest levels of the public mind. If ever Love, as poets sing, delights to visit a cottage, it must be the cottage of an English peasant.

The fondness for rural life among the higher classes of the English has had a great and salutary effect upon the national character. I do not know a finer race of men than the English gentlemen. Instead of the softness and effeminacy which characterise the men of rank in most countries, they exhibit a union of elegance and strength, a robustness of frame and freshness of complexion, which I am inclined to attribute to their living so much in the open air, and pursuing so eagerly the invigorating recreations of the country. These hardy exercises produce also a healthful tone of mind and spirits, and a manliness and simplicity of manners, which even the follies and dissipations of the town cannot easily pervert, and can never entirely destroy. In the country, too, the different orders of society seem to approach more freely, to be more disposed to blend and operate favourably upon each other. The distinctions between them do not appear to be so marked and impassable as in the cities. The manner in which property has been distributed into small estates and farms, has established a regular gradation from the nobleman, through the glasses of gentry, small landed proprietors, and substantial farmers, down to the labouring peasantry; and while it has thus banded the extremes of society together, has infused into each intermediate rank a spirit of independence. This, it must be confessed, is not universally the case at present as it was formerly; the larger estates having, in late years of distress, absorbed the smaller, and, in some parts of the country, almost annihilated the sturdy race of small farmers. These, however, I believe, are but casual breaks in the general system I have mentioned.

In rural occupation there is nothing mean and debasing. It leads a man forth among scenes of natural grandeur and beauty; it leaves him to the workings of his own mind, operated upon by the purest and most elevating of external influences. Such a man may be simple and tough, but he cannot be vulgar. The man of refinement, therefore, finds nothing revolting in an intercourse with the lower orders of rural life, as he does when he casually mingles with the lower orders of cities. He lays aside his distance and reserve, and is glad to waive the distinctions of rank, and to enter into the honest, heartfelt enjoyments of common life. Indeed the very amusements of the country bring men more and more together; and the sound of hound and horn blends all feelings into harmony. I believe this is one great reason why the nobility and gentry are more popular among the inferior orders in England than they are in any other country; and why the latter have endured so many excessive pressures and extremities, without repining more generally at the unequal distribution of fortune and privilege.

To this mingling of cultivated and rustic society may also be attributed the rural feeling that runs through British literature: the frequent use of illustrations from rural life; those incomparable descriptions of nature that abound in the British poets — that have continued down from "The Flower and the Leaf" of Chaucer, and have brought into our closets all the freshness and fragrance of the dewy landscape. The pastoral writers of other countries appear as if they had paid nature an occasional visit, and become acquainted with her general charms; but the British poets have lived and revelled with her. — they have wooed her in her most secret haunts, — they have watched her minutest caprices. A spray could not tremble in the breeze — a leaf could not rustle to the ground — a diamond drop could not patter in the stream — a fragrance could not exhale from the humble violet, nor a daisy unfold its crimson tints to the morning, but it has been noticed by these impassioned and delicate observers, and wrought up into some beautiful morality.

The effect of this devotion of elegant minds to rural occupations has been wonderful on the face of the country. A great part of the island is level, and would be monotous, were it not for the charms of culture; but it is studded and gemmed, as it were, with castles and places, and embroidered with parks and gardens. It does not abound in grand and sublime prospects, but rather in little home-scenes of rural repose and sheltered quiet. Every antique farmhouse and moss-grown cottage is a picture; and as the roads are continually winding, and the view is shut in by groves and hedges, the eye is delighted by a continual succession of small landscapes of captivating loveliness.

The great charm, however, of English scenery is the moral feeling that seems to pervade it. It is associated in the mind with ideas of order, of quiet, of sober, well-established principles, of hoary usage and reverend custom. Every thing seems to be the growth of ages of regular and peaceful existence. The old church of remote architecture, with its low massive portal; its Gothic tower; its windows rich with tracery and painted glass; its stately monuments of warriors and worthies of the olden time, ancestors of the present lords of the soil; its tombstones, recording successive generations of sturdy yeomanry, whose progeny still plough the same fields, and kneel at the same altar. — The parsonage, a quaint irregular pile, partly antiquated, but repaired and altered in the tastes of various ages and occupants — the stile and footpath leading from the church-yard, across pleasant fields, and along shady hedgerows, according to an immemorable right of way — the neighbouring village, with its venerable cottages, its public green sheltered by trees, under which the forefathers of the present race have sported — the antique family mansion, standing apart in some little rural domain, but looking down with a protecting air on the surrounding scene: — all these common features of English landscape evince a calm and settled security, and hereditary transmission of home-bred virtues and local attachments, that speak deeply and touchingly for the moral character of the nation.

It is a pleasing sight on a Sunday morning, when the bell is sending its sober melody across the quiet fields, to behold the peasantry in their best finery, with ruddy faces and modest cheerfulness, thronging tranquilly along the green lanes to church; but it is still more pleasing to see them in the evenings, gathering about their cottage doors, and appearing to exult in the humble comforts and embellishments which their own hands have spread around them

It is this sweet home-feeling, this settled repose of affection in the domestic scene, that is, after all, the parent of the steadiest virtues and purest enjoyments: and I cannot close these desultory remarks better, than by quoting the words of a modern English poet (Rann Kennedy), who has depicted it with remarkable felicity: —

> Through each gradation, from the castled hall,
> The city dome, the villa crown'd with shade,
> But chief from modest mansions numberless,
> In town or hamlet, shelt'ring middle life,
> Down to the cottaged vale, and straw-roof'd shed,
> This western isle hath long been famed for scenes
> Where bliss domestic finds a dwelling-place;

Domestic bliss, that, like a harmless dove
(Honour and sweet endearment keeping guard),
Can centre in a little quiet nest
All that desire would fly for through the earth;
That can, the world eluding, be itself
A world enjoy'd; that wants no witnesses
But its own sharers, and approving heaven;
That like a flower deep hid in a rocky cleft,
Smiles, though 'tis looking only at the sky.

II. Christmas Eve.

We had now come in full view of the old family mansion, partly thrown in deep shadow, and partly lit up by the cold moonshine. It was an irregular building of some magnitude, and seemed to be of the architecture of different periods. One wing was evidently very ancient, with heavy stone-shafted bow-windows jutting out and over-run with ivy, from among the foliage of which the small diamond-shaped panes of glass glittered with the moon-beams. The rest of the house was in the French taste of Charles the Second's time, having been repaired and altered, as my friend told me, by one of his ancestors, who returned with that monarch at the Restoration. The grounds about the house were laid out in the old formal manner of artificial flower-beds, clipped shrubberies, raised terraces, and heavy stone balustrades, ornamented with urns, a leaden statue or two, and a jet of water. The old gentleman, I was told, was extremely careful to preserve this obsolete finery in all its original state. He admired this fashion in gardening: it had an air of magnificence, was courtly and noble, and befitting good old family style. The boasted imitation of nature in modern gardening, had sprung up with modern republican notions, but did not suit a monarchical government; it smacked of the levelling system. — I could not help smiling at this introduction of politics into gardening, though I expressed some apprehension that I should find the old gentleman rather intolerant in his creed. — Frank assured me, however, that it was almost the only instance in which he had ever heard his father meddle with politics: and he believed that he had got this notion from a member of parliament who once passed a few weeks with him. The Squire was glad of any argument to defend his clipped yew trees and formal terraces, which had been occasionally attacked by modern landscape-gardeners.

As we approached the house, we heard the sound of music, and now and then a burst of laughter, from one end of the building. This, Bracebridge said, must proceed from the servants' hall, where a great deal of revelry was permitted, and even encouraged, by the

Squire, throughout the twelve days of Christmas: provided every thing was done conformably to ancient usage. Here were kept up the old games of hoodman blind, shoe the wild mare, hot-cockles, steal the white loaf, bob apple, and snap-dragon: the Yule-log, and Christmas candle, were regularly burnt, and the mistletoe, with its white berries, hung up, to the imminent peril of all the pretty housemaids.

So intent were the servants upon their sports that we had to ring repeatedly before we could make ourselves heard. On our arrival being announced, the Squire came out to receive us, accompanied by his two other sons: one a young officer in the army, home on leave of absence; the other an Oxonian, just from the university. The Squire was a fine healthy-looking old gentleman, with silver hair curling lightly round an open florid countenance; in which a physiognomist, with the advantage, like myself, of a previous hint or two, might discover a singular mixture of whim and benevolence.

The family meeting was warm and affectionate: as the evening was far advanced, the Squire would not permit us to change our travelling dresses, but ushered us at once to the company, which was assembled in a large old-fashioned hall. It was composed of different branches of a numerous family connexion, where there were the usual proportion of old uncles and aunts, comfortably married dames, superannuated spinsters, blooming country cousins, half-fledged striplings, and bright-eyed boarding-school hoydens. They were variously occupied; some at a round game of cards; others conversing around the fire-place: at one end of the hall was a group of the young folks, some nearly grown up, others of a more tender and budding age, fully engrossed by a merry game: and a profusion of wooden horses, penny trumpets, and tattered dolls, about the floor, showed traces of a troop of little fairy beings, who, having frolicked through a happy day, had been carried off to slumber through a peaceful night.

While the mutual greetings were going on between Bracebridge and his relatives, I had time to scan the apartment. I have called it a hall, for so it had certainly been in old times, and the Squire had evidently endeavoured to restore it to something of its primitive state. Over the heavy projecting fire-place was suspended a picture of a warrior in armour, standing by a white horse, and on the opposite wall hung a helmet, buckler, and lance. At one end an enormous pair of antlers were inserted in the wall, the branches serving as hooks on which to suspend hats, whips, and spurs; and in the corners of the apartment were fowling-pieces, fishing-rods, and other sporting implements. The furniture was of the cumbrous workmanship of former days, though some articles of modern convenience had been added, and the oaken floor had been carpeted: so that the whole presented an odd mixture of parlour and hall.

5 The grate had been removed from the wide overwhelming fireplace, to make way for a fire of wood, in the midst of which was an enormous log glowing and blazing, and sending forth a vast volume of light and heat: this I understood was the Yule-log, which the Squire was particular in having brought in and illumined on a 10 Christmas eve, according to ancient custom.

It was really delightful to see the old Squire seated in his hereditary elbow-chair, by the hospitable fireside of his ancestors, and looking around him like the sun of a system, beaming warmth and gladness to every heart. Even the very dog that lay stretched at 15 his feet, as he lazily shifted his position and yawned, would look fondly up in his master's face, wag his tail against the floor, and stretch himself again to sleep, confident of kindness and protection. There is an emanation from the heart in genuine hospitality which cannot be described, but is immediately felt, and puts the stranger 20 at once at his ease. I had not been seated many minutes by the comfortable hearth of the worthy old cavalier, before I found myself as much at home as if I had been one of the family.

Supper was announced shortly after our arrival. It was served up in a spacious oaken chamber, the panels of which shone with 25 wax, and around which were several family portraits decorated with holly and ivy. Beside the accustomed lights, two great wax tapers, called Christmas candles, wreathed with greens, were placed on a highly-polished buffet among the family plate. The table was abundantly spread with substantial fare: but the Squire made his supper 30 of frumenty, a dish made of wheat cakes boiled in milk with rich spices, being a standing dish in old times for Christmas eve. I was happy to find my old friend, minced-pie, in the retinue of the feast; and finding him to be perfectly orthodox, and that I need not be ashamed of my predilection, I greeted him with all the warmth 35 wherewith we usually greet an old and very genteel acquaintance.

The mirth of the company was greatly promoted by the humours of an eccentric personage whom Mr. Bracebridge always addressed with the quaint appellation of Master Simon. He was a tight brisk little man, with the air of an arrant old bachelor. His 40 nose was shaped like the bill of a parrot, his face slightly pitted with the small-pox, with a dry perpetual bloom on it, like a frostbitten leaf in autumn. He had an eye of great quickness and viva-

city, with a drollery and lurking waggery of expression that was
irresistible. He was evidently the wit of the family, dealing very
much in sly jokes and innuendoes with the ladies, and making infinite merriment by harpings upon old themes; which, unfortunately,
my ignorance of the family chronicles did not permit me to enjoy.
It seemed to be his great delight during supper to keep a young
girl next him in a continual agony of stifled laughter, in spite of
her awe of the reproving looks of her mother, who sat opposite.
Indeed he was the idol of the younger part of the company, who
laughed at everything he said or did, and at every turn of his countenance. I could not wonder at it; for he must have been a miracle
of accomplishments in their eyes. He could imitate Punch and Judy;
make an old woman of his hand, with the assistance of a burnt cork
and pocket-handkerchief; and cut an orange into such a ludicrous
caricature, that the young folks were ready to die with laughing.

No sooner was supper removed, and spiced wines and other
beverages peculiar to the season introduced, than Master Simon was
called on for a good old Christmas song. He bethought himself for a
moment, and then, with a sparkle of the eye, and a voice that was
by no means bad, excepting that it ran occasionally into a falsetto,
like the notes of a split reed, he quavered forth a quaint old ditty. —

> Now Christmas is come,
> Let us beat up the drum,
> And call all our neighbours together;
> And when they appear,
> Let us make them such cheer,
> As will keep out the wind and the weather, &c.

The supper had disposed every one to gaiety, and an old harper
was summoned from the servants' hall, where he had been strumming
all the evening, and to all appearance comforting himself with some
of the Squire's home-brewed. He was a kind of hanger-on, I was
told, of the establishment, and though ostensibly a resident of the
village, was oftener to be found in the Squire's kitchen than his
own home, the old gentleman being fond of the sound of "harp
in hall."

The dance, like most dances after supper, was a merry one;
some of the older folks joined in it, and the Squire himself figured
down several couple with a partner with whom he affirmed he had
danced at every Christmas for nearly half a century. Master Simon,
who seemed to be a kind of connecting link between the old times
and the new, and to be withal a little antiquated in the taste of
his accomplishments, evidently piqued himself on his dancing, and

was endeavouring to gain credit by the heel and toe, rigadoon, and other graces of the ancient school; but he had unluckily assorted himself with a little romping girl from boarding-school, who, by her wild vivacity, kept him continually on the stretch, and defeated all his sober attempts at elegance: — such are the ill-sorted matches to which antique gentlemen are unfortunately prone!

The young Oxonian, on the contrary, had led out one of his maiden aunts, on whom the rogue played a thousand little knaveries with impunity: he was full of practical jokes, and his delight was to tease his aunts and cousins; yet, like all madcap youngsters, he was a universal favourite among the women.

The party now broke up for the night with the kind-hearted old custom of shaking hands. As I passed through the hall, on the way to my chamber, the dying embers of the Yule-log still sent forth a dusky glow, and had it not been the season when "no spirit dares stir abroad," I should have been half tempted to steal from my room at midnight, and peep whether the fairies might not be at their revels about the hearth.

My chamber was in the old part of the mansion, the ponderous furniture of which might have been fabricated in the days of the giants. The room was panelled with cornices of heavy carved work, in which flowers and grotesque faces were strangely intermingled; and a row of black-looking portraits stared mournfully at me from the walls. The bed was of rich though faded damask, with a lofty tester, and stood in a niche opposite a bow-window. I had scarcely got into bed when a strain of music seemed to break forth in the air just below the window. I listened, and found it proceeded from a band, which I concluded to be the waits from some neighbouring village. They went round the house, playing under the windows. I drew aside the curtains, to hear them more distinctly. The moonbeams fell through the upper part of the casement, partially lighting up the antiquated apartment. The sounds, as they receded, became more soft and aërial, and seemed to accord with quiet and moonlight. I listened and listened — they became more and more tender and remote, and, as they gradually died away, my head sank upon the pillow and I fell asleep.

III. John Bull.

One would think that, in personifying itself, a nation would be apt to picture something grand, heroic, and imposing; but it is characteristic of the peculiar humour of the English, and of their love for what is blunt, comic, and familiar, that they have embodied their

national oddities in the figure of a sturdy, corpulent old fellow, with
a three-cornered hat, red waistcoat, leather breeches, and stout oaken
cudgel. Thus they have taken a singular delight in exhibiting their
most private foibles in a laughable point of view, and have been so
successful in their delineations, that there is scarcely a being in
actual existence more absolutely present to the public mind, than
that eccentric personage, John Bull.

John Bull, to all appearance, is a plain downright matter-of-
fact fellow, with much less of poetry about him than rich prose.
There is little of romance in his nature, but a vast deal of strong
natural feeling. He excels in humour more than in wit: is jolly rather
than gay; melancholy rather than morose: can easily be moved to
a sudden tear, or surprised into a broad laugh; but he loathes
sentiment, and has no turn for light pleasantry. He is a boon
companion, if you allow him to have his humour, and to talk about
himself; and he will stand by a friend in a quarrel, with life and
purse, however soundly he may be cudgelled.

In this last respect, to tell the truth, he has a propensity to
be somewhat too ready. He is a busy-minded personage, who thinks
not merely for himself and family, but for all the country round, and
is most generously disposed to be everybody's champion. He is
continually volunteering his services to settle his neighbours' affairs,
and takes it in great dudgeon if they engage in any matter of consequence without asking his advice; though he seldom engages in
any friendly office of the kind without finishing by getting into a
squabble with all parties, and then railing bitterly at their ingratitude. He cannot hear of a quarrel between the most distant of his
neighbours, but he begins incontinently to fumble with the edge of
his cudgel, and consider whether his interest or honour does not require that he should meddle in the broil. Indeed he has extended his
relations of pride and policy so completely over the whole country,
that no event can take place, without infringing some of his finely-
spun rights and dignities.

Though really a good-hearted, good-tempered old fellow at
bottom, yet he is singularly fond of being in the midst of contention.
It is one of his peculiarities, however, that he only relishes the
beginning of an affray; he always goes into a fight with alacrity,
but comes out of it grumbling even when victorious; and though no
one fights with more obstinacy to carry a contested point, yet when
the battle is over, and he comes to the reconciliation, he is so much
taken up with the mere shaking of hands, that he is apt to let his
antagonist pocket all they have been quarrelling about. It is not,

therefore, fighting that he ought so much to be on his guard against, as making friends. It is difficult to cudgel him out of a farthing; but put him in a good humour, and you may bargain him out of all the money in his pocket.

He is a little fond of playing the magnifico abroad: of pulling out a long purse; flinging his money bravely about at boxing matches, horse races, cock fights, and carrying a high head among "gentlemen of the fancy"; but immediately after one of these fits of extravagance, he will be taken with violent qualms of economy: stop short at the most trivial expenditure; talk desperately of being ruined and brought upon the parish; and, in such moods, will not pay the smallest tradesman's bill, without violent altercation. He is, in fact, the most punctual and discontented paymaster in the world; drawing his coin out of his breeches' pocket with infinite reluctance; paying to the uttermost farthing, but accompanying every guinea with a growl.

With all his talk of economy, however, he is a bountiful provider, and a hospitable housekeeper. His economy is of a whimsical kind, its chief object being to devise how he may afford to be extravagant; for he will begrudge himself a beefsteak and a pint of port one day, that he may roast an ox whole, broach a hogshead of ale, and treat all his neighbours on the next.

His domestic establishment is enormously expensive: not so much from any great outward parade, as from the great consumption of solid beef and pudding; the vast number of followers he feeds and clothes; and his singular disposition to pay hugely for small services. He is a most kind and indulgent master. Everything that lives on him seems to thrive and grow fat. His house-servants are well paid, and pampered, and have little to do. His horses are sleek and lazy, and prance slowly before his state-carriage; and his house-dogs sleep quietly about the door, and will hardly bark at a house-breaker.

His family mansion is an old castellated manor-house, grey with age, and of a most venerable though weather-beaten appearance. It has been built upon no regular plan, but is a vast accumulation of parts, erected in various tastes and ages. The centre bears evident traces of Saxon architecture, and is as solid as ponderous stone and old English oak can make it. Like all the relics of that style, it is full of obscure passages, intricate mazes, and dusky chambers; and though these have been partially lighted up in modern days, yet there are many places where you must still grope in the dark. Additions have been made to the original edifice from time to time,

and great alterations have taken place; towers and battlements have
been erected during war and tumults; wings built in times of peace;
and outhouses, lodges, and offices, run up according to the whim or
convenience of different generations, until it has become one of the
most spacious, rambling tenements imaginable. An entire wing is
taken up with the family chapel; a reverend pile, that must once
have been exceedingly sumptuous, and, indeed, in spite of having been
altered and simplified at various periods, has still a look of solemn
religious pomp. Its walls within are stored with the monuments
of John's ancestors; and it is snugly fitted up with soft cushions and
well-lined chairs, where such of his family as are inclined to church
services may doze comfortably in the discharge of their duties.

The family apartments are in a very antiquated taste, somewhat
heavy, and often inconvenient, but full of the solemn magnificence
of former times: fitted up with rich, though faded, tapestry, unwieldy
furniture, and loads of massy gorgeous old plate. The vast fire-places,
ample kitchens, extensive cellars, and sumptuous banqueting halls,
all speak of the roaring hospitality of days of yore, of which the
modern festivity at the manor-house is but a shadow. There are
however, complete suites of rooms apparently deserted and time-
worn; and towers and turrets that are tottering to decay; so that
in high winds there is danger of their tumbling about the ears of
the household.

John is given to indulge his veneration for family usages and
family encumbrances to a whimsical extent. His manor is infested
by gangs of gipsies; yet he will not suffer them to be driven off,
because they have infested the place time out of mind, and been
regular poachers upon every generation of the family. He will scarcely
permit a dry branch to be lopped from the great trees that surround
the house, lest it should molest the rooks that have bred there for
centuries. Owls have taken possession of the dove-cot; but they are
hereditary owls, and must not be disturbed. Swallows have nearly
choked up every chimney with their nests; martins build in every
frieze and cornice; crows flutter about the towers, and perch on
every weather-cock; and old grey-headed rats may be seen in every
quarter of the house, running in and out of their holes undauntedly
in broad daylight. In short, John has such a reverence for
everything that has been long in the family, that he will not
hear even of abuses being reformed, because they are good old
family abuses.

All these whims and habits have concurred woefully to drain
the old gentleman's purse; and as he prides himself on punctuality

in money matters, and wishes to maintain his credit in the neighbourhood, they have caused him great perplexity in meeting his engagements. This, too, has been increased by the altercations and heart-burnings which are continually taking place in his family. His children have been brought up to different callings, and are of different ways of thinking; and as they have always been allowed to speak their minds freely, they do not fail to exercise the privilege most clamorously in the present posture of his affairs. Some stand up for the honour of the race, and are clear that the old establishment should be kept up in all its state, whatever may be the cost; others, who are more prudent and considerate, entreat the old gentleman to retrench his expenses, and to put his old system of house-keeping on a more moderate footing.

These family dissensions, as usual, have got abroad, and are rare food for scandal in John's neighbourhood. People begin to look wise, and shake their heads, whenever his affairs are mentioned. They all "hope that matters are not so bad with him as represented; but when a man's own children begin to rail at his extravagance, things must be badly managed. They understand he is mortgaged over head and ears, and is continually dabbling with money-lenders. He is certainly an open-handed old gentleman, but they fear he has lived too fast; indeed, they never knew any good come of this fondness for hunting, racing, revelling, and prize-fighting. In short, Mr. Bull's estate is a very fine one, and has been in the family a long while; but for all that, they have known many finer estates come to the hammer".

Instead of strutting about as formerly, with his three-cornered hat on one side; flourishing his cudgel, and bringing it down every moment with a hearty thump upon the ground; looking every one sturdily in the face, and trolling out a stave of a catch or a drinking song; he now goes about whistling thoughtfully to himself, with his head drooping down, his cudgel tucked under his arm, and his hands thrust to the bottom of his breeches' pockets, which are evidently empty.

Such is the plight of honest John Bull, at present; yet for all this the old fellow's spirit is as tall and as gallant as ever. If you drop the least expression of sympathy or concern, he takes fire in an instant; swears that he is the richest and stoutest fellow in the country; talks of laying out large sums to adorn his house or to buy another estate; and with a valiant swagger and grasping of his cudgel, longs exceedingly to have another bout at quarter-staff.

Though there may be something rather whimsical in all this, yet
I confess I cannot look upon John's situation without strong feelings
of interest. With all his odd humours, and obstinate prejudices, he
is a sterling-hearted old blade. He may not be so wonderfully fine a
fellow as he thinks himself, but he is at least twice as good as his
neighbours represent him. His virtues are all his own; all plain,
home-bred, and unaffected. His very faults smack of the raciness of
his good qualities. His extravagance savours of his generosity; his
quarrelsomeness, of his courage; his credulity, of his open faith; his
vanity, of his pride; and his bluntness, of his sincerity. They are all
the redundancies of a rich and liberal character. He is like his own
oak, rough without, but sound and solid within; whose bark abounds
with excrescences in proportion to the growth and grandeur of the
timber, and whose branches make a fearful groaning and murmuring
in the least storm, from their very magnitude and luxuriance.

WASHINGTON IRVING.

II. Hyde Park.

Five o'clock, and Rotten Row alive with equestrians! Far away
between majestic elms, now gently dipping into the hollow, now
slightly ascending the uneven ground, made as soft and as full as
horse-traps can make it, runs, in the very eye of the setting sun,
this superb horse promenade. And here comes a goodly company, seven
abreast, sweeping along with slackened rein: the young athletes on
the Elgin marbles yonder upon the frieze of the screen, do not seem
more a portion of their horses than these gay young fellows, whispering courtesies to the ladies so bright-eyed and supple of waist,
who gently govern with delicate small hands their fiery-eyed steeds.
Single riders trot steadily past as though they were doing it for a
wager. Dandies drawl along, superbly indifferent to everything about
them, with riding-sticks "based on hip." And when I reach Albert
Gate, all Belgravia seems pouring out through the narrow streets on
prancing, dancing, arch-necked steeds. Where all the horses come
from is the wonder to me. As far as the eye can see, out far into
Kensington, where the perspective of the road is lost in feathery
birch-trees, I see nothing but prancing, dancing horses, tossing their
heads, caracolling, humbly obeying the directions of delicate wrists, or
chafing at the curb of powerful bridle hands. Nor do they end here:
over the bridge and round the drive, the contingents from Tyburnia
pour along in troops; and now, as I come to the corner of Kensington
Gardens, there is a perfect congestion of equestrians, listening to the
band of the Life Guards playing a waltz. There they are, ranged

round the great trees, English men and maidens, and English horses, all thorough-bred — as noble a group as the wide world can show, whilst over all the thick fan-like green leaves of the chestnut trees cast a pleasant shade. Meanwhile the drive is gorged with carriages moving along at a footpace. Let me constitute myself (for the nonce) a young man about town, and comfortably resting my arms over the railings, take a good stare at the passing beauty. I need not feel bashful. As far as I can see, for hundreds of feet on each side of me, there is nothing but young men leaning over the railing, tapping their teeth with their dandy little sticks, and making the most powerful use of their eyes. Here I watch moving before me the great portrait gallery of living British beauties. Every instant a fresh profile passes in review, framed and glazed by the carriage window. Onward rolls the tide of vehicles — of dashing cabs with pendent tigers — of chariots with highly-groomed horses — of open phaetons, the reins of faultless white, guided by lady whips — of family coaches ancient and respectable. Now and then some countryman and his "missus," in a home-made chaise-cart, seem to have got accidentally entangled among the gay throng, and move along sheepishly enough. On they all go to where Kensington Gardens leans, like a sister, beside her bolder brother, Hyde Park; and here all alight, and pour in a bright flood of moving colour upon the emerald turf. Country people pity us poor town-people, and wonder how we can exist! Did anybody ever see such a public park as this in the country? I never did.

HOUSEHOLD WORDS.

12. The Marylebone Match.

To-day the great event of the cricketing year, the Marylebone match, is being played. What a match it has been! The London eleven came down by an afternoon train yesterday, in time to see the end of the Wellesburn match; and as soon as it was over, their leading men and umpire inspected the ground, criticising it rather unmercifully. The Captain of the School eleven, and one or two others, who had played the Lord's match before, and knew old Mr. Aislabie and several of the Lord's men, accompanied them: while the rest of the eleven looked on from under the Three Trees with admiring eyes, and asked one another the names of the illustrious strangers, and recounted how many runs each of them had made in the late matches in 'Bell's Life'. They looked such hard-bitten, wiry, whiskered fellows, that their young adversaries felt rather desponding as to the result of the morrow's match. The ground was at last chosen, and two men set to work upon it to water and roll; and then, there being yet some half-hour of daylight, some one had suggested a dance on the turf. The close was half full of citizens and their families, and the idea was hailed with enthusiasm. The cornopean-player was still on the ground; in five minutes the eleven and half-a-dozen of the Wellesburn and Marylebone men got partners somehow or another, and a merry country dance was going on to which every one flocked, and new couples joined in every minute, till there were a hundred of them going down the middle and up again — and the long line of School buildings looked gravely down on them, every window glowing with the last rays of the western sun, and the rooks clanged about in the tops of the old elms, greatly excited, and resolved on having their country dance too, and the great flag flapped lazily in the gentle western breeze. Altogether it was a sight which would have made glad the heart of our brave old founder, Lawrence Sheriff, if he were half as good a fellow as I take him to have been. It was a cheerful sight to see; but what made it so valuable in the sight of the Captain of the School eleven was, that he there saw his young hands shaking off their shyness and awe of the Lord's men, as they crossed hands and capered about on the grass together; for the strangers entered into it all, and threw away their cigars, and danced and shouted like boys: while old Mr. Aislabie stood by looking on in his white hat, leaning on a bat, in benevolent enjoyment. "This hop will be worth thirty runs to us to-morrow, and will be the making of Raggles and Johnson," thinks the young leader, as he revolves many things in his mind, standing by the side of Mr. Aislabie, whom he will not leave for a minute, for he feels that the character of the School for courtesy is resting on his shoulders.

But when a quarter to nine struck, and he saw old Thomas beginning to fidget about with the keys in his hand, he thought of the Doctor's parting monition, and stopped the cornopean at once, notwithstanding the loud-voiced remonstrances from all sides; and the crowd scattered away from the close, the eleven all going into the School-house, where supper and beds were provided for them by the Doctor's orders.

Deep had been the consultations at supper as to the order of going in, who should bowl the first over, whether it would be best to play steady or freely; and the youngest hands declared that they shouldn't be a bit nervous, and praised their opponents as the jolliest fellows in the world, except perhaps their old friends the Wellesburn men. How far a little good-nature from their elders will go with the right sort of boys!

The morning had dawned bright and warm, to the intense relief of many an anxious youngster, up betimes to mark the signs of the weather. The eleven went down in a body before breakfast, for a plunge in the cold bath in the corner of the close. The ground was in splendid order, and soon after ten o'clock, before spectators had arrived, all was ready, and two of the Lord's men took their places at the wicket; the School, with the usual liberality of young hands, having put their adversaries in first. Old Bailey stepped up to the wicket, and called play, and the match has begun.

* * *

"Oh, well bowled! well bowled, Johnson!" cries the Captain, catching up the ball and sending it high above the rook trees, while the third Marylebone man walks away from the wicket, and old Bailey gravely sets up the middle stump again and puts the bails on.

"How many runs?" Away scamper three boys to the scoring-table, and are back again in a minute amongst the rest of the eleven, who are collected together in a knot between wicket. "Only eighteen runs, and three wickets down!" "Huzza for old Rugby!" sings out Jak Raggles the long-stop, toughest and burliest of boys, commonly called 'Swiper Jack'; and forthwith stands on his head, and brandishes his legs in the air in triumph, till the next boy catches hold of his heels and throws him over on to his back.

"Steady there, don't be such an ass, Jack," says the Captain, "we haven't got the best wicket yet. Ah, look out now at cover-point," adds he, as he sees a long-armed, bareheaded, slashing-looking player coming to the wicket. "And, Jack, mind your hits; he steals more runs than any man in England."

And they all find that they have got their work to do now; the new-comer's off-hitting is tremendous, and his running like a flash of lightning. He is never in his ground, except when his wicket is down. Nothing in the whole game so trying to boys; he has stolen three byes in the first ten minutes, and Jack Raggles is furious, and begins throwing over savagely to the further wicket, until he is sternly stopped by the Captain. It is all that young gentleman can do to keep his team steady, but he knows that everything depends on it, and faces his work bravely. The score creeps up to fifty, the boys begin to look blank, and the spectators, who are now mustering strong, are very silent. The ball flies off his bat to all parts of the field, and he gives no rest and no catches to any one. But cricket is full of glorious chances, and the goddess who presides over it loves to bring down the most skilful players. Johnson, the young bowler, is getting wild, and bowls a ball almost wide to the off; the batter steps out and cuts it beautifully to where cover-point is standing, very deep, in fact almost off the ground. The ball comes skimming and twisting along about three feet from the ground; he rushes at it, and it sticks somehow or other in the fingers of his left hand, to the utter astonishment of himself and the whole field. Such a catch hasn't been made in the close for years, and the cheering is maddening. "Pretty cricket," says the Captain, throwing himself on the ground by the deserted wicket with a long breath; he feels that a crisis has passed.

I wish I had space to describe the whole match; how the Captain stumped the next man off a leg-shooter; and bowled slow lobs to old Mr. Aislabie, who came in for the last wicket. How the Lord's men were out by half-past twelve o'clock for ninety-eight runs. How the Captain of the School eleven went in first to give his men pluck, and scored twenty-five in beautiful style; how Rugby was only four behind in the first innings. What a glorious dinner they had in the fourth-form School, and how the cover-point hitter sang the most topping comic songs, and old Mr. Aislabie made the best speeches that ever were heard, afterwards. But I haven't space, that's the fact, and so you must fancy it all; and carry yourselves on to half-past seven o'clock, when the School are again in, with five wickets down and only thirty-two runs to make to win. The Marylebone men played carelessly in their second innings, but they are working like horses now to save the match.

* * *

"Oh, Brown, mayn't I go in next?" shouts the Swiper.

"Whose name is next on the list?" says the Captain.

"Winter's, and then Arthur's," answers the boy who carries it; "but there are only twenty-six runs to get, and no time to lose. I heard Mr. Aislabie say that the stumps must be drawn at a quarter past eight exactly."

"Oh, do let the Swiper go in," chorus the boys; so Tom yields against his better judgment.

"I dare say now I've lost the match by this nonsense," he says, as he sits down again; "they'll be sure to get Jack's wicket in three or four minutes; however, you'll have the chance, sir, of seeing a hard hit or two," adds he, smiling and turning to the master.

"Come, none of your irony, Brown," answers the master. "I'm beginning to understand the game scientifically. What a noble game it is too!"

"Isn't it? But it's more than a game. It's an institution," said Tom.

"Yes," said Arthur, "the birthright of British boys old and young, as *habeas corpus* and trial by jury are of British men."

"The discipline and reliance on one another which it teaches is so valuable, I think," went on the master, "it ought to be such an unselfish game. It merges the individual in the eleven; he doesn't play that he may win, but that his side may."

"That's very true," said Tom, "and that's why foot-ball and cricket, now one comes to think of it, are such much better games than fives' or hare-and-hounds, or any others where the object is to come in first or to win for oneself, and not that one's side may win."

"And then the Captain of the eleven!" said the master, "what a post is his in our School-world! almost as hard as the Doctor's; requiring skill and gentleness and firmness, and I know not what other rare qualities."

"Which don't he wish he may get?" said Tom, laughing: "at any rate he hasn't got them yet, or he wouldn't have been such a flat to-night as to let Jack Raggles go in out of his turn."

* * *

Meantime Jack Raggles, with his sleeves tucked up above his great brown elbows, scorning pads and gloves, has presented himself at the wicket; and having run one for a forward drive of Johnson's, is about to receive his first ball. There are only twenty-four runs to make, and four wickets to go down, a winning match if they play decently steady. The ball is a very swift one, and rises fast, catching Jack on the outside of the thigh, and bounding away as if from india-rubber, while they run two for a leg-bye amidst great applause, and shouts from Jack's many admirers. The next ball is a beautifully pitched ball for the outer stump, which the reckless and unfeeling Jack catches hold of, and hits right round to leg for five, while the applause becomes deafening: only seventeen runs to get with four wickets — the game is all but ours!

It is "over" now, and Jack walks swaggering about his wicket, with the bat over his shoulder, while Mr. Aislabie holds a short parley with his men. Then the cover-point hitter, that cunning man, goes on to bowl slow twisters. Jack waves his hand triumphantly towards the tent, as much as to say, "See if I don't finish it all off now in three hits."

Alas, my son Jack! the enemy is too old for thee. The first ball of the over Jack steps out and meets, swiping with all his force.

If he had only allowed for the twist! but he hasn't, and so the ball goes spinning up straight into the air, as if it would never come down again. Away runs Jack, shouting and trusting to the chapter of accidents, but the bowler runs steadily under it, judging every spin, and calling out "I have it," catches it, and playfully pitches it on to the back of the stalwart Jack, who is departing with a rueful countenance.

"I knew how it would be," says Tom, rising. "Come along, the game's getting very serious."

So they go to the tent, and after deep consultation Arthur is sent in, and goes off to the wicket with a last exhortation from Tom to play steady and keep his bat straight. To the suggestions that Winter is the best bat left, Tom only replies, "Arthur is the steadiest, and Johnson will make the runs if the wicket is only kept up."

"I am surprised to see Arthur in the eleven," said the master, as they stood together in front of the dense crowd, which was now closing in round the ground.

"Well, I'm not quite sure that he ought to be in for his play," said Tom, "but I couldn't help putting him in. It will do him so much good, and you can't think what I owe him."

The master smiled. The clock strikes eight, and the whole field becomes fevered with excitement. Arthur, after two narrow escapes, scores one; and Johnson gets the ball. The bowling and fielding are superb, and Johnson's batting worthy the occasion. He makes here a two, and there a one, managing to keep the ball to himself, and Arthur backs up and runs perfectly: only eleven runs to make now, and the crowd scarcely breathe. At last Arthur gets the ball again, and actually drives it forward for two, and feels prouder than when he got the three best prizes, at hearing Tom's shout of joy, "Well played, well played, young 'un!"

But the next ball is too much for a young hand, and his bails fly different ways. Nine runs to make, and two wickets to go down — it is too much for human nerves.

Before Winter can get in, the omnibus which is to take the Lord's men to the train pulls up at the side of the close, and Mr. Aislabie and Tom consult, and give out that the stumps will be drawn after the next over. And so ends the great match. Winter and Johnson carry out their bats, and, it being a one day's match, the Lord's men are declared the winners, they having scored the most in the first innings.

But such a defeat is a victory: so think Tom and all the School eleven, as they accompany their conquerors to the omnibus, and send them off with three ringing cheers, after Mr. Aislabie has shaken hands all round, saying to Tom, "I must compliment you, sir, on your eleven, and I hope we shall have you for a member, if you come up to town." THOMAS HUGHES.

13. English Attendance.

You are going off by railway, from any Terminus. You have twenty minutes for dinner, and, like Doctor Johnson, sir, you like to dine. You present to your mind a picture of the refreshment-table at that terminus. The conventional shabby evening party supper — accepted as the model for all termini and all refreshment stations, because it is the last repast known to this state of existence of which any human creature would partake, but in the direst extremity — sickens your contemplation, and your words are these: "I cannot dine on stale sponge-cakes that turn to sand in the mouth. I cannot dine on shining brown patties, composed of unknown animals within, and offering to my view the device of an indigestible star-fish in leaden pie crust without. I cannot dine on a sandwich that has long been pining under an exhausted receiver. I cannot dine on barley-sugar. I cannot dine on toffee." You repair to the nearest hotel and arrive, agitated, in the coffee-room.

It is a most astonishing fact that the waiter is very cold to you. Account for it how you may, smooth it over how you will, you cannot deny that he is cold to you. He is not glad to see you, he would much rather you hadn't come. He opposes to your flushed condition an immovable composure. As if this were not enough, another waiter, born, as it would seem, expressly to look at you in this passage of your life, stands at a little distance, with his napkin under his arm and his hands folded, looking at you with all his might. You impress on your waiter that you have ten minutes for dinner, and he proposes that you shall begin with a bit of fish which will be ready in twenty. That proposal declined, he suggests — as a neat originality — "a 'weal' or mutton cutlet." You close with either cutlet, any cutlet, any thing. He goes, leisurely, behind a door and calls down some unseen shaft. A ventriloquial dialogue ensues, tending finally to the effect that 'weal' only, is available on the spur of the moment. You anxiously call out "Veal then!" Your waiter, having settled that point, returns to array your table cloth, with a table napkin folded cocked-hat-wise (slowly, for something out of window engages his eye), a white wine-glass, a green wine-glass, a blue finger-glass, a tumbler, and a powerful field battery of fourteen castors with nothing in them; or at all events — which is enough for your purpose — with nothing in them that will comeout.

All this thime, the other waiter looks at you — with an air of mental comparison and curiosity, now, as if it had occurred to him that you are rather like his brother.

Half your time gone and nothing come but the jug of ale and the bread, you implore your waiter to "see after that cutlet, waiter; pray do!" He cannot go at once, for he is carrying in seventeen pounds of American cheese for you to finish with, and a small Landed Estate of celery and watercress. The other waiter changes his leg, and takes a new view of you — doubtfully, now, as if he had rejected the resemblance to his brother, and had begun to think you more like his aunt or his grandmother. Again you beseech your waiter with pathetic indignation to "see after that cutlet!" He steps out to see after it, and by-and-by, when you are going away without it, comes back with it. Even then, he will not take the sham silver-cover off, without a pause for a flourish, and a look at the musty cutlet as if he were surprised to see it — which cannot possibly be the case, he must have seen it often before. A sort of fur has been produced upon its surface by the cook's art, and, in a sham silver vessel staggering on two feet instead of three, is a cutaneous kind of sauce, of brown pimples and pickled cucumber. You order the bill, but your waiter cannot bring your bill yet, because he is bringing, instead, three flinty-hearted potatoes and two grim head of broccoli, like the occasional ornaments on area-railings, badly boiled. You know that you will never come to this pass, any more than to the cheese, and you imperatively demand your bill; but it takes time to get, even when gone for, because your waiter has to communicate with a lady who lives behind a sash-window in a corner, and who appears to have to refer to several Ledgers before she can make it out — as if you had been staying there a year. You become distracted to get away, and the other waiter, once more changing his leg, still looks at you — but suspiciously now, as if you had begun to remind him of the party who took the great-coats last winter.

Your bill at last brought and paid, at the rate of sixpence a mouthful, your waiter reproachfully reminds you that "attendance is not charged for a single meal," and you have to search in all your pockets for sixpence more. He has a worse opinion of you than ever when you have given it to him, and lets you out into the street with the air of one saying to himself, as you cannot doubt he is, "I hope we shall never see you here again!"

CHARLES DICKENS.

14. The British Islands and their Population.

The peculiarities of the physical structure of the British Islands have told on their political history.

To them are due the social and political differences which so long parted Ireland from Great Britain, and which still retard their practical union. Ireland is distinguished from Great Britain by its size, as well as by the characteristics both of its position and of its physical structure. Its area amounts to 30,000 square miles; its greatest length is 290 miles, and its greatest breadth 175 miles. It is thus little more than a third as large as the Island of Great Britain. It differs from it as strongly in position as in structure. While it is separated from America by the whole width of the Atlantic Ocean, it is cut off from Europe by the greater island to the eastward of it. This isolated position has to a great extent protected it from foreign invasion, and has preserved in the country its ancient inhabitants with but little change. But at the same time the island has been in a great measure shut out from direct contact with the general civilizing influences of Europe, and it was only in comparatively late times that its wandering tribes were brought within the full scope of European civilization. The remarkable unity of its physical structure, so strongly in contrast with the variety of that of Great Britain, has had even greater social results. It is in fact reflected in the unvaried character of its industry. The centre of the island forms a broad, level plain, broken only by lakes, and traversed by one large river, round which runs a circle of hills and low mountains, which form a wide belt along the northern and southern shores, and a narrower belt along the eastern and western coasts. The moisture of the Irish climate, which results from the position of this island in the Atlantic Ocean, produces a constant rainfall which makes pasture more profitable than tillage; and this vast central plain has in all ages been mainly a grazing ground for cattle. Manufactures, save in the north, there are none. The uniform character of the rocks, from which coal is absent, and which contain metals in but small quantities, has prevented any general growth of manufacturing industry, and thus restricted the great bulk of the inhabitants to agricultural employments.

While physical characteristics thus distinguish Ireland from Great Britain as a whole, they have also been the chief causes which have brought about the division of Great Britain itself into three separate realms, and which have to a great extent determined the social and political character of each of these portions. Taken as a whole, Britain covers an area of 84,000 square miles, its length is about 600 miles from north to south, while its breadth varies from 33 to 367 miles. But it is only in comparatively recent times that the island has become a single nation. For many centuries it was divided into three separate countries, that of Scotland to the north, and Wales to the west, while the southern mass of the island bore the name of England.

Scotland owed its separate existence partly to the form of Great Britain, and partly to the physical differences between the northern and the bulk of the southern parts of the island. The disproportion between the length and the breadth of Britain threw a great obstacle in the way of political unity in times when communications were slow and difficult. Still greater obstacles were interposed by the physical difference between the districts to the north of the Cheviots — the hills which formed the frontier between Scotland and England — and those to the south of them. While the latter consisted for the most part of low hills and open plains, Scotland was little more than a continuous mass of high mountains separated by a strip of level ground from another mass of bare and lofty hills which extend to the border. This natural division of the country into Highlands, or the mountain district, and Lowlands, or the district of the hills and the plains, was reflected in the twofold character of its population, the Gael of the Highlands being distinguished from the Englishman of the Lowlands by differences of race and speech which long held them apart as two separate peoples. Within each district too the broken character of the country tended to promote the division of its inhabitants into separate clans or bodies obeying their special chieftains, and hindered all efforts to bring them to any real national oneness. The barrenness also of their soil, and the inclemency of their climate long doomed the Scotch to extreme poverty; while their position, which cut them off from the civilizing influence of Europe, kept them in a state of barbarism. On the other hand, these hardships helped in creating a thrift and endurance which enabled the smaller country to hold its own against its greater neighbour. Scotland is only about half the size of England, its area being but 24,000 square miles, its extreme length 286, and its breadth varying from 33 to 160 miles; while in wealth and population it was greatly inferior. But in spite of this disproportion it preserved its independence till a peaceful union was brought about by one of the Scotch kings mounting the English throne. Since this union its physical structure has again played a great part in its social history. Whilst the general progress of civilization has removed much of the dissociating effects of its mountainous character, the discovery of rich coal-beds in the level strip between Highlands and Lowlands has given birth to manufactures and large towns, and, with the upgrowth of agriculture in the south through the energy of its people, has turned the poverty of the country into comparative wealth.

The severance of Wales from the mass of the country was due to only one of the circumstances which promoted the separate existence of Scotland. Wales consists of a tract of rugged, mountainous country projecting into the Irish Sea from the western coast of Southern Britain, whose boundary-line on the eastern side runs where these mountains sink into the plains of which Central England is made up. It thus resembles Scotland in its general features, save that its mountains nowhere rise so high as those of Scotland, and that it is far smaller, being only a seventh the size of England and covering an area of but 7,400 square miles. It was in fact a small mountain fastness in which the older, or Celtic, peoples of Northern Britain took refuge when the more open country was conquered by the English invaders, and where they long preserved their independence. Wales, like Scotland, remained for ages poor and barbarous; it was in the same way cut off by England from contact with civilized Europe, while the bleak moorlands and slaty hills which cover most of its surface long afforded only a thin pasture for small sheep and cattle, and supported but a few inhabitants. But again, like Scotland, Wales has in more recent times owed a vast social change to its physical structure. In the northern and southern parts of the country rich beds of coal, iron, and slate have been found and worked; and in these districts the general solitude and poverty of the country is now exchanged for busy industry and a teeming population.

The rest of the island, south of the Cheviots and east of Wales, formed the kingdom of England. It is far the largest of the three, for it is 350 miles long, and has an area of 50,000 square miles. In appearance it at once resembles and differs from the neighbouring countries, for its mountains are less bold than those of Scotland or Wales, while its plains are less monotonous than those of Ireland. In fertility and general wealth it is far more favoured than any. Its surface is more varied; it consists mainly of wide undulating plains, but these are broken by low uplands in the north and south-west. The undulating character of most of its surface not only facilitates communication and road-making; but promotes the gathering together of the waters of the

country into streams and rivers. No other part of the British Isles
can compare with England in the completeness of its system of
rivers, which are spread over the face of the land in an order more
perfect than that of almost any other European country. Unlike the
mere mountain torrents which are so common in Scotland and Wales,
these rivers form a network of navigable waters and carry fertility
to all its plains. The fruitfulness of England is aided by its climate,
a climate less damp than that of Ireland and less cold than that of
Scotland, but sufficiently varied in the amount of its rainfall to
allow the growth of grain over the eastern half of the country, while
it provides rich pastures through the western. To these advantages
we may add that of mineral wealth, in a vast extent of coal-beds
and rich deposits of iron and other metals, as well as salt-mines
and beds of valuable clay. But much as it owes to its physical
structure, England owes hardly less to its geographical position. It
lies closer to Europe than either Scotland, Ireland, or Wales, and
thus possesses greater advantages for trade and commerce, while its
harbours are situated in more sheltered seas than those of its fellow-
countries.

Both its structure and position have combined to shape its
political history. Easy communication with the Continent has brought
England within reach of its civilizing influences, as it has left her
open to descents of invaders, who have driven before them her
older inhabitants to the mountains of the north and west. Thus it
has come about that the Englishmen of Southern Britain are more
recent incomers into the land than the Gael of the Highlands or the
Cymry of Wales. That their conquest of the country was possible was
due in great measure to the absence of mountain-barriers such as
checked their progress in these latter districts; but it is the absence
of such barriers which in later days enabled government to act easily
over the whole face of the land, and soon drew its various tribes
together into one people and a highly organized realm. With such
advantages of structure and position, and with the far greater wealth
and population that came of them, it was inevitable that England
should in the long run gather the neighbouring realms round it, and
that it should form by far the most important element in the political body which has resulted from their union — the United Kingdom
of Great Britain and Ireland. R. J. GREEN.

15. The English Constitution.

The Government of the British Empire is vested in the Sovereign
and the two Houses of Parliament, — the House of Lords and

the House of Commons. It is thus a mixed government, — not pure monarchy, or pure aristocracy, or pure democracy, but a compound of all three. In this composite character lies its chief strength. Every grade of society, every interest in the country, is represented in it. The power of the landed aristocracy has its due weight in the House of Lords. That of the great middle class, and of the industrial classes who cooperate with them in producing wealth, is supreme in the House of Commons. The influence of an ancient hereditary monarchy is preserved in the Sovereign, who crowns the edifice.

The chief business of the two Houses of Parliament is to make laws, and to vote money for the public service. In theory, the power of carrying out the laws belongs to the Sovereign alone; but in practice, this is done in the Sovereign's name by the Ministry, — a body of advisers chosen from both Houses of Parliament. Now, the Ministry is responsible to Parliament for the conduct of affairs, and whenever it ceases to have the confidence of Parliament, the Sovereign must choose another body of advisers. Thus Parliament is virtually supreme.

The crown is hereditary, and may be worn either by a King or by a Queen, who must be a Protestant of the Church of England. The Sovereign has power to make war or peace; to pardon a convicted criminal; to summon, prorogue, or dissolve Parliament; to coin money; and to confer nobility. The assent of the Sovereign is also necessary to every new law. But, as already explained, these prerogatives are now exercised by the Sovereign under the advice of the Ministry for the time being; or by the Ministry in the name of the Sovereign.

The House of Lords, or Upper House of Parliament, comprises Lords Spiritual and Lords Temporal. The Lord Chancellor, sitting on the woolsack, acts as president or chairman of the Lords. The Upper House forms the highest court of justice, to decide appeals from the inferior courts. Any bill, except a money bill, may originate in the House of Lords.

The House of Commons, or Lower House of Parliament, consists of representatives of the counties, boroughs, and universities in England and Wales, Scotland, and Ireland. The electors are — in boroughs, all householders rated for relief of the poor, and lodgers who have occupied for a year rooms valued at £10 a year unfurnished; in counties, owners of freehold property worth £2 a year and of other holdings worth £5 a year, and tenants of lands or houses rated at £12 a year (in Scotland £14). The chairman of the Commons is called the Speaker, because he is their spokesman or representative in approaching the Sovereign. A new Speaker is elected at the beginning of each new Parliament. Money bills can originate in the House of Commons alone; and thus commanding the sources of supply, it can effectually control the Sovereign.

In great emergencies it also practically controls the Upper House; for a Ministry, strongly supported in the House of Commons, may advise the Sovereign to create a sufficient number of new peers to give its party a majority in the House of Lords. The threat of this measure has generally induced the Lords to yield to the wishes of the Commons.

The process of law-making is conducted as follows: — The proposed law is introduced in either House, after leave has been given, in the form of a Bill. It is then read for the first time, without opposition, and is ordered to be printed, to acquaint the members with its details. It is then circulated; and a day is fixed for the second reading. The first debate and voting take place on the question whether the bill shall pass this reading or not. If it pass the second reading, the House proceeds to consider and vote upon each clause in the bill separately. For this purpose, the House goes "into committee." This committee consists of the same members as the House; but the chairman of committee takes the place of the Speaker, and the strict rules of debate and forms of procedure observed in the House are considerably relaxed. After the bill has passed through committee, it is "reported" to the House in its amended form, and is ready for the third reading. If it pass this reading, it is then sent to the other House.

There it undergoes an exactly similar process; three readings, with a careful examination in committee between the second and the third. If amended or altered there, the bill is sent back to the House in which it originated, which either agrees to these amendments or not, and may demand a conference with the other House to settle differences.

When the bill has finally passed both Houses, the royal assent is required before it becomes an Act or law. This is given either personally or by commission. No Sovereign has ventured to exercise the right of veto — that is, of withholding the royal assent — since 1707.

From very early times, the advisers of the Sovereign have been known as the Privy Council, the members of which are dignified with the title of Right Honourable. But this body was found to be too numerous, and too widely scattered, for the systematic transaction of business. It moreover consists of men of different parties and conflicting views. It therefore became customary, after the Revolution of 1688, to intrust the government to a committee of the Privy Council, called the Ministry, or the Cabinet. But now ministers are not selected from the Privy Council, but from Parliament, and become Privy Councillors afterwards.

The head of the Ministry is the Prime Minister, or Premier. He used to owe his office to the good-will or favour of the Sovereign, but now he owes it to the confidence of his supporters in Parliament. The Sovereign chooses as Premier the recognized leader of that political party which has a majority in the House of Commons for the time, and intrusts him with the task of forming a Ministry from among his own supporters.

The chief ministers form the Cabinet, which determines the general policy of the Ministry, and the measures which are to be proposed to Parliament.

When a Ministry loses the confidence of the majority of the House of Commons, it is customary for it to resign. The Sovereign then intrusts the leader of the opposite party with the formation of a Ministry. But, instead of resigning, a defeated Ministry may advise the Sovereign to dissolve the Parliament and call a new one, in the hope that the constituencies may return a majority of members favourable to its views. This is called an "appeal tho the country."

Each House of Parliament may adjourn its meetings from day to day. The Sovereign, advised by the Ministry, prorogues Parliament from session to session; and dissolves it, when a new Parliament is to be elected. Parliament is also dissolved by the Sovereign's death. The duration of a Parliament is limited by law to seven years; but no Parliament since that law passed (1716) has exceeded six years in duration. During the present reign, the average length of the Parliaments has been under five years. ROYAL READERS.

III. HISTORY AND LITERATURE.

1. The Romans in Britain.

It was the afternoon of a September day, and the forest leaves were already touched with the first tints of autumn, when Julius Caesar's fleet of eighty ships drew up off the shore of Kent. The natives lined the beach with horse, foot, and chariots, and stood prepared to defend their island home. The Romans soldiers, clad as they were in heavy plate-armour of brass, and afraid of being struck down before they could gain firm footing, hesitated to leap into the water.

Caesar opened on the Britons a heavy discharge of stones and darts from the engines used in sieges, which his galleys had on board. This made the enemy give back a little. Still the soldiers hesitated to leap from the ships. Then the standard-bearer of the tenth legion, crying "Leap, comrades, unless you wish to see your standard taken by the enemy!" sprang overboard, and began to carry forward the standard.

Roused by his example, the whole twelve thousand soldiers dashed at once into the sea. The Britons met them in the water. A fierce and deadly struggle took place, and much brave blood reddened the waves. Gradually the Romans fought their way to land. They formed and charged, and the terrible rush of their disciplined battalions swept the Britons before them.

This was the beginning of the Roman invasion of Britain. Nearly a century and a half passed after this, however, before they invaded Scotland. Up to the year 80 after Christ, while nearly the whole of England had been reduced to the condition of a Roman province, the Romans possessed no land north of the Solway Firth.

In that year, Agricola, governor of the province, led an army across the border, and began to hew his way into the Caledonian forests. The wary general advanced slowly, and secured his ground as he advanced, by building forts in commanding situations. The native tribes struggled bravely against the formidable invader, but having little union or combination among themselves, they were taken singly, and overcome in detail.

The Romans carried on their operations with merciless vigour. Tacitus, Agricola's son-in-law, who writes an account of his life, tells us that it was his policy to overcome the Britons by the terror of his ravages. We understand what that means.

Yonder, for example, in a forest clearing, is a native village, fenced with its ditch and stockade of posts. It has children playing, cattle feeding, and patches of growing corn. The women sing the quern-song as they grind the meal for the evening repast in the quern or hand-mill. Some of the men are doing a little smith-work, or bit of homely carpentry; others are away hunting.

Suddenly, at the edge of the forest, there is a gleam as of the sun's rays on polished metal. A body of armed men, sheathed in brass, issue from the wood, and sweep across the clearing, their burnished mail flashing as they go. The lightsome quern-song changes into shrieks of terror. The villagers close the gate of their stockade, and grasp their bows. The arrows shot through the openings of the posts rattle vainly against the strong plate-armour of the assailants.

The gate goes down before the strokes of the axe; sword and torch do the rest. The cattle are driven away, and the crops destroyed.

The village hunters, alarmed by the smoke seen rising high over the forest, hasten back, and find a waste of blackened ruin, with the women and children wailing over the slain.

Yonder, again, is a British hill-fort. It is provided with ditch and rampart, and the natives have gathered their families and most valuable effects into it for security. The Romans have come to the foot of the hill, and prepare to carry the fort by storm. They form a "tortoise" as they called it; that is to say, they advance to the attack covered with their great shields overlapping each other like the plates in the shell of the tortoise, or as slates do on a roof.

They take their way up the hill with swift and firm tread. The shower of darts and arrows, from the rampart above, falls harmless on the roof of shields. The defenders loosen a block of stone on the hill-top, and roll it over. The mass comes thundering down, crashes through the "tortoise," and leaves behind it a ghastly and bloody lane. The stern assailants close up their cleft roof without delaying their rapid advance for a moment. They reach the ditch, push planks and ladders across it, storm over the rampart, and put the defenders to the sword to the last man.

Such, no doubt, was the style of the Roman doings. In three of these stern campaigns Agricola penetrated to the Firths of Forth and Clyde. These two arms of the sea run so far inland that the distance between them, from water to water, is less than forty miles. Across this neck of land Agricola built a chain of forts at regular intervals. This line of fortified posts was meant to defend the conquered territory against the warlike tribes of the north.

Dreading an attack from the northern tribes, Agricola resolved to strike them within their own bounds. Leaving his fortified line, and crossing the Forth at Queensferry, he advanced northward through Fife. The clans rose for the defence of their country against the fierce people whose lust of dominion had brought them so far; and they put a chief named Galgacus at their head.

What manner of man he was who has come down to us under this name, what life he lived, or what death he died, we have no means of knowing; but the man around whom these old clans gathered, to bleed and die for country and freedom, must have had in him some of the stuff of which heroes are made.

The Romans found the Caledonian army drawn up on the moor of Ardoch, in Perthshire, at the foot of the Grampian mountains (A. D. 84). Tacitus says that they were 30,000 strong — the Romans

26.000. The Caledonians fought with desperate courage, but the vastly superior discipline and arms of the Romans gave them every advantage.

They fought with a large, oblong shield, and a short, heavy sword, formed either to thrust or to cut. The Caledonians fought with small, round shields, and long, heavy swords without a point. The mighty downward stroke of the Caledonian sword was received on the upper edge of the Roman shield. Pushing it up, the Roman plunged his short keen sword into the body of his adversary.

The Caledonians were defeated with great slaughter. Night alone put a stop to the carnage. Next morning 10.000 dead lay on the face of the moor. Agricola led back his army to the south. Then, when the retiring host was out of sight, the natives would venture down to search for their dead on the field of slaughter. The raven beat his wings and croaked hoarsely when disturbed in his feast; and the wolf looked up and growled fiercely when the widow tried to scare him from the corpse of her husband. H. MACKENZIE.

2. CHARACTERS FROM ENGLISH HISTORY.

1. Alfred the Great (871—901).

The merit of this prince, both in private and public life, may with advantage be set in opposition to that of any monarch or citizen which the annals of any age or any nation can present to us. He seems indeed to be the complete model of that perfect character, which under the denomination of a sage or wise man, the philosophers have been fond of delineating rather as a fiction of their imagination, than in hopes of ever seeing it reduced to practice; so happily were all his virtues tempered together, so justly were they blended, and so powerfully did each prevent the other from exceeding its proper bounds. He knew how to conciliate the most enterprising spirit with the coolest moderation; the most obstinate perseverance with the easiest flexibility; the most severe justice with the greatest lenity; the greatest rigour in command with the greatest affability of deportment; the highest capacity and inclination for science, with the most shining talents for action. His civil and his military virtues are almost equally the objects of our admiration, excepting only, that the former being more rare among princes, as well as more useful, seem chiefly to challenge our applause. Nature also, as if desirous that so bright a production of her skill should be set in the fairest light, had bestowed on him all bodily accomplishments, vigour of limbs, dignity of shape and air, and a pleasant, engaging, and open countenance. Fortune alone, by throwing him into that barbarous age, deprived him of historians worthy to transmit his fame to posterity; and we wish to see him delineated in more lively colours, and with more particular strokes, that we may at least perceive some of those small specks and blemishes, from which, as a man, it is impossible he could be entirely exempted.

DAVID HUME.

II. William the Conqueror (1066—1087).

Few princes have been more fortunate than this great monarch, or were better entitled to prosperity and grandeur, for the abilities and vigour of mind which he displayed in all his conduct. His spirit was bold and enterprising, yet guided by prudence. His ambition, which was exorbitant, and lay little under the restraints of justice, and still less under those of humanity, ever submitted to the dictates of reason and sound policy. Born in an age when the minds of men were intractable and unacquainted with submission, he was yet able to direct them to his purposes; and, partly from the ascendant of his vehement disposition, partly from art and dissimulation, to establish an unlimited monarchy. Though not insensible to generosity, he was hardened against compassion, and seemed equally ostentatious and ambitious of eclat in his clemency and his severity. The maxims of his administration were severe: but might have been useful, had they been solely employed in preserving order in an established government; they were ill calculated for softening the rigours which under the most gentle management are inseparable from conquest. His attempt against England was the last enterprise of this kind, which during the course of seven hundred years, has fully succeeded in Europe; and the greatness of his genius broke through those limits, which first the feudal institutions, then the refined policy of princes, have fixed on the several states of Christendom. Though he rendered himself infinitely odious to his English subjects, he transmitted his power to his posterity, and the throne is still filled by his descendants: a proof that the foundation which he laid was firm and solid, and that amongst all his violences, while he seemed only to gratify the present passion, he had still an eye towards futurity.

DAVID HUME.

3. The Battle of Hastings (1066).

William had been most actively employed. As a preliminary to further proceedings he had caused all the vessels to be drawn on shore and rendered unserviceable. He told his men that they must prepare to conquer or to die — flight was impossible. He had occupied the Roman castle of Pevensey, whose walls are yet existing, flanked by Anglo-Norman towers, and he had personally surveyed all the adjoining country, for he never trusted this part of a general's duty to any eyes but his own. One Robert, a Norman thane who was settled in the neighbourhood, advised him to cast up intrenchments for the purpose of resisting Harold. William replied, that his best defence was in the valour of his army and the goodness of his cause.

When William first set foot on shore, he stumbled, and fell forward on the palms of his hands. 'Mal signe est ci!' exclaimed his troops, affrighted at the omen. 'No,' answered William, as he rose; 'I have taken seizin of the country,' showing the clod of earth which he had grasped. One of his soldiers, with the quickness of a modern Frenchman, instantly followed up the idea; he ran to a cottage, and pulled out a bundle of reeds from the thatch, telling him to receive that symbol also, as the seizin of the realm with which he was invested. These little anecdotes display the turn and temper of the Normans, and the alacrity by which the army was pervaded.

Some fruitless attempts are said to have been made at negotiation. Harold despatched a monk to the enemy's camp, who was to exhort William to abandon his enterprise. The duke insisted on his right; but, as some historians relate, he offered to submit his claim to a legal decision, to be pronounced by the pope, either according to the law of Normandy, or according to the law of England, or if this mode of adjustment did not please Harold, that the question should be decided by single combat, the crown becoming the meed of the victor. The propositions of William are stated, by other authorities, to have contained a proposition for a compromise — namely that Harold should take Northumbria, and William the rest of the Anglo-Saxon dominions. All or any of these proposals are such as may very probably have been made; but they were not minuted down in formal protocols, or couched in diplomatic notes, they were verbal messages, sent to and fro on the eve of a bloody battle.

Fear prevailed in both camps. The English, in addition to the apprehensions which even the most stout-hearted feel on the eve of a morrow whose close they may never see, dreaded the papal excommunication, the curse encountered in support of the unlawful authority of a usurper. When they were informed that battle had been decided upon, they stormed and swore; and now cowardice of conscience spurred them on to riot and revelry. The whole night was passed in debauch. Wæs-heal and Drink-heal resounded from the tents; the wine-cups passed gaily round and round by the smoky blaze of the red watch-fires, while the ballad of ribald mirth was loudly sung by the carousers.

In the Norman Leaguer, far otherwise had the dread of the approaching morn affected the hearts of William's soldiery. No voice was heard excepting the solemn response of the litany and the chant of the psalm. The penitents confessed their sins, the masses were said, and the sense of the imminent peril of the morrow was tranquillised by penance and prayer. Each of the nations, as we are told by one of our most trustworthy English historians, acted according to their 'national custom;' and severe is the censure which the English thus receive.

The English were strongly fortified in their position by lines of trenches and palisades; and within these defences they were marshalled according to the Danish fashion — shield against shield, presenting an impenetrable front to the enemy. The men of Kent formed the vanguard, for it was their privilege to be the first in the strife. The burgesses of London, in like manner, claimed and obtained the honour of being the royal body-guard, and they were drawn up around the standard. At the foot of this banner stood Harold, with this brothers, Leofwin and Gurth, and a chosen body of the bravest thanes.

Before the Normans began their march, and very early in the morning of the feast of St. Calixtus, William had assembled his barons around him, and exhorted them to maintain his righteous cause. As the invaders drew nigh, Harold saw a divison, advancing, composed of the volunteers from the country of Boulogne and from he Amiennois, under the command of William Fitz-Osbern and Roger Montgomery. 'It is the duke,' exclaimed Harold, 'and little shall I fear him. By my forces will his be four times outnumbered!' Gurth shook his head, and expatiated on the strength of the Norman cavalry, as opposed to the footsoldiers of England; but their discourse was stopped by the appearance of the combined cohorts under Aimeric, Viscount of Thouars, and Alan Fergant of Brittany. Harold's heart sank at the sight, and he broke out into passionate exclamations of fear and dismay. But now the third and last division of the Norman army was drawing nigh. The consecrated Gonfanon floats amidst the forest of spears, and Harold is now too well aware that he beholds the ranks which are commanded in person by the Duke of Normandy.

Immediately before the duke rode Taillefer, the minstrel, singing. with a loud and clear voice, the lay of Charlemagne and Roland, and the emprises of the Paladins who had fallen in the dolorous pass of Roncevaux. Taillefer, as his guerdon, had craved permission to strike

the first blow, for he was a valiant warrior, emulating the deeds
which he sang. his appellation, Taille-fer, is probably to be considered not as his real name, but as an epithet derived from his
strength and prowess; and he fully justified his demand, by transfixing the first Englishman whom he attacked, and by felling the 5
second to the ground. The battle now became general, and raged with
the greatest fury The Normans advanced beyond the English lines,
but they were driven back, and forced into a trench, where horses
and riders fell upon each other in fearful confusion. More Normans
were slain here than in any other part of the field. The alarm 10
spread; the light troops left in charge of the baggage and the stores
thought that all was lost, and were about to take flight; but the
fierce Odo, bishop of Bayeux, the duke's halfbrother, and who was
better fitted for the shield than for the mitre, succeeded in reassuring
them, and then, returning to the field, and rushing into that part 15
where the battle was hottest, he fought as the stoutest of the warriors
engaged in the conflict.

From nine in the morning till three in the afternoon, the successes on either side were nearly balanced. The charges of the
Norman cavalry gave them great advantage, but the English phalanx 20
repelled their enemies; and the soldiers were so well protected by
their targets, that the artillery of the Normans was long discharged
in vain. The bowmen, seeing that they had failed to make any impression, altered the direction of their shafts, and instead of shooting
point-blank, the flights of arrows were directed upwards, so that the 25
points came down upon the heads of the men of England, and the
iron shower fell with murderous effect. The English ranks were exceedingly distressed by the volleys, yet they still stood firm; and the
Normans now employed a stratagem to decoy their opponents out of
their intrenchments. A feigned retreat on their part, induced the 30
English to pursue them with great heat. The Normans suddenly
wheeled about, and a new and fiercer battle was urged. The field was
covered with separate bands of foemen, each engaged with one
another. Here, the English yielded — there, they conquered. One
English thane, armed with a battle-axe, spread dismay amongst the 35
Frenchmen. He was cut down by Roger de Montgomery. The Normans
have preserved the name of the Norman baron, but that of the Englishman is lost in oblivion. Some other English thanes are also
praised as having singly, and by their personal prowess, delayed the
ruin of their countrymen and country. 40

At one period of the battle, the Normans were nearly routed.
The cry was raised that the duke was slain, and they began to fly

in every direction. William threw off his helmet, and galloping through
the squadrons, rallied his barons, though not without great difficulty.
Harold, on his part, used every possible exertion, and was distinguished as the most active and bravest amongst the soldiers in the
host which he led on to destruction. A Norman arrow wounded him
in the left eye: he dropped from his steed in agony, and was borne
to the foot of the standard. The English began to give way, or rather
to retreat to the standard as their rallying-point. The Normans en-
circled them, and fought desperately to reach this goal. Robert Fitz-
Ernest had almost seized the banner, but he was killed in the attempt.
William led his troops on with the intention, it is said, of measuring
his sword with Harold. He did encounter an English horseman, from
whom he received such a stroke upon his helmet, that he was nearly
brought to the ground.

The Normans flew to the aid of their sovereign, and the bold
Englishman was pierced by their lances. About the same time the tide
of battle took a momentary turn. The Kentish men and East-Saxons
rallied, and repelled the Norman barons; but Harold was not amongst
them; and William led on his troops with desperate intrepidity. In
the thick crowd of the assailants and the assailed, the hoofs of the
horses were plunged deep into the gore of the dead and the dying.
Gurth was at the foot of the standard, without hope, but without
fear: he fell by the falchion of William. The English banner was
cast down, and the Gonfanon planted in its place announced that
William of Normandy was the conqueror. It was now late in the
evening. The English troops were entirely broken, yet no Englishman
would surrender. The conflict continued in many parts of the bloody
field long after dark.   SIR FRANCIS PALGRAVE.

4. The Amalgamation of the English and the Normans.

Here commences the history of the English nation. The history
of the preceding events is the history of wrongs inflicted and sustained
by various tribes, which indeed all dwelt on English ground, but
which regarded each other with aversion such as has scarcely ever
existed between communities separated by physical barriers. For
even mutual animosity of countries at war with each other is languid
when compared with the animosity of nations which, morally separated,
are yet locally intermingled. In no country has the enmity of race
been carried farther than in England. In no country has that enmity
been more completely effaced. The stages of the process by which
the hostile elements were melted down into one homogeneous mass
are not accurately known to us. But it is certain that, when John

became King, the distinction between Saxons and Normans was strongly marked, and that before the end of the reign of his grandson it had almost disappeared. In the time of Richard the First, the ordinary imprecation of a Norman gentleman was "May I become an Englishman!" His ordinary form of indignant denial was "Do you take me for an Englishman?" The descendant of such a gentleman a hundred years later was proud of the English name.

The sources of the noblest rivers which spread fertility over continents, and bear richly laden fleets to the sea, are to be sought in wild and barren mountain tracts, incorrectly laid down in maps, and rarely explored by travellers. To such a tract the history of our country during the thirteenth century may not unaptly be compared. Sterile and obscure as is that portion of our annals, it is there that we must seek for the origin of our freedom, our prosperity, and our glory. Then it was that the great English people was formed, that the national character began to exhibit those peculiarities which it has ever since retained, and that our fathers became emphatically islanders, islanders not merely in geographical position, but in their politics, their feelings, and their manners. Then first appeared with distinctness that constitution which has ever since, through all changes, preserved its identity; that constitution of which all the other free constitutions in the world are copies, and which, in spite of some defects, deserves to be regarded as the best under which any great society has ever yet existed during many ages. Then it was that the House of Commons, the archetype of all the representative assemblies which now meet, either in the old or in the new world, held its first sittings. Then it was that the common law rose to the dignity of a science, and rapidly became a not unworthy rival of the imperial jurisprudence. Then it was that the courage of those sailors who manned the rude barks of the Cinque Ports first made the flag of England terrible on the seas. Then it was that the most ancient colleges which still exist at both the great national seats of learning were founded. Then was formed that language, less musical indeed than the languages of the south, but in force, in richness, in aptitude for all the highest purposes of the poet, the philosopher, and the orator inferior to the tongue of Greece alone. Then too appeared the first faint dawn of that noble literature, the most splendid and the most durable of the many glories of England.

Early in the fourteenth century the amalgamation of the races was all but complete; and it was soon made manifest, by signs not to be mistaken, that a people inferior to none existing in the world had been formed by the mixture of the three branches of the great

Teutonic family with each other, and with the aboriginal Britons. There was, indeed, scarcely any thing in common between the England to which John had been chased by Philip Augustus, and the England from which the armies of Edward the Third went forth to conquer France.   Th. B. Macaulay.

5. Richard Coeur de Lion in Palestine (1190—1192).

At length, in the spring of the second year, the royal fleets of France and England cast anchor in the bay of Acre, and the siege was more vigorously prosecuted by the youthful emulation of the two kings, Philip Augustus and Richard Plantagenet. After every resource had been tried, and every hope was exhausted, the defenders of Acre submitted to their fate; a capitulation was granted, but their lives and liberties were taxed at the hard conditions of a ransom of two hundred thousand pieces of gold, the deliverance of one hundred nobles and fifteen hundred inferior captives, and the restoration of the wood of the holy cross. Some doubts in the agreement, and some delay in the execution, rekindled the fury of the Franks, and three thousand Moslems, almost in the sultan's view, were beheaded by the command of the sanguinary Richard. By the conquest of Acre, the Latin powers acquired a strong town and a convenient harbour; but the advantage was most dearly purchased. The minister and historian of Saladin computes, from the reports of the enemy, that their numbers, at different periods, amounted to five or six hundred thousand; that more than one hundred thousand Christians were slain; that a far greater number was lost by disease or shipwreck; and that a small portion of this mighty host could return in safety to their native countries.

Philip Augustus, and Richard the First, are the only kings of France and England, who have fought under the same banners; but the holy service, in which they were enlisted, was incessantly disturbed by their national jealousy; and the two factions, which they protected in Palestine, were more averse to each other than to the common enemy. In the eyes of the Orientals, the French monarch was superior in dignity and power; and, in the emperor's absence, the Latins revered him as their temporal chief. His exploits were not adequate to his fame. Philip was brave, but the statesman predominated in his character; he was soon weary of sacrificing his health and interest on a barren coast; the surrender of Acre became the signal of his departure; nor could he justify this unpopular desertion, by leaving the duke of Burgundy, with five hundred knights and ten thousand foot, for the service of the Holy Land. The king of England, though inferior in dignity, surpassed his rival in wealth, and military renown; and if heroism be confined to brutal and ferocious valour, Richard Plantagenet will stand high among the heroes of the age. The memory of Coeur de Lion, of the lion-hearted prince, was long dear and glorious to his English subjects: and, at the distance of sixty years, it was celebrated in proverbial sayings by the grandsons of the Turks and Saracens, against whom he had fought:. his tremendous name was employed by the Syrian mothers to silence their infants; and if a horse suddenly started from the way, his rider was wont to exclaim, "Dost thou think king Richard is in that bush?" His cruelty to the Mahometans was the effect of temper and zeal; but I cannot believe that a soldier, so free and fearless in the use of his lance, would have descended to whet a dagger against his valiant brother Conrad of Montferrat, who was slain at Tyre by some secret assassins. After the surrender of Acre, and the departure of Philip, the king of England led the crusaders to the recovery of the sea-coast: and the cities of Caesarea and Jaffa were added to the fragments of the kingdom of Lusignan. A march of one hundred miles from Acre to Ascalon was a great and perpetual battle of eleven days. In the disorder of his troops, Saladin remained on the field with seventeen guards, without lowering his standard, or suspending the sound of his brazen kettle-drum: he again rallied and renewed the charge: and his preachers or heralds called aloud on the Unitarians, manfully to stand up against the Christians. But the progress of the Christians was irresistible: and it was only by demolishing the walls and buildings of Ascalon, that the sultan could prevent them from occupying an important fortress on the confines of Egypt. During a severe winter, the armies slept: but in the spring, the Franks advanced within a day's march of Jerusalem, under the leading standard of the English king, and his active spirit intercepted a convoy, or caravan, of seven thousand camels. Saladin had fixed his station in the holy city; but the city was struck with consternation and discord: he fasted; he prayed; he preached: he offered to share the dangers of the siege; but his Mamalukes, who remembered the fate of their companions at Acre, pressed the sultan with loyal or seditious clamours, to reserve his person and their courage, for the future defence of their religion and empire. The Moslems were delivered by the sudden, or, as they deemed, the miraculous, retreat of the Christians: and the laurels of Richard were blasted by the prudence, or envy, of his companions. The hero, ascending a hill, and veiling his face, exclaimed with an indignant face, "Those who are unwilling to rescue, are unworthy to view the sepulchre of Christ!" After his return to Acre,

on the news that Jaffa was surprised by the sultan, he sailed with
some merchant vessels, and leaped foremost on the beach; the castle
was relieved by his presence: and sixty thousand Turks and Saracens
fled before his arms. The discovery of his weakness provoked them
to return in the morning; and they found him carelessly encamped
before the gates with only seventeen knights and three hundred
archers. Without counting their numbers, he sustained the charge;
and we learn, from the evidence of his enemies, that the king of
England, grasping his lance, rode furiously along their front, from
the right to the left wing, without meeting an adversary who dared
to encounter his career. Am I writing the history of Orlando or
Armadis?

During the hostilities, a languid and tedious negotiation between the Franks and Moslems was started, and continued, and
broken, and again resumed and again broken. Some acts of royal
courtesy, the gift of snow and fruit, the exchange of Norway hawks
and Arabian horses, softened the asperity of religious war; nor, after
the trial of each other, could either hope for a decisive victory. The
health both of Richard and Saladin appeared to be in a declining
state, and they respectively suffered the evils of distant and domestic
warfare: Plantagenet was impatient to punish a perfidious rival who
had invaded Normandy in his absence, and the indefatigable sultan
was subdued by the cries of the people, who was the victim, and of
the soldiers, who were the instruments, of his martial zeal. The first
demands of the king of England were the restitution of Jerusalem,
Palestine, and the true cross: and he firmly declared, that himself
and his brother pilgrims would end their lives in the pious labour,
rather than return to Europe with ignominy and remorse. But Saladin
asserted, with equal firmness, his religious and civil claim to the
sovereignty of Palestine; descanted on the importance and sanctity
of Jerusalem; and rejected all terms of the establishment, or par-
tition, of the Latins. The marriage which Richard proposed, of his
sister with the sultan's brother, was defeated by the difference of
faith. A personal interview was declined by Saladin, who alleged
their mutual ignorance of each other's language; and the negotiation
was managed with much art and delay by their interpreters and
envoys. The final agreement was equally disapproved by the zealots
of both parties.

It was stipulated that Jerusalem and the holy sepulchre should
be open, without tribute or vexation, to the pilgrimage of the Latin
Christians; that after the demolition of Ascalon, they should in-
clusively possess the sea-coast from Jaffa to Tyre; that the count of

Tripoli and the prince of Antioch should be comprised in the truce, and that, during three years and three months, all hostilities should cease. The principal chiefs of the two armies swore to the observance of the treaty; but the monarchs were satisfied with giving their word and their right-hand; and the royal majesty was excused from an oath, which always implies some suspicion of falsehood and dishonour. Richard embarked for Europe, to seek a long captivity and a premature grave; and the space of a few months concluded the life and glories of Saladin. EDWARD GIBBON.

6. Magna Charta (1215).

A conference between the king and the barons was appointed at Runnymede, between Windsor and Staines, a place which has ever since been celebrated on account of this great event. The two parties encamped apart, like open enemies, the barons on the field of Runnymede, the king on a little shady island on the Buckinghamshire side of the river; and after a debate of a few days, the king, with a facility somewhat suspicious, signed and sealed the charter which was required of him (19th June, 1215). This famous deed, commonly called the Magna Charta, or Great Charter, either granted or secured very important liberties and privileges to every order of men in the kingdom — to the clergy, to the barons, and to the people. The privileges granted to the clergy in the preceding February are confirmed by the Great Charter.

The barons were relieved from the chief grievances to which they had been subject by the crown. The "reliefs" of heirs of the tenants in chief, succeeding to an inheritance, were limited to a certain sum, according to the rank of the tenant; the guardians in chivalry were restrained from wasting the lands of their wards; heirs were to be married without disparagement, and widows secured from compulsory marriages. The next clause was still more important. It enacted that no "scutage" or "aid" should be imposed without the consent of the great council of the kingdom, except in the three feudal cases of the king's ransom, the knighting of his eldest son, and the marriage of his eldest daughter; and it provided that the prelates, earls, and greater barons, should be summoned to this great council, each by a particular writ, and all other tenants in chief by a general summons of the sheriff. All the privileges and immunities granted to the tenants in chief were extended to the inferior vassals. The franchises of the city of London, and of all other cities and boroughs, were declared inviolable; and aids in like manner were not to be required of them, except by the consent of the great council. One weight and one measure were extended throughout the kingdom. The freedom of commerce was granted to alien merchants. The court of Common Pleas was to be stationary instead of following the king's person.

But the essential clauses of Magna Charta are those which protect the personal liberty and property of all freemen, by giving security from arbitrary imprisonment and arbitrary spoliation. "No freeman shall be taken or imprisoned, or be disseized of his freehold, or liberties, or free customs, or be outlawed, or exiled, or any otherwise destroyed; nor will we pass upon him, nor send upon him, but by lawful judgment of his peers, or by the law of the land. We will sell to no man, we will not deny or delay to any man, justice or right." DAVID HUME.

7. Queen Elizabeth (1558—1603).

There are few great personages in history who have been more exposed to the calumny of enemies, and the adulation of friends, than Queen Elizabeth: and yet there is scarce any whose reputation has been more certainly determined by the unanimous consent of posterity. The unusual length of her administration, and the strong features of her character, were able to overcome all prejudices; and obliging her detractors to abate much of their invectives, and her admirers somewhat of their panegyrics, have at last, in spite of political factions, and, what is more, of religious animosities, produced a uniform judgment with regard to her conduct. Her vigour, her constancy, her magnanimity, her penetration, and vigilance, are allowed to merit the highest praise, and appear not to have been surpassed by any person who ever filled a throne: a conduct less vigorous, less imperious, more sincere, more indulgent to her people, would have been requisite to form a perfect character. By the force of her mind, she controlled all her more active and stronger qualities, and prevented them from running into excess: her heroism was exempt from all temerity, her frugality from avarice, her friendship from partiality, her active spirit from turbulency and a vain ambition. She did not guard herself with equal care, or equal success from lesser infirmities; the rivalship of beauty, the desire of admiration, the jealousy of love, and the sallies of anger.

Her singular talents for government were founded equally on her temper and on her capacity. Endowed with a great command over herself, she obtained an uncontrolled ascendant over the people; and while she merited all their esteem by her real virtues, she also engaged their affection by her pretended ones. Few sovereigns of

England succeeded to the throne in more difficult circumstances: and none ever conducted the government with such uniform success and felicity. Though unacquainted with the practice of toleration, the true secret for managing religious factions, she preserved her people by her superior prudence, from those confusions in which theological controversy had involved all the neighbouring nations; and though her enemies were the most powerful princes in Europe, the most active, the most enterprizing, the least scrupulous, she was able by her vigour to make deep impressions on their states; her own greatness meanwhile remained untouched and unimpaired.

The wise ministers and brave warriors, who flourished during her reign, share the praise of her success; but, instead of lessening the applause due to her, they make great addition to it: they owed, all of them, their advancement to her choice; they were supported by her constancy; and with all their ability, they were never able to acquire any undue ascendant over her. In her family, in her court, in her kingdom, she remained equally mistress.

The fame of this princess, though it has surmounted the prejudices, both of faction and bigotry, yet lies still exposed to another prejudice, which is more durable, because more natural, and which, according to the different views in which we survey her, is capable either of exalting beyond measure, or diminishing the lustre of her character. This prejudice is founded in consideration of her sex. When we contemplate her as a woman, we are apt to be struck with the highest admiration of her qualities and extensive capacity; but we are also apt to require some more softness of disposition, some greater lenity of temper, some of those amiable weaknesses by which her sex is distinguished. But the true method of estimating her merit, is to lay aside all those considerations, and consider her merely as a rational being, placed in authority, and intrusted with the government of mankind. We may find it difficult to reconcile our fancy to her as a woman; but her qualities as a sovereign, though with some considerable exceptions, are the object of undisputed applause and approbation. DAVID HUME.

8. Mary, Queen of Scots (1542—1587).

To all the charms of beauty, and the utmost elegance of external form, Mary adding those accomplishments which render their impression irresistible, was polite, affable, insinuating, sprightly, and capable of speaking and writing with equal ease and dignity; sudden, however, and violent in all her attachments, because she had been accustomed from her infancy to be treated as a queen: no stranger, on some occasions, to dissimulation, which, in that perfidious court where she received her education, was reckoned among the necessary arts of government; not insensible to flattery, or unconscious of that pleasure with which almost every woman beholds the influence of her own beauty. Formed with the qualities that we love, not with the talents that we admire, she was an agreeable woman rather than an illustrious queen. The vivacity of her spirit, not sufficiently tempered with sound judgment, and the warmth of her heart, which was not at all times under the restraint of discretion, betrayed her both into errors and crimes. To say that she was most unfortunate, will not account for that long and almost uninterrupted succession of calamities which befell her: we must likewise add, that she was often imprudent. Her passion for Darnley was rash, youthful, and excessive. And though the sudden transition to the opposite extreme was the natural effect of her ill-requited love, and of his ingratitude, insolence, and brutality; yet neither these, nor Bothwell's artful address and important services, can justify her attachment to that nobleman. Even the manners of the age, licentious as they were, are no apology for this unhappy passion; nor can they induce us to look on that tragical and infamous scene which followed upon it, with less abhorrence. Humanity will draw a veil over this part of her character, which it cannot approve, and may, perhaps, prompt some to impute her actions to her situation, more than to her disposition; and to lament the unhappiness of the former rather than accuse the perverseness of the latter. Mary's sufferings exceed, both in degree and duration, those tragical distresses which fancy has feigned to excite sorrow and commiseration; and while we survey them, we are apt altogether to forget her frailties; we think of her faults with less indignation, and approve of our tears, as if they were shed for a person who had attained much nearer to pure virtue.

With regard to the queen's person, a circumstance not to be omitted in writing the history of a female reign, all contemporary authors agree in ascribing to Mary the utmost beauty of countenance and elegance of shape of which the human form is capable. Her hair was black: though, according to the fashion of the age, she frequently wore borrowed locks, and of different colours. Her eyes were a dark grey, her complexion was exquisitely fine, and her hands and arms remarkably delicate, both as to shape and colour. Her stature was of a height that rose to the majestic. She danced, walked, and rode with equal grace. Her taste for music was just, and she sang, and played upon the lute with uncommon skill. Towards the end of her life she began to grow fat; and her long confinement, and the coldness of the house in which she was imprisoned, brought on a rheumatism, which deprived her of the use of her limbs. 'No man,' says Brantome, 'ever beheld her person without admiration and love, or will read her history without sorrow.' WILLIAM ROBERTSON.

9. The Armada (1588).

To Philip of Spain, as to the nearest heir in blood who was of the Catholic Faith, Mary Stuart bequeathed her rights to the Crown, and the hopes of her adherents were from that moment bound up in the success of Spain. The presence of an English army in Flanders only convinced Philip that the road to the conquest of the States lay through England itself; and the operations of Parma in the Low Countries were suspended with a view to the great enterprise. Vessels and supplies for the great fleet of invasion, which was to take the name of the Armada, and which had for three years been gathering in the Tagus, were collected from every port of the Spanish coast. It was time for Elizabeth to strike, and the news of the coming Armada called Drake again to sea. He had sailed a year before for the Indies at the head of twenty-five vessels; had requited the wrongs inflicted by the Inquisition on English seamen by plundering Vigo on his way; and avenged his disappointment at the escape of the gold fleet by the sack of Santiago, and by ravaging San Domingo and Cartagena. He now set sail again with thirty small barks, burnt the storeships and galleys in the harbour of Cadiz, stormed the ports of the Faro, and was only foiled in his aim of attacking the Armada itself by orders from home. A descent upon Corunna, however, completed what Drake called his "singeing of the Spanish King's beard." Elizabeth used the daring blow to back her negotiations for peace; but the Spanish pride had been touched to the quick. Amidst the exchange of protocols Parma gathered thirty thousand men for the coming invasion, collected a fleet of flat-bottomed transports at Dunkirk, and waited impatiently for the Armada to protect his crossing. But the attack of Drake, the death of its first admiral, and the winter storms delayed the fleet from sailing till the spring; and it had hardly started when a gale in the Bay of Biscay drove its scattered vessels into Ferrol. It was only on the twenty-ninth of July that the sails of the Armada were seen from the Lizard, and the English beacons flared out their alarm along the coast.

The news found England ready. An army was mustering under Leicester at Tilbury, the militia of the midland counties were gathering to London, while those of the south and east were held in readiness to meet a descent on either shore. Had Parma landed on

the earliest day he purposed, he would have found his way to London
barred by a force stronger than his own, a force too of men who
had already crossed pikes on equal terms with his best infantry in
Flanders. "When I shall have landed," he warned his master, "I must
fight battle after battle, I shall lose men by wounds and disease, I
must leave detachments behind me to keep open my communications;
and in a short time the body of my army will become so weak that
not only I may be unable to advance in the face of the enemy, and
time may be given to the heretics and your Majesty's other enemies
to interfere, but there may fall out some notable inconveniences,
with the loss of everything, and I be unable to remedy it." Even
had the Prince landed, in fact, the only real chance of Spanish success lay in a Catholic rising: and at this crisis patriotism proved
stronger than religious fanaticism in the hearts of the English
Catholics. Catholic gentry brought their vessels up alongside of Drake
and Lord Howard, and Catholic lords led their tenantry to the muster
at Tilbury.

But to secure a landing at all, the Spaniards had to be masters
of the Channel; and in the Channel lay an English fleet resolved to
struggle hard for the mastery. As the Armada sailed on in a broad
crescent past Plymouth, moving towards its point of junction with
Parma at Dunkirk, the vessels which had gathered under Lord Howard
of Effingham slipped out of the bay and hung with the wind upon
their rear. In numbers the two forces were strangely unequal; the
English fleet counted only 80 vessels against the 130 which composed the Armada. In size of ships the disproportion was even
greater. Fifty of the English vessels, including the squadron of Lord
Howard and the craft of the volunteers, were little bigger than yachts
of the present day. Even of the thirty Queen's ships which formed
its main body, there were only four which equalled in tonnage the
smallest of the Spanish galleons. Sixty-five of these galleons formed
the most formidable half of the Spanish fleet; and four galleasses,
or gigantic galleys, armed with 50 guns apiece, fifty-six armed
merchantmen, and twenty pinnaces, made up the rest. The Armada
was provided with 2,500 cannons, and a vast store of provisions; it
had on board 8,000 seamen and 20,000 soldiers; and if a court-
favourite, the Duke of Medina Sidonia, had been placed at its head,
he was supported by the ablest staff of naval officers which Spain
possessed. Small, however, as the English ships were, they were
manned with 9,000 hardy seamen, and their Admiral was backed by
a crowd of captains who had won fame in the Spanish seas. With
him was Hawkins, who had been the first to break into the charmed

circle of the Indies: Frobisher, the hero of the North-West passage; and above all Drake, who held command of the privateers. They had won, too, the advantage of the wind: and, closing in or drawing off as they would, the lightly-handled English vessels, which fired four shots to the Spaniard's one, hung boldly on the rear of the great fleet as it moved along the Channel. "The feathers of the Spaniard," in the phrase of the English seamen, were "plucked one by one." Galleon after galleon was sunk, boarded, driven on shore; and yet Medina Sidonia failed in bringing his pursuers to a close engagement. Now halting, now moving slowly on, the running fight between the two fleets lasted throughout the week, till the Armada dropped anchor in Calais roads.

The time had now come for sharper work if the junction of the Armada with Parma was to be prevented; for, demoralized as the Spaniards had been by the merciless chase, their loss in ships had not been great, while the English supplies of food and ammunition were fast running out. Howard resolved to force an engagement; and lighting eight fire-ships at midnight, sent them down with the tide upon the Spanish line. The galleons at once cut their cables, and, stood out in panic to sea, drifting with the wind in a long line off Gravelines. Drake resolved at all costs to prevent their return. At dawn the English ships closed fairly in, and almost their last cartridge was spent ere the sun went down. Three great galleons had sunk, three had drifted helplessly on the Flemish coast; but the bulk of the Spanish vessels remained, and even to Drake the fleet seemed "wonderful great and strong." Within the Armada itself, however, all hope was gone. Huddled together by the wind and the deadly English fire, their sails torn, their masts shot away, the crowded galleons had become mere slaughter-houses. Four thousand men had fallen, and bravely as the seamen fought they were cowed by the terrible butchery. Medina himself was in despair. "We are lost, Señor Oquenda," he cried to his bravest captain; "what are we to do?" "Let others talk of being lost," replied Oquenda, "your Excellency has only to order up fresh cartridge." But Oquenda stood alone, and a council of war resolved on retreat to Spain by the one course open, that of a circuit round the Orkneys. "Never anything pleased me better," wrote Drake, "than seeing the enemy fly with a southerly wind to the northwards. Have a good eye to the Prince of Parma, for, with the grace of God, if we like, I doubt not ere it be long so to handle the matter with the Duke of Sidonia, as he shall wish himself at St. Mary Port among his orange trees." But the work of destruction was reserved for a mightier foe than Drake. Supplies fell

short, and the English vessels were forced to give up the chase; but the Spanish ships which remained had no sooner reached the Orkneys than the storms of the northern seas broke on them with a fury before which all concert and union disappeared. Fifty reached Corunna, bearing ten thousand men stricken with pestilence and death; of the rest some were sunk, some dashed to pieces against the Irish cliffs. The wreckers of the Orkneys and the Faroes, the clansmen of the Scottish Isles, the kerns of Donegal and Galway, all had their part in the work of murder and robbery. Eight thousand Spaniards perished between the Giant's Causeway and the Blaskets. On a strand near Sligo an English captain numbered eleven hundred corpses which had been cast up by the sea. The flower of the Spanish nobility, who had been sent on the new crusade under Alonzo da Leyva, after twice suffering shipwreck, put a third time to sea to founder on a reef near Dunluce.
J. R. GREEN.

10. The Gunpowder Plot.

By the Elizabethan legislation, the Recusants, as the Catholics who refused to go to church were called, were in evil case. The richest amongst them were liable to a fine of 20*l.* a month. Landowners who could not afford to pay this were deprived of two-thirds of their estates. Persons who had no lands might have the furniture of their houses seized and sold for the benefit of the exchequer. Any one of these men was liable to excommunication, and an excommunicated man could be sent to prison without any further formality. To say mass as a priest, or to assist a priest in doing so, was punishable with death. Of course these harsh penalties were considerably modified in practice. But every man who did not come to church knew that they were suspended over his head, perhaps to fall without a moment's warning.

Before his accession, James, being anxious to secure adherents, had given hopes of lightening the burthens which pressed upon the Catholics. Not long after his arrival in England he informed the principal Catholics that, as long as they behaved as loyal subjects, the fines would no longer be exacted. But he still had reason for disquietude. There had been plots and rumours of plots, and the number of the recusants had largely increased as soon as the legal penalties had been suspended. In February 1604 James banished all priests from England, though as yet he took no active measures against the laity.

There were Catholics in England who were ready to dare anything for the triumph of their Church. As soon as the proclamation for the banishment of the priests appeared, Robert Catesby, a man steeped in plots and conspiracies, proposed to one or two friends to blow up King, Lords, and Commons with gunpowder. Guy Fawkes, a cool and daring soldier, was sent for from Flanders to assist in the execution of the scheme. Others were by degrees admitted to the secret. They took a house adjoining the House of Lords, and proceeded to dig through the wall, in order that they might place their barrels of powder under the floor before the opening of the next session. The wall was nine feet thick, and after some weeks work they had made but little way. Water flowed in and hindered their operations. Superstitious fancies gathered thickly round them, and they imagined that they were accompanied in their labours by unearthly sounds.

In the spring of 1605 James, frightened at the increase in the number of recusants, put the laws again in force against the Roman Catholic laity. The conspirators felt a fresh spur to their enterprise. At the same time an accident relieved them from further trouble. An adjoining cellar, reaching under the House of Lords without any intervening wall, was found to be for hire. It was taken in the name of one of the conspirators. The powder which they needed was safely lodged in it, and was covered with faggots in order to conceal it from any chance visitant. All that remained was to prepare for the insurrection which was to follow after the fatal deed had been accomplished.

To hire a cellar and to buy a few barrels of powder, was an exploit within the means of the conspirators. More money than they could command was needed to prepare for an insurrection. Three rich Catholics were informed of the project, and their purses were laid under contribution. One of them, anxious for the safety of a relative who was a member of the House of Lords, contrived that information should be given to the government in such a way that the conspirators might be themselves warned in time to fly.

The conspirators received the warning, but they refused to believe it to be true. Parliament was to be opened on November the 5th. On the night of the 4th Fawkes was seized watching over the powder barrels. The next morning the other plotters were flying for their lives. Some were killed before they could be taken. Others were captured and died a traitor's death.

The detected conspiracy was fatal to the hopes of the Catholics. The laws against them were made harsher than ever, and the fines were more unremittingly exacted. The door of mercy seemed closed against them for many a year.   J. R. GARDINER.

II. Cromwell.

He was one of those men, whom his very enemies could not condemn without commending him at the same time; for he could never have done half that mischief without great parts of courage, industry, and judgment. He must have had a wonderful understanding in the natures and humours of men, and as great a dexterity in applying them; who, from a private and obscure birth (though of a good family), without interest or estate, alliance or friendship, could raise himself to such a height, and compound and knead such opposite and contradictory tempers, humours, and interests into a consistence that contributed to his designs and to their own destruction; whilst himself grew insensibly powerful enough to cut off those by whom he had climbed, in the instant that they projected to demolish their own building. What was said of Cinna may very justly be said of him, he attempted those things which no good man durst have ventured on; and achieved those in which none but a valiant and great man could have succeeded. Without doubt, no man with more wickedness ever attempted any thing, or brought to pass what he desired more wickedly, more in the face and contempt of religion and moral honesty; yet wickedness as great as his could never have accomplished these designs, without the assistance of a great spirit, an admirable circumspection and sagacity, and a most magnanimous resolution.

When he appeared first in the parliament, he seemed to have a person in no degree gracious, no ornament of discourse, none of those talents which used to conciliate the affections of the stander-by: yet as he grew into place and authority, his parts seemed to be raised as he had occasion to use them; and when he was to act the part of a great man, he did it without any indecency, notwithstanding the want of custom.

After he was confirmed and invested Protector by the humble Petition and Advice, he consulted with very few upon any action of importance, nor communicated any enterprise he resolved upon, with more than those who were to have principal parts in the execution of it; nor with them sooner than was absolutely necessary. What he once resolved, in which he was not rash, he would not be dissuaded from, nor endure any contradiction of his power and authority; but extorted obedience from them who were not willing to yield it.

One time, when he had laid some very extraordinary tax upon the city, one Cony, an eminent fanatic, and one who had heretofore served him very notably, positively refused to pay his part; and loudly

dissuaded others from submitting to it, 'as an imposition notoriously
against the law, and the property of the subject, which all honest
men were bound to defend.' Cromwell sent for him, and cajoled him
with the memory of 'the old kindness and friendship that had been
between them; and that of all men he did not expect this opposition
from him, in a matter that was so necessary for the good of the
commonwealth.' It had been always his fortune to meet with the most
rude and obstinate behaviour from those who had formerly been absolutely governed by him; and they commonly put him in mind of
some expressions and sayings of his own, in cases of the like nature.
so this man remembered him how great an enemy he had expressed
himself to such grievances, and had declared, 'that all who submitted
to them, and paid illegal taxes, were more to blame, and greater
enemies to their country, than they who had imposed them.' When
Cromwell saw that he could not convert him, he told him, 'that he
had a will as stubborn as his, and he would try which of them two
should be master.' Thereupon, with some expressions of reproach and
contempt, he committed the man to prison; whose courage was
nothing abated by it; but as soon as the term came, he brought his
Habeas Corpus in the King's Bench, which they then called the
Upper Bench. Maynard, who was of council with the prisoner,
demanded his liberty with great confidence, both upon the illegality of
the commitment, and the illegality of the imposition, as being laid
without any lawful authority. The judges could not maintain or defend
either, and enough declared what their sentence would be; and therefore the protector's attorney required a further day, to answer what
had been urged. Before that day, Maynard was committed to the
Tower for presuming to question or make doubt of his authority;
and the judges were sent for, and severely reprehended for suffering
that licence; when they, with all humility, mentioned the law and
Magna Charta, Cromwell told them, with terms of contempt and
derision, 'their Magna Charta should not control his actions; which he
knew were for the safety of the commonwealth.' He asked them,
'who made them judges? whether they had any authority to sit
there; but what he gave them? and if his authority were at an
end, they knew well enough what would become of themselves; and
therefore advised them to be more tender of that which could only
preserve them;' and so dismissed them with caution 'that they
should not suffer the lawyers to prate what it would not become them
to hear.'

    Thus he subdued a spirit that had been often troublesome to
the most sovereign power, and made Westminster Hall as obedient

and subservient to his commands as any of the rest of his quarters. In all other matters, which did not concern the life of his jurisdiction, he seemed to have great reverence for the law, rarely interposing between party and party. As he proceeded with this kind of indignation and haughtiness with those who were refractory, and durst contend with his greatness, so towards all who complied with his good pleasure, and courted his protection, he used great civility, generosity, and bounty.

To reduce three nations, which perfectly hated him, to an entire obedience to all his dictates; to awe and govern those nations by an army that was indevoted to him, and wished his ruin, was an instance of a very prodigious address. But his greatness at home was but a shadow of the glory he had abroad. It was hard to discover which feared him most, France, Spain, or the Low Countries, where his friendship was current at the value he put upon it. As they did all sacrifice their honour and their interest to his pleasure, so there is nothing he could have demanded that either of them would have denied him. To manifest which there needs only one instance. When those of the valley of Lucerne had unwarily risen in arms against the Duke of Savoy, which gave occasion to the Pope and the neighbour princes of Italy, to call and solicit for their extirpation, and their prince positively resolved upon it, Cromwell sent his agent to the Duke of Savoy, a prince with whom he had no correspondence or commerce, and so engaged the cardinal, and even terrified the pope himself, without so much as doing any grace to the English Roman Catholics (nothing being more usual than his saying, 'that his ships in the Mediterranean should visit Civita Vecchia; and that the sound of his cannon should be heard in Rome'), that the duke of Savoy thought it necessary to restore all that he had taken from them, and did renew all those privileges they had formerly enjoyed and newly forfeited.

To conclude his character, Cromwell was not so far a man of blood as to follow Macchiavel's method, which prescribes, upon a total alteration of government, as a thing absolutely necessary, to cut off all the heads of those, and extirpate their families, who are friends to the old one. It was confidently reported that, in the council of officers, it was more than once proposed, 'That there might be a general massacre of all the royal party, as the only expedient to secure the government;' but that Cromwell would never consent to it, it may be, out of too great a contempt of his enemies. In a word, as he was guilty of many crimes, against which damnation is denounced, and for which hell-fire is prepared, so he had some good qualities which have caused the memory of some men in all ages to be celebrated: and he will be looked upon by posterity as a brave wicked man. EDWARD HYDE, EARL OF CLARENDON.

12. Cromwell and Napoleon.

Between Cromwell and Napoleon Mr. Hallam has instituted a parallel, scarcely less ingenious than that which Burke has drawn between Richard Coeur de Lion and Charles the Twelfth of Sweden. In this parallel, however, and indeed throughout his work, we think that he hardly gives Cromwell fair measure. "Cromwell," says he, "far unlike his antitype, never showed any signs of a legislative mind, or any desire to place his renown on that noblest basis, the amelioration of social institutions." The difference in this respect, we conceive, was not in the character of the men, but in the character of the revolutions by means of which they rose to power. The civil war in England had been undertaken to defend and restore; the republicans of France set themselves to destroy. In England, the principles of the common law had never been disturbed, and most even of its forms had been held sacred. In France, the law and its ministers had been swept away together. In France, therefore, legislation necessarily became the first business of the first settled government which rose on the ruins of the old system. The admirers of Inigo Jones have always maintained that his works are inferior to those of Sir Christopher Wren, only because the great fire of London gave Wren such a field for the display of his powers as no architect in the history of the world ever possessed. Similar allowance must be made for Cromwell. If he erected little that was new, it was because there had been no general devastation to clear a space for him. As it was, he reformed the representative system in a most judicious manner. He rendered the administration of justice uniform throughout the island. We will quote a passage from his speech to the Parliament in September, 1656, which contains, we think, simple and rude as the diction is, stronger indications of legislative mind, than are to be found in the whole range of orations delivered on such occasions before or since.

"There is one general grievance in the nation. It is the law. I think, I may say it, I have as eminent judges in this land as have been had, or that the nation has had for these many years. Truly, I could be particular as to the executive part, to the administration; but that would trouble you. But the truth of it is, there are wicked and abominable laws that will be in your power to alter. To hang a man for sixpence, threepence, I know not what, — to hang for a trifle, and pardon murder, is in the ministration of the law through the ill framing of it. I have known in my experience abominable murders quitted: and to see men lose their lives for petty matters! This is a thing that God will reckon for; and I wish it may not lie upon this nation a day longer than you have an opportunity to give a remedy; and I hope I shall cheerfully join with you in it."

Mr. Hallam truly says that, though it is impossible to rank Cromwell with Napoleon as a general, yet "his exploits were as much above the level of his contemporaries, and more the effects of an original uneducated capacity." Bonaparte was trained in the best military schools; the army which he led to Italy was one of the finest that ever existed. Cromwell passed his youth and the prime of his manhood in a civil situation. He never looked on war till he was more than forty years old. He had first to form himself, and then to form his troops. Out of raw levies he created an army, the bravest and the best disciplined, the most orderly in peace, and the most terrible in war, that Europe had seen. He called this body into existence. He led it to conquest. He never fought a battle without gaining it. He never gained a battle without annihilating the force opposed to him. Yet his victories were not the highest glory of his military system. The respect which his troops paid to property, their attachment to the laws and religion of their country, their submission to the civil power, their temperance, their intelligence, their industry are without parallel. It was after the Restoration that the spirit which their great leader had infused into them was most signally displayed. At the command of the established government, an established government which had no means of enforcing obedience, fifty thousand soldiers, whose backs no enemy had ever seen, either in domestic or in continental war, laid down their arms, and retired into the mass of the people, thenceforward to be distinguished only by superior diligence, sobriety, and regularity in the pursuits of peace, from the other members of the community which they had saved.

In the general spirit and character of his administration, we think Cromwell far superior to Napoleon. "In civil government," says Mr. Hallam, "there can be no adequate parallel between one who had sucked only the dregs of a besotted fanaticism, and one to whom the stores of reason and philosophy were open." These expressions, it seems to us, convey the highest eulogium on our great countryman. Reason and philosophy did not teach the conqueror of Europe to command his passions, or to pursue, as a first object, the happiness of his people. They did not prevent him from risking his fame and his power in a frantic contest against the principles of human nature and the laws of the physical world, against the rage of the winter and the liberty of the sea. They did not exempt him from the influence of that most pernicious of superstitions, a presumptuous fatalism. They did not preserve him from the inebriation of prosperity, or restrain him from indecent querulousness in adversity. On the other hand, the fanaticism of Cromwell never urged him on impracticable undertakings, or confused his perception of the public good. Our countryman, inferior to Bonaparte in invention, was far superior to him in wisdom. The French Emperor is among conquerors what Voltaire is among writers, a miraculous child. His splendid genius was frequently clouded by fits of humour as absurdly perverse as those of the pet of the nursery, who quarrels with his food, and dashes his playthings to pieces. Cromwell was emphatically a man. He possessed, in an eminent degree, that masculine and full-grown robustness of mind, that equally diffused intellectual health, which, if our national partiality does not mislead us, has peculiarly characterized the great men of England. Never was any ruler so conspicuously born for sovereignty. The cup which has intoxicated almost all others, sobered him. His spirit, restless from its own buoyancy in a lower sphere, reposed in majestic placidity as soon as it had reached the level congenial to it. He had nothing in common with that large class of men who distinguish themselves in subordinate posts, and whose incapacity becomes obvious as soon as the public voice summons them to take the lead. Rapidly as his fortunes grew, his mind expanded more rapidly still. Insignificant as a private citizen, he was a great general; he was a still greater prince. Napoleon had a theatrical manner, in which the coarseness of a revolutionary guard-room was blended with the ceremony of the old Court of Versailles. Cromwell, by the confession even of his enemies, exhibited in his demeanour the simple and natural nobleness of a man neither ashamed of his origin nor vain of his elevation, of a man who had found his proper place in society, and who felt secure that he was competent to fill it. Easy, even to familiarity, where his own dignity was concerned, he was punctilious only for his country. His own character he left to take care of itself; he left it to be defended by his victories in war, and his reforms in peace. But he was a jealous and implacable guardian of the public honour. He suffered a crazy Quaker to insult him in the gallery of Whitehall, and revenged himself only by liberating him and giving him a dinner. But he was prepared to risk the chances of war to avenge the blood of a private Englishman.

No sovereign ever carried to the throne so large a portion of the best qualities of the middling orders, so strong a sympathy with the feelings and interests of his people. He was sometimes driven to arbitrary measures: but he had a high, stout, honest, English heart. Hence it was that he loved to surround his throne with such men as Hale and Blake. Hence it was that he allowed so large a share of political liberty to his subjects, and that, even when an opposition dangerous to his power and to his person almost compelled him to govern by the sword, he was still anxious to leave a germ from which, at a more favourable season, free institutions might spring. We firmly believe that, if his first Parliament had not commenced its debates by disputing his title, his government would have been as mild at home as it was energetic and able abroad. He was a soldier; he had risen by war. Had his ambition been of an impure or selfish kind, it would have been easy for him to plunge his country into continental hostilities on a large scale, and to dazzle the restless factions which he ruled, by the splendour of his victories. Some of his enemies have sneeringly remarked that in the successes obtained under his administration he had no personal share; as if a man who had raised himself from obscurity to empire solely by his military talent could have any unworthy reason for shrinking from military enterprise. This reproach is his highest glory. In the success of the English navy he could have no selfish interest. Its triumphs added nothing to his fame: its increase added nothing to his means of overawing his enemies; its great leader was not his friend. Yet he took a peculiar pleasure in encouraging that noble service which, of all the instruments employed by an English government, is the most impotent for mischief, and the most powerful for good. His administration was glorious, but with no vulgar glory. It was not one of those periods of overstrained and convulsive exertion which necessarily produce debility and languor. Its energy was natural, healthful, temperate. He placed England at the head of the Protestant interest, and in the first rank of Christian powers. He taught every nation to value her friendship and to dread her enmity. But he did not squander her resources in a vain attempt to invest her with that supremacy which no power, in the modern system of Europe, can safely affect, or can long retain.

This noble and sober wisdom had its reward. If he did not carry the banners of the Commonwealth in triumph to distant capitals, if he did not adorn Whitehall with the spoils of the Stadthouse and the Louvre, if he did not portion out Flanders and Germany into principalities for his kinsmen and his generals, he did not, on the other hand, see his country overrun by the armies of nations which his ambition had provoked. He did not drag out the last years of his life an exile and a prisoner, in an unhealthy climate and under an ungenerous gaoler, raging with the impotent desire of vengeance, and brooding over visions of departed glory. He went down to his grave in the fulness of power and fame; and he left to his son an autoritby which any man of ordinary firmness and prudence would have retained.   TH. B. MACAULAY.

13. Cromwell's Face and Figure.

"His highness," says Whitelocke, "was in a rich but plain suit — black velvet, with cloak of the same: about his hat a broad band of gold." Does the reader see him? A rather likely figure, I think. Stands some five feet ten or more: a man of strong, solid stature, and dignified, now partly military carriage: the expression of him valour and devout intelligence — energy and delicacy on a basis of simplicity. Fifty-four years old, gone April last; brown hair and moustache are getting gray. A figure of sufficient impressiveness — not lovely to the man-milliner species, nor pretending to be so. Massive stature: big, massive head, of somewhat leonine aspect; wart above the right eyebrow: nose of considerable blunt-aquiline proportions: strict yet copious lips, full of all tremulous sensibilities, and also, if need were, of all fiercenesses and rigours: deep, loving eyes, call them grave, call them stern — looking from under those craggy brows as if in life-long sorrow, and yet not thinking it sorrow, thinking it only labour and endeavour: on the whole, a right noble lion-face and hero-face; and to me royal enough.

THOMAS CARLYLE.

14. The Battle of Culloden.

In the beginning of April 1743 the duke of Cumberland began to march from Aberdeen; and on the 12th passed the deep and rapid river Spey, without opposition from the rebels, though a detachment of them appeared on the opposite side. Why they did not dispute the passage is not easy to be conceived; but, indeed, from this instance of neglect, and their subsequent conduct, we may conclude they were under a total infatuation. His royal highness proceeded to Nairn, where he received intelligence that the enemy had advanced from Inverness to Culloden, about the distance of nine miles from the royal army, with intention to give him battle. The design of Charles was to march in the night from Culloden, and surprise the duke's army at day-break: for this purpose the English camp had been reconnoitred: and on the night of the 15th the Highland army began to march in two columns. Their design was to surround the enemy, and attack them at once on all quarters: but the length of the columns embarrassed the march, so that the army was obliged to make many halts: the men had been under arms during the whole preceding night, were faint with hunger and fatigue, and many of them overpowered with sleep. Some were unable to proceed; others dropped off unperceived in the dark; and the march was retarded in such a manner that it would have been impossible to reach the duke's camp before sunrise. The design being thus frustrated, the prince-pretender was with great reluctance prevailed upon by his general officers to measure back his way to Culloden; at which place they had no sooner arrived, than great numbers of his followers dispersed in quest of provision; and many, overcome with weariness and sleep, threw themselves down on the heath, and along the park walls. Their repose, however, was soon interrupted in a very disagreeable manner. Their prince receiving intelligence that his enemies were in full march to attack him, resolved to hazard an engagement, and ordered his troops to be formed for that purpose. On the 16th day of April, the duke of Cumberland having made the proper dispositions, decamped from Nairn early in the morning, and after a march of nine miles perceived the Highlanders drawn up in order of battle, to the number of 4000 men in thirteen divisions, supplied with some pieces of artillery. The royal army, which was much more numerous, the duke immediately formed into three lines, disposed in excellent order; and about one o'clock in the afternoon the cannonading began. The artillery of the rebels was ill served, and did very little execution: but that of the king's troops made dreadful havoc among the enemy. Impatient of this fire their front-line advanced to the attack, and about 500 of the clans charged the duke's left wing with their usual impetuosity. One regiment was disordered by the weight of this column; but two battalions advancing from the second line, sustained the first, and soon put a stop to their career, by a severe fire, that killed a great number. At the same time, the dragoons under Hawley, and the Argyleshire militia, pulled down a park-wall that covered their right flank, and the cavalry falling in among the rebels, sword in hand, completed their confusion. The French pickets on their left covered the retreat of the Highlanders by a close and regular fire; and then retired to Inverness, where they surrendered themselves prisoners of war. An entire body of the rebels marched off the field in order, with their pipes playing, and the pretender's standard displayed: the rest were routed with great slaughter: and their prince was with reluctance prevailed upon to retire. In less than thirty minutes, they were totally defeated and the field covered with the slain. The road, as far as Inverness, was strewed with dead bodies; and a great number of people, who, from motives of curiosity, had come to see the battle, were sacrificed to the undistinguishing vengeance of the victors. Twelve hundred rebels were slain or wounded on the field and in the pursuit. The earl of Kilmarnock was taken; and in a few days Lord Balmerino surrendered to a country gentleman, at whose house he presented himself for this purpose. The glory of the victory was sullied by the barbarity of the soldiers. They had been provoked by their former disgraces to the most savage thirst of revenge. Not contented with the blood which was so profusely shed in the heat of action, they traversed the field after the battle, and massacred those miserable wretches who lay maimed and expired; nay, some officers acted a part in this cruel scene of assassination; the triumph of low illiberal minds, uninspired by sentiment, untinctured by humanity. The vanquished adventurer rode off the field, accompanied by the duke of Perth, Lord Elcho, and a few horsemen; he crossed the water of Nairn, and retired to the house of a gentleman in Strutharrick, where he conferred with old Lord Lovat: then he dismissed his followers, and wandered about a wretched and solitary fugitive among the isles and mountains, for the space of five months, during which he underwent such a series of dangers, hardships, and misery, as no other person outlived: at length, on the 20th day of September, this unfortunate prince embarked for France, and arrived in safety at Roscau, near Morlaix, in Bretagne.

Thus, in one short hour, all his hope vanished, and the rebellion was entirely extinguished. One would almost imagine the conductors of this desperate enterprise had conspired their own destruction, as they certainly neglected every step that might have contributed to their safety or success. They might have opposed the duke of Cumberland at the passage of the Spey; they might, by proper conduct, have afterwards attacked his camp in the night, with a good prospect of success. As they were greatly inferior to him in number, and weakened with hunger and fatigue, they might have retired to the hills and fastnesses, where they would have found plenty of live cattle for provision, recruited their regiments, and been joined by a strong reinforcement, which was actually in full march to their assistance. But they were distracted by dissensions and jealousies; they obeyed the dictates of despair, and wilfully devoted themselves to ruin and death. When the news of the battle arrived in England,

the nation was transported with joy, and extolled the duke of Cumberland as a hero and deliverer. Both houses of parliament congratulated his Majesty on the auspicious event. They decreed, in the most solemn manner, their public thanks to his royal highness, which were
5 transmitted to him by the speakers; and the Commons, by bill, added 25,000 *l.* per annum to his former revenue.   TOBIAS SMOLLETT.

15. The Trial of Warren Hastings.

The place was worthy of such a trial. It was the great hall of William Rufus, the hall which had resounded with acclamations at
10 the inauguration of thirty kings, the hall which had witnessed the just sentence of Bacon and the just absolution of Somers, the hall where the eloquence of Strafford had for a moment awed and melted a victorious party inflamed with just resentment, the hall where Charles had confronted the High Court of Justice with the placid
15 courage which has half redeemed his fame. Neither military nor civil pomp was wanting. The avenues were lined with grenadiers. The streets were kept clear by cavalry. The peers, robed in gold and ermine, were marshalled by the heralds, under Garter King-at-arms. The judges in their vestments of state attended to give advice on
20 points of law. Near a hundred and seventy lords, three fourths of the Upper House as the Upper House then was, walked in solemn order from their usual place of assembling to the tribunal. The junior baron present led the way. George Eliott, Lord Heathfield, recently ennobled for his memorable defence of Gibraltar against the fleets
25 and armies of France and Spain. The long procession was closed by the Duke of Norfolk, Earl Marshal of the realm, by the great dignitaries, and by the brothers and sons of the King. Last of all came the Prince of Wales, conspicuous by his fine person and noble bearing. The grey old walls were hung with scarlet. The long
30 galleries were crowded by an audience such as has rarely excited the fears or the emulation of an orator There were gathered together, from all parts of a great, free, enlightened, and prosperous empire, grace and female loveliness, wit and learning, the representatives of every science and of every art. There were seated round the Queen
35 the fair-haired young daughters of the house of Brunswick. There the Ambassadors of great Kings and Commonwealths gazed with admiration on a spectacle which no other country in the world could present. There Siddons, in the prime of her majestic beauty, looked with emotion on a scene surpassing all the imitations of the stage.
40 There the historian of the Roman Empire thought of the days when Cicero pleaded the cause of Sicily against Verres, and when,

before a senate which still retained some show of freedom, Tacitus thundered against the oppressor of Africa. There were seen, side by side, the greatest painter and the greatest scholar of the age. The spectacle had allured Reynolds from that easel which has preserved to us the thoughtful foreheads of so many writers and statesmen, and the sweet smiles of so many noble matrons.

It had induced Parr to suspend his labours in that dark and profound mine from which he had extracted a vast treasury of erudition, a treasure too often buried in the earth, too often paraded with injudicious and inelegant ostentation, but still precious, massive, and splendid. There appeared the charms of her to whom the heir of the throne had in secret plighted his faith. There too was she, the beautiful mother of a beautiful race, the Saint Cecilia whose delicate features, lighted up by love and music, art has rescued from the common decay.

The Sergeants made proclamation. Hastings advanced to the bar, and bent his knee. The culprit was indeed not unworthy of that great presence. He had ruled an extensive and populous country, and made laws and treaties, had sent forth armies, had set up and pulled down princes. And in his high place he had so borne himself, that all had feared him, that most had loved him, and that hatred itself could deny him no title to glory, except virtue. He looked like a great man, and not like a bad man. A person small and emaciated, yet deriving dignity from a carriage which, while it indicated deference to the court, indicated also habitual self-possession and self-respect, a high and intellectual forehead, a brow pensive, but not gloomy, a mouth of inflexible decision, a face pale and worn, but serene, on which was written, as legibly as under the picture in the council-chamber at Calcutta, *mens aequa in arduis;* such was the aspect with which the great proconsul presented himself to his judges.

The charges and the answers of Hastings were first read. The ceremony occupied two whole days: on the third day Burke rose. Four sittings were occupied by his opening speech, which was intended to be a general introduction to all the charges. With an exuberance of thought and a splendour of diction which more than satisfied the highly raised expectation of the audience, he described the character and institutions of the natives of India, recounted the circumstances in which the Asiatic empire of Britain had originated, and set forth the constitution of the Company and of the English Presidencies. Having thus attempted to communicate to his hearers an idea of Eastern society, as vivid as that which existed in his own mind, he proceeded to arraign the administration of Hastings as systematically conducted in defiance of morality and public law. The energy and pathos of the great orator extorted expressions of unwonted admiration from the stern and hostile Chancellor, and, for a moment, seemed to pierce even the resolute heart of the defendant. At length the orator concluded. Raising his voice till the old arches of Irish oak resounded, "Therefore," said he, "hath it with all confidence been ordered by the Commons of Great Britain, that I impeach Warren Hastings of High Crimes and Misdemeanours. I impeach him in the name of the Commons' House of Parliament, whose trust he has betrayed. I impeach him in the name of the English nation, whose ancient honour he has sullied. I impeach him in the name of the people of India, whose rights he has trodden under foot, and whose country he has turned into a desert. Lastly, in the name of human nature itself, in the name of both sexes, in the name of every age, in the name of every rank, I impeach the common enemy and oppressor of all!"

When the deep murmur of various emotions had subsided, Mr. Fox rose to address the Lords respecting the course of proceeding to be followed. The wish of the accusers was that the Court would bring to a close the investigation of the first charge before the second was opened. The wish of Hastings and of his counsel was that the managers should open all the charges, and produce all the evidence for the prosecution, before the defence began. The Lords retired to their own House to consider the question. The Chancellor took the side of Hastings. Lord Loughborough, who was now in opposition, supported the demand of the managers. The division showed which way the inclination of the tribunal leaned. A majority of near three to one decided in favour of the course for which Hastings contended.

When the Court sat again, Mr. Fox, assisted by Mr. Grey, opened the charge respecting Cheyte Sing, and several days were spent in reading papers and hearing witnesses. The next article was that relating to the Princesses of Oude. The conduct of this part of the case was intrusted to Sheridan. The curiosity of the public to hear him was unbounded. His sparkling and highly finished declamation lasted two days; but the Hall was crowded to suffocation during the whole time. It was said that fifty guineas had been paid for a single ticket. Sheridan, when he concluded, contrived, with a knowledge of stage-effect which his father might have envied, to sink back, as if exhausted, into the arms of Burke, who hugged him with the energy of generous admiration.

June was now far advanced. The session could not last much longer; and the progress which had been made in the impeachment was not very satisfactory. There were twenty charges. On two only of these had even the case for the prosecution been heard; and it was now a year since Hastings had been admitted to bail.

The interest taken by the public in the trial was great when the Court began to sit, and rose to the height when Sheridan spoke on the charge relating to the Begums. From that time the excitement went down fast. The spectacle had lost the attraction of novelty. The great displays of rhetoric were over.   Th. B. Macaulay.

16. The American War of Independence.

The hour of the American Revolution was come. The people of the continent with irresistible energy obeyed one general impulse, as the earth in spring listens to the command of nature, and without the appearance of effort bursts forth to life in perfect harmony. The change which Divine wisdom ordained and which no human policy or force could hold back, proceeded as uniformly and as majestically as the laws of being, and was as certain as the degrees of eternity. The movement was quickened, even when it was most resisted; and its fiercest adversaries worked together effectually for its fulfilment. The indestructible elements of freedom in the colonies asked room for expansion and growth. Standing in manifold relations with the governments, the culture, and the experience of the past, the Americans seized as their peculiar inheritance the tradition of liberty. Beyond any other nation they had made trial of the possible forms of popular representation, and respected the activity of individual conscience and thought. The resources of the vast country in agriculture and commerce, forests and fisheries, mines and materials for manufactures, were so diversified and complete, that their development could neither be guided nor circumscribed by a government beyond the ocean; the numbers, purity, culture, industry, and daring of its inhabitants proclaimed the existence of a people, rich in creative energy, and ripe for institutions of their own.

They were rushing towards revolution, and they knew it not. They refused to acknowledge even to themselves the hope that was swelling within them; and yet they were possessed by the truth that man holds inherent and indefeasible rights; and as their religion had its witness coeval and coextensive with intelligence, so in their political aspirations, they deduced from universal principles a bill of rights, as old as creation and as wide as humanity. The idea of freedom had never been wholly unknown; it had always revealed itself at least to a few of the wise, whose prophetic instincts were quickened by love of their kind; its rising light flashed joy across the darkest centuries: and its growing energy can be traced in the tendency of the ages. In America it was the breath of life to the people. For the first time it found a region and race where it could be professed with the earnestness of an indwelling conviction, and be defended with enthusiasm that heretofore had marked no wars but those for religion. When all Europe slumbered over questions of liberty, a band of exiles, keeping watch by night, heard the glad tidings which promised the political regeneration of the world. A revolution, unexpected, in the moment of its coming but prepared by glorious forerunners, grew naturally and necessarily out of the series of past events by the formative principle of a living belief. And why should man organize resistance to the grand design of Providence? Why should not the consent of the ancestral land and the gratulations of every other call the young nation to its place among the powers of the earth? Britain was the mighty mother who bred and formed men capable of laying the foundation of so noble an empire: and she alone could have formed them.

She had excelled all nations of the world as the planter of colonies. The condition which entitled her colonies to independence was now more than fulfilled. Their vigorous vitality refused conformity to foreign laws and external rule. They could take no other way to perfection than by the unconstrained development of that which was within them. They were not only able to govern themselves, they alone were able to do so; subordination visibly repressed their energies. It was only by self-direction that they could at all times and in entireness freely employ in action their collective and individual powers to the fullest extent of their ever increasing intelligence. Could not the illustrious nation which had gained no distinction in war, in literature, or in science, comparable to that of having wisely founded distant settlements on a system of liberty, willingly perfect its beneficent work, now when no more was required than the acknowledgement that its offspring was come of age, and its own duty accomplished? Why must the ripening of lineal virtue be struck at as rebellion in the lawful sons? Why is their unwavering attachment to the essential principle of their existence to be persecuted as treason, rather than viewed with delight as the crowning glory of the country from which they sprang? If the institutions of Britain were so deeply fixed in the usages and opinions of its people, that their deviations from justice could not as yet be rectified; if the old continent was pining under systems of authority which were not fit to be borne,

and which as yet no way opened to amend, why should not a people
be heartened to build a commonwealth in the wilderness, which alone
offered it a home?

So reasoned a few Britons who were jeered "as visionary enthu-
siasts," deserving no weight in public affairs. Parliament had asserted
an absolute lordship over the colonies in all cases whatsoever: and
fretting itself into a frenzy at the denial of its unlimited dominion,
was blindly destroying all its recognised authority in the madness of
its zeal for more. The majority of the ministers, including the most
active and determined, were bent on the immediate employment of
force. Lord North, who recoiled from civil war, exercised no control
over his colleagues, leaving the government to be conducted by the
several departments. As a consequence, the king became the only
point of administrative union, and ruled as well as reigned. In him
an approving conscience had no misgiving as to his duty. His heart
knew no relenting; his will never wavered. Though America were to
be drenched in blood and its towns reduced to ashes, though its
people were to be driven to struggle for total independence, though he
himself should find it necessary to bid high for hosts of mercenaries
from the Scheld to Moscow, and in quest of savage allies, go tapping
at every wigwam from Lake Huron to the Gulf of Mexico, he was
resolved to coerce the thirteen colonies into submission. The people
of Great Britain identified themselves, though but for the moment,
with his anger and talked like so many kings of their subjects beyond
the Atlantic. Of their ability to crush resistance they refused to
doubt: nor did they, nor the ministers, nor George the Third, apprehend interference, except from that great neighbouring kingdom whose
vast colonial system Britain had just overthrown.

GEORGE BANCROFT.

17. The Death of Nelson.

A long swell was setting into the Bay of Cadiz. Our ships,
crowding all sail, moved majestically before it, with light winds from
the south-west. The sun shone on the sails of the enemy, and their
well-formed line, with their numerous three-deckers, made an appearance which any other assailants would have thought formidable; but
the British sailors only admired the beauty and the splendour of the
spectacle: and, in full confidence of winning what they saw, remarked
to each other what a fine sight yonder ships would make at Spithead!
Ten minutes before twelve the enemy opened his fire. Eight or nine
of the ships immediately ahead of the Victory, and across her bows,
fired single guns at her, to ascertain, whether she was yet within

their range. As soon as Nelson perceived that their shot passed over him, he desired Blackwood, and Capt. Prowse, of the Sirius, to repair to their respective frigates, and on their way to tell all the Captains that he depended on their exertions; and that if by the prescribed mode of attack they found it impracticable to get into action immediately, they might adopt whatever they thought best, provided it led them quickly and closely alongside an enemy. As they were standing on the front of the poop, Blackwood took him by the hand, saying he hoped soon to return and find him in possession of twenty prizes. He replied, "God bless you, Blackwood: I shall never speak to you again."

Nelson's column was steered about two points more to the north than Collingwood's, in order to cut off the enemy's escape into Cadiz; the lee line, therefore, was first engaged. "See," cried Nelson, pointing to the Royal Sovereign, as she steered right for the centre of the enemy's line, cut through it astern of the Santa Anna, three-decker, and engaged her at the muzzle of her guns on the starboard side, "See how that noble fellow Collingwood carries his ship into action." Collingwood, delighted at being first in the heat of the fire, and knowing the feelings of his commander and old friend, turned to his Captain, and exclaimed, "Rotherham, what would Nelson give to be here!" Both these brave officers, perhaps at this moment thought of Nelson with gratitude, for a circumstance which had occurred on the preceding day. Admiral Collingwood, with some of the Captains, having gone on board the Victory to receive instructions, Nelson inquired of him where his Captain was, and was told in reply that they were not upon good terms with each other. "Terms!" said Nelson; "good terms with each other." Immediately he sent a boat for Capt. Rotherham; led him, as soon as he arrived, to Collingwood, and saying, "Look! yonder are the enemy," bade them shake hands like Englishmen.

The enemy continued to fire a gun at a time at the Victory, till they saw that a shot had passed through her main-topgallant sail; then they opened their broadsides aiming chiefly at her rigging, in the hope of disabling her before she could close with them. Nelson, as usual, had hoisted several flags, lest one should be shot away. The enemy showed no colours till late in the action, when they began to feel the necessity of having them to strike. For this reason the Santissima Trinidad, Nelson's old acquaintance, was distinguishable only by her four decks, and to the bow of this opponent he ordered the Victory to be steered. Meantime an incessant raking fire was kept up upon the Victory. The Admiral's Secretary was one of the first who fell; he was killed by a cannon-shot while conversing with Hardy. Presently a double-headed shot struck a party of marines who were drawn up on the poop and killed eight of them, upon which Nelson immediately desired Capt. Adair to disperse his men round the ship, that they might not suffer so much from being together. A few minutes afterwards a shot struck the fore-brace bits on the quarter-deck and passed between Nelson and Hardy, a splinter from the bit tearing off Hardy's buckle, and bruising his foot. Both stopped, and looked anxiously at each other; each supposed the other to be wounded. Nelson then smiled and said, "This is too warm work, Hardy, to last long." The Victory had not yet returned a single gun. Fifty of her men had been by this time killed or wounded, and her main-topmast, with all her studding sails and her booms, shot away. Nelson declared that in all his battles he had seen nothing which surpassed the cool courage of his crew on this occasion. At four minutes after twelve she opened her fire from both sides of her deck. It was not possible to break the enemy's line without running on board one of their ships. Hardy informed him of this, and asked him which he would prefer. Nelson replied: "Take your choice, Hardy, it does not signify much." The Master was ordered to put the helm to port, and the Victory ran on board the Redoutable, just as her tiller ropes were shot away. The French ship received her with a broadside; then instantly let down her lower-deck ports, for fear of being boarded through them, and never afterwards fired a great gun during the action. Her tops, like those of all the enemy's ships, were filled with riflemen. Nelson never placed musketry in his tops. He had a strong dislike to the practice, not merely because it is a murderous sort of warfare, by which individuals may suffer, and a commander now and then be picked off, but which never can decide the fate of a general engagement.

Capt. Harvey, in the Téméraire, fell on board the Redoutable on the other side. Another enemy was in like manner on board the Téméraire; so that these four ships formed as compact a tier as if they had been moored together, their heads lying all the same way. The Lieutenants of the Victory, seeing this, depressed their guns of the middle and lower decks and fired with a diminished charge, lest the shot should pass through and injure the Téméraire. And because there was danger that the Redoutable might take fire from the lower-deck guns, the muzzles of which touched her side when they were run out, the fireman of each gun stood ready with a bucket of water, which, as soon as the gun was discharged, he dashed into the hole made by the shot. An incessant fire was kept up from the Victory from both sides, her larboard guns playing upon the Bucentaure, and the huge Santissima Trinidad.

Nelson setting an example of his humanity, twice gave orders to cease firing upon the Redoutable, supposing that she had struck, because her great guns were silent; for as she carried no flag, there was no means of instantly ascertaining the fact. From this ship, which he had thus twice spared, he received his death. A ball fired from her mizzen-top, which in the then situation of the two vessels was not more than fifteen yards from that part of the deck where he was standing, struck the epaulette on his left shoulder, about a quarter after one, just in the heat of the action. He fell upon his face, on the spot which was covered with his poor Secretary's blood; Hardy, who was a few steps from him, turning round, saw three men raising him up. "They have done for me at last, Hardy," said he. "I hope not," cried Hardy. "Yes," he replied, "my backbone is shot through." Yet even now, not for a moment losing his presence of mind, he observed, as they were carrying him down the ladder, that the tiller ropes, which had been shot away, were not yet replaced, and ordered that new ones should be rove immediately; then, that he might not be seen by the crew, he took out his handkerchief, and covered his face and his stars. Had he but concealed these badges of honour from the enemy, England perhaps would not have had cause to receive with sorrow the news of the battle of Trafalgar. The cockpit was crowded with wounded and dying men, over whose bodies he was with some difficulty conveyed, and laid upon a pallet in the Midshipmen's berth. It was soon perceived, upon examination, that the wound was mortal. This, however, was concealed from all except Captain Hardy, the Chaplain, and the medical attendants. He himself being certain, from the sensation in his back and the gush of blood he felt momently within his breast, that no human care could avail him, insisted that the surgeon should leave him, and attend to those to whom he might be useful; "for," said he, "you can do nothing for me." All that could be done was to fan him with paper, and frequently to give him lemonade to alleviate his intense thirst.

He was in great pain, and expressed much anxiety for the event of the action, which now began to declare itself. As often as a ship struck, the crew of the Victory hurraed, and at every hurrah a visible expression of joy gleamed in the eye and marked the countenance of the dying hero. But he became impatient to see Capt. Hardy: and as that officer, though often sent for, could not leave the deck, Nelson feared that some fatal cause prevented him and repeatedly cried. "Will no one bring Hardy to me? He must be killed!

He is surely dead!" An hour and ten minutes elapsed from the time when Nelson received his wound before Hardy could come to him. They shook hands in silence, Hardy in vain struggling to suppress the feeling of that most painful and yet sublimest moment. "Well Hardy," said Nelson; "how goes the day with us?" "Very well," replied Hardy; "ten ships have struck, but five of the van have tacked, and show an intention to bear down upon the Victory. I have called two or three of our fresh ships round, and have no doubt of giving them a drubbing." "I hope," said Nelson, "none of our ships have struck." Hardy answered, "there was no fear of that." Then, and not till then, Nelson spoke of himself. "I am a dead man, Hardy," said he; "I am going fast; it will be all over with me soon. Come nearer to me." Hardy observed, that he hoped Mr. Beatty could yet hold out some prospect of life. "Oh, no!" he replied: "it is impossible. My back is shot through. Beatty will tell you so." Capt. Hardy then once more shook hands with him, and, with a heart, almost bursting, hastened upon deck. — By this time all feeling below the breast was gone: and Nelson, having made the Surgeon ascertain this, said to him, "You know I am gone, I know it. I feel something rising in my breast," — putting his hand on his left side, — "which tells me so." Capt. Hardy, some fifty minutes after he had left the cock-pit, returned; and again taking the hand of his dying friend and commander, congratulated him on having gained a complete victory. How many of the enemy were taken he did not know, as it was impossible to perceive them distinctly; but fourteen or fifteen at least. "That's well," cried Nelson, "but I bargained for twenty:" and then in a stronger voice, he said! "Anchor, Hardy, anchor." Presently, calling Hardy back, he said to him in a low voice, "Don't throw me overboard," and he desired that he might be buried by his parents, unless it should please the King to order otherwise. "Kiss me, Hardy." He knelt down and kissed his cheek. "Now I am satisfied," said Nelson. "Thank God, I have done my duty." Hardy stood over him in silence for a moment or two, then knelt again and kissed his forehead. "Who is that?" said Nelson; and being informed, he replied, "God bless you, Hardy." And Hardy then left him — for ever.

Nelson now desired to be turned upon his right side, and said, "I wish I had not left the deck; for I shall soon be gone." Death was, indeed, rapidly approaching. His articulation now became difficult: but he was distinctly heard to say, "Thank God, I have done my duty." These words he repeatedly pronounced; and they were the last words which he uttered. He expired at thirty minutes after four — three hours and a quarter after he had received his wound.

ROBERT SOUTHEY.

18. Beowulf.

The only English national epic which has been preserved entire is Beowulf. Its argument is briefly as follows:

The poem opens with a few verses in praise of the Danish kings, especially Scild, the son of Sceaf. His death is related, and his descendants briefly traced down to Hrothgar. Hrothgar, elated with his prosperity and success in war, builds a magnificent hall, which he calls Heorot. In this hall Hrothgar and his retainers live in joy and festivity, until a malignant fiend, called Grendel, jealous of their happiness, carries off by night thirty of Hrothgar's men, and devours them in his moorland retreat. These ravages go on for twelve years. Beowulf, a thane of Hygelac, king of the Goths, hearing of Hrothgar's calamities, sails from Sweden with fourteen warriors to help him. They reach the Danish coast in safety, and, after an animated parley with Hrothgar's coast-guard, who at first takes them for pirates, they are allowed to proceed to the royal hall, where they are well received by Hrothgar. A banquet ensues, during which Beowulf is taunted by the envious Hunferhth about his swimming-match with Breca, king of the Brondings. Beowulf gives the true account of the contest, and silences Hunferhth. At nightfall the king departs, leaving Beowulf in charge of the hall. Grendel soon breaks in, seizes and devours one of Beowulf's companions, is attacked by Beowulf, and after losing an arm, which is torn off by Beowulf, escapes to the fens. The joy of Hrothgar and the Danes, and their festivities, are described, various episodes are introduced, and Beowulf, and his companions receive splendid gifts. The next night Grendel's mother revenges her son by carrying off Aeschere, the friend and councillor of Hrothgar, during the absence of Beowulf. Hrothgar appeals to Beowulf for vengeance, and describes the haunts of Grendel and his mother. They all proceed thither; the scenery of the lake, and the monsters that dwell in it are described. Beowulf plunges into the water, and attacks Grendel's mother in her dwelling at the bottom of the lake. He at length overcomes her, and cuts off her head, together with that of Grendel, and brings the heads to Hrothgar. He then takes leave of Hrothgar, sails back to Sweden, and relates his adventures to Hygelac. Here the first half of the poem ends. The second begins with the accession of Beowulf to the throne after the fall of Hygelac and his son Heardred. He rules prosperously for fifty years, till a dragon, brooding over a hidden treasure, begins to ravage the country, and destroys Beowulf's palace with fire. Beowulf sets out in quest of its hiding place with twelve men. Having a presentment of his approaching end, he pauses and recalls to mind his past life and exploits. He then takes leave of his followers one by one, and advances alone to attack the dragon. Unable from the heat to enter the cavern, he shouts aloud, and the dragon comes forth. The dragon's scaly hide is proof against Beowulf's sword, and he is reduced to great straits, when Wiglaf, one of his followers, advances to help him. Wiglaf's shield is consumed by the dragon's fiery breath, and he is compelled to seek shelter under Beowulf's shield of iron. Beowulf's sword snaps asunder, and he is seized by the dragon. Wiglaf stabs the dragon from underneath, and Beowulf cuts it in two with his dagger. Feeling that his end is near, he bids Wiglaf bring out the treasures from the cavern, that he may see them before he dies. Wiglaf enters the dragon's den, which is described, returns to Beowulf, and receives his last commands. Beowulf dies, and Wiglaf bitterly reproaches his companions for their cowardice. The disastrous consequences of Beowulf's death are then foretold, and the poem ends with his funeral. HENRY SWEET.

19. Chaucer.

The most illustrious ornament of the reign of Edward III. and of his successor Richard II. was Geoffrey Chaucer, a poet with whom the history of our poetry is by many supposed to have commenced, and who has been pronounced, by a critic of unquestionable taste and discernment, to be the first English versifier who wrote poetically. He was born about the year 1340, and was probably in his youth a page of Elizabeth, wife of Prince Lionel, third son of Edward III.; but the liveliness of his parts, and the native gaiety of his disposition, soon recommended him to the patronage of a magnificent monarch, and rendered him a very popular and acceptable character in his brilliant court. In the meantime he added to his accomplishments by frequent tours into France and Italy, which he sometimes visited under the advantage of a public character. Hitherto our poets had been persons of a private and circumscribed education, and the art of versifying, like every other kind of composition, had been confined to recluse scholars. But Chaucer was a man of the world; and from this circumstance we are to account, in great measure, for the many new embellishments which he conferred on our language and our poetry. The descriptions of splendid processions and gallant carousals with which his works abound are a proof that he was conversant with the practices and diversions of polite life. Familiarity with a variety of things and objects, opportunities of acquiring the fashionable and courtly modes of speech, connections with the great at home, and a personal acquaintance with the vernacular poets of foreign countries, opened his mind, and furnished him with new lights. In Italy he is said to have met Petrarch, at the wedding of Violante, daughter of Galeazzo, duke of Milan, with the duke of Clarence; and it is even alleged that Boccaccio was of the party. Although Chaucer had undoubtedly studied the works of these celebrated writers, and particularly of Dante, before this, yet it seems likely that these excursions gave him a new relish for their compositions, and enlarged his knowledge of the Italian fables. His travels likewise enabled him to cultivate the Italian and French languages with the greatest success, and induced him to polish the asperity, and enrich the sterility of his native versification with softer cadences, and a more copious and variegated phraseology. This attempt was authorized by the recent and popular examples of Petrarch in Italy and Jean de Meun and others in France. The revival of learning in most countries appears to have first owed its rise to translation. At rude periods the modes of original thinking are unknown, and the arts of original composition have not yet been studied. The writers, therefore, of such periods are chiefly and very usefully employed in importing the ideas of other languages into their own. They do not venture to think for themselves, nor aim at the merit of inventors, but they are laying the foundation of the literature; and while they are naturalizing the knowledge of more learned ages and countries by translation, they are imperceptibly improving the national language. This has been remarkably the case, not only in England, but in France and Italy. In the year 1387, John Trevisa, canon of Westbury in Gloucestershire and a great traveller, not only finished a translation of the Old and New Testaments at the command of his munificent patron, Thomas Lord Berkley, but also translated Higden's Polychronicon and other Latin pieces. But the translations would have been alone insufficient to have produced or sustained any considerable revolution in our language: the great work was reserved for Gower and Chaucer. Wickliffe had also translated the Bible; and in other respects his attempts to bring about a reformation in religion at this time proved beneficial to English literature. The orthodox divines of this period generally wrote in Latin: but Wickliffe, that his arguments might be familiarized to common readers and the bulk of the people, was obliged to compose in English his numerous theological treatises against the Pope. Edward III. while he perhaps intended only to banish a badge of conquest, greatly contributed to establish the national dialect, by abolishing the use of the Norman tongue in public acts and judicial proceedings, and by substituting the natural language of the country. But Chaucer manifestly first taught his countrymen to write English, and formed a style by naturalizing words from the Langue d'Oye at that time the richest dialect of any in Europe, and the best adapted to the purposes of poetical expression.

It is certain that Chaucer abounds in classical allusions, but his poetry is not formed to ancient models. He appears to have been a universal reader, and his learning is sometimes mistaken for genius; but his chief sources were the French and Italian poets. —

Nothing can be more ingeniously contrived than the occasion on which Chaucer's Canterbury Tales are supposed to be recited. A company of pilgrims, on their journey to visit the shrine of Thomas à Becket at Canterbury, lodge at the Tabard Inn in Southwark. Although strangers to each other, they are assembled in one room at supper, as was then the custom; and agree, not only to travel together the next morning, but to relieve the fatigue of the journey by telling each a story. Chaucer undoubtedly intended to imitate Boccaccio, whose Decameron was then the most popular of books, in writing a set of tales.

But the circumstance invented by Boccaccio, as the cause which gave rise to his Decameron, or the relation of his hundred stories, is by no means so happily conceived as that of Chaucer for a similar purpose. Boccaccio supposes that, when the plague began to abate at Florence, ten young persons of both sexes retired to a country house, two miles from the city, with a design of enjoying fresh air, and passing ten days agreeably. Their principal and established amusement, instead of playing at chess after dinner, was for each to tell a tale. One superiority which, among others, Chaucer's plan afforded above that of Boccaccio, was the opportunity of displaying a variety of striking and dramatic characters, which would not have easily met but on such an expedition: — a circumstance which also contributed to give a variety to the stories. And for a number of persons in their situation, so natural, so practicable, so pleasant, I add so rational, a mode of entertainment could not have been imagined.

The Canterbury Tales are unequal, and of various merit. Few perhaps, if any, of the stories are the invention of Chaucer.

Chaucer's vein of humour, although conspicuous in the Canterbury Tales, is chiefly displayed in the characters with which they are introduced. In these his knowledge of the world availed him in a peculiar degree, and enabled him to give such an accurate picture of ancient manners as no contemporary nation has transmitted to posterity. It is here that we view the pursuits and employments, the customs and diversions of our ancestors, copied from the life, and represented with equal truth and spirit, by a judge of mankind whose penetration qualified him to discern their foibles or discriminating peculiarities, and by an artist, who understood that proper selection of circumstances and those predominant characteristics, which form a finished portrait. We are surprised to find, in so gross and ignorant an age, such talents for satire and for observation on life: qualities which usually exert themselves at more civilized periods, when the improved state of society, by subtilising our speculations, and establishing uniform modes of behaviour, disposes mankind to study themselves, and renders deviations of conduct and singularities of character more immediately and necessarily the objects of censure and ridicule. These curious and valuable remains are specimens of Chaucer's native genius, unassisted and unalloyed. The figures are all British, and bear comparatively faint marks of Classical, Italian, or French imitation. WARTON-HAZLITT.

20. The Rise of English Literature in the Age of Queen Elizabeth.

The age of Elizabeth was distinguished, beyond, perhaps, any other in our history, by a number of great men, famous in different ways, and whose names have come down to us with unblemished honours, — statesmen, warriors, divines, scholars, poets, and philosophers: Raleigh, Drake, Coke, Hooker, and higher and more sounding still, and still more frequent in our mouths, Shakespeare, Spenser, Sidney, Bacon, Jonson, Beaumont and Fletcher — men whom fame has eternised in her long and lasting scroll, and who, by their words and acts, were benefactors of their country, and ornaments of human nature. Their attainments of different kinds bore the same general stamp, and it was sterling: what they did had the mark of their age and country upon it. Perhaps the genius of Great Britain (if I may so speak without offence or flattery) never shone out fuller or brighter, or looked more like itself, than at this period.

For such an extraordinary combination and development of fancy and genius many causes may be assigned; and we may seek for the chief of them in religion, in politics, in the circumstances of the time, the recent diffusion of letters, in local situation, and in the character of the men who adorned that period, and availed themselves so nobly of the advantages placed within their reach.

I shall here attempt to give a general sketch of these causes, and of the manner in which they operated to mould and stamp the poetry of the country at the period of which I have to treat: independently of incidental and fortuitous causes, for which there is no accounting, but which, after all, have often the greatest share in determining the most important results.

The first cause I shall mention, as contributing to this general effect, was the Reformation, which had just then taken place. This event gave a mighty impulse and increased activity to thought and inquiry, and agitated the inert mass of accumulated prejudices throughout Europe. The effect of the concussion was general; but the shock was greatest in this country. It toppled down the full-grown intolerable abuses of centuries at a blow: and the roar and dashing of opinions, loosened from their accustomed hold, might be heard like the noise of an angry sea, and has never yet subsided. Germany first broke the spell, and gave the watchword; but England joined the shout, and echoed it back, with her island voice, from her thousand cliffs and craggy shores, in a longer and a louder strain. With that cry, the genius of Great Britain rose, and threw down the gauntlet to the nations. There was a mighty fermentation: the waters were out: public opinion was in a state of projection. Liberty was held out to all to think and speak the truth. Men's brains were busy; their spirits stirring; their hearts full; and their hands not idle. Their eyes were opened to expect the greatest things, and their ears burned with curiosity and zeal to know the truth, that the truth might make them free.

The translation of the Bible was the chief engine in the great work. It threw open, by a secret spring, the rich treasures of religion and morality, which had been there locked up as in a shrine. It revealed the visions of the prophets, and conveyed the lessons of inspired teachers to the meanest of the people. It gave them a common interest in a common cause. Their hearts burnt within them as they read. It gave a mind to the people, by giving them common subjects of thought and feeling. It cemented their union of character and sentiment; it created endless diversity and collision of opinion. They found objects to employ their faculties, and a motive in the magnitude of the consequences attached to them, to exert the utmost eagerness in the pursuit of truth, and the most daring intrepidity in maintaining it. Religious controversy sharpens the understanding by the subtlety and remoteness of the topics it discusses, and embraces the will by their infinite importance. We perceive in the history of this period a nervous masculine intellect. No levity, no feebleness, no indifference; or, if there were, it is a relaxation from the intense activity which gives a tone to its general character. But there is a gravity approaching to piety; a seriousness of impression, a conscientious severity of argument, an habitual fervour and enthusiasm in their method of handling almost every subject. The debates of the schoolmen were sharp and subtle enough; but they want interest and grandeur, and were besides confined to a few: they did not affect the general mass of the community. But the Bible was thrown open to all ranks and conditions 'to run and read,' with its wonderful table of contents from Genesis to the Revelations. Every village in England would present the scene so well described in Burns' 'Cotter's Saturday Night.' I cannot think that all this variety and weight of knowledge could be thrown in all at once upon the minds of the people and not make some impression upon it, the traces of which might be discerned in the manners and literature of the age. For, to leave more disputable points, and take only the historical parts of the Old Testament, or the moral sentiments of the New, there is nothing like them in the power of exciting awe and admiration. or of riveting sympathy. We see what Milton has made of the account of the Creation, from the manner in which he has treated it, imbued and impregnated with the spirit of the time of which we speak.

The literature of this age then, I would say, was strongly influenced (among other causes). first by the spirit of Christianity and secondly by the spirit of Protestantism.

The effects of the Reformation on politics and philosophy may be seen in the writings and history of the next and of the following ages. They are still at work, and will continue to be so. The effects on the poetry of the time were chiefly confined to the moulding of the character, and giving a powerful impulse to the intellect of the country. The immediate use or application that was made of religion to subjects of imagination and fiction was not (from an obvious ground of separation) so direct or frequent, as that which was made of the classical and romantic literature.

For, much about the same time, the rich and fascinating stories of the Greek and Roman mythology, and those of the romantic poetry of Spain and Italy, were eagerly explored by the curious, and thrown open in translations to the admiring gaze of the vulgar. This last circumstance could hardly have afforded so much advantage to the poets of that day, who were themselves, in fact, the translators, as it shows the general curiosity and increasing interest in such subjects as a prevailing feature of the times. There were translations of Tasso by Fairfax, and of Ariosto by Harrington, of Homer and Hesiod by Chapman, and of Virgil long before, and Ovid soon after; there was Sir Thomas North's translation of Plutarch, of which Shake-

speare has made such admirable use in his Coriolanus and Julius
Caesar; and Ben Jonson's tragedies of Catiline and Sejanus may
themselves be considered as almost literal translations into verse
of Tacitus, Sallust, and Cicero's Orations in his consulship. Petrarch,
Dante, the satirst Aretine, Machiavel, Castiglion, and others, were 5
familiar to our writers, and they make occasional mention of some
few French authors, as Ronsard and Du Bartas; for the French
literature had not at this stage arrived at its Augustan period, and
it was the imitation of their literature a century afterwards, when
it had arrived at its greatest height (itself copied from the Greek 10
and Latin), that enfeebled and impoverished our own. But of the
time that we are considering it might be said, without much extravagance, that every breath that blew, that every wave that rolled
to our shores, brought with it some accession to our knowledge
which was engrafted on the national genius. 15

What also gave an unusual impetus to the mind of men at this
period was the discovery of the New World, and the reading of
voyages and travels. Green islands and golden sands seemed to arise,
as by enchantment, out of the bosom of the watery waste, and
invite the cupidity, or wing the imagination of the dreaming specu- 20
lator. Fairy land was realized in new and unknown worlds. 'Fortunate
fields, and groves, and flowery vales, thrice happy isles,' were found
floating, 'like those Hesperian gardens famed of old,' beyond Atlantic
seas, as dropt from the zenith. The people, the soil, the clime, every
thing gave unlimited scope to the curiosity of the traveller and reader. 25
Other manners might be said to enlarge the bounds of knowledge,
and new mines of wealth were tumbled at our feet. It is from
a voyage to the Straits of Magellan that Shakespeare has taken the
hint of Prospero's Enchanted Island, and of the savage Caliban with
his god Setebos. Spenser seems to have had the same feeling in 30
his mind in the production of his Fairy Queen.

WILLIAM HAZLITT.

21. Bacon.

What has been the fame of Bacon, "the wisest, greatest of
mankind," it is needless to say. What has been his real influence 35
over mankind, how much of our enlarged and exact knowledge may
be attributed to his inductive method, what of this again has been
due to a thorough study of his writings, and what to an indirect
and secondary acquaintance with them, are questions of another
kind, and less easily solved. Stewart, the philosopher who has dwelt 40
most on the praises of Bacon, while he conceives him to have ex-

ercised a considerable influence over the English men of science in the seventeenth century, supposes, on the authority of Montucla, that he did not "command the general admiration of Europe" till the publication of the preliminary discourse to the French Encyclopaedia by Diderot and D'Alembert. This, however, is by much too precipitate a conclusion. He became almost immediately known on the Continent. Gassendi was one of his most ardent admirers. Descartes mentions him, I believe, once only, in a letter to Mersenne in 1632; but he was of all men the most unwilling to praise a contemporary. It may be said that these were philosophers, and that their testimony does not imply the admiration of mankind. But writers of a very different character mention him in a familiar manner. Richelieu is said to have highly esteemed Lord Bacon. And it may in some measure be due to this, that in the *Sentimens de l'Académie Française sur le Cid,* he is alluded to simply by the name of Bacon, as one well known. Voiture, in a letter to Costar, about the same time, bestows high eulogy on some passages of Bacon which his correspondent had sent to him, and observes that Horace would have been astonished to hear a barbarian Briton discourse in such a style. The treatise *De Augmentis* was republished in France in 1624, the year after its appearance in England. It was translated into French as early as 1632: no great proofs of neglect. Editions came out in Holland, 1645, 1652, and 1662. Even the *Novum Organum*, which, as has been said, never became so popular as his other writings, was thrice printed in Holland, in 1645, 1650, and 1660. Leibnitz and Puffendorf are loud in their expressions of admiration, the former ascribing to him the revival of true philosophy as fully as we can at present. I should be more inclined to doubt whether he were adequately valued by his countrymen in his own time, or in the immediately subsequent period. Under the first Stuarts, there was little taste among studious men but for theology, and chiefly for a theology which, proceeding with an extreme deference to authority, could not but generate a disposition of mind, even upon other subjects, alien to the progressive and inquisitive spirit of the inductive philosophy. The institution of the Royal Society, or rather the love of physical science out of which that institution arose, in the second part of the seventeenth century, made England resound with the name of her illustrious chancellor. Few now spoke of him without a kind of homage that only the greatest men receive. Yet still it was by natural philosophers alone that the writings of Bacon were much studied. The editions of his works, except the Essays, were few; the *Novum Organum* never came separately from the English press. They were not even frequently quoted; for I believe it will be found that the fashion of referring to the brilliant passages of the *De Augmentis* and the *Novum Organum*, at least in books designed for the general reader, is not much older than the close of the last century. Scotland has the merit of having led the way; Reid, Stewart, Robinson, and Playfair turned that which had been a blind veneration into a rational worship; and I should suspect that more have read Lord Bacon within these thirty years than in the two preceding centuries. It may be a usual consequence of the enthusiastic panegyrics lately poured upon his name, that a more positive efficacy has sometimes been attributed to his philosophical writings than they really possessed, and it might be asked whether Italy, where he was probably not much known, were not the true school of experimental philosophy in Europe, whether his methods of investigation were not chiefly such as men of sagacity and lovers of truth might simultaneously have devised. But, whatever may have been the case with respect to actual discoveries in science, we must give to written wisdom its proper meed; no books prior to those of Lord Bacon carried mankind so far on the road to truth: none have obtained so thorough a triumph over arrogant usurpation without seeking to substitute another; and he may be compared to those liberators of nations, who have given them laws by which they might govern themselves, and retained no homage but their gratitude.

HENRY HALLAM.

22. William Shakespeare.

Close by the river Avon in Warwickshire, a tall grey spire, springing from amid embowering elms and lime-trees, marks the position of the parish church of Stratford, in the chancel of which sleeps the body of our greatest poet. The proud roof of Westminster has been deemed by England the fitting vault for her illustrious dead; but Shakespeare's dust rests in a humbler tomb. By his own loved river, whose gentle music fell sweet upon his childish ear, he dropped into his last long sleep, and still its melancholy murmur, as it sweeps between its willowy banks, seems to sing the poet's dirge. Four lines, carved upon the flat stone which lies over the grave, are ascribed to his own pen. Whoever wrote them, they have served their purpose well, for a religious horror of disturbing the honoured dust has ever since hung about the place:

> Good friend, for Jesus' sake, forbear,
> To dig the dust enclosed here:
> Blest be the man that spares these stones,
> And curst be he that moves my bones.

A niche in the wall above holds a bust of the poet, whose high arching brow, and sweet oval face, fringed with a peaked beard and small moustache, are so familiar to us all. How well we know his face and his spirit; and yet, how little of the man's real life has descended to our day!

Not very far from Shakespeare's tomb part of the house in which he was born still stands. Sun and rain and air have gradually reduced the plastered timber of its old neighbours into powder: but its wood and lime still hold together, and the room is still shown in which baby Shakespeare's voice uttered its first feeble wail. The dingy walls of the little chamber are scribbled all over with the names of visitors, known and unknown to fame. It is pleasant to think that this shrine, sacred to the memory of the greatest English writer, has been lately purchased by the English nation; so that lovers of Shakespeare have now the satisfaction of feeling that the relics, which tell so picturesque a story of the poet's earliest days, are in safe and careful keeping. Here, then, was born in April 1564 William, son of John Shakespeare and Mary Arden, his wife. The gossiping Aubrey, no great authority, certainly, who came into the world about ten years after Shakespeare's death, says that the poet's father was a butcher: others make out the honest man to have been a wool-comber or a glover, while an ingenious writer strives to reconcile all accounts by supposing that since good John held some land in the neighbourhood of Stratford, whenever he killed a sheep, he sold the mutton, the wool, and the skin, adding to his other occupations the occasional dressing of leather and fashioning of gloves. Perhaps John Shakespeare's chief occupation was dealing in wool. At any rate, whatever may have been his calling, he ranked high enough among the burgesses of Stratford to sit on the bench as High Bailiff or Mayor of the town. Mary Arden, who should perhaps interest us more, if the commonly received rule be true, that men more strongly resemble their mothers in nature and genius, seems to have belonged to an old country family, and to have possessed what was then a considerable fortune.

From Hunt and Jenkins, then the masters of the school, Shakespeare received that education which his friend Jonson characterizes as consisting of "little Latin and less Greek".

How he spent his life after he had left school, and before he went to London, we know as dimly as we know the calling of his father. Aubrey says he helped his father the butcher, and that he acted also as a teacher. It is thought, from the constant recurrence of law terms in his writings, that he spent some of these years in an attorney's office. Nor was he free from youthful faults. To tell the truth, he appears to have engaged in many wild pranks, of which two stories have floated down to our day. One relates to an ale-drinking bout at the neighbouring village of Bidford, by which he was so overcome that, with his companions, he was obliged to spend the night by the road-side under the sheltering boughs of a large crab-tree. The other story is that of a poaching affair. It seems that the wild youths of Stratford could not resist the temptation of hunting deer and rabbits in the park of Sir Thomas Lucy, who lived at Charlecote, about three miles off. Shakespeare got into the poaching set, was detected one night, and locked up in the keeper's lodge till morning. His examination before the offended justice, and whatever punishment followed it, awoke the anger of the boyish poet, who in revenge wrote some doggerel, punning rhymes upon Sir Thomas, and stuck them on the park gate. This was throwing oil upon flame; and the knight's rage grew so violent that Shakespeare had to flee from Stratford. — His early marriage, too, contracted when he was but a raw boy of eighteen, with Anne Hathaway of Shottery, a yeoman's daughter, some eight years older than himself, affords additional evidence of youthful indiscretion.

Driven either by the fear of Sir Thomas Lucy's vengeance, or, more probably, by the need of providing daily bread for his wife and children, Shakespeare went up to London in 1586 or 1587; and then began that wonderful theatrical life of six and twenty years, whose great creations form the chief glory of our dramatic literature. The brightest day at noon is that whose dawn is wrapped in heavy mists; and so upon the opening of this brilliant time — the midsummer of English poetry — thick clouds of darkness rest.

How Shakespeare lived when first he arrived in London, we do not certainly know. Three Warwickshire men, one a native of his own town, then held a prominent place among the metropolitan players, and this, no doubt, coupled with his poetical tastes, led him to the theatre. Here, too, there are vague traditions of his life. According to one, he was call-boy or deputy-prompter; according to another, he held horses at the theatre door. However he may have earned his first shillings in London, it is certain that he soon became prosperous, and even wealthy. In the year 1589 he held a share in the Blackfriars Theatre, having previously, by his acting, by the adaption of old plays, and the production of new ones, proved himself worthy to be much more than a mere sleeping partner in the concern. As his fame brightened, his purse filled. He became also a part-owner of the Globe Theatre; and at one time drew from all sources a yearly income fully equivalent to £ 1500 of our money. Thus acting, writing and managing, he lived among the fine London folks, honoured with the special notice of his Queen, and associating every day with the noblest and wittiest Englishmen of that brilliant time, yet never snapping the link which bound him to the sweet banks of Avon. Every year he ran down to Stratford, where his family continued to reside; and there he bought a house and land for the rest and solace of his waning life.

The year 1612 is given as the date of the poet's final retirement from London life. He was then only forty-eight, and might reasonably hope for a full score of years, in which to grow his flowers, his mulberries, and his apple-trees, to treat his friends to sack and claret under the hospitable roof of New-Place, and to continue that series of Roman plays which had so noble a beginning in "Julius Caesar" and "Coriolanus". But four years more brought this great life to an untimely close. He died on the 23rd of April 1616, of what disease we have no certain knowledge.

His wife survived him seven years; his only son had gone to the grave before him; and long before the close of the century that saw this great poet die, all the descendants of William Shakespeare had perished from the face of the earth.

The thirty-seven plays of Shakespeare are classed as Tragedies, Comedies, and Histories. His great Tragedies are five — Macbeth, King Lear, Romeo and Juliet, Hamlet, and Othello. A Midsummer Night's Dream, As You Like It, and The Merchant of Venice, are perhaps the finest Comedies; while Richard III., Coriolanus, and Julius Caesar, stand prominently out among the noble series of Histories. The student who knows these eleven plays, knows Shakespeare in his finest vein. Besides his plays, Shakespeare gave to the world various poems: Venus and Adonis, Lucrece, The Passionate Pilgrim, A Lover's Complaint, and one hundred and fifty-four Sonnets.   W. F. COLLIER.

23. Milton's Paradise Lost.

By the general consent of critics, the first praise of genius is due to the writer of an epic poem, as it requires an assemblage of all the powers which are singly sufficient for other compositions. Poetry is the art of uniting pleasure with truth, by calling imagination to the help of reason. Epic poetry undertakes to teach the most important truths by the most pleasing precepts, and therefore relates some great event in the most affecting manner. History must supply the writer with the rudiments of narration, which he must improve and exalt by a nobler art, must animate by dramatic energy, and diversify by retrospection and anticipation; morality must teach him the exact bounds, and different shades of vice and virtue; from policy, and the practice of life, he has to learn the discriminations of character, and the tendency of the passions, either single or combined; and physiology must supply him with illustrations and images. To put these materials to poetical use, is required an imagination capable of painting nature, and realizing fiction. Nor is he yet a poet till he has attained the whole extension of his language, distinguished all the delicacies of phrase, and all the colours of words, and learned to adjust their different sounds to all the varieties of metrical modulation.

Bossu is of opinion, that the poet's first work is to find a moral, which his fable is afterwards to illustrate and establish. This seems to have been the process only of Milton; the moral of other poems is incidental and consequent; in Milton's only it is essential and intrinsic. His purpose was the most useful and the most arduous: "to vindicate the ways of God to man;" to show the reasonableness of religion, and the necessity of obedience to the Divine law.

To convey this moral there must be a fable, a narration artfully constructed, so as to excite curiosity, and surprise expectation. In this part of his work, Milton must be confessed to have equalled every other poet. He has involved in his account of the fall of man the events which preceded, and those that were to follow it: he has interwoven the whole system of theology with such propriety, that every part appears to be necessary; and scarcely any recital is wished shorter for the sake of quickening the progress of the main action.

The subject of an epic poem is naturally an event of great importance. That of Milton is not the destruction of a city, the conduct of a colony, or the foundation of an empire. His subject is the fate of worlds, the revolutions of heaven and of earth; rebellion against the supreme King, raised by the highest order of created beings: the overthrow of their host, and the punishment of their crime; the creation of a new race of reasonable creatures, their original happiness and innocence, their forfeiture of immortality, and their restoration to hope and peace.

The characteristic quality of his poem is sublimity. He sometimes descends to the elegant, but his element is the great. He can occasionally invest himself with grace; but his natural port is gigantic loftiness. He can please when pleasure is required; but it is his peculiar power to astonish.

He seems to have been well acquainted with his own genius, and to know what it was that Nature had bestowed upon him more bountifully than upon others: the power of displaying the vast, illuminating the splendid, enforcing the awful, darkening the gloomy, and aggravating the dreadful; he therefore chose a subject on which too much could not be said, on which he might tire his fancy without the censure of extravagance.

The appearance of nature, and the occurences of life, did not satiate his appetite for greatness. To paint things as they are, requires a minute attention, and employs the memory rather than the fancy. Milton's delight was to sport in the wide regions of possibility; reality was a scene too narrow for his mind. He sent his faculties out upon discovery, into worlds where only imagination can travel, and delighted to form new modes of existence, and furnish sentiment and action to superior beings, to trace the counsels of hell, or accompany the choirs of heaven.

But he could not be always in other worlds; he must sometimes revisit earth, and tell of things visible and known. When he cannot raise wonder by the sublimity of his mind, he gives delight by its fertility.

Whatever be his subject, he never fails to fill the imagination: but his images and descriptions of the scenes or operations of Nature do not seem to be always copied from original form, nor to have the freshness, raciness, and energy of immediate observation. He saw Nature, as Dryden expresses it, "through the spectacles of books;" and on most occasions calls learning to his assistance. The garden of Eden brings to his mind the vale of Enna, where Proserpine was gathering flowers. Satan makes his way through fighting elements, like Argo between the Cyanean rocks; or Ulysses, between the two Sicilian whirlpools, when he shunned Charybdis on the larboard. The mythological allusions have been justly censured, as not being always used with notice of their vanity; but they contribute variety to the narration, and produce an alternate exercise of the memory and the fancy.

His similes are less numerous, and more various, than those of his predecessors. But he does not confine himself within the limits of rigorous comparison: his great excellence is amplitude; and he expands the adventitious image beyond the dimensions which the occasion required. Thus, comparing the shield of Satan to the orb of the moon, he crowds the imagination with the discovery of the telescope, and all the wonders which the telescope discovers.

The defects and faults of "Paradise Lost", for faults and defects every work of man must have, it is the business of impartial criticism to discover. As, in displaying the excellence of Milton, I have not made long quotations, because of selecting beauties there had been no end, I shall in the same general manner mention that which seems to deserve censure; for what Englishman can take delight in transcribing passages, which, if they lessen the reputation of Milton, diminish in some degree the honour of our country?

The plan of "Paradise Lost" has this inconvenience, that it comprises neither human actions nor human manners. The man and woman who act and suffer are in a state which no other man or woman can ever know. The reader finds no transaction in which he can be engaged; beholds no condition in which he can by any effort of imagination place himself; he has, therefore, little natural curiosity or sympathy.

We all, indeed, feel the effects of Adam's disobedience; we all sin like Adam, and like him must all bewail our offences: we have restless and insidious enemies in the fallen angels; and in the blessed spirits we have guardians and friends: in the redemption of mankind we hope to be included; and in the description of heaven and hell we are surely interested, as we are all to reside hereafter either in the regions of horror or of bliss.

But these truths are too important to be new; they have been taught to our infancy; they have mingled with our solitary thoughts and familiar conversations, and are habitually interwoven with the whole texture of life. Being therefore not new, they raise no unaccustomed emotion in the mind; what we knew before, we cannot learn; what is not unexpected, cannot surprise.

Known truths, however, may take a different appearance, and be conveyed to the mind by a new train of intermediate images. This Milton has undertaken, and performed with pregnancy and vigour of mind peculiar to himself. Whoever considers the few radical positions which the Scriptures afforded him, will wonder by what energetic operation he expanded them to such extent, and ramified them to so much variety, restrained as he was by religious reverence from licentiousness of fiction.

Here is a full display of the united force of study and genius; of a great accumulation of materials, with judgment to digest, and fancy to combine them: Milton was able to select from nature, or from story, from ancient fable, or from modern science, whatever could illustrate or adorn his thoughts. An accumulation of knowledge impregnated his mind, fermented by study, and exalted by imagination.

It has been therefore said, without an indecent hyperbole, by one of his encomiasts, that in reading "Paradise Lost", we read a book of universal knowledge.

But original deficience cannot be supplied. The want of human interest is always felt. "Paradise Lost" is one of the books which the reader admires and lays down, and forgets to take up again. None ever wished it longer than it is. Its perusal is a duty rather than a pleasure. We read Milton for instruction, retire harassed and overburdened, and look elsewhere for recreation; we desert our master, and seek for companions.

The highest praise of genius is original invention. Milton cannot be said to have contrived the structure of an epic poem. But, of all the borrowers from Homer, Milton is perhaps the least indebted. He was naturally a thinker for himself, confident of his own abilities, and disdainful of help or hinderance: he did not refuse admission to the thoughts or images of his predecessors, but he did not seek them. From his contemporaries he neither courted nor received support; there is in his writings nothing by which the pride of other authors might be gratified, or favour gained, no exchange of praise, nor solicitation of support. His great works were performed under discountenance, and in blindness; but difficulties vanished at his touch; he was born for whatever is arduous; and his work is not the greatest of heroic poems, only because it is not the first.   SAMUEL JOHNSON.

24. On English Literature in the Age of Queen Anne.

It was the ambition of the authors of Queen Anne's time to improve and perfect the new style introduced at the Restoration, rather than to return to the old one; and it cannot be denied that they did improve it. They corrected its gross indecency — increased its precision and correctness — made its pleasantry and sarcasm more polished and elegant — and spread through the whole of its irony, its narration, and its reflection, a tone of clear and condensed good sense, which recommended itself to all who had, and all who had not, any relish for higher beauties. This is the praise of Queen Anne's wits, and to this praise they are justly entitled. This was left for them to do, and they did it well. They were invited to it by the circumstances of their situation, and do not seem to have been possessed of any such bold or vigorous spirit as either to neglect, or to outgo the invitation. Coming into life immediately after the consummation of a bloodless revolution, effected much more by the cool sense than the angry passions of the nation, they seem to have felt that they were born in an age of reason, rather than

of feeling or fancy; and that men's minds, though considerably divided
and unsettled upon many points, were in a much better temper to
relish judicious argument and cutting satire, than the glow of enthusiastic passion, or the richness of a luxuriant imagination. To
these, accordingly, they made no pretensions; but writing with infinite
good sense, and great grace and vivacity, and, above all, writing for
the first time in a tone that was peculiar to the upper ranks of
society, and upon subjects that were almost exclusively interesting
to them, they naturally figured, at least while the manner was new,
as the most accomplished, fashionable, and perfect writers which the
world had ever seen, and made the wild, luxuriant, and humble
sweetness of our earlier authors appear rude and untutored in the
comparison. Men grew ashamed of admiring, and afraid of imitating,
writers of so little skill and smartness; and the opinion became
general, not only that their faults were intolerable, but that even
their beauties were puerile and barbarous, and unworthy the serious
regard of a polite and distinguishing age.

These, and similar considerations, will go far to account for the
celebrity which those authors acquired in their day: but it is not
quite so easy to explain how they should have so long retained their
ascendant. One cause, undoubtedly, was the real excellence of their
productions, in the style which they had adopted. It was hopeless to
think of surpassing them in that style; and, recommended as it was
by the felicity of their execution, it required some courage to depart
from it, and to recur to another, which seemed to have been so
lately abandoned for its sake. The age which succeeded, too, was not
the age of courage or adventure. There never was, on the whole, a
quieter time than the reigns of the two first Georges, and the greater
part of that which ensued. There were two little provincial rebellions,
indeed, and a fair proportion of foreign war; but there was nothing
to stir the minds of the people at large, to rouse their passions, or
excite their imaginations — nothing like the agitations of the Reformation in the sixteenth century, or of the civil wars in the seventeenth. They went on, accordingly, minding their old business, and
reading their old books, with great patience and stupidity; and certainly there never was so remarkable a dearth of original talent —
so long an interregnum of native genius — as during about sixty
years in the middle of the last century. The dramatic art was dead
fifty years before, and poetry seemed verging to a similar extinction.
The few sparks that appeared, too, showed that the old fire was
burnt out, and that the altar must hereafter be heaped with fuel of
another quality. Gray, with the talents rather of a critic than a

poet, — with learning, fastidiousness, and scrupulous delicacy of taste, instead of fire, tenderness, or invention, — began and ended a small school, which we could scarcely have wished to become permanent, admirable in many respects as some of its productions are, being far too elaborate and artifical either for grace or for fluency, and fitter to excite the admiration of scholars than the delight of ordinary men. However, he had the merit of not being in any degree French, and of restoring to our poetry the dignity of seriousness, and the tone at least of force and energy. The Wartons, both as critics and as poets, were of considerable service in discrediting the high pretensions of the former race, and in bringing back to public notice the great stores and treasures of poetry which lay hid in the records of our older literature. Akenside attempted a sort of classical and philosophical rapture, which no elegance of language could easily have rendered popular, but which had merits of no vulgar order for those who could study it. Goldsmith wrote with perfect elegance and beauty, in a style of mellow tenderness and elaborate simplicity. He had the harmony of Pope without his quaintness, and his selectness of diction without his coldness and eternal vivacity. And last of all came Cowper, with a style of complete originality, and, for the first time, made it apparent to readers of all descriptions that Pope and Addison were not longer to be the models of English poetry.

In philosophy and prose writing in general, the case was nearly parallel. The name of Hume is by far the most considerable which occurs in the period to which we have alluded. But, though his thinking was English, his style is entirely French: and, being naturally of a cold fancy, there is nothing of that eloquence or richness about him which characterizes the writings of Taylor, and Hooker, and Bacon, and continues, with less weight of matter, to please in those of Cowley and Clarendon. Warburton had great powers, and wrote with more force and freedom than the wits to whom he succeeded; but his faculties were perverted by a paltry love of paradox, and rendered useless to mankind by an unlucky choice of subjects, and the arrogance and dogmatism of his temper. Adam Smith was nearly the first who made deeper reasonings and more exact knowledge popular among us, and Junius and Johnson the first who again familiarized us with more glowing and sonorous diction, and made us feel the tameness and poorness of the serious style of Addison and Swift.

FRANCIS JEFFREY.

25. Oliver Goldsmith.

Goldsmith's father was no doubt the good Doctor Primrose, whom we all of us know. Swift was yet alive, when the little Oliver was born at Pallas, or Pallasmore, in the county of Longford, in Ireland. In 1730, two years after the child's birth, Charles Goldsmith removed his family to Lissoy, in the county Westmeath, that sweet 'Auburn,' which every person who hears me has seen in fancy. Here the kind parson brought up his eight children: and loving all the world, as his son says, fancied all the world loved him. He had a crowd of poor dependents besides those hungry children. He kept an open table; round which sat flatterers and poor friends, who laughed at the honest rector's many jokes, and ate the produce of his seventy acres of farm. Those who have seen an Irish house in the present day, can fancy that one of Lissoy. The old beggar still has his allotted corner by the kitchen turf; the maimed old soldier still gets his potatoes and buttermilk; the poor cottier still asks his honour's charity, and prays God bless his Reverence for the sixpence; the ragged pensioner still takes his place by right and sufferance. There's still a crowd in the kitchen, and a crowd round the parlour-table; profusion, confusion, kindness, poverty. If an Irishman comes to London to make his fortune, he has half a dozen of Irish dependents who take a percentage of his earnings. The good Charles Goldsmith left but little provision for his hungry race when death summoned him: and, one of his daughters being engaged to a Squire of rather superior dignity, Charles Goldsmith impoverished the rest of his family to provide the girl with a dowry.

The small-pox, which scourged all Europe at that time, and ravaged the roses off the cheeks of half the world, fell foul of poor little Oliver's face, when the child was eight years old, and left him scarred and disfigured for his life. An old woman in his father's village taught him his letters, and pronounced him a dunce: Paddy Byrne, the hedge-schoolmaster, took him in hand: and from Paddy Byrne, he was transmitted to a clergyman at Elphin. When a child was sent to school in those days, the classic phrase was that he was placed under Mr. So and So's ferule. Poor little ancestors! It is hard to think how ruthlessly you were birched; and how much of needless whipping and tears our small forefathers had to undergo! A relative, kind uncle Contarine, took the main charge of little Noll; who went through his schooldays righteously doing as little work as he could: robbing orchards, playing at ball, and making his pocket money fly about whenever fortune sent it to him. Everybody knows the story

of that famous 'Mistake of a Night', when the young schoolboy, provided with a guinea and a nag, rode up to the 'best house' in Ardagh, called for the landlord's company over a bottle of wine at supper, and for a hot cake for breakfast in the morning; and found
5 when he asked for the bill, that the best house was Squire Featherstone's, and not the inn for which he mistook it. Who does not know every story about Goldsmith? That is a delightful and fantastic picture of the child dancing and capering about in the kitchen at home, when the old fiddler gibed at him for his ugliness — and
10 called him Æsop, and little Noll made his repartee of 'Heralds proclaim aloud this saying — see Æsop dancing and his monkey playing.' One can fancy a queer pitiful look of humour and appeal upon that little scarred face — the funny little dancing figure, the funny little brogue. In his life, and his writings which are the honest
15 expression of it, he is constantly bewailing that homely face and person; anon he surveys them in the glass ruefully; and presently assumes the most comical dignity. He likes to deck out his little person in splendour and fine colours. He presented himself to be examined for ordination in a pair of scarlet breeches, and said
20 honestly that he did not like to go into the church because he was fond of coloured clothes. When he tried to practise as a doctor, he got by hook or by crook a black-velvet suit, and looked as big and grand as he could, and kept his hat over a patch on the old coat: in better days he bloomed out in plum-colour, in blue silk, and in
25 new velvet. For some of those splendours the heirs and assignees of Mr. Filby, the tailor, have never been paid to this day; perhaps the kind tailor and his creditor have met and settled the little account in Hades.

They showed until lately a window at Trinity College, Dublin,
30 on which the name of O. Goldsmith was engraved with a diamond. Whose diamond was it? Not the young Sizar's who made but a poor figure in that place of learning. He was idle, penniless, and fond of pleasure: he learned his way early to the pawnbroker's shop. He wrote ballads, they say, for the street singers, who paid him a crown
35 for a poem; and his pleasure was to steal out at night and hear his verses sung. He was chastised by his tutor for giving a dance in his rooms, and took the box on the ear so much to heart, that he packed up his all, pawned his books and little property, and disappeared from college and family. He said he intended to go to America,
40 but when his money was spent, the young prodigal came home ruefully, and the good folks there killed their calf — it was but a lean one — and welcomed him back.

After College, he hung about his mother's house and lived for some years the life of a buckeen — passed a month with this relation and that, a year with one patron, a great deal of time at the public-house. Tired of this life, it was resolved that he should go to London, and study at the Temple: but he got no farther on the road to London and the woolsack than Dublin, where he gambled away the fifty pounds given him for his outfit, and whence he returned to the indefatigable forgiveness of home. Then he determined to be a doctor, and Uncle Contarine helped him to a couple of years at Edinburgh. Then from Edinburgh he felt that he ought to hear the famous professors of Leyden and Paris, and wrote most amusing pompous letters to his uncle about the great Farheim, Du Petit and Duhamel du Monceau, whose lectures he proposed to follow. If Uncle Contarine believed those letters — if Oliver's mother believed that story which the youth related of his going to Cork, with the purpose of embarking for America, of his having paid his passage-money, and having sent his kit on board: of the anonymous captain sailing away with Oliver's valuable luggage, in a nameless ship, never to return; if Uncle Contarine and the mother at Ballymahon believed his stories, they must have been a very simple pair; as it was a very simple rogue indeed who cheated them. When the lad, after failing in his clerical examination, after failing in his plan for studying the law, took leave of these projects and of his parents, and set out for Edinburgh, he saw mother, and uncle, and lazy Ballymahon, and green native turf, and sparkling river for the last time. He was never to look on old Ireland more, and only in fancy revisit her.

> 'But me not destined such delights to share,
> My prime of life in wandering spent and care,
> Impelled, with step unceasing, to pursue
> Some fleeting good that mocks me with the view;
> That like the circle bounding earth and skies
> Allures from far, yet, as I follow, flies:
> My fortune leads to traverse realms unknown,
> And find no spot of all the world my own.'

I spoke in a former lecture of that high courage which enabled Fielding, in spite of disease, remorse, and poverty, always to retain a cheerful spirit and to keep his manly benevolence and love of truth intact, as if these treasures had been confided to him for the public benefit, and he was accountable to posterity for their honourable employ; and a constancy equally happy and admirable I think was shown by Goldsmith, whose sweet and friendly nature bloomed kindly always in the midst of a life's storm, and rain, and bitter weather. The poor fellow was never so friendless but he could

befriend some one; never so pinched and wretched but he could give
of his crust, and speak his word of compassion. If he had but his
flute left, he could give that, and make the children happy in the
dreary London court. He could pawn his coat to save his landlord
from gaol: when he was a school-usher, he spent his earnings in
treats for the boys, and the good-natured schoolmaster's wife said
justly that she ought to keep Mr. Goldsmith's money as well as the
young gentlemen's. When he met his pupils in later life, nothing
would satisfy the Doctor but he must treat them still. 'Have you
seen the print of me after Sir Joshua Reynolds?' he asked of one
of his old pupils. 'Not seen it? not bought it? Sure, Jack, if your
picture had been published, I'd not have been without it half-an-
hour.' His purse and his heart were everybody's, and his friends' as
much as his own. When he was at the height of his reputation, and
the Earl of Northumberland, going as Lord-Lieutenant to Ireland,
asked if he could be of any service to Dr. Goldsmith. Goldsmith recommended his brother, and not himself, to the great man. 'My patrons,'
he gallantly said, 'are the booksellers, and I want no others.' Hard
patrons they were, and hard work he did; but he did not complain
much: if in his early writings some bitter words escaped him, some
allusions to neglect and poverty, he withdrew these expressions, when
his works were republished, and better days seemed to open for him:
and he did not care to complain that printer or publisher had overlooked his merit, or left him poor. The Court face was turned from
honest Oliver, the Court patronised Beattie; the fashion did not
shine on him — fashion adored Sterne. Fashion pronounced Kelly to
be the great writer of comedy of his day. A little — not ill humour,
but plaintiveness — a little betrayal of wounded pride which he
showed rendered him not the less amiable. The author of the 'Vicar
of Wakefield' had a right to protest when Newbery kept back the
MS. for two years; had a right to be a little peevish with Sterne; a
little angry when Colman's actors declined their parts in his delightful
comedy, when the manager refused to have a scene painted for it,
and pronounced its damnation before hearing. He had not the great
public with him; but he had the noble Johnson, and the admirable
Reynolds, and the great Gibbon, and the great Fox — friends and
admirers illustrious indeed, as famous as those who, fifty years before,
sat round Pope's table.

Nobody knows, and I dare say Goldsmith's buoyant temper kept
no account of the pains which he endured during the early period
of his literary career. Should any man of letter in our day have to
bear up against such, Heaven grant he may come out of the period

of misfortune with such a pure kind heart as that which Goldsmith obstinately bore in his breast. The insults to which he had to submit are shocking to read of, — slander, contumely, vulgar satire, brutal malignity perverting his commonest motives and actions: he had his share of these, and one's anger is roused at reading of them, as it is at seeing a woman insulted or a child assaulted, at the notion that a creature so very gentle and weak, and full of love, should have had to suffer so. And he had worse than insult to undergo — to own to fault, and deprecate the anger of ruffians. There is a letter of his extant to one Griffiths: a bookseller, in which poor Goldsmith is forced to confess, that certain books sent by Griffiths are in the hands of a friend from whom Goldsmith had been forced to borrow money. 'He was wild, Sir,' Johnson said, speaking of Goldsmith to Boswell, with his great, wise benevolence and noble mercifulness of heart. 'Dr. Goldsmith was wild, Sir; but he is so no more.' Ah! if we pity the good and weak man who suffers undeservedly, let us deal very gently with him from whom misery extorts not only tears, but shame; let us think humbly and charitably of the human nature that suffers so sadly and falls so low. Whose turn may it be to-morrow? What weak heart, confident before trial, may not succumb under temptation invincible? Cover the good man who has been vanquished — cover his face and pass on.

For the last half dozen years of his life, Goldsmith was far removed from the pressure of any ignoble necessity: and in the receipt, indeed, of a pretty large income from the booksellers, his patrons. Had he lived but a few years more, his public fame would have been as great as his private reputation, and he might have enjoyed alive a part of that esteem which his country has ever since paid to the vivid and versatile genius who has touched on almost every subject of literature, and touched nothing that he did not adorn. Except in rare instances a man is known in our profession, and esteemed as a skilful workman, years before the lucky hit, which trebles his usual gains, and stamps him a popular author. In the strength of his age, and the dawn of his reputation, having for backers and friends the most illustrious literary men of his time, fame and prosperity might have been in store for Goldsmith, had fate so willed: and, at forty-six, had not sudden disease carried him off. I say prosperity rather than competence, for it is probable that no sum could have put order into his affairs, or sufficed for his irreclaimable habits of dissipation. It must be remembered that he owed 2000 *l*. when he died. 'Was ever poet,' Johnson asked, 'so trusted before?' As has been the case with many another good fellow of his nation, his life was tracked and his substance wasted by crowds of hungry beggars and lazy dependents. If they came at a lucky time, (and be sure they knew his affairs better than he did himself, and watched his pay day) he gave them of his money: if they begged on empty-purse days he gave them his promissory bills: or he treated them to a tavern where he had credit; or he obliged them with an order upon honest Mr. Filby for coats, for which he paid as long as he could earn, and until the shears of Filby were to cut for him no more. Staggering under a load of debt and labour, tracked by bailiffs and reproachful creditors, running from a hundred poor dependents, whose appealing looks were perhaps the hardest of all pains for him to bear, devising fevered plans for the morrow, new histories, new comedies, all sorts of new literary schemes, flying from all these into seclusion, and out of seclusion into pleasure — at last, at five and forty, death seized him and closed his career. I have been many a time in the chambers in the Temple which were his, and passed up the stair-case, which Johnson, and Burke, and Reynolds trod to see their friend, their poet, their kind Goldsmith — the stair on which the poor women sat weeping bitterly when they heard that greatest and most generous of all men was dead within the black oak door. Ah, it was a different lot from that for which the poor fellow sighed, when he wrote with heart yearning for home those most charming of all fond verses, in which he fancies he revisits Auburn —

> 'Here as I take my solitary rounds,
> Amidst thy tangled walks and ruined grounds,
> And, many a year elapsed, return to view
> Where once the cottage stood, the hawthorn grew,
> Remembrance wakes, with all her busy train,
> Swells at my heart, and turns the past to pain.
> In all my wanderings round this world of care,
> In all my griefs — and God has given my share,
> I still had hopes my latest hours to crown.
> Amidst these humble bowers to lay me down;
> To husband out life's taper at the close,
> And keep the flame from wasting by repose;
> I still had hopes — for pride attends us still —
> Amidst the swains to show my book-learned skill,
> Around my fire an evening group to draw,
> And tell of all I felt and all I saw;
> And, as a hare, whom hounds and horns pursue,
> Pants to the place from whence at first she flew —
> I still had hopes — my long vexations past,
> Here to return, and die at home at last.'

W. M. THACKERAY.

26. Byron.

Immediately on Lord Byron's arrival in London, Mr. Dallas called upon him. "On the 15th of July," says this gentleman, "I had the pleasure of shaking hands with him at Redish's Hotel in St. James's Street. I thought his looks belied the report he had given me of his bodily health, and his countenance did not betoken melancholy, or displeasure at his return. He was very animated in the account of his travels, but assured me he had never had the least idea of writing them. He said he believed satire to be his *forte*, and to that he had adhered, having written, during his stay at different places abroad, a Paraphrase of Horace's Art of Poetry, which would be a good finish to 'English Bards and Scotch Reviewers'. He seemed to promise himself additional fame from it, and I undertook to superintend its publication, as I had done that of the Satire. I had chosen the time ill for my visit, and we had hardly any time to converse uninterruptedly; he therefore engaged me to breakfast with him next morning."

In the interval, Mr. Dallas looked over this Paraphrase, which he had been permitted by Lord Byron to take home with him for the purpose, and his disappointment was, as he himself describes it, "grievous". on finding that a pilgrimage of two years to the inspiring lands of the East had been attended with no richer poetical result. On their meeting again next morning, though unwilling to speak disparagingly of the work, he could not refrain, as he informs us, from expressing some surprise that his noble friend should have produced nothing else during his absence. "Upon this," he continues, "Lord Byron told me that he had occasionally written short poems, besides a great many stanzas in Spenser's measure, relative to the countries he had visited. 'They are not worth troubling you with, but you shall have them all with you, if you like.' So came I by Childe Harold's Pilgrimage. He took it from a small trunk, with a number of verses. He said they had been read but by one person, who had found very little to commend, and much to condemn: that he himself was of that opinion, and he was sure I should be so too. Such as it was, however, it was at my service: but he was urgent that 'The Hints from Horace' should be immediately put in train — which I promised to have done."

The value of the treasure thus presented to him, Mr. Dallas was not slow in discovering. That very evening he dispatched a letter to his noble friend, saying — "You have written one of the most delightful poems I ever read. If I wrote this in flattery, I should deserve your contempt rather than your friendship. I have been so fascinated with Childe Harold that I have not been able to lay it down. I would almost pledge my life on its advancing the reputation of your poetical powers, and on its gaining you great honour and regard, if you will do me the credit and favour of attending to my suggestions respecting," etc. etc. etc.

Notwithstanding this just praise, and the secret echo it must have found in a heart so awake to the slightest whisper of fame, it was some time before Lord Byron's obstinate repugnance to the idea of publishing Childe Harold could be removed.

"Attentive," says Mr. Dallas, "as he had hitherto been to my opinions and suggestions, and natural as it was that he should be swayed by such decided praise, I was surprised to find that I could not at first obtain credit with him for my judgment on Childe Harold's Pilgrimage. "It was any thing but poetry — it had been condemned by a good critic — had I not myself seen the sentences on the margin of the manuscript?" He dwelt upon the Paraphrase of the Art of Poetry with pleasure, and the manuscript of that was given to Cawthorn, the publisher of the Satire, to be brought forth without delay. I did not, however, leave him so: before I quitted him I returned to the charge, and told him that I was so convinced of the merit of Childe Harold's Pilgrimage, that, as he had given it to me, I should certainly publish it, if he would have the kindness to attend to some corrections and alterations."

In tracing the fortunes of men, it is not a little curious to observe how often the course of a whole life has depended on a single step.

Had Lord Byron now persisted in his original purpose of giving this Poem to the press instead of Childe Harold, it is more than probable that he would have been lost, as a great poet, to the world. Happily, the better judgment of his friends averted such a risk; and he, at length, consented to the immediate publication of Childe Harold, still, however, to the last, expressing his doubts of its merits, and his alarm at the sort of reception it might meet with in the world.

The publication being now determined upon, there arose some doubts and difficulties as to a publisher. At length Mr. Murray, who at this period resided in Fleet Street, having, some time before, expressed a desire to be allowed to publish some work of Lord Byron, it was in his hands that Mr. Dallas now placed the manuscript of Childe Harold.

While thus busily engaged in his literary projects, and having, besides, some law affairs to transact with his agent, he was called suddenly away to Newstead, by the intelligence of his mother's illness; an event which seems to have affected his mind far more deeply than, considering all the circumstances of the case, could have been expected. Mrs. Byron had been of late indisposed, but not to any alarming degree: on his going abroad, she had conceived a sort of superstitious fancy that she should never see him again; and when he returned, safe and well, and wrote to inform her that he should soon see her at Newstead, she said to her waiting-woman, "If I should be dead before Byron comes down, what a strange thing it would be!" — and so, in fact, it happened. At the end of July, her illness took a new and fatal turn, and so sadly characteristic was the close of the poor lady's life, that a fit of rage, brought on, it is said, by reading over the upholsterer's bills, was the ultimate cause of her death. Lord Byron had, of course, prompt intelligence of the attack; but though he started instantly from town, he was too late — she had breathed her last.

The manuscripts of both his poems having been shown, much against his own will, to Mr. Gifford, the opinion of that gentleman was thus reported to him by Mr. Dallas: — "Of your Satire he spoke highly: but this poem (Childe Harold) he pronounces not only the best you have written, but equal to any of the present age."

At the same time with Childe Harold, he had three other works in the press — his "Hints from Horace", the "Curse of Minerva", and a fifth edition of "English Bards and Scotch Reviewers".

In the month of January 1812, the whole of the two Cantos being printed off, some of the poet's friends, and among others, Mr. Rogers and myself, were so far favoured as to be indulged with a perusal of the sheets. In adverting to this period in "his Memoranda", Lord Byron, I remember, mentioned, — as one of the ill omens which preceded the publication of the Poem, — that some of the literary friends to whom it was shown expressed doubts of its success, and that one among them had told him that "it was too good for the age".

Whoever may have pronounced this opinion, — and I have some suspicion that I am, myself, the guilty person, — the age has, it must be owned, most triumphantly refuted the calumny upon its taste which the remark implied.

On the 27th of February, he made the first trial of his eloquence in the House of Lords, and it was on this occasion he had the good fortune to become acquainted with Lord Holland, — an acquaintance no less honourable than gratifying to both, as having originated in feelings the most generous, perhaps, of our nature, a ready forgiveness of injuries on the one side, and a frank and unqualified atonement for them on the other. It was within two days after his speech in the House of Lords, that Childe Harold appeared, — and the impression it produced upon the public was as instantaneous as it has proved deep and lasting. The permanence of such success genius alone could secure, but to its instant and enthusiastic burst, other causes besides the merit of the work concurred.

There are those who trace in the peculiar character of Lord Byron's genius, strong features of relationship to the times in which he lived; who think that the great events which marked the close of the last century, by giving a new impulse to men's minds, by habituating them to the daring and the free, and allowing full vent to "the flash and outbreak of fiery spirits," had led naturally to the production of such a poet as Byron; and that he was, in short, as much the child and representative of Revolution, in poesy, as another great man of the age, Napoleon, was in statesmanship and warfare. Without going the full length of this notion, it will at least be conceded that the free loose which had been given to all the passions and energies of the human mind, in the great struggle of that period, together with the constant spectacle of such astounding vicissitudes as were passing almost daily on the theatre of the world, had created in all minds, and in every work of intellect, a taste for strong excitement, which the stimulants supplied from ordinary sources were insufficient to gratify; — that a tame deference to established authorities had fallen into disrepute, no less in literature than in politics; and that the poet who should breathe into his songs the fierce and passionate spirit of the age, and assert, untrammelled and unawed, the high dominion of genius, would be the most sure of an audience toned in sympathy with his strains.

Another and not the least of those causes which concurred with the intrinsic claims of his genius to give an impulse to the tide of success that now flowed upon him, was, unquestionably, the peculiarity of his personal character. There had been, in his very first introduction of himself to the public, a sufficient portion of singularity to excite strong attention and interest. While all other youths of talent, in his high station, are heralded into life by the applauses and anticipations of a host of friends, young Byron stood forth alone, unannounced by either praise or promise, — the representative of an ancient house, whose name, long lost in the gloomy solitudes of Newstead, seemed to have just awakened from the sleep

of half a century in his person. The circumstances that in succession
followed, — the prompt vigour of his reprisals upon the assailants
of his fame, — his disappearance after this achievement from the scene
of his triumph, without deigning even to wait for the laurels which
he had earned, and his departure on a far pilgrimage, whose limits
he left to chance and fancy, — all the successive incidents had
thrown an air of adventure round the character of the young poet,
which prepared his readers to meet half way the impressions of his
genius. Instead of finding him, on a nearer view, fall short of their
imaginations — the new features of his disposition now disclosed to
them far outwent, in peculiarity and interest, whatever they might
have preconceived; while the curiosity and sympathy awakened by
what he suffered to transpire of his history were still more heightened
by the mystery of his allusions to much that yet remained untold.
The late losses by death which he had sustained, and mourned, it
was manifest, so deeply, gave a reality to the notion formed of him
by his admirers which seemed to authorize them in imagining still
more: and what has been said of the poet Young, that he found out
the art of "making the public a party to his private sorrows," may
be, with infinitely more force and truth, applied to Lord Byron.

That his rank was also to be numbered among these extrinsic
advantages, appears to have been his own persuasion. "I may place
a great deal of it," said he to Mr. Dallas, "to my being a Lord."
— It was also natural that, in that circle, the admiration of the new
poet should be at least quickened by the consideration that he had
sprung up among themselves, and that their order had, at length,
produced a man of genius, by whom the arrears of contribution, long
due from them to the treasury of English literature, would be at
once fully and splendidly discharged.

Altogether, taking in consideration the various points I have
here enumerated, it may be asserted, that never did there exist
before, and, it is most probable, never will exist again, a combination
of such vast mental power and surprising genius, with so many
others of those advantages and attractions, by which the world is in
general dazzled and captivated. The effect was accordingly electric:
— his fame had not to wait for any of the ordinary gradations, but
seemed to spring up, like the palace of a fairy tale, in a night. As
he himself briefly described in his Memoranda, — "I awoke one
morning and found myself famous." The first edition of his work
was disposed of instantly; and, as the echoes of its reputation multiplied on all sides, "Childe Harold" and "Lord Byron" became the
theme of every tongue. At his door, most of the leading names of

the day presented themselves, — some of them persons whom he had much wronged in his Satire, but who now forgot their resentment in generous admiration. From morning till night, the most flattering testimonies of his success crowded his table, — from the grave tributes of the statesman and philosopher down to (what flattered him still more) the romantic billet of some *incognita,* or the pressing note of invitation from some fair leader of fashion; and, in place of the desert which London had been to him but a few weeks before, he now, not only saw the whole splendid interior of High Life thrown open to receive him, but found himself, among its illustrious crowds, the most distinguished object.

The copyright of the Poem, which was purchased by Mr. Murray for £ 600, he presented, in the most delicate and unostentatious manner to Mr. Dallas, saying, at the same time, that he "never would receive money for his writings;" — a resolution, the mixed result of generosity and pride, which he afterwards wisely abandoned.

Among the tributes to his fame this spring (1812), it should have been mentioned that, at some evening party, he had the honour of being presented, at that royal personage's own desire, to the Prince Regent. "The Regent," says Mr. Dallas, "expressed his admiration of Childe Harold's Pilgrimage, and continued a conversation, which so fascinated the poet, that, had it not been for an accidental deferring of the next levee, he bade fair to become a visitor at Carlton House, if not a complete courtier." THOMAS MOORE.

IV. ESSAYS AND MEDITATIONS.

I. On Studies.

Studies serve for delight, for ornament, and for ability. Their chief use for delight, is in privateness and retiring; for ornament, is in discourse; and for ability, is in the judgment and disposition of business: for expert men can execute, and perhaps judge of particulars, one by one: but the general counsels, and the plots and marshalling of affairs come best from those that are learned. To spend too much time in studies, is sloth; to use them too much for ornament, is affectation; to make judgment wholly by their rules, is the humour of a scholar: they perfect nature, and are perfected by experience: for natural abilities are like natural plants, that need pruning by study; and studies themselves do give forth directions too much at large, except they be bounded in by experience. Crafty men contemn studies, simple men admire them, and wise men use them;

for they teach not their own use; but that is a wisdom without them, and above them, won by observation. Read not to contradict and confute, nor to believe and take for granted, nor to find talk and discourse, but to weigh and consider. Some books are to be tasted, others to be swallowed, and some few to be chewed and digested; that is, some books are to be read only in parts; others to be read, but not curiously: and some few to be read wholly, and with diligence and attention.

Some books also may be read by deputy, and extracts made of them by others; but that would be only in the less important arguments and the meaner sort of book; else distilled books are, like common distilled waters, flashy things. Reading maketh a full man, conference a ready man; and writing an exact man; and, therefore, if a man write little, he had need have a great memory; if he confer little, he had need have a present wit; and if he read little, he had need have much cunning, to seem to know that he doth not. Histories make men wise; poets, witty: the mathematics, subtile: natural philosophy, deep; moral, grave; logic and rhetoric, able to contend. There is no stond or impediment in the wit, but may be wrought out by fit studies: like as diseases of the body may have appropriate exercises; shooting is good for the lungs and breast, gentle walking for the stomach, riding for the head and the like; so if a man's wit be wandering, let him study the mathematics: for in demonstrations, if his wit be called away never so little, he must begin again: if his wit be not apt to distinguish or find differences, let him study the schoolmen, for they are "Cymini sectores;" if he be not apt to beat over matters, and to call up one thing to prove and illustrate another, let him study the lawyers' cases: so every defect of the mind may have a special receipt. FRANCIS BACON.

2. Precision in Speech.

Seeing that truth consisteth in the right ordering of names in our affirmations, a man that seeketh precise truth had need to remember what every name he useth stands for, and to place it accordingly, or else he will find himself entangled in words as a bird in lime twigs — the more he struggles the more belimed. And therefore in geometry, which is the only science that it hath pleased God hitherto to bestow on mankind, men begin at settling the significations of their words: which settling of significations they call definitions, and place them in the beginning of their reckoning.

By this it appears how necessary it is for any man that aspires to true knowledge to examine the definitions of former authors: and either to correct them where they are negligently set down, or to make them himself. For the errors of definitions multiply themselves according as the reckoning proceeds, and lead men into absurdities, which at last they see, but cannot avoid without reckoning anew from the beginning, in which lies the foundation of their errors. From whence it happens that they which trust to books do as they that cast up many little sums into a greater, without considering whether those little sums were rightly cast up or not: and at last finding the error visible and not mistrusting their first grounds, know not which way to clear themselves, but spend time in fluttering over their books, as birds that, entering by the chimney, flutter at the false light of a glass window, for want of wit to consider which way they came in. So that in the right definition of names lies the first use of speech, which is the acquisition of science, and in wrong or no definitions lies the first abuse; from which proceed all false and senseless tenets, which make those men that take their instruction from the authority of books, and not from their own meditation, to be as much below the condition of ignorant men as men endowed with true science are above it. For between true science and erroneous doctrines, ignorance is in the middle. Natural sense and imagination are not subject to absurdity. Nature itself cannot err; and as men abound in copiousness of language, so they become more wise or more mad than ordinary. Nor is it possible without letters for any man to become either excellently wise, or, unless his memory be hurt by disease or ill constitution of organs, excellently foolish. For words are wise men's counters — they do but reckon by them: but they are the money of fools, that value them by the authority of an Aristotle, a Cicero, or a Thomas, or any other doctor whatsoever, if but a man. THOMAS HOBBES.

3. On Reading.

Those who have read of every thing are thought to understand every thing too, but it is not always so. Reading furnishes the mind only with materials of knowledge: it is thinking makes what we read ours. We are of the ruminating kind, and it is not enough to cram ourselves with a great load of collections; unless we chew them over again, they will not give us strength and nourishment. There are indeed in some writers visible instances of deep thought, close and acute reasoning, and ideas well pursued. The light these would give, would be of great use, if their readers would observe and imitate them: all the rest, at best are but particularly fit to be turned into knowledge; but that can be done only by our own meditation, and examining the reach, force, and coherence, of what is said; and then, as far as we apprehend and see the connexion of ideas, so far is it ours: without that, it is but so much loose matter floating in our brain. The memory may be stored, but the judgment is little better, and the stock of knowledge not increased by being able to repeat what others have said, or produce the arguments we have found in them. Such a knowledge as this is but knowledge by hearsay, and the ostentation of it is at best but talking by rote, and very often upon weak and wrong principles. For all that is to be found in books, is not built upon true foundations, nor always rightly deduced from the principles it is pretended to be built on. Such an examen as is requisite to discover that, every reader's mind is not forward to make: especially in those who have given themselves up to a party, and only hunt for what they can scrape together, that may favour and support the tenets of it. Such men willfully exclude themselves from truth, and from all true benefit to be received by reading. Others of more indifferency often want attention and industry. The mind is backward in itself to be at the pains to trace every argument to its original, and to see upon what basis it stands, and how firmly; but yet it is this that gives so much the advantage to one man more than another in reading. The mind should, by severe rules, be tied down to this, at first uneasy, task; use and exercise will give it facility. So that those who are accustomed to it, readily, as it were with one cast of the eye, take a view of the argument, and presently, in most cases, see where it bottoms. Those who have got this faculty, one may say, have got the true key of books, and the clue to lead them through the mizmaze of a variety of opinions and authors to truth and certainty. This young beginners should be entered in, and showed the use of, that they might profit by their reading. Those who are strangers to it, will be apt to think it too great a clog in the way of men's studies; and they will suspect they shall make but small progress, if, in the books they read, they must stand to examine and unravel every argument, and follow it step by step up to its original.

I answer, this is a good objection, and ought to weigh with those whose reading is designed for much talk and little knowledge, and I have nothing to say to it. But I am here inquiring into the conduct of the understanding in its progress towards knowledge; and to those who aim at that, I may say, that he who fair and softly goes steadily forward in a course that points right, will sooner be at his journey's end, than he that runs after every one he meets, though he gallop all day full speed.

To which let me add, that this way of thinking on and profiting by what we read, will be a clog and rub to any one only in the beginning; when custom and exercise has made it familiar, it will be dispatched, in the most occasions, without resting or interruption in the course of our reading. The motions and views of a mind exercised that way, are wonderfully quick; and a man used to such sort of reflections, sees as much at one glimpse, as would require a long discourse to lay before another, and make out in an entire and gradual deduction. Besides, when the first difficulties are over, the delight and sensible advantage it brings, mightily encourages and enlivens the mind in reading, which, without this, is very improperly called study. JOHN LOCKE.

4. On Discontentment.

It is a celebrated thought of Socrates, that if all the misfortunes of mankind were cast into a public stock, in order to be equally distributed among the whole species, those who now think themselves the most unhappy, would prefer the share they are already possessed of, before that which would fall to them by such a division. Horace has carried this thought a great deal further: he says that the hardships or misfortunes which we lie under, are more easy to us than those of any other person would be, in case we could change conditions with him.

As I was ruminating on these two remarks, and seated in my elbow-chair, I insensibly fell asleep; when, on a sudden, I thought there was a proclamation made by Jupiter, that every mortal should bring in his griefs and calamities, and throw them together in a heap. There was a large plain appointed for this purpose. I took my stand in the centre of it, and saw, with a great deal of pleasure, the whole human species marching one after another, and throwing down their several loads, which immediately grew up into a prodigious mountain, that seemed to rise above the clouds.

There was a certain lady of a thin airy shape, who was very active in this solemnity. She carried a magnifying glass in one of her hands, and was clothed in a loose flowing robe, embroidered with several figures of fiends and spectres, that discovered themselves in a thousand chimerical shapes, as her garment hovered in the wind. There was something wild and distracted in her looks. Her name was Fancy. She led up every mortal to the appointed place, after having very officiously assisted him in making up his pack, and laying it upon his shoulders. My heart melted within me, to see my fellow-creatures groaning under their respective burdens, and to consider that prodigious bulk of human calamities which lay before me.

There were, however, several persons, who gave me great diversion upon this occasion. I observed one bringing in a fardel very carefully concealed under an old embroidered cloak, which, upon his throwing it into the heap, I discovered to be Poverty. Another, after a great deal of puffing, threw down his luggage, which, upon examining, I found to be his wife.

There were multitudes of lovers saddled with very whimsical burdens composed of darts and flames: but, what was very odd, though they sighed as if their hearts would break under these bundles of calamities, they could not persuade themselves to cast them into the heap, when they came up to it: but, after a few faint efforts, shook their heads, and marched away as heavy laden as they came. I saw multitudes of old women throw down their wrinkles, and several young ones who stripped themselves of a tawny skin. There were very great heaps of red noses, large lips, and rusty teeth. The truth of it is, I was surprised to see the greatest part of the mountain made up of bodily deformities. Observing one advancing towards the heap, with a larger cargo than ordinary upon his back, I found, upon his near approach, that it was only a natural hump, which he disposed of, with great joy of heart, among this collection of human miseries. There were likewise distempers of all sorts; though I could not but observe, that there were many more imaginary than real. One little packet I could not but take notice of, which was a complication of all the diseases incident to human nature, and was in the hand of a great many fine people: this was called the spleen. But what most of all surprised me, was a remark I made, that there was not a single vice or folly thrown into the whole heap; at which I was very much astonished, having concluded within myself, that every one would take this opportunity of getting rid of his passions, prejudices, and frailties.

I took notice in particular of a very profligate fellow, who I did not question came loaded with his crimes: but upon searching into his bundle, I found that, instead of throwing his guilt from him, he had only laid down his memory. He was followed by another worthless rogue, who flung away his modesty instead of his ignorance.

When the whole race of mankind had thus cast their burdens, the phantom which had been so busy on this occasion, seeing me an idle spectator of what had passed, approached toward me. I grew uneasy at her presence, when of a sudden she held her magnifying glass full before my eyes. I no sooner saw my face in it, but I was startled at the shortness of it, which now appeared to me in its upmost aggravation. The immoderate breadth of the features made me very much out of humour with my own countenance; upon which I threw it from me like a mask. It happened very luckily, that one who stood by me had just before thrown down his visage, which it seems was too long for him. It was indeed extended to a shameful length: I believe the very chin was, modestly speaking, as long as my whole face. We had both of us an opportunity of mending ourselves; and all the contributions being now brought in, every man was at liberty to exchange his misfortunes for those of another person. But as there arose many new incidents in the sequel of my vision, I shall reserve them for the subject of my next paper.

* * *

In my last paper, I gave my reader a sight of that mountain of miseries, which was made up of those several calamities that afflict the minds of men. I saw, with unspeakable pleasure, the whole species thus delivered from its sorrow; though at the same time, as we stood round the heap, and surveyed the several materials of which it was composed, there was scarcely a mortal, in this vast multitude, who did not discover what he thought pleasures of life: and wondered how the owners of them ever came to look upon them as burdens and grievances.

As we were regarding very attentively this confusion of miseries, this chaos of calamity, Jupiter issued out a second proclamation, that every one was now at liberty to exchange his affliction, and to return to his habitation with any such other bundle as should be delivered to him.

Upon this, Fancy began again to bestir herself, and parcelling out the whole heap with incredible activity, recommended to every one his particular packet. The hurry and confusion at this time were not to be expressed. Some observations which I made upon this occasion I shall communicate to the public. A venerable gray-headed man, who had laid down the colic, and who I found wanted an heir to his estate, snatched up an undutiful son, that had been thrown into the heap by an angry father. The graceless youth, in less than a quarter of an hour, pulled the old gentleman by the beard, and had like to have knocked his brains out; so that meeting the true father, who came towards him with a fit of the gripes, he begged him to take his son again, and give him back his colic; but they were incapable either of them to recede from the choice they had made. A poor galley slave who had thrown down his chains, took up the gout in their stead, but made such wry faces, that one might easily perceive he was no great gainer by the bargain. It was pleasant enough to see the several exchanges that were made, for sickness against poverty, hunger against want of appetite, and care against pain.

The female world were very busy among themselves in bartering for features; but there was not one of them who did not think the new blemish, as soon as she had got it into her possession, much more disagreeable than the old one. I made the same observation on every other misfortune or calamity, which every one in the assembly brought upon himself, in lieu of what he had parted with; whether it be that all the evils which befall us are in some measure suited and proportioned to our strength, or that every evil becomes more supportable by our being accustomed to it, I shall not determine.

I must not omit my own particular adventure. My friend with the long visage had no sooner taken upon him my short face, but he made so grotesque a figure, that as I looked upon him I could not forbear laughing at myself, insomuch that I put my own face out of countenance. The poor gentleman was so sensible of the ridicule, that I found he was ashamed of what he had done: on the other side, I found that I myself had no great reason to triumph, for as I went to touch my forehead I missed the place, and clapped my finger upon my upper lip. Besides, as my nose was exceedingly prominent, I gave it two or three unlucky knocks as I was playing my hand about my face, and aiming at some other part of it. I saw two other gentlemen by me, who were in the same ridiculous circumstances. These had made a foolish exchange between a couple of thick bandy-legs, and two long trap-sticks that had no calves to them. One of these looked like a man walking upon stilts, and was so lifted up into the air, above his ordinary height, that his head turned round with it: while the other made so awkward circles, as he attempted to walk, that he scarcely knew how to move forward upon his new supporters. Observing him to be a pleasant kind of fellow, I stuck my cane in the ground, and told him I would lay him a bottle of wine, that he did not march up to it, on a line that I drew for him, in a quarter of an hour.

The heap was at last distributed among the two sexes, who made a most piteous sight, as they wandered up and down under the pressure of their several burdens. The whole plain was filled with murmurs and complaints, groans and lamentations. Jupiter, at length, taking compassion on the poor mortals, ordered them a second time to lay down their loads, with a design to give every one his own again. They discharged themselves with a great deal of pleasure: after which, the phantom who had led them into such gross delusions, was commanded to disappear. There was sent in her stead a goddess of a quite different figure: her motions were steady and composed, and her aspect serious, but cheerful. She every now and then cast her eyes towards heaven, and fixed them upon Jupiter: her name was Patience. She had no sooner placed herself by the Mount of Sorrows, but, what I thought very remarkable, the whole heap sank to such a degree, that it did not appear a third part so big as it was before. She afterwards returned every man his own proper calamity, and, teaching him how to bear it in the most commodious manner, he marched off with it contentedly, being very well pleased that he had not been left to his own choice, as to the kind of evils which fell to his lot.

Besides the several pieces of morality to be drawn out of this vision, I learned from it never to repine at my own misfortunes, or to envy the happiness of another, since it is impossible for any man to form a right judgment of his neighbour's sufferings; for which reason also, I have determined never to think too lightly of another's complaints, but to regard the sorrows of my fellow-creatures with sentiments of humanity and compassion. JOSEPH ADDISON.

5. London, an Emporium for the Whole Earth.

There is no place in the town which I so much love to frequent as the Royal Exchange. It gives me a secret satisfaction, and, in some measure, gratifies my vanity, as I am an Englishman, to see so rich an assembly of countrymen and foreigners consulting together upon the private business of mankind, and making this metropolis a kind of emporium for the whole earth. I must confess I look upon High-Change to be a great council, in which all considerable nations have their representatives. Factors in the trading world are what ambassadors are in the politic world: they negotiate affairs, conclude treaties, and maintain a good correspondence between those wealthy societies of men that are divided from one another by seas and oceans, or live on the different extremities of a continent. I have often been pleased to hear disputes adjusted between an inhabitant of Japan, and an alderman of London, or to see a subject of the great Mogul entering into a league with one of the Czar of Muscovy. I am infinitely delighted in mixing with these several ministers of commerce, as they are distinguished by their different walks, and different languages: sometimes I am justled among a body of Armenians: sometimes I am lost in a crowd of Jews: and sometimes make one in a group of Dutchmen. I am a Dane, Swede, or Frenchman, at different times: or rather fancy myself like the old philosopher, who, upon being asked what countryman he was, replied, that he was a citizen of the world.

Though I very frequently visit this busy multitude of people, I am known to nobody there but my friend Sir Andrew, who often smiles upon me as he sees me bustling in the crowd, but at the same time connives at my presence without taking any further notice of me. There is indeed a merchant of Egypt, who just knows me by sight, having formerly remitted me some money to Grand Cairo; but as I am not versed in the modern Coptic, our conferences go no further than a bow and a grimace.

This grand scene of business gives me an infinite variety of solid and substantial entertainments. As I am a great lover of mankind, my heart naturally overflows with pleasure at the sight of a prosperous and happy multitude, insomuch that at many public solemnities I cannot forbear expressing my joy with tears that have stolen down my cheeks. For this reason I am wonderfully delighted to see such a body of men thriving in their own private fortunes, and at the same time promoting the public stock; or, in other words, raising estates for their own families, by bringing into their own country whatever is wanting, and carrying out of it whatever is superfluous.

Nature seems to have taken a particular care to disseminate her blessings among the different regions of the world with an eye to this mutual intercourse and traffic among mankind, that the natives of the several parts of the globe might have a kind of dependence upon one another and be united together by their common interest. Almost every degree produces something peculiar to it. The food often grows in one country, and the sauce in another. The fruits of Portugal are corrected by the products of Barbadoes: the infusion of a China plant sweetened with the pith of an Indian cane. The Philippine Islands give a flavour to our European bowls. The single dress of a woman of quality is often the product of a hundred climates. The muff and the fan come together from the different ends of the earth. The scarf is sent from the Torrid Zone, and the tippet from beneath the Pole. The brocade petticoat rises out of the mines of Peru, and the diamond necklace out of the bowels of Hindoostan.

If we consider our own country in its natural prospect without any of the benefits and advantages of commerce, what a barren uncomfortable spot of earth falls to our share! Natural historians tell us, that no fruit grows originally among us, besides hips and haws, acorns and pignuts, with other delicacies of the like nature; that our

climate of itself, and without the assistances of art, can make no
further advances towards a plum than to a sloe, and carries an apple
to no greater perfection than a crab; that our melons, our peaches,
our figs, our apricots, and cherries, are strangers among us, imported
in different ages and naturalized in our English gardens: and that
they would all degenerate and fall away into the trash of our own
country, if they were wholly neglected by the planter, and left to
the mercy of our sun and soil. Nor has traffic more enriched our
vegetable world, than it has improved the whole face of nature among
us. Our ships are laden with the harvest of every climate: our tables
are stored with spices, and oils, and wines: our rooms are filled
with pyramids of China, and adorned with the workmanship of Japan:
our morning's draught comes to us from the remotest corners of the
earth: we repair our bodies by the drugs of America, and repose
ourselves under Indian canopies. My friend Sir Andrew calls the vineyards of France our gardens; the Spice Islands our hot-beds; the
Persians our silk-weavers; and the Chinese our potters. Nature indeed
furnishes us with the bare necessaries of life: but traffic gives us a
great variety of what is useful, and at the same time supplies us
with every thing that is convenient and ornamental. Nor is it the
least part of this our happiness, that whilst we enjoy the remotest
products of the North and South, we are free from those extremities
of weather which give them birth; that our eyes are refreshed with
the green fields of Britain, at the same time that our palates are
feasted with fruits that rise between the tropics.

For these reasons, there are no more useful members in a
commonwealth than merchants. They knit mankind together in a
mutual intercourse of good offices, distribute the gifts of nature, find
work for the poor, add wealth to the rich, and magnificence to the
great. Our English merchant converts the tin of his country into
gold, and exchanges his wool for rubies. The Mohametans are clothed
in our British manufacture, and the inhabitants of the Frozen Zone
warmed with the fleeces of our sheep.

When I have been upon the 'Change, I have often fancied one
of our old kings standing in person, where he is represented in effigy,
and looking down upon the wealthy concourse of people with which
that place is every day filled. In this case, how would he be surprised to hear all the languages of Europe spoken in this little spot
of his former dominions, and to see so many private men, who in
his time would have been the vassals of some powerful baron, nego-
tiating like princes for greater sums of money than were formerly
to be met with in the royal treasury! Trade, without enlarging the

British territories, has given us a kind of additional empire: it has multiplied the number of the rich, made our landed estates infinitely more valuable than they were formerly, and added to them an accession of other estates as valuable as the lands themselves.

JOSEPH ADDISON.

6. The Story-Teller.

I look upon a tedious talker, or what is generally known by the name of a story-teller, to be much more insufferable than even a prolix writer. An author may be tossed out of our hand, and thrown aside when he grows dull and tiresome, but such liberties are so far from being allowed towards your orators in common conversation, that I have known a challenge sent a person for going out of the room abruptly, and leaving a man of honour in the midst of a dissertation. This evil is at present so very common and epidemical, that there is scarce a coffee-house in town that has not some speakers belonging to it, who utter their political essays, and draw parallels out of Baker's "Chronicle" to almost every part of her Majesty's reign. It was said of two ancient authors, who had very different beauties in their style, "that if you took a word from one of them, you only spoiled his eloquence; but if you took a word from the other, you spoiled his sense." I have often applied the first part of this criticism to several of these coffee-house speakers whom I have at present in my thoughts, though the character that is given to the last of those authors is what I would recommend to the imitation of my loving countrymen. But it is not only public places of resort, but private clubs and conversations over a bottle, that are infested with this loquacious kind of animal, especially with that species which I comprehend under the name of a story-teller. I would earnestly desire these gentlemen to consider, that no point of wit or mirth at the end of a story can atone for the half-hour that has been lost before they come at it. I would likewise lay it home to their serious consideration, whether they think that every man in the company has not a right to speak as well as themselves? and whether they do not think they are invading another man's property, when they engross the time which should be divided equally among the company to their own private use?

What makes this evil so much greater in conversation is, that these humdrum companions seldom endeavour to wind up their narrations into a point of mirth or instruction, which might make some amends for the tediousness of them, but think they have a right to tell anything that has happened within their memory. They look upon matter of fact to be a sufficient foundation for a story, and give us a long account of things, not because they are entertaining or surprising, but because they are true.

My ingenious kinsman, Mr. Humphrey Wagstaff, used to say, "The life of man is too short for a story-teller."

Methusalem might be half an hour in telling what o'clock it was; but as for us postdiluvians, we ought to do everything in haste; and in our speeches, as well as actions, remember that our time is short. A man that talks for a quarter of an hour together in company, if I meet him frequently, takes up a great part of my span. A quarter of an hour daily may be reckoned the eight-and-fortieth part of a year, and a year the three score and tenth part of life. By this moral arithmetic, supposing a man to be in the talking world one-third part of the day, whoever gives another a quarter of an hour's hearing, makes him a sacrifice of more than the four hundred thousandth part of his conversable life.

I would establish but one great general rule to be observed in all conversation, which is this, "That men should not talk to please themselves, but those that hear them." This would make them consider whether what they speak be worth hearing; whether there be either wit or sense in what they are about to say; and whether it be adapted to the time when, the place where, and the person to whom, it is spoken. For the utter extirpation of these orators and story-tellers, which I look upon as very great pests of society, I have invented a watch which divides the minute into twelve parts, after the same manner that the ordinary watches are divided into hours; and will endeavour to get a patent, which shall oblige every club or company to provide themselves with one of these watches, that shall lie upon the table, as an hour-glass is often placed near the pulpit, to measure out the length of a discourse.

I shall be willing to allow a man one round of my watch, that is, a whole minute to speak in: but if he exceeds that time, it shall be lawful for any of the company to look upon the watch, or to call him down to order. Provided, however, that if any one can make it appear he is turned of threescore, he may take two, or, if he pleases three rounds of the watch without giving offence. Provided, also, that this rule be not construed to extend to the fair sex, who shall still be at liberty to talk by the ordinary watch that is now in use. I would likewise earnestly recommend this little automaton, which may easily be carried in the pocket without any incumbrance, to all such as are troubled with this infirmity of speech, that upon pulling out their watches, they may have frequent occasion to consider what they are doing, and by that means cut the thread of the story short, and hurry to a conclusion. RICHARD STEELE.

7. On the Love of Life.

Age. that lessens the enjoyment of life, increases our desire of living. Those dangers which, in the vigour of youth, we had learned to despise, assume new terrors as we grow old. Our caution increasing as our years increase, fear becomes at last the prevailing passion of the mind; and the small remainder of life is taken up in useless efforts to keep off our end, or provide for a continued existence.

Strange contradiction in our nature, and to which even the wise are liable! If I should judge of that part of life which lies before me by that which I have already seen, the prospect is hideous.

Experience tells me, that my past enjoyments have brought no real felicity; and sensation assures me, that those I have felt are stronger than those which are yet to come. Yet experience and sensation in vain persuade: hope, more powerful than either, dresses out the distant prospect in fancied beauty; some happines, in long prospective, still beckons me to pursue; and like a losing gamester, every disappointment increases my ardour to continue the game.

Whence then is this increased love of life, which grows upon us with our years? — whence comes it, that we thus make greater efforts to preserve our existence, at a period when it becomes scarce worth the keeping? —

Is it that Nature, attentive to the preservation of mankind, increases our wishes to live, while she lessens our enjoyments: and as she robs the senses of every pleasure, equips Imagination in the spoils? Life would be insupportable to an old man, who, loaded with infirmities, feared death no more than when in the vigour of manhood; the numberless calamities of decaying nature, and the consciousness of surviving every pleasure, would at once induce him, with his own hand, to terminate the scene of misery; but happily the contempt of death forsakes him at a time when it could only be prejudicial; and life acquires an imaginary value, in proportion as its real value is no more.

Our attachment to every object around us, increases, in general, from the length of our acquaintance with it. "I would not choose," says a French philosopher, "to see an old post pulled up, with which I had been long acquainted." A mind long habituated to a certain set of objects, insensibly becomes fond of seeing them; visits them from habit, and parts from them with reluctance; from hence proceeds the avarice of the old in every kind of possession: they love the world and all that it produces: they love life and all its advantages: not because it gives them pleasure, but because they have known it long.

Chinvang the Chaste, ascending the throne of China, commanded that all who were unjustly detained in prison during the preceding reigns should be set free. Among the number who came to thank their deliverer on this occasion, there appeared a majestic old man, who falling at the emperor's feet, addressed him as follows: "Great father of China, behold a wretch, now eighty-five years old, who was shut up in a dungeon at the age of twenty-two. I was imprisoned, though a stranger to crime, or without being even confronted by my accusers. I have now lived in solitude and darkness for more than fifty years, and am grown familiar with distress. As yet, dazzled with the splendour of that sun to which you have restored me, I have been wandering the streets to find out some friend that would assist, or relieve, or remember me: but my friends, my family, and relations, are all dead; and I am forgotten. Permit me then, O Chinvang, to wear out the wretched remains of life in my former prison: the walls of my dungeon are to me more pleasing than the most splendid palace: I have not long to live, and shall be unhappy except I spend the rest of my days where my youth was passed; in that prison from whence you were pleased to release me."

The old man's passion for confinement is similar to that we all have for life. We are habituated to the prison, we look round with discontent, are displeased with the abode, and yet the length of our captivity only increases our fondness for the cell. The trees we have planted, the houses we have built, or the posterity we have begotten, shall serve to bind us closer to the earth, and embitter our parting. Life sues the young like a new acquaintance; the companion, as yet unexhausted, is at once instructive and amusing: its company pleases, yet, for all this, it is but little regarded. To us, who are declined in years, life appears like an old friend; its jests have been anticipated in former conversation: it has no new story to make us smile, no new improvement with which to surprise, yet still we love it; destitute of every enjoyment, still we love it, husband the wasting treasure with increasing frugality, and feel all the poignancy of anguish in the fatal separation.

Sir Philip Mordaunt was a young, beautiful, sincere, brave Englishman. He had a complete fortune of his own, and the love of the king his master, which was equivalent to riches. Life opened all her treasures before him, and promised a long succession of happiness. He came, tasted of the entertainment, but was disgusted even at the beginning. He professed an aversion to living; was tired of walking round the same circle; had tried every enjoyment, and found them all grow weaker at every repetition. "If life be, in youth, so displeasing." cried he to himself. "what will it appear when age comes on? if it be at present indifferent, sure it will then be execrable." This thought embittered every reflection; till at last, with all the serenity of perverted reason, he ended the debate with a pistol. Had this self-deluded man been apprized, that existence grows more desirable to us the longer we exist, he would then have faced old age without shrinking; he would have boldly dared to live; and served that society by his future assiduity, which he basely injured by his desertion. OLIVER GOLDSMITH.

8. On Supernatural Agents in Poetry.

The only supernatural agents which can in any manner be allowed to us moderns, are ghosts; but of these I would advise an author to be extremely sparing. These are, indeed, like arsenic, and other dangerous drugs in physic, to be used with the utmost caution; nor would I advise the introduction of them at all in those works, or by those authors, to which, or to whom, a horse-laugh in the reader would be any great prejudice or mortification.

As for elves and fairies, and other such mummery, I purposely omit the mention of them, as I should be very unwilling to confine within any bounds those surprising imaginations, for whose vast capacity the limits of human nature are too narrow; whose works are to be considered as a new creation; and who have, consequently just right to do what they will with their own.

Man, therefore, is the highest subject (unless on very extraordinary occasions indeed) which presents itself to the pen of our historian, or of our poet; and in relating his actions, great care is to be taken that we do not exceed the capacity of the agent we describe.

Nor is possibility alone sufficient to justify us: we must keep likewise within the rules of probability. It is, I think, the opinion of Aristotle, or, if not, it is the opinion of some wise man, whose authority will be as weighty when it is as old, 'That it is no excuse for a poet who relates what is incredible, that the thing related is matter of fact.' This may, perhaps, be allowed true with regard to poetry, but it may be thought impracticable to extend it to the historian: for he is obliged to record matters as he finds them, though they may be of so extraordinary a nature as will require no small degree of historical faith to swallow them. Such was the successless armament of Xerxes, described by Herodotus, or the successful expedition of Alexander, related by Arrian. Such of later years was the victory of Agincourt, obtained by Harry the Fifth; or that of Narva, won by Charles the Twelfth of Sweden. All which instances, the more we reflect on them, appear still the more astonishing.

Such facts, however, as they occur in the thread of the story, nay, indeed, as they constitute the essential part of it, the historian is not only justifiable in recording as they really happened, but indeed would be unpardonable should he omit or alter them. But there are other facts not of such consequence nor so necessary, which, though ever so well attested, may nevertheless be sacrificed to oblivion, in complaisance to the scepticism of a reader. Such is that memorable story of the ghost of George Villiers, which might with more propriety have been made a present of to Dr. Drelincourt, to have kept the ghost of Mrs. Veale company, at the head of his Discourse upon Death, than have been introduced into so solemn a work as the History of the Rebellion.

To say the truth, if the historian will confine himself to what really happened, and utterly reject any circumstance which, though ever so well attested, he must be well assured is false, he will sometimes fall into the marvellous, but never into the incredible. He will often raise the wonder and surprise of his reader, but never that incredulous hatred mentioned by Horace. It is by falling into fiction, therefore, that we generally offend against this rule of deserting probability, which the historian seldom, if ever, quits, till he forsakes his character, and commences a writer of romance. In this, however, those historians, who relate public transactions, have the advantage of us who confine ourselves to scenes of private life. The credit of the former is by common notoriety supported for a long time; and public records, with the concurrent testimony of many authors, bear evidence to their truth in future ages. Thus a Trajan and an Antonius, a Nero and a Caligula, have all met with the belief of posterity; and no one doubts but that men so very good and so very bad, were once the masters of mankind.

But we, who deal in private character, who search into the most retired recesses, and draw forth examples of virtue and vice from holes and corners of the world, are in a more dangerous situation. As we have no public notoriety, no concurrent testimony, no records to support and corroborate what we deliver, it becomes us to keep within the limits not only of possibility, but of probability too; and this more especially in painting what is greatly good and amiable. Knavery and folly, though ever so exorbitant, will more easily meet with assent; for ill-nature adds great support and strength to faith.

Thus we may, perhaps, with little danger, relate the history of Fisher; who having long owed his bread to the generosity of Mr. Derby, and having one morning received a considerable bounty from his hands, yet, in order to possess himself of what remained in his friend's scrutoire, concealed himself in a public office of the Temple, through which there was a passage into Mr. Derby's chambers. Here he overheard Mr. Derby for many hours solacing himself at an entertainment which he that evening gave his friends, and to which Fisher had been invited. During all this time, no tender, no grateful reflections arose to restrain his purpose, but when the poor gentleman had let his company out through the office, Fisher came suddenly from his lurking-place, and walking softly behind his friend into his chamber, discharged a pistol-ball into his head. This may be believed when the bones of Fisher are as rotten as his heart. Nay, perhaps, it will be credited, that the villain went two days afterwards with some young ladies to the play of Hamlet; and with an unaltered countenance heard one of the ladies, who little suspected how near she was to the person, cry out, 'Good God! if the man that murdered Mr. Derby was now present;' manifesting in this a more seared and callous conscience than even Nero himself; of whom we are told by Suetonius, that the consciousness of his guilt, after the death of his mother, became immediately intolerable, and so continued; nor could all the congratulations of the soldiers, of the senate, and the people, allay the horrors of his conscience.

But now, on the other hand, should I tell my reader, that I had kown a man whose penetrating genius had enabled him to raise a large fortune in a way where no beginning was chalked out to him; that he had done this with the most perfect preservation of his integrity, and not only without the least injustice or injury to any one individual person, but with the highest advantage to trade, and a vast increase of the public revenue; that he had expended one part of the income of this fortune in discovering a taste superior to most, by works where the highest dignity was united with the purest simplicity, and another part in displaying a degree of goodness superior to all men, by acts of charity to objects whose only recommendations were their merits or their wants; that he was most industrious in searching after merit in distress, most eager to relieve it, and then as careful (perhaps too careful) to conceal what he had done; that his house, his furniture, his gardens, his table, his private hospitality, and his public beneficence, all denoted the mind from which they flowed, and were all intrinsically rich and noble, without tinsel, or external ostentation; that he filled every relation in life with the most adequate virtue; that he was most piously religious to his creator, most zealously loyal to his sovereign; a most tender husband to his wife, a kind relation, a munificent patron, a warm and firm friend, a knowing and a cheerful companion, indulgent to his servants, hospitable to his neighbours, charitable to the poor, and benevolent to all mankind. Should I add to these the epithets of wise, brave, elegant, and indeed every other epithet in our language; I might surely say.

— Quis credet? nemo Hercule! nemo;
Vel duo, vel nemo.

And yet I know a man who is all I have here described. But a single instance (and I really know not such another) is not sufficient to justify us, while we are writing to thousands who never heard of the person, nor of any thing like him. Such *rarae aves* should be remitted to the epitaph writer, or to some poet, who may condescend to hitch him in a distich, or to slide him into a rhyme with an air of carelessness and neglect, without giving any offence to the reader.

In the last place, the actions should be such as may not only be within the compass of human agency, and which human agents may probably be supposed to do: but they should be likely for the very actors and characters themselves to have performed; for what may be only wonderful and surprising in one man, may become improbable, or indeed impossible, when related of another.

This last requisite is what the dramatic critics call conservation of character; and it requires a very extraordinary degree of judgment. and a most exact knowledge of human nature.

It is admirably remarked by a most excellent writer that zeal can no more hurry a man to act in direct opposition to itself, than a rapid stream can carry a boat against its own current. I will venture to say, that for a man to act in direct contradiction to the dictates of his nature, is, if not impossible, as improbable and as miraculous as any thing which can be well conceived. Should the best parts of the story of Mr. Antoninus be ascribed to Nero, or should the worst incidents of Nero's life be imputed to Antoninus, what would be more shocking to belief than either instance; whereas both these, being related of their proper agent, constitute the truly marvellous.

Our modern authors of comedy have fallen almost universally into the error here hinted at: their heroes generally are notorious rogues, during the first four acts; but in the fifth, they become very

worthy gentlemen; nor is the writer often so kind as to give himself
the least trouble to reconcile or account for this monstrous change
and incongruity. There is, indeed, no other reason, to be assigned
for it, than because the play is drawing to a conclusion: as if
it was no less natural in a rogue to repent in the last act of a
play, than in the last of his life: which we perceive to be generally
the case at Tyburn, a place which might indeed close the scene
of some comedies with much propriety, as the heroes in these are
commonly eminent for those very talents which not only bring men
to the gallows, but enable them to make a heroic figure when they
are there.

Within these few restrictions, I think, every writer may be
permitted to deal as much in the wonderful as he pleases; nay, if
he thus keeps within the rules of credibility, the more he can surprise the reader, the more he will engage his attention, and the
more he will charm him. As a genius of the highest rank observes
in his fifth chapter of the Bathos, 'The great art of all poetry is
to mix truth with fiction: in order to join the credible with the
surprising.'

For though every good author will confine himself within the
bounds of probability, it is by no means necessary that his characters,
or his incidents, should be trite, common, or vulgar: such as happen
in every street, in every house, or which may be met with in
the home articles of a newspaper. Nor must he be inhibited from
showing many persons and things, which may possibly have never
fallen within the knowledge of great part of his readers. If the
writer stricly observes the rules above mentioned, he has discharged
his part; and is then entitled to some faith from his reader, who is
indeed guilty of critical infidelity if he disbelieves him. For want of
a portion of such faith, I remember the character of a young lady
of quality was condemned on the stage for being unnatural, by the
unanimous voice of a very large assembly of clerks and apprentices;
though it had the previous suffrages of many ladies of the first rank:
one of whom. very eminent for her understanding, declared it was
the picture of half the young people of her acquaintance.

HENRY FIELDING.

9. On the Knowledge of the World.

Nothing has so much exposed men of learning to contempt and
ridicule, as their ignorance of things which are known to all but
themselves. Those who have been taught to consider the institutions

of the schools as giving the last perfection to human abilities, are surprised to see men wrinkled with study, yet wanting to be instructed in the minute circumstances of propriety, or the necessary forms of daily transaction; and quickly shake off their reverences for modes of education, which they find to produce no ability above the rest of mankind.

Books, says Bacon, can never teach the use of books. The student must learn by commerce with mankind to reduce his speculations to practice, and accommodate his knowledge to the purposes of life.

It is too common for those who have been bred to scholastic professions, and passed much of their time in academies, where nothing but learning confers honours, to disregard every other qualification, and to imagine, that they shall find mankind ready to pay homage to their knowledge, and to crowd about them for instruction. They therefore step out from their cells into the open world, with all the confidence of authority, and dignity of importance; they look round about them at once with ignorance and scorn on a race of beings, to whom they are equally unknown and equally contemptible, but whose manners they must imitate, and with whose opinions they must comply, if they desire to pass their time happily among them.

To lessen that disdain with which scholars are inclined to look on the common business of the world, and the unwillingness with which they condescend to learn what is not to be found in any system of philosophy, it may be necessary to consider, that though admiration is excited by abstruse researches, and remote discoveries, yet pleasure is not given, or affection conciliated, but by softer accomplishments, and qualities more easily communicable to those about us. He that can only converse upon questions, about which only a small part of mankind has knowledge sufficient to make them curious, must lose his days in unsocial silence, and live in the crowd of life without a companion. He that can only be useful on great occasions may die without exerting his abilities and stand a helpless spectator of a thousand vexations, which fret away happiness, and which nothing is required to remove but a little dexterity of conduct and readiness of expedients.

No degree of knowledge attainable by man is able to set him above the want of hourly assistance, or to extinguish the desire of fond endearments, and tender officiousness; and therefore no one should think it unnecessary to learn those arts, by which friendship may be gained. Kindness is preserved by a constant reciprocation of benefits or interchange of pleasures; but such benefits only can be bestowed, as others are capable of receiving, and such pleasures only imparted, as others are qualified to enjoy.

By this descent from the pinnacles of art, no honour will be
lost: for the condescensions of learning are always overpaid by gratitude. An elevated genius employed in little things appears, to use
the simile of Longinus, like the sun in his evening declination; he
remits his splendour, but retains his magnitude; and pleases more,
though he dazzles less.   SAMUEL JOHNSON.

10. On the Choice of our Situation in Life.

The influence of a new situation of external fortune is so great,
it gives so different a turn to our temper and affections, to our views
and desires, that no man can foretell what his character would prove,
should he be either raised or depressed in his circumstances, in a
remarkable degree; or placed in some sphere of action, widely different
from that to which he has been accustomed in former life.

The seeds of various qualities, good and bad, lie in all our
hearts. But until proper occasions ripen, and bring them forward,
they lie there inactive and dead. They are covered up and concealed
within the recesses of our nature: or, if they spring up at all, it is
under such an appearance as is frequently mistaken, even by ourselves. Pride, for instance, in certain situations, has no opportunity
of displaying itself, but as magnanimity, or sense of honour. Avarice
appears as necessary and laudable economy. What in one station of
life would discover itself to be cowardice and baseness of mind,
passes in another for prudent circumspection. What in the fulness
of power would prove to be cruelty and oppression, is reputed, in a
subordinate rank, no more than the exercise of proper discipline.
For a while, the man is known neither by the world, nor by himself
to be what he truly is. But bring him into a new situation of life,
which accords with his predominant disposition; which strikes on
certain latent qualities of his soul, and awakens them into action;
and as the leaves of a flower gradually unfold to the sun, so shall
all his true character open full to view.

This may, in one light, be accounted not so much an alteration
of character, produced by a change of circumstances, as a discovery
brought forth of the real character, which formerly lay concealed.
Yet, at the same time, it is true that the man himself undergoes a
change. For opportunity being given for certain dispositions, which
had been dormant, to exert themselves without restraint, they of
course gather strength. By means of the ascendency which they gain,
other parts of the temper are borne down; and thus an alteration is
made in the whole structure and system of the soul. He is a truly
wise and good man, who, through Divine assistance, remains superior

to this influence of fortune on his character; who, having once imbibed worthy sentiments, and established proper principles of action, continues constant to these, whatever his circumstances be; maintains throughout all the changes of his life, one uniform and supported tenor of conduct: and what he abhorred as evil and wicked in the beginning of his days, continues to abhor to the end. But how rare is it to meet with this honourable consistency among men, while they are passing through the different stations and periods of life! When they are setting out in the world, before their minds have been greatly misled or debased, they glow with generous emotions, and look with contempt on what is sordid and guilty.

But advancing farther in life, and inured by degrees to the crooked ways of men; pressing through the crowd, and the bustle of the world; obliged to contend with this man's craft, and that man's scorn: accustomed, sometimes, to conceal their sentiments, and often to stifle their feelings, they become at last hardened in heart, and familiar with corruption. Who would not drop a tear over this sad but frequent fall of human probity and honour? Who is not humbled, when he beholds the refined sentiments and high principles on which we are so ready to value ourselves brought to such a shameful issue; and man, with all his boasted attainments of reason, discovered so often to be the creature of his external fortune, moulded and formed by the incidents of his life?

Let us for a moment reflect on the dangers which arise from stations of power and greatness; especially when the elevation of men to these has been rapid and sudden. Few have the strength of mind which is requisite for bearing such a change with temperance and self-command. The respect which is paid to the great, and the scope which their condition affords for the indulgence of pleasure, are perilous circumstances to virtue.

When men live among their equals, and are accustomed to encounter the hardships of life, they are of course reminded of their mutual dependence on each other, and of the dependence of all upon God. But when they are highly exalted above their fellows, they meet with few objects to awaken serious reflection, and with many to feed and inflame their passions. They are apt to separate their interest from that of all around them: to wrap themselves up in their vain grandeur; and, in the lap of indolence and selfish pleasure, to acquire a cold indifference to the concerns even of those whom they call their friends. The fancied independence into which they are lifted up, is adverse to sentiments of piety, as well as of humanity, in their heart.

But we are not to imagine, that elevated stations in the world
furnish the only formidable trials to which our virtue is exposed. It
will be found, that we are liable to no fewer, nor less dangerous
temptations, from the opposite extreme of poverty and depression.
When men who have known better days are thrown down into abject
situations of fortune, their spirits are broken, and their tempers
soured: envy rankles in their breast at such as are more successful;
the providence of Heaven is accused in secret murmurs; and the
sense of misery is ready to push them into atrocious crimes, in order
to better their state. Among the inferior classes of mankind, craft
and dishonesty are too often found to prevail. Low and penurious
circumstances depress the human powers. They deprive men of the
proper means of knowledge and improvement; and where ignorance
is gross, it is always in hazard of engendering profligacy.

Hence it has been, generally, the opinion of wise men in all
ages, that there is a certain middle condition of life, equally remote
from either of those extremes of fortune, which, though it wants not
also its own dangers, yet is, on the whole, the state most favourable
both to virtue and to happiness. For there, luxury and pride on the
one hand, have no opportunity to enervate or intoxicate the mind,
nor want and dependence on the other, to sink and debase it; there,
all the native affections of the soul have the freest and fairest exercise, the equality of men is felt, friendships are formed, and improvements of every sort are pursued with most success: there, men
are prompted to industry without being overcome by toil, and their
powers called forth into exertion, without being either superseded by
too much abundance, or baffled by insuperable difficulties; there, a
mixture of comforts and of wants, at once awakens their gratitude
to God, and reminds them of their dependence on his aid; and therefore, in this state, men seem to enjoy life to most advantage, and
to be least exposed to the snares of vice.

From what has been said, we learn the importance of attending,
with the utmost care, to the choice which we make of our employment and condition in life. It has been shown, that our external
situation frequently operates powerfully on our moral character; and
by consequence that it is strictly connected, not only with our temporal welfare, but with our everlasting happiness or misery. He who
might have passed unblamed, and upright, through certain walks of
life, by unhappily choosing a road where he meets with temptations
too strong for his virtue, precipitates himself into shame here, and
into endless ruin hereafter. Yet how often is the determination of
this most important article left to the chance of accidental connexions,

or submitted to the option of youthful fancy and humour! When it is made the subject of serious deliberation, how seldom have they on whom the decision of it depends, any further view than so to dispose of one who is coming out into life, as that he may the soonest become rich, or, as it is expressed, make his way to most advantage in the world! Are there no other objects than this to be attended to, in fixing the plan of life? Are there not sacred and important interests which deserve to be consulted? — We would not willingly place one whose welfare we studied, in a situation for which we were convinced that his abilities were unequal. These, therefore, we examine with care; and on them we rest the ground of our decision. It is, however, certain, that not abilities merely, but the turn of the temper and the heart, require to be examined with equal attention, in forming the plan of future establishment. Every one has some peculiar weakness, some predominant passion, which exposes him to temptations of one kind more than of another. Early this may be discerned to shoot; and from its first risings its future growth may be inferred. Anticipate its progress. Consider how it is likely to be affected, by succeeding occurrences in life. If we bring one whom we are rearing up, into a situation, where all the surrounding circumstances shall cherish and mature this fatal principle in his nature, we become, in a great measure, answerable for the consequences that follow. In vain we trust to his abilities and powers. Vice and corruption, when they have tainted the heart, are sufficient to overset the greatest abilities. Nay, too frequently they turn them against the possessor, and render them the instruments of his more speedy ruin.

Hugh Blair.

II. The Novelist and the Dramatist.

It is the object of the novel-writer to place before the reader as full and accurate a representation of the events which he relates as can be done by the mere force of an excited imagination, without the assistance of material objects. His sole appeal is made to the world of fancy and ideas, and in this consists his strength and his weakness, his poverty and his wealth. He cannot, like the painter, present a visible and tangible representation of his towns and his woods, his palaces and his castles: but, by awakening the imagination of a congenial reader, he places before his mind's eye landscapes fairer than those of Claude, and wilder than those of Salvator. He cannot, like the dramatist, present before our living eyes the heroes of former days, or the beautiful creations of his own fancy, embodied in the grace and majesty of Kemble or of Siddons; but he

can teach his reader to conjure up forms even more dignified and
beautiful than theirs. The same difference follows him through every
branch of his art. The author of a novel, in short, has neither stage,
nor scene-painter, nor company of comedians, nor dresses, nor wardrobe: words, applied with the best of his skill, must supply all that
these bring to the assistance of the dramatist. Action, and tone, and
gesture, the smile of the lover, the frown of the tyrant, the grimace
of the buffoon, — all must be told, for nothing can be shown. Thus the
very dialogue becomes mixed with the narration; for he must not
only tell what the characters actually said, in which his task is the
same as that of the dramatic author, but must also describe the
tone, the look, the gesture, with which their speech was accompanied
— telling, in short, all which in the drama it becomes the province
of the actor to express. It must, therefore, frequently happen, that
the author best qualified for a province in which all depends on the
communication of his own ideas and feelings to the reader, without
any intervening medium, may fall short of the skill necessary to
adapt his compositions to the medium of the stage, where the very
qualities most excellent in a novelist are out of place, and an impediment to success. Description and narration, which form the very
essence of the novel, must be very sparingly introduced into dramatic
composition, and scarce ever have a good effect upon the stage.
Even Puff, in 'The Critic,' has the good sense to leave out "all about
gilding the eastern hemisphere;" and the very first thing which the
players struck out of his memorable tragedy, was the description of
Queen Elizabeth, her palfrey, and her side-saddle. The drama speaks
to the eye and ear; and when it ceases to address the bodily organs,
and would exact from a theatrical audience that exercise of the
imagination which is necessary to follow forth and embody circumstances neither spoken nor exhibited, there is an immediate failure,
though it may be the failure of a man of genius. Hence it follows,
that though a good acting play may be made by selecting a plot
and characters from a novel, yet scarce any effort of genius could
render a play into a narrative romance. In the former case, the
author has only to contract the events within the space necessary
for representation, to choose the most striking characters, and exhibit
them in the most forcible contrast, discard from the dialogue whatever is redundant or tedious, and so dramatize the whole. But we
know not any effort of genius which could successfully insert into a
good play those accessories of description and delineation which are
necessary to dilate it into a readable novel. It may thus easily
be conceived, that he whose chief talent lies in addressing the imagina-

tion only, and whose style, therefore, must be expanded and circumstantial, may fail in a kind of composition where so much must be left to the efforts of the actor, with his allies and assistants, the scene-painter and property-man, and where every attempt to interfere with their province is an error unfavourable to the success of the piece. Besides, it must further be remembered that in fictitious narrative an author carries on his manufacture alone, and upon his own account, whereas, in dramatic writing, he enters into partnership with the performers, and it is by their joint efforts that the piece is to succeed. Copartnery is called, by civilians, the mother of discord; and, how likely it is to prove so in the present instance, may be illustrated by reference to the admirable dialogue between the player and poet in 'Joseph Andrews,' book III, chap. 10. The poet must either be contented to fail, or to make great condescensions to the experience, and pay much attention to the peculiar qualifications of those by whom his piece is to be represented. And he who, in a novel, had only to fit sentiments, action, and character, to ideal beings, is now compelled to assume the much more difficult task of adapting all these to real existing persons, who, unless their parts are exactly suited to their own taste, and their peculiar capacities have, each in his line, the means, and not unfrequently the inclination, to ruin the success of the play. Such are, amongst many others, the peculiar difficulties of the dramatic art, and they seem impediments which lie peculiarly in the way of the novelist who aspires to extend his sway over the stage.   WALTER SCOTT.

12. Poetry and Civilisation.

We think that, as civilisation advances, poetry almost necessarily declines. Therefore, though we fervently admire those great works of imagination which have appeared in dark ages, we do not admire them the more because they have appeared in dark ages. On the contrary, we hold that the most wonderful and splendid proof of genius is a great poem produced in a civilised age. We cannot understand why those who believe in that most orthodox article of literary faith, that the earliest poets are generally the best, should wonder at the rule as if it were the exception. Surely the uniformity of the phænomenon indicates a corresponding uniformity in the cause.

The fact is, that common observers reason from the progress of the experimental sciences to that of the imitative arts. The improvement of the former is gradual and slow. Ages are spent in collecting materials, ages more in separating and combining them. Even when a system has been formed, there is still something to add, to alter, or to reject. Every generation enjoys the use of a vast hoard bequeathed to it by antiquity, and transmits that hoard, augmented by fresh acquisitions, to future ages. In these pursuits, therefore the first speculators lie under great disadvantages, and even when they fail, are entitled to praise. Their pupils, with far inferior intellectual powers, speedily surpass them in actual attainments. Every girl who has read Mrs. Marcet's little dialogues on Political Economy could teach Montague or Walpole many lessons in finance. Any intelligent man may now, by resolutely applying himself for a few years to mathematics, learn more than the great Newton knew after half a century of study and meditation.

But it is not thus with music, with painting, or with sculpture. Still less is it thus with poetry. The progress of refinement rarely supplies these arts with better objects of imitation. It may indeed improve the instruments which are necessary to the mechanical operations of the musician, the sculptor, and the painter. But language, the machine of the poet, is best fitted for his purpose in its rudest state. Nations, like individuals, first perceive, and then abstract. They advance from particular images to general terms. Hence the vocabulary of an enlightened society is philosophical, that of a half-civilised people is poetical.

This change in the language of men is partly the cause and partly the effect of a corresponding change in the nature of their intellectual operations, of a change by which science gains, and poetry loses. Generalisation is necessary to the advancement of knowledge; but particularity is indispensable to the creations of the imagination. In proportion as men know more and think more, they look less at individuals and more at classes. They therefore make better theories and worse poems. They give us vague phrases instead of images, and personified qualities instead of men. They may be better able to analyse human nature than their predecessors. But analysis is not the business of the poet. His office is to portray, not to dissect. He may believe in a moral sense, like Shaftesbury; he may refer all human actions to self-interest, like Helvetius; or he may never think about the matter at all. His creed on such subjects will no more influence his poetry, properly so called, than the notions which a painter may have conceived respecting the lacrymal glands, or the circulation of the blood, will affect the tears of his Niobe, or the blushes of his Aurora. If Shakespeare had written a book on the motives of human actions, it is by no means certain that it would have been a good one. It is extremely improbable that it would have contained half so much able reasoning on the subject as is to be found in the 'Fable of the Bees'. But could Mandeville have created an Iago? Well as he knew how to resolve characters into their elements, would he have been able to combine those elements in such a manner as to make up a man, a real, living, individual man?

Perhaps no person can be a poet, or can even enjoy poetry. without a certain unsoundness of mind, if any thing which gives so much pleasure ought to be called unsoundness. By poetry we mean not all writing in verse, nor even all good writing in verse. Our definition excludes many metrical compositions which, on other grounds, deserve the highest praise. By poetry we mean the art of employing words in such a manner as to produce an illusion on the imagination, the art of doing by means of words what the painter does by means of colours. Thus the greatest of poets has described it, in lines universally admired for the vigour and felicity of their diction, and still more valuable on account of the just notion which they convey of the art in which he excelled:

> "As imagination bodies forth
> The forms of things unknown, the poet's pen
> Turns them to shapes, and gives to airy nothing
> A local habitation and a name."

These are the fruits of the "fine frenzy" which he ascribes to the poet — a fine frenzy doubtless, but still a frenzy. Truth, indeed, is essential to poetry; but it is the truth of madness. The reasonings are just; but the premises are false. After the first suppositions have been made, every thing ought to be consistent; but those first suppositions require a degree of credulity which almost amounts to a partial and temporary derangement of the intellect. Hence of all people children are the most imaginative. They abandon themselves without reserve to every illusion. Every image which is strongly presented to their mental eye produces on them the effect of reality. No man, whatever his sensibility may be, is ever affected by Hamlet or Lear, as a little girl is affected by the story of poor Red Ridinghood. She knows that it is all false, that wolves cannot speak, that there are no wolves in England. Yet in spite of her knowledge she believes; she weeps; she trembles; she dares not go into a dark room lest she should feel the teeth of the monster at her throat. Such is the despotism of the imagination over uncultivated minds.

In a rude state of society men are children with a greater variety of ideas. It is therefore in such a state of society that we may expect to find the poetical temperament in its highest perfection. In an enlightened age there will be much intelligence, much science, much philosophy, abundance of just classification and subtle analysis, abundance of wit and eloquence, abundance of verses, and even of good ones: but little poetry. Men will judge and compare; but they will not create. They will talk about the old poets, and comment on them, and to a certain degree enjoy them. But they will scarcely be able to conceive the effect which poetry produced on their ruder ancestors, the agony, the ecstacy, the plenitude of belief. The Greek Rhapsodist, according to Plato, could scarce recite Homer without falling into convulsions. The Mohawk hardly feels the scalping knife while he shouts his death-song. The power which the ancient bards of Wales and Germany exercised over their auditors seems to modern readers almost miraculous. Such feelings are very rare in a civilised community, and most rare among those who participate most in its improvements. They linger longest among the peasantry.

Poetry produces an illusion on the eye of the mind, as a magic lantern produces an illusion on the eye of the body. And, as the magic lantern acts best in a dark room, poetry effects its purpose most completely in a dark age. As the light of knowledge breaks in upon its exhibitions, as the outlines of certainty become more and more distinct, the hues and lineaments of the phantoms which the poet calls up grow fainter and fainter. We cannot unite the incompatible advantages of reality and deception, the clear discernment of truth and the exquisite enjoyment of fiction.

He who, in an enlightened and literary society, aspires to be a great poet, must first become a little child. He must take to pieces the whole web of his mind. He must unlearn much of that knowledge which has perhaps constituted hitherto his chief title to superiority. His very talents will be a hindrance to him. His difficulties will be proportioned to his proficiency in the pursuits which are fashionable among his contemporaries; and that proficiency will in general be proportioned to the vigour and activity of his mind. And it is well if, after all his sacrifices and exertions, his works do not resemble a lisping man, or a modern ruin. We have seen in our own time great talents, intense labour, and long meditation, employed in this struggle against the spirit of the age, and employed, we will not say absolutely in vain, but with dubious success and feeble applause.

TH. B. MACAULAY.

13. The Character of Cordelia.

It appears to me that the whole character rests upon the two sublimest principles of human action — the love of truth, and the sense of duty; but these, when they stand alone (as in the "Antigone"), are apt to strike us as severe and cold.

Shakespeare has, therefore, wreathed them round with the dearest attributes of our feminine nature, the power of feeling and inspiring affection. The first part of the play shows us how Cordelia is loved, the second part how she can love. To her father she is the object of a secret preference; his agony at her supposed unkindness draws from him the confession that he had loved her most, and "thought to set his rest on her kind nursery." Till then she had been "his best object, the argument of his praise, balm of his age, most best, most dearest!" The faithful and worthy Kent is ready to brave death and exile in her defence; and afterwards a further impression of her benign sweetness is conveyed in a simple and beautiful manner, when we are told that "since the Lady Cordelia went to France, her father's poor fool had much pined away." We have her sensibility "when patience and sorrow strove which should express her goodliest;" and all her filial tenderness when she commits her poor father to the care of the physician, when she hangs over him as he is sleeping, and kisses him as she contemplates the wreck of grief and majesty. — Her mild magnanimity shines out in her farewell to her sisters, of whose real character she is perfectly aware. — The modest pride with which she replies to the Duke of Burgundy is admirable. —

To complete the picture, her very voice is characteristic, "ever soft, gentle, and low; an excellent thing in woman."

But it will be said that the qualities here exemplified — as sensibility, gentleness, magnanimity, fortitude, generous affection — are qualities which belong, in their perfection, to others of Shakespeare's characters; to Imogen, for instance, who unites them all; and yet Imogen and Cordelia are wholly unlike each other. Even though we should reverse their situations, and give to Imogen the filial devotion of Cordelia, and Cordelia the conjugal virtues of Imogen, still they would remain perfectly distinct as women.

What is it, then, which lends to Cordelia that peculiar and individual truth of character which distinguishes her from every other human being? It is a natural reserve, a tardiness of disposition, "which often leaves the history unspoke which it intends to do;" a subdued quietness of deportment and expression, a veiled shyness thrown over all her emotions, her language and her manner, making the outward demonstration invariably fall short of what we know to be the feeling within. Not only is the portrait singularly beautiful and interesting in itself, but the conduct of Cordelia, and the part which she bears in the beginning of the story, is rendered consistent and natural by the wonderful truth and delicacy with which this peculiar disposition is sustained throughout the play. How many such are there in the world! How many to sympathize with the fiery, fond old man, when he shrinks, as if petrified, from Cordelia's quiet calm reply!

> Lear. Now, our joy,
> Although our last and least,
> What can you say to draw
> A third more opulent than your sisters? Speak!
> Cord. Nothing, my lord.
> Lear. Nothing!
> Cord. Nothing.
> Lear. Nothing will come of nothing: speak again.
> Cord. Unhappy that I am! I cannot heave
> My heart into my mouth: I love your majesty
> According to my bond; nor more nor less.

Now this is perfectly natural. Cordelia has penetrated the vile characters of her sister. Is it not obvious that in proportion as her own mind is pure and guileless, she must be disgusted with their gross hypocrisy and exaggeration, their empty protestation, their "plighted cunning;" and would retire from all competition with what she so disdains and abhors, — even into the opposite extreme? In such a case, as she says herself,

> What should Cordelia do? — love and be silent.

For the very expressions of Lear —

> what can you say to draw
> A third more opulent than your sisters?

are enough to strike dumb for ever a generous, delicate, but shy disposition, such as is Cordelia's, by holding out a bribe for professions.

If Cordelia were not thus portrayed, this deliberate coolness would strike as verging on harshness or obstinacy: but it is beautifully represented as a certain modification of character, the necessary result of feelings habitually, if not naturally, repressed; and through the whole play we trace the same peculiar and individual disposition — the same absence of all display — the same sobriety of speech veiling the most profound affections — the same quiet steadiness of purpose — the same shrinking from all exhibition of emotion.

"*Tous les sentiments naturels ont leur pudeur*" was a *vivâ voce* observation of Madame de Staël, when disgusted by the sentimental affection of her imitators. This "*pudeur*," carried to an excess, appears to me the peculiar characteristic of Cordelia. ANNA JAMESON.

V. LETTERS.

1. Raleigh's Last Letter.

You shall receive, my dear wife, my last words, in these my last lines; my love I send you, that you may keep when I am dead: and my counsel, that you may remember it when I am no more. I would not, with my will, present you sorrows, dear Bess; let them go to the grave with me, and be buried in the dust. And seeing that it is not the will of God that I shall see you any more, bear my destruction patiently, and with a heart like yourself.

First, I send all the thanks which my heart can conceive, or my words express, for your many cares for me, which, though they have not taken effect as you wished, yet my debt to you is not the less: but pay it I never shall, in this world.

Secondly, I beseech you, for the love you bear me living, that you do not hide yourself many days, but by your patience seek to help my miserable fortunes, and the right of your poor child. Your mourning cannot avail me, that am but dust.

When I am dead, no doubt you shall be much sought unto; for the world thinks I was very rich: have a care to fair pretences of men: for no greater misery can befall you, in this life, than to become a prey unto the world, and after to be despised. I speak, God knows, not to dissuade you from marriage: for it will be best for you, both in respect of God and the world. As for me, I am no more yours, nor you mine; death has cut us asunder, and God has divided me from the world, and you from me.

Remember your poor child for his father's sake, who loved you in his happiest estate. I sued for my life, but God knows, it was for you and yours that I desired it; for know it, my dear wife, your child is the child of a true man, who, in his own respect, despiseth death and his misshapen and ugly forms. I cannot write much, (God knows how hardly I steal this time, when all sleep!) and it is also time for me to separate my thoughts from the world. Beg my dead body, which, living, was denied you, and either lay it in Sherburne or Exeter church, by my father and mother. I can say no more; time and death call me away.

The everlasting God, powerful, infinite, and inscrutable, God Almighty, who is goodness itself, the true light and life, keep you and yours, and have mercy upon me, and forgive my persecutors and false accusers, and send us to meet in his glorious kingdom! My dear wife, farewell: bless my boy: pray for me, and let my true God hold you both in his arms.

2. John Locke to Mr. Molyneux.

Sir, — You look with the eyes, and speak the language of friendship, when you make my life of much more concern to the world than your own; I take it, as it is, for an effect of your kindness, and so shall not accuse you of compliment; the mistakes and overvaluings of good-will being always sincere, even when they exceed what common truth allows. Thus, on my side, I must beg you to believe that my life would be much more pleasant and useful to me if you were within my reach, that I might sometimes enjoy your conversation, and upon twenty occasions, lay my thoughts before you, and have the advantage of your judgment. I cannot complain that I have not my share of friends of all ranks, and such whose interest, assistance, affection, and opinions too, in fit cases, I can rely on. But methinks, for all this, there is one place vacant, that I know nobody that would fill so well as yourself: I want one near me to talk freely with, *de quolibet ente;* to propose to the extravagancies, that rise in my mind; one with whom I would debate several doubts and questions, to see what was in them. Meditating by one's-self is like digging in the mine; it often, perhaps, brings up maiden earth, which never came near the light before; but whether it contain any metal in it, is never so well tried as in conversation with a knowing judicious friend, who carries about him the true touchstone, which is love of truth in a clear thinking head. Men of parts and judgment the world generally gets hold of, and by a great mistake, that their abilities of mind are lost, if not employed in the pursuit of wealth and power, engages them in the ways of fortune and interest, which usually leave but little freedom or leisure of thought for pure disinterested truth. And such who give themselves up frankly, and in earnest, to the full latitude of real knowledge, are not everywhere to be met with. Wonder not, therefore, that I wish so much for you in my neighbourhood. I should be too happy in a friend of your make, were you within my reach. But yet I cannot but wish that some business would once bring you within distance; and it is a pain to think of leaving the world, without the happiness of seeing you.

I do not wonder that a kinsman of yours should magnify civilities that scarce deserve that name; I know not wherein they consisted, but in being glad to see one who was any way related to you, and was himself a very ingenious man; either of those was a title to more than I did, or could show him. I am sorry I have not yet had an opportunity to wait on him in London, and I fear he should be gone before I am able to get thither. This long winter and cold spring has hung very heavy upon my lungs, and they are not yet in a case to be ventured in London air, which must be my excuse, for not waiting upon him and Dr. Ashe yet.

3. Richardson to Aaron Hill.

I will now write to your question — whether there was any original ground-work of fact for the general foundation of Pamela's story.

About twenty-five years ago, a gentleman, with whom I was intimately acquainted, but, who, alas, is now no more! met with such a story as that of Pamela, in one of the summer tours which he used to take for his pleasure, attended with one servant only. At every inn he put up at, it was his way to inquire after curiosities in its neighbourhood, either ancient or modern; and particularly he asked who was the owner of a fine house, as it seemed to him, beautifully situated, which he had passed by (describing it), within a mile or two of the inn.

It was a fine house, the landlord said; the owner was Mr. B., a gentleman of a large estate in more counties than one. That his and his lady's history engaged the attention of everybody who came that way, and put a stop to all other inquiries, though the house and the gardens were well worth seeing. The lady, he said, was one of the greatest beauties in England; but the qualities of her mind had no equal; beneficent, prudent, and equally beloved and admired by high and low. That she had been taken at twelve years of age, for the sweetness of her manners and modesty, and for an understanding above her years, by Mr. B—'s mother, a truly worthy lady, to wait upon her person. Her parents, ruined by suretiships, were remarkably honest and pious, and had instilled into their daughter's mind the best principles. When the misfortunes happened first, they attempted a little school, in their village, where they were much beloved; he teaching writing and the first rules of arithmetic to boys; his wife plain needle-work to girls, and to knit and spin; but that it answered not; and when the lady took their child, the industrious man earned his bread by day-labour, and the lowest kind of husbandry.

That the girl, improving daily in beauty, modesty, and genteel and good behaviour, by the time she was fifteen, engaged the attention of her lady's son; that her noble and excellent qualities subdued him, and he thought fit to make her his wife. That she behaved herself with so much dignity, sweetness, and humility, that she made herself beloved of everybody, and even by his relations, who at first despised her; and now had the blessings both of rich and poor, and the love of her husband.

The gentleman who told me this added that he had the curiosity to stay in the neighbourhood from Friday to Sunday, that he might see this happy couple at church, from which they never absented themselves: that, in short he did see them; that her deportment was all sweetness, ease, and dignity mingled; that he never saw a lovelier woman: that her husband was as fine a man, and seemed even proud of his choice; and that she attracted the respects of the persons of rank present, and had the blessings of the poor. — The relator of the story told me all this with transport.

This, sir, was the foundation of Pamela's story; but little did I think to make a story of it for the press. That was owing to this occasion.

Mr. Rivington and Mr. Osborne, whose names are on the title-page, had long been urging me to give them a little book (which, they said, they were often asked after) of familiar letters on the useful concerns in common life: and at last I yielded to their importunity, and began to recollect such subjects as I thought would be useful in such a design, and formed several letters accordingly, and, among the rest, I thought of giving one or two as cautions to young folks circumstanced as Pamela was. Little did I think, at first, of making one, much less two volumes of it. But, when I began to recollect what had, so many years before, been told me by my friend, I thought the story, if written in an easy and natural manner, suitable to the simplicity of it, might possibly introduce a new species of writing, that might possibly turn young people into a course of reading different from the pomp and parade of romance-writing, and, dismissing the improbable and marvellous, with which novels generally abound, might tend to promote the cause of religion and virtue. I therefore gave way to enlargement; and so Pamela became as you see her. But so little did I hope for the approbation of judges, that I had not the courage to send the two volumes to your ladies, until I found the books well received by the public.

While I was writing the two volumes, my worthy-hearted wife, and the young lady who is with us, when I had read them some part of the story, which I had begun without their knowing it, used to come into my little closet every night, with — "Have you any more of Pamela, Mr. R.? we are come to hear a little more of Pamela," etc. This encouraged me to prosecute it, which I did so diligently, through all my other business, that, by a memorandum on my copy, I began it November 10, 1739, and finished it January

10. 1739—40. And I have often, censurable as I might be thought for my vanity for it, and lessening to the taste of my two female friends, had the story of Molière's Old Woman in my thoughts upon the occasion.

4. Chesterfield to His Son.

My dear friend,

Very few people are good economists of their fortune, and still fewer of their time; and yet, of the two, the latter is the most precious. I heartily wish you to be a good economist of both; and you are now of age, to begin to think seriously of these two important articles. Young people are not to think they have so much time before them, that they may squander what they please of it, and yet have enough left; as very great fortunes have frequently seduced people to a ruinous profusion. Fatal mistakes, always repented of, but always too late! Old Mr. Lowndes, the famous Secretary of the Treasury in the reigns of King William, Queen Anne, and King George the First, used to say, 'take care of the pence, and the pounds will take care of themselves.' To this maxim, which he not only preached, but practised, his two grandsons, at this time, owe the very considerable fortunes that he left them.

This holds equally true as to time; and I most earnestly recommend to you the care of those minutes and quarters of hours, in the course of the day, which people think too short to deserve their attention; and yet, if summed up at the end of the year, would amount to a very considerable portion of time. For example, you are to be at such a place at twelve, by appointment: you go out at eleven, to make two or three visits first; those persons are not at home; instead of sauntering away that intermediate time at a coffee-house and possibly alone, return home, write a letter before-hand for the ensuing post, or take up a good book, I do not mean Descartes, Mallebranche, Locke or Newton, by way of dipping, but some book of rational amusement, and detached pieces, as Horace, Boileau, Waller, La Bruyère etc. This will be so much time saved, and by no means ill-employed. Many people lose a great deal of time by reading; for they read frivolous and idle books, such as the absurd romances of the two last centuries where characters, that never existed, are insipidly displayed, and sentiments, that were never felt, pompously described. Stick to the best established books in every language; the celebrated poets, historians, orators, or philosophers. By these means (to use a city metaphor) you will make fifty per cent of that time, of which others do not make above three or four, or probably nothing at all.

Many people lose a great deal of their time by laziness; they loll and yawn in a great chair, tell themselves that they have not time to begin any thing then, and that it will do as well another time. This is a most unfortunate disposition, and the greatest obstruction to both knowledge and business. At your age you have no right nor claim to laziness; I have, if I please, being *emeritus*. You are but just listed in the world, and must be active, diligent and indefatigable. If ever you propose commanding with dignity, you must serve up to it with diligence. Never put off till to-morrow what you can do to-day.

Dispatch is the soul of business; and nothing contributes more to dispatch than method. Lay down a method for every thing, and stick to it inviolably as far as unexpected incidents may allow. Fix one certain hour and day in the week for your accompts, and keep them together in their proper order; by which means they will require very little time, and you can never be much cheated. Whatever letters and papers you keep, docket and tie them up in their respective classes, so that you may have instantly recourse to any one. Lay down a method also for your reading, for which you allot a certain share of your mornings. Let it be in a consistent and consecutive course, and not in that desultory and immethodical manner, in which many people read scraps of different authors upon different subjects. Keep a useful and short common-place book of what you read to help your memory only, and not for pedantic quotations. Never read history without having maps, and a chronological book or tables, lying by you and constantly recurred to; without which history is only a confused heap of facts. One method more I recommend to you, by which I have found great benefit, even in the most dissipated part of my life; this is, to rise early, and at the same hour every morning, how late soever you may have sat up the night before. This secures you an hour or two, at least, of reading or reflection, before the common interruptions of the morning begin; and it will save your constitution, by forcing you to go to bed early, at least one night in three.

You will say, it may be, as many young people would, that all this order and method is very troublesome, only fit for dull people, and a disagreeable restraint upon the noble spirit and fire of youth. I deny it: and assert, on the contrary, that it will procure you both more time and more taste of your pleasures: and so far from being troublesome to you, that after you have pursued it a month, it would be troublesome to you to lay it aside. Business whets the appetite, and gives a taste to pleasures, as exercise does to food: and business can never be done without method; it raises the spirits for pleasures; and a spectacle, a ball, an assembly will much more sensibly affect a man who has employed, than a man who has lost, the preceding part of the day. The same listlessness runs through his whole conduct, and he is as insipid in his pleasures, as inefficient in every thing else.

I wish to God that you had as much pleasure in following my advice, as I have in giving it you! and you may the more easily have it, as I give you none that is inconsistent with your pleasure. In all that I say to you, it is your interest alone that I consider; trust to my experience, you know you may to my affection. Adieu.

5. Johnson to Chesterfield.

Feb. 7. 1755.

My Lord, — I have been lately informed, by the proprietor of the 'World,' that two papers, in which my Dictionary is recommended to the public, were written by your lordship. To be so distinguished, is an honour, which, being very little accustomed to favours from the great, I know not well how to receive, or in what terms to acknowledge.

When, upon some slight encouragement, I first visited your Lordship, I was overpowered, like the rest of mankind, by the enchantment of your address, and could not forbear to wish that I might boast myself *Le vainqueur du vainqueur de la terre:* that I might obtain that regard for which I saw the world contending; but I found my attendance so little encouraged, that neither pride nor modesty would suffer me to continue it. When I had once addressed your Lordship in public. I had exhausted all the art of pleasing which a retired and uncourtly scholar can possess. I had done all that I could; and no man is well pleased to have his all neglected, be it ever so little.

Seven years, my Lord, have now passed since I waited in your outward rooms, or was repulsed from your door; during which time I have been pushing on my work through difficulties, of which it is useless to complain, and have brought it, at last, to the verge of publication, without one act of assistance. one word of encouragement, or one smile of favour. Such treatment I did not expect, for I never had a patron before.

The shepherd in Virgil grew at last acquainted with Love, and found him a native of the rocks.

Is not a patron, my Lord, one who looks with unconcern on a man struggling for life in the water, and when he has reached the ground, encumbers him with help? The notice which you have been pleased to take of my labours, had it been early, had been kind: but it has been delayed till I am indifferent, and cannot enjoy it: till I am solitary, and cannot impart it; till I am known, and do not want it. I hope it is no very cynical asperity not to confess obligations where no benefit has been received, or to be unwilling that the public should consider me as owing that to a patron, which Providence has enabled me to do for myself.

Having carried on my work thus far with so little obligation to any favourer of learning, I shall not be disappointed, though I should conclude it, if less be possible, with less, for I have been long wakened from that dream of hope, in which I once boasted myself with so much exultation.

My Lord,
    Your Lordship's most humble,
        Most obedient servant.
            Samuel Johnson.

6. Lady Montagu to Pope.

Adrianople, April 1st, O. S. 1717.

I dare say you expect at least something very new in this letter, after I have gone a journey not undertaken by any Christian for some hundred years. The most remarkable accident that happened to me, was my being very near overturned into the Hebrus; and, if I had much regard for the glories that one's name enjoys after death, I should certainly be sorry for having missed the romantic conclusion of swimming down the same river in which the musical head of Orpheus repeated verses so many ages since.

Who knows but some of your bright wits might have found it a subject affording many poetical turns, and have told the world, in a heroic elegy, that,

    "As equal were our souls, so equal were our fates?"

I despair of ever having so many fine things said of me, as so extraordinary a death would have given occasion for.

I am at this present writing in a house situated on the banks of the Hebrus, which runs under my chamber window. The summer is already far advanced in this part of the world; and for some miles round Adrianople, the whole ground is laid out in gardens, and the banks of the river set with rows of fruit-trees, under which all the most considerable Turks divert themselves every evening; not with walking, that is not one of their pleasures, but a set party of them choose out a green spot, where the shade is very thick, and there they spread a carpet, on which they sit drinking their coffee, and generally attended by some slave with a fine voice, or that plays on some instrument. Every twenty paces you may see one of these little companies listening to the dashing of the river; and this taste is so universal, that the very gardeners are not without it. I have often seen them and their children sitting on the banks, and playing on a rural instrument, perfectly answering the description of the ancient *fistula*, being composed of unequal reeds, with a simple but agreeable softness in the sound.

Mr. Addison might here make the experiment he speaks of in his travels; there not being one instrument of music among the Greek or Roman statues, that is not to be found in the hands of the people of this country. The young lads generally divert themselves with making garlands for their favourite lambs, which I have often seen painted and adorned with flowers, lying at their feet while they sang or played. It is not that they ever read romances, but these are the ancient amusements here, and as natural to them as cudgel-playing and foot-ball to our British swains; the softness and warmth of the climate forbidding all rough exercises, which were never so much as heard of amongst them, and naturally inspiring a laziness and aversion to labour, which the great plenty indulges. These gardeners are the only happy race of country people in Turkey. They furnish all the city with fruit and herbs, and seem to live very easily. They are most of them Greeks, and have little houses in the midst of their gardens, where their wives and daughters take a liberty not permitted in the town, I mean, to go unveiled. These wenches are very neat and handsome, and pass their time at their looms under the shade of their trees.

I no longer look upon Theocritus as a romantic writer; he has only given a plain image of the way of life amongst the peasants of his country; who, before oppression had reduced them to want, were, I suppose, all employed as the better sort of them are now. I don't doubt, had he been born a Briton, his *Idyllions* had been filled with descriptions of threshing and churning, both which are unknown here, the corn being all trod out by oxen; and butter (I speak it with sorrow) unheard of.

I read over your Homer here with an infinite pleasure, and find several little passages explained, that I did not before entirely comprehend the beauty of; many of the customs, and much of the dress then in fashion, being yet retained, and I don't wonder to find more remains here of an age so distant, than is to be found in any other country, the Turks not taking that pains to introduce their own manners as has been generally practised by other nations, that imagine themselves more polite. It would be too tedious to you to point out all the passages that relate to the present customs. But I can assure you that the princesses and great ladies pass their time at their looms, embroidering veils and robes, surrounded by their maids, who are always very numerous, in the same manner as we find Andromache and Helen described. The description of the belt of Menelaus exactly resembles those that are now worn by the great men, fastened before with broad golden clasps, and embroidered round with rich work. The snowy veil that Helen throws over her face, is still fashionable; and I never see (as I do very often) half a dozen of old pashas with their reverend beards, sitting basking in the sun, but I recollect good King Priam and his counsellors. Their manner of dancing is certainly the same that Diana is sung to have danced on the banks of the Eurotas. The great lady still leads the dance, and is followed by a troop of young girls, who imitate her steps. and, if she sings, make up the chorus. The tunes are extremely gay and lively, yet with something in them wonderfully soft. The steps are varied according to the pleasure of her that leads the dance, but always in exact time, and infinitely more agreeable than any of our dances, at least in my opinion. I sometimes make one in the train, but am not skilful enough to lead; these are Grecian dances, the Turkish being very different.

7. Burke to Richard Shackleton.

Tuesday Night, June 1780

My dear Shackleton, — I feel as I ought for your friendly solicitude about me and this family. Yesterday our furniture was entirely replaced, and my wife, for the first time since the beginning of this strange tumult, lay at home. During that week of havoc and destruction, we were under the roof of my worthy and valuable friend General Burgoyne. who did everything that could be done to make her situation comfortable to her. You will hear with satisfaction that she went through the whole with no small degree of fortitude. On Monday se'nnight, about nine o'clock, I received undoubted intelligence that immediately after the destruction of Savile House, mine was to suffer the same fate. I instantly came hence (for Mrs. Burke and I were both abroad when we received this intelligence) and I removed such papers as I thought of most importance. In about an hour after, sixteen soldiers, without my knowledge or desire, took possession of the house. Government had, it seems, been apprized of the design, at the time when they were informed of the same ill-intention with regard to houses of so much more consideration than my little tenement: and they obligingly afforded me this protection, by means of which, under God, I think the house was saved. The next day I had my books and furniture removed, and the guards dismissed. I thought, in the then scarcity of troops, they might be better employed than in looking after my paltry remains. My wife being safely lodged, I spent part of the next day in the street, amidst this wild assembly, into whose hands I delivered myself, informing them who I was. Some of them were malignant and fanatical; but I think the far greater part of those whom I saw were rather dissolute and unruly than very ill-disposed. I even found friends and well-wishers among the blue cockades. My friends had come to me to persuade me to go out of town, representing (from their kindness to me) the danger to be much greater than it was. But I thought, that if my liberty was once gone, and that I could not walk the streets of the town with tranquillity, I was in no condition to perform the duties for which I ought alone to wish for life. I therefore resolved they should see that, for one, I was neither to be forced nor intimidated from the straight line of what was right; and I returned, on foot, quite through the multitude to the House, which was covered by a strong body of horse and foot. I spoke my sentiments in such a way that I do not think I have ever, on any occasion, seemed to affect the House more forcibly. However, such was the confusion, that they could not be kept from coming to a resolution which I thought unbecoming and pusillanimous, — which was, that we should take that flagitious petition, which came from that base gang called "The Protestant Association," into our serious consideration. I am now glad that we did so; for if we had refused it, the subsequent ravages would have been charged upon our obstinacy. For four nights I kept watch at Lord Rockingham's, or Sir George Savile's, whose houses were garrisoned by a strong body of soldiers, together with numbers of true friends of the first rank, who were willing to share their danger. Savile House, Rockingham House, Devonshire House, to be turned into garrisons! *O tempora!* We have all served the country for several years — some of us for near thirty — with fidelity, labour, and affection; and we are obliged to put ourselves under military protection for our houses and our persons. The bell rings, and I have filled my time and paper with a mere account of this house: but it is what you will first inquire about, though of the least concern to others. God bless you: — remember me to your worthy host. We can hardly think of leaving town; — there is much to be done to repair the ruins of our country and its reputation, as well as to

console the number of families ruined by wickedness, masking itself
under the colour of religious zeal. Adieu, my dear friend, — our
best regards to your daughter.

                      Yours ever,

                              Edm. Burke.

8. Robert Burns to Moore.

Sir, — Mrs. Dunlop has been so kind as to send me extracts of
letters she has had from you, where you do the rustic bard the
honour of noticing him and his works. Those who have felt the
anxieties and solicitudes of authorship, can only know what pleasure
it gives to be noticed in such a manner by judges of the first
character. Your criticisms, sir, I receive with reverence: only I am
sorry they mostly came too late: a peccant passage or two, that I
would certainly have altered, were gone to the press.

The hope to be admired for ages is, in by far the greater part
of those even who are authors of repute, an unsubstantial dream.
For my part, my first ambition was, and still my strongest wish is,
to please my compeers, the rustic inmates of the hamlet, while ever-
changing language and manners shall allow me to be relished and
understood. I am very willing to admit that I have some poetical
abilities; and as few, if any writers, either moral or poetical,
are intimately acquainted with the classes of mankind among whom
I have chiefly mingled. I may have seen men and manners in a
different phasis from what is common; which may assist originality
of thought. Still I know very well the novelty of my character has
by far the greatest share in the learned and polite notice I have
lately had; and in a language where Pope and Churchill have raised
the laugh, and Shenstone and Gray drawn the tear — where Thomson
and Beattie have painted the landscape, and Lyttleton and Collins
described the heart, I am not vain enough to hope for distinguished
fame.

9. Byron to His Mother.

                              Athens, January 14, 1811.

My dear Madam,

I seize an occasion to write as usual, shortly, but frequently,
as the arrival of letters, where there exists no regular communication,
is, of course, very precarious. I have lately made several small tours
of some hundred or two miles about the Morea, Attica etc., as I
have finished my grand giro by the Troad, Constantinople etc. and am
returned down again to Athens. I believe I have mentioned to you

more than once that I swam (in imitation of Leander, though without his lady) across the Hellespont, from Sestos to Abydos. Of this, and all other particulars, Fletcher, whom I have sent home with papers etc., will apprise you. I cannot find that he is any loss; being tolerably master of the Italian and modern Greek languages, which last I am also studying with a master, I can order and discourse more than enough for a reasonable man. Besides, the perpetual lamentations after beef and beer, the stupid, bigoted contempt for every thing foreign, and insurmountable incapacity of acquiring even a few words of any language, rendered him, like all other English servants, an encumbrance. I do assure you, the plague of speaking for him, the comforts he required (more than myself by far), the pilaws (a Turkish dish of rice and meat) which he could not eat, the wines which he could not drink, the beds where he could not sleep, and the long list of calamities, such as stumbling horses, want of tea!!! etc., which assailed him, would have made a lasting source of laughter to a spectator, and inconvenience to a master. After all, the man is honest enough, and, in Christendom, capable enough; but in Turkey, Lord forgive me! my Albanian soldiers, my Tartars and Janissary, worked for him and us too, as my friend Hobhouse can testify.

It is probable I may steer homewards in spring; but to enable me to do that, I must have remittances. At present, I do not care ro venture a winter's voyage, even if I were otherwise tired of avelling; but I am so convinced of the a dvantages of looking at mankind instead of reading about them, and the bitter effects of staying at home with all the narrow prejudices of an islander, that I think there should be a law amongst us, to set our young men abroad, for a term, among the few allies our wars have left us. Here I see and have conversed with French, Italians, Germans, Danes, Greeks, Turks, Americans, etc. etc.; and without losing sight of my own, I can judge of the countries and manners of others. Where I see the superiority of England (which, by the bye, we are a good deal mistaken about in many things), I am pleased, and where I find her inferior, I am at least enlightened. Now, I might have stayed, smoked in your towns, or fogged in your country, a century, without being sure of this, and without acquiring any thing more useful or amusing at home. I keep no journal, nor have I any intention of scribbling my travels. I have done with authorship; and if, in my last production, I have convinced the critics or the world I was something more than they took me for, I am satisfied; nor will I hazard that reputation by a future effort. It is true I

have some others in manuscript, but I leave them for those who
come after me; and, if deemed worth publishing, they may serve to
prolong my memory when I myself shall cease to remember. I have
a famous Bavarian artist taking some views of Athens etc. etc. for
me. This will be better than scribbling, a disease I hope myself
cured of. I hope, on my return, to lead a quiet, recluse life, but
God knows and does best for us all; at least, so they say, and I
have nothing to object, as, on the whole, I have no reason to complain of my lot. I am convinced, however, that men do more harm
to themselves than ever the devil could do to them. I trust this will
find you well, and as happy as we can be; you will, at least, be
pleased to hear I am so, and yours ever.

10. Byron to Walter Scott.

St. James's Street, July 6, 1812.

Sir — I have just been honoured with your letter — I feel sorry
that you should have thought it worth while to notice the "evil
works of my non-age," as the thing is suppressed voluntarily, and
your explanation is too kind not to give me pain. The satire was
written when I was very young and very angry, and fully bent on
displaying my wrath and my wit, and now I am haunted by the
ghosts of my wholesale assertions. I cannot sufficiently thank you
for your praise; and now, waving myself, let me talk to you of the
Prince Regent. He ordered me to be presented to him at a ball; and
after some sayings peculiarly pleasing from royal lips, as to my own
attempts, he talked to me of you and your immortalities: he preferred you to every bard past and present, and asked which of your
works pleased me most. It was a difficult question. I answered, I
thought the "Lay." He said his own opinion was nearly similar. In
speaking of the others I told him that I thought you more particularly the poet of Princes, as they never appeared more fascinating
than in "Marmion" and the "Lady of the Lake." He was pleased
to coincide, and to dwell on the description of your Jameses as no
less royal than poetical. He spoke alternately of Homer and yourself,
and seemed well acquainted with both; so that (with the exceptions
of the Turks and your humble servant) you were in very good company. I defy Murray to have exaggerated his royal highness's opinion
of your powers, nor can I pretend to enumerate all he said on the
subject; but it may give you pleasure to hear that it was conveyed
in a language which would only suffer by my attempting to transcribe
it, and with a tone and taste which gave me a very high idea of his
abilities and accomplishments, which I had hitherto considered as

confined to manners, certainly superior to those of any living gentleman. This interview was accidental. I never went to the levee; for having seen the courts of Mussulman and Catholic sovereigns, my curiosity was sufficiently allayed; and my politics being as perverse as my rhymes, I had, in fact, "no business there." To be thus praised by your sovereign must be gratifying to you; and if that gratification is not alloyed by the communication being made through me, the bearer of it will consider himself very fortunately and sincerely

    Your obliged and obedient servant,

                    Byron.

II. Dickens to Thomas Mitton.

Baltimore, United States, March 22, 1842.

My dear Friend,

We have been as far south as Richmond in Virginia (where they grow and manufacture tobacco, and where the labour is all performed by slaves), but the season in those latitudes in so intensely and prematurely hot, that it was considered a matter of doubtful expediency to go on to Charleston. For this unexpected reason, and because the country between Richmond and Charleston is but a desolate swamp the whole way, and because slavery is anything but a cheerful thing to live amidst, I have altered my route by the advice of Mr. Clay (the great political leader in this country), and have returned here previous to diving into the far West. We start for that part of the country — which includes mountain travelling, and lake travelling, and prairie travelling — the day after to-morrow, at eight o'clock in the morning; and shall be in the West, and from there going northward again, until the 30th of April or 1st of May, when we shall halt for a week at Niagara, before going further into Canada. We have taken our passage home (God bless the word) in the George Washington packet-ship from New York. She sails on the 7th of June.

I have departed from my resolution not to accept any more public entertainments; they have been proposed in every town I have visited — in favour of the people of St. Louis, my utmost western point. That town is on the borders of the Indian territory, a trifling distance from this place — only two thousand miles! At my second halting place I shall be able to write to fix the day; I suppose it will be somewhere about the 12th of April. Think of my going so far towards the setting sun to dinner!

In every town where we stay, though it be only for a day, we hold a regular levee or drawing-room, where I shake hands on an

average with five or six hundred people, who pass on from me to
Kate, and are shaken again by her. Maclise's picture of our darlings
stands upon a table or sideboard the while; and my travelling secretary, assisted very often by a committee belonging to the place,
presents the people in due form. Think of two hours of this every
day, and the people coming in by hundreds, all fresh, and piping hot,
and full of questions, when we are literally exhausted and can hardly
stand. I really do believe that if I had not a lady with me, I should
have been obliged to leave the country and go back to England. But
for her they never would leave me alone by day or night, and as it
is, a slave comes to me now and then in the middle of the night
with a letter, and waits at the bedroom door for an answer.

It was so hot at Richmond that we could scarcely breathe, and
the peach and other fruit trees were in full blossom; it was so cold
at Washington next day that we were shivering; but even in the
same town you might often wear nothing but a shirt and trousers
in the morning, and two greatcoats at night, the thermometer very
frequently taking a little trip of thirty degrees between sunrise and
sunset.

They do lay it on at the hotels in such a style! They charge by
the day, so that whether one dines out or dines at home makes no
manner of difference. T'other day I wrote to order our rooms at
Philadelphia to be ready on a certain day, and was detained a week
longer than I expected in New York. The Philadelphia landlord not
only charged me half rent for the rooms during the whole of that
time, but board for myself and Kate and Anne during the whole
time too, though we were actually boarding at the same expense
during the same time in New York! What do you say to that?
If I remonstrated, the whole virtue of the newspapers would be
aroused directly.

We were at the President's drawing-room while we were in
Washington. I had a private audience besides, and was asked to
dinner, but couldn't stay.

Parties — parties — parties — of course, every day and night.
But it's not all parties. I go into the prisons, the police-offices, the
watch-houses, the hospitals, the work-houses. I was out half the
night in New York with two of their most famous constables; started
at midnight, and went into every thieves' house, murdering hovel,
sailors' dancing-place, and abode of villany, both black and white, in
the town. I went incog. behind the scenes to the little theatre where
Mitchell is making a fortune. He has been rearing a little dog for
me, and has called him "Boz." I am going to bring him home. In

a word I go everywhere, and a hard life it is. But I am careful to drink hardly anything, and not to smoke at all. I have recourse to my medicine-chest whenever I feel at all bilious, and am, thank God, thoroughly well.

When I next write to you, I shall have begun, I hope, to turn my face homeward. I have a great store of oddity and whimsicality. and am going now into the oddest and most characteristic part of this most queer country.

Always direct to the care of David Colden, Esq., 28, Laight Street. Hudson Square, New York. I received your Caledonia letter with the greatest joy.

Kate sends her best remembrances.

And I am always etc.

P. S. — Richmond was my extreme southern point, and I turn from the South altogether the day after to-morrow. Will you let the Britannia know of this change — if needful?

VI. SPEECHES.

I. Representatives and Constituents.

I am sorry I cannot conclude without saying a word on a topic touched upon by my worthy colleague. I wish that topic had been passed by at a time when I have so little leisure to discuss it. But since he has thought proper to throw it out, I owe you a clear explanation of my poor sentiments on that subject.

He tells you. that "the topic of instructions has occasioned much altercation and uneasiness in this city;" and he expresses himself (if I understand him rightly) in favour of the coercive authority of such instructions.

Certainly, gentlemen, it ought to be the happiness and glory of a representative to live in the strictest union. the closest correspondence, and the most unreserved communication with his constituents. Their wishes ought to have great weight with him: their opinion high respect; their business unremitted attention. It is his duty to sacrifice his repose, his pleasures, his satisfactions, to theirs; and above all, ever, and in all cases, to prefer their interest to his own. But, his unbiassed opinion. his mature judgment, his enlightened conscience, he ought not to sacrifice to you, to any man, or to any set of men living. These he does not derive from your pleasure; no, nor from the law and the constitution. They are a trust from Providence, for the abuse of which he is deeply answerable. Your representative owes you, not his industry only, but his judgment; and he betrays, instead of serving you, if he sacrifices it to your opinion.

My worthy colleague says, his will ought to be subservient to yours. If that be all, the thing is innocent. If government were a matter of will upon any side, yours, without question, ought to be superior. But government and legislation are matters of reason and judgment, and not of inclination: and what sort of reason is that, in which the determination precedes the discussion; in which one set of men deliberate, and another decide; and where those who form the conclusion are perhaps three hundred miles distant from those who hear the arguments?

To deliver an opinion, is the right of all men; that of constituents is a weighty and respectable opinion, which a representative ought always to rejoice to hear; and which he ought always most seriously to consider. But authoritative instructions; mandates issued, which the member is bound blindly and implicitly to obey, to vote, and to argue for, though contrary to the clearest conviction of his judgment and conscience, — these are things utterly unknown to the laws of this land, and which arise from a fundamental mistake of the whole order and tenor of our constitution.

Parliament is not a congress of ambassadors from different and hostile interests; which interests each must maintain, as an agent and advocate, against other agents and advocates; but parliament is a deliberative assembly of one nation, with one interest, that of the whole; where, not local purposes, not local prejudices, ought to guide, but the general good, resulting from the general reason of the whole. You choose a member indeed: but when you have chosen him, he is not member of Bristol, but he is a member of parliament. If the local constituent should have an interest, or should form a hasty opinion, evidently opposite to the real good of the rest of the community, the member for that place ought to be as far, as any other, from any endeavour to give it effect. I beg pardon for saying so much on this subject. I have been unwillingly drawn into it; but I shall ever use a respectful frankness of communication with you. Your faithful friend, your devoted servant, I shall be to the end of my life; a flatterer you do not wish for. On this point of instructions, however, I think it scarcely possible we ever can have any sort of difference. Perhaps I may give you too much, rather than too little, trouble.

From the first hour I was encouraged to court your favour, to this happy day of obtaining it, I have never promised you any thing but humble and persevering endeavours to do my duty. The weight

of that duty, I confess, makes me tremble; and whoever well considers what it is, of all things in the world, will fly from what has the least likeness to a positive and precipitate engagement. To be a good member of parliament, is, let me tell you, no easy task; especially
5 at this time, when there is so strong a disposition to run into the perilous extremes of servile compliance or wild popularity. To unite circumspection with vigour, is absolutely necessary; but it is extremely difficult. We are now members for a rich commercial city; this city, however, is but a part of a rich commercial nation, the interests
10 of which are various, multiform, and intricate. We are members for that great nation, which, however, is itself but part of a great empire, extended by our virtue and our fortune to the farthest limits of the east and of the west. All these wide-spread interests must be considered; must be compared; must be reconciled, if possible. We
15 are members for a free country; and surely we all know, that the machine of free constitution is no simple thing; but as intricate and as delicate as it is valuable. We are members in a great and ancient monarchy and we must preserve religiously the true legal rights of the sovereign, which form the key-stone that binds together the noble
20 and well-constructed arch of our empire and our constitution. A constitution made up of balanced powers must ever be a critical thing. As such I mean to touch that part of it which comes within my reach. I know my inability, and I wish for support from every quarter. In particular I shall aim at the friendship, and shall culti-
25 vate the best correspondence, of the worthy colleague you have given me.   EDMUND BURKE.

2. Against Warren Hastings.

In the name of the Commons of England, I charge all this villany upon Warren Hastings, in this last moment of my applica-
30 tion to you.

My Lords, what is it that we want here to a great act of national justice? Do we want a cause, my Lords? You have the cause of oppressed princes, of undone women of the first rank, of desolated provinces, and of wasted kingdoms.

35 Do you want a criminal, my Lords? When was there so much iniquity ever laid to the charge of any one? No, my Lords, you must not look to punish any other such delinquent from India. Warren Hastings has not left substance enough in India to nourish such another delinquent.

40 My Lords, is it a prosecutor you want? You have before you the Commons of Great Britain as prosecutors, and I believe, my

Lords, that the sun, in his beneficent progress round the world, does not behold a more glorious sight than that of men, separated from a remote people by the material bounds and barriers of nature, united by the bond of a social and moral community; all the Commons of England resenting, as their own, the indignities and cruelties that are offered to all the people of India.

Do you want a tribunal? My Lords, no example of antiquity, nothing in the modern world, nothing in the range of human imagination, can supply us with a tribunal like this. My Lords, here we see virtually in the mind's eye that sacred majesty of the crown, under whose authority you sit and whose power you exercise. We see in that invisible authority what we all feel in reality and life, the beneficent powers and protecting justice of his Majesty. We have here the heir apparent of the crown, such as the fond wishes of the people of England wish an heir apparent of the crown to be. We have here all the branches of the royal family in a situation between majesty and subjection, between the sovereign and the subject, offering a pledge in that situation for the support of the rights of the crown and the liberties of the people, both which extremities they touch. My Lords, we have a great hereditary peerage here; those who have their own honour, the honour of their ancestors and of their posterity to guard: and who will justify, as they have always justified, that provision in the constitution by which justice is made an hereditary office. My Lords, we have here a new nobility, who have risen and exalted themselves by various merits, by great military services, which have extended the fame of this country from the rising to the setting sun: we have those who, by various merits and various civil talents, have been exalted to a situation which they well deserve, and in which they will justify the favour of their sovereign and the good opinion of their fellow-subjects, and make them rejoice to see those virtuous characters, that were the other day upon a level with them, now exalted above them in rank, but feeling with them in sympathy what they felt in common with them before. We have persons exalted from the practice of the law, from the place in which they administered high, though subordinate justice, to a seat here, to enlighten with their knowledge, and to strengthen with their votes, those principles which have distinguished the courts in which they have presided.

My Lords, you have here also the lights of our religion: you have the bishops of England. You have the representatives of that religion which says, that their God is love, that the very vital spirit of their institution is charity; a religion which so much hates oppression, that, when the God whom we adore appeared in human form, he did not appear in a form of greatness and majesty, but in sympathy with the lowest of the people, and thereby made it a firm and ruling principle, that their welfare was the object of all government, since the person who was the Master of Nature chose to appear himself in a subordinate situation. These are the considerations which influence them, which animate them, and will animate them, against all oppression; knowing that He, who is called first among them, and first among us all, both of the flock that is fed and of those who feed it, made himself "the servant of all."

My Lords, these are the securities which we have in all the constituent parts of the body of this house. We know them, we reckon, we rest upon them, and commit safely the interest of India and of humanity into your hands. Therefore, it is with confidence that, ordered by the Commons,

I impeach Warren Hastings, Esquire, of high crimes and misdemeanours.

I impeach him in the name of the Commons of Great Britain in parliament assembled, whose parliamentary trust he has betrayed.

I impeach him in the name of all the Commons of Great Britain, whose national character he has dishonoured.

I impeach him in the name of the people of India, whose laws, rights, and liberties, he has subverted, whose properties he has destroyed, whose country he has laid waste and desolate.

I impeach him in the name and by virtue of those eternal laws of justice which he has violated.

I impeach him in the name of human nature itself, which he has cruelly outraged, injured, and oppressed, in both sexes, in every age, rank, situation, and condition of life. EDMUND BURKE.

3. On the War with America.

My Lords, this ruinous and ignominious situation where we cannot act with success, nor suffer with honour, calls upon us to remonstrate in the strongest and loudest language of truth to rescue the ear of Majesty from the delusions which surround it. The desperate state of our arms abroad is in part known. No man thinks more highly of them than I do: I love and honour the English troops; I know their virtues and their valour; I know they can achieve anything except impossibilities, and I know that the conquest of America is an impossibility. You cannot, I venture to say it, you cannot conquer America. Your armies in the last war effected every thing that could be effected; and what was it? It cost a numerous army, under the command of a most able general, now a noble Lord in this House, a long and laborious campaign, to expel 5000 Frenchmen from French America. My Lords, you cannot conquer America. What is your pressent situation there? We do not know the worst, but we know that in three campaigns we have done nothing, and suffered much. Besides the sufferings, perhaps total loss, of the northern force, the best appointed army that ever took the field, commanded by Sir William Howe, has retired from the American lines; he was obliged to relinqnish his attempt, and, with great delay and danger, to adopt a new and distant plan of operations. We shall soon kuow, and in any event have reason to lament, what may have happened since. As to conquest, therefore, my Lords, I repeat, it is impossible. You may swell every expense, and every effort still more extravagantly, pile and accumulate every assistance you can buy or borrow, traffic and barter with every little pitiful German prince that sells his subjects to the shambles of a foreign prince: your efforts are for ever vain and impotent, doubly so from this mercenary aid on which you rely, for it irritates to an incurable resentment the minds of your enemies. To overrun them with the mercenary sons of rapine and plunder, devoting them and their possessions to the rapacity of hireling cruelty! If I were an American, as I am an Englishman, while a foreign troop was landed in my country, I never would lay down my arms — never, never, never!

Your own army is infected with the contagion of these illiberal allies. The spirit of plunder and of rapine is gone forth among them. I know it, and notwithstanding what the noble Earl who moved the address has given as his opinion of our American army, I know from authentic information and the most experienced officers that our discipline is deeply wounded. Whilst this is notoriously our sinking situation, America grows and flourishes; whilst our strength and discipline is lowered, theirs rises and improves.

But, my Lords, who is the man that, in addition to these disgraces and mischiefs of our army, has dared to authorize and associate to our arms the tomahawk and the scalping-knife of the savage, to call into civilized alliance the wild and inhuman savage of the woods; to delegate to the merciless Indians the defence of disputed rights, and to wage the horrors of this barbarous war against our brethren? My Lords, these enormities cry aloud for redress and punishment. Unless thoroughly done away, it will be a stain on the national character, it is a violation of the constitution, I believe it is against law. It is not the least of our national misfortunes, that the strength and character of our army are thus impaired. Infected with the mercenary spirit of robbery and rapine, familiarized to the horrid scenes of savage cruelty, it can no longer boast of the noble and generous principles which dignify a soldier; no longer sympathize with the dignity of the royal banner, nor feel the pride, pomp, and circumstance of glorious war that "make ambition virtue." What makes ambition virtue? The sense of honour. But is the sense of honour consistent with a spirit of plunder, or the practice of murder? Besides these murderers and plunderers, let me ask our ministers, what other allies have they acquired? What other powers have they associated to their cause? Have they entered into alliance with the king of the gipsies? Nothing, my Lords, is too low or too ludicrous to be consistent with their counsels.

The independent views of America have been stated and asserted as the foundation of this address. My Lords, no man wishes more for due dependence of America on this country than I do. To preserve it, and not to confirm that state of independence into which your measures hitherto have driven them, is the object we ought to unite in attaining. The Americans, contending for their rights against arbitrary exaction, I love and admire; but contending for independency and total disconnection from England, as an Englishman, I cannot wish them success; for, in a due constitutional dependency, including the ancient supremacy of this country in regulating their commerce and navigation, consists the mutual happiness and prosperity both of England and America. She derived assistance and protection from us, and we reaped from her the most important advantages: she was, indeed, the fountain of our wealth, the nerve of our strength, the nursery and basis of our moral power. It is our duty, therefore, my Lords, if we wish to save our country, most seriously to endeavour the recovery of these most beneficial subjects. And in this perilous crisis, perhaps the present moment may be the only one in which we can hope for success. For in their negotiations with France, they have, or think, they have, reason to complain. Though it be notorious that they have received from that power important supplies and assistance of various kinds, yet it is certain they expected it in a more decisive and immediate degree. America is in ill humour with France on some points that have not entirely answered her expectation. Let us wisely take advantage of every possible moment of reconciliation. Besides, the natural disposition of America herself still leans towards England; to the old habits of connection and mutual interest that united both countries. This was the established sentiment of all the continent; and still, my Lords, in the great and principal part, the sound part of America, this wise and affectionate disposition prevails. And there is a very considerable part of America yet sound, the middle and the southern provinces. Some parts may be factious and blind to their true interests; but if we express a wise and benevolent disposition to communicate with them those immutable rights of nature, and those constitutional liberties to which they are equally entitled with ourselves by a conduct so just and humane, we shall confirm the favourable and conciliate the adverse. I say, my Lords, the rights and liberties to which they are equally entitled with ourselves, but no more. I would participate to them every enjoyment and freedom which the colonizing subjects of a free state can possess, or wish to possess; and I do not see why they should not enjoy every fundamental right in their property, and every original substantial liberty which Devonshire or Surrey, or the county I live in, or any other county in England, can claim, reserving always, as the sacred right of the mother country, the true constitutional dependency of the colonies. The inherent supremacy of the state in regulating and protecting the navigation and commerce of all her subjects, is necessary for the mutual benefit and preservation of every part to constitute and preserve the prosperous arrangement of the whole empire.

The sound parts of America, of which I have spoken, must be sensible of these great truths, and of their real interests. America is not in that state of desperate and contemptible rebellion which this country has been deluded to believe. It is not a wild and lawless banditto, who, having nothing to lose, might hope to snatch something from public convulsions. Many of their leaders and great men have a great stake in this contest. The gentleman who conducts their armies, I am told, has an estate of £ 4 or 5000 a year. And when I consider these things, I cannot but lament the inconsiderate violence of our penal acts, our declarations of treason and rebellion, with all the fatal effects of attainder and confiscation.

As to the disposition of foreign powers, which is asserted in the Speech from the throne to be pacific and friendly, let us judge. my Lords, rather by their actions and the nature of things than by interested assertions. The uniform assistance, supplied to America by France, suggests a different conclusion: the most important interests of France in aggrandizing and enriching herself with what she most wants, supplies of every naval store from America, must inspire her with different sentiments. The extraordinary preparations of the House of Bourbon, by land and by sea, from Dunkirk to the Streights, equally ready and willing to overwhelm these defenceless islands, should rouse us to a sense of their real disposition and our own danger. Not 5000 troops in England! hardly 3000 in Ireland! What can we oppose to the combined force of our enemies? Scarcely 20 ships of the line, fully or sufficiently manned, that any admiral's reputation would permit him to take the command of. The river of Lisbon in the possession of our enemies! The seas swept by American privateers, our Channel trade torn to pieces by them! In this complicated crisis of danger, weakness at home, and calamity abroad, terrified and insulted by the neighbouring powers, unable to act in America, or acting only to be destroyed: where is the man with the forehead to promise or hope for success in such a situation? Who has the forehead to do so? Where is that man? I should be glad to see his face.

You cannot conciliate America by your present measures, you cannot subdue her by your present, or by any measures. What, then, can you do? You cannot conquer, you cannot gain, but you can address: you can lull the fears and anxieties of the moment into an ignorance of the danger that should produce them. But, my Lords, the time demands the language of truth, we must not now apply the flattering unction of servile compliance, or blind complaisance. In a just and necessary war, to maintain the rights or honour of my country, I would strip the shirt from my back to support it. But in such a war as this, unjust in its principle, impracticable in its means, and ruinous in its consequences, I would not contribute a single effort, nor a single shilling. I do not call for vengeance on the heads of those who have been guilty, I only recommend to them to make their retreat. Let them walk off, and let them make haste, or they may be assured that speedy and condign punishment will overtake them.

My Lords, I have submitted to you, with the freedom and truth which I think my duty, my sentiments on the present awful situation. I have laid before you the ruin of your power, the disgrace of your reputation, the pollution of your discipline, the contamination of your morals, the complication of calamities, foreign and domestic, that overwhelm your sinking country. Your dearest interests, your own liberties, the constitution itself, totters to the foundation. All this disgraceful danger, this multitude of misery, is the monstrous offspring of this unnatural war. We have been deceived and deluded too long. Let us now stop short. This is the crisis, may be the only crisis, of time and situation to give us a possibility of escape from the fatal effects of our delusions. But if, in an obstinate and infatuated perseverance in folly, we slavishly echo the peremptory words this day presented to us. nothing can save this devoted country from complete and final ruin. We madly rush into multiplied miseries and "confusion worse confounded." WILLIAM PITT THE ELDER

4. On the Abolition of the Slave-Trade.

Now, Sir, I come to Africa. That is the ground on which I rest, and here it is that I say my right honourable friends do not carry their principles to their full extent. Why ought the slave-trade to be abolished? Because it is incurable injustice. How much stronger then is the argument for immediate than gradual abolition! By allowing it to continue even for one hour, do not my right honourable friends weaken, do not they desert their own argument of its injustice? If on the ground of injustice it ought to be abolished at last, why ought it not now? Why is injustice to be suffered to remain for a single hour? From what I hear without doors, it is evident that there is a general conviction entertained of its being far from just; and from that very conviction of its injustice, some men have been led, I fear, to the supposition, that the slave-trade never could have been permitted to begin, but from some strong and irresistible necessity: a necessity, however, which, if it was fancied to exist at first, I have shown cannot be thought by any man whatever to exist now. This plea of necessity thus presumed, and presumed, as I suspect, from the circumstance of injustice itself, has caused a sort of acquiescence in the continuance of this evil. Men have been led to place it among the rank of those necessary evils, which are supposed to be the lot of human creatures, and to be permitted to fall upon some countries or individuals rather than upon others, by that Being, whose ways are inscrutable to us, and whose dispensations, it is conceived, we ought not to look into. The origin of evil is indeed a subject beyond the reach of human understanding: and the permission of it by a Supreme Being, is a subject into which it belongs not to us to inquire. But where the evil in question is a moral evil which a man can scrutinize, and where that moral evil has its origin with ourselves, let us not imagine that we can clear our consciences by this general, not to say irreligious and impious way of laying aside the question. If we reflect at all on this subject, we must see that every necessary evil supposes that some other and greater evil would be incurred were it removed; I therefore desire to ask, what can be that greater evil, which can be stated to over-balance the one in question?

I know of no evil that ever has existed, nor can imagine any evil to exist, worse than the tearing of seventy or eighty thousand persons annually from their native land by a combination of the most civilized nations, inhabiting the most enlightened part of the globe, but more especially under the sanction of the laws of that nation which calls herself the most free and the most happy of them all. Even if these miserable beings were proved guilty of every crime before you take them off (of which, however, not a single proof is adduced), ought we to take upon ourselves the office of executioners? And even if we condescend so far, still can we be justified in taking them, unless we have clear proof that they are criminals? But if we go much further, — if we ourselves tempt them to sell their fellow-creatures to us, we may rest assured, that they will take care to provide by every method, by kidnapping, by village-breaking, by unjust wars, by iniquitous condemnations, by rendering Africa a scene of bloodshed and misery, a supply of victims increasing in proportion to our demand. Can we then hesitate in deciding whether the wars in Africa are their wars or ours? It was our arms in the river Cameroon put into the hands of the trader, that furnished him with the means of pushing his trade; and I have no more doubt that they are British arms, put into the hands of Africans, which promote universal war and desolation, than I can doubt their having done so in that individual instance.

I have shown how great is the enormity of this evil, even on the supposition that we take only convicts and prisoners of war. But take the subject in the other way; take it on the grounds stated by the right honourable gentleman over the way, and how does it stand? Think of eighty thousand persons carried away out of their country by we know not what means! for crimes imputed! for light or inconsiderable faults; for debt perhaps! for the crime of witchcraft! or a thousand other weak and scandalous pretexts; besides all the fraud and kidnapping, the villanies and perfidy, by which the slave-trade is supplied! Reflect on these eighty thousand persons thus annually taken off! There is something in the horror of it that surpasses all the bounds of imagination. Admitting that there exists in Africa something like to courts of justice; yet what an office of humiliation and meanness is it in us, to take upon ourselves to carry into execution the partial, the cruel, iniquitous sentences of such courts, as if we also were strangers to all religion, and to the first principles of justice! But that country, it is said, has been in some degree civilized, and civilized by us. It is said they have gained some knowledge of the principles of justice. What, Sir, have they gained principles of justice from us? Their civilization brought about by us! Yes, we give them enough of our intercourse to convey to them the means, and to initiate them in the study, of mutual destruction. We give them just enough of the forms of justice to enable them to add the pretext of legal trials to their other modes of perpetrating the most atrocious iniquity. We give them just enough of European improvements to enable them the more effectually to turn Africa into a ravaged wilderness. Some evidences say that the Africans are addicted to the practice of gambling; that they even sell their wives and children, and ultimately themselves. Are these then the legitimate sources of slavery? Shall we pretend that we can thus acquire an honest right to exact the labour of these people? Can we pretend that we have a right to carry away to distant regions men of whom we know nothing by authentic inquiry, and of whom there is every reasonable presumption to think that those who sell them to us, have no right to do so?

But the evil does not stop here. I feel that there is not time for me to make all the remarks which the subject deserves, and I refrain from attempting to enumerate half the dreadful consequences of this system. Do you think nothing of the ruin and the miseries in which so many other individuals, still remaining in Africa, are involved in consequence of carrying off so many myriads of people? Do you think nothing of their families which are left behind? of the connexions which are broken? of the friendships, attachments, and relationships that are burst asunder? Do you think nothing of the miseries in consequence, that are felt from generation to generation? of the privation of that happiness which might be communicated to them by the introduction of civilization, and of mental and moral improvement? A happiness which you withhold from them so long as you permit the slave-trade to continue.

Thus, Sir, has the perversion of British commerce carried misery instead of happiness to one whole quarter of the globe. False to the very principles of trade, misguided in our policy, and unmindful of our duty, what astonishing — I had almost said, what irreparable mischief, have we brought upon that Continent! I would apply this thought to the present question. How shall we ever repair this mischief? How shall we hope to obtain, if it be possible, forgiveness from Heaven for those enormous evils we have committed, if we refuse to make use of those means which the mercy of Providence hath still reserved to us for wiping away the guilt and shame with which we are now covered? If we refuse even this degree of compensation, if, knowing the miseries we have caused, we refuse even now to put a stop to them, how greatly aggravated will be the guilt of Great Britain! and what a blot will the history of these transactions for ever be in the history of this country! Shall we then delay to repair these injuries, and to begin rendering this justice to Africa? Shall we not count the days and hours that are suffered to intervene and to delay the accomplishment of such a work? Reflect, what an immense object is before you — what an object for a nation to have in view, and to have a prospect, under the favour of Providence, of being now permitted to attain! I think the house will agree with me in cherishing the ardent wish to enter without delay upon the measures necessary for these great ends: and I am sure that the immediate abolition of the slave-trade is the first, the principal, the most indispensable act of policy, of duty, and of justice, that the legislature of this country has to take, if it is indeed their wish to secure those important objects to which I have alluded, and which we are bound to pursue by the most solemn obligations.

WILLIAM PITT THE YOUNGER.

5. On the Overtures of Peace from the First Consul.

— But, Sir, I should think that it is the interest of Bonaparte to make peace. A lover of military glory as that General must necessarily be, may he not think that his measure of glory is full — that it may be tarnished by a reverse of fortune, and can hardly be increased by any new laurels? He must feel, that, in the situation to which he is now raised, he can no longer depend on his own fortune, his own genius, and his own talents, for a continuance of his success; he must be under the necessity of employing other generals, whose misconduct or incapacity might endanger his power, or whose triumphs even might affect the interest which he holds in the opinion of the French. Peace, then, would secure to him what he had achieved, and fix the inconstancy of fortune. But this will not be his only motive. He must see that France also requires a respite — a breathing interval, to recruit her wasted strength. To procure her this respite would be, perhaps, the attainment of more solid glory, as well as the means of acquiring more solid power than anything which he can hope to gain from arms, and from the proudest triumphs. May he not then be zealous to gain this fame, the only species of fame, perhaps, that is worth acquiring? — Nay, granting that his soul may still burn with the thirst of military exploits, is it not likely that he is disposed to yield to the feelings of the French people, and consolidate his power by consulting their interest! I have a right to argue in this way, when suppositions of his sincerity are reasoned upon on the other side. Sir, these aspersions are in truth always idle, and even mischievous. I have been too long accustomed to hear imputation and calumnies thrown out upon great and honourable characters, to be much influenced by them. My hon. and learned friend. Mr. Erskine, has paid this night a most just, deserved, and honourable tribute of applause to the memory of that great and unparalleled character, who is so recently lost to the world. I must, like him, beg leave a moment to dwell on the venerable George Washington, though I know that it is impossible for me to bestow anything like adequate praise on a character which gave us, more than any other human being, the example of a perfect man; yet, good, great, and unexampled as General Washington was, I can remember the time, when he was not better spoken of in this House than Bonaparte is now. The right hon. gentleman who opened this debate may remember in what terms of disdain, of virulence, even of contempt, General Washington was spoken of by gentlemen on that side of the House. Does he not recollect with what marks of indignation any member was stigmatized as an enemy to his country, who mentioned, with common respect, the name of General Washington? — If a negotiation had then been proposed to be opened with that great man, what would have been said? — Would you treat with a rebel, a traitor! What an example would you not give by such an act? I do not know whether the right hon. gentleman may not yet possess some of his old prejudices on the subject. I hope not: I hope by this time we are all convinced that a republican government, like that of America, may exist without danger or injury to social order or to established monarchies.

They have happily shown that they can maintain the relations of peace and amity with other states. They have shown too that they are alive to the feelings of honour; but they do not lose sight of good sense and discretion. They have not refused to negotiate with the French, and have accordingly the hopes of a speedy termination of every difference.

* * *

Where then, Sir, is this war, which on every side is pregnant with such horrors, to be carried? Where is it to stop? Not till you establish the House of Bourbon! And this you cherish the hope of doing, because you have had a successful campaign.

Why, Sir, before this you have had a successful campaign. The situation of the allies, with all they have gained, is surely not to be compared now to what it was when you had taken Valenciennes, Quesnoy, Condé etc. which induced some gentlemen in this House to prepare themselves for a march to Paris. With all that you have gained, you surely will not say that the prospect is brighter now than it was then.

What have you gained but the recovery of a part of what you before lost? One campaign is successful to you — another to them — and in this way, animated by the vindictive passions of revenge, hatred, and rancour, which are infinitely more flagitious even than those of ambition and the thirst of power, you may go on for ever: as, with such black incentives, I see no end to human misery.

And all this without an intelligible motive — all this because you may gain a better peace a year or two hence! So that we are called upon to go on merely as a speculation. — "We must keep Bonaparte for some time longer at a war, as a state of probation." Gracious God, Sir, is a war a state of probation? Is peace a rash system? Is it dangerous for nations to live in amity with each other? — Is your vigilance, your policy, your common powers of observation, to be extinguished by putting an end to the horrors of war? Cannot this state of probation be as well undergone without adding to the catalogue of human sufferings? "But we must pause!" What! must the bowels of Great Britain be torn out — her best blood be spilt — her treasure wasted — that you may make an experiment? Put yourselves, oh! that you would put yourselves in the field of battle and learn to judge of the sort of horrors that you excite.

In former wars a man might, at least, have some feeling, some interest, that served to balance in his mind the impressions which a scene of carnage and of death must inflict. If a man had been present at the battle of Blenheim for instance, and had enquired the motive of the battle there was not a soldier engaged who could not have satisfied his curiosity, and even perhaps, allayed his feelings — they were fighting to repress the uncontrolled ambiton of the Grand Monarque. — But if a man were present now at a field of slaughter, and were to enquire for what they are fighting, they are pausing! — "Why is that man expiring? Why is that other writhing with agony? What means this implacable fury?" The answer must be, "You are quite wrong — Sir, you deceive yourself — They are not fighting — Do not disturb them — they are merely pausing — this man is not expiring with agony — that man is not dead — he is only pausing! Lord help you, Sir, they are not angry with one another. They have now no cause of quarrel — but their country thinks that there should be a pause. All that you see, Sir, is nothing like fighting — there is no harm, nor cruelty, nor bloodshed in it whatever — it is nothing more than a political pause — it is merely to try an experiment — to see whether Bonaparte will not behave himself better than heretofore, and in the mean time we have agreed to pause in pure friendship." And is this the way, Sir, that you are to show yourselves the advocates of order! You take up a system calculated to uncivilize the world — to destroy order — to trample on religion — to stifle in the heart, not merely the generosity of noble sentiments, but the affections of social nature; and in the prosecution of this system, you spread terror and devastation all around you. CHARLES FOX.

6. On Parliamentary Reform.

I am asked what great practical benefits are to be expected from this measure? And is it no benefit to have the Government strike its roots into the hearts of the people? Is it no benefit to have a calm and deliberative, but a real organ of the public opinion, by which its course may be known, and its influence exerted upon State affairs regularly and temperately, instead of acting convulsively, and as it were by starts and shocks? I will only appeal to one advantage, which is as certain to result from this salutary improvement of our system, as it is certain that I am addressing your Lordships.

A Noble Earl inveighed strongly against the licentiousness of the Press; complained of its insolence; and asserted that there was no tyranny more intolerable than that which its conductors now exercised. It is most true, that the Press has great influence from expressing, more or less correctly, the opinion of the country. Let it run counter to the prevailing course, and its power is at an end. But I will also admit that, going in the same general direction with public opinion, the Press is oftentimes armed with too much power in particular instances; and such power is always liable to be abused. But I will tell the Noble Earl upon what foundation this overgrown power is built. The Press is now the only organ of public opinion. This title it assumes; but it is not by usurpation; it is rendered legitimate by the defects of your Parliamentary constitution; it is erected upon the ruins of real representation. The periodical Press is the rival of the House of Commons; and it is, and it will be, the successful rival, as long as that House does not represent the people — but not one day longer. If ever I felt confident in any prediction, it is in this, that the restoration of Parliament to its legitimate office of representing truly the public opinion will overthrow the tyranny of which Noble Lords are so ready to complain, who, by keeping out the lawful sovereign, in truth, support the usurper. It is you who have placed this unlawful authority on a rock: pass the Bill, it is built on a quicksand. Let but the country have a full and free representation, and to that will men look for the expression of public opinion, and the Press will no more be able to dictate, as now, when none else can speak the sense of the people.

Will its influence wholly cease? God forbid! Its just influence will continue, but confined within safe and proper bounds. It will continue — long may it continue — to watch the conduct of public men — to watch the proceedings even of a reformed legislature — to watch the people themselves — a safe, an innoxious, a useful instrument, to enligthen and improve mankind! But its overgrown power — its assumption to speak in the name of the nation — its pretension to dictate and to command, will cease with the abuse upon which alone it is founded, and will be swept away, together with the other creatures of the same abuse, which now 'fright our Isle from its propriety.'

Those portentous appearances, the growth of later times, those figures that stalk abroad, of unknown stature, and strange form — unions, and leagues, and musterings of men in myriads, and conspiracies against the Exchequer — whence do they spring, and how come they to haunt our shores? What power engendered those uncouth shapes — what multiplied the monstrous births, till they people the land? Trust me, the same power which called into frightful existence, and armed with resistless force, the Irish volunteers of 1782 — the same power which rent in twain your empire, and raised up thirteen republics — the same power which created the Catholic Association, and gave it Ireland for a portion. What power is that? Justice denied — rights withheld — wrongs perpetrated — the force which common injuries lend to millions — the wickedness of using the sacred trust of Government as a means of indulging private caprice — the idiotcy of treating Englishmen like the children of the South Sea Islands — the phrenzy of believing, or making believe, that the adults of the nineteenth century can be led like children, or driven like barbarians! This it is that has conjured up the strange sights at which we now stand aghast! And shall we persist in the fatal error of combating the giant progeny, instead of extirpating the execrable parent? Good God! Will men never learn wisdom, even from their own experience? Will they never believe, till it be too late, that the surest way to prevent immoderate desires being formed, aye, and unjust demands enforced, is to grant in due season the moderate requests of justice? You stand, my Lords, on the brink of a great event — you are in the crisis of a whole nation's hopes and fears. An awful importance hangs over your decision. Pause, ere you plunge!

I hear it constantly said, that the Bill is rejected by all the Aristocracy. Favour, and a good number of supporters, our adversaries allow it has among the people; the Ministers, too, are for it; but

the Aristocracy, say they, is strenuously opposed to it. I broadly
deny this silly, thoughtless assertion. What! My Lords, the Aristocracy set themselves in a mass against the people — they who
sprang from the people — are inseparably connected with the people
— are the natural chiefs of the people!

They set themselves against the people, for whom Peers are
ennobled — Bishops consecrated — Kings anointed — the people,
to serve whom Parliament itself has an existence, and the Monarch and all its institutions are constituted, and without whom none
of them could exist for an hour? This assertion of reflecting men is
too monstrous to be endured — as a member of this House, I deny
it with indignation. I repel it with scorn, as a calumny upon us all.
And yet are there those who even within these walls speak of the
Bill, augmenting so much the strength of the democracy, as to
endanger the other orders of the State: and so they charge its
authors with promoting anarchy and rapine. Why, my Lords, have
its authors nothing to fear from democratic spoliation? The fact is,
that there are Members of the present Cabinet, who possess, one or
two of them alone, far more property than any two administrations
within my recollection; and all of them have ample wealth. I need
hardly say, I include not myself, who have little or none. But even
of myself I will say, that whatever I have depends on the stability
of existing institutions; and it is as dear to me as the princely
possessions of any amongst you. Permit me to say, that, in becoming
a Member of your House, I staked my all on the aristocratic institutions of the State. I abandoned certain wealth, a large income, and
much real power in the State for an office of great trouble, heavy
responsibility, and very uncertain duration. I say, I gave up substantial
power for the shadow of it, and for distinction depending upon
accident. I quitted the elevated station of Representative for Yorkshire,
and a leading Member of the Commons. I descended from a position
quite lofty enough to gratify any man's ambition; and my lot became
bound up in the stability of this House. Then, have I not a right to
throw myself on your justice, and to desire that you will not put in
jeopardy all I have now left?

But the populace only, the rabble, the ignoble vulgar, are for
the Bill. Then what is the Duke of Norfolk, Earl Marshal of England?
What the Duke of Devonshire? What the Duke of Bedford? *(Cries of
Order from the opposition.)* I am aware it is irregular in any Noble
Lord that is a friend to the measure; its adversaries are patiently
suffered to call peers even by their christian and surnames. Then
I shall be as regular as they were, and ask, does my friend John

Russell, my friend William Cavendish, my friend Harry Vane, belong to the mob, or to the Aristocracy? Have they no possessions? Are they modern names? Are they wanting in Norman blood, or whatever else you pride yourselves on? The idea is too ludicrous to be seriously refuted: — that the Bill is only a favourite with the democracy, is a delusion so wild as to point a man's destiny towards St. Luke's. Yet many, both here and elsewhere, by dint of constantly repeating the same cry, or hearing it repeated, have almost made themselves believe that none of the nobility are for the measure. A Noble Friend of mine has had the curiosity to examine the List of Peers, opposing and supporting it, with respect to the dates of their creation, and the result is somewhat remarkable. A large majority of the Peers, created before Mr. Pitt's time, are for the Bill; the bulk of those against it are of recent creation; and if you divide the whole into two classes, those ennobled before the reign of George III. and those since, of the former, fifty-six are friends and only twenty-one enemies, of the Reform. So much for the vain and saucy boast, that the real nobility of the country are against Reform I have dwelt upon this matter more than its intrinsic importance deserves, only through my desire to set right the fact, and to vindicate the ancient Aristocracy from a most groundless imputation. LORD BROUGHAM.

7. Education and the State.

I believe, Sir, that it is the right and the duty of the State to provide means of education for the common people. This proposition seems to me to be implied in every definition that has ever yet been given of the functions of a government. About the extent of those functions there has been much difference of opinion among ingenious men. There are some who hold that it is the business of a government to meddle with every part of the system of human life, to regulate trade by bounties and prohibitions, to regulate expenditure by sumptuary laws, to regulate literature by a censorship, to regulate religion by an inquisition. Others go to the opposite extreme, and assign to Government a very narrow sphere of action. But the very narrowest sphere that ever was assigned to governments by any school of political philosophy is quite wide enough for my purpose. On one point all the disputants are agreed. They unanimously acknowledge that it is the duty of every government to take order for giving security to the persons and property of the members of the community.

This being admitted, can it be denied that the education of the common people is a most effectual means of securing our persons and our property? Let Adam Smith answer that question for me. His authority, always high, is, on this subject, entitled to peculiar respect, because he extremely disliked busy, prying, interfering governments. He was for leaving literature, arts, sciences, to take care of themselves. He was not friendly to ecclesiastical estabishments. He was of opinion, that the State ought not to meddle with the education of the rich. But he has expressly told us that a distinction is to be made, particularly in a commercial and highly civilized society, between the education of the rich and the education of the poor. The education of the poor, he says, is a matter which deeply concerns the commonwealth. Just as the magistrate ought to interfere for the purpose of preventing the leprosy from spreading among the people, he ought to interfere for the purpose of stopping the progress of the moral distempers which are inseparable from ignorance. Nor can this duty be neglected without danger to the public peace. If you leave the multitude uninstructed, there is serious risk that religious animosities may produce the most dreadful disorders. The most dreadful disorders! Those are Adam Smith's own words; and prophetic words they were. Scarcely had he given this warning to our rulers when his prediction was fulfilled in a manner never to be forgotten. I speak of the No Popery riots o 1780. I do not know that I could find in all history a stronger proof of the proposition, that the ignorance of the common people makes the property, the limbs, the lives of all classes insecure. Without the shadow of a grievance, at the summons of a madman, a hundred thousand people rise in insurrection. During a whole week, there is anarchy in the greatest and wealthiest of European cities. The parliament is besieged. Your predecessor sits trembling in his chair, and expects every moment to see the door beaten in by the ruffians whose roar he hears all round the house. The peers are pulled out of their coaches. The bishops in their lawn are forced to fly over the tiles. The chapels of foreign ambassadors, buildings made sacred by the law of nations, are destroyed. The house of the Chief Justice is demolished. The little children of the Prime Minister are taken out of their beds and laid in their night clothes on the table of the Horse Guards, the only safe asylum from the fury of the rabble. The prisons are opened. Highwaymen, housebreakers, murderers, come forth to swell the mob by which they have been set free. Thirty-six fires are blazing at once in London. Then comes the retribution. Count up all the wretches who were shot, who were hanged, who were crushed, who drank themselves to death at the rivers of gin which ran down Holborn Hill; and you will find that battles have been lost and won with a smaller sacrifice of life. And what was the cause of this calamity, a calamity which, in the history of London, ranks with the great plague and the great fire? The cause was the ignorance of a population which had been suffered, in the neighbourhood of palaces, theatres, temples, to grow up as rude and stupid as any tribe of tattooed cannibals in New Zealand, I might say as any drove of beasts in Smithfield Market.

The instance is striking: but it is not solitary. To the same cause are to be ascribed the riots of Nottingham, the sack of Bristol, all the outrages of Ludd, and Swing, and Rebecca, beautiful and costly machinery broken to pieces in Yorkshire, barns and haystacks blazing in Kent, fences and buildings pulled down in Wales. Could such things have been done in a country in which the mind of the labourer had been opened by education, in which he had been taught to find pleasure in the exercise of his intellect, taught to revere his Maker, taught to respect legitimate authority, and taught at the same time to seek the redress of real wrongs by peaceful and constitutional means?

This then is my argument, It is the duty of Government to protect our persons and property from danger. The gross ignorance of the common people is a principal cause of danger to our persons and property. Therefore, it is the duty of the Government to take care that the common people shall not be grossly ignorant.

And what is the alternative? It is universally allowed that, by some means, Government must protect our persons and property. If you take away education, what means do you leave? You leave means such as only necessity can justify, means which inflict a fearful amount of pain, not only on the guilty, but on the innocent who are connected with the guilty. You leave guns and bayonets, stocks and whipping-posts, treadmills, solitary cells, penal colonies, gibbets. See hen how the case stands. Here is an end which, as we all agree, governments are bound to attain. There are only two ways of attaining it. One of those ways is by making men better, and wiser, and happier. The other way is by making them infamous and miserable. Can it be doubted which way we ought to prefer? Is it not strange, is it not almost incredible, that pious and benevolent men should gravely propound the doctrine that the magistrate is bound to punish and at the same time bound not to teach? To me it seems quite clear that whoever has a right to hang has a right to educate. Can we think without shame and remorse that more than half of those wretches who have been tied up at Newgate in our time might have been living happily, that more than half of those who are now in our gaols might have been enjoying liberty and using that liberty well, that such a hell on earth as Norfolk Island need never have existed, if we had expended in training honest men but a small part of what we have expended in hunting and torturing rogues.

I would earnestly entreat every gentleman to look at a report which is contained in the Appendix to the First Volume of the Minutes of the Committee of Council. I speak of the report made by Mr. Seymour Tremenheare on the state of that part of Monmouthshire which is inhabited by a population chiefly employed in mining. He found that, in this district, towards the close of 1839, out of eleven thousand children who were of an age to attend school, eight thousand never went to any school at all, and that most of the remaining three thousand might almost as well have gone to no school as to the squalid hovels in which men who ought themselves to have been learners pretended to teach. In general these men had only one qualification for their employment; and that was their utter unfitness for every other employment. They were disabled miners, or broken hucksters. In their schools all was stench, and noise, and confusion. Now and then the clamour of the boy was silenced for two minutes by the furious menaces of the master; but it soon broke out again. The instruction given was of the lowest kind. Not one school in ten was provided with a single map. This is the way in which you suffered the minds of a great population to be formed. And now for the effects of your negligence. The barbarian inhabitants of this region rise in an insane rebellion against the Government. They come pouring down their valleys to Newport. They fire on the Queen's troops. They wound a magistrate. The soldiers fire in return; and too many of these wretched men pay with their lives the penalty of their crime. But is the crime theirs alone? Is it strange that they should listen to the only teaching that they had? How can you, who took no pains to instruct them, blame them for giving ear to the demagogue who took pains to delude them? We put them down, of course. We punished them. We had no choice. Order must be maintained; property must be protected; and, since we had omitted to take the best way of keeping these people quiet, we were under the necessity of keeping them quiet by the dread of the sword and the halter. But could any necessity be more cruel? And which of us would run the risk of being placed under such necessity a second time?

I say, therefore, that the education of the people is not only a means, but the best means, of attaining that which all allow to be a chief end of government; and, if this be so, it passes my faculties to understand how any man can gravely contend that Government has nothing to do with the education of the people.

My confidence in my opinion is strengthened when I recollect that I hold that opinion in common with all the greatest lawgivers, statesmen, and political philosophers of all nations and ages, with all the most illustrious champions of civil and spiritual freedom, and especially with those men whose names were once held in the highest veneration by the Protestant Dissenters of England. I might cite many of the most venerable names of the old world; but I would rather cite the example of that country which the supporters of the Voluntary system here are always recommending to us as a pattern. Go back to the days when the little society which has expanded into the opulent and enlightened commonwealth of Massachusetts began to exist. Our modern Dissenters will scarcely, I think, venture to speak contumeliously of those Puritans whose spirit Laud and his High Commission Court could not subdue, of those Puritans who were willing to leave home and kindred, and all the comforts and refinements of civilized life, to cross the ocean, to fix their abode in forests among wild beasts and wild men, rather than commit the sin of performing, in the House of God, one gesture which they believed to be displeasing to Him. Did those brave exiles think it inconsistent with civil or religious freedom that the State should take charge of the education of the people? No, Sir; one of the earliest laws enacted by the Puritan colonists was that every township, as soon as the Lord had increased it to the number of fifty houses, should appoint one to teach all children to write and read, and that every township of a hundred houses should set up a grammar school. Nor have the descendants of those who made this law ever ceased to hold that the public authorities were bound to provide the means of public instruction. Nor is this doctrine confined to New England. "Educate the people," was the first admonition addressed by Penn to the colony which he founded. "Educate the people," was the legacy of Washington to the nation which he had saved. "Educate the people," was the unceasing exhortation of Jefferson: and I quote Jefferson with peculiar pleasure, because, of all the eminent men that have ever lived, Adam Smith himself not excepted. Jefferson was the one who most abhorred everything like meddling on the part of governments. Yet the chief business of his later years was to establish a good system of State education in Virginia.

And, against such authority as this, what have you who take the other side to show? Can you mention a single great philosopher, a single man distinguished by his zeal for liberty, humanity, and truth, who, from the beginning of the world down to the time of this present Parliament, ever held your doctrines? You can oppose to the unanimous voice of all the wise and good, of all ages, and of both hemispheres, nothing but a clamour which was first heard a few months ago, a clamour in which you cannot join without condemning, not only all whose memory you profess to hold in reverence, but even your former selves.

This new theory of politics has at least the merit of originality. It may be fairly stated thus. All men have hitherto been utterly in the wrong as to the nature and objects of civil government. The great truth, hidden from every preceding generation, and at length revealed, in the year 1846, to some highly respectable ministers and elders of dissenting congregations, is this, Government is simply a great hangman. Government ought to do nothing except by harsh and degrading means. The one business of government is to handcuff, and lock up, and scourge, and shoot, and stab, and strangle. It is odious tyranny in a Government to attempt to prevent crime by informing the understanding and elevating the moral feeling of a people. A statesman may see hamlets turned, in the course of one generation, into great seaport towns and manufacturing towns. He may know that on the character of the vast population which is collected in those wonderful towns, depends the prosperity, the peace, the very existence of society. But he must not think of forming that character. He is an enemy of public liberty if he attempts to prevent those hundreds of thousands of his countrymen from becoming mere Yahoos. He may, indeed, build barrack after barrack to overawe them. If they break out into insurrection, he may send cavalry to sabre them: he may mow them down with grape shot: he may hang them, draw them, quarter them, anything but teach them. He may see, and may shudder as he sees, throughout large rural districts, millions of infants growing up from infancy to manhood as ignorant, as mere slaves of sensual appetite, as the beasts that perish. No matter. He is a traitor to the cause of civil and religious freedom if he does not look on with folded arms, while absurd hopes and evil passions ripen in that rank soil. He must wait for the day of his harvest. He must wait till the Jacquerie comes, till farm houses are burning, till threshing machines are broken in pieces; and then begins his business, which is simply to send one poor ignorant savage to the country gaol, and another to the antipodes, and a third to the gallows.

Such, Sir, is the new theory of government which was first propounded, in the year 1846, by some men of high note among the Nonconformists of England. It is difficult to understand how men of excellent abilities and excellent intentions, — and there are, I readily admit, such men among those who hold this theory, — can have fallen into so absurd and pernicious an error. One explanation only occurs to me. This is, I am inclined to believe, an instance of the operation of the great law of reaction. We have just come victorious out of a long and fierce contest for the liberty of trade. While that contest was undecided, much was said and written about the advantages of free competition, and about the danger of suffering the State to regulate matters which should be left to individuals. There has consequently arisen in the minds of persons who are led by words, and who are little in the habit of making distinctions, a disposition to apply to political questions and moral questions principles which are sound only when applied to commercial questions. These people, not content with having forced the Government to surrender a province wrongfully usurped, now wish to wrest from the Government a domain held by a right which was never before questioned, and which cannot be questioned with the smallest show of reason. "If," they say, "free competition is a good thing in trade, it must surely be a good thing in education. The supply of other commodities, of sugar, for example, is left to adjust itself to the demand; and the consequence is, that we are better supplied with sugar than if the Government undertook to supply us. Why then should we doubt that the supply of instruction will, without the intervention of the Government, be found equal to the demand?"

Never was there a more false analogy. Whether a man is well supplied with sugar is a matter which concerns himself alone. But whether he is well supplied with instruction is a matter which concerns his neighbours and the State. If he cannot afford to pay for sugar, he must go without sugar. But it is by no means fit that, because he cannot afford to pay for education, he should go without education. Between the rich and their instructors there may, as Adam Smith says, be free trade. The supply of music masters and Italian masters may be left to adjust itself to the demand. But what is to become of the millions who are too poor to procure without assistance the services of a decent schoolmaster? We have indeed heard it said that even these millions will be supplied with teachers by the free competition of benevolent individuals who will vie with each other in rendering this service to mankind. No doubt there are many benevolent individuals who spend their time and money most laudably in setting up and supporting schools; and you may say, if you please, that there is, among these respectable persons, a competition to do good. But do not be imposed upon by words. Do not believe that this competition resembles the competition which is produced by the desire of wealth and by the fear of ruin. There is a great difference, be assured, between the rivalry of philanthropists and the rivalry of grocers. The grocer knows that, if his wares are worse than those of other grocers, he shall soon go before the Bankrupt Court, and his wife and children will have no refuge but the workhouse: he knows that, if his shop obtains an honorable celebrity, he shall be able to set up a carriage and buy a villa: and this knowledge impels him to exertions compared with which the exertions of even very charitable people to serve the poor are but languid. It would be strange infatuation indeed to legislate on the supposition that a man cares for his fellow creatures as much as he cares for himself.

Unless, Sir, I greatly deceive myself, those arguments, which show that the Government ought not to leave to private people the task of providing for the national defence, will equally show that the Government ought not to leave to private people the task of providing for national education. On this subject, Mr. Hume has laid down the general law with admirable good sense and perspicuity. I mean David Hume, not the Member for Montrose, though that honorable gentleman will, I am confident, assent to the doctrine propounded by his illustrious namesake. David Hume, Sir, justly says that most of the arts and trades which exist in the world produce so much advantage and pleasure to individuals, that the magistrate may safely leave it to individuals to encourage those arts and trades. But he adds that there are callings which, though they are highly useful, nay, absolutely necessary to society, yet do not administer to the peculiar pleasure or profit of any individual. The military calling is an instance. Here, says Hume, the government must interfere. It must take on itself to regulate these callings, and to stimulate the industry of the persons who follow these callings by pecuniary and honorary rewards.

Now, Sir, it seems to me that, on the same principle on which Government ought to superintend and to reward the soldier, Government ought to superintend and to reward the schoolmaster. I mean, of course, the schoolmaster of the common people. That his calling is useful, that his calling is necessary, will hardly be denied. Yet it is clear that his services will not be adequately remunerated if he is left to be remunerated by those whom he teaches, or by the voluntary contributions of the charitable. Is this disputed? Look at the facts. You tell us that schools will multiply and flourish exceedingly, if the Government will only abstain from interfering with them? Has not the Government long abstained from interfering with them? Has not everything been left, through many years, to individual exertion? If it were true that education, like trade, thrives most where the magistrate meddles least, the common people of England would now be the best educated in the world. Our schools would be model schools. Every one would have a well chosen little library, excellent maps, a small but neat apparatus for experiments in natural philosophy. A grown person unable to read and write would be pointed at like Giant O'Brien or the Polish Count. Our schoolmaster would be as eminently expert in all that relates to teaching as our cutlers, our cotton-spinners, our engineers are allowed to be in their respective callings. They would, as a class, be held in high consideration; and their gains would be such that it would be easy to find men of respectable character and attainments to fill up vacancies.

Now, is this the case? Look at the charges of the judges, at the resolutions of the grand juries, at the reports of public officers, at the reports of voluntary associations. All tell the same sad and ignominious story. Take the reports of the Inspectors of Prisons. In the House of Correction at Hertford, of seven hundred prisoners one half could not read at all; only eight could read and write well. Of eight thousand prisoners who had passed through Maidstone gaol only fifty could read and write well. In Coldbath Fields Prison, the proportion that could read and write well seems to have been still smaller. Turn from the registers of prisoners to the registers of marriages. You will find that about a hundred and thirty thousand couples were married in the year 1844. More than forty thousand of the bridegrooms and more than sixty thousand of the brides did not sign their names, but made their marks. Nearly one third of the men and nearly one half of the women, who are in the prime of life, who are to be the parents of the Englishmen of the next generation, who are to bear a chief part in forming the minds of the next generation, cannot write their own names. Remember, too, that though people who cannot write their own names must be grossly ignorant, people may write their own names and yet have very little knowledge. Tens of thousands who were able to write their names had in all probability received only the wretched education of a common day school. We know what such a school too often is; a room crusted with filth, without light, without air, with a heap of fuel in one corner and a brood of chickens in another; the only machinery of instruction a dog-eared spelling-book and a broken slate; the masters the refuse of all other callings, discarded footmen, ruined pedlars, men who cannot work a sum in the rule of three, men who cannot write a common letter without blunders, men who do not know whether the earth is a sphere or a cube, men who do not know whether Jerusalem is in Asia or America. And to such men, men to whom none of us would entrust the key of his cellar, we have entrusted the mind of the rising generation, and, with the mind of the rising generation, the freedom, the happiness, the glory of our country.

Do you question the accuracy of this description? I will produce evidence to which I am sure that you will not venture to take an exception. Every gentleman here knows, I suppose, how important a place the Congregational Union holds among the Nonconformists, and how prominent a part Mr. Edward Baines has taken in opposition to State education. A Committee of the Congregational Union drew up last year a report on the subject of education. That report was received by the Union; and the person who moved that it should be received was Mr. Edward Baines. That report contains the following passage: "If it were necessary to disclose facts to such an assembly as this, as to the ignorance and debasement of the neglected portions of our population in towns and rural districts, both adult and juvenile, it could easily be done. Private information communicated to the Board, personal observation and investigation of the various localities, with the published documents of the Registrar General, and the reports of the state of prisons in England and Wales, published by order of the House of Commons, would furnish enough to make us modest in speaking of what has been done for the humbler classes, and make us ashamed that the sons of the soil of England should have been so long neglected, and should present to the enlightened traveller from other shores such a sad spectacle of neglected cultivation, lost mental power, and spiritual degradation." Nothing can be more just. All the information which I have been able to obtain bears out the statements of the Congregational Union. I do believe that the ignorance and degradation of a large part of the community to which we belong ought to make us ashamed of ourselves. I do believe that an enlightened traveller from New York, from Geneva, or from Berlin, would be shocked to see so much barbarism in the close neighbourhood of so much wealth and civilization. But is it not strange that the very gentlemen who tell us in such emphathic language that the people are shamefully ill educated, should yet persist in telling us that under a system of free competition the people are certain to be excellently educated? Only this morning the opponents of our plan circulated a paper in which they confidently predict that free competition will do all that is necessary, if we will only wait with patience! Wait with patience! Why, we have been waiting ever since the Heptarchy. How much longer are we to wait? Till the year 2847? Or till the year 3847? That the experiment has as yet failed you do not deny. And why should it have failed? Has it been tried in unfavourable circumstances? Not so; it has been tried in the richest and in the freeest, and in the most charitable country in all Europe. Has it been tried on too small a scale? Not so: millions have been subjected to it. Has it been tried during too short a time? Not so: it has been going on during ages. The cause of the failure then is plain. Our whole system has been unsound. We have applied the principle of free competition to a case to which that principle is not applicable.

But, Sir, if the state of the southern part of your island has furnished me with one strong argument, the state of the northern part furnishes me with another argument, which is, if possible, still more decisive. A hundred and fifty years ago England was one of the best governed and most prosperous countries in the world; Scotland was perhaps the rudest and poorest country that could lay any claim to civilization. The name of Scotchman was then uttered in this part of the island with contempt. The ablest Scotch statesmen contemplated the degraded state of their poorer countrymen with a feeling approaching to despair. It is well known that Fletcher of Saltoun, a brave and accomplished man, a man, who had drawn his sword for liberty, who had suffered proscription and exile for liberty, was so much disgusted and dismayed by the misery, the ignorance, the idleness, the lawlessness of the common people, that he proposed to make many thousands of them slaves. Nothing, he thought but the discipline which kept order and enforced exertion among the negroes of a sugar colony, nothing but the lash and the stocks, could reclaim the vagabonds who infested every part of Scotland from their indolent and predatory habits, and compel them to support themselves by steady labour. He, therefore, soon after the Revolution, published a pamphlet, in which he earnestly, and, as I believe, from the mere impulse of humanity and patriotism, recommended to the Estates of the Realm this sharp remedy, which alone, as he conceived, could remove the evil. Within a few months after the publication of that pamphlet a very different remedy was applied. The Parliament which sat at Edinburgh passed an act for the establishment of parochial schools. What followed? An improvement such as the world had never seen took place in the moral and intellectual character of the people. Soon, in spite of the rigour of the climate, in spite of the sterility of the earth, Scotland became a country which had no reason to envy the fairest portions of the globe. Wherever the Scotchman went, — and there were few parts of the world to which he did not go, — he carried his superiority with him. If he was admitted into a public office, he worked his way up to the highest post. If he got employment in a brewery or a factory, he was soon the foreman. If he took a shop, his trade was the best in the street. If he enlisted in the army, he became a colour-sergeant. If he went to a colony, he was the most thriving planter there. The Scotchman of the seventeenth century had been spoken of in London as we speak of the Esquimaux. The Scotchman of the eighteenth century was an object, not of scorn, but of envy. The cry was that, whereever he came, he got more than his share; that, mixed with Englishmen or mixed with Irishmen, he rose to the top as surely as oil rises to the top of water. And what had produced this great revolution? The Scotch air was still as cold, the Scotch rocks were still as bare as ever. All the natural qualities of the Scotchman were still what they had been when learned and benevolent men advised that he should be flogged, like a beast of burden, to his daily task. But the State had given him an education. That education was not, it is true, in all respects what it should have been. But, such as it was, it had done more for the bleak and dreary shores of the Forth and the Clyde than the richest of soils and the most genial of climates had done for Capua and Tarentum. Is there one member of this House, however strongly he may hold the doctrine that the Government ought not to interfere with the education of the people, who will stand up and say that, in his opinon, the Scotch would now have been a happier and a more enlightened people if they had been left, during the last five generations, to find instruction for themselves?

I say then, Sir, that if the science of Government be an experimental science, this question is decided. We are in a condition to perform the inductive process according to the rules laid down in the Novum Organum. We have two nations closely connected, inhabiting the same island, sprung from the same blood, speaking the same language, governed by the same Sovereign and the same Legislature, holding essentially the same religious faith, having the same allies and the same enemies. Of these two nations one was, a hundred and fifty years ago, as respects opulence and civilization, in the highest rank among European communities, the other in the lowest rank. The opulent and highly civilized nation leaves the education of the people to free competition. In the poor and half barbarous nation the eduction of the people is undertaken by the State. The result is that the first are last and the last first. The common people of Scotland, — it is vain to disguise the truth, — have passed the common people of England. Free competition, tried with every advantage, has produced effects of which, as the Congregational Union tells us, we ought to be ashamed, and which must lower us in the opinion of every intelligent foreigner. State education, tried under every disadvantage, has produced an improvement to which it would be difficult to find a parallel in any age or country. Such an experiment as this would be regarded as conclusive in surgery or chemistry, and ought, I think, to be regarded as equally conclusive in politics.

These, Sir, are the reasons which have satisfied me that it is the duty of the State to educate the people.   TH. B. MACAULAY.

8. On the State of Ireland.

First, I hold that Ireland is in a most unsatisfactory, indeed in a most dangerous state.

Secondly, I hold that for the state in which Ireland is Her Majesty's Ministers are in a great measure accountable, and that they have not shown, either as legislators or as administrators, that they are capable of remedying the evils which they have caused.

Now, Sir, if I make out these two propositions, it will follow that it is the constitutional right and duty of the representatives of the nation to interfere; and I conceive that my noble friend, by moving for a Committee of the whole House, has proposed a mode of interference which is both parliamentary and convenient. My first proposition, Sir, will scarcely be disputed. Both sides of the House are fully agreed in thinking that the condition of Ireland may well excite great anxiety and apprehension. That island, in extent about one fourth of the United Kingdom, in population more than one fourth, superior probably in natural fertility to any area of equal size in Europe, possessed of natural facilities for trade such as can nowhere else be found in an equal extent of coast, an inexhaustible nursery of gallant soldiers, a country far more important to the prosperity, the strength, the dignity of this great empire than all our distant dependencies together, than the Canadas and the West Indies added to Southern Africa, to Australasia, to Ceylon, and to the vast dominions of the Moguls, that island, Sir, is acknowledged by all to be so ill affected and so turbulent that it must, in any estimate of our power, be not added but deducted. You admit that you govern that island, not as you govern England and Scotland, but as you govern your new conquests in Scinde, not by means of the respect which the people feel for the laws, but by means of bayonets, of artillery, of entrenched camps.

My first proposition, then, I take to be conceded. Ireland is in a dangerous state. The question which remains to be considered is, whether for the state in which Ireland is Her Majesty's Ministers are to be held accountable.

Now, Sir, I at once admit that the distempers of Ireland must in part be attributed to causes for which neither Her Majesty's present Ministers nor any public men now living can justly be held accountable. I will not trouble the House with a long dissertation on those causes. But it is necessary, I think, to take at least a rapid glance at them. ...... And now, Sir, I must stop. I have said enough to justify the vote which I shall give in favour of the motion of my noble friend. I have shown, unless I deceive myself, that the extraordinary disorders which now alarm us in Ireland have been produced by the fatal policy of the Government. I have shown that the mode in which the Government is now dealing with those disorders is far more likely to inflame than to allay them. While this system lasts, Ireland can never be tranquil; and till Ireland is tranquil, England can never hold her proper place among the nations of the world. To the dignity, to the strength, to the safety of this great country, internal peace is indispensably necessary. In every negotiation, whether with France on the right of search, or with America on the line of boundary, the fact that Ireland is discontented is uppermost in the minds of the diplomatists on both sides; making the representative of the British Crown timorous, and making his adversary bold. And no wonder. This is indeed a great and splendid empire, well provided with the means both of annoyance and of defence. England can do many things which are beyond the power of any other nation in the world. She has dictated peace to China. She rules Caffraria and Australasia. She could again sweep from the ocean all commerce but her own. She could again blockade every port from the Baltic to the Adriatic. She is able to guard her vast Indian dominions against all hostility by land or sea. But in this gigantic body there is one vulnerable spot near to the heart. At that spot forty-six years ago a blow was aimed which narrowly missed, and which, if it had not missed, might have been deadly. The government and the legislature, each in its own sphere, is deeply responsible for the continuance of a state of things which is fraught with danger to the State. From my share of that responsibility I shall clear myself by the vote which I am about to give; and I trust that the number and the respectability of those in whose company I shall go into the lobby will be such as to convince the Roman Catholics of Ireland that they need not yet relinquish all hope of obtaining relief from the wisdom and justice of an Imperial Parliament. TH. B. MACAULAY.

9. On English Literature.

Some of the objections which have been made to such institutions as ours have been so happily and completely refuted by my friend the Lord Provost, and by the Most Reverend Prelate who has honoured us with his presence this evening, that it would be idle to say again what has been so well said. There is, however, one objection which, with your permission, I will notice. Some men, of whom I wish to speak with great respect, are haunted, as it seems to me, with an unreasonable fear of what they call superficial knowledge. Knowledge, they say, which really deserves the name, is a great blessing to mankind, the ally of virtue, the harbinger of freedom. But such knowledge must be profound. A crowd of people who have a smattering of mathematics, a smattering of astronomy, a smattering of chemistry, who have read a little poetry and a little history, is dangerous to the commonwealth. Such half knowledge is worse than ignorance. And then the authority of Pope is vouched. Drink deep or taste not; shallow draughts intoxicate: drink largely; and that will sober you. I must confess that the danger which alarms these gentlemen never seemed to me very serious; and my reason is this: that I never could prevail on any person who pronounced superficial knowledge a curse, and profound knowledge a blessing, to tell me what was his standard of profundity. The argument proceeds on the supposition that there is some line between profound and superficial knowledge similar to that which separates truth from falsehood. I know of no such line. When we talk of men of deep science, do we mean that they have got to the bottom or near the bottom of science? Do we mean that they know all that is capable of being known? Do we mean even that they know, in their own especial department, all that the smatterers of the next generation will know? Why, if we compare the little truth that we know with the infinite mass of truth which we do not know, we are all shallow together; and the greatest philosophers that ever lived would be the first to confess their shallowness.

If we could call up the first of human beings, if we could call up Newton, ask him whether, even in those sciences in which he had no rival he considered himself as profoundly knowing, he would have told us that he was but a smatterer like ourselves, and that the difference between his knowledge and ours vanished, when compared with the quantity of truth still undiscovered, just as the distance between a person at the foot of Ben Lomond and at the top of Ben Lomond vanishes when compared with the distance of the fixed stars.

It is evident then that those who are afraid of superficial knowledge do not mean by superficial knowledge, knowledge which is superficial when compared with the whole quantity of truth capable of being known. For, in that sense, all human knowledge is, and always has been, and always must be, superficial. What then is the standard? Is it the same two years together in any country? Is it the same, at the same moment, in any two countries? Is it not notorious that the profundity of one age is the shallowness of the next; that the profundity of one nation is the shallowness of a neighbouring nation? Ramohun Roy passed, among Hindoos, for a man of profound western learning; but he would have been but a very superficial member of this institute. Strabo was justly entitled to be called a profound geographer eighteen hundred years ago. But a teacher of geography, who had never heard of America, would now be laughed at by the girls of a boarding-school. What would now be thought of the greatest chemist of 1749, or of the greatest geologist of 1746? The truth is that, in all experimental science, mankind is, of necessity, constantly advancing. Every generation, of course, has its front rank and its rear rank; but the rear rank of a later generation occupies the ground which was occupied by the front rank of a former generation. You remember Gulliver's adventures. First he is shipwrecked in a country of little men; and he is a Colossus among them. He strides over the walls of their capital: he stands higher than the cupola of their great temple; he tugs after him a royal fleet: he stretches his legs; and a royal army, with drums beating and colours flying, marches through the gigantic arch: he devours a whole granary for breakfast, eats a herd of cattle for dinner, and washes down his meal with all the hogsheads of a cellar. In his next voyage he is among men sixty feet high. He who, in Lilliput, used to take people up in his hand in order that he might be able to hear them, is himself taken up in the hands and held to the ears of his masters. It is all that he can do to defend himself with his hanger against the rats and mice. The court ladies amuse themselves with seeing him fight wasps and frogs: the monkey runs off with him to the chimney top: the dwarf drops him into the cream jug and leaves him to swim for his life. Now, was Gulliver a tall or a short man? Why, in his own house at Rotherhithe, he was thought a man of the ordinary stature. Take him to Lilliput; and he is Quinbus Flestrin, the man Mountain. Take him to Brobdingnag, and he is Grildrig, the little Manikin. It is the same in science. The pygmies of one society would have passed for giants in another.

It might be amusing to institute a comparison between one of the profoundly learned men of the thirteenth century and one of the superficial students who will frequent our library. Take the great philosopher of the time of Henry the Third of England, or Alexander the Third of Scotland, the man renowned all over the island, and

even as far as Italy and Spain, as the first of astronomers and
chemists. What is his astronomy? He is a firm believer in the
Ptolemaic system. He never heard of the law of gravitation. Tell him
that the succession of day and night is caused by the turning of
the earth on its axis, tell him that, in consequence of this motion,
the polar diameter of the earth is shorter than the equatorial diameter, tell him that the succession of summer and winter is
caused by the revolution of the earth round the sun, — and he
will set you down for an idiot. To do him justice, however, if he
is ill informed on these points, there are other points on which
Newton and Laplace were mere children when compared with him.
He can cast your nativity. He knows what will happen when Saturn
is in the House of Life, and what will happen when Mars is in conjunction with the Dragon's Tail. He can read in the stars whether
an expedition will be successful, whether the next harvest will be
plentiful, which of your children will be fortunate in marriage, and
which will be lost at sea. Happy the State, happy the family, which
is guided by the counsels of so profound a man! And what but
mischief, public and private, can we expect from the temerity and
conceit of sciolists who know no more about the heavenly bodies
than what they have learned from Sir John Herschel's beautiful little
volume. But, to speak seriously, is not a little truth better than a
great deal of falsehood? Is not the man who in the evenings of
a fortnight, has acquired a correct notion of the solar system, a
more profound astronomer than a man who has passed thirty years in
reading lectures about the *primum mobile* and in drawing schemes of
horoscopes? Or take chemistry. Our philosopher of the thirteenth century
shall be, if you please, a universal genius, chemist as well as astronomer. He has perhaps got so far as to know that, if he mixes
charcoal and saltpetre in certain proportions and then applies fire,
there will be an explosion which will shatter all his retorts and
aludels, and he is proud of knowing what will in a later age be
familiar to all the idle boys in the kingdom. But there are departments of science in which he need not fear the rivalry of Black, or
Lavoisier, or Cavendish, or Davy. He is in hot pursuit of the philosopher's stone, of the stone that is to bestow wealth, and health,
and longevity. He has a long array of strangely shaped vessels, filled
with red oil and white oil, constantly boiling. The moment of projection is at hand: and soon all his kettles and gridirons will be
turned into pure gold. Poor Professor Faraday can do nothing of the
sort. I should deceive you if I held out to you the smallest hope
that he will ever turn your halfpence into sovereigns. But if you can

induce him to give at our Institute a course of lectures such as I once heard him give at the Royal Institution to children in the Christmas holidays, I can promise you that you will know more about the effects produced on bodies by heat and moisture than was known to some alchemists who, in the middle ages, were thought worthy of the patronage of kings.

As it has been in science so it has been in literature. Compare the literary acquirements of the great men of the thirteenth century with those which will be within the reach of many who will frequent our reading room. As to Greek learning, the profound man of the thirteenth century was absolutely on a par with the superficial man of the nineteenth. In the modern languages, there was not, six hundred years ago, a single volume which is now read. The library of our profound scholar must have consisted entirely of Latin books. We will suppose him to have had both a large and a choice collection. We will allow him thirty, nay forty manuscripts, and among them a Virgil, a Terence, a Lucan, an Ovid, a Statius, a great deal of Livy, a great deal of Cicero. In allowing him all this, we are dealing most liberally with him; for it is much more likely that his shelves were filled with treatises on school divinity and canon law, composed by writers whose names the world has very wisely forgotten. But, even if we suppose him to have possessed all that is most valuable in the literature of Rome, I say with perfect confidence that, both in respect of intellectual improvement, and in respect of intellectual pleasures, he was far less favourably situated than a man who now, knowing only the English language, has a bookcase filled with the best English works. Our great man of the Middle Ages could not form any conception of any tragedy approaching Macbeth or Lear, or of any comedy equal to Henry the Fourth or Twelfth Night. The best epic poem that he had read was far inferior to the Paradise Lost, and all the tomes of his philosophers were not worth a page of the Novum Organum.

The Novum Organum, it is true, persons who know only English must read in a translation: and this reminds me of one great advantage which such persons will derive from our institution. They will, in our library, be able to form some acquaintance with the master minds of remote ages and foreign countries. A large part of what is best worth knowing in ancient literature, and in the literature of France, Italy, Germany, and Spain, has been translated into our own tongue. It is scarcely possible that the translation of any book of the highest class can be equal to the original. But, though the finer touches may be lost in the copy, the great outlines will remain. An Englishman who never saw the frescoes in the Vatican may yet, from engravings, form some notion of the exquisite grace of Raphael, and of the sublimity and energy of Michael Angelo. And so the genius of Homer is seen in the poorest version of the Iliad; the genius of Cervantes is seen in the poorest version of Don Quixote. Let it not be supposed that I wish to dissuade any person from studying either the ancient languages or the languages of modern Europe. Far from it. I prize most highly those keys of knowledge; and I think that no man who has leisure for study ought to be content until he possesses several of them. I always much admired a saying of the Emperor Charles the Fifth. "When I learn a new language," he said, "I feel as if I had got a new soul." But I would console those who have not time to make themselves linguists, by assuring them that, by means of their own mother tongue, they may obtain ready access to vast intellectual treasures, to treasures such as might have been envied by the greatest linguists of the age of Charles the Fifth, to treasures surpassing those which were possessed by Aldus, by Erasmus, and by Melanchthon. And thus I am brought back to the point from which I started, I have been requested to invite you to fill your glasses to the Literature of Britain; to that literature, the brightest, the purest, the most durable of all the glories of our country; to that literature, so rich in precious truth and precious fiction; to that literature which boasts of the prince of all poets and of the prince of all philosophers; to that literature which has exercised an influence wider than that of our commerce, and mightier than that of our arms; to that literature which has taught France the principles of liberty, and has furnished Germany with models of art; to that literature which forms a tie closer than the tie of consanguinity between us and the commonwealths of the valley of the Mississippi; to that literature before the light of which impious and cruel superstitions are fast taking flight on the banks of the Ganges; to that literature which will in future ages, instruct and delight the unborn millions who will have turned the Australasian and Caffrarian deserts into cities and gardens. To the Literature of Britain, then! And wherever British literature spreads, may it be attended by British virtue and by British freedom! TH. B. MACAULAY.

10. Against Materialism.

The wants of this age, Gentlemen, are very special and very urgent. It is a time of rapid progress, and rapid progress is in itself a good. But when the velocity is great, then, as in the physical so in the moral world, the conditions of equilibrium are more severe,

and the consequences of losing it are more disastrous. The changes
that have taken place among us within the compass of a generation
as to the external and material conditions of life have been far
greater changes than at any previous period of recorded history have
been crowded into a similar space of time. Capital and Industry, if
they could be regarded as persons, and as persons who had gone to
sleep 40 years back and were now suddenly awakened, would be at
a loss to identify the world they remembered with the world they
found. At the commencement of that period the laws which were
miscalled Protection, and which were really laws for the promotion
of scarcity and the prevention of abundance, had so completely
attained their purpose that, notwithstanding the growth of population
and of mechanical invention, notwithstanding a few initial efforts of
enlightened statesmen, never to be sufficiently commended, the exchange of British produce with the produce of other countries
remained at the point where it had stood at the commencement of
the century. At the close of the period the commerce of the country
was multiplied fivefold. Our shipping, which at the close of the war
in 1815 had amounted to two millions and a half tons, and by dint
of "protective" fostering stood at the same figure in 1830, in 1873
passed six millions and a half tons; navigated at a much smaller
expense per ton, and also, through the agency of steam, performing
relatively to tonnage from twice to three times the amount of work.
Goods which had been used to travel from place to place at two
miles an hour now principally go at 20. Persons who travelled at
four, six, or ten, now, at one-third or one-fourth the cost, accomplish
four times the speed. Private correspondence had been a luxury forbidden to the less wealthy classes, for a letter from Edinburgh to
London paid, I think, fifteen-pence halfpenny for each separate piece
of paper it contained, while it now passes, in a fourth part of the
time, for a penny or halfpenny. Messages while I speak are passing
with the speed of lightning along a thousand wires: and further, we
are cheered or threatened, as according to our several temperaments
the case may be regarded, with inventions of which the joint effect
seems likely to be that everybody will speak to everybody at all
times, in and to all places, and upon all subjects. Materials and instruments of production which nature had supplied to us grudgingly,
and from a distance, are now produced at will by art in quantities
only limited by demand. But it would be vain to attempt a complete
enumeration of the changes which — often, it must be sorrowfully
confessed, deforming the fair face of creation — have during this
wonderful period passed upon our industry and trade; I will only

sum up the results by stating that the annual income taxable to income-tax, which was 130 millions in 1813, was 571 millions in 1874-5; that the annual increment of personal property, without allowing for capital laid out upon the soil, is 150 millions; that the amount added in a decade is greater than the entire amount of personal property in 1814, and that if there had not been any property at all in the country 50 years back, if we had then started from zero and could have made it at the rate at which we are now making it, nearly the whole of what we now possess would by this time have been accumulated in that brief time.

A review, even upon paper, of these enormous changes seems to make the head giddy, and suggests the need of knowing something of their actual and probable effect, upon the entire, and especially upon the higher, destinies of man; and this the more gravely because there is not the least reason to suppose that we have reached, or have even approached, the close of this great epoch of industrial and material development. It has been owing to two great causes. The first of them has been the removal of fetters from human thought and human action by the repeal of unwise laws which hampered and restrained at every point interchange among men both of mental and material products. The other has been the progress of the natural sciences and the inventive arts. The former of these causes is negative. It is, speaking generally, not the doing of good so much as the undoing of mischief, and it has among other effects provided enormous scope and field for the positive action of the second cause. To the operation of the latter cause, whether here or elsewhere, it seems hard to set any limit whatever. Let us now, therefore, attempt a more general survey from a somewhat higher point of view. The great salient feature of the age is, on a first view, the constant discovery of the secrets of nature and the progressive subjugation of her forces to the purposes and will of man. These conquests over nature have enormously multiplied the means of enjoyment. Had that multiplication been so distributed as either wholly or principally to sweeten the cup of those for whom this life is habitually a life of care and labour and daily pressure in a thousand forms, it might have seemed rather to redress a painful inequality than to create an excess or threaten a disturbance. We may contemplate with unmixed satisfaction that rise of wages and that increased command of the necessaries and conveniences of life for the many which have marked our time. But these have not been the only, perhaps not the principal, results of the conquests I have described. If they have done much for industry, they have done more for capital; if much for labour, more for luxury. They have enormously extended the numbers — they have, I believe, extended even the relative numbers — of the leisured and wealthy classes; they have variously and vastly multiplied the incitements to gain, the avenues of excitement, the solicitations to pleasure among those for whom all these had been at the very least sufficient in the more quiet and stationary times that went before. These tendencies to excess, these activities beyond the means, have acted upon the classes that mainly govern affairs, and, what is more, that mainly form and propagate the current opinion of the day. Among these the pursuit of material enjoyment, and of wealth as the means of it, has made a progress wholly out of proportion to any advancement they may have effected during the last quarter of a century in mental resources or pursuits. Disproportioned growth, if large in degree, is in the physical world deformity: in the moral and social world it is derangement that answers to deformity and partakes of its nature. Among the signs of this derangement has been the growth of a new class — a class unknown to the past, and on whose existence the future will have cause to deplore. It is the class of hybrid or bastard men of business, men of family, men of rank, men of title, men gallant by courtesy and perhaps by nature, country gentlemen, members of both Houses of Parliament, members of various professions, generally alike in being unsuited for apprenticeship to commercial enterprise. It is made up from the scattered and less considerate members of all classes. The bond that unites them is the bond of gain, not the legitimate produce of toil by hand or brain; in most cases not fenced off from rashness, as in former times, by liability to ruinous loss in the event of failure but to be had without the conditions which alone make profit truly honourable. In giving their names to speculations which they neither understand nor examine as directors or trustees, or in other like responsible positions, these spurious representatives of British enterprise are merely used as decoys, to allure the unwary and entrap them into the subscription list: for it is a serious truth that there is a proportion of the free people inhabiting these islands who are ever ready to accept merely decorative names as guarantees for the soundness of a project, without the presence or the presumption of knowledge, or skill, or judgment, or proud and hardy integrity. I do not enter into the question whether and how this social and economic romance, with all the loss, discredit, and demoralization it entails, may be abated but I note its existence as a salient proof that we live in a time when, among the objects offered to the desire of a man, wealth and the direct accompaniments and fruits of wealth have of late years augmented their always dangerous preponderance.

In all times and all places and all stages of its existence, it is the office of the University as such to embody a protest and to work a comprehensive and powerful machinery in rebuke and in abatement of this preponderance — in all times, ancient, mediæval, modern; in all places, in Athens and Alexandria, in the Padua and Bologna and the Paris and Oxford of the Middle Ages, and in the German, Scottish, English and all the other Universities of to-day; in all stages of their existence, for the ancients do not seem to have had more than the rudiment of our University, which it was reserved for the Christian period to bring up to its full maturity and development. It is not from this source that the age has derived its tendencies to excess in money-making pursuits and in material enjoyment. This is the home of hard labour and of modest emoluments. Here, undoubtedly, it is that many a Scottish youth obtains the means of advancement in life, but the improvement in his condition to which they lead him flows from the improvement of his mind, from the exercise and expansion of his power to perceive and to reflect, from the formation of habits of attention and application, from a bias given to character in favour of cultivating intelligence for its own sake as well as for the sake of the direct advantages it brings. These advantages lie in the far future, and do not administer to the feverish excitements which are of necessity in various degrees incidental to the pursuits of the modern commercial world. The habits of mind formed by Universities are founded on sobriety and tranquillity; they help to settle the spirits of a man firmly upon the centre of gravity; they tend to self-command, self-government, and that genuine self-respect which has in it nothing of self-worship, for it is the reverence that each man ought to feel for the nature that God has given him and for the laws of nature. It is one thing to plough and sow with the expectation of the harvest in due season when the year shall have come round; it is another to ransack the ground in the gold-field with the heated hope and craving for vast returns to-morrow or to-day. All honour, then, to the University; because, while it prepares young men in the most useful manner for the practical purposes of life, it embodies a protest against the excessive dominion of wordly appetites, and supplies a powerful agency for neutralizing the specific dangers of this age. W. E. GLADSTONE.

B. POETRY.

I. LYRIC AND EPIC POEMS.

1. The National Anthem.

1. God save our gracious Queen,
   Long live our noble Queen,
     God save the Queen!
   Send her victorious,
   Happy and glorious,
   Long to reign over us,
     God save the Queen.

2. O Lord, our God, arise,
   Scatter her enemies,
     And let them fall!
   Confound their politics,
   Frustrate their knavish tricks!
   On her our hope we fix:
     God save us all.

3. Thy choicest gifts in store,
   On her be pleased to pour,
     Long may she reign!
   May she defend our laws,
   And ever give us cause
   To sing, with heart and voice,
     God save the Queen.

4. O grant her long to see
   Friendship and amity
     Always increase!
   May she her scepter sway,
   All loyal souls obey,
   Join heart and voice, Huzza!
     God save the Queen.

   ANONYMOUS.

2. "Rule, Britannia."

1. When Britain first, at Heaven's command,
     Arose from out the azure main;
   This was the charter of the land,
     And guardian angels sung this strain:
       "Rule, Britannia, rule the waves:
       Britons never will be slaves!"

2. The nations not so blest as thee.
   Must, in their turns, to tyrants fall:
   While thou shalt flourish great and free,
   The dread and envy of them all.
       "Rule," etc.

3. Still more majestic shalt thou rise,
   More dreadful from each foreign stroke:
   As the loud blast that tears the skies
   Serves but to root thy native oak.
       "Rule," etc.

4. Thee haughty tyrants ne'er shall tame:
   All their attempts to bend thee down
   Will but arouse thy generous flame;
   But work their woe, and thy renown.
       "Rule," etc.

5. To thee belongs the rural reign;
   Thy cities shall with commerce shine:
   All thine shall be the subject main,
   And every shore it circles thine.
       "Rule," etc.

6. The Muses, still with freedom found,
   Shall to thy happy coast repair:
   Blest isle! with matchless beauty crowned,
   And manly hearts to guard the fair.
       "Rule, Britannia, rule the waves;
       Britons never will be slaves!"

JAMES THOMSON.

3. The Last Rose of Summer.

1. 'Tis the last rose of summer
   Left blooming alone;
   All her lovely companions
   Are faded and gone;
   No flower of her kindred,
   No rose-bud is nigh,
   To reflect back her blushes,
   Or give sigh for sigh.

2. I'll not leave thee, thou lone one!
   To pine on the stem;
   Since the lovely are sleeping,
   Go, sleep thou with them.
   Thus kindly I scatter
   Thy leaves o'er the bed,
   Where thy mates of the garden
   Lie scentless and dead.

3. So soon may I follow,
   When friendships decay,
   And from Love's shining circle
   The gems drop away!
   When true hearts lie withered,
   And fond ones are flown,
   Oh! who would inhabit
   This bleak world alone?

THOMAS MOORE.

4. All that's Bright Must Fade.

1. All that's bright must fade, —
 The brightest still the fleetest;
 All that's sweet was made
 But to be lost when sweetest.
 Stars that shine and fall; —
 The flower that drops in spring-
 ing: —
 These, alas! are types of all
 To which our hearts are clinging.
 All that's bright must fade, —
 The brightest still the fleetest;
 All that's sweet was made
 But to be lost when sweetest!

2. Who would seek or prize
 Delights that end in aching?
 Who would trust to ties
 That every hour are breaking?
 Better far to be
 In utter darkness lying,
 Than to be blessed with light and
 see
 That light for ever flying.
 All that's bright must fade, —
 The brightest still the fleetest;
 All that's sweet was made
 But to be lost when sweetest!

THOMAS MOORE.

5. Those Evening Bells.

1. Those evening bells! those evening bells!
 How many a tale their music tells,
 Of youth, and home, and that sweet time,
 When last I heard their soothing chime.

2. Those joyous hours are past away,
 And many a heart, that then was gay,
 Within the tomb now darkly dwells,
 And hears no more those evening bells.

3. And so 'twill be when I am gone;
 That tuneful peal will still ring on,
 While other bards shall walk the dells,
 And sing your praise, sweet evening bells!

THOMAS MOORE.

6. That Dream of Home.

1. Who has not felt how sadly sweet
 The dream of home, the dream of home
 Steals o'er the heart, too soon to fleet,
 When far o'er sea or land we roam?
 Sunlight more soft may o'er us fall,
 To greener shores our bark may come;
 But far more bright, more dear than all,
 That dream of home, that dream of home.

2. Ask of the sailor youth, when far
    His light bark bounds o'er ocean's foam,
   What charms him most, when evening's star
    Smiles o'er the wave? — to dream of home.
   Fond thoughts of absent friends and loves
    At that sweet hour around him come;
   His heart's best joy where'er he roves,
    That dream of home, that dream of home.
                                    THOMAS MOORE.

7. John Barleycorn.

1. There was three kings into the east,
    Three kings both great and high,
   And they had sworn a solemn oath
    John Barleycorn should die.

2. They took a plough and ploughed him down,
    Put clods upon his head;
   And they ha'e sworn a solemn oath
    John Barleycorn was dead.

3. But the cheerful Spring came kindly on,
    And show'rs began to fall;
   John Barleycorn got up again,
    And sore surprised them all.

4. The sultry suns of Summer came,
    And he grew thick and strong,
   His head weel armed wi' pointed spears,
    That no one should him wrong.

5. The sober Autumn entered mild,
    When he grew wan and pale;
   His bending joints and drooping head
    Showed he began to fail.

6. His colour sickened more and more,
    He faded into age,
   And then his enemies began
    To shew their deadly rage.

7. They've ta'en a weapon, long and sharp,
    And cut him by the knee;
   Then tied him fast upon a cart,
    Like a rogue for forgery.

8. They laid him down upon his back,
    And cudgelled him full sore;
  They hung him up before the storm,
    And turned him o'er and o'er.

9. They filléd up a darksome pit
    With water to the brim,
  They heavéd in John Barleycorn,
    There let him sink or swim.

10. They laid him out upon the floor,
     To work him farther woe,
   And still, as signs of life appeared,
     They tossed him to and fro.

11. They wasted o'er a scorching flame
     The marrow of his bones;
   But a miller used him worst of all,
     For he crushed him 'tween two stones.

12. And they ha'e ta'en his very heart's blood,
     And drank it round and round;
   And still the more and more they drank,
     Their joy did more abound.

13. John Barleycorn was a hero bold,
     Of noble enterprise,
   For if you do but taste his blood,
     'Twill make your courage rise.

14. 'Twill make a man forget his woe:
     'Twill heighten all his joy:
   'Twill make the widow's heart to sing,
     Tho' the tear were in her eye.

15. Then let us toast John Barleycorn,
     Each man a glass in hand;
   And may his great posterity
     Ne'er fail in old Scotland.

ROBERT BURNS.

8. Farewell to the Highlands.

1. My heart's in the Highlands, my heart is not here;
My heart's in the Highlands, a chasing the deer:
Chasing the wild deer, and following the roe,
My heart's in the Highlands wherever I go.

Farewell to the Highlands, farewell to the North,
The birth-place of valour, the country of worth;
Wherever I wander, wherever I rove,
The hills of the Highlands for ever I love.

2. Farewell to the mountains high covered with snow;
Farewell to the straths and green valleys below:
Farewell to the forests and wild-hanging woods;
Farewell to the torrents and loud-pouring floods;
My heart's in the Highlands, my heart is not here;
My heart's in the Highlands, a chasing the deer;
Chasing the wild deer, and following the roe,
My heart's in the Highlands wherever I go.

ROBERT BURNS.

9. A Song of Spring.

1. The cock is crowing,
The stream is flowing,
The small birds twitter,
The lake doth glitter,
The green field sleeps in the sun;
The oldest and youngest
Are at work with the strongest;
The cattle are grazing,
Their heads never raising;
There are forty feeding like one.

2. Like an army defeated
The snow has retreated,
And now doth fare ill
On the top of the bare hill:
The ploughboy is whooping — anon
— anon:
There's joy in the mountains;
There's life in the fountains;
Small clouds are sailing,
Blue sky prevailing;
The rain is over and gone!

WILLIAM WORDSWORTH.

10. We are Seven.

1. A simple child, dear brother Jim,
That lightly draws its breath,
And feels its life in every limb,
What should it know of death?

2. I met a little cottage girl:
She was eight years old, she said;
Her hair was thick with many a curl
That clustered round her head.

3. She had a rustic, woodland air,
And she was wildly clad:
Her eyes were fair, and very fair; —
Her beauty made me glad.

4. 'Sisters and brothers, little maid,
How many may you be?'
'How many? Seven in all,' she said,
And, wondering, looked at me.

5. 'And where are they? I pray you tell.'
She answered, 'Seven are we;

And two of us at Conway dwell,
And two are gone to sea.

6. Two of us in the churchyard lie,
My sister and my brother,
And, in the churchyard cottage, I
Dwell near them, with my mother.'

7. 'You say that two at Conway dwell,
And two are gone to sea,
Yet ye are seven! — I pray you tell,
Sweet maid, how this may be.'

8. Then did the little maid reply,
'Seven boys and girls are we:
Two of us in the churchyard lie,
Beneath the churchyard tree.'

9. 'You run about, my little maid,
Your limbs they are alive:
If two are in the churchyard laid,
Then ye are only five.'

10. 'Their graves are green, they may be seen,'
The little maid replied,
'Twelve steps, or more, from mother's door,
And they are side by side.

11. My stockings there I often knit,
My kerchief there I hem:
And there upon the ground I sit,
And sing a song to them.

12. And often after sunset, sir,
When it is light and fair,
I take my little porringer,
And eat my supper there.

13. The first that died was sister Jane;
In bed she moaning lay,
Till God released her of her pain;
And then she went away.

14. So in the churchyard she was laid;
And when the grass was dry,
Together round her grave we played,
My brother John, and I.

15. And when the ground was white with snow,
And I could run and slide,
My brother John was forced to go,
And he lies by her side.'

16. 'How many are you then,' said I,
'If they two are in heaven?'
Quick was the little maid's reply,
'O, master! we are seven.'

17. 'But they are dead; those two are dead!
Their spirits are in heaven!'
'Twas throwing words away;
for still
The little maid would have her will,
And said, 'Nay, master! we are seven!'

WILLIAM WORDSWORTH.

II. To Milton.

Milton! thou shouldst be living at this hour;
England hath need of thee! she is a fen
Of stagnant waters; altar, sword and pen,

5 Fire-side, the heroic wealth of hall and bower,
   Have forfeited their ancient English dower
   Of inward happiness. We are selfish men;
   Oh! raise us up, return to us again:
   And give us manners, virtue, freedom, power.
10 Thy soul was like a star, and dwelt apart;
   Thou hadst a voice whose sound was like the sea!
   Pure as the naked heavens, majestic, free,
   So didst thou travel on life's common way
   In cheerful godliness; and yet thy heart
15 The lowliest duties on herself did lay.

        WILLIAM WORDSWORTH.

12. The Homes of England.

1. The stately Homes of England,
   How beautiful they stand!
   Amidst their tall ancestral trees,
   O'er all the pleasant land.
   The deer across their greensward bound,
   Through shade and sunny gleam;
   And the swan glides past them with the sound
   Of some rejoicing stream.

2. The merry Homes of England!
   Around their hearths by night,
   What gladsome looks of Household love
   Meet in the ruddy light!
   There woman's voice flows forth in song,
   Or childhood's tale is told,
   Or lips move tunefully along
   Some glorious page of old.

3. The blessed Homes of England!
   How softly on their bowers
   Is laid the holy quietness
   That breathes from Sabbath-hours!
   Solemn, yet sweet, the church-bells' chime
   Floats through their woods at morn;
   All other sounds, in that still time,
   Of breeze and leaf are born.

4. The cottage Homes of England!
   By thousands on her plains,

They are smiling o'er the silvery brooks,
And round the hamlet-fanes,
Through glowing orchards forth they peep,
Each from its nook of leaves;
And fearless there the lowly sleep,
As the bird beneath the eaves.

5. The free, fair Homes of England!
Long, long, in hut and hall,
May hearts of native proof be reared
To guard each hallowed wall!
And green for ever be the groves,
And bright the flowery sod,
Where first the child's glad spirit loves
Its country and its God!

FELICIA HEMANS.

13. A Psalm of Life.

1. Tell me not, in mournful numbers,
    "Life is but an empty dream!"
For the soul is dead that slumbers,
    And things are not what they seem.

2. Life is real! Life is earnest!
    And the grave is not its goal;
"Dust thou art, to dust returnest,"
    Was not spoken of the soul.

3. Not enjoyment, and not sorrow,
    Is our destined end or way;
But to act, that each to-morrow
    Find us farther than to-day.

4. Art is long, and Time is fleeting;
    And our hearts, though stout and brave,
Still, like muffled drums, are beating
    Funeral marches to the grave.

5. In the world's broad field of battle,
    In the bivouac of Life,
Be not like dumb, driven cattle!
    Be a hero in the strife!

6. Trust no Future, howe'er pleasant!
    Let the dead Past bury its dead!
Act, — act in the living Present!
    Heart within, and God o'erhead!

7. Lives of great men all remind us
    We can make our lives sublime,
    And, departing, leave behind us
    Footprints on the sands of time;

8. Footprints, that perhaps another,
    Sailing o'er life's solemn main,
    A forlorn and shipwrecked brother,
    Seeing, shall take heart again.

9. Let us, then, be up and doing,
    With a heart for any fate;
    Still achieving, still pursuing,
    Learn to labour and to wait.
                                H. W. LONGFELLOW.

14. The Village Blacksmith.

1. Under a spreading chestnut-tree
    The village smithy stands:
    The smith, a migthy man is he,
    With large and sinewy hands;
    And the muscles of his brawny arms
    Are strong as iron bands.

2. His hair is crisp, and black, and long,
    His face is like the tan;
    His brow is wet with honest sweat,
    He earns whate'er he can,
    And looks the whole world in the face,
    For he owes not any man.

3. Week in, week out, from morn till night,
    You can hear his bellows blow;
    You can hear him swing his heavy sledge,
    With measured beat and slow,
    Like a sexton ringing the village bell,
    When the evening sun is low.

4. And children coming home from school
    Look in at the open door:
    They love to see the flaming forge,
    And hear the bellows roar,
    And catch the burning sparks that fly
    Like chaff from a thrashing-floor.

5. He goes on Sunday to the church,
   And sits among his boys;
He hears the parson pray and preach,
   He hears his daughter's voice
Singing in the village choir,
   And it makes his heart rejoice.

6. It sounds to him like her mother's voice,
   Singing in Paradise!
He needs must think of her once more,
   How in the grave she lies;
And with his hard, rough hand he wipes
   A tear out of his eyes.

7. Toiling, — rejoicing, — sorrowing,
   Onward through life he goes:
Each morning sees some task begin,
   Each evening sees it close:
Something attempted, something done,
   Has earned a night's repose.

8. Thanks, thanks to thee, my worthy friend,
   For the lesson thou hast taught!
Thus at the flaming forge of life
   Our fortunes must be wrought;
Thus on its sounding anvil shaped
   Each burning deed and thought!

H. W. LONGFELLOW.

15. The Slave's Dream.

1. Beside the ungathered rice he lay,
   His sickle in his hand;
His breast was bare, his matted hair
   Was buried in the sand.
Again, in the mist and shadow of sleep,
   He saw his Native Land.

2. Wide through the landscape of his dreams
   The lordly Niger flowed;
Beneath the palm-trees on the plain
   Once more a king he strode,
And heard the tinkling caravans
   Descend the mountain-road.

3. He saw once more his dark-eyed queen
    Among her children stand;
  They clasped his neck, they kissed his cheeks,
    They held him by the hand! —
  A tear burst from the sleeper's lids,
    And fell into the sand.

4. And then at furious speed he rode
    Along the Niger's bank;
  His bridle-reins were golden chains,
    And, with a martial clank,
  At each leap he could feel his scabbard of steel,
    Smiting his stallion's flank.

5. Before him, like a blood-red flag,
    The bright flamingoes flew;
  From morn till night he followed their flight,
    O'er plains where the tamarind grew,
  Till he saw the roofs of Caffre huts,
    And the ocean rose to view.

6. At night he heard the lion roar,
    And the hyena scream;
  And the river-horse, as he crushed the reeds
    Beside some hidden stream;
  And it passed, like a glorious roll of drums,
    Through the triumph of his dream.

7. The forests with their myriad tongues,
    Shouted of liberty;
  And the Blast of the Desert cried aloud,
    With a voice so wild and free,
  That he started in his sleep and smiled
    At their tempestuous glee.

8. He did not feel the driver's whip,
    Nor the burning heat of day;
  For death had illumined the Land of Sleep,
    And his lifeless body lay
  A worn-out fetter, that the soul
    Had broken and thrown away!

H. W. LONGFELLOW.

16. The Luck of Edenhall.

1. Of Edenhall, the youthful Lord
   Bids sound the festal trumpet's call,
   He rises at the banquet board,
   And cries, 'mid the drunken revellers all,
   "Now bring me the Luck of Edenhall!"

2. The butler hears the words with pain,
   The house's oldest seneschal,
   Takes slow from its silken cloth again
   The drinking glass of crystal tall:
   They call it the Luck of Edenhall.

3. Then said the Lord: "This glass to praise,
   Fill with red wine from Portugal!"
   The gray-beard with trembling hand obeys;
   A purple light shines over all,
   It beams from the Luck of Edenhall.

4. Then speaks the Lord, and waves it light,
   "This glass of flashing crystal tall
   Gave to my sires the Fountain-Sprite;
   She wrote in it: *If this glass doth fall,
   Farewell then, O Luck of Edenhall!*

5. 'Twas right a goblet the Fate should be
   Of the joyous race of Edenhall!
   Deep draughts drink we right willingly;
   And willingly ring, with merry call,
   Kling! klang! to the Luck of Edenhall!"

6. First rings it deep, and full, and mild,
   Like to the song of a nightingale;
   Then like the roar of a torrent wild:
   Then mutters at last like the thunder's fall,
   The glorious Luck of Edenhall.

7. "For its Keeper takes a race of might
   The fragile goblet of crystal tall;
   It has lasted longer than is right;
   Kling! klang! — with a harder blow than all
   Will I try the Luck of Edenhall!"

8. As the goblet ringing flies apart,
   Suddenly cracks the vaulted hall;
   And through the rift, the wild flames start;
   The guests in dust are scattered all,
   With the Breaking Luck of Edenhall!

9. In storms the foe, with fire and sword;
   He in the night had scaled the wall,
   Slain by the sword lies the youthful Lord,
   But holds in his hand the crystal tall,
   The shattered Luck of Edenhall.

10. On the morrow the butler gropes alone,
    The gray-beard in the desert hall,
    He seeks his Lord's burnt skeleton,
    He seeks in the dismal ruin's fall
    The shards of the Luck of Edenhall.

11. "The stone wall," saith he, "doth fall aside,
    Down must the stately columns fall;
    Glass is this earth's Luck and Pride;
    In atoms shall fall this earthly ball
    One day like the Luck of Edenhall!"

    H. W. LONGFELLOW.

17. Beowulf's Expedition to the Danes.

Thus then, much care-worn, The son of Healfden
Sorrowed evermore, Nor might the prudent hero
His woe avert. The war was too hard.
5 Too loath and longsome, That on the people came,
Dire wrath and grim, Of night-woes the worst.
This from home heard Higelac's Thane,
Good among the Goths, Grendel's deeds.
He was of mankind In might the strongest,
10 At that day Of this life,
Noble and stalwart. He bade him a sea-ship,
A goodly one, prepare. Quoth he, the war-king,
Over the swan's road, Seek he would
The mighty monarch, Since he wanted men.
15 For him that journey His prudent fellows
Straight made ready, Those that loved him,
Had the good-man Of the Gothic people
Champions chosen, Of those that keenest

He might find, Some fifteen men.
20 The sea-wood sought he, The warrior showed,
Sea-crafty man! The landmarks,
And first went forth. The ship was on the waves,
Boat under the cliffs. The barons ready
To the prow mounted. The streams they whirled
25 The sea against the sands. The chieftains bore
On the naked breast Bright ornaments,
War-gear, Goth-like. The men shoved off,
Men on their willing-way, The bounden wood.
Then went over the sea-waves, Hurried by the wind,
30 The ship with foamy neck, Most like a sea-fowl,
Till about one hour Of the second day
The curved prow Had passed onward
So that the sailors The land saw,
The shore-cliffs shining, Mountains steep,
35 And broad sea-noses. Then was the sea-sailing
Of the earl at an end. Then up speedily
The Weather people On the land went,
The sea-bark moored, Their mail-sarks shook,
Their war-weeds. God thanked they,
40 That to them the sea-journey Easy had been.
Then from the wall beheld The warden of the Scyldings,
He who the sea-cliffs Had in his keeping,
Bear o'er the balks The bright shields,
The war-weapons speedily. Him the doubt disturbed
45 In his mind's thought, What these men might be.
Went then to the shore, On his steed riding,
The Thane of Hrothgar. Before the host he shook
His warden's staff in hand, In measured words demanded,
"What men are ye, War-gear wearing,
50 Host in harness, Who thus the brown keel
Over the water-street Leading come
Hither over the sea? I these boundaries
As shore-warden hold; That in the Land of the Danes
Nothing loathsome With a ship-crew
55 Scathe us might. Ne'er saw I mightier
Earl upon earth Than is your own,
Hero in harness. Not seldom this warrior
Is in weapons distinguished; Never his beauty belies him,
His peerless countenance! Now would I fain
60 Your origin know, Ere ye forth

      As false spies Into the Land of the Danes
      Farther fare, Now, ye dwellers afar off!
      Ye sailors of the sea! Listen to my
      One-fold thought. Quickest is best
65 To make known Whence your coming may be."
                                H. W. LONGFELLOW.

18. Belshazzar.

1. The King was on his throne,
   The Satraps thronged the hall;
   A thousand bright lamps shone
   O'er that high festival.
   A thousand cups of gold,
   In Judah deemed divine —
   Jehovah's vessels hold
   The godless heathen's wine!

2. In that same hour and hall,
   The fingers of a hand
   Came forth against the wall,
   And wrote as if on sand:
   The fingers of a man; —
   A solitary hand
   Along the letters ran,
   And traced them like a wand.

3. The monarch saw, and shook,
   And bade no more rejoice;
   All bloodless waxed his look
   And tremulous his voice.
   'Let the men of lore appear,
   The wisest of the earth,
   And expound the words of fear,
   Which mar our royal mirth.'

4. Chaldea's seers are good,
   But here they have no skill!
   And the unknown letters stood
   Untold and awful still.
   And Babel's men of age
   Are wise and deep in lore;
   But now they were not sage,
   They saw — but knew no more.

5. A captive in the land,
   A stranger and a youth,
   He heard the king's command,
   He saw that writing's truth.
   The lamps around were bright,
   The prophecy in view;
   He read it on that night, —
   The morrow proved it true.

6. 'Belshazzar's grave is made,
   His kingdom passed away,
   He in the balance weighed,
   Is light and worthless clay,
   The shroud, his robe of state,
   His canopy, the stone;
   The Mede is at his gate!
   The Persian on his throne!'
                      LORD BYRON.

19. The Destruction of Sennacherib's Army.

1. The Assyrian came down like the wolf on the fold,
   And his cohorts were gleaming in purple and gold:
   And the sheen of their spears was like stars on the sea,
   When the blue wave rolls nightly on deep Galilee.

2. Like the leaves of the forest when Summer is green,
   That host with their banners at sunset were seen:
   Like the leaves of the forest when Autumn hath blown,
   That host on the morrow lay withered and strown.

3. For the Angel of Death spread his wings on the blast.
And breathed in the face of the foe as he passed;
And the eyes of the sleepers waxed deadly and chill,
And their hearts but once heaved, and for ever grew still!

4. And there lay the steed with his nostrils all wide,
But through it there rolled not the breath of his pride;
And the foam of his gasping lay white on the turf,
And cold as the spray of the rock-beating surf.

5. And there lay the rider, distorted and pale,
With the dew on his brow and the rust on his mail;
And the tents were all silent, the banners alone,
The lances unlifted, the trumpet unblown.

6. And the widows of Asshur are loud in their wail,
And the idols are broke in the temple of Baal;
And the might of the Gentile, unsmote by the sword,
Hath melted like snow in the glance of the Lord!

LORD BYRON.

20. Time.

Unfathomable Sea, whose waves are years!
 Ocean of Time, whose waters of deep woe
Are brackish with the salt of human tears!
 Thou shoreless flood which in thy ebb and flow
Claspest the limits of mortality,
 And, sick of prey, yet howling on for more,
Vomitest thy wrecks on its inhospitable shore;
 Treacherous in calm, and terrible in storm,
  Who shall put forth on thee,
  Unfathomable Sea?

PERCY BYSSHE SHELLEY.

21. To the Night.

1. Swiftly walk over the western wave,
  Spirit of Night!
 Out of the misty eastern cave
 Where, all the long and lone daylight,
 Thou wovest dreams of joy and fear
 Which make thee terrible and dear, —
  Swift be thy flight!

2. Wrap thy form in a mantle grey,
 Star-inwrought!
Blind with thine hair the eyes of day,
Kiss her until she be wearied out,
Then wander o'er city, and sea, and land
Touching all with thine opiate wand —
 Come, long-sought!

3. When I arose and saw the dawn,
 I sighed for thee;
When light rode high, and the dew was gone,
And noon lay heavy on flower and tree,
And the weary Day turned to her rest,
Lingering like an unloved guest,
 I sighed for thee.

4. Thy brother Death came, and cried,
 Wouldst thou me?
Thy sweet child Sleep, the filmy-eyed,
Murmured like a noontide bee,
Shall I nestle near thy side?
Wouldst thou me? — And I replied,
 No, not thee.

5. Death will come when thou art dead,
 Soon, too soon —
Sleep will come when thou art fled;
Of neither would I ask the boon
I ask of thee, beloved Night —
Swift be thine approaching flight,
 Come soon, soon!

PERCY BYSSHE SHELLEY.

22. The Wanderers of the World.

1. Tell me, thou star, whose wings of light
Speed thee in thy fiery flight,
In what cavern of the night
 Will thy pinions close now?

2. Tell me, moon, thou pale and grey
Pilgrim of heaven's homeless way,
In what depth of night or day
 Seekest thou repose now?

3. Weary wind who wanderest
   Like the world's rejected guest,
   Hast thou still some secret nest
   On the tree or billow?

   PERCY BYSSHE SHELLEY.

23. Complaints of the Poor.

1. 'And wherefore do the poor complain?' the rich man asked of me.
   'Come walk abroad with me,' I said, 'and I will answer thee.'
   'Twas evening, and the frozen streets were cheerless to behold,
   And we were wrapt and coated well, and yet we were a-cold.

2. We met an old bareheaded man — his locks were few and white:
   I asked him what he did abroad in that cold winter's night.
   'Twas bitter keen, indeed, he said, but at home no fire had he,
   And therefore he had come abroad to ask for charity.

3. We met a young barefooted child, and she begged loud and bold:
   I asked her what she did abroad when the wind it blew so cold.
   She said her father was at home, and he lay sick a-bed;
   And therefore was it she was sent abroad to beg for bread.

4. We saw a woman sitting down upon a stone to rest;
   She had a baby at her back, and another at her breast.
   I asked her why she loitered there, when the night-wind was so chill; —
   She turned her head, and bade the child that screamed behind be still.

5. She told us that her husband served, a soldier, far away,
   And therefore to her parish she was begging back her way.
   I turned me to the rich man then, for silently stood he; —
   'You asked me why the poor complain, and these have answered thee.

   ROBERT SOUTHEY.

24. My Days among the Dead are Passed.

1. My days among the Dead are passed;
     Around me I behold,
   Where'er these casual eyes are cast.
     The mighty minds of old;
   My never-failing friends are they,
   With whom I converse day by day.

2. With them I take delight in weal,
   And seek relief in woe;
   And while I understand and feel
   How much to them I owe,
   My cheeks have often been bedewed
   With tears of thoughtful gratitude.

3. My thoughts are with the Dead; with them
   I live in long-past years,
   Their virtues love, their faults condemn
   Partake their hopes and fears,
   And from their lessons seek and find
   Instruction with an humble mind.

4. My hopes are with the Dead; anon
   My place with them will be,
   And I with them shall travel on
   Through all Futurity,
   Yet leaving here a name, I trust,
   That will not perish in the dust.
                                   ROBERT SOUTHEY

25. The Well of St. Keyne.

1. A Well there is in the West country,
   And a clearer one never was seen;
   There is not a wife in the west country
   But has heard of the Well of St. Keyne.

2. And oak and an elm tree stand beside,
   And behind does an ash tree grow;
   And a willow from the bank above
   Droops to the water below.

3. A traveller came to the Well of St. Keyne.
   Joyfully he drew nigh:
   For from cock-crow he had been travelling,
   And there was not a cloud in the sky.

4. He drank of the water so cool and clear,
   For hot and thirsty was he;
   And he sat down upon the bank,
   Under the willow tree.

5. There came a man from the neighbouring town,
   At the well to fill his pail;

By the well-side he rested it,
    And he bade the stranger hail.

6. "Now, art thou a bachelor, stranger?" quoth he,
    "For an if thou hast a wife,
The happiest draught thou hast drunk this day
    That ever thou didst in thy life.

7. Or has thy good woman, if one thou hast,
    Ever here in Cornwall been?
For an if she have I'll venture my life
    She has drunk of the Well of St. Keyne."

8. "I have left a good woman who never was here,"
    The stranger he made reply;
"But that my draught should be better for that,
    I pray you answer me why."

9. "St. Keyne," quoth the Cornishman, "many a time
    Drank of this crystal Well;
And before the angel summoned her
    She laid on the water a spell: —

10. If the husband, of this gifted Well
    Shall drink before his wife,
A happy man henceforth is he,
    For he shall be master for life.

11. But if the wife should drink of it first,
    Woe be to the husband then!" —
The stranger stooped to the Well of St. Keyne,
    And drank of the water again.

12. "You drank of the Well, I warrant, betimes,"
    He to the Cornishman said;
But the Cornishman smiled as the stranger spake,
    And sheepishly shook his head.

13. "I hastened as soon as the wedding was done,
    And left my wife in the porch;
But in truth she had been wiser than I,
    For she took a bottle to church."

ROBERT SOUTHEY.

26. The Soldier's Dream.

1. Our bugles sung truce; for the night-cloud had lowered,
   And the sentinel stars set their watch in the sky;
   And thousands had sunk on the ground overpowered,
   The weary to sleep, and the wounded to die.

2. When reposing, that night on my pallet of straw,
   By the wolf-scaring faggot that guarded the slain,
   At the dead of the night a sweet vision I saw;
   And thrice, ere the morning, I dreamt it again.

3. Methought from the battle-field's dreadful array,
   Far, far I had roamed on a desolate track:
   'Twas autumn, and sunshine arose on the way
   To the home of my fathers, that welcomed me back.

4. I flew to the pleasant fields traversed so oft
   In life's morning march, when my bosom was young;
   I heard my own mountain-goats bleating aloft,
   And knew the sweet strain that the corn-reapers sung.

5. Then pledged we the wine-cup; and fondly I swore,
   From my home and my weeping friends never to part,
   My little ones kissed me a thousand times o'er;
   And my wife sobbed aloud, in her fulness of heart:

6. "Stay — stay with us; rest: thou art weary, and worn."
   And fain was their war-broken soldier to stay;
   But sorrow returned with the dawning of morn,
   And the voice in my dreaming ear melted away.

   THOMAS CAMPBELL.

27. Ye Mariners of England.

1. Ye Mariners of England,
   That guard our native seas;
   Whose flag has braved, a thousand years,
   The battle and the breeze!
   Your glorious standard launch again,
   To match another foe!
   And sweep through the deep,
   While the stormy tempests blow;
   While the battle rages loud and long,
   And the stormy tempests blow.

2. The spirits of your fathers
　　Shall start from every wave! —
　　For the Deck it was their field of fame,
　　And Ocean was their grave:
　　Where Blake and mighty Nelson fell,
　　Your manly hearts shall glow,
　　As ye sweep through the deep,
　　While the stormy tempests blow;
　　While the battle rages loud and long,
　　And the stormy tempests blow.

3. Britannia needs no bulwarks —
　　No towers along the steep;
　　Her march is o'er the mountain waves,
　　Her home is on the deep.
　　With thunders from her native oak,
　　She quells the floods below,
　　As they roar on the shore,
　　When the stormy tempests blow:
　　When the battle rages loud and long,
　　And the stormy tempests blow.

4. The meteor flag of England
　　Shall yet terrific burn;
　　Till danger's troubled night depart,
　　And the star of peace return.
　　Then, then, ye ocean warriors!
　　Our song and feast shall flow
　　To the fame of your name,
　　When the storm has ceased to blow;
　　When the fiery fight is heard no more,
　　And the storm has ceased to blow.
　　　　　　　　THOMAS CAMPBELL.

28. William the Conqueror.

1. Great King William spread before him
　　All his stores of wealth untold,
　　Diamonds, emeralds, and rubies,
　　Heaps on heaps of minted gold.
　Mournfully he gazed upon it,
　　As it glittered in the sun,
　Sighing to himself, "Oh, treasure!
　　Held in care, by sorrow won;

Millions think me rich and happy,
  But, alas! before me piled,
I would give thee ten times over
  For the slumbers of a child."

2. Great King William from his turret
  Heard the martial trumpets blow,
Saw the crimson banners floating
  Of a countless host below:
Saw their weapons flash in sunlight,
  As the squadrons trod the sward;
And he sighed, "Oh, mighty army,
  Hear thy miserable lord:
At my word thy legions gather —
  At my nod thy captains bend —
But with all thy power and splendour
  I would give thee for a friend!"

3. Great King William stood on Windsor,
  Looking from its castled height,
O'er his wide-spread realm of England,
  Glittering in the morning light;
Looking on the tranquil river
  And the forest waving free.
And he sighed, "Oh, land of beauty,
  Fondled by the circling sea,
Mine thou art, but I would yield thee,
  And be happy, could I gain,
In exchange, a peasant's garden
  And a conscience free from stain."

C. MACKAY.

29. Lullaby.

1. O, hush thee, my baby! — thy sire was a knight,
Thy mother a lady, both lovely and bright;
The woods and the glens, from the towers which we see,
They all are belonging, dear baby, to thee.

2. O, fear not the bugle, though loudly it blows,
It calls but the warders that guard thy repose;
Their bows would be bended, their blades would be red,
Ere the step of a foemann draws near to thy bed.

3. O, hush thee, my baby! — the time soon will come,
When thy sleep shall be broken by trumpet and drum;
Then hush thee, my darling, take rest while you may,
For strife comes with manhood, and waking with day!
Walter Scott.

30. Lady Clare.

1. It was the time when lilies blow,
    And clouds are highest up in air,
Lord Ronald brought a lily-white doe
    To give his cousin, Lady Clare.

2. I trow they did not part in scorn;
    Lovers long betrothed were they:
They two will wed to-morrow morn;
    God's blessing on the day.

3. "He does not love me for my birth,
    Nor for my lands, so broad and fair; —
He loves me for my own true worth,
    And that is well," said Lady Clare.

4. In there came old Alice the nurse;
    Said, "Who was this that went from thee?"
"It was my cousin," said Lady Clare;
    "To-morrow he weds with me."

5. "O God be thanked!" said Alice the nurse,
    "That all comes round so just and fair:
Lord Ronald is heir of all your lands,
    And you are not the Lady Clare."

6. "Are ye out of your mind, my nurse, my nurse,"
    Said Lady Clare, "that ye speak so wild?"
"As God's above," said Alice the nurse,
    "I speak the truth — you are my child.

7. The old Earl's daughter died at my breast
    I speak the truth, as I live by bread!
I buried her like my own sweet child,
    And put my child in her stead."

8. "Falsely, falsely have ye done,
    O mother," she said, "if this be true:
To keep the best man under the sun
    So many years from his due."

9. "Nay, now, my child," said Alice the nurse;
   "But keep the secret for your life,
   And all you have will be Lord Ronald's
   When you are man and wife."

10. "If I'm a beggar born," she said,
    "I will speak out, for I dare not lie; —
    Pull off, pull off the brooch of gold,
    And fling the diamond necklace by!"

11. "Nay, now, my child," said Alice the nurse;
    "But keep the secret all ye can."
    She said, "Not so; but I will know
    If there be any faith in man."

12. "Nay, now, what faith?" said Alice the nurse;
    "The man will cleave unto his right." —
    "And he shall have it," the lady replied,
    "Though I should die, to-night!"

13. "Yet give one kiss to your mother dear!
    Alas, my child, I sinned for thee." —
    "O mother, mother, mother," she said,
    "So strange it seems to me.

14. Yet here's a kiss for my mother dear, —
    My mother dear, if this be so;
    And lay your hand upon my head,
    And bless me, mother, ere I go."

15. She clad herself in a russet gown;
    She was no longer Lady Clare:
    She went by dale, and she went by down,
    With a single rose in her hair.

16. The lily-white doe Lord Ronald had brought
    Leapt up from where she lay,
    Dropt her head in the maiden's hand,
    And followed her all the way.

17. Down stept Lord Ronald from his tower:
    "O Lady Clare, you shame your worth?
    Why come you drest like a village maid,
    That are the flower of the earth?"

18. "If I come drest like a village maid,
    I am but as my fortunes are;

I am a beggar born," she said,
"And not the Lady Clare."

19. "Play me no tricks," said Lord Ronald,
"For I am yours in word and deed; —
Play me no tricks," said Lord Ronald:
"Your riddle is hard to read."

20. O, and proudly stood she up!
Her heart within her did not fail;
She looked into Lord Ronald's eyes,
And told him all her nurse's tale.

21. He laughed a laugh of merry scorn;
He turned and kissed her where she stood:
"If you are not the heiress born,
And I," said he, "the next in blood —

22. If you are not the heiress born,
And I," said he, "the lawful heir,
We two will wed to-morrow morn,
And you shall still be Lady Clare."

ALFRED TENNYSON.

31. Ring out, Wild Bells.

1. Ring out, wild bells, to the wild sky,
The flying cloud, the frosty light:
The year is dying in the night;
Ring out, wild bells, and let him die.

2. Ring out the old, ring in the new:
Ring happy bells, across the snow:
The year is going, let him go;
Ring out the false, ring in the true.

3. Ring out the grief that saps the mind,
For those that here we see no more;
Ring out the feud of rich and poor,
Ring in redress to all mankind.

4. Ring out a slowly dying cause,
And ancient forms of party strife;
Ring in the nobler modes of life,
With sweeter manners, purer laws.

5. Ring out the want, the care, the sin,
The faithless coldness of the times:

Ring out, ring out my mournful rhymes,
But ring the fuller minstrel in.

6. Ring out false pride in place and blood,
The civic scandal and the spite;
Ring in the love of truth and right,
Ring in the common love of good.

7. Ring out old shapes of foul disease;
Ring out the narrowing lust of gold;
Ring out the thousand wars of old,
Ring in the thousand years of peace.

8. Ring in the valiant man and free,
The larger heart, the kindlier hand;
Ring out the darkness, of the land, —
Ring in the Christ that is to be.

ALFRED TENNYSON.

32. Alexander Selkirk.

1. I am monarch of all I survey:
My right there is none to dispute;
From the centre all round to the sea
I am lord of the fowl and the brute.
O solitude! where are the charms
That sages have seen in thy face?
Better in the midst of alarms
Than reign in this horrible place.

2. I am out of humanity's reach,
I must finish my journey alone,
Never hear the sweet music of speech;
I start at the sound of my own.
The beasts that roam over the plain
My form with indifference see;
They are so unacquainted with man,
Their tameness is shocking to me.

3. Society, friendship, and love,
Divinely bestowed upon man,
O had I the wings of a dove,
How soon would I taste you again!

My sorrows I then might assuage
    In the ways of religion and truth,
Might learn from the wisdom of age,
    And be cheered by the sallies of youth.

4. Religion, what treasure untold
    Resides in that heavenly word!
More precious than silver and gold,
    Or all that this earth can afford.
But the sound of the church-going bell
    These valleys and rocks never heard,
Never sighed at the sound of a knell,
    Or smiled when a sabbath appeared.

5. Ye winds, that have made me your sport,
    Convey to this desolate shore
Some cordial, endearing report
    Of a land I shall visit no more.
My friends, do they now and then send
    A wish or a thought after me?
O tell me I yet have a friend,
    Though a friend I am never to see.

6. How fleet is a glance of the mind!
    Compared with the speed of its flight,
The tempest itself lags behind,
    And the swift-winged arrows of light.
When I think of my own native land,
    In a moment I seem to be there;
But alas! recollection at hand
    Soon hurries me back to despair.

7. But the sea-fowl is gone to her nest,
    The beast is laid down in his lair;
Even here is a season of rest,
    And I to my cabin repair.
There's mercy in every place,
    And mercy, encouraging thought!
Gives even affliction a grace,
    And reconciles man to his lot.

                        W. COWPER.

33. Hymn Before Sunrise in the Vale Chamouni.

 Hast thou a charm to stay the morning-star
In his steep course? So long he seems to pause
On thy bald, awful head, O sovereign Blanc!
The Arve and Arveiron at thy base
5 Rave ceaselessly: but thou, most awful form!
Risest from forth thy silent sea of pines,
How silently! Around thee, and above,
Deep is the air and dark, substantial, black,
An ebon mass: methinks thou piercest it,
10 As with a wedge! But when I look again,
It is thine own calm home, thy crystal shrine,
Thy habitation from eternity!
O dread and silent mount! I gazed upon thee,
Till thou, still present to the bodily sense,
15 Didst vanish from my thought: entranced in prayer,
I worshipped the Invisible alone.

 Yet, like some sweet beguiling melody,
So sweet we know not we are listening to it,
Thou, the meanwhile, wast blending with my thought,
20 Yea, with my life, and life's own secret joy:
Till the dilating soul, enrapt, transfused,
Into the mighty vision passing — there,
As in her natural form, swelled vast to heaven!

 Awake, my soul! not only passive praise
25 Thou owest! not alone these swelling tears,
Mute thanks, and secret ecstasy! Awake,
Voice of sweet song! Awake, my heart, awake!
Green vales and icy cliffs, all join my hymn!

 Thou first and chief, sole sovereign of the vale!
30 Oh, struggling with the darkness all the night,
And visited all night by troops of stars,
Or when they climb the sky, or when they sink, —
Companion of the morning-star at dawn,
Thyself Earth's rosy star, and of the dawn
35 Co-herald! wake, O wake, and utter praise!
Who sank thy sunless pillars deep in earth?
Who filled thy countenance with rosy light?
Who made thee parent of perpetual streams?

      And you, ye five wild torrents fiercely glad!
40 Who called you forth from night and utter death,
    From dark and icy caverns called you forth,
    Down those precipitous, black, jagged rocks,
    For ever shattered, and the same for ever?
    Who gave you your unvulnerable life,
45 Your strength, your speed, your fury, and your joy,
    Unceasing thunder, and eternal foam?
    And who commanded (and the silence came), —
    "Here let the billows stiffen and have rest?"

    Ye ice-falls! ye that from the mountain's brow
50 Adown enormous ravines slope amain —
    Torrents, methinks, that heard a mighty voice,
    And stopped at once amid their maddest plunge!
    Motionless torrents! silent cataracts!
    Who made you glorious as the gates of heaven
55 Beneath the keen full moon? Who bade the sun
    Clothe you with rainbows? Who, with living flowers
    Of loveliest blue, spread garlands at your feet? —
    GOD! let the torrents, like a shout of nations,
    Answer! and let the ice-plains echo, GOD!
60 GOD! sing, ye meadow-streams, with gladsome voice!
    Ye pine-groves, with your soft and soul-like sounds!
    And they, too, have a voice, yon piles of snow,
    And in their perilous fall shall thunder, GOD!
    Ye living flowers that skirt th'eternal frost!
65 Ye wild goats sporting round the eagle's nest!
    Ye eagles, playmates of the mountain-storm!
    Ye lightnings, the dread arrows of the clouds!
    Ye signs and wonders of the element!
    Utter forth GOD, and fill the hills with praise!

70   Thou too, hoar mount! with thy sky-pointing peaks,
    Oft from whose feet the avalanche, unheard,
    Shoots downward, glittering through the pure serene
    Into the depth of clouds, that veil thy breast —
    Thou too, again, stupendous mountain! thou,
75 That, as I raise my head, awhile bowed low
    In adoration, upward from thy base
    Slow travelling, with dim eyes suffused with tears,
    Solemnly seemest, like a vapoury cloud,

To rise before me, — Rise, oh, ever rise,
80 Rise like a cloud of incense, from the earth!
Thou kingly spirit, throned among the hills,
Thou dread ambassador from earth to heaven,
Great Hierarch! tell thou the silent sky,
And tell the stars, and tell yon rising sun:
85 Earth, with her thousand voices, praises GOD.

S. T. COLERIDGE.

34. On the Last Day.

The fatal period, the great hour is come,
And nature shrinks at her approaching doom;
Loud peals of thunder give the sign, and all
Heaven's terrors in array surround the ball:
5 Sharp lightnings with the meteor's blaze conspire,
And darted downward, set the world on fire;
Black rising clouds the thickened ether choke,
And spiry flames dart thro' the rolling smoke,
With keen vibration, cut the sullen night.
10 And strike the darkened sky with dreadful light;
From Heaven's four regions, with immortal force,
Angels drive on the wind's impetuous course,
T' enrage the flame; it spreads, it soars on high,
Swells in the storm and billows through the sky:
15 Here winding pyramids of fire ascend.
Cities and deserts in one ruin blend;
Here blazing volumes wafted overwhelm
The spacious face of a far distant realm:
There, undermined, down rush eternal hills,
20 The neighb'ring vales the vast destruction fills.

Hear'st thou that dreadful crack? that sound which broke
Like peals of thunder, and the centre shook?
What wonders must that groan of nature tell!
Olympus there, and mightier Atlas fell:
25 Which seemed above the reach of fate to stand,
A tow'ring monument of God's right hand:
Now dust and smoke, whose brow so lately spread
O'er sheltered countries its diffusive shade.
Some angel say, where ran proud Asia's bound?
30 Or where with fruits was fair Europa crowned?
Where stretched waste Libya, where did India's store
Sparkle in diamonds, and her golden ore?

    Each lost in each, their mingled kingdoms glow
    And all dissolved, one fiery deluge flow:
35 Thus Earth's contending monarchies are joined,
    And a full period for ambition find.

    And now whate'er or swims, or walks, or flies,
    Inhabitants of sea, or earth, or skies;
    All on whom Adam's wisdom fixed a name,
40 All plunge and perish in the conqu'ring flame.

    This globe alone would but defraud the fire,
    Starve its devouring rage; the flakes aspire,
    And catch the cloud, and make the heavens their prey.
    The sun, the moon, the stars, all melt away:
45 All, all is lost; no monument, no sign,
    Where once so proudly blazed the gay machine.
    So bubbles on the foaming stream expire,
    So sparks that scatter from the kindling fire;
    The devastations of one dreadful hour
50 The Great Creator's six days' work devour.

                              EDWARD YOUNG.

35. Alexander's Feast.

    'Twas at the royal feast, for Persia won
        By Philip's warlike son:
    Aloft in awful state
    The godlike hero sate
5   On his imperial throne:
      His valiant peers were placed around,
    Their brows with roses and with myrtle bound:
    So should desert in arms be crowned.
    The lovely Thais by his side
10 Sate, like a blooming Eastern bride,
    In flower of youth and beauty's pride.
        Happy, happy, happy pair!
          None but the brave,
          None but the brave,
15   None but the brave deserves the fair.

    Timotheus, placed on high
        Amid the tuneful quire,
        With flying fingers touched the lyre:
    The trembling notes ascend the sky,
20   And heavenly joys inspire.

    The song began from Jove,
    Who left his blissful seats above.
    The listening crowd admire the lofty sound;
    A present deity! they shout around:
25 A present deity! the vaulted roofs rebound.
        With ravished ears
        The monarch hears,
        Assumes the god,
        Affects to nod,
30 And seems to shake the spheres.
    The praise of Bacchus then the sweet musician sung:
      Of Bacchus ever fair, and ever young:
      The jolly god in triumph comes;
      Sound the trumpets, beat the drums:
35   Flushed with a purple grace
      He shews his honest face.
    Now give the hautboys breath; he comes, he comes!
      Bacchus, ever fair and young,
      Drinking joys did first ordain;
40   Bacchus' blessings are a treasure,
      Drinking is the soldier's pleasure;
      Rich the treasure,
        Sweet the pleasure;
      Sweet is pleasure after pain.
45 Soothed with the sound, the king grew vain,
    Fought all his battles o'er again,
    And thrice he routed all his foes, and thrice he slew the slain.
      The master saw the madness rise;
    His glowing cheeks, his ardent eyes;
50 And, while he heaven and earth defied,
    Changed his hand, and checked his pride.
    He chose a mournful Muse,
    Soft pity to infuse:
    He sung Darius great and good,
55 By too severe a fate
    Fallen, fallen, fallen, fallen,
    Fallen from his high estate,
    And weltering in his blood;
    Deserted, at his utmost need,
60 By those his former bounty fed,
    On the bare earth exposed he lies,
    With not a friend to close his eyes.

With downcast look the joyless victor sate,
Revolving in his altered soul
65   The various turns of fate below;
And now and then a sigh he stole,
And tears began to flow.

The mighty master smiled to see
That love was in the next degree:
70 'Twas but a kindred sound to move;
For pity melts the mind to love.
    Softly sweet, in Lydian measures,
    Soon he soothed his soul to pleasures,
    War, he sung, is toil and trouble;
75   Honour but an empty bubble;
      Never ending, still beginning,
    Fighting still, and still destroying:
    If the world be worth thy winning,
    Think, oh think it worth enjoying!
80   Lovely Thais sits beside thee,
    Take the good the gods provide thee.
The many rend the skies with loud applause:
So love was crowned, but Music won the cause.
    The prince, unable to conceal his pain,
85   Gazed on the fair
      Who caused his care,
    And sighed and looked, sighed and looked,
    Sighed and looked, and sighed again. —

Now strike the golden lyre again;
90   And louder yet, and yet a louder strain. —
    Hark, hark, the horrid sound
    Has raised up his head;
    As awaked from the dead
    And amazed, he stares around.
95   Revenge, revenge, Timotheus cries,
    See the Furies arise,
    See the snakes that they rear,
    How they hiss in their hair,
    And the sparkles that flash from their eyes!
100   Behold a ghastly band,
    Each a torch in his hand!
Those are Grecian ghosts, that in battle were slain,
    And unburied remain,

    Inglorious on the plain;
105 Give the vengeance due
    To the valiant crew.
  Behold how they toss their torches on high,
    How they point to the Persian abodes,
  And glitt'ring temples of their hostile gods!
110 The princes applaud with a furious joy;
  And the King seized a flambeau, with zeal to destroy;
    Thais led the way,
    To light him to his prey,
  And, like another Helen, fired another Troy.

115 Thus, long ago,
    Ere heaving bellows learned to blow,
    While organs yet were mute,
    Timotheus to his breathing flute
    And sounding lyre
120 Could swell the soul to rage, or kindle soft desire.
    At last divine Cecilia came,
    Inventress of the vocal frame;
  The sweet enthusiast, from her sacred store,
    Enlarged the former narrow bounds,
125 And added length to solemn sounds,
  With nature's mother-wit, and arts unknown before.
    Let old Timotheus yield the prize,
    Or both divide the crown;
    He raised a mortal to the skies:
130 She drew an angel down. JOHN DRYDEN.

36. London.

 London thou great emporium of our isle,
 O thou too-bounteous, thou too-fruitful Nile!
 How shall I praise or curse to thy desert?
 Or separate thy sound from thy corrupted part?
5 I called thee Nile; the parallel will stand:
 Thy tides of wealth o'erflow the fattened land;
 Yet monsters from thy large increase we find,
 Engendered on the slime thou leavest behind.
 Sedition has not wholly seized on thee,
10 Thy nobler parts are from infection free.
 Thy military chiefs are brave and true;
 Nor are thy disenchanted burghers few.

  The head is loyal which thy heart commands,
  But what's a head with two such gouty hands?
15 The wise and wealthy love the surest way,
  And are content to thrive and to obey.
  But wisdom is to sloth too great a slave:
  None are so busy as the fool and knave.
  Those let me curse: what vengeance will they urge,
20 Whose ordures neither plague nor fire can purge?
  Nor sharp experience can to duty bring,
  Nor angry heaven, nor a forgiving king!
  In gospel-phrase their chapmen they betray,
  Their shops are dens, the buyer is their prey.
25 The knack of trades is living on the spoil;
  They boast ev'n when each other they beguile.
  Customs to steal is such a trivial thing,
  That 'tis their charter to defraud their king.
  All hands unite of every jarring sect;
30 They cheat the country first and then infect.
  They for God's cause their monarchs dare dethrone
  And they'll be sure to make his cause their own.
  Such impious axioms foolishly they show,
  For in some soils republics will not grow:
35 Our temperate isle will no extremes sustain.
  Of popular sway or arbitrary reign:
  But slides between them both into the best,
  Secure in freedom, in a monarch blest.
  And though the climate vexed with various winds,
40 Works through our yielding bodies on our minds,
  The wholesome tempest purges what it breeds,
  To recommend the calmness that succeeds.
        JOHN DRYDEN.

37. London after the Great Fire.

1. Methinks already from this chymic flame,
 I see a city of more precious mould:
 Rich as the town which gives the Indies name,
 With silver paved and all divine with gold.

2. Already labouring with a mighty fate,
 She shakes the rubbish from her mounting brow.
 And seems to have renewed her charters' date,
 Which heaven will to the death of time allow.

3. More great than human now, and more august,
   Now deified she from her fires does rise:
   Her widening streets on new foundations trust,
   And opening into larger parts she flies.

4. Before, she like some shepherdess did show,
   Who sat to bathe her by a river's side:
   Not answering to her fame, but rude and low,
   Nor taught the beautious arts of modern pride.

5. Now like a maiden queen she will behold,
   From her high turrets, hourly suitors come;
   The East with incense, and the West with gold,
   Will stand like suppliants to receive her doom.

6. The silver Thames, her own domestic flood,
   Shall bear her vessels like a sweeping train;
   And often wind, as of his mistress proud,
   With longing eyes to meet her face again.
   JOHN DRYDEN.

38. Universal Prayer.

1. Father of All! in every age,
      In every clime adored,
     By saint, by savage, and by sage,
      Jehovah, Jove, or Lord.

2. Thou great first cause, least understood;
      Who all my sense confined
     To know but this, that thou art good,
      And that myself am blind;

3. Yet gave me, in this dark estate,
      To see the good from ill;
     And, binding nature fast in fate,
      Left free the human will.

4. What conscience dictates to be done,
      Or warns me not to do,
     This, teach me more than hell to shun,
      That more than heaven pursue.

5. What blessings thy free bounty gives,
      Let me not cast away;
     For God is paid when man receives,
      T'enjoy is to obey.

6. Yet not to earth's contracted span
    Thy goodness let me bound,
    Or think thee Lord alone of man,
    When thousand worlds are round.

7. Let not this weak, unknowing hand
    Presume thy bolts to throw,
    And deal damnation round the land
    On each I judge thy foe.

8. If I am right, thy grace impart,
    Still in the right to stay!
    If I am wrong, oh, teach my heart
    To find that better way!

9. Save me alike from foolish pride,
    Or impious discontent,
    At aught thy wisdom has denied,
    Or aught thy goodness lent.

10. Teach me to feel another's woe,
    To hide the fault I see;
    That mercy I to others show,
    That mercy show to me.

11. Mean though I am, not wholly so,
    Since quickened by thy breath;
    O, lead me wheresoe'er I go,
    Through this day's life or death.

12. This day, be bread and peace my lot:
    All else beneath the sun,
    Thou knowst if best bestowed or not,
    And let thy will be done.

13. To thee, whose temple is all space,
    Whose altar, earth, sea, skies!
    One chorus let all beings raise,
    All nature's incense rise!
                    ALEXANDER POPE.

39. Windsor Forest in the Time of William Rufus.

A dreary desert, and a gloomy waste,
To savage beasts and savage laws a prey,
And kings more furious and severe than they;
Who claimed the skies, dispeopled air and floods,

5 The lonely lords of empty wilds and woods:
　Cities laid waste, they stormed the dens and caves
　(For wiser brutes were backward to be slaves).
　What could be free, when lawless beasts obeyed,
　And e'en the elements a tyrant swayed?
10 In vain kind seasons swelled the teeming grain;
　Soft showers distilled, and suns grew warm in vain;
　The swain with tears his frustrate labour yields,
　And, famished, dies amidst his ripened fields.
　What wonder then, a beast or subject slain
15 Were equal crimes in a despotic reign?
　Both doomed alike for sportive tyrants bled,
　But, while the subject starved, the beast was fed.
　Proud Nimrod first the bloody chase began,
　A mighty hunter, and his prey was man:
20 Our haughty Norman boasts that barbarous name,
　And makes his trembling slaves the royal game.
　The fields are ravished from the industrious swains,
　From men their cities, and from gods their fanes:
　The levelled towns with weeds lie covered o'er;
25 The hollow winds through naked temples roar;
　Round broken columns clasping ivy twined;
　O'er heaps of ruin stalked the stately hind;
　The fox obscene to gaping tombs retires,
　And savage howlings fill the sacred quires.
30 Awed by his nobles, by his commons curst,
　The oppressor ruled tyrannic where he durst,
　Stretched o'er the poor and church his iron rod,
　And served alike his vassals and his God.
　Whom e'en the Saxon spared, and bloody Dane,
35 The wanton victims of his sport remain.
　But see, the man who spacious regions gave
　A waste for beasts, himself denied a grave!
　Stretched on the lawn his second hope survey,
　At once the chaser, and at once the prey:
40 Lo Rufus, tugging at the deadly dart,
　Bleeds in the forest like a wounded hart.

　　　　　　　　　　ALEXANDER POPE.

40. King Leir and his Three Daughters.

1. King Leir once ruled in this land
　With princely power and peace;

And had all things with heart's content,
    That might his joys increase.
Amongst those things that nature gave,
    Three daughters fair had he,
So princely seeming beautiful,
    As fairer could not be.

2. So on a time it pleased the king
    A question thus to move,
Which of his daughters to his grace
    Could shew the dearest love:
For to my age you bring content,
    Quoth he, then let me hear,
Which of you three in plighted troth
    The kindest will appear.

3. To whom the eldest thus began;
    Dear father, mind, quoth she,
Before your face, to do you good,
    My blood shall rendered be:
And for your sake my bleeding heart
    Shall here be cut in twain,
Ere that I see your reverend age
    The smallest grief sustain.

4. And so will I, the second said;
    Dear father, for your sake,
The worst of all extremities
    I'll gently undertake:
And serve your highness night and day
    With diligence and love;
That sweet content and quietness
    Discomforts may remove.

5. In doing so, you glad my soul,
    The aged king replied:
But what sayst thou, my youngest girl,
    How is thy love allied?
My love (quoth young Cordelia then)
    Which to your grace I owe,
Shall be the duty of a child,
    And that is all I'll show.

6. And wilt thou show no more, quoth he,
    Than doth thy duty bind,
I well perceive thy love is small,

When as no more I find.
Henceforth I banish thee my court,
Thou art no child of mine;
Nor any part of this my realm
By favour shall be thine.

7. Thy elder sisters' loves are more
Than well I can demand,
To whom I equally bestow
My kingdom and my land,
My pompal state and all my goods,
That lovingly I may
With those thy sisters be maintained
Until my dying day.

8. Thus flattering speeches won renown,
By these two sisters here;
The third had causeless banishment,
Yet was her love more dear:
For poor Cordelia patiently
Went wand'ring up and down,
Unhelped, unpitied, gentle maid,
Through many an English town.

9. Until at last in famous France
She gentler fortunes found;
Though poor and bare, yet she was deemed
The fairest on the ground:
Where when the king her virtues heard,
And this fair lady seen,
With full consent of all his court
He made his wife and queen.

10. Her father King Leir this while
With his two daughters staid:
Forgetful of their promised loves,
Full soon the same decayed:
And living in Queen Ragan's court,
The eldest of the twain,
She took from him his chiefest means,
And most of all his train.

11. For whereas twenty men were wont
To wait with bended knee:

She gave allowance but to ten,
　　　　And after scarce to three;
　　　Nay, one she thought too much for him;
　　　　So took she all away,
　　　In hope that in her court, good king,
　　　　He would no longer stay.

12. Am I rewarded thus, quoth he,
　　　　In giving all I have
　　　Unto my children, and to beg
　　　　For what I lately gave?
　　　I'll go unto my Gonorell:
　　　　My second child, I know,
　　　Will be more kind and pitiful,
　　　　And will relieve my woe.

13. Full fast he hies then to her court;
　　　　Where when she heard his moan,
　　　Returned him answer, That she grieved,
　　　　That all his means were gone;
　　　But no way could relieve his wants;
　　　　Yet if that he would stay
　　　Within her kitchen, he should have
　　　　What scullions gave away.

14. When he had heard, with bitter tears,
　　　　He made his answer then;
　　　In what I did let me be made
　　　　Example to all men.
　　　I will return again, quoth he,
　　　　Unto my Ragan's court;
　　　She will not use me thus, I hope,
　　　　But in a kinder sort.

15. Where when he came, she gave command
　　　　To drive him thence away;
　　　When he was well within her court
　　　　(She said) he would not stay.
　　　Then back again to Gonorell
　　　　The woeful king did hie,
　　　That in her kitchen he might have
　　　　What scullion boys set by.

16. But there of that he was denied
　　　　Which she had promised late:

      For once refusing, he should not
         Come after to her gate,
      Thus twixt his daughters, for relief
         He wandered up and down;
      Being glad to feed on beggar's food,
         That lately wore a crown.

17. And calling to remembrance then
         His youngest daughter's words,
      That said the duty of a child
         Was all that love affords:
      But doubting to repair to her,
         Whom he had banished so,
      Grew frantic mad; for in his mind
         He bore the wounds of woe:

18. Which made him rend his milk-white locks,
         And tresses from his head,
      And all with blood bestain his cheeks,
         With age and honour spread.
      To hills and woods and wat'ry founts
         He made his hourly moan,
      Till hills and woods and senseless things,
         Did seem to sigh and groan.

19. Even thus possest with discontents,
         He passed o'er to France,
      In hopes from fair Cordelia there,
         To find some gentler chance;
      Most virtuous dame! which when she heard
         Of this her father's grief,
      As duty bound, she quickly sent
         Him comfort and relief.

20. And by a train of noble peers,
         In brave and gallant sort,
      She gave in charge he should be brought
         To Aganippus' court;
      Whose royal king, with noble mind
         So freely gave consent,
      To muster up his knights at arms,
         To fame and courage bent.

21. And so to England came with speed,
         To repossess King Leir,

And drive his daughters from their thrones
  By his Cordelia dear.
Where she, true-hearted noble queen,
  Was in the battle slain;
Yet he good king, in his old days,
  Possest his crown again.

22. But when he heard Cordelia's death,
  Who died indeed for love
Of her dear father, in whose cause
  She did this battle move;
He swooning fell upon her breast,
  From whence he never parted:
But on her bosom left his life,
  That was so truly hearted.

23. The lords and nobles when they saw
  The end of these events,
The other sisters unto death
  They doomed by consents;
And being dead, their crowns they left
  Unto the next of kin:
Thus have you seen the fall of pride,
  And disobedient sin.

PERCY, *Reliques of Ancient English Poetry.*

II.
EPIC AND DRAMATIC FRAGMENTS.

I. FROM 'PARADISE LOST.'

I. Satan and the Fallen Angels.

Of man's first disobedience, and the fruit
Of that forbidden tree, whose mortal taste
Brought death into the world, and all our woe,
With loss of Eden, till one greater man
5 Restore us, and regain the blissful seat,
Sing Heav'nly Muse, that on the secret top
Of Oreb, or of Sinai, didst inspire
That Shepherd, who first taught the chosen seed
In the beginning, how the heav'ns and earth

10 Rose out of Chaos. Or if Sion hill
　Delight thee more, and Siloa's brook that flow'd
　Fast by the oracle of God; I thence
　Invoke thy aid to my advent'rous song,
　That with no middle flight intends to soar
15 Above th'Aonian mount, while it pursues
　Things unattempted yet, in prose or rhyme.
　And chiefly Thou, O Sp'rit, that dost prefer
　Before all temples th'upright heart and pure.
　Instruct me, for Thou know'st: Thou from the first
20 Wast present, and with mighty wings outspread
　Dove-like sat'st brooding on the vast abyss.
　And mad'st it pregnant. What in me is dark
　Illumine, what is low raise and support,
　That to the height of this great argument
25 I may assert eternal Providence,
　And justify the ways of God to Men.
　　Say first, for Heav'n hides nothing from thy view,
　Nor the deep tract of Hell; say first what cause
　Moved our grand parents, in that happy state,
30 Favour'd of Heav'n so highly, to fall off
　From their Creator, and transgress his will
　For one restraint, lords of the world besides?
　Who first seduced them to that foul revolt?
　Th'infernal Serpent: he it was whose guile.
35 Stirr'd up with envy and revenge, deceived
　The mother of mankind, what time his pride
　Had cast him out from Heav'n, with all his host
　Of rebel Angels; by whose aid aspiring
　To set himself in glory 'bove his peers,
40 He trusted to have equall'd the Most High,
　If he opposed; and with ambitious aim
　Against the throne and monarchy of God,
　Raised impious war in Heav'n, and battle proud
　With vain attempt. Him the Almighty Power
45 Hurl'd headlong flaming from th'ethereal sky,
　With hideous ruin and combustion, down
　To bottomless perdition; there to dwell
　In adamantine chains and penal fire,
　Who durst defy th'Omnipotent to arms.
50　Nine times the space that measures day and night
　To mortal men, he with his horrid crew

Lay vanquish'd, rolling in the fiery gulf,
Confounded though immortal: But his doom
Reserved him to more wrath; for now the thought
55 Both of lost happiness and lasting pain
Torments him: round he throws his baleful eyes,
That witness'd huge affliction and dismay,
Mix'd with obdurate pride and steadfast hate:
At once, as far as angels ken, he views
60 The dismal situation waste and wild:
A dungeon horrible on all sides round,
As one great furnace flamed; yet from those flames
No light; but rather darkness visible
Served only to discover sights of woe,
65 Regions of sorrow, doleful shades, where peace
And rest can never dwell; hope never comes,
That comes to all: but torture without end
Still urges, and a fiery deluge, fed
With ever-burning sulphur unconsumed:
70 Such place eternal justice had prepared
For those rebellious; here their pris'n ordain'd
In utter darkness, and their portion set
As far removed from God and light of heaven,
As from the centre thrice to th' utmost pole.
75 O how unlike the place from whence they fell!
There the companions of his fall, o'erwhelm'd
With floods and whirlwinds of tempestuous fire,
He soon discerns, and welt'ring by his side
One next himself in power, and next in crime,
80 Long after known in Palestine, and named
Beëlzebub. To whom th' Arch-Enemy,
And thence in Heav'n call'd Satan, with bold words
Breaking the horrid silence thus began:
If thou beest he; (but O how fallen! how changed
85 From him who, in the happy realms of light
Cloth'd with transcendent brightness didst outshine
Myriads though bright!) if he whom mutual league,
United thoughts and counsels, equal hope
And hazard in the glorious enterprise,
90 Join'd with me once, now misery hath join'd
In equal ruin: into what pit thou seest
From what height fall'n, so much the stronger proved
He with his thunder: and till then who knew
The force of those dire arms? yet not for those

95 Nor what the potent victor in his rage
　　Can else inflict, do I repent or change
　　Though changed in outward lustre, that fix'd mind
　　And high disdain from sense of injured merit,
　　That with the Mightiest raised me to contend,
100 And to the fierce contention brought along
　　Innumerable force of Spirits arm'd,
　　That durst dislike his reign, and me preferring,
　　His utmost pow'r with adverse pow'r opposed
　　In dubious battle on the plains of Heav'n,
105 And shook his throne. What though the field be lost?
　　All is not lost; th'unconquerable will
　　And study of revenge, immortal hate,
　　And courage never to submit or yield:
　　And what is else not to be overcome?
110 That glory never shall his wrath or might
　　Extort from me. To bow and sue for grace
　　With suppliant knee, and deify his pow'r,
　　Who from the terror of this arm so late
　　Doubted his empire; that were low indeed!
115 That were an ignominy and shame beneath
　　This downfall; since by fate the strength of Gods
　　And this empyreal substance cannot fail,
　　Since through experience of this great event
　　In arms not worse, in foresight much advanced,
120 We may with more successful hope resolve
　　To wage by force or guile eternal war,
　　Irreconcileable to our grand foe,
　　Who now triumphs, and in th'excess of joy
　　Sole reigning holds the tyranny of heav'n.
125　So spake th'apostate Angel, though in pain,
　　Vaunting aloud, but rack'd with deep despair:
　　And him thus answer'd soon his bold compeer:
　　　O Prince, O Chief of many throned powers!
　　That led th'embattled Seraphim to war
130 Under thy conduct, and in dreadful deeds
　　Fearless, endanger'd heaven's perpetual King,
　　And put to proof his high supremacy,
　　Whether upheld by strength, or chance, or fate!
　　Too well I see and rue the dire event,
135 That with sad overthrow and foul defeat
　　Hath lost us heav'n, and all this mighty host
　　In horrible destruction laid thus low,

As far as Gods and heav'nly essences
Can perish: for the mind and spirit remains
140 Invincible, and vigour soon returns,
    Though all our glory extinct, and happy state
    Here swallow'd up in endless misery.
    But what if he our conqu'ror (whom I now
    Of force believe almighty, since no less
145 Than such could have o'erpower'd such force as ours)
    Have left us this our spirit and strength entire
    Strongly to suffer and support our pains,
    That we may so suffice his vengeful ire,
    Or do him mightier service as his thralls
150 By right of war, whate'er his business be
    Here in the heart of Hell to work in fire,
    Or do his errands in the gloomy deep;
    What can it then avail, though yet we feel
    Strength undiminish'd, or eternal being
155 To undergo eternal punishment?
    Whereto with speedy words th'Arch-Fiend reply'd:
    Fall'n Cherub, to be weak is miserable
    Doing or suffering: but of this be sure,
    To do aught good never will be our task,
160 But ever to do ill our sole delight,
    As being the contrary to his high will
    Whom we resist. If then his providence
    Out of our evil seek to bring forth good,
    Our labour must be to pervert that end,
165 And out of good still to find means of evil;
    Which oft-times may succeed, so as perhaps
    Shall grieve him, if I fail not, and disturb
    His inmost counsels from their destined aim.
    But see, the angry victor hath recall'd
170 His ministers of vengeance and pursuit
    Back to the gates of Heav'n: the sulph'rous hail
    Shot after us in storm, o'erblown hath laid
    The fiery surge, that from the precipice
    Of Heav'n received us falling; and the thunder,
175 Wing'd with red lightning and impetuous rage,
    Perhaps hath spent his shafts, and ceases now
    To bellow through the vast and boundless deep.
    Let us not slip th'occasion, whether scorn
    Or satiate fury yield it from our foe.
180 Seest thou yon dreary plain, forlorn and wild,

The seat of desolation, void of light,
Save what the glimm'ring of these livid flames
Casts pale and dreadful? Thither let us tend
From off the tossing of these fiery waves,
185 There rest, if any rest can harbour there,
And reassembling our afflicted powers,
Consult how we may henceforth most offend
Our enemy, our own loss how repair,
How overcome this dire calamity,
190 What reinforcement we may gain from hope.
If not what resolution from despair.

II. The Son of God in Battle.

And the third sacred morn began to shine.
Dawning through Heav'n. Forth rush'd with whirlwind sound
The chariot of paternal Deity,
Flashing thick flames, wheel within wheel undrawn,
5 Itself instinct with Spirit, but convoy'd
By four Cherubic shapes: four faces each
Had wondrous; as with stars their bodies all
And wings were set with eyes, with eyes the wheels
Of beryl, and careering fires between;
10 Over their heads a crystal firmament,
Whereon a sapphire throne inlaid with pure
Amber, and colours of the show'ry arch.
He in celestial panoply all arm'd
Of radiant Urim, work divinely wrought,
15 Ascended. At his right hand victory
Sat eagle-wing'd: beside him hung his bow
And quiver with three-bolted thunder stored;
And from about him fierce effusion roll'd
Of smoke and bick'ring flame and sparkles dire:
20 Attended with ten thousand Saints,
He onward came: far off his coming shone;
And twenty thousand (I their number heard)
Chariots of God, half on each hand were seen.
He on the wings of Cherub rode sublime
25 On the crystalline sky, in sapphire throned,
Illustrious far and wide, but by his own
First seen; them unexpected joy surprised,
When the great ensign of Messiah blazed
Aloft, by Angels borne, his sign in Heav'n;

30 Under whose conduct Michael soon reduced
　His army, circumfused on either wing,
　Under their Head embody'd all in one.
　Before him pow'r divine his way prepared;
　At his command th'uprooted hills retired
35 Each to his place: they heard his voice, and went
　Obsequious: Heav'n his wonted face renew'd,
　And with fresh flow'rets hill and valley smiled.
　This saw his hapless foes, but stood obdured,
　And to rebellious fight rallied their Pow'rs
40 Insensate, hope conceiving from despair.
　In Heav'nly Spirits could such perverseness dwell?
　But to convince the proud what signs avail,
　Or wonders move th' obdurate to relent?
　They, harden'd more by what might most reclaim,
45 Grieving to see his glory, at the sight
　Took envy; and aspiring to his height,
　Stood re-embattled fierce, by force or fraud
　Weening to prosper, and at length prevail
　Against God and Messiah, or to fall
50 In universal ruin last: and now
　To final battle drew, disdaining flight
　Or faint retreat: when the great Son of God
　To all his host on either hand thus spake:
　　Stand still in bright array, ye Saints; here stand
55 Ye Angels arm'd, this day from battle rest:
　Faithful hath been your warfare, and of God
　Accepted, fearless in his righteous cause;
　And as ye have received, so have ye done
　Invincibly: but of this cursed crew
60 The punishment to other hand belongs:
　Vengeance is his, or whose he sole appoints;
　Number to this day's work is not ordain'd,
　Nor multitude; stand only and behold
　God's indignation on these Godless pour'd
65 By me; not you, but me, they have despised,
　Yet envy'd. Against me is all their rage,
　Because the Father, t' whom in Heav'n supreme
　Kingdom, and pow'r, and glory appertains,
　Hath honour'd me according to his will.
70 Therefore to me their doom he hath assign'd;
　That they may have their wish, to try with me
　In battle which the stronger proves; they all,

  Or I alone against them, since by strength
  They measure all, of other excellence
75 Not emulous, nor care who them excels;
  Nor other strife with them do I vouchsafe.
   So spake the Son, and into terror changed
  His count'nance, too severe to be beheld,
  And full of wrath bent on his enemies.
80 At once the Four spread out their starry wings
  With dreadful shade contiguous, and the orbs
  Of his fierce chariot roll'd, as with the sound
  Of torrent floods, or of a num'rous host.
  He on his impious foes right onward drove,
85 Gloomy as night: under his burning wheels
  The steadfast empyrean shook throughout,
  All but the throne itself of God. Full soon
  Among them he arrived; in his right hand
  Grasping ten thousand thunders, which he sent
90 Before him, such as in their souls infix'd
  Plagues. They astonish'd all resistance lost,
  All courage; down their idle weapons dropt;
  O'er shields and helms and helmed heads he rode
  Of Thrones and mighty Seraphim prostrate,
95 That wish'd the mountains now might be again
  Thrown on them, as a shelter from his ire.
  Nor less on either side tempestuous fell
  His arrows, from the fourfold-visaged Four,
  Distinct with eyes, and from the living wheels
100 Distinct alike with multitude of eyes;
  One Spirit in them ruled, and ev'ry eye
  Glared lightning, and shot forth pernicious fire
  Among th' accursed, that wither'd all their strength,
  And of their wonted vigour left them drain'd,
105 Exhausted, spiritless, afflicted, fall'n.
  Yet half his strength he put not forth, but check'd
  His thunder in mid volley; for he meant
  Not to destroy, but root them out of Heav'n.
  The overthrown he raised, and, as a herd
110 Of goats or tim'rous flock together throng'd,
  Drove them before him thunder-struck, pursued
  With terrors and with furies to the bounds
  And crystal wall of Heav'n; which opening wide,
  Roll'd inward, and a spacious gap disclosed
115 Into the wasteful deep. The monstrous sight

  Struck them with horror backward, but far worse
  Urged them behind: headlong themselves they threw
  Down from the verge of Heav'n; eternal wrath
  Burnt after them to the bottomless pit.
120 Hell heard th' unsufferable noise: Hell saw
  Heav'n ruining from Heav'n, and would have fled
  Affrighted; but strict Fate had cast too deep
  Her dark foundations, and too fast had bound.
  Nine days they fell; confounded Chaos roar'd,
125 And felt tenfold confusion in their fall
  Through his wild anarchy, so huge a rout
  Incumber'd him with ruin. Hell at last
  Yawning, received them whole, and on them closed;
  Hell, their fit habitation, fraught with fire
130 Unquenchable, the house of woe and pain.
  Disburden'd Heav'n rejoiced, and soon repair'd
  Her mural breach, returning whence it roll'd.
  Sole victor from th'expulsion of his foes,
  Messiah his triumphal chariot turn'd:
135 To meet him, all his saints, who silent stood
  Eye-witnesses of his almighty acts,
  With jubilee advanced; and as they went,
  Shaded with branching palm, each order bright,
  Sung triumph, and him sung victorious King,
140 Son, Heir, and Lord, to him dominion given,
  Worthiest to reign. He celebrated rode
  Triumphant through mid Heav'n into the courts
  And temple of his Mighty Father throned
  On high: who into glory him received;
145 Where now he sits at the right hand of bliss.

            J. MILTON.

2. FROM 'THE LAY OF THE LAST MINSTREL.'
I.

  The way was long, the wind was cold,
  The Minstrel was infirm and old;
  His wither'd cheek, and tresses grey,
  Seem'd to have known a better day;
5 The harp, his sole remaining joy,
  Was carried by an orphan boy.
  The last of all the bards was he,
  Who sung of Border chivalry;
  For, welladay! their date was fled,

10 His tuneful brethren all were dead;
   And he, neglected and oppress'd,
   Wish'd to be with them, and at rest.
   No more on prancing palfrey borne,
   He caroll'd light as lark at morn;
15 No longer courted and caress'd,
   High placed in hall, a welcome guest,
   He pour'd, to lord and lady gay,
   The unpremeditated lay:
   Old times were changed, old manners gone:
20 A stranger fill'd the Stuarts' throne:
   The bigots of the iron time
   Had call'd his harmless art a crime.
   A wandering harper, scorn'd and poor,
   He begg'd his bread from door to door.
25 And tuned, to please a peasant's ear,
   The harp, a king had loved to hear.
       He pass'd where Newark's stately tower
   Looks out from Yarrow's birchen bower:
   The Minstrel gazed with wistful eye —
30 No humbler resting-place was nigh;
   With hesitating step at last,
   The embattled portal arch he pass'd,
   Whose ponderous grate and massy bar
   Had oft roll'd back the tide of war,
35 But never closed the iron door
   Against the desolate and poor.
   The Duchess mark'd his weary pace,
   His timid mien, and reverend face,
   And bade her page the menials tell
40 That they should tend the old man well:
   For she had known adversity,
   Though born in such a high degree;
   In pride of dower, in beauty's bloom,
   Had wept o'er Monmouth's bloody tomb!
45   When kindness had his wants supplied,
   And the old man was gratified,
   Began to rise his minstrel pride;
   And he began to talk anon,
   Of good Earl Francis, dead and gone,
50 And of Earl Walter, rest him God!
   A braver ne'er to battle rode;

And how full many a tale he knew,
Of the old warriors of Buccleuch:
And, would the noble Duchess deign
55 To listen to an old man's strain.
Though stiff his hand, his voice though weak,
He thought even yet, the sooth to speak,
That, if she loved the harp to hear,
He could make music to her ear.

60 The humble boon was soon obtain'd;
The aged Minstrel audience gain'd.
But, when he reach'd the room of state,
Where she, with all her ladies, sate,
Perchance he wish'd his boon denied;
65 For, when to tune his harp he tried,
His trembling hand had lost the ease,
Which marks security to please:
And scenes, long past, of joy and pain,
Came wildering o'er his aged brain —
70 He tried to tune his harp in vain!
The pitying Duchess praised its chime,
And gave him heart, and gave him time,
Till every string's according glee
Was blended into harmony.
75 And then, he said, he would full fain
He could recall an ancient strain,
He never thought to sing again.
It was not framed for village churls,
But for high dames and mighty earls;
80 He had play'd it to King Charles the good,
When he kept court in Holyrood:
And much he wish'd, yet fear'd, to try
The long-forgotten melody.
Amid the strings his finger stray'd,
85 And an uncertain warbling made,
And oft he shook his hoary head.
But when he caught the measure wild,
The old man raised his face and smiled;
And lighten'd up his faded eye,
90 With all a poet's ecstasy!
In varying cadence, soft or strong,
He swept the sounding chords along:
The present scene, the future lot,

His toils, his wants, were all forgot:
95 Cold diffidence, and age's frost,
In the full tide of song were lost;
Each blank in faithless memory void,
The poet's glowing thought supplied;
And while his harp responsive rung,
100 'Twas thus the Latest Minstrel sung.

II.

Breathes there the man, with soul so dead
Who never to himself hath said,
This is my own, my native land!
Whose heart hath ne'er within him burn'd,
5 As home his footsteps he hath turn'd,
From wandering on a foreign strand!
If such there breathe, go, mark him well;
For him no minstrel raptures swell:
High though his titles, proud his name,
10 Boundless his wealth as wish can claim;
Despite those titles, power, and pelf,
The wretch, concentred all in self,
Living, shall forfeit fair renown,
And, doubly dying, shall go down
15 To the vile dust, from whence he sprung,
Unwept, unhonour'd and unsung.

O Caledonia! stern and wild,
Meet nurse for a poetic child!
Land of brown heath and shaggy wood,
20 Land of the mountain and the flood,
Land of my sires! what mortal hand
Can e'er untie the filial band,
That knits me to thy rugged strand!
Still, as I view each well-known scene,
25 Think what is now, and what hath been,
Seems as, to me, of all bereft,
Sole friends thy woods and streams were left;
And thus I love them better still,
Even in extremity of ill.
30 By Yarrow's streams still let me stray,
Though none should guide my feeble way;
Still feel the breeze down Ettrick break,

Although it chill my wither'd cheek;
Still lay my head by Teviot stone.
35 Though there, forgotten and alone,
The bard may draw his parting groan.

Not scorn'd like me! to Branksome Hall
The minstrels came, at festive call;
Trooping they came from near and far,
40 The jovial priests of mirth and war;
Alike for feast and fight prepared,
Battle and banquet both they shared.
Of late, before each martial clan,
They blew their death-note in the van,
45 But now, for every merry mate,
Rose the portcullis' iron grate;
They sound the pipe, they strike the string,
They dance, they revel, and they sing,
Till the rude turrets shake and ring.

50 Me lists not at this tide declare
The splendour of the spousal rite,
How muster'd in the chapel fair
Both maid and matron, squire and knight;
Me lists not tell of owches rare,
55 Of mantels green, and braided hair,
And kirtles furr'd with miniver;
What plumage waved the altar round,
How spurs and ringing chainlets sound:
And hard it were for bard to speak
60 The changeful hue of Margaret's cheek:
That lovely hue which comes and flies,
As awe and shame alternate rise!

The spousal rites were ended soon:
'Twas now the merry hour of noon.
65 And in the lofty arched hall
Was spread the gorgeous festival.
Steward and squire, with heedful haste,
Marshall'd the rank of every guest;
Pages, with ready blade, were there,
70 The mighty meal to carve and share.

Then rose the riot and the din,
Above, beneath, without, within!

  For, from the lofty balcony,
  Rung trumpet, shalm, and psaltery:
75 Their clanging bowls old warriors quaff'd,
  Loudly they spoke, and loudly laugh'd;
  Whisper'd young knights, in tone more mild,
  To ladies fair, and ladies smiled.
  The hooded hawks, high perch'd on beam,
80 The clamour join'd with whistling scream,
  And flapp'd their wings, and shook their bells,
  In concert with the stag-hounds' yells.
  Round go the flasks of ruddy wine,
  From Bourdeaux, Orleans, or the Rhine;
85 Their tasks the busy sewers ply,
  And all is mirth and revelry.

III.

  By this, the Dame
  Had bid the minstrels tune their lay.
  And first stept forth old Albert Graeme,
  The minstrel of that ancient name:
5 Was none who struck the harp so well,
  Within the land debateable;
  Well friended, too, his hardy kin,
  Whoever lost, were sure to win;
  They sought the beeves that made their broth,
10 In Scotland and in England both.
  In homely guise, as nature bade,
  His simple song the Borderer said:

1. It was an English ladye bright,
  (The sun shines fair on Carlisle wall,)
 And she would marry a Scottish knight,
  For Love will still be lord of all.

2. Blithely they saw the rising sun,
  When he shone fair on Carlisle wall.
 But they were sad ere day was done,
  Though Love was still the lord of all.

3. Her sire gave brooch and jewel fine,
  Where the sun shines fair on Carlisle wall;
 Her brother gave but a flask of wine,
  For ire that Love was lord of all.

4. For she had lands, both meadow and lea,
 Where the sun shines fair on Carlisle wall,
 And he swore her death, ere he would see
 A Scottish knight the lord of all.

5. That wine she had not tasted well,
 (The sun shines fair on Carlisle wall,)
 When dead, in her true love's arms, she fell,
 For Love was still the lord of all!

6. He pierced her brother to the heart,
 Where the sun shines fair on Carlisle wall:
 So perish all would true love part,
 That Love may still be lord of all!

7. And then he took the cross divine,
 (Where the sun shines fair on Carlisle wall,)
 And died for her sake in Palestine;
 So Love was still the lord of all.

8. Now all ye lovers that faithful prove,
 (The sun shines fair on Carlisle wall,)
 Pray for their souls who died for love,
 For Love shall still be lord of all.

IV.

Then, from his seat, with lofty air,
Rose Harold, bard of brave St. Clair;
St. Clair, who, feasting high at Home,
Had with that lord to battle come.
5 Harold was born where restless seas
Howl round the storm-swept Orcades;
Where erst St. Clair held princely sway
O'er isle and islet, strait and bay; —
Still nods their palace to its fall,
10 Thy pride and sorrow, fair Kirkwall! —
Thence oft he mark'd fierce Pentland rave,
As if grim Odin rode her wave;
And watch'd, the whilst, with visage pale,
And throbbing heart, the struggling sail;
15 For all of wonderful and wild
Had rapture for the lonely child.

    And much of wild and wonderful
    In these rude isles might fancy cull;
    For thither came, in times afar,
20 Stern Lochlin's sons of roving war,
    The Norsemen, train'd to spoil and blood,
    Skilled to prepare the raven's food:
    Kings of the main their leaders brave,
    Their barks the dragons of the wave.
25 And there, in many a stormy vale,
    The Scald had told his wondrous tale;
    And many a Runic column high
    Had witness'd grim idolatry.
    And thus had Harold, in his youth,
30 Learn'd many a Saga's rhyme uncouth, —
    Of that sea-snake, tremendous curl'd,
    Whose monstrous circle girds the world:
    Of those dread maids, whose hideous yell
    Maddens the battle's bloody swell;
35 Of chiefs who, guided through the gloom
    By the pale death-lights of the tomb,
    Ransack'd the graves of warriors old,
    Their falchions wrench'd from corpses' hold,
    Waked the deaf tomb with war's alarms,
40 And bade the dead arise to arms!
    With war and wonder all on flame,
    To Roslin's bowers young Harold came,
    Where, by sweet glen and greenwood tree,
    He learn'd a milder minstrelsy;
45 Yet something of the Northern spell
    Mix'd with the softer numbers well.

1. O listen, listen, ladies gay;
    No haughty feat of arms I tell;
  Soft is the note, and sad the lay,
    That mourns the lovely Rosabelle.

2. "Moor, moor the barge, ye gallant crew!
    And, gentle ladye, deign to stay!
  Rest thee in Castle Ravensheuch,
    Nor tempt the stormy firth to-day.

3. "The blackening wave is edged with white:
    To inch and rock the sea-mews fly;

  The fishers have heard the water-sprite,
   Whose screams forebode that wreck is nigh.

4. "Last night the gifted seer did view
  A wet shroud swathed round ladye gay:
Then stay thee, fair, in Ravensheuch;
  Why cross the gloomy firth to-day?" —

5. "'Tis not because Lord Lindesay's heir
  To-night at Roslin leads the ball,
But that my ladye mother there
  Sits lonely in her castle hall.

6. "'Tis not because the ring they ride,
  And Lindesay at the ring rides well,
But that my sire the wine will chide,
  If 'tis not fill'd by Rosabelle." —

7. O'er Roslin all that dreary night,
  A wondrous blaze was seen to gleam!
'Twas broader than the watch-fire's light,
  And redder than the bright moon-beam.

8. It glared on Roslin's castled rock,
  It ruddied all the copse-wood glen;
'Twas seen from Dryden's groves of oak,
  And seen from cavern'd Hawthornden.

9. Seem'd all on fire that chapel proud,
  Where Roslin's chiefs uncoffin'd lie,
Each baron, for a sable shroud,
  Sheathed in his iron panoply.

10. Seem'd all on fire within, around,
  Deep sacristy and altar's pale;
Shone every pillar foliage-bound,
  And glimmer'd all the dead men's mail.

11. Blazed battlement and pinnet high,
  Blazed every rose-carved buttress fair —
So still they blaze, when fate is nigh
  The lordly line of high St. Clair.

12. There are twenty of Roslin's barons bold
  Lie buried within that proud chapelle;
Each one the holy vault doth hold —
  But the sea holds lovely Rosabelle!

13. And each St. Clair was buried there,
    With candle, with book, and with knell;
  But the sea-caves sung, and the wild winds sung,
    The dirge of lovely Rosabelle.

V.

  Hush'd is the harp — the Minstrel gone.
  And did he wander forth alone?
  Alone in indigence and age,
  To linger out his pilgrimage?
5 No! — close beneath proud Newark's tower,
  Arose the Minstrel's lowly bower!
  A simple hut; but there was seen
  The little garden hedged with green,
  The cheerful hearth, and lattice clean.
10 There shelter'd wanderers, by the blaze,
  Oft heard the tale of other days;
  For much he loved to ope his door,
  And give the aid he begg'd before.
  So pass'd the winter's day; but still,
15 When Summer smiled on sweet Bowhill,
  And July's eve, with balmy breath,
  Waved the blue-bells on Newark heath;
  When throstles sung in Hairhead-shaw,
  And corn was green on Carterhaugh,
20 And flourish'd, broad, Blackandro's oak,
  The aged harper's soul awoke!
  Then would he sing achievements high,
  And circumstance of chivalry,
  Till the rapt traveller would stay,
25 Forgetful of the closing day.
  And noble youths, the strain to hear,
  Forsook the hunting of the deer;
  And Yarrow, as he roll'd along,
  Bore burden to the Minstrel song.

                          W. SCOTT.

3. FROM "CHILDE HAROLD'S PILGRIMAGE."

1. My Native Land — Good Night!

1. Adieu, adieu! my native shore
   Fades o'er the waters blue;
   The Night-winds sigh, the breakers roar,
   And shrieks the wild sea-mew.
   Yon Sun that sets upon the sea
   We follow in his flight;
   Farewell awhile to him and thee,
   My native Land — Good Night!

2. A few short hours and He will rise
   To give the morrow birth;
   And I shall hail the main and skies,
   But not my mother earth.
   Deserted is my own good hall,
   Its hearth is desolate:
   Wild weeds are gathering on the wall;
   My dog howls at the gate.

3. "Come hither, hither, my little page!
   Why dost thou weep and wail?
   Or dost thou dread the billow's rage,
   Or tremble at the gale?
   But dash the tear-drop from thine eye;
   Our ship is swift and strong:
   Our fleetest falcon scarce can fly
   More merrily along."

4. 'Let winds be shrill, let waves roll high,
   I fear not wave nor wind;
   Yet marvel not, Sir Childe, that I
   Am sorrowful in mind:
   For I have from my father gone,
   A mother whom I love,
   And have no friend, save these alone,
   But thee — and one above.

5. My father blessed me fervently,
   Yet did not much complain;
   But sorely will my mother sigh
   Till I come back again.' —

"Enough, enough, my little lad,
  Such tears become thine eye:
If I thy guileless bosom had,
  Mine own would not be dry.

6. Come hither, hither, my staunch yeoman,
  Why dost thou look so pale?
Or dost thou dread a French foeman?
  Or shiver at the gale?" —
'Deemst thou I tremble for my life?
  Sir Childe, I'm not so weak;
But thinking on an absent wife
  Will blanch a faithful cheek.

7. My spouse and boys dwell near thy hall,
  Along the bordering lake,
And when they on their father call,
  What answer shall she make?' —
"Enough, enough, my yeoman good,
  Thy grief let none gainsay;
But I, who am of lighter mood,
  Will laugh to flee away."

8. For who would trust the seeming sighs
  Of wife or paramour?
Fresh feres will dry the bright blue eyes
  We late saw streaming o'er.
For pleasures past I do not grieve,
  Nor perils gathering near;
My greatest grief is that I leave
  No thing that claims a tear.

9. And now I'm in the world alone,
  Upon the wide, wide sea:
But why should I for others groan,
  When none will sigh for me?
Perchance my dog will whine in vain,
  Till fed by stranger hands:
But long ere I come back again
  He'd tear me where he stands.

10. With thee, my bark, I'll swiftly go
  Athwart the foaming brine:
Nor care what land thou bearst me to,
  So not again to mine.

          Welcome, welcome, ye dark-blue waves!
            And when you fail my sight,
          Welcome, ye deserts, and ye caves!
            My native Land — Good Night!

II. The Battle of Waterloo.

1. Stop! — for thy tread is on an Empire's dust!
   An Earthquake's spoil is sepulchred below!
   Is the spot marked with no colossal bust?
   Nor column trophied for triumphal show?
   None; but the moral's truth tells simpler so.
   As the ground was before, thus let it be; —
   How that red rain hath made the harvest grow!
   And is this all the world has gained by thee,
   Thou first and last of fields! king-making Victory!

2. And Harold stands upon this place of skulls,
   The grave of France, the deadly Waterloo;
   How in an hour the power which gave annuls
   Its gifts, transferring fame as fleeting too!
   In "pride of place" here last the eagle flew,
   Then tore with bloody talon the rent plain,
   Pierced by the shaft of banded nations through;
   Ambition's life and labours all were vain;
   He wears the shatter'd links of the world's broken chain.

3. There was a sound of revelry by night,
   And Belgium's capital had gathered then
   Her Beauty and her Chivalry, and bright
   The lamps shone o'er fair women and brave men:
   A thousand hearts beat happily; and when
   Music arose with its voluptuous swell,
   Soft eyes looked love to eyes which spake again,
   And all went merry as a marriage-bell;
   But hush! hark! a deep sound strikes like a rising knell!

4. Did ye not hear it? — No; 'twas but the wind
   Or the car rattling o'er the stony street;
   On with the dance! let joy be unconfined;
   No sleep till morn, when Youth and Pleasure meet
   To chase the glowing Hours with flying feet —
   But, hark! — that heavy sound breaks in once more,

As if the clouds its echo would repeat;
And nearer, clearer, deadlier than before;
Arm! Arm! it is — it is — the cannon's opening roar!

5. Within a windowed niche of that high hall
Sat Brunswick's fated chieftain; he did hear
That sound the first amidst the festival,
And caught its tone with Death's prophetic ear;
And when they smiled because he deemed it near,
His heart more truly knew that peal too well
Which stretched his father on a bloody bier,
And roused the vengeance blood alone could quell:
He rushed into the field, and, foremost fighting, fell.

6. Ah! then and there was hurrying to and fro,
And gathering tears, and tremblings of distress,
And cheeks all pale, which but an hour ago
Blushed at the praise of their own loveliness;
And there were sudden partings, such as press
The life from out young hearts, and choking sighs
Which ne'er might be repeated; who could guess
If ever more should meet those mutual eyes,
Since upon night so sweet such awful morn could rise!

7. And there was mounting in hot haste: the steed,
The mustering squadron, and the clattering car,
Went pouring forward with impetuous speed,
And swiftly forming in the ranks of war;
And the deep thunder peal on peal afar;
And near, the beat of the alarming drum
Roused up the soldier ere the morning star;
While thronged the citizens with terror dumb,
Or whispering, with white lips — "The foe! They
    come! they come!"

8. And wild and high the "Cameron's gathering" rose!
The war-note of Lochiel, which Albyn's hills
Have heard, and heard, too, have her Saxon foes: —
How in the noon of night that pibroch thrills,
Savage and shrill! But with the breath which fills
Their mountain-pipe, so fill the mountaineers
With the fierce native daring which instils
The stirring memory of a thousand years,
And Evan's, Donald's fame rings in each clansman's ears.

9. And Ardennes waves above them her green leaves,
Dewy with nature's tear-drops, as they pass,
Grieving, if aught inanimate e'er grieves,
Over the unreturning brave, — alas!
Ere evening to be trodden like the grass
Which now beneath them, but above shall grow
In its next verdure, when this fiery mass
Of living valour, rolling on the foe
And burning with high hope, shall moulder cold and low.

10. Last noon beheld them full of lusty life,
Last eve in Beauty's circle proudly gay,
The midnight brought the signal-sound of strife,
The morn the marshalling in arms, — the day
Battle's magnificently-stern array!
The thunder-clouds close o'er it, which when rent
The earth is covered thick with other clay,
Which her own clay shall cover, heaped and pent,
Rider and horse, — friend, foe, — in one red burial blent!

11. There sunk the greatest, nor the worst of men,
Whose spirit antithetically mixt
One moment of the mightiest, and again
On little objects with like firmness fixt,
Extreme in all things! hadst thou been betwixt,
Thy throne had still been thine, or never been;
For daring made thy rise as fall: thou seekst
Even now to re-assume the imperial mien,
And shake again the world, the Thunderer of the scene!

12. Conqueror and captive of the earth art thou!
She trembles at thee still, and thy wild name
Was ne'er more bruited in men's minds than now
That thou art nothing, save the jest of Fame,
Who wooed thee once, thy vassal, and became
The flatterer of thy fierceness, till thou wert
A god unto thyself; nor less the same
To the astounded kingdoms all inert,
Who deemed thee for a time whate'er thou didst assert.

13. Oh, more or less than man — in high or low,
Battling with nations, flying from the field;
Now making monarchs' necks thy footstool, now,
More than thy meanest soldier taught to yield:

An empire thou couldst crush, command, rebuild.
But govern not thy pettiest passion, nor,
However deeply in men's spirits skilled,
Look through thine own, nor curb the lust of war.
Nor learn that tempted Fate will leave the loftiest star.

III. To the Ocean.

1. Roll on, thou deep and dark blue Ocean — roll!
Ten thousand fleets sweep over thee in vain;
Man marks the earth with ruin — his control
Stops with the shore: — upon the watery plain
The wrecks are all thy deed, nor doth remain
A shadow of man's ravage, save his own,
When, for a moment, like a drop of rain,
He sinks into thy depths with bubbling groan,
Without a grave, unknelled, uncoffined, and unknown.

2. His steps are not upon thy paths, thy fields
Are not a spoil for him, — thou dost arise
And shake him from thee; the vile strength he wields
For earth's destruction thou dost all despise,
Spurning him from thy bosom to the skies,
And sendst him, shivering in thy playful spray
And howling, to his Gods, where haply lies
His petty hope in some near port or bay,
And dashest him again to earth: — there let him lay.

3. The armaments which thunderstrike the walls
Of rock-built cities, bidding nations quake,
And monarchs tremble in their capitals,
The oak leviathans, whose huge ribs make
Their clay creator the vain title take
Of lord of thee, and arbiter of war;
These are thy toys, and, as the snowy flake,
They melt into thy yeast of waves, which mar
Alike the Armada's pride, or spoils of Trafalgar.

4. Thy shores are empires, changed in all save thee —
Assyria, Greece, Rome, Carthage, what are they?
Thy waters wasted them while they were free,
And many a tyrant since: their shores obey

  The stranger, slave, or savage: their decay
  Has dried up realms to deserts: — not so thou,
  Unchangeable save to thy wild waves' play —
  Time writes no wrinkle on thine azure brow —
 Such as creation's dawn beheld, thou rollest now.

5. Thou glorious mirror, where the Almighty's form
  Glasses itself in tempests; in all time,
  Calm or convulsed — in breeze, or gale, or storm,
  Icing the pole, or in the torrid clime
  Dark-heaving; — boundless, endless, and sublime —
  The image of Eternity — the throne
  Of the Invisible; even from out thy slime
  The monsters of the deep are made; each zone
 Obeys thee; thou goest forth, dread, fathomless, alone.

6. And I have loved thee, Ocean! and my joy
  Of youthful sports was on thy breast to be
  Borne, like thy bubbles, onward: from a boy
  I wantoned with thy breakers — they to me
  Were a delight; and if the freshening sea
  Made them a terror — 'twas a pleasing fear.
  For I was as it were a child of thee,
  And trusted to thy billows far and near,
 And laid my hand upon thy mane — as I do here.
          Lord Byron.

4. THE LOTOSEATERS.

1. "Courage!" he said, and pointed toward the land,
  "This mounting wave will roll us shoreward soon."
  In the afternoon they came unto a land,
  In which it seemed always afternoon.
  All round the coast the languid air did swoon,
  Breathing like one that hath a weary dream.
  Full-faced above the valley stood the moon;
  And like a downward smoke, the slender stream
  Along the cliff to fall, and pause, and fall did seem.

2. A land of streams! some, like a downward smoke,
  Slow-dropping veils of thinnest lawn, did go;
  And some thro' wavering lights and shadows broke,
  Rolling a slumb'rous sheet of foam below.
  They saw the gleaming river seaward flow
  From the inner land: far off, three mountain-tops,

Three silent pinnacles of aged snow,
Stood sunset-flushed: and, dewed with showery drops,
Up-clomb the shadowy pine above the woven copse.

3. The charmed sunset lingered low adown
In the red West: thro' mountain clefts the dale
Was seen far inland, and the yellow down
Bordered with palm. and many a winding vale
And meadow, set with slender galingale;
A land where all things always seemed the same!
And round about the keel with faces pale,
Dark faces pale against that rosy flame,
The mild-eyed melancholy Lotos-eaters came.

4. Branches they bore of that enchanted stem,
Laden with flower and fruit, whereof they gave
To each, but whoso did receive of them,
And taste, to him the gushing of the wave
Far, far away did seem to mourn and rave
On alien shores; and if his fellow spake,
His voice was thin, as voices from the grave;
And deep-asleep he seemed, yet all awake,
And music in his ears his beating heart did make.

5. They sat them down upon the yellow sand,
Between the sun and moon upon the shore;
And sweet it was to dream of Father-land,
Of child, and wife, and slave; but evermore
Most weary seemed the sea, weary the oar,
Weary the wandering fields of barren foam.
Then some one said, "We will return no more;"
And all at once they sang, "Our island home
Is far beyond the wave; we will no longer roam."

Choric Song.

There is sweet music here that softer falls
Than petals from blown roses on the grass,
Or night-dews on still waters between walls
Of shadowy granite, in a gleaming pass;
5 Music that gentlier on the spirit lies,
Than tired eyelids upon tired eyes;
Music that brings sweet sleep down from the blissful skies.

Here are cool mosses deep,
And thro' the moss the ivies creep,
10 And in the stream the long-leaved flowers weep,
And from the craggy ledge the poppy hangs in sleep.

Why are we weighed upon with heaviness,
And utterly consumed with sharp distress,
While all things else have rest from weariness?
15 All things have rest: why should we toil alone,
We only toil, who are the first of things,
And make perpetual moan,
Still from one sorrow to another thrown:
Nor ever fold our wings,
20 And cease from wanderings,
Nor steep our brows in slumber's holy balm;
Nor harken what the inner spirit sings,
"There is no joy but calm!"
Why should we only toil, the roof and crown of things?

25 Lo! in the middle of the wood,
The folded leaf is wooed from out the bud
With winds upon the branch, and there
Grows green and broad, and takes no care,
Sun-steeped at noon, and in the moon
30 Nightly dew-fed; and turning yellow
Falls, and floats adown the air.
Lo! sweetened with the summer light,
The full-juiced apple, waxing over-mellow,
Drops in a silent autumn night.
35 All its allotted length of days,
The flower ripens in its place,
Ripens and fades, and falls, and hath no toil,
Fast-rooted in the fruitful soil.

Hateful is the dark-blue sky,
40 Vaulted o'er the dark-blue sea.
Death is the end of life; ah, why
Should life all labour be?
Let us alone. Time driveth onward fast,
And in a little while our lips are dumb.
45 Let us alone. What is it that will last?
All things are taken from us, and become

Portions and parcels of the dreadful Past.
Let us alone. What pleasure can we have
To war with evil? Is there any peace
50 In ever climbing up the climbing wave?
All things have rest, and ripen toward the grave
In silence; ripen, fall and cease:
Give us long rest or death, dark death, or dreamful ease.

How sweet it were, hearing the downward stream,
55 With half-shut eyes ever to seem
Falling asleep in a half-dream!
To dream and dream, like yonder amber light,
Which will not leave the myrrh-bush on the height;
To hear each other's whispered speech;
60 Eating the Lotos day by day,
To watch the crisping ripples on the beach,
And tender curving lines of creamy spray;
To lend our hearts and spirits wholly
To the influence of mild-minded melancholy!
65 To muse and brood and live again in memory,
With those old faces of our infancy
Heaped over with a mound of grass,
Two handfuls of white dust, shut in an urn of brass!

Dear is the memory of our wedded lives,
70 And dear the last embraces of our wives
And their warm tears: but all hath suffered change:
For surely now our household hearths are cold:
Our sons inherit us: our looks are strange:
And we should come like ghosts to trouble joy:
75 Or else the island princes over-bold
Have eat our substance, and the minstrel sings
Before them of the ten years' war in Troy,
And our great deeds, as half-forgotten things.
Is there confusion in the little isle?
80 Let what is broken so remain
The Gods are hard to reconcile:
'Tis hard to settle order once again.
There is confusion worse than death,
Trouble on trouble, pain on pain,
85 Long labour unto aged breath,
Sore task to hearts worn out with many wars,
And eyes grown dim with gazing on the pilot-stars.

But, propt on beds of amaranth and moly,
How sweet (while warm airs lull us, blowing lowly)
90 With half dropt eyelids still,
Beneath a heaven dark and holy,
To watch the long bright river drawing slowly
His waters from the purple hill —
To hear the dewy echoes calling
95 From cave to cave thro' the thick-twined vine —
To watch the emerald-coloured water falling
Thro' many a woven acanthus-wreath divine!
Only to hear and see the far-off sparkling brine,
Only to hear were sweet, stretched out beneath the pine.

100 The Lotos blooms below the barren peak:
The Lotos blows by every winding creek:
All day the wind breathes low with mellower tone:
Thro' every hollow cave and alley lone
Round and round the spicy downs the yellow Lotos-dust is blown.
105 We have had enough of action, and of motion we,
Rolled to starboard, rolled to larboard, when the surge was seething free,
Where the wallowing monster spouted his foam-fountains in the sea.
Let us swear an oath, and keep it with an equal mind,
In the hollow Lotos-land to live and lie reclined
110 On the hills like Gods together, careless of mankind.
For they lie beside their nectar, and the bolts are hurled
Far below them in the valleys, and the clouds are lightly curled
Round their golden houses, girdled with the gleaming world:
Where they smile in secret, looking over wasted lands,
115 Blight and famine, plague and earthquake, roaring deeps and fiery sands,
Clanging fights, and flaming towns, and sinking ships, and praying hands.
But they smile, they find a music centred in a doleful song
Steaming up, a lamentation and an ancient tale of wrong,
Like a tale of little meaning tho' the words are strong:
120 Chanted from an ill-used race of men that cleave the soil,
Sow the seed, and reap the harvest with enduring toil,
Storing yearly little dues of wheat, and wine and oil:
Till they perish and they suffer — some, 'tis whispered — down in hell
Suffer endless anguish, others in Elysian valleys dwell,
125 Resting weary limbs at last on beds of asphodel.
Surely, surely, slumber is more sweet than toil, the shore
Than labour in the deep mid-ocean, wind, and wave, and oar:
Oh rest ye, brother mariners, we will not wander more.

ALFRED TENNYSON.

5. KING LEAR.

Act I. Scene I.

Enter Lear, Cornwall, Albany, Goneril, Regan, Cordelia and Attendants.

    Lear. Attend the Lords of France and Burgundy, Gloster!
    Glo. I shall, my liege.   (Exit Gloster.)
    Lear. Meantime we shall express our darker purpose. —
Give me the map there. — Know that we have divided
5 In three our kingdom: and 'tis our fast intent
To shake all cares and business from our age;
Conferring them on younger strengths, while we
Unburden'd crawl toward death. — Our son of Cornwall,
And you, our no less loving son of Albany,
10 We have this hour a constant will to publish
Our daughters' several dowers, that future strife
May be prevented now. The princes France and Burgundy,
Great rivals in our youngest daughter's love,
Long in our court have made their amorous sojourn,
15 And here are to be answer'd. — Tell me, my daughters. —
Since now we will divest us both of rule,
Interest of territory, cares of state, —
Which of you shall we say doth love us most?
That we our largest bounty may extend
20 Where nature doth with merit challenge. — Goneril,
Our eldest-born, speak first.
    Gon. Sir, I love you more than words can wield the matter:
Dearer than eyesight, space, and liberty:
Beyond what can be valu'd, rich or rare;
25 No less than life, with grace, health, beauty, honour:
As much as child e'er lov'd, or father found:
A love that makes breath poor, and speech unable:
Beyond all manner of "so much" I love you.
    Cor. (aside) What shall Cordelia do? Love, and be silent.
30   *Lear.* Of all these bounds, even from this line to this,
With shadowy forests and with champains rich'd,
With plenteous rivers and wide-skirted meads,
We make thee lady: to thine and Albany's issue
Be this perpetual. — What says our second daughter,
35 Our dearest Regan, wife to Cornwall? Speak.

Reg. I'm made of that self metal as my sister,
And prize me at her worth. In my true heart
I find she names my very deed of love;
Only she comes too short, — that I profess
40 Myself an enemy to all other joys,
Which the most precious square of sense professes;
And find I am alone felicitate
In your dear highness' love.
    Cor. (aside)   Then poor Cordelia!
And yet not so; since, I am sure, my love's
45 More richer than my tongue.
    Lear. To thee and thine hereditary ever
Remain this ample third of our fair kingdom:
No less in space, validity, and pleasure,
Than that conferr'd on Goneril. — Now, our joy,
50 Although our last and least; to whose young love
The vines of France and milk of Burgundy
Strive to be interest, what can you say to draw.
A third more opulent than your sisters? Speak.
    Cor. Nothing, my lord.
55   *Lear.* Nothing!
    Cor. Nothing.
    Lear. Nothing will come of nothing: speak again.
    Cor. Unhappy that I am, I cannot heave
My heart into my mouth: I love your majesty
60 According to my bond; nor more nor less.
    Lear. How, How, Cordelia! mend your speech a little,
Lest it may mar your fortunes.
    Cor.   Good my lord,
You have begot me, bred me, lov'd me: I
Return those duties back as are right fit,
65 Obey you, love you, and most honour you.
Why have my sisters husbands, if they say
They love you all? Haply, when I shall wed,
That lord whose hand must take my plight shall carry
Half my love with him, half my care and duty:
70 Sure, I shall never marry like my sisters.
    Lear. But goes thy heart with this?
    Cor.   Ay, good my lord.
    Lear. So young, and so untender?
    Cor.   So young, my lord, and true.
    Lear. Let it be so, — thy truth then, be thy dower:

   For, by the sacred radiance of the sun,
75 The mysteries of Hecate, and the night;
   By all the operation of the orbs
   From whom we do exist, and cease to be;
   Here I disclaim all my paternal care,
   Propinquity and property of blood,
80 And as a stranger to my heart and me
   Hold thee, from this, for ever. The barbarous Scythian,
   Or he that makes his generation messes
   To gorge his appetite, shall to my bosom
   Be as well neighbour'd, pitied, and reliev'd,
85 As thou my sometime daughter.
    Kent.   Good my liege, —
    Lear. Peace, Kent;
   Come not between the dragon and his wrath. —
   I lov'd her most, and thought to set my rest
   On her kind nursery. — Hence and avoid my sight! —
90 So be my grave my peace, as here I give
   Her father's heart from her! — Call France: — who stirs?
   Call Burgundy. — Cornwall and Albany.
   With my two daughters' dowers digest this third:
   Let pride, which she calls plainness, marry her.
95 I do invest you jointly with my power,
   Pre-eminence, and all the large effects
   That troop with majesty. — Ourself, by monthly course,
   With reservation of an hundred knights,
   By you to be sustain'd, shall our abode
100 Make with you by due turn. Only we still retain
   The name, and all th'additions to a king;
   The sway, revenue, execution of the rest,
   Beloved sons, be yours: which to confirm,
   This coronet part between you.
    Kent.   Royal Lear,
105 Whom I have ever honour'd as my king,
   Lov'd as my father, as my master follow'd,
   As my great patron thought on in my prayers,—
    Lear. The bow is bent and drawn, make from the shaft.
    Kent. Let it fall rather, though the fork invade
110 The region of my heart: be Kent unmannerly,
   When Lear is mad. What wouldst thou do, old man?
   Think'st thou that duty shall have dread to speak,
   When power to flattery bows? To plainness honour's bound,

When majesty falls to folly. Reserve thy state
115 And, in thy best consideration, check
This hideous rashness: answer my life my judgment,
Thy youngest daughter does not love thee least:
Nor are those empty-hearted whose low sound
Reverbs no hollowness.

  Lear.   Kent, on thy life, not more.
120 *Kent.* My life I never held but as a pawn
To wage against thine enemies: nor fear to lose it,
Thy safety being the motive.
  Lear.   Out of my sight!
  Kent. See better, Lear; and let me still remain
The true blank of thine eye.
125 *Lear.* Now, by Apollo, —
  Kent.   Now, by Apollo, king,
Thou swear'st thy gods in vain.
  Lear.   O, vassal! miscreant!
  Alb., Corn. Dear sir, forbear.
  Kent.   Kill thy physician, and the fee bestow
Upon the foul disease. Revoke thy gift;
130 Or, whilst I can vent clamour from my throat,
I'll tell thee thou dost evil.
  Lear.   Hear me, recreant!
On thine allegiance, hear me! —
Since thou hast sought to make us break our vow, —
Which we durst never yet, — and with strain'd pride
135 To come between our sentence and our power, —
Which nor our nature nor our place can bear, —
Our potency made good, take thy reward.
Five days we do allot thee, for provision
To shield thee from diseases of the world;
140 And, on the sixth, to turn thy hated back
Upon our kingdom: if, on the tenth day following,
Thy banish'd trunk be found in our dominions,
The moment is thy death. Away! by Jupiter,
This shall not be revok'd.
145 *Kent.* Fare thee well, king: sith thus thou wilt appear,
Freedom lives hence, and banishment is here. —
(To Cordelia) The gods to their dear shelter take thee, maid,
That justly think'st, and hast most rightly said! —
(To Regan and Goneril) And your large speeches may your deeds approve,

150 That good effects may spring from words of love. —
Thus Kent, O princes, bids you all adieu;
He'll shape his old course in a country new. (Exit.)

Flourish, Re-enter Gloster, with France, Burgundy, and Attendants.
    Glo. Here's France and Burgundy, my noble lord.
    Lear. My Lord of Burgundy,
155 We first address towards you, who with this king
Hath rivall'd for our daughter: what, in the least,
Will you require in present dower with her,
Or cease your quest of love?
    Bur.   Most royal majesty,
I crave no more than hath your highness offer'd,
160 Nor will you tender less.
    Lear.   Right noble Burgundy,
When she was dear to us, we did hold her so;
But now her price is fall'n. Sir, there she stands:
If aught within that little seeming substance,
Or all of it, with our displeasure piec'd,
165 And nothing more, may fitly like your grace,
She's there, and she is yours.
    Bur.   I know no answer.
    Lear. Will you, with those infirmities she owes,
Unfriended, new-adopted to our hate,
Dower'd with our curse, and stranger'd with our oath,
170 Take her, or leave her?
    Bur.   Pardon me, royal sir;
Election makes not up on such conditions.
    Lear. Then leave her, sir; for, by the power that made me,
I tell you all her wealth. (To France) For you, great king,
I would not from your love make such a stray,
175 To match you where I hate; therefore beseech you
T'avert your liking a more worthier way
Than on a wretch whom nature is asham'd
Almost t' acknowledge hers.
    France.   This is most strange,
That she, who even but now was your best object,
180 The argument of your praise, balm of your age,
Most best, most dear'st, should in this trice of time
Commit a thing so monstrous, to dismantle
So many folds of favour. Sure, her offence
Must be of such unnatural degree,
185 That monsters it, or your fore-vouch'd affection

Fall'n into taint: which to believe of her,
Must be a faith that reason without miracle
Should never plant in me.
    Cor.   I yet beseech your majesty. —
If for I want that glib and oily art,
190 To speak and purpose not: since what I will intend,
I'll do't before I speak, — that you make known
It is no vicious blot, murther, or foulness,
No unchaste action, or dishonour'd step,
That hath depriv'd me of your grace and favour:
195 But even for want of that for which I'm richer, —
A still-soliciting eye, and such a tongue
As I am glad I have not, though not to have it
Hath lost me in your liking.
    Lear.   Better thou
Hadst not been born than not t'have pleas'd me better.
200   *France.* Is it but this, — a tardiness in nature
Which often leaves the history unspoke
That it intends to do? — My Lord of Burgundy,
What say you to the lady? Love's not love
When it is mingled with regards that stands
205 Aloof from th' entire point. Will you have her?
She is herself a dowry.
    Bur.   Royal Lear,
Give but that portion which yourself propos'd,
And here I take Cordelia by the hand,
Duchess of Burgundy.
    Lear. Nothing: I have sworn; I am firm.
210   *Bur.* I'm sorry then, you have so lost a father
That you must lose a husband.
    Cor.   Peace be with Burgundy!
Since that respect and fortunes are his love,
I shall not be his wife.
    France.   Fairest Cordelia, that art most rich, being poor;
215 Most choice, forsaken; and most lov'd, despis'd!
Thee and thy virtues here I seize upon:
Be't lawful I take up what's cast away.
Gods, gods! 'tis strange that from their cold'st neglect
My love should kindle to inflam'd respect. —
220 Thy dowerless daughter, king, thrown to my chance,
Is queen of us, of ours, and our fair France:
Not all the dukes of waterish Burgundy
Can buy this unpriz'd precious maid of me. —

Bid them farewell, Cordelia, though unkind:
225 Thou losest here, a better where to find.
    Lear. Thou hast her, France: let her be thine; for we
Have no such daughter, nor shall ever see
That face of hers again: — Therefore be gone
Without our grace, our love, our benison. —
230 Come. noble Burgundy. (Flourish, Exeunt Lear, Burgundy, Cornwall, Albany
                                                                                Gloster, and Attendants.)
    France. Bid farewell to your sisters.
    Cor. The jewels of our father, with wash'd eyes
Cordelia leaves you: I know you what you are;
And like a sister, am most loth to call
235 Your faults as they are nam'd. Love well our father:
To your professed bosoms I commit him:
But yet, alas, stood I within his grace.
I would prefer him to a better place.
So, farewell to you both.
240   *Reg.* Prescribe not us our duties.
    Gon.   Let your study
Be to content your lord, who hath receiv'd you
At fortune's alms. You have obedience scanted,
And well are worth the want that you have wanted.
    Cor. Time shall unfold what plighted cunning hides:
245 Who covers faults, at last with shame derides.
Well may you prosper!
    France.   Come my fair Cordelia.
                                        (Exeunt France and Cordelia.)
    Gon. Sister, it is not little I have to say of what most nearly
appertains to us both. I think our father will hence to-night.
    Reg. That's most certain, and with you; next month with us.
250   *Gon.* You see how full of changes his age is; the observation
we have made of it hath not been little: he always loved our sister
most; and with what poor judgment he hath now cast her off appears
too grossly.
    Reg. 'Tis the infirmity of his age: yet he hath ever but slen-
255 derly known himself.
    Gon. The best and soundest of his time hath been but rash;
then must we look to receive from his age, not alone the imper-
fections of long-engraffed condition, but therewithal the unruly waywardness that infirm and choleric years bring with them.
260   *Reg.* Such unconstant starts are we like to have from him as
this of Kent's banishment.
    Gon. There is further compliment of leave-taking between France

and him. Pray you, let us hit together: if our father carry authority
with such dispositions as he bears, this last surrender of his will but
265 offend us.
    Reg. We shall further think of it.
    Gon. We must do something, and i' the heat.   (*Exeunt.*)

Act III. Scene II.
Another part of the heath. Storm continues.
Enter Lear and Fool.

    Lear. Blow, winds, and crack your cheeks! rage! blow!
You cataracts and hurricanoes, spout
Till you have drench'd our steeples, drown'd the cocks!
You sulphurous and thought-executing fires,
5 Vaunt-couriers to oak-cleaving thunderbolts,
Singe my white head! And thou, all-shaking thunder,
Strike flat the thick rotundity o' the world!
Crack nature's moulds, all germens spill at once,
That makes ingrateful man!
10   *Fool.* O nuncle, court holy-water in a dry house is better than
this rain-water out o'door. Good nuncle, in, and ask thy daughters'
blessing: here's a night pities neither wise men nor fools.
    Lear. Rumble thy bellyful! Spit, fire! spout, rain!
Nor rain, wind, thunder, fire, are my daughters:
15 I tax not you, you elements, with unkindness;
I never gave you kingdom, call'd you children,
You owe me no subscription: then let fall
Your horrible pleasure: here I stand, your slave,
A poor, infirm, weak, and despis'd old man:
20 But yet I call you servile ministers,
That have with two pernicious daughters join'd
Your high-engender'd battles 'gainst a head
So old and white as this! O! O! 'tis foul!
    Fool. He that has a house to put 's head in has a good head-
25 piece.

        The man that makes his toe
        What he his heart should make,
        Shall of a corn cry woe,
        And turn his sleep to wake:
30 for there was never yet fair woman but she made mouths in a glass.
    Lear. No, I will be the pattern of all patience;
I will say nothing.
        Enter Kent.

Kent. Who's there?

Fool. Marry, that's a wise man and a fool.

35   *Kent.* Alas, sir, are you here? things that love night
Love not such nights as these; the wrathful skies
Gallow the very wanderers of the dark,
And make them keep their caves: since I was man,
Such sheets of fire, such bursts of horrid thunder,
40 Such groans of roaring wind and rain, I never
Remember to have heard; man's nature cannot carry
Th' affliction nor the fear.

    Lear.   Let the great gods,
That keep this dreadful pother o'er our heads,
Find out their enemies now. Tremble, thou wretch,
45 That hast within thee undivulged crimes,
Unwhipp'd of justice: hide thee, thou bloody hand:
Thou perjur'd, and thou simular of virtue
That under covert and convenient seeming
Has practis'd on man's life: close pent-up guilts,
50 Rive your concealing continents, and cry
These dreadful summoners grace. — I am a man
More sinn'd against than sinning.

    Kent.   Alack, bare-headed!
Gracious my lord, hard by here is a hovel;
Some friendship will it lend you 'gainst the tempest:
55 Repose you there; while I to this hard house —
More harder than the stones whereof 'tis rais'd;
Which even but now, demanding after you,
Denied me to come in — return, and force
Their scanted courtesy.

    Lear.   My wits begin to turn. —
60 Come on, my boy: how dost, my boy? art cold?
I'm cold myself. — — Where is this straw, my fellow?
The art of our necessities is strange,
That can make vild things precious. Come, your hovel. —
Poor fool and knave, I've one part in my heart
65 That's sorry yet for thee.

    Fool.   *He that has and a little tiny wit,* —   (Singing.)
        With hey, ho the wind and the rain, —
        Must make content with his fortunes fit,
        Though the rain it raineth every day.

70   *Lear.* True, my good boy. — Come, bring us to this hovel.
(Exeunt Lear and Kent.)

   Fool. I'll speak a prophecy ere I go:
When brewers mar their malt with water;
When nobles are their tailors' tutors;
75   When every case in law is right:
No squire in debt, nor no poor knight;
When slanders do not live in tongues;
Nor cutpurses come not to throngs:
When usurers tell their gold i' the field;
80   Then shall the realm of Albion
Come to great confusion:
Then comes the time, who lives to see't,
That going shall be us'd with feet.
This prophecy Merlin shall make; for I live before his time. *(Exit.)*

Scene IV.

A part of the heath, with a hovel. Storm continues.

Enter Lear, Kent, and Fool.

   Kent. Here is the place, my lord; good my lord, enter:
The tyranny of the open night's to rough
For nature to endure.
   Lear.   Let me alone.
   Kent. Good my lord, enter here.
   Lear.   Wilt break my heart?
5   *Kent.* I had rather break mine own. Good my lord, enter.
   Lear. Thou think'st 'tis much that this contentious storm
Invades us to the skin: so 'tis to thee;
But where the greater malady is fix'd,
The lesser is scarce felt. Thou'dst shun a bear;
10 But if thy flight lay toward the roaring sea,
Thou'dst meet the bear i' the mouth. When the mind's free,
The body's delicate: the tempest in my mind
Doth from my senses take all feeling else
Save what beats there. — Filial ingratitude!
15 Is it not as this mouth should tear this hand
For lifting food to't? — But I will punish home: —
No, I will weep no more. — In such a night
To shut me out! — Pour on; I will endure: —

In such a night as this! O Regan, Goneril!
20 Your old kind father, whose frank heart gave all. —
O, that way madness lies; let me shun that:
No more of that.

    Kent. Good my lord, enter here.

    Lear. Prithee, go in thyself; seek thine own ease:
This tempest will not give me leave to ponder
25 On things would hurt me more. — But I'll go in. —
(To the Fool) In, boy, go first. You houseless poverty, —
Nay, get thee in. I'll pray, and then I'll sleep. —   (Fool goes in.)
Poor naked wretches, wheresoe'er you are,
That bide the pelting of this pitiless storm,
30 How shall your houseless heads and unfed sides,
Your loop'd and window'd raggedness, defend you
From seasons such as these? O, I have ta'en
Too little care of this! Take physic, pomp;
Expose thyself to feel what wretches feel,
35 That thou mayst shake the superflux to them,
And show the heavens more just.

    Edg. (within) Fathom and half, fathom and half! Poor Tom!
                                 (The Fool runs out from the hovel.)

    Fool. Come not in here, nuncle, here's a spirit. Help me, help me!

40   *Kent.* Give me thy hand. — Who's there?

    Fool. A spirit, a spirit: he says his name's poor Tom.

    Kent. What art thou that dost grumble there i' the straw? Come forth.

              Enter Edgar disguised as a madman.

    Edg. Away! the foul fiend follows me. Through the sharp haw-
45 thorn blow the winds. — Hum! go to thy bed, and warm thee.

    Lear. Didst thou give all to thy daughters? And art thou come to this?

    Edg. Who gives any thing to poor Tom? whom the foul fiend hath led through fire and through flame, through ford and whirlpool,
50 o'er bog and quagmire; that hath laid knives under his pillow, and halters in his pew; set ratsbane by his porridge; made him proud of heart, to ride on a bay trotting horse over four-inched bridges, to course his own shadow for a traitor. — Bless thy five wits! — Tom's a-cold. — O, do de, do de, do de. — Bless thee from whirl-
55 winds, star-blasting and taking! Do poor Tom some charity, whom the foul fiend vexes: — there could I have him now, — and there, — and there again, and there.   (Storm continues.)

Lear. What, have his daughters brought him to this pass? — Couldst thou save nothing? Didst thou give 'em all?

60 *Fool.* Nay, he reserved a blanket.

Lear. Now, all the plagues that in the pendulous air
Hang fated o'er men's faults light on thy daughters!

Kent. He hath no daughters, sir.

Lear. Death, traitor! nothing could have subdu'd nature
65 To such a lowness but his unkind daughters. —
Is it the fashion, that discarded fathers
Should have thus little mercy on their flesh?
Judicious punishment! 'twas this flesh begot
Those pelican daughters.

70 *Fool.* This cold night will turn us all to fools and madmen.

Edg. Take heed o' the foul fiend; obey thy parents; keep thy word's justice: swear not; set not thy sweet heart on proud array. Tom's a-cold.

Lear. What hast thou been?

75 *Edg.* A serving-man, proud in heart and mind; that curled my hair; wore gloves in my cap.
  Still through the hawthorn blows the cold wind:
  Says suum, mun, nonny.
  Dolphin my boy, my boy, sessa! let him trot by.
80   (Storm continues.)

Lear. Why, thou wert better in thy grave than to answer with thy uncovered body this extremity of the skies. — Is man no more than this? Consider him well. Thou owest the worm no silk, the beast no hide, the sheep no wool, the cat no perfume. — Ha! here's
85 three on 's are sophisticated! — Thou art the thing itself: unaccommodated man is no more but such a poor, bare, forked animal as thou art. — Off, off, you lendings! — come, unbutton here.

Fool. Prithee, nuncle, be contented; 'tis a naughty night to swim in. — Now a little fire in a wild field were like an old
90 sinner's heart, — a small spark, all the rest on's body cold. — Look, here comes a walking fire.

Enter Gloster with a torch.

Edg. This is the foul fiend Flibbertigibbet: he begins at curfew, and walks at first cock: he gives the web and the pin, squints the
95 eye, and makes the hare-lip; mildews the white wheat, and hurts the poor creature of earth.

*Swithold footed thrice the wold,
He met the night-mare, and her nine-fold;
    Bid her alight,*
100   *And her troth plight,
And aroint thee, witch, aroint thee!*
    Kent. How fares your grace?
    Lear. What's he?
    Kent. Who's there? What is't you seek?
105   *Glo.* What are you there? Your names?
    Edg. Poor Tom; that eats the swimming frog, the toad, the tadpole, the wall-newt and the water: that in the fury of his heart, when the foul fiend rages, eats cow-dung for sallets; swallows the old rat and the ditch-dog; drinks the green mantle of the standing
110 pool; who is whipped from tithing to tithing, and stock-punished, and imprisoned; who hath three suits to his back, six shirts to his body, horse to ride, and weapon to wear;
    But mice and rats, and such small deer,
    Have been Tom's food for seven long year.
115 Beware my follower. — Peace, Smulkin; peace, thou fiend!
    Glo. What, hath your grace no better company?
    Edg. The prince of darkness is a gentleman. Modo he's call'd, and Mahu.
    Glo. Our flesh and blood, my lord, is grown so vild,
120 That it doth hate what gets it.
    Edg. Poor Tom's a-cold.
    Glo. Go in with me: my duty cannot suffer
T' obey in all your daughters' hard commands:
Though their injunction be to bar my doors,
125 And let this tyrannous night take hold upon you,
Yet have I ventur'd to come seek you out,
And bring you where both fire and food is ready.
    Lear. First let me talk with this philosopher. —
What is the cause of thunder?
130   *Kent.* Good my lord, take his offer: go into the house.
    Lear. I'll talk a word with this same learned Theban. —
What is your study?
    Edg. How to prevent the fiend, and to kill vermin.
    Lear. Let me ask you one word in private.
135   *Kent.* Importune him once more to go, my lord;
His wits begin t' unsettle.
    Glo.   Canst thou blame him?
His daughters seek his death: — ah, that good Kent! —

He said it would be thus, — poor banish'd man! —
Thou say'st the king grows mad: I'll tell thee, friend.
140 I'm almost mad myself: I had a son,
Now outlaw'd from my blood; he sought my life,
But lately, very late: I lov'd him, friend,
No father his son dearer: true to tell thee, (Storm continues.)
The grief hath craz'd my wits. — What a night's this! —
145 I do beseech your grace, —
  Lear.   O, cry you mercy, sir. —
Noble philosopher, your company.
  Edg. Tom's a-cold.
  Glo. In, fellow, there, into the hovel: keep thee warm.
  Lear. Come, let's in all.
  Kent.   This way, my lord.
  Lear.   With him:
150 I will keep still with my philosopher.
  Kent. Good my lord, soothe him; let him take the fellow.
  Glo. Take him you on.
  Kent. Sirrah, come on; go along with us.
  Lear. Come, good Athenian.
155   *Glo.* No words, no words: hush.
  Edg. *Child Rowland to the dark tower came:*
    His word was still, — Fie, foh, and fum,
    I smell the blood of a British man. (Exeunt.)

Act IV, Scene VII.

Cordelia's head-quarters.

Enter Cordelia, Kent, Doctor and a Gentleman.

  Cor. O thou good Kent, how shall I live and work,
To match thy goodness? My life will be too short,
5 And every measure fail me.
  Kent. To be acknowledg'd, madam, is o'erpaid.
All my reports go with the modest truth;
Nor more nor clipp'd, but so.
  Cor.   Be better suited:
These weeds are memories of those worser hours:
I prithee, put them off.
  Kent.   Pardon, dear madam:
Yet to be known shortens my made intent:
10 My boon I make it, that you know me not
Till time and I think meet.

  Cor. Then be't so, my good lord. — (To the Doctor) How does
                  the king?
  Doct. Madam, sleeps still.
  Cor. O you kind gods,
15 Cure this great breach in his abused nature!
Th' untun'd and jarring senses, O, wind up
Of this child-changed father!
  Doct.   So please your majesty
That we may wake the king: he hath slept long.
  Cor. Be govern'd by your knowledge, and proceed
20 I' the sway of your own will. Is he array'd?
  Kent. Ay, madam; in the heaviness of sleep
We put fresh garments on him.
      (Enter Lear in a chair carried by servants.)
  Doct. Be by, good madam, when we do awake him:
I doubt not of his temperance.
  Cor.   Very well.
25   *Doct.* Please you, draw near. — Louder the music there!
  Cor. O my dear father! Restoration hang
Thy medicine on my lips; and let this kiss
Repair those violent harms that my two sisters
Have in thy reverence made!
  Kent.   Kind and dear princess!
30   *Cor.* Had you not been their father, these white flakes
Had challeng'd pity of them. Was this a face
To be oppos'd against the warring winds?
To stand against the deep dread-bolted thunder?
In the most terrible and nimble stroke
35 Of quick, cross lightning? to watch — poor perdu! —
With this thin helm? Mine enemy's dog,
Though he had bit me, should have stood that night
Against my fire; and wast thou fain, poor father,
To hovel thee with swine, and rogues forlorn,
40 In short and musty straw? Alack, alack!
'Tis wonder that thy life and wits at once
Had not concluded all. — He wakes; speak to him.
  Doct. Madam, do you; 'tis fittest.
  Cor. How does my royal lord? how fares your majesty?
45   *Lear.* You do me wrong to take me out o' the grave: —
Thou art a soul in bliss; but I am bound
Upon a wheel of fire, that mine own tears
Do scald like molten lead.
  Cor.   Sir, do you know me?

Lear. You are a spirit, I know: when did you die?
50   *Cor.* Still, still, far wide!
Doct. He's scarce awake: let him alone awhile.
Lear. Where have I been? Where am I? — Fair daylight? —
I'm mightily abus'd. — I should e'en die with pity,
To see another thus. — I know not what to say. —
55 I will not swear these are my hands: — let's see;
I feel this pin prick. Would I were assur'd
Of my condition!
  Cor.   O, look upon me, sir,
And hold your hands in benediction o'er me: —
No, sir, you must not kneel.
  Lear.   Pray, do not mock me: —
60 I am a very foolish fond old man,
Fourscore and upward, not an hour more nor less:
And, to deal plainly,
I fear I am not in my perfect mind.
Methinks I should know you, and know this man;
65 Yet I am doubtful: for I'm mainly ignorant
What place this is; and all the skill I have
Remembers not these garments; nor I know not
Where I did lodge last night. Do not laugh at me;
For, as I am a man, I think this lady
70 To be my child Cordelia.
  Cor.   And so I am, I am.
Lear. Be your tears wet? yes, faith. I pray, weep not:
If you have poison for me, I will drink it.
I know you do not love me; for your sisters
Have, as I do remember, done me wrong:
75 You have some cause, they have not.
  Cor.   No cause, no cause.
Lear. Am I in France?
  Kent.   In your own kingdom, sir.
Lear. Do not abuse me.
Doct. Be comforted, good madam: the great rage,
You see, is kill'd in him: and yet 'tis danger
80 To make him even o'er the time he has lost.
Desire him to go in; trouble him no more
Till further settling.
  Cor. Will't please your highness walk?
  Lear.   You must bear with me:
Pray you now, forget and forgive: I'm old and foolish.   (Exeunt.)

WILLIAM SHAKESPEARE.

6. THE CRITIC.

Act I, Scene I.

Servant. Sir Fretful Plagiary, sir.

Dangle. Beg him to walk up. — (Exit Servant.) Now, Mrs. Dangle, Sir Fretful Plagiary is an author to your own taste.

Mrs. Dangle. I confess he is a favourite of mine, because everybody else abuses him.

Sneer. Very much to the credit of your charity, madam, if not of your judgment.

Dang. But, egad, he allows no merit to any author but himself, that's the truth on't — though he's my friend.

Sneer. Never. — He is as envious as an old maid verging on the desperation of six-and-thirty: and then the insidious humility with which he seduces you to give a free opinion on any of his works, can be exceeded only by the petulant arrogance with which he is sure to reject your observations.

Dang. Very true, egad — though he's my friend.

Sneer. Then his affected contempt of all newspaper strictures; though, at the same time, he is the sorest man alive, and shrinks like scorched parchment from the fiery ordeal of true criticism: yet is he so covetous of popularity, that he had rather be abused than not mentioned at all.

Dang. There's no denying it — though he is my friend.

Sneer. You have read the tragedy he has just finished, haven't you?

Dang. O yes; he sent it to me yesterday.

Sneer. Well, and you think it execrable, don't you?

Dang. Why, between ourselves, egad, I must own — though he is my friend — that it is one of the most — He's here — (Aside) — finished and most admirable perform —

Sir Fret. (Without) Mr. Sneer with him, did you say?

(Enter Sir Fretful Plagiary.)

Dang. Ah, my dear friend! — Egad, we were just speaking of your tragedy. — Admirable, Sir Fretful, admirable!

Sneer. You never did any thing beyond it, Sir Fretful — never in your life.

Sir Fret. You make me extremely happy; for without a compliment, my dear Sneer, there isn't a man in the world whose judgment I value as I do yours and Mr. Dangle's.

Mrs. Dang. They are only laughing at you, Sir Fretful: for it was but just now that —

Dang. Mrs. Dangle! — Ah, Sir Fretful, you know Mrs. Dangle. — My friend Sneer was rallying just now: — he knows how she admires you, and —

Sir Fret. O Lord, I am sure Mr. Sneer has more taste and sincerity than to — (Aside.) A damned double faced fellow!

Dang. Yes, yes — Sneer will jest — but a better humoured —

Sir Fret. Oh, I know —

Dang. He has a ready turn for ridicule — his wit costs him nothing.

Sir Fret. No, egad — or I should wonder how he came by it. (Aside.)

Mrs. Dang. Because his jest is always at the expense of his friend. (Aside.)

Dang. But, Sir Fretful, have you sent your play to the managers yet? — or can I be of any service to you?

Sir Fret. No, no, I thank you: I believe the piece had sufficient recommendation with it. — I thank you though. — I sent it to the manager of Covent Garden Theatre this morning.

Sneer. I should have thought now, that it might have been cast (as the actors call it) better at Drury Lane.

Sir Fret. O lud! — never send a play there while I live — hark'ee! (Whispers Sneer.)

Sneer. Writes himself! — I know he does!

Sir Fret. I say nothing — I take away from no man's merit — am hurt at no man's good fortune — I say nothing. — But this I will say — through all my knowledge of life, I have observed — that there is not a passion so strongly rooted in the human heart as envy.

Sneer. I believe you have reason for what you say, indeed.

Sir Fret. Besides — I can tell you it is not always so safe to leave a play in the hands of those who write themselves.

Sneer. What, they may steal from them, hey, my dear Plagiary?

Sir Fret. Steal! — to be sure they may; and, egad, serve your best thoughts as gypsies do stolen children, disfigure them to make 'em pass for their own.

Sneer. But your present work is a sacrifice to Melpomene, and he, you know, never —

Sir Fret. That's no security: a dexterous plagiarist may do any thing. Why, sir, for aught I know, he might take out some of the best things in my tragedy, and put them into his own comedy.

Sneer. That might be done, I dare be sworn.

Sir Fret. And then, if such a person gives you the least hint or assistance, he is devilish apt to take the merit of the whole —

Dang. If it succeeds.

Sir Fret. Ay, but with regard to this piece, I think I can hit that gentleman, for I can safely swear he never read it.

Sneer. I'll tell you how you may hurt him more.

Sir Fret. How?

Sneer. Swear he wrote it.

Sir Fret. Plague on't now, Sneer, I shall take it ill! — I believe you want to take away my character as an author.

Sneer. Then I am sure you ought to be very much obliged to me.

Sir Fret. Hey! — sir! —

Dang. Oh, you know, he never means what he says.

Sir Fret. Sincerely then — you do like the piece?

Sneer. Wonderfully!

Sir Fret. But come now, there must be something that you think might be mended, hey? — Mr. Dangle, has nothing struck you?

Dang. Why, faith, it is but an ungracious thing, for the most part, to —

Sir Fret. With most authors it is just so indeed; they are in general strangely tenacious! But, for my part. I am never so well pleased as when a judicious critic points out any defect to me; for what is the purpose of showing a work to a friend, if you don't mean to profit by his opinion?

Sneer. Very true. — Why then, though I seriously admire the piece upon the whole, yet there is one small objection: which, if you'll give me leave, I'll mention.

Sir Fret. Sir, you can't oblige me more.

Sneer. I think it wants incident.

Sir Fret. Good God! you surprise me! — wants incident!

Sneer. Yes: I own I think the incidents are too few.

Sir Fret. Good God! Believe me, Mr. Sneer, there is no person for whose judgment I have a more implicit deference. But I protest to you, Mr. Sneer, I am only apprehensive that the incidents are too crowded. — My dear Dangle, how does it strike you?

Dang. Really I can't agree with my friend Sneer. I think the plot quite sufficient; and the four first acts by many degrees the best I ever read or saw in my life. If I might venture to suggest any thing, it is that the interest rather falls off in the fifth.

Sir Fret. Rises, I believe you mean, sir.

Dang. No, I don't, upon my word.

Sir Fret. Yes, yes, you do, upon my soul! — it certainly don't fall off, I assure you. No, no; it don't fall off.

Dang. Now, Mrs. Dangle, didn't you say it struck you in the same light?

Mrs. Dang. No. indeed, I did not see a fault in any part of the play, from the beginning to the end.

Sir Fret. Upon my soul, the women are the best judges after all!

Mrs. Dang. Or, if I made any objection, I am sure it was to nothing in the piece; but that I was afraid it was, on the whole, a little too long.

Sir Fret. Pray, madam, do you speak as to duration of time; or do you mean that the story is tediously spun out?

Mrs. Dang. O lud! no. — I speak only with reference to the usual length of acting plays.

Sir Fret. Then I am very happy — very happy indeed — because the play is a short play, a remarkably short play. I should not venture to differ with a lady on a point of taste; but, on these occasions, the watch, you know, is the critic.

Mrs. Dang. Then, I suppose, it must have been Mr. Dangle's drawling manner of reading it to me.

Sir Fret. Oh, if Mr. Dangle read it, that's quite another affair! — But I assure you, Mrs. Dangle, the first evening you can spare me three hours and a half, I'll undertake to read you the whole from beginning to end, with the prologue and epilogue; and allow time for the music between the acts.

Mrs. Dang. I hope to see it on the stage next.

Dang. Well, Sir Fretful, I wish you may be able to get rid as easily of the newspaper criticisms as you do of ours

Sir Fret. The newspapers! Sir, they are the most villanous licentious abominable — infernal — Not that I ever read them — no — I make it a rule never to look into a newspaper.

Dang. You are quite right; for it certainly must hurt an author of delicate feelings to see the liberties they take.

Sir Fret. No, quite the contrary! their abuse is, in fact, the best panegyric — I like it of all things. An author's reputation is only in danger from their support.

Sneer. Why that's true — and that attack, now, on you the other day —

Sir Fret. What? where?

Dang. Ay, you mean in a paper of Thursday: it was completely ill-natured, to be sure.

Sir Fret. Oh, so much the better. — Ha! ha! ha! I wouldn't have it otherwise.

Dang. Certainly it is only to be laughed at; for —

Sir Fret. You don't happen to recollect what the fellow said; do you?

Sneer. Pray, Dangle, — Sir Fretful seems a little anxious —

Sir Fret. O lud, — no! — anxious! — not I, — not the least. — 1 — but one may as well hear, you know.

Dang. Sneer, do you recollect? — (Aside to Sneer.) Make out something.

Sneer. (Aside to Dangle.) I will. — (Aloud.) Yes, yes, I remember perfectly.

Sir Fret. Well, — and pray now — not that it signifies — what might the gentleman say?

Sneer. Why, he roundly asserts that you have not the slightest invention or original genius whatever; though you are the greatest traducer of all other authors living.

Sir Fret. Ha! ha! ha! — very good.

Sneer. That as to comedy, you have not one idea of your own, he believes, even in your common place-book — where stray jokes and pilfered witticisms are kept with as much method as the ledger of the lost and stolen office.

Sir Fret. Ha! ha! ha! very pleasant!

Sneer. Nay, that you are so unlucky as not to have the skill even to steal with taste: — but that you glean from the refuse of obscure volumes, where more judicious plagiarists have been before you: so that the body of your work is a composition of dregs and sediments — like a bad tavern's worst wine.

Sir Fret. Ha! ha!

Sneer. In your more serious efforts, he says, your bombast would be less intolerable, if the thoughts were ever suited to the expression: but the homeliness of the sentiment stares through the fantastic encumbrance of its fine language, like a clown in one of the new uniforms!

Sir Fret. Ha! ha!

Sneer. That your occasional tropes and flowers suit the general coarseness of your style, as tambour sprigs would a ground of linsey-woolsey; while your imitations of Shakespeare resemble the mimicry of Fallstaff's page, and are about as near the standard of the original.

Sir Fret. Ha!

Sneer. In short, that even the finest passages you steal are of no service to you; for the poverty of your own language prevents their assimilating; so that they lie on the surface like lumps of marl on a barren moor, encumbering what it is not in their power to fertilise!

Sir Fret. (After great agitation.) Now, another person would be vexed at this.

Sneer. Oh! but I wouldn't have told you — only to divert you.

Sir Fretful. I know it — I am diverted. — Ha! ha! ha! — not the least invention! — Ha! ha! ha! — very good — very good!

Sneer. Yes — no genius! ha! ha! ha!

15 *Dang.* A severe rogue! ha! ha! ha! But you are quite right, Sir Fretful, never to read such nonsense.

Sir Fret. To be sure — for if there is anything to one's praise, it is a foolish vanity to be gratified at it; and, if it is abuse, — why one is always sure to hear of it from one damned good-
20 natured friend or another! R. B. SHERIDAN.

7. SOCIETY.

Act I, Scene I.

Sidney Daryl's Chambers, in Lincoln's Inn; two doors; the room to present the appearance of belonging to a sporting literary barrister, books, pictures, whips, the mirror stuck full of cards, a table, chairs etc.

(As the curtain rises a knock heard, and Doddles discovered opening door.)

Tom. (without) Mr. Daryl in?

Dodd. Not up yet.

(Enter Tom Stylus, Chodd, jun., and Chodd, sen.)

Chodd, jun. (a supercilious, bad swell — glass in eye, hooked stick — vulgar and uneasy — looking at watch). Ten minutes to twelve, eh, guv?

5 *Tom.* Late into bed; up after he oughter: out for brandy and sobering water.

Sidney. (within) Doddles.

Dodd. Yes, sir.

Sidney. Brandy and soda.

10 *Dodd.* Yes, sir!

Tom. I said so! Tell Mr. Daryl two gentlemen wish to see him on particular business.

Chodd, jun. So this is an author's crib — is it? — don't think much of it, eh, guv?

15 *Chodd, sen.* (a common old man, with a dialect). Seems comfortable enough to me, Johnny.

Chodd, jun. Don't call me Johnny! — I hope he won't be long! (looking at watch.) Don't seem to me the right sort of thing for two gentlemen to be kept waiting for a man they are going to
20 employ.

Chodd, sen. Gently, Johnny. (Chodd, jun., looks annoyed) I mean gently without the Johnny. — Mister —

Tom. Daryl — Sidney Dary

Chodd, sen. Daryl didn't know as we was coming!

25   *Chodd, jun.* (rudely to Tom). Why didn't you let him know?

Tom. (fiercely). How the devil could I? — I didn't see you till last night. (Chodd, jun., retires into himself). You'll find Sidney Daryl just the man for you; young — full of talent — what I was thirty years ago; — I'm old now, and not full of talent, if ever I was; I've 30 emptied myself; — I've missed my tip. You see I wasn't a swell — he is!

Chodd, jun. A swell — what? a man who writes for his living?

(Doddles enters.)

Dodd. Mr. Daryl will be with you directly; will you please to 35 sit down?

(Chodd, sen., and Tom sit. Chodd, jun., waits to have a chair given to him, is annoyed that no one does so, and sits on table — Doddles goes round the table.)

Chodd, jun. Where is Mr. Daryl?

Dodd. In his bath.

Chodd, jun. (jumping off table). What! you don't mean to say he keeps us here while he's washing himself?

(Enter Sidney Daryl in morning jacket.)

40   *Sidney.* Sorry to have detained you; how are you, Tom?

(Tom and Chodd, sen., rise, Chodd, jun. sits again on table and sucks cane.)

Chodd, sen. Not at all.

Chodd, jun. (with watch). Fifteen minutes.

Sidney (crossing, handing chair to Chodd, jun.) Take a chair!

Chodd, jun. This'll do.

45   *Sidney.* But you're sitting on the steel pens.

Tom. Dangerous things! pens.

(Chodd, jun., takes a chair.)

Sidney. Yes! loaded with ink, percussion powder's nothing to 'em.

Chodd, jun. We came here to talk business. (to Doddles.) Here, you get out!

50   *Sidney.* (surprised). Doddles — I expect a lot of people this morning, be kind enough to take them into the library.

Dodd. Yes, sir! (aside looking at Chodd, jun.) Young rhinoceros!

(Exit.)

Sidney. Now, gentlemen, I am — (crossing behind table.)

Tom. Then I'll begin, — first let me introduce Mr. Sidney 55 Daryl, to Mr. John Chodd of Snoggerston, also to Mr. John Chodd, jun., of the same place; Mr. John Chodd of Snoggerston is very rich; — he made a fortune by —

Chodd, sen. No! — my brother Joe made the fortune in Australey, by gold digging and then spec'lating; which he then died, and left all to me.

Chodd, jun. (aside). Guv! cut it!

Chodd, sen. I shan't, — I ain't ashamed of what I was, nor what I am; — it never was my way. Well, sir. I have lots of brass!

Sidney. Brass!

Chodd, sen. Money!

Chodd, jun. Heaps!

Chodd, sen. Heaps! but having begun by being a poor man without education, and not being a gentleman —

Chodd, jun. (aside). Guv! — cut it.

Chodd, sen. I shan't — I know I'm not, and I'm proud of it, that is proud of knowing I'm not, and I won't pretend to be. Johnny, don't put me out — I say I'm not a gentleman, but my son is.

Sidney (looking at him). Evidently.

Chodd, sen. And I wish him to cut a figure in the world — to get into Parliament.

Sidney. Very difficult.

Chodd, sen. To get a wife.

Sidney. Very easy.

Chodd, sen. And in short, to be a — a real gentleman.

Sidney. Very difficult.

Chodd, sen. } Eh?
Chodd, jun. }

Sidney. I mean very easy.

Chodd, sen. Now, as I'm anxious he should be an M. P. as soon as

Sidney. As he can.

Chodd, sen. Just so, and as I have lots of capital unemployed, I mean to invest it in —

Tom. (slapping Sidney on knees). A new daily paper?

Sidney. By Jove!

Chodd, sen. A cheap daily paper, that could — that will — What will a cheap daily paper do?

Sidney. Bring the "Court Circular" within the knowledge of the humblest.

Tom. Educate the masses — raise them morally, socially, politically, scientifically, geologically, and horizontally.

Chodd, sen. (delighted). That's it — that's it, only it looks better in print.

Tom. (spouting). Bring the glad and solemn tidings of the day to the labourer at his plough — the spinner at his wheel — the swart forger at his furnace — the sailor, on the giddy mast — the lighthouse keeper, as he trims his beacon lamp — the housewife, at her paste-board — the mother at her needle — the lowly lucifer seller, as he plashes his wet and weary way through the damp, steaming, stony streets, eh? — you know (slapping Sidney Daryl on the knee — they both laugh.)

Chodd, sen. (to Chodd, jun.). What are they a laughing at?

Tom. So my old friend, Johnny Prothero, who lives hard by Mr. Chodd, knowing that I have started lots of papers, sent the two Mr. Chodds, or the Messrs. Chodd — which is it? you're a great grammarian — to me. I can find them an efficient staff, and you are the first man we've called upon.

Sidney. Thanks, old fellow. When do you propose to start it?

Chodd, sen. At once.

Sidney. What is it to be called?

Chodd, sen. We don't know.

Chodd, jun. We leave that to the fellows we pay for their time and trouble.

Sidney. You want something —

Chodd, sen. Strong.

Tom. And sensational.

Sidney. I have it.

Tom.
Chodd, sen. } What?
Chodd, jun.

Sidney (rising). The "Morning Earthquake!"

Tom. (rising). Capital!

Chodd, sen. (rising). First rate!

Chodd, jun. (still seated). Not so bad (goes up during next speech).

Sidney. Don't you see? In place of the clock, a mass of houses — factories, and palaces tumbling one over the other: and then the prospectus! "At a time when thrones are tottering, dynasties dissolving — while the old world is displacing to make room for the new" —

Tom. Bravo!

Chodd, sen. (enthusiastically). Hurray!

Tom. A second edition at 4 o'clock, p.m. The "Evening Earthquake," eh? Placard the walls. "The Earthquake," one note of admiration: "The Earthquake," two notes of admiration: "The Earthquake", three notes of admiration. Posters: "'The Earthquake' delivered every morning with your hot rolls." "With coffee, toast, and eggs, enjoy your 'Earthquake!'"

Chodd, sen. (with pocket book). I've got your name and address.

Chodd, jun. (who has been looking at cards stuck in glass.) Guv! (takes old Chodd up and whispers to him.)

Tom. (to Sidney.) Don't like this young man!

Sidney. No.

140 *Tom.* Cub.

Sidney. Cad.

Tom. Never mind. The old un's not a bad 'un. We're off to a printer's.

Sidney. Good bye, Tom, and thank ye.

145 *Chodd. sen.* Good morning. (Exeunt Chodd, sen., and Tom.)

Sidney. (filling pipe.) Have a pipe?

Chodd, jun. (taking out a magnificent case.) I always smoke cigars.

Sidney. Gracious creature! Have some bitter beer? (getting it from locker.)

Chodd, jun. I never drink anything in the morning.

150 *Sidney.* Oh!

Chodd, jun. But champagne.

Sidney. I haven't got any.

Chodd, jun. Then I'll take beer. (They sit.) Business is business — so I'd best begin at once. The present age is as you are aware — a 155 practical age. I come to the point — it's my way. Capital commands the world. The capitalist commands capital, therefore the capitalist commands the world.

Sidney. But you don't quite command the world, do you?

Chodd, jun. Practically I do. I wish for the highest honours —
160 I bring out my cheque book. I want to get into the House of Commons — cheque book. I want the best legal opinion in the House of Lords — cheque book. The best house — cheque book. The best turn-out — cheque book. The best friends, the best wife, the best trained children — cheque book, cheque book, and cheque book.

165 *Sidney.* You mean to say with money you can purchase anything?

Chodd, jun. Exactly. This life is a matter of bargain.

Sidney. But "honour, love, obedience, troops of friends."

Chodd, jun. Can buy 'em all, sir, in lots as at an auction.

Sidney. Love, too?

170 *Chodd, jun.* Marriage means a union mutually advantageous. It is a civil contract like a partnership.

Sidney. And the old-fashioned virtues of honour and chivalry?

Chodd, jun. Honour means not being a bankrupt. I know nothing at all about chivalry, and I don't want to.

175 *Sidney.* Well, yours is quite a new creed to me, and I confess I don't like it.

Act III, Scene III.

The Wells at Springmead-le-Beau. — An avenue of elms; — house with windows &c. on to lawn — railings at back of stage.

Garden-seats, chairs, lounges, small tables etc. discovered near house — Lord Ptarmigant discovered asleep in garden-chair against house, his feet resting on another — Enter Chodd, sen., down avenue.

Chodd. sen. Oh, dear! oh, dear! What a day this is! There's Johnny to be elected, and I'm expecting the first copy of the "Morning Earthquake," — my paper! my own paper! — by the next train. Then here's Lady Ptarmigant says that positively her niece will have
5 Johnny for her wedded husband, an M. P., and part proprietor of a daily paper! Whew! how hot it is! It's lucky that the wells are so near the hustings — one can run under the shade and get a cooler. Here's my lord! (waking him.) My lord!

Lord P. (waking). Oh! eh! Mr. Chodd — good morning! — how
10 de do!

Chodd, sen. (sitting on stool). Oh, flurried, and flurried, and flustered, and worritted. You know to-day's the election.

Lord P. Yes, I believe there is an election going on somewhere. (calling.) A tumbler of the waters No. 2.

Enter Waitress from house, places tumbler of water on table, and exit.

15 *Chodd, sen.* Oh, what a blessing there is no opposition! If my boy is returned — (rising).

Enter Chodd, jun., agitated, a placard in his hand.

Chodd, jun. Look here, guv! look here!

Chodd. sen. What is it, my Johnny!

Chodd. jun. Don't call me Johnny! Look here! (shows electioneering
20 placard, "Vote for Daryl!")

Chodd. sen. What?

Chodd. jun. That vagabond has put up as candidate! His brother used to represent the borough.

Chodd, sen. Then the election will be contested?

25 *Chodd, jun.* Yes. (Chodd, sen., sinks on garden chair.)

Enter Country Boy with newspaper.

Boy. Mr. Chodd?

Chodd. sen.
Chodd. jun. } Here!

Boy. Just arrived.

Chodd, jun. "The Morning Earthquake." (they both clutch at it eagerly — each secures a paper, and sit under tree.)

Chodd, sen. (reading.) "The borough of Springmead-le-Beau has for centuries been represented by the house of Daryl."

Chodd, jun. (reading.) "A worthy scion of that ancient race intends to offer himself as candidate at the forthcoming election, and, indeed, who will dare to oppose him?"

Chodd, sen. "Surely not a Mister —"

Chodd, jun. "Chodd." (they rise and come down.)

Chodd, sen. "Whoever he may be."

Chodd, jun. "What are the Choddian antecedents?"

Chodd, sen. "Whoever heard of Chodd?"

Chodd, jun. "To be sure a young man of that name has recently been the cause of considerable laughter at the clubs on account of his absurd attempts to become a man of fashion."

Chodd, sen. "And to wriggle himself into Society."

Chodd, jun. Why, it's all in his favour. (in a rage.)

Chodd, sen. In our own paper too. Oh, that villain Stylus!

Chodd, jun. There are no more of these in the town, are there?

Boy. Yes, sir. A man came down with two thousand: he's giving them away everywhere.

Chodd, jun. Confound you! (pushes him off and follows.)

T. W. ROBERTSON.

Litterarhistorische Anmerkungen.

Die englische Sprache hat wie jede andere Kultursprache im Laufe der Zeiten bedeutende lautliche Wandlungen durchgemacht. Das Streben aller dieser Veränderungen geht im wesentlichen auf Vereinfachung der Formen, auf Kürzung der Wörter. Wie im Deutschen nach dem Grade dieser Veränderungen eine alt-, mittel- und neuhochdeutsche, so wird auch im Englischen eine alt-, mittel- und neuenglische Periode unterschieden; die erste reicht bis etwa 1100, die zweite bis 1500. Die in der vorliegenden Sammlung aufgenommenen Lesestücke sind selbstverständlich in neuenglischer Sprache geschrieben; durch ihren Inhalt weisen aber einige derselben auf die zwei wichtigsten Erscheinungen der alt- und mittelenglischen Periode. Diese sollen daher im folgenden zunächst kurz besprochen werden.

Altenglische Periode.

Das wichtigste Denkmal der altenglischen Litteratur, ja der Litteratur aller altgermanischen Dialekte ist das Epos, **Beowulf.** (s. S. 184 und S. 316.) — Über die Entstehung der Beowulfsage schreibt ten Brink in seiner Geschichte der englischen Litteratur: "Im ersten Viertel des sechsten Jahrhunderts, zu einer Zeit also, wo ein Teil der englischen Stämme mit den Briten in blutigen Kämpfen rang, ein grofser Teil aber noch daheim safs, da ereignete sich in den Küstenländern der Nord- und Ostsee eine Reihe von Begebenheiten, welche die Einbildungskraft der Meeranwohner mächtig ergriffen. Vor allem ein Ereignis erregte gewaltiges Aufsehen. In den Jahren 512—520 unternahm der Geatenkönig Hygelak (aus dem jetzigen schwedischen Götaland) einen Raubzug nach dem Niederrhein. Da rückte des fränkischen Königs Thenderich Sohn Thendebert ihm mit einem Heere von Franken und Friesen entgegen. Ein heifser Kampf fand statt, der auf beiden Seiten zahlreiche Opfer verschlang; den Franken aber blieb der Sieg. Hygelak fiel, sein Heer wurde zu Wasser und zu Lande aufgerieben, die schon auf den Schiffen befindliche Beute von dem Feinde zurückgewonnen. In diesem Kampfe zeichnete sich ein Gefolgsmann und Verwandter Hygelak's vor allen aus, zumal durch die Kühnheit, mit der er schliefslich seinen Rückzug bewerkstelligte. Er scheint ein Mann von riesiger Körperkraft, ein vorzüglicher Schwimmer gewesen zu sein. Die Kunde von diesem Kampfe, der Ruhm dieses Degens erscholl weit und breit zu beiden Ufern des Meeres, das die kimbrische Halbinsel von dem schwedischen Festlande trennt, bei Geaten, Inseldänen und Angeln. Die Thaten des Neffen Hygelak's, des Sohnes Ecgtheow's, wurden in Liedern gefeiert. Allmählich gewann die Heldengestalt sagenhafte Proportionen, er trat in das Erbe göttlicher Heroen ein. Beowulf, der Sohn des Ecgtheow, trat an die Stelle Beowa's, des Siegers über Grendel." — Von den germanischen Einwanderern, wahrscheinlich von den Angeln, wurde die Sage von dem mythisch-geschichtlichen Beowulf nach England verpflanzt. In England fand um diese Zeit (Anfang des 7. Jahrh.) das Christentum Eingang, und auch dieses äufserte seinen Einflufs auf die Beowulf-Dichtung.

Die einzige Handschrift, die wir vom Beowulflied besitzen, stammt aus dem Anfang des 10. Jahrhunderts; sie bildet einen Schatz des Britischen Museums. — Müllenhoff hat, indem er auf die Beowulf-Dichtung die Liedertheorie anwandte, gezeigt, dafs wir im Beowulf das Werk mehrerer Verfasser vor uns haben; selbst für den Laien unverkennbare Einschiebsel sind die reflektierenden Stellen, welche von einem christlichen Geistlichen — dem Schlufs-Redactor — herrühren.

Neben Longfellow's metrischer Übertragung einer Episode aus dem Beowulf möge die folgende wörtliche Übersetzung des Schlusses der Dichtung als Probe des altenglischen epischen Stiles dienen. "Then the men of the Goths wrought a mound on the hill, high and broad, easily seen from afar by all wave-farers, and built in ten days the warrior's beacon: they raised a wall round his ashes, as honourably as the wisest men could devise it. They placed in the mound rings and gems, all the treasures, of which hostile men had spoiled the hoard. They let the earth hold the treasure, the heritage of earls, where it still remains, as useless to men as it was before. Then round the mound rode a troop of nobles, twelve in all they wished to mourn the king with fitting words: they praised his courage and deeds of valour, as is right for a man to praise his dear lord with words, and love him in his heart, when his soul has departed from his body. So the Goths mourned their lord's fall, his hearth-companions said that he was the mildest and most humane of world-kings, the gentlest to his people, and most eager for glory." (Sweet.)

Die besten deutschen Übersetzungen des Beowulf sind die von Simrock (mit Anmerkungen), Grein und Heyne.

Mittelenglische Periode.

Durch die Schlacht bei Hastings (1066) waren die Normannen zur Herrschaft in England gelangt; daher war die Sprache der herrschenden Klasse, die sich in den Besitz der höheren Ämter und Würden gesetzt hatte, durch einige Jahrhunderte die französische, und in dieser entwickelte sich eine nicht unbedeutende Litteratur in England. Aber der Grundstock und die Masse der Bevölkerung war und blieb germanisch, und unter Eduard III. wurde ihre Sprache, die inzwischen allerdings manche romanische Bestandteile aufgenommen und ihre Endungen geschwächt hatte, wieder die Sprache des Gerichtes (1362), des Parlaments und der Schulen (vgl. Pauli, Geschichte von England, IV. 698 ff.). Dies konnte um so leichter geschehen, als sich durch die wiederholten Kriege mit Frankreich in den beiden Volksstämmen Englands ein Gefühl der Zusammengehörigkeit in dem Mafse entwickelt hatte, dafs sich nun auch die Normannen als Engländer betrachteten. Vgl. S. 150. Dazu kam, dafs Eduard III. im Frieden zu Brétigny (1360) auf Krone, Titel und Wappen von Frankreich und auf alle Ansprüche in Normandie, Touraine, Anjou, Maine, Bretagne und Flandern verzichtet hatte, und dafs auch die übrigen englischen Besitzungen in Frankreich in der Folgezeit allmählich verloren gingen. — Die englische Sprache befand sich im 14. Jahrhundert in einem Übergangsstadium. Wörter und Formen waren nicht bestimmt und fest. Chaucer, der gröfste Dichter der mittelenglischen Periode, 'der Vater der englischen Poesie,' hat, um Hertzberg's Worte zu gebrauchen, das Verdienst, durch seine unsterblichen Werke "die Sprache und mit der Sprache die Nationalität selbst fixiert zu haben. Die Umwandlungen, welche das Englische seit seiner Zeit und bis zu Shakespeare erlitten hat, sind zwar nicht unbedeutend gewesen, sie haben sich aber durchaus innerhalb der Demarkationspunkte bewegt, die wir bereits von Chaucer abgesteckt finden. — Darum darf noch nach zwei Jahrhunderten Spenser, der ältere Zeitgenosse des grofsen britischen Dramatikers, auf Chaucer als auf den 'reinen Born des ungetrübten Englisch' (well of English undefiled) hinweisen."

Geoffrey Chaucer wurde 1340 in London geboren. Sein Vater, ein wohlhabender Weinhändler, liefs ihm eine sorgfältige Erziehung angedeihen und schickte ihn wahrscheinlich auch auf eine der beiden Universitäten, wo sich Chaucer seine beträchtliche Belesenheit in den Schriftstellern des Altertums und Mittelalters aneignete. Im Jahre 1357 ist Chaucer Page bei der Gemahlin Lionel's, des dritten Sohnes Eduard's III., hierauf tritt er in den Kriegsdienst und nimmt 1359 an dem Zuge gegen Frankreich teil. Auf dem Rückzuge von Paris nach der Bretagne, welcher am 12. April 1360 angetreten wurde, gerät er in Gefangenschaft, aus welcher er aber bald wieder gelöst wird, denn schon im Mai wird Friede geschlossen. In der Folgezeit (1367) treffen wir Chaucer, der sich inzwischen vermählt hat, am Hofe Eduard's III. als Kammerdiener des Königs. Auf den diplomatischen Sendungen, zu welchen er vom König verwendet wird, kommt er nach seiner Ernennung zum Knappen (squire) 1372 nach Genua; ob er dort mit Petrarca zusammenkam, ist zweifelhaft. Dafs er die diplomatische Mission zur Zufriedenheit seines Herrn ausführte, dafür spricht die besondere Gunst, welche ihm der König 1374 erwies, indem er ihm für seine ganze Lebenszeit einen Krug Wein täglich bewilligte (statt dessen er unter Richard II. 20 Mark jährlich erhielt) und zum Steuerkontrolor über die Abgabe von Fellen und gegerbten Häuten, sowie über die kleineren Weinzölle im Londoner Hafen ernannte, eine Stellung, die, wenn sie auch mit beträchtlichen Einnahmen verbunden war, des Dichters Zeit viel in Anspruch nahm, da er sich im Dienst nicht vertreten lassen durfte. In den Jahren 1376 und 77 wurde er wieder zu diplomatischen Sendungen (nach Flandern und Frankreich) verwendet. — Auch bei Eduard's († 1377) Nachfolger Richard II. steht Chaucer in Gunst; er wird Anfang 1378 mit einer Gesandtschaft nach Paris geschickt, um für seinen König um die Hand einer französischen Prinzessin zu werben; im Mai desselben Jahres ist er als Gesandter in Oberitalien. 1386 wird Chaucer von der Grafschaft Kent ins Parlament gewählt. Die Majorität desselben ist gegen das zur Partei des John von Gaunt, des Protektors Chaucer's, gehörige Ministerium. Bald darauf verliert Chaucer seine Stellen, wohl nur deswegen, weil er zur gestürzten Lancaster-Partei hielt. Es begannen nun trübe Zeiten für den Dichter. Als aber Richard im Jahre 1389 selbst die Zügel der Regierung ergriff, wurde Chaucer zum Aufseher über die königlichen Bauten ernannt, mit der Ermächtigung, sich vertreten zu lassen; doch führte er dies Amt nur bis 1391. Wenn ihm auch der König gewogen blieb und ihm 1394 einen Gnadengehalt von 20 Pfund und 1398 eine Tonne Wein jährlich bewilligte, so blieben des Dichters Verhältnisse doch äufserst dürftige. Eine der ersten Regierungsthaten Heinrich's IV. (1399), des Sohnes John's v. Gaunt, war, dafs er Chaucer's Pension um 40 Mark jährlich erhöhte. Aber der Dichter genofs diese Unterstützung kaum ein Jahr, er starb 1400 und wurde in der Westminster-Abtei begraben, wo sein Grabmal das älteste im Poets' Corner ist.

Chaucer gewann durch seine köstlichen Canterbury Tales und durch seine zahlreichen übrigen Werke das Interesse der vornehmen Welt seiner Heimat für die englische Litteratur, die bis dahin von den höheren Kreisen mit Geringschätzung betrachtet worden war, und wirkte, wie Hertzberg ausführt, in dieser Beziehung ähnlich, wiewohl unendlich eindringender und umfassender wie im 18. Jahrhundert Wieland auf die französisch redenden aristokratischen Kreise Deutschlands.

Neuenglische Periode.

Shakespeare. Zur Ergänzung des in den Lesestücken (S. 98, 100, 188, 193) über den Dichter, seine Werke und seine Zeit Beigebrachten folgen hier einige Bemerkungen. Zunächst über den Druck der Werke Sh's. Der Dichter verkaufte seine Dramen an Schauspieler-Gesellschaften, in deren Interesse es lag, dafs jene nicht durch den Druck bekannt würden. Die grofse Beliebtheit der Shakespeare'schen Stücke veranlafste aber unrechtmäfsige Ausgaben, zu welchen der Text durch Nachschreiben während der Vorstellungen beschafft wurde. Von 16 Stücken Sh's kamen Raubausgaben (in Quarto) zu stande. Eine rechtmäfsige (Folio-)Ausgabe der gesamten Werke Sh's erschien erst 1623, besorgt von seinen ehemaligen Kollegen, den Schauspielern John Heminge und Henry Condell. Die erste Folio giebt 36 Stücke — Pericles fehlt — und teilt sie ein in Comedies (14), Histories (10) und Tragedies (11); dazu kamen in den zwei letzten Folios (3 u. 4) aufser dem als echt anerkannten Pericles noch sechs unechte Stücke. — Sh's Quellen. Den Stoff zu seinen Dramen hat Sh. italienischen Novellen und englischen Erzählungen, der englischen und schottischen Chronik Holinshed's (und Hall's), North's englischer Übersetzung des Plutarch u. a. entnommen; dem Sommernachtstraum und Troilus und Cressida liegen Erzählungen Chaucer's und dem Pericles ein Abschnitt aus einem Werke Gower's, eines Zeitgenossen Chaucer's, zu grunde. Einige Dramen sind Überarbeitungen älterer Stücke, nur zu einer Komödie (Love's Labour's Lost) soll Sh. den Stoff frei erfunden haben. Vgl. K Simrock. 'Die Quellen des Shakespeare'.
    Perioden der dramatischen Thätigkeit Sh's. Gervinus teilt die Dramen Sh's in drei Gruppen. I. Die Dramen der ersten Periode, von Sh's Ankunft in London (1585 oder 87) bis 1592 oder 93. Ältere zeitgenössische Dichter, besonders Marlowe und Greene, sind Sh's Vorbilder, er bearbeitet zum Teil ältere Stücke für die Bühne, "mehr oder weniger verraten alle den ungebildeten Volksgeschmack der vorshakespeare'schen Zeit in Stoffen und Formen." Hierher gehören: Titus Andronicus, Pericles (vgl. Elze, 409 ff.), Henry VI. (in drei Teilen), Comedy of Errors, Taming of the Shrew. (Von anderen später angesetzt: 1594—1600; vgl. Elze, 387 f., Dowden X u. XVII.) II. Die Dramen der zweiten Periode, von 1592—1600. "In dieser kurzen Zeit schwingt sich der Dichter in einer fast unbegreiflichen Thätigkeit vom Schüler zum Meister auf." Charakteristisch ist die grofse Vielseitigkeit in der Wahl der Stoffe; "die Stücke drehen sich vorzugsweise um Liebe, Freundschaft, Vaterland und alle die heiligsten Regungen, die einen Jüngling zumeist zu beschäftigen pflegen." Es sind teils Stücke erotischen Inhalts: Two Gentlemen of Verona, Love's Labour's Lost (meist in eine frühere Zeit verwiesen 1588—92, Elze 384; Dowden XVI u. X), All's Well that Ends Well, Midsummer Night's Dream, Romeo and Juliet; — teils Historien: Richard II., Richard III., King John, Henry IV. (in zwei Teilen), Henry V.; -- teils Lustspiele: The Merry Wives of Windsor, As You Like It, Much Ado about Nothing, Twelfth Night or What you Will, The Merchant of Venice. III. Die Dramen der dritten Periode, von 1600—1610 (1612), sind ernsten Inhalts. Während in der vorhergehenden Periode zwölf Lustspiele und heitere Schauspiele vier eigentlichen Trauerspielen gegenüberstehen, "folgen nun acht Tragödien des schwersten Inhalts und eigentlich keine Komödie mehr." Schwierige psychologische Probleme, tragische Konflikte, herbe Charaktere ziehen nun das Hauptinteresse des Dichters auf sich. "Die unnatürliche Lösung natürlicher Bande, Unterdrückung, Falschheit, Verrat und Undank gegen Wohlthäter, Freunde, Familienglieder gekehrt, welchen die heiligsten Pflichten gerade geweiht sein sollten, dies ist der neue, der tragische Vorwurf, der jetzt den Dichter in den verschiedensten

Werken dieses Zeitabschnittes am gewaltigsten und tiefsten bewegt." Aufser den Römer-Dramen: Julius Caesar, Anthony and Cleopatra, Coriolanus gehören hierher die Tragödien: Hamlet, Othello, Lear und Macbeth; ferner die Dramen: Timon of Athens, Troilus and Cressida, Measure for Measure, Cymbeline, The Winter's Tale, The Tempest und endlich die Historie Henry VIII.

Shakespeare in Deutschland. Die wichtigsten Übersetzungen. Nachdem schon im 17. Jahrhundert, ja vielleicht schon zu Ende des 16., wandernde 'englische Komödianten' Shakespeare'sche Stücke, freilich sehr verstümmelt und ohne seinen Namen in Deutschland aufgeführt hatten (vgl. Scherer, Gesch. d. deutsch. Literatur, S. 311 u. 314), wuchs sein Ansehen im 18. Jahrhundert immer mehr. Bodmer preist ihn in der Vorrede zu seiner prosaischen Verdeutschung von Milton's 'verlorenem Paradiese' (1732) als den 'engelländischen Sophokles.' Wieland übersetzt 1762 bis 1766 einundzwanzig Dramen Sh's in Prosa und eines, den Sommernachtstraum, im Versmafs des Originals; vor ihm hatten schon andere einzelne Stücke ins Deutsche übertragen. Lessing weist im 17. Literaturbriefe auf Sh., den er den deutschen Dramatikern zum Vorbild empfiehlt, und stellt in der Dramaturgie die Kunst des Briten der Künstelei der Franzosen gegenüber. Hamann macht Herder'n auf Sh. aufmerksam, und Herder's Begeisterung für Sh., den er noch in den Briefen zur Beförderung der Humanität IX, 113 'als Gebein von unserem Gebein, als Menschen unserer Art, als den auf eine Insel verpflanzten Deutschen fühlt,' — Herder's Begeisterung verkündigt in den "Blättern von deutscher Art und Kunst" das Evangelium von der Herrlichkeit Sh's und teilt sich Goethe (vgl. Dichtung und Wahrheit, 11. Buch) und den Stürmern und Drängern mit, die ihn als höchstes Muster der Dichtkunst verehren und auf ihre Art nachahmen. (Vgl. Scherer, S. 485 ff.) Bald darauf erscheint eine vollständige, prosaische Übersetzung Sh's von Eschenburg (1775—77). Mehrere Jahre später (1784) bearbeitet Bürger den Macbeth. — Schiller lernt auf der Karls-Akademie Shakespeare (in Wieland's Übersetzung) kennen, "er ist von ihm bezaubert und studiert ihn mit ununterbrochenem Eifer." Auf seine wie auf Goethe's Jugendwerke ist Sh's Einflufs bestimmend; in späteren Jahren versenken sich unsere Dichterfürsten in die Werke des kongenialen Engländers mit liebevoller Hingebung, Beweis dafür Schiller's Bearbeitung des Macbeth (1801, nach Eschenburg), viele Stellen in seinen ästhetischen Schriften, in seinem Briefwechsel mit Goethe, in Goethe's Wilhelm Meister, Goethe's Bearbeitung von Romeo und Julia (1811), sein Aufsatz 'Shakespeare und kein Ende' (1813 und 1826), u. a. — In den Jahren 1797—1801 liefert A. W. Schlegel seine meisterhaften Verdeutschungen von sechzehn Dramen Sh's, woran sich 1810 noch ein siebzehntes schliefst. Tieck, der in seinem 'Dichterleben' eine poetische Jugendgeschichte Sh's bietet, vollendet Schlegel's Werk, indem er teils selbst übersetzt, teils, und zwar hauptsächlich die von seiner Tochter Dorothea und dem Grafen Wolf von Baudissin gefertigten Übersetzungen durchsieht (1826—1833). Auch Joh. Heinrich Vofs verdeutscht 1818—1839 einzelne Dramen Sh's, wobei ihm seine Söhne an die Hand gehen. — Die Schlegel-Tieck'sche Übersetzung, durch welche Sh. zum Gemeingut der Deutschen geworden ist, wurde in neuerer Zeit (1867 ff.) durch die deutsche Shakespeare-Gesellschaft unter Redaktion von H. Ulrici sorgfältig revidiert und teilweise neu bearbeitet und mit Einleitungen und Noten versehen, an welchem Werke sich aufser dem genannten Gelehrten noch K. Elze, W. Hertzberg, A. Schmidt, Leo Herwegh u. a. beteiligten. Von dieser Übersetzung wurde 1891 durch W. Öchelhäuser, den Gründer der deutschen Shakespeare-Gesellschaft, eine Volksausgabe veranstaltet. — Zwei neuere Übersetzungen der gesamten dramatischen Werke Sh's sind noch als treffliche Leistungen zu nennen: die von Dingelstedt

Jordan, Seeger. Simrock, Viehoff und Genée (1865—67) — und die von Bodenstedt, Delius, Gildemeister, Herwegh, Heyse, Kurz, Wilbrandt (1867). In neuester Zeit wurden Sh's dramatische Werke nach der Übersetzung von A. W. Schlegel, Ph. Kaufmann und Vofs, revidiert und teilweise neu bearbeitet, mit Einleitungen versehen und herausgegeben von Max Koch (Stuttgart 1882—84).

Die Litteratur über Sh. ist fast unübersehbar. — Wir beschränken uns hier auf die Angabe einiger weniger Werke. K. Elze, 'William Shakespeare.' 1876. Dies die beste Shakespeare-Biographie. R. Genée, 'Shakespeare's Leben und Werke.' 1872. Von demselben Verfasser haben wir auch eine wertvolle 'Geschichte der Shakespeare'schen Dramen in Deutschland.' 1870. Max Koch, 'Shakespeare.' 1884. (Preis geb. 1 M.) Die ästhetische Betrachtung steht im Vordergrund in G. Gervinus' 'Shakespeare,' H. Ulrici's 'Shakespeare's dramatische Kunst. Fr. Kreyssig's 'Vorlesungen über Shakespeare, seine Zeit und seine Werke' und E. Dowden's 'Shakespeare: A Critical Study of His Mind and Art' (7th ed. 1883), dessen 'Shakespeare' in den Literature Primers in das Studium des Dichters einführt. — Von älteren englischen Schriftstellern seien hier genannt: William Hazlitt, geb. 1780 in Maidstone in Kent, gest. 1830, berühmter Kritiker und Essayist, sein Hauptwerk ist 'Characters of Shakespeare's Plays' (1817). — Charles Lamb, geb. zu London 1775, gest. 1835, veröffentlichte 1807 im Verein mit seiner Schwester Mary 'Tales from Shakespeare,' im folgenden Jahre erschienen seine 'Specimens of English Dramatic Poets who lived about the time of Shakespeare.' — Mrs. Anna Jameson, geb. 1797 in Dublin als die Tochter des Malers Murphy, gest. 1860, schrieb nebst zahlreichen anderen Werken: 'Characteristics of Women,' 2 Bde., 1832, woraus das Lestück S. 243 genommen ist.

Hilfsmittel zur Lektüre. Der Unterschied zwischen der Sprache Sh's und der modern-englischen ist viel gröfser, als man sich gewöhnlich vorstellt, und die Veränderung vollzog sich namentlich im Laufe des 17. Jahrhunderts. Der Abstand zwischen Shakespeare und Addison ist gröfser als der zwischen Addison und Macaulay, oder als der zwischen Goldsmith und Dickens (Storm). Zum richtigen Verständnis Sh's bedarf man daher des Wörterbuches, des Kommentars und der Grammatik. Es kommen in Betracht: 1. Dr. Alexander Schmidt, Shakespeare-Lexikon 1875. — 2. Shakespeare's Werke. Herausgegeben und erklärt von Nikolaus Delius (5. Aufl. 1882). Aufserdem die Kommentare von Alexander Schmidt zu Coriolan, Lear, Caesar; und die in der Clarendon Press Series erschienenen Select Plays, edited by W. G. Clark und W. A. Wright; erschienen sind: Hamlet, The Tempest. As You Like It, Julius Caesar, Richard III., King Lear, A Midsummer Night's Dream, Coriolanus, Henry V., The Merchant of Venice, Richard II., Macbeth, Twelfth Night. King John, Henry VIII. Hier möge auch die von denselben Gelehrten besorgte, unkommentierte, Globe Edition of Shakespeare genannt sein, weil darnach gewöhnlich citiert wird. — 3. E. A. Abbott, A Shakespearian Grammar. — C. Deutschbein, Shakespeare-Grammatik für Deutsche. 1882.

Sir Walter Raleigh (1552—1618) leistete seinem Lande unter der Regierung Elisabeth's, bei der er in grofser Gunst stand, und der er auch seinen vertrauten Freund Spenser, den Verfasser der Fairy Queen, vorstellte, grofse Dienste als Krieger, Seefahrer und Staatsmann. Unter Jakob I. wurde er fälschlich des Hochverrates angeklagt und nach vierzehnjähriger Gefangenschaft im Tower enthauptet. Von Raleigh besitzen wir anmutige Gedichte und eine für ihre Zeit verdienstliche History of the World (bis zum Sturze des macedonischen Reiches gehend), die er während seiner Gefangenschaft abfafste.

Francis Bacon wurde 1561 in London geboren. Er war der jüngste Sohn Sir Nicholas Bacon's, des Grofssiegelbewahrers der Königin Elisabeth. Als Kind zeichnete er sich durch seinen frühreifen Geist aus. Im Alter von dreizehn Jahren wurde er auf die Universität Cambridge geschickt, wo er drei Jahre zubrachte, hierauf nach Frankreich, um sich unter der Anleitung des englischen Gesandten in Paris, Sir Amyas Paulet, für den Staatsdienst vorzubereiten. Infolge des plötzlichen Todes seines Vaters kehrte er nach einer Abwesenheit von drei Jahren nach England zurück. Im Jahre 1590 erhielt er eine Anstellung als juridischer Ratgeber (Counsel Extraordinary) bei der Königin, mit welchem Posten kein fester Gehalt verbunden war.

Nach Jakob's Thronbesteigung verbesserten sich Bacon's Aussichten, und er stieg, von Villiers, dem nachmaligen Herzog von Buckingham, unterstützt, von Stufe zu Stufe, bis er 1617 das Ziel seines Ehrgeizes, den Posten des Grofssiegelbewahrers (Lord Keeper of the Great Seal) erreichte; im folgenden Jahre wurde er Lordkanzler und erhielt die Pairswürde als Baron von Verulam. Die Stellung als Lordkanzler hatte er drei Jahre inne und stand nun auf der Höhe seines Glückes, geehrt und angesehen nicht blofs als Richter und Staatsmann, sondern auch als Philosoph. Schon 1605 kam seine Schrift Of the Advancement of Learning heraus, welche in der später umgearbeiteten lateinischen Form den ersten Teil seines philosophischen Systems bildet, dem er den stolzen Namen Instauratio magna, die grofse Reform, gab; 1620 veröffentlichte er das Novum Organum, welches den zweiten Teil der Instauratio ausmacht; es ist in lateinischer Sprache verfafst und wie der erste Teil dem König gewidmet. Im Jahre 1621 wurde Bacon zum Viscount of St. Albans erhoben — und drei Monate später war er Gefangener im Tower. Im neuen Parlament, zu dessen Einberufung er selbst geraten hatte, wurde er vom Unterhause der Bestechlichkeit bei seiner Amtsführung angeklagt und von den Lords einstimmig schuldig erkannt. Das Urteil lautete auf Amtsentsetzung, Bezahlung von 40,000 l. und Gefangenhaltung im Tower auf unbestimmte Zeit; überdies wurde er für unwürdig erklärt, in Zukunft irgend ein Amt zu bekleiden oder im Parlament zu sitzen. Bacon, der sich damit verteidigte, dafs es von jeher Sitte gewesen sei, Geschenke anzunehmen, ohne sich dadurch beeinflussen zu lassen, wurde bald auf freien Fufs gesetzt, desgleichen wurde ihm die Geldstrafe erlassen; in den übrigen Punkten trat erst später eine Milderung und endlich eine vollständige Begnadigung ein.

Nun von seiner Höhe gestürzt, wendete er sich vollständig seinen Studien zu. Im Jahre 1622 erschien seine History of Henry VII., 1623 De Dignitate et Augmentis Scientiarum, eine neue, sehr erweiterte, lateinische Ausgabe des Advancement of Learning; 1625 eine neue und vermehrte Ausgabe seiner Essays oder politischen und moralischen Gedanken; ferner eine Sammlung von Anekdoten und Witzen nach Caesar's Vorbilde. u. e. a. Aber seine Hoffnung, wieder zur Macht zu gelangen, erfüllte sich nicht. Da entsagte er endlich der Politik gänzlich, und als er von Jakob's Nachfolger Karl ins Parlament berufen werden sollte, lehnte er ab mit den Worten: "I have done with such vanities." Er starb in der Zurückgezogenheit am 9. April 1626. In seinem Testamente hatte er kurz vorher geschrieben: "My Name and memory I leave to men's charitable speeches, and to foreign nations and the next ages." — Seit Bacon datiert eine neue Periode der Philosophie. Während die bis zu seiner Zeit herrschende Scholastik sich von Natur und Erfahrung losgerissen hatte und in Wortklauberei und Formelwesen ausgeartet war, lehrte Bacon, dafs unser Wissen nur auf Empirie, auf Beobachtung und Sichtung der Thatsachen basiere, und dafs man, nach Ablegung aller überkommenen Vorurteile, nur durch Induction zu neuen Erkenntnissen gelangen könne.

Thomas Hobbes (1588—1679) schrieb philosophische Werke (De cive 1642, Leviathan 1651, Elementorum philosophiae sectio I: de corpore, 1655, s. II: de homine, 1658), in denen er das absolute Königtum, das nach seiner Ansicht ursprünglich durch einen Vertrag zwischen Regierenden und Regierten zu stande kam, als die einzig richtige Staatsform erklärte. Sein Stil zeichnet sich durch Kürze, Klarheit und Präcision aus.

John Milton wurde am 9. Dezember 1608 in London geboren, wo sein Vater ein angesehener Notar war. Er studierte an der Universität Cambridge und zeigte schon während dieser Zeit grofse poetische Anlagen. Im Jahre 1638 ging er über Frankreich nach Italien. Nach einer Abwesenheit von fünf Vierteljahren kehrte er nach England zurück, um in dem zwischen König und Parlament ausgebrochenen Streite seine Stellung auf Seite der Freiheit zu nehmen, zu deren Verteidigung er mehrere Schriften verfafste; am bemerkenswertesten darunter ist seine Staatsrede über die Presse, Areopagitica (1644), die zum Bollwerk der englischen Prefsfreiheit geworden ist. — Durch sein angestrengtes Arbeiten im Dienste der Republik, zu deren lateinischem Sekretär der auswärtigen Angelegenheiten er im Jahre 1649 ernannt worden war, erblindete der Dichter, dessen Augen immer schwach gewesen waren, im Jahre 1652 vollständig. — Nach der Restauration wurden zwei von Milton's Schriften (Defensio pro populo anglicano und Iconoclastes) von Henkers Hand verbrannt, er selbst aber am 15. December 1660 durch den Einfluſs mächtiger Gönner begnadigt.

Schon während der Zeit der Republik war er von seinem ursprünglichen Plane, der Abfassung eines Epos, dessen Held König Arthur sein sollte, abgekommen und hatte sich für den religiösen Stoff entschieden, mit dessen Bearbeitung er im Jahre der Pest in London (1665) fertig wurde; im Jahre 1667, ein Jahr nach dem grofsen Brande in der Metropole, veröffentlichte er dies Werk: Paradise Lost, ursprünglich in 10, von der zweiten Auflage an in 12 Gesängen. Der Fall des ersten Menschenpaares und vor diesem der Sturz Satans und seiner Scharen, die sich wider den Sohn Gottes empört hatten, bilden den Stoff der Dichtung. Das Gedicht ist, wie Hettner sagt, voll der ergreifendsten Schönheiten. Himmel, Hölle und Erde thun sich vor uns auf mit all ihren Wundern und Schrecken. Dort der kühne Titanentrotz des rebellischen Satan, hier die liebliche Zartheit des schuldlosen Menschenpaares, und über diesem wirksamen Gegensatz des Erhabenen und Zarten die ruhig thronende Milde und Hoheit Gottes, des Sohnes und der himmlischen Heerscharen. Wie vielstimmiger Orgelklang rauscht das hohe Lied daher "in gewaltigen, herzrührenden, reizvoll wechselnden Tönen"; bald laut aufschmetternd, bald leise flüsternd, immer aber ein voller und inbrünstiger Hymnus zum Preise des Allmächtigen. — Interessant ist Goethe's und Schiller's Urteil über Milton, s. Briefwechsel 31. Juli bis 3. August 1799. (Ed. Speemann II, 197—200.)

Milton's Paradise Lost erlebte unzählige Auflagen. Schon im Jahre 1682 wurde es von Berge ins Deutsche übertragen (in Jamben); 1732 verdeutschte es Bodmer in Prosa, angeregt durch Addison's Kritik und Charakteristik des Gedichtes im Spectator. Für alle ästhetischen Schriften, die Bodmer und sein Genosse Breitinger herausgaben, bildet Milton, wie Scherer sich ausdrückt, den idealen Mittelpunkt. Immer soll er verteidigt, seine Schönheiten sollen ins Licht gesetzt, seine Verächter zurückgewiesen werden. — Bekannt ist Milton's mächtige, bestimmende Wirkung auf Klopstock und seine Schule.

Als Fortsetzung des Paradise Lost schrieb Milton das kurze Epos Paradise Regained (1671), das die Versuchung Christi durch Satan zum Gegenstande hat. Im selben Jahre erschien auch sein Samson Agonistes (Samson der Kämpfer), ein Trauerspiel in antiker Form und Haltung.

Milton starb am 5. November 1674, arm und verlassen, aber voll Ergebenheit und Gottvertrauen. Die Nachwelt verehrt in ihm einen der gröfsten Epiker der neueren Zeit. Vgl. auch Moriz Carriere: Milton als Staatsmann und Dichter. Westermann's Mtsh. XXIX (1870), S. 293—314.

Edward Hyde, Earl of Clarendon wurde 1609 zu Dinton in Wiltshire geboren. Nach kurzem Aufenthalt in Oxford studierte er in London die Rechte. Im Jahre 1640 wurde er ins Unterhaus gewählt und war Mitglied des kurzen und langen Parlaments. Er gehörte anfangs der gemäfsigten Opposition gegen des Königs Willkürlichkeiten an; als aber das Parlament einen Weg einschlug, der die bestehende Verfassung bedrohte, trat er entschieden dagegen auf und wurde von dieser Zeit ein treuer Anhänger der Sache des Königs und dessen vornehmster Ratgeber. Bei der grofsen Secession im Mai 1642 trat er aus dem Parlament aus und begab sich zum König nach York.

Später vertrat er die Sache der Stuarts an den fremden Höfen, und nach Cromwell's Tod leitete er die Unterhandlungen, die zur Wiedereinsetzung der Stuarts führten. Er wurde nun 1660 Lordkanzler und Earl von Clarendon und leitete sieben Jahre die Geschicke seines Landes; er hatte aber einen schweren Stand, und als England von Holland besiegt wurde, benützte der König den allgemeinen Unwillen und liefs Clarendon fallen (1667). Von einer Anklage wegen Hochverrats bedroht, verliefs dieser England, in das er nie wieder zurückkehren sollte. Ein Schreiben, das er an den König richtete mit der Bitte, es möge ihm gestattet werden, im Vaterlande zu sterben, blieb unbeantwortet. Er starb zu Rouen 1674. — Seine älteste Tochter Anna heiratete den Herzog von York, den nachmaligen König Jakob II., und so wurde sie Mutter der Königinnen Maria und Anna.

Clarendon's Hauptwerk ist: The History of the Rebellion and Civil Wars in England; es beginnt mit dem Jahre 1641 und endet mit der Restauration. Das Werk ist in zwei weit auseinander liegenden Lebensperioden geschrieben, der erste Teil (die ersten acht Bücher, bis Ausgang 1644) während seines Aufenthaltes in Jersey (1646—47), wohin er den Thronfolger begleitet hatte; das übrige während des letzten Exils. Veröffentlicht wurde es erst 1702, unter der Regierung der Königin Anna, der es gewidmet ist. Seine Autobiographie erschien gar erst 1759. — Eine Charakteristik Clarendon's als Historiker giebt Ranke in seiner englischen Geschichte. Clarendon's Werk ist vom royalistischen Standpunkt geschrieben, zeigt aber nichtsdestoweniger das Streben, auch dem Gegner gerecht zu werden, und ist eine Fundgrube der Belehrung über seine Zeitgenossen.

John Dryden wurde 1631 in dem Dorfe Oldwinkle All-Saints in Northamptonshire geboren, seine Mittelschulbildung erhielt er in der berühmten Westminster School, die er bis zu seinem 18. Jahre besuchte, worauf er 1650 die Universität Cambridge bezog, wo er 7 Jahre blieb. Nach dem Tode seines Vaters war er auf die Unterstützung wohlhabender Verwandter und auf die Verwertung seiner poetischen Anlagen angewiesen, die sich schon auf dem Gymnasium in Westminster in Übersetzungen und Gelegenheitsgedichten gezeigt hatten. Sein erstes Gedicht, mit dem er vor die Öffentlichkeit trat, war eine volltönende Ode auf den Tod Cromwell's; zwei Jahre darauf folgte ein Jubelgedicht auf die Rückkehr der Stuarts: Astraea redux. Im Interesse der nun herrschenden Partei verfafste er mehrere politische Streitschriften satirischen Inhalts. Nach der Thronbesteigung Jakob's II., der Katholik war, trat Dryden zum Katholicismus über. Dryden hat eine Reihe von Dramen geschrieben, deren Schwulst von dem Herzog von Buckingham in der Komödie 'The Rehearsal' (1671) geistreich parodiert wurde. Noch heute berühmt ist aber Dryden's wohlklingende Ode auf den Tag der heiligen Cäcilie oder, wie sie gewöhnlich genannt wird, das Alexanderfest, und sein Gedicht Annus mirabilis (1667), in welchem er die Pest und die Feuersbrunst, welche 1665 und 1666 London verheert hatten, besang. Umfassend war Dryden's Thätigkeit als Übersetzer und Bearbeiter antiker Dichter; auch Boccaccio und Chaucer bildete er einzelne Erzählungen in seinen vortrefflichen Fables Ancient and Modern (1699) nach.

Dryden starb am 1. Mai 1700 in London. Hettner vergleicht Dryden nicht unpassend mit Opitz, dem Dichter der ersten schlesischen Schule. Wie dieser, ist er ohne alle schöpferische Phantasie, seine Dichtung ist reine Verstandesdichtung; aber auch er führt, wie Opitz, mit grundsätzlicher Bewusstheit ein neues Formgesetz ein und wird damit der Begründer einer neuen, lange nachwirkenden Dichterschule. Als Kritiker stand Dryden bei seinen Zeitgenossen in unbestrittenem Ansehen, auf das er sich durch sein Essay on Dramatic Poesy ein Anrecht erworben hatte. Gottsched in seiner besten Zeit läfst sich in dieser Beziehung mit Dryden vergleichen, mit welchem er auch die Werthaltung und Nachahmung der französischen Klassik gemein hat.

John Locke (1632—1704), einer der bedeutendsten Philosophen Englands, verfolgte die von Bacon zuerst betretenen Bahnen, indem auch er die Erfahrung als den Grund alles menschlichen Wissens erklärte. Sein Hauptwerk ist Essay Concerning Human Understanding. Locke's Bedeutung als Philosoph besteht vor allem darin, dafs er, wie die von ihm angeregten Philosophen Hume und Kant, es sich zur Aufgabe stellte, die Tragweite der menschlichen Erkenntnisfähigkeiten zu prüfen. Das Resultat seiner Untersuchung war der Satz, dafs alle unsere Erkenntnis durch die Sinne vermittelt werde. Von seinen kleinen Schriften sind besonders seine Letters Concerning Toleration und Thoughts Concerning Education zu nennen.

Joseph Addison, 1672 als der Sohn eines Landpfarrers bei Amesbury in Wiltshire geboren, besuchte die Schule in Salisbury und dann Charterhouse-School in London; im Alter von 15 Jahren kam er auf die Universität Oxford, wo er sich bald durch seine lateinischen Verse auszeichnete. Während der zehn Jahre, die er sich (zum Teil als fellow, d. h. im Genusse eines ausgiebigen Stipendiums nach abgelegter Prüfung) in Oxford aufhielt, erwarb er sich gründliche Kenntnisse in der lateinischen Litteratur. Im Jahre 1697 verschaffte ihm Montague eine jährliche Pension von 300 *l.* (für ein Gedicht auf den Frieden von Ryswick). Addison ging nun auf Reisen und besuchte Frankreich und Italien. Als er 1702 zurückkam, war eben William III. gestorben und Montague aus dem Ministerium geschieden. Addison verlor daher seine Pension und war einige Zeit in bedrängter Lage. Ein Gedicht, Campaign, das bei ihm auf den Sieg Marlbourough's bei Blenheim bestellt wurde, fand solchen Beifall, dafs er sogleich (1705) eine Sinecure erhielt und bald darauf Unter-Staats-Sekretär wurde. Im Jahre 1717 wurde er Staats-Sekretär (Minister), doch legte er seinen Posten bald nieder und zog sich mit einer Pension von 1500 *l.* ins Privatleben zurück. Im Jahre 1718 erschien seine, nach den Regeln der französischen Klassizität gebaute Tragödie Cato, die mit allgemeinem Beifall aufgenommen, 35mal nacheinander gegeben und 1732 von Gottsched nachgeahmt wurde. — Addison starb in Holland House, dem Palais seiner Gattin, der Gräfin von Warwick, im Jahre 1719.

Während der Cato und die kleineren Gedichte Addison's heute vergessen sind, lebt sein Name fort als der des Hauptmitarbeiters an dem Spectator, welchen sein Freund Steele vom März 1711 bis Ende 1712 täglich (mit Ausnahme des Sonntags) erscheinen liefs. Der Spectator und die anderen von Steele (s. d.) herausgegebenen Zeitschriften enthielten sich der eigentlichen Politik und behandelten Themen von allgemeinem Interesse, Tagesbegebenheiten, Litteraturerscheinungen, Theater, Sitten und Moden in kurzen, ernsthaft oder humoristisch, satirisch oder ironisch gehaltenen Aufsätzen. Muster für diese Art der Litteratur waren Montaigne's Essais und La Bruyère's Caractères. Die moralischen Wochenschriften trugen viel dazu bei, das englische Leben zu verfeinern und in die unter den letzten Stuarts verwilderte Litteratur den Ton des Anstandes und der Zucht wieder einzuführen. Die verschiedenen Aufsätze wurden in der Regel durch einen novellistischen Rahmen zusammengehalten.

Sir Richard Steele wurde im Jahre 1672 zu Dublin von englischen Eltern geboren; sein Vater, Sekretär des Lord-Lieutenants von Irland, liefs ihn in Charterhouse in London, wo er mit Addison, dem head-boy der Schule, Freundschaft schlofs, und in Oxford, wo er wieder Addison traf, erziehen. Wie Goldsmith, so verleugnete auch Steele nie seine irische Abkunft: er war treuherzig und gutmütig, aber dabei so grenzenlos leichtsinnig, dafs er selbst in einträglichen Posten immer in Geldverlegenheit war und mehrmals mit dem Schuldenarrest Bekanntschaft machte. Gegen den Willen seiner Eltern trat er 1699, seine Studien in Oxford verlassend, in die Horse-Guards ein, wo er sich bei den Officieren rasch so beliebt machte, dafs sie ihm eine Fähnrichstelle verschafften, von der er bald zum Hauptmann vorrückte. Als Gegengewicht gegen seinen lockeren Lebenswandel verfafste er damals eine kleine Schrift: The Christian Hero, durch die er die Heiterkeit aller erregte, die sein Leben mit den frommen, ernstgemeinten, aber nicht befolgten Grundsätzen verglichen. Steele hat mehrere Lustspiele geschrieben, die (mit Ausnahme eines einzigen, in welchem die Moral zu vordringlich betont war) zu ihrer Zeit mit Beifall aufgenommen wurden; dauernden Ruhm hat er sich aber erworben durch die Begründung der sogenannten moralischen Wochenschriften in England. Schon seit 1602 waren in England politische und hie und da wohl auch theologische Zeitschriften erschienen, ja Daniel Defoe, der später als Verfasser des Robinson Crusoe bekannt wurde, hatte in seiner 'Review' von 1704 an sogar den Versuch gemacht, eine von ihm als Scandal-Club bezeichnete Unterabteilung einzuführen, in der er moralische und dichterische Fragen behandelte. Aber Steele war der erste, der für diese moralischen und dichterischen Fragen eine eigene und ausschliefsliche Zeitschrift zu gründen wagte. Dieser erste Versuch war der Tatler (Plauderer), der vom 12. April 1709 bis 2. Januar 1711 wöchentlich dreimal erschien. Die nächste Veranlassung des Tatler war eine zufällige. Steele war der Herausgeber der 'Gazette,' das heifst der amtlichen Regierungszeitung. In dieser konnte er sich nicht so frei bewegen, wie er wünschte. Daher gründete er ein besonderes Blatt, den Tatler, in welchem er, neben den mehr in den Hintergrund tretenden politischen Neuigkeiten, Theater- und Kunstkritiken und (seinem Hange zum Moralisieren, den er im Christian Hero bethätigt hatte, nachgebend) Sittenschilderungen und erbauliche Betrachtungen bringen konnte. Von allen Seiten kamen Mitarbeiter; der bedeutendste unter ihnen war Steele's alter Schulfreund Addison. Als im Jahre 1710 die Partei der Whigs, der Steele und Addison angehörten, gestürzt wurde und Steele die Redaktion der 'Gazette' verlor, verschwinden die politischen Betrachtungen gänzlich aus dem Tatler; auch die Theater- und Tageserscheinungen der Litteratur treten immer mehr zurück, und es werden nun Schilderungen von Welt und Menschen, Sitten und Gewohnheiten, Thorheiten, Lastern und Tugenden der hauptsächlichste, wenn nicht ausschliefsliche Gegenstand. Die Zeitschrift wird in der That eine 'moralische' Zeitschrift. Auf den Tatler liefs Steele den Spectator und auf diesen den Guardian folgen. Vom Juni bis December 1814 führte die Zeitschrift wieder den Titel Spectator. — Der Erfolg dieser Wochenschriften war glänzend. Nicht nur, dafs diese Blätter sogleich als Zeitschrift eine unerwartet weite Verbreitung gewannen, sondern sie wurden auch alsbald gesammelt und in stattlichen Oktavbänden verkauft. — Steele schrieb noch eine Zeit lang politische Flugschriften; er starb, geachtet und gefeiert, im Jahre 1729.

Der Einflufs der englischen Wochenschriften auf die deutsche Litteratur ist nicht zu unterschätzen. Gottsched liefs die wichtigsten derselben, den Spectator als 'Zuschauer' und den Guardian als 'Aufseher oder Vormund,' übersetzen. Gellert und Wieland haben ihnen manchen Stoff entnommen, Rabener hat von ihnen gelernt. Ähnliche Wochenschriften erschienen in Deutschland, wo man von 1714 bis 1800 deren nicht weniger als fünfhundert zählt. Am bekanntesten sind davon Bodmer's 'Discourse der Maler' (1721) und Gottsched's 'Vernünftige Tadlerinnen' (1725) und 'Der Biedermann' (1727). Vgl. Scherer, S. 371 f.

Alexander Pope wurde im Jahre 1688, wenige Monate vor der Vertreibung des Königs Jakob II., in London geboren. Da sein Vater, ein wohlhabender Leinwarenhändler, strenger Katholik und Anhänger der Stuarts war, so blieb Pope das Universitätsstudium und jeder Staatsdienst verschlossen. Er wurde zuerst durch Priester und dann in einem katholischen Seminar zu Twyford (in der Nähe von Windsor) unterrichtet, aber schon mit zwölf Jahren verliefs er die Anstalt und besorgte seine Weiterbildung durch fleifsige Lektüre. In kurzer Zeit hatte er die meisten englischen, französischen, italienischen, lateinischen und griechischen Dichter gelesen und sich in ihren Manieren geübt. Sechzehn Jahre alt, verfafste er seine Pastorals, Schäfergedichte, die er 1709 herausgab. Zwei Jahre später erschien sein Essay on Criticism, schon 1709 in vortrefflichen Versen geschrieben. Dieses Lehrgedicht ist Boileau's Gedichte über die Dichtkunst nachgeahmt und empfiehlt die steife Unnatur der französischen Renaissance. Die schönste Dichtung Pope's ist der Lockenraub, The Rape of the Lock (1712), in welchem er sein Vorbild, Boileau's 'Lutrin,' an Zierlichkeit und Anmut übertrifft. Von 1713—25 übersetzte er Homer, eine Arbeit, die, obgleich mehr von seinen Zeitgenossen anerkannt, als Dryden's Übersetzung der Vergil'schen Aeneis, gleichfalls sehr weit von dem Geiste des Originals entfernt ist. Die dafür erhaltene glänzende Bezahlung (5000 *l.*) setzte ihn in stand, das väterliche Haus in Windsor Forest zu verlassen und seinen Wohnsitz in dem reizend gelegenen Twickenham (bei Richmond) aufzuschlagen, wodurch er seinen Londoner Freunden, ausgezeichneten Staatsmännern und Schriftstellern — Bolingbroke, Addison, Steele, Swift, Lady Montagu u. a. — die Besuche bei ihm erleichterte. Im Jahre 1725 liefs Pope eine Ausgabe Shakespeare's erscheinen. Lewis Theobald, der 1733 selbst Shakespeare's Werke herausgab, deckte die Mängel des Pope'schen Werkes auf; dadurch wurde Pope so gereizt, dafs er in einer satirischen Dichtung The Dunciad, Lied von den Dummköpfen (1728), Theobald und andere ihm mifsliebige Schriftsteller scharf angriff. Von Pope's übrigen Werken sei noch das 1733-34 erschienene philosophische Lehrgedicht Essay on Man genannt. Pope starb am 30. Mai 1744.

Zur Charakterisierung der Dichtungen Pope's und der des Zeitalters der Königin Anna, das sich gern das augusteische Zeitalter der englischen Litteratur nennen liefs, seien einige Sätze aus Hettner angeführt. — Die Engländer nennen Pope *the prince of rhyme and the grand poet of reason*. Und in der That ist damit sein ganzes Wesen bezeichnet. In seiner Sprechweise fein und witzig, gelang es ihm zugleich, eine Kunst des Versbaues zu erreichen, die selbst die Kunst Dryden's weit überragte. Der kräftige, wohllautende Reim Pope's ist noch heute ein Stolz der englischen Dichtung; selbst Voltaire, dem die englische Sprache ein Greuel ist, vergleicht ihn mit dem Ton einer Flöte. Der Gehalt der Dichtungen der *Wits*, so nennen sich die Dichter jener Zeit mit Vorliebe, ist aber kein rein poetischer. Sie wollen unterrichten und aufklären oder höchstens durch geistreichen Witz, durch sprühenden Esprit in Erstaunen setzen und blenden. Nirgends ein warmer Hauch, der sich warm ins Gemüt senkt; überall nur das städtische, vornehme, witzig feine Leben, das sich ruhmredig bespiegelt und nichts Höheres als sich selbst kennt. Vgl. S. 200. — 'Pope's Lockenraub hat,' wie uns Goethe im sechsten Buche von Dichtung und Wahrheit erzählt, 'viele Nachahmungen erweckt; Zachariä kultivierte diese Dichtart — am bekanntesten ist sein 'Renommist.' — auf deutschem Grund und Boden, und jedermann gefiel sie, weil der gewöhnliche Gegenstand derselben irgend ein täppischer Mensch war, den die Genien zum besten hatten, indem sie den besseren begünstigten'; und im siebenten Buche von Dichtung und Wahrheit lesen wir, dass Goethe's nachmaliger Schwager Schlosser, 'im Widerstreit mit Pope's Versuch über den Menschen, ein Gedicht in gleicher Form und Silbenmafs geschrieben, welches der christlichen Religion über jenen Deismus den Sieg verschaffen sollte.' Auch Haller und Hagedorn, die einen Teil ihrer litterarischen Bildung in England erwarben, berühren sich mit Pope: beide verfafsten Lehrgedichte und Satiren (Scherer, 372). Die Aufstellung einer Preisfrage über Pope's philosophisches System von Seiten der Berliner Akademie veranlafste Lessing und Mendelssohn zu der Abhandlung: 'Pope ein Metaphysiker' (1755), in welcher in Verspottung der Akademie gezeigt wird, 'dass ein philosophischer Dichter kein Philosoph, und ein poetischer Weltweiser kein Poet' sei (Gervinus, IV, 378).

Daniel Defoe, eigentlich **Foe**, wurde 1661 in London geboren. Sein Vater, ein wohlhabender Fleischer, liefs ihm eine sorgfältige Erziehung geben und wollte ihn zum puritanischen Geistlichen ausbilden lassen. Foe fühlte sich aber für diesen Beruf nicht geschaffen, er ergriff ein bürgerliches Gewerbe, das eines Strumpfwarenhändlers. Schon unter Karl II. veröffentlichte er seine erste, gegen die unduldsame Hochkirche gerichtete politische Schrift. Als Prinz Monmouth nach der Thronbesteigung seines Oheims, Jakob's II., einen Einfall nach England machte, schlofs sich Foe dem Heere der Rebellen an und kämpfte tapfer bei Bristol und Bath. Der Aufstand war bald unterdrückt. Foe flüchtete nach dem Kontinent und durchwanderte Spanien, Frankreich und Deutschland. Bald kehrte er zurück, und nahm, wohl vorsichtshalber, den Namen de Foe oder Defoe an. — An William von Oranien schlofs er sich mit Begeisterung an, und der König, der schon auf Defoe's bedeutendes, für die Entwicklung der neueren Volkswirtschaftslehre grundlegendes Buch Essay on Projects aufmerksam geworden war, wandte dem Dichter des Trueborn Englishman (1701), der die Grundlosigkeit der Abneigung der Engländer gegen den fremdländischen Regenten zeigte, seine Gunst zu. Unter der Regierung der Königin Anna schrieb Defoe seine glänzende Satire gegen die die Dissenters von neuem bedrückende Hochkirche, The Shortest Way with the Dissenters (1703). Infolge dessen wurde er zu Pranger und Gefängnis verurteilt. Das Volk drängte sich aber an den Pranger, um den unerschrockenen Vorkämpfer der religiösen Toleranz mit Rosen zu schmücken. Am

19. Februar begann Defoe mit der Herausgabe einer Zeitschrift Review, die bis 1705 zweimal, und von da bis 1713 dreimal wöchentlich erschien und Sir Richard Steele das Vorbild zu seinem 'Tatler' gab. — Noch einmal mufste Defoe ins Gefängnis wandern, als er gegen die jakobitischen Umtriebe gegen Ende der Regierung Anna's seine Stimme erhob, doch wurde er noch von der Königin begnadigt.

Man hätte erwarten sollen, dafs Georg I. die Verdienste Defoe's belohnen würde. Dieser war aber zu bescheiden, sich vorzudrängen und blieb unbemerkt. Im April 1719 veröffentlichte Defoe The Life and Surprising Adventures of Robinson Crusoe, ein Buch, durch das der Dichter am meisten bekannt geworden ist. Der Geschichte Robinson's liegt eine wahre Begebenheit zu Grunde. Alexander Selderaig (1676 in Schottland geb.), ein wilder Bursche, verliefs seine Heimat und abenteuerte in der Welt herum. Nach einer Abwesenheit von sechs Jahren in die Heimat zurückgekehrt, legte er sich, um nicht erkannt zu werden, den Namen Selkirk bei und ging bald darauf mit dem berühmten Seefahrer Dampier in das Südmeer. Wegen offener Widerspenstigkeit wurde er mehrmals gezüchtigt; als das Schiff an der Insel Juan Fernandez anlegte, verbarg sich der Starrkopf in den Wäldern, liefs das Schiff absegeln und brachte über vier Jahre allein auf der Insel zu. Im Jahre 1709 kehrte er auf Kapitän Rogers' Schiff nach England zurück. Die Erlebnisse Selkirk's, über die u. a. Steele's Zeitschrift 'The Englishman' i. J. 1712 berichtet, gaben dem Dichter nur einige dürftige Umrisse. Was Robinson zum Robinson macht — um Hettner wieder das Wort zu geben — die entzückende Meisterschaft der künstlerischen Form und die überraschende Tiefe des Inhalts, gehören einzig und allein unserem Defoe, der sich durch diese Schöpfung den bedeutendsten Dichtern aller Zeiten anreiht. Walter Scott, der sich Defoe in vielen Dingen zum Muster nahm, bemerkt in Betreff der Form sehr richtig, die peinliche Umständlichkeit auch bei der Erzählung des scheinbar Geringfügigen und Gleichgiltigen verscheuche in uns jeden Zweifel an der Wahrheit des Erzählten; wir denken, wenn die Sache nicht wahr wäre, da hätte der Erzähler schwerlich so viel Mühe an sie verschwendet. Und bezüglich des Inhalts ist Hettner's Wort bezeichnend, der den Robinson eine Art Philosophie der Geschichte nennt. Wir sehen, wie der Mensch mit innerer Notwendigkeit Stufe um Stufe aus dem ersten rohen Naturzustande zur Bildung und Civilisation kommt.

Das Buch, das dem Geschmack jener Zeit an fabelhaften Reisebeschreibungen entgegenkam, wurde fast in alle Sprachen der Welt übersetzt. Namentlich in Deutschland, wo Grimmelshausen schon 1668 am Schlusse seines Simplicissimus ein ähnliches Motiv verwendet hatte, wurde der Robinson sehr beliebt. Er wurde bereits 1721 übersetzt und dann vielfältig und noch lange nachgeahmt. Die fremden Nationen und die heimischen Landschaften mufsten sich, wie Scherer erzählt, gebrauchen lassen, um alle diese Robinsons oder Aventuriers zu benennen. Da gab es einen italienischen, französischen, holländischen, nordischen, einen sächsischen, schlesischen, thüringischen, schwäbischen, brandenburgischen, kurpfälzischen Robinson, einen schweizerischen, dänischen, Dresdener, Leipziger Aventurier und viele andere. Diese Litteratur der Robinsonaden zog sich bis in das Zeitalter Friedrich's II. hinein, und das berühmteste Stück derselben ist eine vierbändige Erzählung, welche 1731 bis 1743 erschien und die man nach ihrem Schauplatze die Insel Felsenburg zu nennen pflegt.

Defoe, dem auch Swift manches für Gulliver's Reisen verdankt, hat noch eine Reihe anderer Erzählungen geschrieben, die als die ersten Vorläufer des englischen Familien- und Sittenromans betrachtet werden können. Besonders genannt sei The Journal of the Great Plague of London, ein erdichtetes Tagebuch eines Londoner Bürgers aus der Pest-Zeit, das infolge seiner realistischen Darstellung sogar als Geschichtsquelle betrachtet worden ist, und The Apparition of one Mrs. Veal to Her Friend Mrs. Bargrave at Canterbury, eine spannende Erzählung einer angeblichen Geistererscheinung, welche von Defoe zur Empfehlung von Drelincourt's Erbauungsbuch 'On Death', das keinen Absatz hatte finden können, geschrieben wurde. Defoe starb am 24. April 1731.

Jonathan Swift wurde im Jahre 1667 in Dublin geboren. Sein Vater, ein Engländer, war schon vor der Geburt des Sohnes gestorben und hatte nichts hinterlassen. Die Entbehrungen, die Swift so von seiner frühesten Kindheit an zu erleiden hatte, legten den Grund zu seiner verbitterten Stimmung, die sich in seinen Werken ausspricht. Ein Oheim liefs ihn erziehen, und durch seine — spärliche — Unterstützung wurde ihm auch der Besuch der Universität in Dublin ermöglicht; Swift brachte es aber nur bis zum Baccalaureus. Als im Jahre 1688 in Irland ein Aufstand zu Gunsten des abgesetzten Königs ausbrach, ging Swift nach England und wandte sich an einen entfernten Verwandten, den Staatsmann Sir William Temple, auf dessen Landgute Moor Park in Surrey er 11 Jahre zubrachte. Durch Sir William wurde er in die politischen Verhältnisse Englands eingeweiht. In Moor Park nahm Swift seine Studien wieder auf und erwarb sich im Jahre 1692 den Magistergrad in Oxford. Infolge eines Zerwürfnisses mit Sir William reiste er nach Irland, liefs sich zum Priester weihen und übernahm eine Landpfarre; doch diese Stellung wurde ihm bald unerträglich, er kehrte nach England zurück, versöhnte sich mit Sir William und blieb bis zu dessen Tode im Jahre 1699 bei ihm.

Da sich Swift in seinen Hoffnungen auf eine Anstellung in England getäuscht sah, ging er wieder nach Irland und nahm den Posten eines Kaplans und Sekretärs bei Lord Berkeley, einem hohen irischen Beamten, an. Die Probstwürde, die ihm dieser versprochen hatte, wurde anderweitig verliehen, und Swift mufste sich mit der Stelle eines Pastors in Laracor — einem Orte nicht weit von Dublin — begnügen. Dort blieb er von 1700—1713. Diese 13 Jahre können als die glücklichsten in Swift's Leben bezeichnet werden. Er unternahm regelmäfsig wenigstens einmal im Jahre eine Reise nach England, wo er mit den berühmtesten Schriftstellern Bekanntschaft schlofs. Im Jahre 1701 gab er (anonym, wie alle seine Schriften) seine erste politische Abhandlung: Discourse on the Contests and Dissensions between the Nobles and Commons in Athens and Rome heraus, in welcher er die Partei des vom Unterhause angeklagten Whig-Ministeriums Somers-Halifax ergriff. Im Jahre 1704 erschien seine Satire The Tale of a Tub, die, schon während seines Aufenthaltes bei Sir William Temple abgefafst, sich gegen die katholische, lutherische und calvinische Religion kehrt. Die Satire soll, wie Swift behauptet, zu Gunsten der anglikanischen Kirche geschrieben sein; sie war aber, da sie vor Religion überhaupt wenig Ehrfurcht zeigt, später der Grund, dafs Swift nie zur Bischofswürde erhoben wurde, was er so eifrig anstrebte, um ins Haus der Lords gelangen zu können; denn als Geistlichen war ihm der Weg ins Unterhaus versperrt. — Da die Whigs seine Hoffnung auf Beförderung nicht erfüllten, trat er zu ihren Gegnern, den Tories, über, die im Jahre 1710 ans Ruder kamen. Swift war der einflufsreichste Ratgeber der Regierung, deren Grundsätze er in Flugblättern und in seiner Wochenschrift The Examiner (2. Nov. 1710 bis 7. Juni 1711) verfocht. Aber selbst der mächtige Bolingbroke war nicht im Stande, Swift einen Bischofssitz zu verschaffen; die Königin konnte ihm sein Märchen von der Tonne nicht vergessen. Nur die Stelle eines Dechanten an der St. Patricks-Kirche in Dublin (Dean of St. Patrick's) wurde ihm im Jahre 1713 verliehen. Verstimmt und verbittert trat er im folgenden Jahre dieses Amt an, als mit dem Tode der Königin Anna das Tory-Ministerium stürzte. Er betrachtete seinen Aufenthalt in Irland nun als eine Verbannung und betrat das Land nach längerer Abwesenheit mit Unwillen und Hafs gegen dessen Bewohner, ein Gefühl, das ihm auch von diesen entgegengebracht wurde, war er doch der vertraute Freund der den Irländern feindlichen Minister gewesen.

Es dauerte aber keine zehn Jahre, so war Swift der Abgott der Irländer. Das kam so. Einem gewissen William Wood war durch den Einfluß verhafster Günstlinge am englischen Hofe das Patent zur Prägung einer Kupferscheidemünze für Irland verliehen worden. Die Irländer, die den Druck Englands nur mit Widerwillen ertrugen, sahen dies als einen Eingriff in ihre Rechte an. Da ließ Swift im Jahre 1723 seine Letters by M. B., Drapier in Dublin erscheinen, in welchen er sich in der schärfsten Weise gegen die englische Regierung aussprach und geradezu zur Erhebung gegen sie aufforderte. Ganz Irland scharte sich um ihn, und die englische Regierung war genötigt, nachzugeben und Wood's Patent zurückzuziehen.

Im Jahre 1727 veröffentlichte Swift sein bedeutendstes Werk: Travels into Several Remote Nations of the World by Lemuel Gulliver. Das Werk ist eine phantastisch-satirische Reisebeschreibung. Es zerfällt in vier Teile. Im ersten wird erzählt, wie Gulliver auf die Insel der Liliputaner verschlagen wird. Höchst ergötzlich ist die Schilderung der Sitten und Einrichtungen dieser kaum sechs Zoll hohen Däumlinge. Englische Verhältnisse: die Parteien der Whigs und Tories (Low-Heels und High-Heels), der Papisten und Protestanten, die Kriege gegen Frankreich u. a. werden *en miniature* vorgeführt und lächerlich gemacht. — Endlich flüchtet er aus diesem Reich der Zwerge. Eine zweite Reise bringt ihn auf die von Riesen bewohnte Insel Brobdingnag (S. 23). Der Bauer, in dessen Hände er dort gerät, zieht mit ihm von Ort zu Ort und läßt ihn für Geld sehen; zuletzt verkauft er ihn an den Hof. Nun setzt wieder die Satire ein.

In einer Reihe von Audienzen hatte Gulliver dem feinsinnigen König von Brobdingnag — dem Ideal eines Monarchen — die Verfassung und die Geschichte Englands geschildert. Gulliver hatte sich hiebei und bei den Fragen und Einwürfen, die der König machte, bestrebt, den Zustand seines Vaterlandes im günstigsten Lichte erscheinen zu lassen — doch der scharfsinnige Herrscher sieht den Dingen auf den Grund und schließt die Unterredung über diesen Gegenstand mit dem Satze: By what I have gathered from your own relation, and the answers I have with much pains wringed and extorted from you, I cannot but conclude the bulk of your natives to be the most pernicious race of little odious vermin that nature ever suffered to crawl upon the surface of the earth.

Wenn aber Gulliver während seines Aufenthaltes auf der Insel Brobdingnag bei solchen und ähnlichen Gelegenheiten England noch scheinbar in Schutz nimmt, wenn er auf dem fliegenden Eiland Laputa und dessen fixem Inselreich (seine dritte Reise brachte ihn dorthin) seine Satire dadurch mildert, daß er sie gegen die Einrichtungen, die er dort antrifft, kehrt, wobei er allerdings die königliche Societät meint — so wird in dem letzten Teil seines Werkes — er wird auf seiner vierten und letzten Reise auf die Insel der edlen Pferde, der Houyhnhnms, verschlagen — seine Satire um so herber und verletzender, als sie die mustergiltigen gesellschaftlichen Zustände in dem Pferdereiche direkt mit denen Englands vergleicht, ein Vergleich, der so ganz zum Nachteile seines Vaterlandes ausfällt, daß Gulliver es für sein größtes Unglück ansieht, wieder in seine Heimat zurückkehren zu müssen.

Mit Recht nennt Hettner Gulliver's Reisen "ein gar nicht genug zu bewunderndes Kunstwerk." Dafs das Werk noch heute mit demselben Vergnügen gelesen wird, wie zur Zeit seines Erscheinens, in der manche das Erzählte für bare Münze nahmen — Arbuthnot, ein Freund Swift's, erzählt, dafs ein alter Herr nach der Lektüre der Reise nach Lilliput die Landkarte zur Hand nahm, um die Insel zu suchen — das ist durch zwei Mittel erreicht: durch den unverwüstlichen Ernst und die Umständlichkeit, mit welcher alle diese abenteuerlichen und absonderlichen Erlebnisse erzählt werden. Gerade wie ja auch Defoe seinem Robinson durch die liebevolle Kleinmalerei den Anschein des Wirklich-Geschehenen gegeben hat.

Nach Gulliver's Reisen hat Swift nur mehr wenig von Bedeutung geschrieben. Ein körperliches Übel (Schwindelanfälle), das er sich in Moor Park zugezogen hatte, verschlimmerte sich immer mehr; dazu wurde sein Gehör immer schlechter. Seine Geisteskräfte verfielen. Im Jahre 1736 begann er sein Gedächtnis zu verlieren. Sein Vermögen, 10,000 l., bestimmte er im Jahre 1740 zur Errichtung eines Irrenhauses in Dublin. Die letzten Jahre litt er an fürchterlichen Schmerzen und sprach kaum ein Wort mehr. Er starb am 19. Oktober 1745.

Swift's schriftstellerische Thätigkeit ist nicht ohne Einflufs auf die deutsche Litteratur geblieben. Die Satiriker Liscow, Rabener, Lichtenberg haben sich an ·der Houymess Freund' (Wingolf II.) gebildet; Wieland, Hippel, Jean Paul (vgl. Gervinus, V. 257) haben ihn eifrig gelesen und gelegentlich neben Fielding, Smollett und Sterne nachgeahmt; Swift steht unter den Lieblings-Schriftstellern Herder's obenan, und Goethe wird durch Herder auf ihn aufmerksam gemacht (Dichtung und Wahrheit. 11. Buch).

Lady Mary Wortley Montagu (1689—1762), bekannt durch ihre Briefe, die als ein Muster der epistolaren Gattung gelten; Macaulay nennt sie 'the brilliant Mary Montagu.' Lady Mary begleitete ihren Gemahl Mr. Wortley (Lady wird sie, die Tochter des Herzogs v. Kingston, genannt zum Unterschied von der Mrs. Montagu, der Gründerin des Blue Stocking Club) auf seiner Gesandtschaftsreise nach Constantinopel, wo er von 1716—18 weilte. Die Briefe aus dieser Epoche haben ein besonderes Interesse. — Zurückgekehrt, trat sie in freundschaftlichen Verkehr mit Addison, Steele, Young und Pope; mit letzterem zerwarf sie sich in der Folgezeit.

Man hat Lady Montagu nicht mit Unrecht mit Madame de Sévigné (1627 bis 1696) verglichen.

Philip Dormer Stanhope, Earl of Chesterfield, wurde 1694 zu London geboren. In Cambridge, das er von seinem achtzehnten Jahre an besuchte, studierte er eifrig die Alten; sein eigentliches Leben aber begann erst, als er im Sommer 1714 in die grofse Welt eingeführt wurde. Er hatte, wie er selbst sagt, das entschiedene Verlangen, allen zu gefallen. Er ging nach Haag und wurde dort Spieler, nicht weil ihm das Spielen Vergnügen machte, sondern weil es zum guten Ton gehörte; dann nach Paris; und wohl niemals haben die Pariser Salons einen gelehrigeren Schüler gefunden. Doch vergafs der junge Gentleman über der leichtfertigen Oberfläche den tieferen Ernst nicht. Er wollte vor allem als Staatsmann glänzen; noch sehr jung trat er ins Unterhaus und ragte bald als Redner hervor. Durch den Tod seines Vaters kam er 1726 ins Oberhaus und wurde in diesem durch seinen Humor, seine grofse Redekunst und sein anmutiges, gewinnendes Wesen ein sehr geachteter Führer. Nachdem er wiederholt Gesandter in Haag gewesen war, wurde er Statthalter *(Lord Lieutenant)* von Irland, und seine Verwaltung war eine für das unglückliche Land segensreiche. Im Oktober 1746 wurde er Staatssekretär; im Januar 1748 aber zog er sich aus Rücksicht auf seine schwankende Gesundheit vom öffentlichen Leben zurück; nur bei sehr wichtigen Fragen, wie z. B. bei der Einführung des neuen Kalenders, trat er dann und wann noch im Parlament auf. Er lebte von jetzt an nur noch seinem Sohne, seinen Freunden und Büchern; die von Dr. Moore 1753—56 herausgegebene fashionable Zeitschrift The World zählte ihn zu ihren Mitarbeitern. Er starb am 24. März 1773.

Am bekanntesten von Chesterfield sind die Briefe an seinen Sohn Sir Philip Stanhope. Sie enthalten einen Schatz von feinen Beobachtungen und Lebensmaximen und sind in einem leichten, anmutigen Stil abgefasst. Doch kann einigen von ihnen der Vorwurf, es mit der Moral gar zu leicht zu nehmen, nicht erspart bleiben. Die Stimmung der Zeit und die Lage der Umstände mag diese, wie Lord Mahon — ebenfalls ein Stanhope — in seiner englischen Geschichte schreibt, entschuldigen. — (Auf dem Gebiete der deutschen Litteratur liefse sich am ehesten Wieland in den Jahren 1760—69 mit Chesterfield vergleichen.)

James Thomson, der Sohn eines schottischen Geistlichen, wurde 1700 zu Ednam in der Grafschaft Roxburgh geboren. Er studierte Theologie in Edinburgh, wo er bereits den 'Winter', den besten Teil seiner Seasons, abfafste; das ganze Gedicht erschien 1726 und fand eine so günstige Aufnahme, dafs Thomson beschloss, fortan völlig der Dichtkunst zu leben. Durch Studiengenossen mit Pope, seinem Vorbilde, bekannt gemacht, fand er bei diesem Rat und Unterstützung. Durch Pope's Empfehlung erhielt er einträgliche Stellen; als Reisebegleiter eines jungen Edelmannes lernte er Frankreich, die Schweiz und Italien kennen. In Nachahmung Spenser's schrieb er eine Allegorie The Castle of Indolence. Seine Trauerspiele sind ohne Wert. Thomson ist auch der Dichter des berühmten Nationalliedes Rule Britannia, welches ursprünglich den Schlusschor seines mit Mallet gemeinschaftlich verfafsten Maskenspiels Alfred bildete. Thomson starb 1748.

Am berühmtesten sind Thomson's Jahreszeiten. Sie sind ein Meisterstück der beschreibenden Dichtung und wurden ihrerzeit allgemein bewundert. Der sentimentale Hang zur Natur, aus dem sie entsprungen sind, sagt Hettner, und die religiöse Feierlichkeit des Grundtones, der dann aber wieder lieblich bald in still-elogische, bald in anmutig-idyllische Klänge hinüberklingt, fanden in dieser Zeit, die von der religiösen Dichtung Milton's und Klopstock's bewegt war, und in der die Vorahnung Rousseau's und des Goethe'schen Werther's schlummerten, den begeistertsten Widerhall. Die Jahreszeiten wurden sogleich in viele Sprachen übersetzt und weckten namentlich auch bei uns Deutschen, die wir unter allen Völkern am meisten zu träumerischer Naturempfindung angelegt sind, in Haller, Klopstock und Ewald von Kleist, tiefempfundene Nachahmung.

Aber nur eine Zeit, die den Begriff der echten Dichtung verloren hatte, konnte Thomson's Seasons unbedingt bewundern. Lessing's Laokoon machte mehrere Decennien später der zweideutigen Zwittergattung der beschreibenden (malenden) Dichtung ein Ende.

Edward Young, der Sohn eines Geistlichen, wurde 1681 geboren. Er studierte zunächst die Rechte, doch schon früh legte er sich auf ein unabhängiges Litteratenleben und suchte nach damaligem Dichterbrauch durch Widmungen und Pensionengesuche den nötigen Unterhalt zu erwerben. Im Alter von einigen vierzig Jahren nahm er plötzlich die geistlichen Weihen, und 1728 wurde er Hofkaplan bei Georg II. Er hatte bereits früher einige fromme Dichtungen geschrieben, die aber heute vergessen sind. Da verlor er nach zehnjähriger glücklicher Ehe 1741 seine Gattin und zwei von ihm sehr geliebte Stiefkinder. Aus dem Schmerz über diese herben Schicksalsschläge ging seine berühmteste Dichtung hervor: The Complaint, or Night-thoughts. Dies Gedicht — mit seinen erhabenen und herzerschütternden Gedanken über die Eitelkeit und Hinfälligkeit des menschlichen Lebens, über Tod und Unsterblichkeit und über die tröstende Kraft des christlichen Glaubens — war eine lange Zeit hindurch das Lieblingsbuch aller Gebildeten, nicht blofs in England, sondern ebenso in Frankreich, Deutschland (und da besonders Klopstock's und seines Kreises) und selbst in Italien. Diese grofsartige Wirkung lag, wie Hettner ausführt, in den geschichtlichen Umständen, unter denen die Nachtgedanken auftraten. Nach langer Winterzeit waren sie der erste erquickende Frühlingstag. Überall war noch Gemachtheit und Künstelei; Young, obwohl wie Klopstock, mit dem er innig befreundet war, oft verschwommen sentimental und unnatürlich gespreizt, sang wieder aus der Tiefe und Inbrunst des eigenen Herzens. In der Zeit der allgemeinen Nachahmung war er ursprünglich und selbstschöpferisch. Young starb 1765.

Samuel Richardson, der Begründer des englischen Familienromanes, wurde im Jahre 1689 in Derbyshire geboren. Seine Eltern waren schlichte Bürgersleute. Schon als Knabe zeichnete er sich durch sein Erzählertalent aus. Da sein Vater, ein Schreiner, nicht die Mittel hatte, ihm eine höhere Bildung zu geben, so mufste er das Buchdruckerhandwerk erlernen; dabei strebte er aber unablässig, die Lücken seiner Bildung zu ergänzen. Durch Fleifs und umsichtige Thätigkeit erwarb er sich, nachdem er selbständig geworden war, ein nicht geringes Vermögen. — Richardson war bereits fünfzig Jahre alt, als er, wie er in dem (S. 248 abgedruckten) Briefe an Aaron Hill erzählt, aus einem rein äufserlichen Anlasse im Jahre 1740 seinen ersten Roman Pamela, or Virtue Rewarded veröffentlichte. Der grofse Erfolg dieses Werkes veranlafste ihn, noch zwei Romane ähnlicher, moralischer Tendenz zu schreiben: Clarissa, oder die Geschichte eines jungen Mädchens, die wichtigsten Beziehungen des Familienlebens umfassend, und Sir Charles Grandison, oder wie es hätte ursprünglich heifsen sollen: The Good Man, London 1753. — Richardson starb am 2. Juli 1761, gefeiert und betrauert von allen, die ihn kannten.

Die grofse Wirkung Richardson's auf seine Zeit wird erklärlich, wenn man bedenkt, wie bis dahin dem Lesepublikum nur schwülstige Romane, in denen Prinzen und Prinzessinnen auftraten, und die Unnatur auf der Tagesordnung war, geboten wurden. Richardson wagte den kühnen Griff ins volle bürgerliche Menschenleben, er setzte die Natur wieder in ihre Rechte ein. Und so sagt Scott: 'Der Leser mufs einigermafsen mit den ungeheuren Foliobänden voller Nichtigkeit bekannt sein, bei denen unsere Vorväter sich in Schlaf gähnten, um sich von der Freude einen Begriff machen zu können, die sie empfanden, als ihnen Wahrheit und Natur so unverhofft geboten wurde.'

In der konsequenten Durchführung der Charaktere, wenn sie auch an sich mitunter verschroben sind, beruht eine Hauptstärke der Erzählungen Richardson's, den man in dieser Hinsicht als den Shakespeare unter den Prosaisten bezeichnet hat. Den Eindruck der Wahrscheinlichkeit erreicht er, wie seine grofsen Vorgänger Defoe und Swift, durch die Ausführlichkeit und Anschaulichkeit, die er auch auf die Schilderung der kleinsten und scheinbar nebensächlichen Dinge und Umstände verwendet. Dazu kommt das Dramatische der Komposition, das Goethe's Ausspruch, es wäre nicht unmöglich, ein Drama in Briefen zu schreiben (Wilhelm Meister's Lehrjahre, V, 7), zur Bestätigung dienen könnte.

Der Einflufs Richardson's auf fremde Litteraturen, auf die französische und deutsche, war ein noch kräftigerer als auf die englische. Diderot vergleicht ihn mit Moses, Sophokles und Euripides und läfst sich von ihm zur Bearbeitung seiner dramatischen Familiengemälde begeistern. Rousseau stellt ihn neben Homer und nimmt ihn in der neuen Heloïse zum Vorbilde. Selbst Voltaire kann sich seinem Einflusse nicht entziehen. Voltaire's 'Nanine' ist nichts anderes als die dramatisierte Pamela, s. Lessing. Dramaturgie, 21. Stück. Und erst die deutsche Literatur! Klopstock, Gellert, Wieland ahmen ihn nach, und Lessing's Dramen Mifs Sara Sampson und Emilia Galotti lehnen sich an Motive in Richardson an, den zu loben er in seiner hamburgischen Dramaturgie wiederholt Gelegenheit findet.

Zwei Grundmängel haften aber den Dichtungen Richardson's an: Die ermüdende Breite — Clarissa hat z. B. acht Bände, jeder zu fünf- bis sechshundert Seiten — und die ausgesprochene aufdringliche Lehrhaftigkeit, der zu Gefallen er z. B. in Grandison einen fehlerlosen Mustermenschen schuf, wie er in der Natur nicht vorkommt. Vgl. Schiller's Xenion über den philosophischen Roman. Dieser trocken moralisierende Ton war dem lebensfrohen Geiste des fröhlichen Altengland zuwider und forderte zur Opposition heraus.

Henry Fielding wurde am 22. April 1707 zu Sharpham-Park in Sommersetshire geboren. Aus einer sehr angesehenen Familie stammend, erhielt er seine Mittelschulbildung in Eton und bezog dann die Universität Leyden, konnte aber aus Mangel an Mitteln seine Studien nicht beendigen. Nach London zurückgekehrt, verschaffte sich der Zwanzigjährige durch Abfassung kleiner Lustspiele die Hilfsquellen zu einem leichtsinnigen Genufsleben. Im Jahre 1736 machte er eine reiche Heirat und hierdurch, sowie durch die Erbschaft seiner Mutter sah er sich in stand gesetzt, ein Landgut zu kaufen. Als er aber sein Vermögen in kürzester Zeit verschwendet hatte, setzte er seine juridischen Studien wieder fort, fand jedoch anfangs keine passende Stellung. Er wendete sich daher der Romanschriftstellerei zu. Im Jahre 1740 veröffentlichte er seinen ersten bedeutenden Roman: The History and Adventures of Joseph Andrews, in welchem er, wie in seinen folgenden Werken, sich in bewufstem Gegensatz zu Richardson befindet, dessen Tugendhelden er lächerlich macht. Endlich im Jahre 1749 erhielt er die Stelle eines Friedensrichters von Westminster und Middlesex, die er gewissenhaft versah. Während der Plackereien dieses Amtes schrieb er seinen zweiten Roman, sein Hauptwerk: The History of Tom Jones, 1750. Auch dieses Werk trägt den parodistischen Zweck offen an der Stirn. Dies ist in den einleitenden Kapiteln, die er den einzelnen Büchern des Romanes voranschickt, mehrmals offen ausgesprochen. Über diese Einleitungen, von denen im Lesebuche eine Probe gegeben ist (S. 229), sei hier ein Urteil Walter Scott's in seinen 'Lives of the Novelists' angeführt.

Fielding considered his works as an experiment in British literature; and therefore, he chose to prefix a preliminary chapter to each book, explanatory of his own views, and of the rules attached to this mode of composition. Those critical introductions, which rather interrupt the course of the story, and the flow of the interest at the first perusal, are found, on a second or third, the mos entertaining chapters of the whole book.

Als dritter bedeutender Roman Fielding's sei noch Amelia genannt, die er 1752 veröffentlichte. — Durch sein leichtsinniges Jugendleben hatte Fielding seine Gesundheit untergraben, vergebens suchte er in Bath Linderung seines Übels; er zog daher in ein wärmeres Klima, nach Portugal. Dort, in Lissabon, ereilte ihn der Tod, im Oktober 1754.

Fielding's Dichtungen kann man mit Hettner in der That in ihrer unnachahmlichen Kunst noch heute unerreichte Meisterwerke nennen. Was sie vor den

Romanen Richardson's so vorteilhaft auszeichnet, ist die Naturwahrheit ihrer Charaktere, die nichts Gemachtes, nichts Überspanntes an sich haben, sondern sich mit all den Fehlern und Gebrechen geben, welche den Menschenkindern anhaften; der Dichter führt uns eine Menschenwelt vor, "so reich bewegt, vielgestaltig und eigentümlich, und dabei doch so getreu aus den Zuständen und Stimmungen der Zeit herausgegriffen, dafs der Sprachgebrauch ganz in seinem Rechte ist, wenn er die Romane Fielding's und die Romane Smollett's, die ebenfalls aus derselben Richtung hervorgegangen sind, als den englischen Sittenroman zu bezeichnen pflegt."

Die Reaktion gegen den rührenden Familienroman, den Gellert durch seine Übersetzung der Pamela und des Grandison und durch seinen viel nachgeahmten Originalroman 'Leben der schwedischen Gräfin' in Deutschland eingeführt hatte, rief Musäus' Parodie 'Grandison der Zweite' (1760) und Wieland's poetische Erzählungen hervor, in denen er, nachdem er sich von Richardson's Tugendseligkeit abgewendet, frohen Lebensgenufs predigt; auf Musäus und Wieland, sowie auf seine Nachahmer ist der Einflufs Fielding's (Smollett's und Sterne's) unverkennbar (vgl. Gervinus, V, 192 f.); und so sagt Goethe zu Eckermann (am 3. Dec. 1824): 'Unsere Romane, unsere Trauerspiele, woher haben wir sie denn als von Goldsmith, Fielding und Shakespeare?'

Tobias George Smollett, ein Schotte, wurde 1721 geboren. Er besuchte die Schule zu Dumbarton und trat später bei einem Wundarzte zu Glasgow in die Lehre. Im Jahre 1740 begab er sich nach London, um dort mit dem Manuskripte eines Trauerspieles: The Regicide sein Glück zu versuchen. In seinen Hoffnungen getäuscht, nahm er im folgenden Jahre die Stelle eines Unterwundarztes auf einem Linienschiffe an, das für die Unternehmung gegen Cartagena bestimmt war. Nach den mannigfachsten Schicksalen forderte er in Westindien seine Entlassung, brachte einige Zeit in Jamaica zu und kehrte 1746 nach London zurück. Der Versuch, sich als Arzt Stellung und Einkommen zu verschaffen, scheiterte. So wurde er Schriftsteller. Von seinen Romanen seien die wichtigsten genannt. Im Jahre 1746 erschien sein erster Roman Roderick Random; 1751 Peregrine Pickle. Aufserdem übersetzte er den Don Quixote und schrieb eine Complete History of England, die als Fortsetzung von Hume's Geschichtswerk zu betrachten ist. Unausgesetzte Kränklichkeit nötigte ihn 1770 nach Italien zu übersiedeln; er wohnte in Montenero, einem Flecken auf einem Bergabhange in der Nähe Livornos. Dort schrieb er seinen letzten und berühmtesten Roman: The Expedition of Humphry Clinker, der 1771 in drei Bänden erschien. Humphry Clinker ist der Diener des Squire Bramble, der auf Anraten seines Arztes eine Reise durch England unternimmt und dabei von seiner Schwester, seiner Nichte und seinem Neffen begleitet wird. Das Werk besteht aus Briefen der einzelnen Mitglieder dieser Gesellschaft, in welchen sie die Reiseerlebnisse erzählen. — Smollett starb am 21. Oktober 1771.

Die Zeit, in der die grofsen Novellisten Richardson, Fielding und Smollett lebten, war sittlich aufserordentlich roh. Die höheren Stände insbesondere ergaben sich einem liederlichen Leben, wie es unter Karl II. im Schwunge war. Die in Ostindien reich gewordenen Engländer trugen nach ihrer Rückkehr in die Heimat zur Verwilderung der Gesellschaft bei. Die öffentliche Sicherheit war dabei in dem bedenklichsten Zustande. Freche Räuber trieben ihr Handwerk abends sogar in den Strafsen der Stadt. — Die Wirklichkeit, romanhafter als der romanhafteste Roman, bot daher Stoff zu litterarischer Verarbeitung in Hülle und Fülle. — Hettner macht mit Recht auf die Abstammung der drei genannten Schriftsteller aufmerksam.

Richardson, aus armer Familie entsprossen, schildert, insbesondere in Clarissa, die sittliche Verkommenheit der höheren Stände mit tiefer Entrüstung, während Fielding und Smollett, die vornehmer Abkunft waren, die Sache leicht nehmen.

Es erübrigen noch einige Bemerkungen über die litterarische Stellung Smollett's. — Künstlerisch steht er weit hinter seinem grofsen Vorgänger Fielding zurück. Seine Charaktere sind meist verwildert und roh, seine Komik wird burleskverzerrt. Der Komposition mangelt die Einheit der Handlung, es ist nur Abenteuer an Abenteuer gereiht. Diese Schwächen werden aber wettgemacht durch den Reichtum und die Kraft der Schilderung; seine lebensvollen Gemälde geben uns von den Sitten und Zuständen jener Zeit einen anschaulichen Begriff, und in der Ausmalung des Seelenlebens ist er noch von keinem der neueren Dichter übertroffen worden.

Lawrence Sterne war der Sohn eines armen englischen Offiziers und wurde am 24. Nov. 1713 zu Clonmell in der Grafschaft Tipperary im südlichen Irland geboren. Er war kränklich und litt beständig an Husten und Blutspeien. Von Verwandten unterstützt, bezog er 1732 die Universität Cambridge, schon dort zeigte er sich als genialer Sonderling. Im Jahre 1740 erhielt er die Pfarre zu Sutton in Yorkshire und eine Pfründe zu York, und nach seiner Verheiratung noch eine dritte Stelle. Er war ein Freund der ländlichen Stille und liebte es, seine freie Zeit mit Lektüre, Malen, Geigenspiel und Jagd auszufüllen. Zweimal unternahm er eine Reise nach Frankreich und Italien. Er starb am 18. März 1768 in London.

Sterne ist Humorist. Wenn Swift die Verkehrtheiten der Welt mit hafserfülltem Herzen betrachtet und sie mit beifsendem Spotte überschüttet, so sieht Sterne die menschlichen Schwächen mit nachsichtigen Augen an und schildert sie mit gutmütigem Scherz. Zwei berühmte Romane stammen aus seiner Feder: Tristram Shandy und A Sentimental Journey, beide sind unvollendet, beide ohne rechten Zusammenhang. Die Geschichte Tristram Shandy's ist, um Hettner's Worte zu gebrauchen, eigentlich gar keine Geschichte, sondern besteht aus einer Reihe von Skizzen und Episoden. Die wichtigsten Personen sind Walter Shandy, der Vater des Tristram, welch letzteren wir übrigens gar nie zu sehen bekommen, ferner Walter's Bruder Toby, ein Officier a. D., und dessen Diener, Korporal Trim. Die Erzählung ist Nebensache, die sprudelnde Ungebundenheit des witzigen oder rührenden Einfalles ist alles. (Vgl. Lesestück S. 36.) Sternes Humor im Tristram Shandy, in jeder andern Beziehung so entzückend und hinreifsend, ist doch launenhaft, willkürlich und abspringend. Künstlerisch steht die "empfindsame Reise" höher. Sie ist reiner in der Form, wenn auch ärmer an innerem Gehalt. Aber selbst Männer wie Lessing und Goethe, denen doch von Seiten der Kunstform gar manches in Sterne widerstehen mufste, waren von der liebevollen Gemütstiefe Sterne's hingerissen. Der Einflufs, den Sterne auf die deutsche Litteratur hatte, ist ein bedeutender; Jean Paul's und Hippel's Stil und Komposition ist Sterne'isch; besonders häufig wurde die empfindsame Reise nachgeahmt. Vgl. darüber Scherer, Geschichte der deutschen Litteratur, S. 663 f. Selbst Goethe verdankt Sterne manche Anregung, so äufsert er sich zu Eckermann (16. Dec. 1828): 'Ich bin Shakespeare, Sterne und Goldsmith Unendliches schuldig geworden,' und ähnlich schreibt er am 25. Dez. 1829 an Zelter: 'Es wäre nicht nachzukommen, was Goldsmith und Sterne gerade im Hauptpunkte der Entwicklung auf mich gewirkt haben.'

Oliver Goldsmith wurde am 10. Nov. 1728 im Dorfe Pallas in der Grafschaft Langford in Irland geboren. Seine Jugend verbrachte er im Dorfe Lissoy in West Meath, wohin sein Vater, ein herzensguter Pfarrer, das Original zu Dr. Primrose im

'Vicar' und des freundlichen alten Predigers im 'Deserted Village,' bald nach Oliver's Geburt versetzt worden war. Sein erster Lehrer war ein alter verabschiedeter Quartiermeister, der unter Marlborough gedient hatte; er unterhielt seine Zöglinge am liebsten mit der Erzählung seiner Abenteuer zu Felde und mit Sagen und Märchen. Nachdem Oliver einige Schulen durchgemacht hatte, kam er auf die Universität in Dublin, wo er wegen seiner Armut sowohl von Lehrern als Schülern manches zu dulden hatte. Seine Fortschritte in den eigentlichen Universitätsstudien, besonders in der Mathematik, waren sehr geringe, dagegen nahm er es in den Klassikern mit jedem auf. Sein Vater hatte ihn für den geistlichen Stand bestimmt, aber da er das Examen vor dem Bischof nicht bestand, konnte er nicht ordiniert werden. Nach einem mifsglückten Versuch mit dem juridischen Studium wurde er nach Edinburgh geschickt, um Medizin zu studieren. Hier hielt er sich zwei Jahre auf, dann reiste er auf den Kontinent und verbrachte noch einige Zeit auf den medizinischen Schulen in Löwen und Leiden. Scott erzählt darüber in seinen 'Lives of English Novelists':

At Leyden, Goldsmith was peculiarly exposed to a temptation which he never, at any period of his life, could easily resist. The opportunities of gambling were frequent, — he seldom declined them, and was at length stripped of every shilling.

In this hopeless condition, Goldsmith commenced his travels, with one shirt in his pocket, and a devout reliance on Providence. It is understood, that in the narrative of George in the Vicar of Wakefield, the author gave a sketch of the resources which enabled him, on foot and without money, to make a tour of Europe. Through Germany and Flanders, he had recourse to his violin, in which he was tolerably skilled; and a lively tune usually procured him a lodging in some peasant's cottage for the evening. In Italy, where his musical skill was held in less esteem, he found hospitality by disputing at the monasteries, in the character of a travelling scholar, upon certain philosophical theses. The foreign universities afford similar facilities to poor scholars with those presented by the monasteries. Goldsmith resided at Padua for several months, and is said to have taken a degree at Louvain. Goldsmith spent about twelve months in these wanderings, and landed in England in the year 1746, after having perambulated France, Italy, and part of Germany.

Poverty was now before our author in all its bitterness. His Irish friends had long renounced or forgotten him; and the wretched post of usher to an academy, of which he has drawn so piteous a picture in George's account of himself, was his refuge from actual starving. Unquestionably, his description was founded on personal recollections, where he says, — "I was up early and late; ... to seek civility abroad." This state of slavery he underwent at Peckham [Map F 7] academy, and had such bitter recollection thereof as to be offended at the slightest allusion to it.

Die übrigen Versuche, die er machte, sich eine feste Lebensstellung zu schaffen, schlugen ebenfalls fehl. Er war eine Zeit lang Laborant in einer Apotheke, praktischer Arzt im Armenviertel an der Themse, Korrektor in Richardson's Druckerei und endlich Recensent für Griffith's Monthly Review. Diese letzte Stellung wurde ihm infolge der Änderungen, die man mit seinen Beiträgen vornahm, so unerträglich, dafs er sich entschlofs, abermals Schulmeister zu werden. Ein darauf folgender neuer Versuch, sich als Arzt seinen Unterhalt zu verschaffen, hatte gleicherweise keinen Erfolg, und so griff er wieder zur Feder. Er lieferte Beiträge zu den Revuen und Magazinen, die damals in England üppig gediehen. In ein Tagblatt schrieb er nach dem Muster von Montesquieu's 'Lettres persannes'

seine Chinesischen Briefe, die er später unter dem Titel The Citizen of
the World sammelte. Eine Wochenschrift The Bee, die er redigierte, brachte
es nur bis zu Nummer acht. Im Jahre 1761 schlofs er durch Vermittlung des
nachmaligen Bischofs Percy, des Herausgebers der 'Relics of Ancient English
Poetry' Bekanntschaft mit Johnson, und mit beiden entwickelte sich eine
Freundschaft, die erst mit Goldsmith's Tode endete.

Den gröfsten Teil seiner Zeit verwendete nun Goldsmith des lieben Brotes
halber auf Arbeiten, die Buchhändler bei ihm bestellten. So entstand seine History of England (in zwei Ausgaben, einer kürzeren und einer ausführlicheren),
seine Histories of Greece and Rome und seine auf Buffon's Werk gegründete
History of the Earth and Animated Nature. Während er mit diesen litterarischen Taglohnsarbeiten beschäftigt war, schrieb er seine unsterblichen Werke,
die dem englischen Schrifttum, ja der Weltlitteratur überhaupt zur Zierde gereichen.
Im Jahre 1764 veröffentlichte er seine poetische, mit sozialen Reflexionen durchwobene
Reisebeschreibung: The Traveller, A Prospect of Society, wozu er sechs
Jahre später ein Gegenstück oder eine Art Fortsetzung lieferte: The Deserted
Village, ein Gedicht, das auch durch seine Tendenz Goldsmith's gutem Herzen
alle Ehre macht, indem es den Reichen die Pflicht einschärft, sich der Besitzlosen anzunehmen. Sein berühmtestes Werk ist aber der idyllische Roman: The
Vicar of Wakefield (1766) — neben Robinson die am weitesten verbreitete
erzählende Dichtung. Es ist überflüssig, auf die grofsen Verdienste dieses Werkes,
aus dem, wie Scherr sagt, der Ruf des Rousseau'schen Naturevangeliums herauszuhören ist, näher einzugehen. Jeder, der den schlichten Landprediger und die
Seinigen kennt, ist von ihnen bezaubert. Hier sei nur auf Goethe's liebevolle
Würdigung des Werkes, mit dem ihn Herder bekannt gemacht hatte, im X. Buche
von Dichtung und Wahrheit hingewiesen.

Von seinen zwei Lustspielen: The Good-Natured Man und She
Stoops to Conquer, or The Mistakes of a Night, wird das letztere noch
heute gegeben.

Obwohl Goldsmith in der späteren Zeit in seiner Schriftstellerei eine nicht
unbeträchtliche Einnahmsquelle hatte, so war er doch infolge seines unpraktischen
Sinnes einerseits, seines guten Herzens, das den Notleidenden keine Bitte abschlagen konnte, andererseits, meist in Geldverlegenheit. Er starb am 4. April 1774,
aufrichtig betrauert von seinen Freunden und beklagt von den vielen Armen,
deren Not er gelindert. Sein Leib ist im Templekirchhof begraben. Sein Monument
befindet sich in der Westminster-Abtei.

Mächtig war der Einflufs Goldsmith's auf die deutsche Litteratur und insbesondere auf Goethe; im 'Wilhelm Meister,' in 'Hermann und Dorothea,' ja auch
im 'Faust' finden sich Reminiscenzen an Goldsmith, vornehmlich an seinen Vicar;
aus der 'liebenswürdigen Romanze' im 8. Kapitel dieses Romanes entstand die
Oper 'Erwin und Elmire' (vgl. Dichtung und Wahrheit, 19. Buch), und Goethe's
'Wanderer' entnimmt dem Traveller Namen und Grundmotiv. Vgl. den Aufsatz
Levy's 'Goethe und Oliver Goldsmith' im VI. Band des Goethe-Jahrbuches.

Samuel Johnson, der Sohn eines Buchhändlers in Lichfield in Staffordshire, wurde 1709 geboren. Schon an dem Kinde waren die physischen und
psychischen Eigentümlichkeiten, die nachher den herangewachsenen Mann auszeichneten, deutlich zu erkennen; grofse Körperkraft, vereint mit linkischem Wesen
und mancherlei Schwächen; ein überaus reger Geist in Verbindung mit einem
krankhaften Hange zur Trägheit; ein gütiges und edles Herz und dazu ein verdüstertes und reizbares Temperament. Der Knabe erwarb sich trotz seiner Trägheit

spielend eine Menge Kenntnisse. Vom sechzehnten bis zum achtzehnten Jahre war er zu Hause und erweiterte seinen geistigen Gesichtskreis durch sprunghafte Lektüre, wozu ihm seines Vaters Gewerbe reichlich Gelegenheit gab; leider war auch dieser mehr Bücherfreund als Buchhändler; er verarmte gänzlich. Nur mit Hilfe eines reichen Nachbars konnte Samuel die Universität Oxford beziehen. Dort war der absonderliche, schlecht gekleidete, aber durch seinen Geist hervorragende Jüngling bald eine bekannte Erscheinung. Da aber die Unterstützungen, die ihm zugesagt worden waren, ausblieben, mufste er 1731 Pembroke College verlassen, ohne einen akademischen Grad erlangt zu haben. Im folgenden Winter starb sein Vater und hinterliefs seiner Familie soviel wie nichts.

Während der dreifsig folgenden Jahre war Johnson's Leben ein unausgesetzter harter Kampf mit der Armut, der ihm um so härter wurde, als sich seine körperliche und geistige Gesundheit sehr verschlimmert hatte. Während fünf Jahren blieb er in Lichfield und den Nachbarorten. In seinem Geburtsorte glückte es ihm nicht, ein Unterkommen zu finden; er wurde nacheinander Usher in einer Grammar-School in Leicestershire, Gesellschafter eines Landedelmannes und schliefslich Lohnschreiber bei einem Buchhändler in Birmingham. Eine Heirat, die er um diese Zeit schlofs, nötigte ihn, eine einträglichere Beschäftigung zu suchen. Er errichtete daher eine Erziehungsanstalt, aber anderthalb Jahre verflossen, und er hatte blofs drei Zöglinge. Da entschlofs er sich, 28 Jahre alt, mit dem unvollendeten Manuskript seiner Tragödie Irene und einigen Guineas in der Tasche nach London zu gehen und sein Glück als Schriftsteller zu versuchen. Aber gerade zu der Zeit waren die wenigsten Aussichten für einen Litteraten. Ein Jahr lang hatte er höchst kümmerlich gelebt, als er von dem Buchhändler Cave für das Gentleman's Magazine beschäftigt wurde. Johnson hatte Parlamentsberichte (aus Lilliput) zu schreiben, in welchen er seinen torystischen Grundsätzen Ausdruck gab. Im Mai 1738 veröffentlichte er anonym ein Gedicht London, in welchem er in Nachahmung einer Satire Juvenal's die Leiden des Schriftstellerlebens beschreibt. Das Gedicht erregte allgemeine Aufmerksamkeit, und Pope, der seine Nachahmung von horazischen Satiren und Episteln hatte erscheinen lassen, nahm sich um den vielversprechenden Autor an, aber ohne Erfolg. Johnson hatte noch mehrere Jahre Not und Entbehrungen zu tragen. Unter seinen damaligen Bekannten befand sich auch der geniale, aber leichtsinnige Richard Savage, der als Sohn eines Earl die mannigfachsten Schicksale durchgemacht hatte und 1743 im Elend starb. Bald nach seinem Tode gab Johnson The Life of Savage heraus, das, obwohl anonym, seinen litterarischen Ruf so steigerte, dafs sich im Jahre 1747 mehrere hervorragende Buchhändler an ihn wandten mit der Aufforderung, ein Wörterbuch der englischen Sprache zu schreiben. Den Prospekt des Wörterbuches richtete er an den Earl von Chesterfield, der wegen seines Geschmackes und seiner feinen Manieren berühmt war, erhielt aber von ihm keinerlei Aufmunterung. Nach sieben Jahren mühsamer Arbeit beendigte Johnson sein Wörterbuch in zwei grofsen Bänden (1755). Während dieser Zeit schrieb er The Vanity of Human Wishes, eine ausgezeichnete Nachahmung der 10. Satire Juvenal's (1749). Im folgenden Jahre begann er mit der Veröffentlichung der Wochenschrift The Rambler, nach dem Muster des 36 Jahre früher erschienenen Spectator; die Wochenschrift erschien durch zwei Jahre (März 1750 bis März 1752) und errang sich allmählich eine grofse Bedeutung. Von anderer Seite redigiert trat die Zeitschrift 'The World' das Erbe des Rambler an. In 'The World' schrieben viele hochgestellte Männer Beiträge, so auch der Earl of Chesterfield, an den Johnson den Prospekt zu seinem Wörterbuche mit so wenig Erfolg gerichtet hatte. Als nun das grofse Werk nahezu beendigt war, hätte Chesterfield es gerne gesehen,

wenn es ihm gewidmet worden wäre. Daher schrieb er mehrere Artikel für 'The
World', in denen er, wie wir sagen würden, für das Wörterbuch Reclame machte, die
Schriften Johnson's warm pries und den Vorschlag that, Johnson solle mit der
Autorität eines Diktators, ja eines Papstes (Pope) über die englische Sprache ausgestattet werden und seine Entscheidung über Bedeutung und Schreibung eines Wortes
solle endgiltig sein. Doch Johnson war nicht zu versöhnen; in einem würdig und
kräftig stilisierten Brief (s. S. 252) lehnte er diese verspätete Gönnerschaft ab und
liefs sein Dictionary ohne Widmung drucken. Das Werk wurde mit beispiellosem
Enthusiasmus aufgenommen. Es war in der That das erste Wörterbuch, das man
mit Vergnügen lesen konnte. Die Definitionen zeigen so viel Schärfe des Geistes
und Herrschaft über die Sprache, und die Belegstellen aus Dichtern und Prosaikern
sind so geschickt gewählt, dafs man eine Mufsestunde immer sehr angenehm mit
der Lektüre derselben zubringen kann. Leider trug dieses Werk dem Verfasser nicht
so viel ein, dafs er vor Mangel geschützt gewesen wäre. Er eröffnete eine Subskription
auf eine Ausgabe Shakespeare's und liefs von 1758—1760 The Idler, eine
neue Wochenschrift, erscheinen. Im Jahre 1759 starb seine Mutter (seine Gattin
war schon 1752 gestorben); um die Begräbniskosten decken zu können, schrieb
er in einer Woche seine philosophische Erzählung Rasselas. Im Jahre 1762 erhielt Johnson vom König eine Pension von 300 Pfund jährlich; so der Sorge um
das tägliche Brot enthoben, dachte er bei seiner angeborenen Lässigkeit wenig daran,
an der versprochenen Ausgabe Shakespeare's weiter zu arbeiten; endlich wurde er
1765 durch eine Satire Churchill's zur Einlösung seines Versprechens gezwungen.
Wenn aber Johnson ungern zur Feder griff, so wuchs seine Bedeutung und sein
Einflufs auf die Litteratur auf eine andere Art. Im Jahre 1764 bildete sich ein
litterarischer Klub, als dessen Haupt Johnson galt. Berühmte Schriftsteller und
Künstler gehörten diesem Klub an. Goldsmith vertrat die Poesie und schöne
Litteratur, der Maler Reynolds die Künste, Burke die politische Beredsamkeit
und Staatswissenschaft; da war ferner Gibbon, der gröfste Historiker, und Jones,
der gröfste Sprachforscher des Zeitalters; Garrick, der berühmte Schauspieler, ein
engerer Landsmann Johnson's, einer von den drei Zöglingen seines Pensionats,
war ein geschätztes Mitglied; ferner gehörte diesem Klub Boswell an, dem
wir ein ausführliches Leben Johnson's verdanken. Bald nach der Gründung
des Klubs wurde Johnson mit der wohlhabenden Familie Thrale bekannt, bei
der er nun viele angenehme Stunden verlebte. Im Jahre 1773 machte er eine
Reise nach den Hebriden, deren Beschreibung er 1775 veröffentlichte. Sein
letztes und (vom Wörterbuch abgesehen) bedeutendstes Werk ist: The Lives
of the English Poets (1781), das er auf Einladung von vierzig hervorragenden Buchhändlern schrieb, die die Dichtungen der englischen Poeten von
Cowley (1618—67) an mit kurzen biographischen Einleitungen herauszugeben beabsich-
tigten. Johnson starb, allgemein betrauert, am 13. Dezember 1784 und wurde in
der Westminster-Abtei begraben, inmitten der Dichter, deren Leben er beschrieben.

Der Bischof **Dr. Thomas Percy** gab 1765 The Relics of Ancient
English Poetry heraus; die Wirkung dieser alten Balladen war eine zündende,
von dem Herausgeber selbst nicht erwartete. Die 'korrekte' Dichtung, die sich an
Pope anlehnte, hatte dadurch den Todesstofs erlitten. Man hatte, wie Hettner sagt,
so lange in trockener Dürre geschmachtet: hier sprang aus reicher Quelle der erquickende Labetrank; hier war wieder frische Natürlichkeit, unbefangene Empfin-
dung, derb zugreifende Handlung. Das alte Regelsystem wurde in seinen Grundfesten
erschüttert. Was kümmern uns die Pope und Boileau? Natur, Natur! Frische und
fröhliche Ursprünglichkeit, — das ist das Geheimnis der Dichtung.

In Deutschland wurde Percy's Sammlung mit Entzücken aufgenommen; der Einfluſs dieser Balladen auf die Dichter von Klopstock bis zu den Stürmern und Drängern ist nicht geringer als der, welchen der fast gleichzeitig erschienene Ossian Macpherson's übte; namentlich wurde Bürger dadurch zu seiner volkstümlichen Balladendichtung begeistert.

Hugh Blair (1718—1800), ein schottischer Geistlicher und Freund Johnson's, ist bekannt durch seine 'Lectures on Rhetoric and the Belles Lettres,' die er als Professor in seinem Geburtsort Edinburgh hielt und dann drucken lieſs. Von Blair besitzen wir auch 'Sermons.'

David Hume, der Sohn eines schottischen Edelmanns, wurde 1711 in Edinburgh geboren. Er studierte die Rechte, aber seine Neigung zog ihn zur Beschäftigung mit der Litteratur. Nach seines Vaters Tode ging er mit dem geringen Erbteil, das er erhielt, nach Frankreich, wo er sich drei Jahre aufhielt und ganz den Studien widmete. Im Jahre 1737 kehrte er nach England zurück und veröffentlichte 1738 eine philosophische Abhandlung über die Natur des Menschen, die er später umarbeitete und Enquiry Concerning Human Understanding betitelte. Im Jahre 1742 gab er Essays Moral, Political, and Literary heraus, zu welchen er zehn Jahre später eine Fortsetzung: Political Discourses erscheinen lieſs. Von 1746—48 begleitete er den General St.-Clair, Gesandten bei den Höfen in Wien und Turin, als Sekretär; über diese Reisen führte er ein Tagebuch, das später der Öffentlichkeit übergeben wurde. Nachdem er sich vergebens um eine Professur in Glasgow und Edinburgh beworben hatte, nahm er in letzterer Stadt die Stelle eines Bibliothekars an der Bibliothek der schottischen Advokaten an. Er benützte die reiche Büchersammlung fleiſsig zu historischen Studien, denn er beabsichtigte die Geschichte Englands von der Zeit der Vereinigung Schottlands mit England (1603) bis zum Tode der Königin Anna (1714) zu schreiben. Diesen Plan führte er nur zum Teil aus, indem die beiden ersten Bände mit Jakob II. schlieſsen. Der erste Band (1754), der die Regierung Jakob's I. und Karl's I. umfaſst, wurde sehr kühl aufgenommen; der zweite (1757) gefiel den Whigs schon besser. Die freundliche Aufnahme des dritten Bandes (1759), der die Zeit der Tudors schildert, bewog ihn, dem Drängen des Buchhändlers nachzugeben und das Werk mit einer Schilderung der Zeit von Cäsar's Einfall bis zu Heinrich VII. abzuschlieſsen (1761—62). Dieser letzte Teil ist der schwächste, da die wichtigsten Akten für diesen Zeitabschnitt damals noch ganz unbekannt und unbearbeitet waren. — Seine Schriftstellerei machte Hume so angesehen und wohlhabend, daſs er nur ungern dem Gesandten am Versailler Hofe, dem Marquis von Hertford, im Jahre 1763 als Gesandtschafts-Sekretär nach Paris folgte. Sein Ruhm war ihm schon vorausgegangen, und Hume war sogleich in der vornehmen Pariser Gesellschaft der Löwe des Tages; aber er war auch ein tüchtiger Diplomat und leitete für eine kurze Zeit als Chargé d'Affaires die Gesandtschaft. Im Jahre 1766 kehrte er nach England zurück und wurde Unter-Staats-Sekretär des Unterrichtsministers General Conway, eines Bruders Lord Hertford's. Im Jahre 1769, als das Ministerium aufgelöst wurde, ging Hume nach Schottland zurück. Er starb 1776 in Edinburgh.

Hume's Englische Geschichte gehört zu den klassischen Werken der englischen Litteratur. In dem Preise seines vortrefflichen historischen Stils, seiner Klarheit, Natürlichkeit und Lebendigkeit ist alles einig, wogegen der Inhalt seines Werkes in England nicht ungeteilten Beifall fand und findet. Die zuerst erschienene Geschichte der Stuarts erregte wegen ihres antipuritanischen Tones bei den Whigs Anstoſs, aber auch die Tories waren damit nicht ganz zufrieden, bei dem folgenden Bande wurde das Verhältnis ein entgegengesetztes. Aber gerade darin, dafs mehrere von den politischen Parteien in England mit Hume unzufrieden waren, liegt, wie Fr. v. Raumer treffend bemerkt, der Beweis, dafs Hume eben kein Parteischriftsteller war, sondern der durch ernste Studien gewonnenen Überzeugung treu blieb. — Hume als Philosoph bezweifelt vor allem die Notwendigkeit des Zusammenhanges von Ursache und Wirkung; weil wir gewohnt sind zu sehen, dafs ein Ding auf ein anderes der Zeit nach folgt, erwarten wir, dafs es jederzeit darauf folgen werde, ohne dabei eine Einsicht in die Notwendigkeit dieser regelmäfsigen Aufeinanderfolge zu gewinnen. Der grofse deutsche Philosoph Kant wurde durch Hume teils zur Opposition, teils zur Nachfolge angeregt.

Dr. William Robertson (1721—93) war wie Hume ein Schotte. Dem Stande seines Vaters folgend, wurde er Geistlicher und brachte es zu hohen Würden, unter anderem war er Kurator der Universität Edinburgh. Seine History of Scotland (1759) wurde gleich bei ihrem Erscheinen mit gröfstem Beifalle begrüfst und trug ihm den Titel eines Hofhistoriographen für Schottland ein. Für seine History of the Reign of Charles V. (1769) erhielt er von seinem Verleger das beträchtliche Honorar von 4500 *l.*; zu seiner History of America waren ihm die besten spanischen Quellen und Hilfsmittel zur Verfügung gestellt.

Seine Werke sind auf fleifsige, genaue Forschungen gegründet und zeugen von gediegenem Urteil und einem mit dem Menschenwohl sympathisierenden Herzen. Sein Stil, obgleich sorgfältig, erreicht nicht die natürliche Feinheit Hume's und die klassische Rundung Gibbon's. — Bekanntlich hat Schiller bei seinen Vorstudien zu 'Maria Stuart' Robertson's History of Scotland, sowie Hume's History of England benützt.

Edward Gibbon wurde im Jahre 1737 als Sohn eines reichen Gutsbesitzers in Putney (damals ein Dorf, jetzt ein südwestlicher Stadtteil von London) geboren. Da er schwächlich war, erhielt er seinen Unterricht zu Hause; gröfstenteils war er indes sich selbst überlassen und beschäftigte sich viel mit Büchern, besonders gern las er geschichtliche Werke. Er hatte sein fünfzehntes Jahr noch nicht zurückgelegt, als er auf die Universität Oxford kam, wo er aber wenig Anregung erhielt. Die Lektüre der Schriften Bossuet's bewog ihn, zum Katholicismus überzutreten; dadurch wurde sein fernerer Aufenthalt am Magdalen College unmöglich. Sein Vater schickte ihn daher nach Lausanne, wo er in dem Hause eines reformierten Geistlichen Aufnahme fand, durch dessen Einflufs er wieder zur protestantischen Kirche zurückkehrte. Während seines fünfjährigen Aufenthaltes in Lausanne trieb er fleifsig das Studium der klassischen Sprachen, des Französischen und der Geschichte. Im Jahre 1758 kehrte er nach England zurück und leistete von 1760—62 Dienste in der Miliz. Wenn auch Gibbon diese zwei Jahre für sich und für die Miliz für verloren hält, so hatten sie doch den Nutzen, dafs sie ihm sein Volk und sein Land, das ihm durch seinen Lausanner Aufenthalt fremd geworden war, wieder näher brachten; dafs die Erfahrungen, die er da machte, später seinem Geschichtswerke zu gute kamen, giebt er selbst zu.

Nach Abschlufs des Friedens (1763) ging er wieder auf den Kontinent, und zwar zunächst nach Paris, dann nach Lausanne, wo er sich elf Monate für das Ziel seiner Reise, Italien, vorbereitete. In Rom entstand in ihm (15. Okt. 1764 abends, als er auf den Ruinen am Kapitol safs und Mönche in Jupiter's Tempel die Vesper sangen) der Plan, die Geschichte der ewigen Stadt zu schreiben. Im Jahre 1765 kehrte er nach England zurück und verwendete nun die folgenden zweiundzwanzig Jahre auf die Sammlung des Stoffes und die Ausarbeitung seines grofsen Geschichtswerkes: The History of the Decline and Fall of the

Roman Empire. Gründlich und allseitig vorbereitet, ging Gibbon an seine Arbeit. Zu seinem umfassenden Quellenstudium und der teilweisen Bekanntschaft mit dem Schauplatz der Begebenheiten, die er schilderte, kam seine Stellung als Offizier in der englischen Miliz, die ihm die für seine Arbeit nötige Einsicht in die Einrichtungen und die Verwendung der bewaffneten Macht verschaffte, ebenso wie ihn seine Stellung als mehrjähriges (1774—82) Parlamentsmitglied mit den Wegen und Weisen bekannt machte, wie ein grofses Gemeinwesen geführt und gelenkt wird. — Im Todesjahre Hume's, 1776, erschien der erste Band von Gibbon's Geschichtswerke; die zwei folgenden kamen 1781 heraus, und damit sollte das Werk, das bis zum Falle des weströmischen Reiches geführt war, nach dem ursprünglichen Plane schliefsen. Drei weitere Bände, die Gibbon in Lausanne, wo er seit 1783 wieder weilte, schrieb, enthalten als Fortsetzung die Geschichte des oströmischen Reiches. Am Abend des 27. Juni 1787 schrieb er in seinem Gartenhause in Lausanne die letzte Zeile des letzten Blattes, wie er selbst erzählt (in seinen Memoiren, die Lord Sheffield nach Gibbon's Tode zusammen mit dessen Briefen unter dem Titel: Miscellaneous Works of Edward Gibbon veröffentlichte). Im Jahre 1793 verliefs er die Schweiz und starb 1794 in England. Gibbon's Geschichtswerk wurde sowohl von Kennern wie Hume und Robertson, als auch vom grofsen Publikum mit aufserordentlichem Beifall aufgenommen; sein sorgfältig durchgearbeiteter Stil gilt als klassisch.

William Pitt, nachmals zum Earl von Chatham erhoben, aber unter dem Ehrennamen des grofsen Commoners in der Geschichte seines Landes und der Menschheit unsterblich, wurde 1708 zu London geboren und hauchte auf seinem Landsitze zu Hayes 1778 mit den zu seinem Freunde Camden gesprochenen Worten: 'Dear Camden, save my country!' seine grofse Seele aus. Er zuerst beherrschte die öffentliche Meinung, das Parlament und den widerwilligen Hof mittelst der Macht des Wortes und drang zwei Königen seine Politik der Freiheit und des Ruhmes auf. Stets auf Seite der Unterdrückten kämpfend, verschönte er den Abend seines Lebens durch seinen standhaften Widerstand gegen die Mafsnahmen jener kurzsichtigen Politik, welche die Unabhängigkeitserklärung der Kolonien von Nordamerika herbeiführte. Er war es, welcher im Januar 1766 bei der grofsen Debatte hinsichtlich der über die Nordamerikaner durch das Kabinet Grenville verhängten und von dem Kabinet Rockingham aufrecht erhaltenen Besteuerung ausrief, er freue sich zu hören, dafs Amerika zum Widerstand gegen diese ungerechte Zumutung entschlossen sei. Bei dieser Gelegenheit, sowie bei seiner neun Jahre später in derselben Sache im Oberhause gehaltenen Rede (s. S. 266) loderte noch einmal die volle Flamme seines Geistes auf. (Scherr.)

Edmund Burke wurde 1729 [?] in Dublin geboren. Sein Vater war Protestant, seine Mutter Katholikin, Erziehung und Unterricht erhielt er von einem Quäker, Abraham Shackleton, einem ausgezeichneten Menschen, und so wurde in Burke frühzeitig der Grund zur religiösen Toleranz gelegt, die er später so warm verfocht. Die juristische Laufbahn, die er nach dem Wunsche seines Vaters, der selbst Advokat war, einschlagen sollte, sagte ihm wegen der mechanischen Art des Studiums weniger zu, als die Beschäftigung mit der schönen Litteratur und der Geschichte und Philosophie. Seine im Jahre 1756 veröffentlichten Schriften: Vindication of Natural Society und Inquiry into our Ideas of the Sublime and Beautiful und ein treffliches Fragment einer Geschichte Englands von Caesar's Einfall bis zu König Johann's Tod — er gab diese Arbeit auf, als er erfuhr, dafs Hume dieselbe Periode behandeln wolle — machten ihm bald einen Namen, und er ward ein hervorragendes Mitglied des Johnson-Klubs. Die

Mitarbeiterschaft an The Annual Registers, einem politisch-litterarischen Jahrbuche, erweiterte Burke's Einsicht in die politischen Verhältnisse Englands und des Kontinents.

Im Jahre 1765 wurde er durch den Einfluſs des Marquis von Rockingham, der eben an die Spitze eines Whig-Kabinetts gelangt war, ins Parlament gewählt. Er trat 1766 ins Unterhaus, zu einer Zeit, da der ältere Pitt (Chatham) ins Haus der Lords kam, und beide lieſsen sich in der Debatte über die Zurücknahme der amerikanischen Stempelakte vernehmen, Burke zum ersten-, Pitt zum letztenmale, 'a splendid sunset and a splendid dawn,' wie Macaulay sagt. Im Jahre 1774 wurde er und ein gewisser Mr. Cruger, ein Kaufmann, der groſse Geschäfte mit Amerika machte, für Bristol gewählt, was insoferne als eine besondere Auszeichnung gelten kann, als Bristol damals die zweit-bedeutendste Stadt in England war. Bei der Gelegenheit hielt Burke zwei Ansprachen an seine Wähler, die eine vor, die andere nach der Wahl — von letzterer ist S. 262 der Schluſs gegeben. Er war im Parlament für eine gerechtere Handelspolitik gegen Irland und für die Aufhebung der härtesten Bestimmung gegen die Katholiken. Im Jahre 1778 wurden mit Parlamentsbeschluſs das berüchtigte Statut Wilhelm's III. gegen die irischen Katholiken aufgehoben. Dies gab der unwissenden Menge Anlaſs zu den unter dem Namen 'Gordon Riots' bekannten Unruhen im Jahre 1780; vgl. den Brief Burke's an Shackleton, den Sohn seines alten Lehrers, S. 255. — Durch diese Haltung zog er sich den Unwillen seiner Wähler zu, so daſs ihn 1780 Bristol fallen lieſs; Rockingham stellte ihm aber einen anderen Wahlkreis zur Verfügung, und Burke blieb bis 1794 Mitglied des Unterhauses. Burke's selbstlose Thätigkeit für das öffentliche Wohl umfaſste ein weites Gebiet, in welchem seine Stellung zu der amerikanischen Frage, der administrativen Reform, den indischen Angelegenheiten und der französischen Revolution besonders hervorragt.

In dem Streite Englands mit seinen amerikanischen Kolonien war Burke von jeher für ein versöhnliches Auftreten, um die Verbindung derselben mit dem Mutterlande zu bewahren. Aber seine warnenden Worte verhallten wirkungslos: 1778 schloſs Frankreich einen Freundschafts- und Handelsvertrag mit den unabhängigen Staaten in Amerika, und 1781 wurde Yorktown von den Amerikanern genommen.

Der von Burke im J. 1780 eingebrachte Vorschlag einer Reform in der Verwaltung (A Plan for the Better Security of the Independence of Parliament, and the Economical Reformation of the Civil and other Establishments) bezweckte die Abschaffung der von der jeweiligen Regierung zu verleihenden Pensionen und Sinekuren, die, zur Bestechung von Parlamentsmitgliedern miſsbraucht, dazu dienten, die Regierungspartei zu verstärken. Wenn Burke auch nicht vollständig durchdrang, so haben seine Anregungen doch für die Folgezeit gewirkt und zur Herstellung eines geordneten Staatshaushaltes beigetragen.

Im Jahre 1786 stellte Burke, der seit mehr als einem Jahrzehnt die indische Frage eingehend studiert hatte, im Unterhause den Antrag auf Vorlage der notwendigen Schriftstücke zur Prüfung der Administration des Warren Hastings in Indien, um ihn vor das Reichsgericht stellen zu können. Burke trat an die Spitze des 1787, nach stürmischen Verhandlungen, aus dem Unterhause gewählten Anklage-Ausschusses und entwickelte eine glänzende rednerische Thätigkeit. Obwohl der siebenjährige Proceſs gegen Warren Hastings, der des Miſsbrauches seiner Gewalt, der Erpressung und der Bedrückung der Eingeborenen (for high crimes and misdemeanours) beschuldigt war, 1795 mit dem Freispruche des Angeklagten endigte, weil er, wie verwerflich auch die von ihm angewandten Mittel waren, England und der ostindischen Kompanie grofse Dienste geleistet, so war der moralische Erfolg, den Burke und seine Genossen errungen hatten, ein bleibender: hinfort waren solche, dem Völkerrecht Hohn sprechende Handlungen, wie sie Hastings als General-Gouverneur in Indien verübt hatte, zu einer Unmöglichkeit geworden.

Die französische Revolution betrachtete Burke vom Anfang an mit mifstrauischen Augen. Für ihn, der nur eine Weiterentwicklung und Besserung der bestehenden Verhältnisse auf gesetzmäfsigem Boden für recht hielt, mufsten die Vorgänge, die sich in Frankreich abspielten, abstofsend sein. In diesem Sinne verfafste er eine Reihe von Schriften, unter welchen seine Reflections on the Revolution in France, die mehrere Entgegnungen hervorriefen, am bedeutendsten sind.

Burke starb am 9. Juli 1797 auf seiner Besitzung im Dorfe Beaconsfield (in der Nähe von Windsor) in Buckinghamshire.

Charles James Fox, der zweite Sohn des ersten Lord Holland, wurde 1749 geboren; er erhielt seine Bildung am Gymnasium in Eton (bei Windsor) und an der Universität Oxford und zeichnete sich besonders durch seine Fortschritte in den alten Sprachen aus. Nachdem er mehrere Reisen auf dem Kontinent gemacht hatte, kam er 1768 ins Parlament, wo er sich infolge seiner aufserordentlichen Beredsamkeit bald zum Führer der Whigs aufschwang. Zwei Jahre nach Fox' Tode (1806) wurde durch seinen Neffen Lord Holland seine 'History of the Early Part of the Reign of James II.' herausgegeben.

William Pitt (1759—1806), eines berühmten Vaters berühmter Sohn, trat 1781 in das Unterhaus und hielt seine Jungfernrede (maiden speech) zu Gunsten eines von Burke eingebrachten Antrages auf Ersparnisse im königlichen Hofhalt. Bei seinem zweiten Auftreten überschüttete ihn Fox (sein nachmaliger Gegner) mit Lob, und Wilberforce, der edle Kämpfer für die Aufhebung der Sklaverei, prophezeite, dafs der junge Mann früher oder später die erste Stelle im Lande einnehmen werde. Die Prophezeiung ging frühzeitig in Erfüllung, denn Pitt war noch nicht fünfundzwanzig Jahre alt, als er erster Lord der Schatzkammer und Leiter des Unterhauses wurde. Diese höchste staatsmännische Stellung in England behauptete er mit einer Unterbrechung von wenigen Jahren bis zu dem Tage, an welchem er den grofsen Toten in der Westminster-Abtei beigesellt wurde. Seine Politik war eine specifisch englische: vom Standpunkte eines englisch-patriotischen Oligarchen aus lenkte er, allen Anstrengungen der Whigpartei zum Trotz, den Staat im widerrevolutionären Sinn und bewaffnete die Koalitionen des monarchischen Europas gegen die französische Republik. Schlagfertige Geistesgegenwart, Klarheit und Leichtigkeit des Ausdrucks zeichneten ihn als Redner aus. (Scherr.)

Richard Brinsley Sheridan wurde als der Sohn des berühmten Schauspielers und Nebenbuhlers Garrick's im Jahre 1751 zu Dublin geboren. Er besuchte bis zu seinem achtzehnten Jahre die Schule in Harrow (10 Meilen nordwestlich von London) und sollte dann, da seines Vaters Verhältnisse ihm den Besuch einer Universität nicht ermöglichten, sich zum Advokaten ausbilden. Aber während eines Besuches in Bath machte er die Bekanntschaft der jungen und schönen Sängerin Mifs Linley, mit der er unter sehr romantischen Umständen im Alter von zwanzig Jahren eine Ehe einging. Im Jahre 1775 trat er mit seinem ersten Lustspiel, The Rivals, auf, das aber ziemlich kühl aufgenommen wurde. Im Jahre 1776 kaufte er mit zwei Teilhabern das Drury Lane Theater von Garrick, der sich damals von der Bühne zurückzog. Hier brachte er 1777 sein zweites Lustspiel, The School for Scandal, zur Aufführung, das sogleich aufserordentlichen Beifall erzielte. Wie einzelne Charaktere in den Rivals mit Personen in Smollett's Humphry Clinker, so haben Joseph und Charles Surface in 'The School for Scandal' Ähnlichkeit mit Fielding's Tom Jones und Blifil. Das wenig günstige Bild, das der Romanschriftsteller und der Dramatiker von der vornehmen englischen Gesellschaft ihrer Zeit entwerfen, ist ein historisch-treues und wird nie sein Interesse verlieren. Grofsen Erfolg hatte auch die komische Oper The Duenna. Mit der witzigen Farce The Critic, einer Nachahmung von Buckingham's Rehearsal (s. Dryden), schlofs Sheridan im J. 1779 seine dramatische Thätigkeit ab.

Durch den Einflufs seines Freundes Fox wurde Sheridan im J. 1780 von dem Flecken Stafford ins Unterhaus gewählt. Er schlofs sich den Whigs an und unterstützte sie in ihrer langen aussichtslosen Opposition. Er arbeitete sich bald zu einem hervorragenden Redner empor. Unter seine besten Reden zählen seine Zeitgenossen den sogenannten Begum Speech, welchen er am 7. Februar 1787 gegen Hastings hielt (vgl. S. 264 und Anm.). Die Rede ist leider nicht erhalten, doch besitzen wir andere berühmte Reden von ihm. In einer derselben (1810 gehalten) kommt der oft citierte Ausspruch über die Presse vor: "Give them a corrupt House of Lords; give them a venal House of Commons; give them a tyrannical Prince; give them a truckling court, — and let me but have an unfettered press: I will defy them to encroach a hair's breadth upon the liberties of England."

Sheridan war eine leichtlebige Natur. Im Jahre 1812 verlor er seinen Sitz im Parlamente, wie er selbst sagt, aus Mangel an Mitteln, um die Ausgaben für seine Wiederwahl in Stafford zu bestreiten, und das vollendete seinen Ruin. Er kam in die gröfste Geldverlegenheit. Während seiner letzten Krankheit kamen Gerichtsdiener, die den Sterbenden ins Schuldgefängnis führen wollten, was aber durch die Dazwischenkunft eines menschenfreundlichen Arztes verhindert wurde. Acht Tage nach seinem Tode (1816) wurde er mit fürstlichem Pomp in der Westminster-Abtei beigesetzt.

Thomas Campbell wurde 1777 in Glasgow geboren, wo sein Vater Kaufmann war. Er studierte an der Universität seiner Vaterstadt und vollendete seine Studien in Deutschland, das er wiederholt besuchte. Am berühmtesten ist sein Lehrgedicht The Pleasures of Hope (1799), in dessen siebenter Auflage er das volkstümlich gewordene Lied Ye Mariners of England brachte. Campbell starb 1844 in Boulogne.

Robert Burns wurde am 25. Januar 1759 in Ayrshire im südwestlichen Schottland geboren. Er war der Sohn eines Pächters und verbrachte selbst den gröfsten Teil seines kurzen Lebens hinter dem Pfluge. Er erhielt eine für seine Verhältnisse gute Bildung, indem er neben der englischen Sprache auch etwas Französisch und Geometrie lernte, aufserdem war er ein eifriger Leser. Früh erwachte in ihm die Liebe zur Dichtkunst. Der Tod seines Vaters nötigte ihn, die Pachtung zu übernehmen; da es damit nicht recht vorwärts gehen wollte, beschlofs er, als Aufseher einer Pflanzung nach Jamaica zu gehen. Um sich das Reisegeld zu verschaffen, veröffentlichte er eine Sammlung seiner Gedichte (1786). Sie wurden sehr beifällig aufgenommen, und Burns erhielt eine Einladung nach Edinburgh, wo er, in den besten Kreisen freundlichst aufgenommen, eine neue Auflage seiner Gedichte erscheinen liefs. Mit dem Ertrage seines dichterischen Erstlingswerkes trat er eine gröfsere Pachtung an, konnte aber auch diesmal nicht vorwärts kommen. Er übernahm daher 1789 den Posten eines Zollbeamten in Dumfries, den ihm seine Edinburgher Gönner verschafften. Die mit seinem Amte verbundenen Plackereien drückten ihn. Sein Freimut zog ihm, dem Jakobiten, statt Beförderung Unannehmlichkeiten zu. Seine Gesundheit fing an zu wanken;

Armut. Sorgen und Unzufriedenheit verschlimmerten das Übel, und schon am 21. Juli 1796 erlag er demselben in einem Seebade am Solway-Ufer.

Burns war eine echte Dichternatur. Seine Gedichte waren, um mit Hettner zu reden, Gelegenheitsgedichte in jenem hohen Sinne, in welchem Goethe dieses Wort auf die aus wirklichen und persönlichen Anlässen entspringende Dichtung anwendet. Was war von den gelehrten Dichtern, von Pope und seinen Nachahmern, über die idyllische Schäferwelt eines erlogenen Traumlandes gesungen und gefabelt worden! Hier steht ein einfacher Landmann, selbst ein Schäfer und Pflüger; und wie ganz anders spiegelt sich hier die Welt! — Nicht über ihm, sondern in ihm und um ihn liegt sein Sehnen und seine Befriedigung. — Der Kreis, in dem sich Burns bewegt, ist nicht grofs. Es ist die Liebe, die Hochlandsnatur und die Freiheit, die sich hier überdies echt patriarchalisch als Sehnsucht nach der Wiederherstellung der angestammten Stuarts darstellt. — Aus dem Volksliede entsprungen — zum Teil im Dialekt geschrieben — ist Burns' Dichtung auch wieder Volkslied geworden. Volkslied im echtesten Sinne! Überall, wo englische Sprache gesprochen wird, erschallen Burns' schöne Gesänge. Walter Scott und Thomas Moore, die Seeschule, selbst Byron und Shelley stehen auf seinen Schultern.

William Cowper wurde 1731 als der Sohn des Kaplans König Georg's II. in Berkhampstead in Hertfordshire geboren. Früh verlor er seine heifsgeliebte Mutter. Er studierte in Temple die Rechte, war aber bei seiner übermäfsigen Schüchternheit und Melancholie, die zuweilen in Wahnsinn ausartete, zur Bekleidung eines Amtes untauglich. Er lebte in dem Hause eines gewissen Mr. Urwin, der ihn zu poetischem Schaffen ermunterte. Cowper's bedeutendstes Werk ist das Lehrgedicht The Task, sehr beliebt ist das humoristische Gedicht John Gilpin. Von Cowper besitzen wir auch eine Übersetzung Homer's. Er starb im Jahre 1800.

Cowper ist für die englische Litteratur insofern epochemachend, als er den glatten, gekünstelten Stil, der sich in Nachahmung Pope's herausgebildet hatte, aufgab und es wagte, natürlich zu schreiben. Die Seeschule — voran Wordsworth — zeigt deutlich den Einflufs Cowper's.

William Wordsworth wurde 1770 zu Cockermouth (25 Meilen südwestlich von Carlisle) in Cumberland geboren. Nach dem Tode seines Vaters, eines Rechtsanwaltes, bezog William mit Unterstützung seiner Verwandten die Universität Cambridge, machte hierauf Reisen nach dem Kontinente und zog sich dann unter bescheidenen Verhältnissen an einen Gebirgssee in Westmoreland zurück. Seine Freunde Samuel Taylor Coleridge (s. d.) und Robert Southey, die sich ebenfalls eine Zeit lang an den Seen Westmorelands und Cumberlands aufhielten — daher der Name Seeschule für die drei Dichter — stimmten in mehreren Punkten seinen von Cowper's Dichtungen beeinflufsten Ansichten über Poesie bei. Sein Hauptgrundsatz war, zu den Zwecken der Dichtkunst die gewöhnliche Umgangssprache der mittleren und niederen Volksklassen zu verwenden, die Stoffe aus der Alltäglichkeit des gewöhnlichen Menschenlebens zu nehmen, um dessen poetische Seiten hervorzukehren, kurz in jeder ländlichen Scene, jedem ländlichen Ton seine Freude zu suchen und zu finden. So anheimelnd diese der Pope'schen Dichtung, dem Perückenstil in der englischen Litteratur, entgegengesetzte Wahl und Behandlung der dichterischen Stoffe auch sein mochte, so liefs sich doch eine Gefahr nicht vermeiden, die: ins Platte und Triviale zu verfallen, dessen Gebiet so nahe an das des Natürlichen, Naiven grenzt. Ein sprechendes Beispiel hierfür ist Wordsworth's bekanntes Gedicht 'We are seven' (s. S. 308), das von manchen reizend naiv, von anderen albern gefunden wird.

Wordsworth's bedeutendstes Werk ist seine philosophische Dichtung The Excursion, in welcher er, wie in seinen übrigen Gedichten — Balladen, Oden, Sonetten — den Zweck verfolgt, menschliches Glück, menschliche Tugend zu fördern, die Macht des Geistes, die Kräfte der Menschennatur zu erhöhen. Nach Southey's Tode wurde Wordsworth Poet Laureate. Er starb 1850 in Rydal Mount (am See von Windermere in Westmoreland).

Samuel Taylor Coleridge wurde als der Sohn eines Pastors am 21. Oktober 1772 in dem Städtchen Ottery St. Mary (10 Meilen nordöstlich von Exeter) in Devonshire geboren. Ein Jahr nach dem Tode seines Vaters erhielt der frühreife Knabe 1782 einen Freiplatz in der bekannten Schule Christ's Hospital in London. Die übertrieben strenge Zucht, unter welcher er hier acht Jahre stand, machte den jugendlichen Dichter für die Ideen der französischen Revolution um so empfänglicher. Nach mehrjährigem Studium an der Universität Cambridge traf er im Sommer 1794 in Oxford mit Southey (s. d.) zusammen, der wie er von revolutionären Gedanken erfüllt war. Die beiden Jünglinge begaben sich nach Bristol, schlossen Freundschaft und verabredeten den Plan, nach Amerika auszuwandern, um dort eine neue Gesellschaft mit völliger Gleichberechtigung aller, eine 'Pant-iso-kratie', zu gründen. Coleridge, der sich auf dem Gebiete der Dichtkunst gegen den Pope'schen Klassizismus auflehnte und Milton und Spenser als seine Muster verehrte, knüpfte um diese Zeit Beziehungen mit der radikalen Presse an, um Pitt sowohl in den Tageblättern als auch in öffentlichen Vorträgen mit hoher Meisterschaft der Rede zu bekämpfen. Zu seinem grofsen Leidwesen zerschlug sich indessen infolge der Absage des praktischeren Southey das Projekt der Auswanderung.

In das Jahr 1796 fällt seine Bekanntschaft mit Wordsworth. Über das Verhältnis der beiden Dichter schreibt Brandl in seinem schönen Buche 'S. T. Coleridge und die englische Romantik': "Wordsworth füllte bei Coleridge den Platz aus, den sich Southey verscherzt hatte. Auch er hafste die modische Gesellschaft mit ihrer äufseren Rangabsonderung und inneren Nivellierung, kämpft für die Wiederkehr natürlicher Zustände, hatte sich für die Revolution begeistert, war gegen die orthodoxe Kirche kühl und für die Romantik ein Bahnbrecher geworden. Er hatte überdies, was Southey nicht besafs und Coleridge doch zu seiner Ergänzung von einem Freunde bedurfte: feste Innigkeit." Zu den Lyrical Ballads, welche Wordsworth 1798 herausgab, steuerte Coleridge mehrere Oden bei, ferner die Ballade The Ancient Mariner und epische Episoden aus seinem Drama Osorio (das er später umarbeitete und Remorse betitelte). Um dieselbe Zeit entstand das unvollendet gebliebene Schauer-Märchen Christabel, das aber erst 1816 — auf Byron's Empfehlung — gedruckt wurde.

Coleridge, der infolge seiner sprunghaften, nicht andauernden Thätigkeit stets mit Sorgen zu kämpfen hatte, fand durch begeisterte Verehrer seines Genius freigebige Unterstützung; zuerst wurde ihm diese durch Thomas Wedgwood, den Sohn des Töpfer-Krösus, zu teil. So konnte der Dichter im Herbste 1798 mit seinem Freunde Wordsworth und dessen feingebildeter Schwester eine Reise nach Deutschland unternehmen, wo er sich acht Monate lang aufhielt, um die Sprache und Sitte des Landes zu studieren. Er versenkte sich insbesondere in die Werke Lessing's, die er ins Englische zu übersetzen beabsichtigte — ein Plan, der wie so viele andere unausgeführt blieb. Auch den deutschen Philosophen, vor allen Kant, trat er näher. Mehrere Gedichte Klopstock's und Stolberg's wurden übersetzt. "Er überarbeitete ferner die klopstockisierende Ode 'Chamouni vor Sonnenaufgang' von derselben Friederike Brun, deren 'Sieben Hügel' auch Wordsworth die Idee zu 'We are seven' gegeben haben soll; allerdings ist Coleridge sehr frei zu Werke gegangen und hat namentlich mancherlei Erinnerungen an seine Harzreise eingefügt." Die schönste und reifste Frucht seiner deutschen Reise ist aber die Übersetzung von Schiller's Wallenstein, die er 1800 innerhalb sechs Wochen vollendete.

Die folgenden zehn Jahre verbrachte er zum gröfsten Teil an den Seen von Cumberland und Westmoreland, wo sich Wordsworth und Southey niedergelassen hatten. Wie diese, so lenkte auch er allgemach in mafsvollere Bahnen. Doch war der Höhepunkt seiner dichterischen Thätigkeit überschritten. Sein Gesundheitszustand war ein ungünstiger; da griff er, um seine gichtischen Schmerzen zu lindern, zur Opiumflasche — und verschlimmerte das Übel. Eine Zeitschrift The Friend, die er gründete, ging wie schon früher The Watchman bald ein. All das drückte ihn nieder.

Im Herbste 1810 zog Coleridge in das Haus eines neuen Gönners John Morgan's in Hammersmith, einem Vorort Londons im Westen von Kensington (Map D 1). Hier liefs man dem Kranken, dem man vor allem das Opium entzog, die freundlichste Pflege angedeihen. Wiedergenesen, entwarf er seine berühmten Lectures on Shakespeare and Milton, zu denen er durch das Studium von Jean Pauls 'Vorschule der Ästhetik' und A. W. Schlegel's 'Vorlesungen über dramatische Litteratur und Kunst' angeregt worden war. In den Schlufs dieser Zeit fällt seine Biographia Literaria, seine tiefsinnigste Prosa-Leistung, und das Drama Zapolya.

Vom Frühjahr 1816 an wohnte Coleridge in Highgate (Map A 3—4) bei der Familie Dr. Gillman's, eines angesehenen Arztes, hauptsächlich mit dem Studium und der Abfassung philosophischer, theologischer und mystischer Schriften beschäftigt. Am 25. Juli 1834 starb Coleridge, 'der am wenigsten productive, aber bei weitem genialste und originellste Dichter der Seeschule' (Körting).

'Coleridge war,' um mit Brandl's Worten zu schliefsen, 'ein mächtiger, hingebungsvoller, durch Mifserfolge unentwegter Erzieher seines Volkes, er durchsetzte den kaufmännisch beschränkten, teils skeptischen, teils frömmelnden Hausverstand seiner damaligen Landsleute mit einer vielseitigen, begeisterten, hellenisch-deutschen Denkmethode und bietet noch heute für manches brennende Übel der Gesellschaft einen beherzigenswerten Rat.' — Noch fruchtbarer als durch seine mannigfachen Schriften wirkte er unmittelbar durch seine Persönlichkeit.

Robert Southey, 1774 als Sohn eines Leinenhändlers in Bristol geboren, besuchte die Westminster School und hierauf die Universität Oxford, wo er Theologie studieren sollte, aber, wie er selbst sagt, nichts lernte als schwimmen und rudern. Im Sommer 1794 vereinigte er sich mit Coleridge (s. d.) zur Gründung der 'Pantisokratie'. Die beiden Freiheitsschwärmer vermählten sich mit zwei Schwestern in Southey's Geburtsort und warben Anhänger für ihren Plan der Auswanderung nach Amerika, der sich aber bald infolge des Rücktrittes Southey's zerschlug. Im Jahre 1796 veröffentlichte Southey ein revolutionäres Gedicht Joan of Arc, an welchem Coleridge mitgearbeitet hatte. Zwischen 1802 und 1814 schrieb Southey eine Reihe von Balladen und längeren epischen Dichtungen, die ihre Stoffe zum Teil entlegenen Ländern entnahmen: Thalaba spielt in Arabien, The Curse of Kehama in Indien, Roderick the Last of the Goths, sein bestes Werk, hat den Untergang des Westgothen-Reiches in Spanien zum Gegenstande.

In späteren Jahren änderte Southey, der sich durch seinen Fleifs aus ärmlichen Verhältnissen emporgerungen und seit 1804 zu Greta Hall bei Keswick

(24 Meilen südwestlich von Carlisle) in Cumberland seinen Sitz aufgeschlagen hatte, seine Gesinnung: er wurde ein Hochtory, wie seine Vision of Judgment bezeugt, in welcher er Georg III. kurz nach dessen Tode verherrlicht.

Aufser seinen Dichtungen hat Southey auch eine Reihe von Prosa-Schriften abgefasst: History of Brazil, History of the Peninsular War, Life of Nelson u. a.

Die letzten vier Jahre seines Lebens verbrachte Southey, der 1813 zum Poet Laureate ernannt worden war, in geistiger Zerrüttung — eine Folge seiner Überanstrengung. Er starb 1843.

Walter Scott wurde am 15. August 1771 als der Sohn eines Rechtsanwalts in Edinburgh geboren. Die Jahre seiner Kindheit verlebte der schwächliche, am rechten Fufse gelähmte Knabe bei seinem Grofsvater, der in der Nähe von Melrose (am Tweed) eine Besitzung hatte, und empfing dort die ersten Eindrücke der Hochlandsnatur und des Hochlandslebens, das er in seinen Werken so poetisch verherrlicht; zugleich machte er sich durch eine ausgedehnte Lektüre mit der Vergangenheit und den Sagen des Landes bekannt. Dem Willen seines Vaters gemäfs studierte er in Edinburgh die Rechtswissenschaft und war im Alter von 21 Jahren Advokat. Im Jahre 1799 wurde er Sheriff in Selkirkshire, der Gegend, in der er seine Jugend verbracht hatte, und 1806 erhielt er die Stelle eines Sekretärs bei dem obersten Gerichtshofe (Court of Sessions) in Edinburgh. Beide Posten verschafften ihm eine sorgenfreie Existenz, ohne ihm zu viel Zeit wegzunehmen, und so konnte er manche Stunde der Beschäftigung mit den Musen widmen. Schon 1796 war er mit einer Übersetzung von Bürger's Lenore und drei Jahre später mit einer Übersetzung von Goethe's Götz vor die Öffentlichkeit getreten. In den Jahren 1802—3 erschien als Frucht seiner wiederholten Reisen, seiner antiquarischen und historischen Studien, die er der Vergangenheit seines geliebten Landes widmete, und zu denen ihn seine Stellung als Sheriff einlud, sein Werk: Minstrelsy of the Scottish Border, eine Sammlung von Volksliedern und Abhandlungen über schottische Sitten und Gebräuche, über historische Personen und Ereignisse, und dieses Werk wurde ihm später eine reiche Fundgrube für Stoffe zu seinen Dichtungen in gebundener und ungebundener Rede. Im Jahre 1805 erschien The Lay of the Last Minstrel, eine Verherrlichung des Geschlechtes der Buccleuch in sprunghaften Balladen — besonders gelungen ist die Gestalt des alten Minstrel — drei Jahre später Marmion, a Tale of Flodden Field (Schlacht zwischen Heinrich VIII. und Jacob IV., 1543) und 1810 The Lady of the Lake. Die folgenden poetischen Erzählungen fanden nicht mehr dieselbe begeisterte Aufnahme, einerseits standen sie nicht mehr auf derselben künstlerischen Höhe wie die genannten, anderseits waren um diese Zeit (im März 1812) die zwei ersten Gesänge von Childe Harold's Pilgrimage erschienen und hatten das Publikum im Sturme gewonnen.

Scott wandte sich daher einem anderen Gebiete zu, dem des historischen Romans, auf welchem er unerreichter Meister wurde. Im Jahre 1815 erschien sein erster Roman: Waverley, or 'Tis Sixty Years Since', den er schon 1805 begonnen, dann aber hatte liegen lassen. Den Stoff zu dem Roman bot eine Episode aus dem jakobitischen Aufstand von 1745. Waverley und die folgenden Erzählungen erschienen anonym, und Scott bewahrte seine Anonymität bis 1857, obschon das Geheimnis von seinen Freunden und Verehrern längst durchschaut war. "Der grofse Unbekannte," wie man Scott nannte, erwarb sich durch seine geniale Feder ein fürstliches Vermögen, das ihn in den Stand setzte, seinen Lieblingswunsch, der Stifter eines adeligen Geschlechtes zu werden, in Ausführung zu bringen. Er kaufte an den Ufern des Tweed ein Stück Land um das andere und baute dort einen glänzenden Herrensitz, Abbotsford, wo er selbst seinen König, von dem er zum Baronet gemacht wurde, bewirtete. — Wir wollen nicht die lange Reihe der Romane, die 74 Bände umfafst, aufzählen. Hier mag ein Urteil Scherr's über die bedeutendsten derselben einen Platz finden: Unter den eigentlich ritterlichen Romanen streiten Ivanhoe (1820), Quentin Durward (1823) und Kenilworth (1821) um den Vorrang. Einen höchst anziehenden Cyklus von Gemälden der Hof- und Volkszustände vor der Revolution, unter Cromwell und während der Restauration bilden The Fortunes of Nigel (1822), Woodstock (1826) und Peveril of the Peak (1823). Hinsichtlich des Humors übertrifft der The Antiquary (1816) (in welchem Schottland zur Zeit Scott's geschildert ist) alle übrigen, hinsichtlich der Charakterzeichnung stehen Guy Mannering (1815), Rob Roy (1818) und Waverley voran, und der mächtigste Hauch von Poesie weht in The Bride of Lammermoor (1819) und in The Heart of Midlothian (1818). — Was Scott's Schreibart durchwegs auszeichnet, ist die sinnliche Plastik in der Schilderung von Menschen, Landschaften und Begebenheiten; geradezu wunderbar ist es, um wieder mit Scherr zu reden, wie er, welche Scene er auch schildere, nicht allein die Form, sondern auch den Geist der Lokalität wiederzugeben vermag.

Aufser seinen poetischen Erzählungen und den Romanen machte sich Scott um die ältere englische Litteratur und deren Geschichte verdient durch die Herausgabe der Werke Dryden's und Swift's und durch seine Lives of the Novelists; er lieferte Beiträge zur Edinburgh Review (einem Whigblatt, 1812 von Francis Jeffrey, dem gefürchteten Kritiker, im Verein mit Brougham u. a. gegründet) und zu dem Toryblatt The Quarterly Review, welches er im Jahre 1809 im Verein mit dem nachmaligen Minister Canning, dem Philologen George Ellis, dem Nationalökonomen Malthus u. a. ins Leben rief. Scott selbst war ein Tory.

Scott war Teilhaber an Ballantyne's Druckerei und Constable's Verlagsfirma in Edinburgh. Als beide Geschäfte im Januar 1826 fallierten, fiel auf Scott eine Schuldenlast von 120,000 l. Diese ungeheure Summe wollte er durch verdoppelte litterarische Thätigkeit abzahlen, und schon hatte er mehr als die Hälfte davon getilgt, als er infolge seiner übermäfsigen Anstrengung im Februar 1830 einen heftigen Schlaganfall erlitt; obwohl er im folgenden Jahre eine Reise nach dem Süden machte, erholte er sich nicht mehr und starb, nach Abbotsford zurückgekehrt, am 21. September 1832, von ganz England betrauert.

Wenn sich Scott an der deutschen Litteratur, vor allen an Goethe gebildet hatte, so fanden andererseits seine Romane wieder in Deutschland viele Nachahmer, unter denen als bedeutendster Zschokke genannt sei, 'der in seinen schweizerischen Lokalbildern und übrigen historischen Gemälden am meisten in Scott's geschichtliche und örtliche Charakteristik einging' (Gervinus V. 774).

George Gordon Byron wurde am 22. Januar 1788 in London geboren. Er stammte väterlicherseits aus einer Familie, deren Glieder sich durch ungebundenes, excentrisches Wesen hervorthaten (vgl. S. 107, Z. 10 ff.); sein Vater zeigte die schlechten Seiten des Familiencharakters in hohem Grade. Er war ein Verschwender und Wüstling, der die reiche Mitgift seiner Gattin in weniger als zwei Jahren durchgebracht hatte und einige Jahre nach der Geburt seines Sohnes starb. Byron's Mutter — mit ihrem Mädchennamen Miss Catharine Gordon of Gight und mit dem schottischen Königshause verwandt — liefs sich 1790 in Aberdeen nieder; sie war zu jähzornig und launisch, um auf seine Erziehung einen wohlthätigen

Einfluſs zu nehmen. Es war unter diesen Umständen noch gut, daſs der frühreife Knabe viel sich selbst überlassen war und seinen Geist durch planlose Lektüre von geschichtlichen und Reisewerken beschäftigte. Nachdem er ein Scharlachfieber überstanden hatte, ging seine Mutter im Sommer 1796 mit ihm in die schottischen Hochlande, deren wilde Schönheit einen so nachhaltigen Eindruck auf sein empfängliches Gemüt machte, daſs er in seinen Werken wiederholt die Hochlandsscenerie schildert.

In seinem zehnten Jahre (1798) erbte er durch den Tod eines Groſsoheims den Lordstitel und die Besitzung Newstead Abbey in Nottinghamshire. Seine Mutter zog nun mit ihm nach London. Im Jahre 1801 kam er auf die von Adeligen besuchte Mittelschule in Harrow (einige Meilen nordwestlich von London); von seinen Mitschülern, mit denen er einen freundschaftlichen Verkehr unterhielt, ist besonders Robert Peel zu nennen. Die Jahre 1805—1808 brachte er auf der Universität Cambridge zu, wo er, die regelmäſsigen Studien verachtend, seine planlose Lektüre weiter trieb und sich, trotz seines Klumpfuſses, in allen Arten der körperlichen Fertigkeiten ausbildete. Im Jahre 1807 veröffentlichte er eine Gedichtsammlung Hours of Idleness; *a Series of Poems, Original and Translated. By George Gordon, Lord Byron, a Minor*, die in der Edinburgh Review so abfällig beurteilt wurden, daſs sich Byron in einer beiſsenden Satire, English Bards and Scotch Reviewers (1809) rächte, in welcher er auch auf solche Dichter, die später zu seinen besten Freunden zählten, wie Moore und Scott, heftige Ausfälle machte.

Von Widerwillen gegen die heimischen Zustände erfüllt, trat Byron am 11. Juni 1809 in Begleitung seines Freundes Hobhouse eine Reise über Spanien nach dem Orient an; seine Excentricität veranlaſste ihn, am 9. Mai 1810 Leander's Wagstück nachzuahmen und von Sestos nach Abydos zu schwimmen. Im folgenden Jahre kehrte er nach London zurück. Über den Erfolg der ersten zwei Gesänge seiner in der Spenserstrophe abgefaſsten poetischen Reisebeschreibung Childe Harold's Pilgrimage berichtet Moore (s. oben S. 209). Byron fühlte sich zu regem poetischen Schaffen angeeifert; in den Jahren 1813—15 erschienen auſser seinen Hebrew Melodies seine prächtigen, morgenländische Glut atmenden Epyllien The Giour, The Bride of Abydos, The Corsair, Lara, The Siege of Corinth, Parisina; woran sich später noch The Prisoner of Chillon (1816), Mazeppa (1818) und The Island (1823) schlossen. Wie Childe Harold nur eine durchsichtige Maske der eigenen Persönlichkeit des Dichters ist, so hat er sich auch in den Helden fast aller seiner Erzählungen selbst geschildert, wenn auch mit übertrieben düsteren Farben. Die energischen, von der Glut wilder Leidenschaften durchtobten Gestalten seiner Helden, die mit sich selbst und der menschlichen Gesellschaft in beständiger Fehde leben, die kein Gesetz auſser ihrer ungezähmten Lust anerkennen, und für deren blasiertes Gemüt nichts auſser dem Gefahrvollen, Schrecklichen Reiz besitzt — sie alle weisen Charakterzüge des jungen englischen Lords auf, der, um Strodtmann's Worte zu gebrauchen, in der kraftlosen Zeit kein Feld für seinen Thatendrang findet, der seine Jugend in excentrischen Tollheiten vergeudet, und der im Kampfe mit sich und der Welt schon in einem seiner frühesten Gedichte sich 'einen lebens- und liebemüden Timon von noch nicht neunzehn Jahren' nennt! — Anfangs 1815 vermählte sich Byron mit Miss Anna Isabella Milbanke, der Tochter eines begüterten Landedelmannes; die Ehe wurde aber nach Ablauf eines Jahres, bald nach der Geburt einer Tochter, Augusta Ada, geschieden. Das bot der englischen Gesellschaft, der das ungebundene Wesen Byron's ein Greuel war, willkommenen

Anlaſs, ihren früheren Günstling fallen zu lassen. Im Parlament und im Salon wandte man ihm kalt den Rücken, selbst auf der Strafse und im Theater wurde er vom Pöbel insultiert; Byron verliefs daher am 25. April 1816 sein undankbares Vaterland, das er nie wieder sehen sollte. Er reiste über Belgien, den Rhein aufwärts, nach der Schweiz. In Genf, wo er mit Frau von Staël und Shelley in vertrautem Verkehr stand, dichtete er den dritten Gesang des Childe Harold und begann das dramatische Gedicht 'Manfred,' das er im folgenden Jahre zugleich mit dem vierten und letzten Gesang von Childe Harold in Venedig vollendete. In der genannten Stadt verbrachte er den gröfsten Teil der Jahre 1817—19 und begann seinen Don Juan, diese Epopöe des verbissensten Weltschmerzes, in der er 'die ganze moderne Civilisation in den Bereich seiner weltverachtenden Satire zieht.' Dem zügellosen Leben, das er in Venedig führte, entrifs ihn der Einfluſs der jungen und schönen Gräfin Therese Guiccioli, die er im Herbst 1818 kennen lernte. In Ravenna, wo Byron in der folgenden Zeit weilte, schrieb er seine Dramen Marino Faliero, Sardanapalus, The Two Foscari, die Mysterien Cain und Heaven and Earth. Wegen der Teilnahme an der Verschwörung der Carbonari mufste Byron und die Familie des Grafen Gamba, aus der Therese Guiccioli stammte, ausgewiesen von Stadt zu Stadt ziehen.

Byron war europamüde geworden und wollte nach Südamerika auswandern. Da brach der Aufstand der Griechen los, jenes Landes, das seine Sympathien von Jugend auf besafs. Begeistert ergriff Byron die Sache der Hellenen. Er schiffte sich am 15. Juli 1823 ein und landete am 3. August auf Kephalonia. Am 4. Januar 1824 traf er in Missolunghi ein und wurde mit fürstlichen Ehren empfangen. Byron entwickelte eine energische Thätigkeit bei der Organisierung des Aufstandes; sein kränklicher Körper hielt aber den Strapazen nicht stand. Ein rutkisches Fieber befiel ihn. Am 19. April 1824 hauchte Byron seine unruhige Seele aus. Sein Herz blieb in der Kirche von Missolunghi, sein Leichnam wurde, da ihm (wie später seiner von Thorwaldsen gemeifselten Büste) das tugendstolze England die Westminster-Abtei und die St. Paul's-Kathedrale verschlofs, in der kleinen Dorfkirche von Hucknall Torkard bei Newstead in der alten Familiengruft beigesetzt. Ein ewig dauerndes Denkmal hat Goethe dem Dichter im Euphorion im zweiten Teil, 3. Act des Faust gesetzt.

Byron, der Goethe's Dichtungen manche Anregung verdankt, ist der gröfste Lyriker der Engländer. Er ist klassisch in Form und Sprache. Seine Weltschmerzpoesie hat, weniger in England als auf dem Kontinent, viele Nachahmer gefunden. Die französische Romantik, das junge Deutschland, besonders Heine, den man mit Recht einen verzerrten Byron genannt hat, wandeln auf Pfaden, die Byron erschlossen.

Percy Bysshe Shelley wurde am 4. August 1792 als der älteste Sohn des Baronets Sir Timothy Shelley zu Fieldplace bei Horsham in Sussex geboren. Seine unerschrockene Wahrheitsliebe, die sich gegen Autoritätsglauben und Tyrannei sperrte, zog ihm schon auf der Schule zu Eton, wo ihn die Roheiten seiner Mitschüler und die grausamen Strafen abstiefsen, mancherlei Verdrufs zu. — Die Universität Oxford mufste er wegen einer atheistischen Schrift im zweiten Jahre verlassen, und auch sein Vater verstiefs ihn. Shelley bezog ein kleines Stübchen in London und widmete sich poetischen und philosophischen Studien, als deren Frucht er, achtzehn Jahre alt, ein philosophisches Gedicht Queen Mab schrieb. — Shelley's äufsere Verhältnisse besserten sich, als er grofsjährig geworden war; er mietete ein Haus am Rande des Windsor Forest, oft lag er tagelang im Schatten der mächtigen Eichen des Parkes, mit dichterischen Plänen beschäftigt. So entstand um diese Zeit (1815) seine tiefsinnige Elegie Alastor, welche, um Strodtmann's Worte zu gebrauchen, in den glühendsten Farben die Reize der Natur und die Qualen einer leidenschaftlich kämpfenden Dichterseele besingt. Der Schatten des Todes, der ihm, dem Kränkelnden, in den letzten Jahren so oftmals als ein Erlöser von aller irdischen Qual erschienen war, wirft ein geheimnisvoll erhabenes Dunkel über das ganze Gedicht.

Nachdem seine erste Ehe gelöst war, vermählte er sich mit Mary Godwin, einem hochherzigen, feingebildeten Mädchen; die Ehe war eine äufserst glückliche. Im Sommer 1816, den Shelley am Genfer See zubrachte, beschäftigte er sich hauptsächlich mit seiner Übersetzung des Prometheus von Aeschylos und verkehrte besonders mit Lord Byron, der ihm manche Anregung, so die Bekanntschaft mit Goethe's Faust, aus dem Shelley Bruchstücke übersetzte, verdankte. Im Frühling 1818 verliefs Shelley, dessen Gesundheitszustand sich nach seiner Rückkehr nach England immer mehr verschlimmert hatte, seine Heimat — er sollte sie nie wiedersehen — um ein wärmeres Klima aufzusuchen. Er ging nach Italien, besuchte Byron in Venedig und liefs sich, nachdem er Neapel gesehen, in Rom nieder. Dort verfafste er seinen Prometheus Unbound, eine symbolische Verherrlichung der welterlösenden Kraft der Humanität, und das Trauerspiel The Cenci. — Die italienischen Revolutionen, sowie den Befreiungskampf Griechenlands verherrlichte Shelley 1821 durch schwungvolle Hymnen und das lyrische Drama Hellas, dessen Schlufschor zu den erhabensten Weissagungen der Poesie gehört.

Shelley, der das Meer sehr liebte, ertrank am 8. Juli 1822 auf einer Bootfahrt von Livorno nach Rezzia, wo er seit April des genannten Jahres gewohnt hatte. Die Leiche, welche einige Tage später an den Strand trieb, wurde in Gegenwart Byron's auf einem Scheiterhaufen am Meeresufer verbrannt, und die Asche auf dem Kirchhofe der Protestanten in Rom neben der Pyramide des Cestius beigesetzt.

Shelley war, um mit Scherr zu reden, der ideellen Bildung seines Landes so weit vorausgeeilt, dafs nur sehr wenige seiner Landsleute dem Fluge seiner Gedanken folgen konnten, einige Mildgesinnte ihm ein mitleidiges Achselzucken widmeten, die ungeheure Mehrzahl aber ihn verwünschte und verfluchte. — Seine Dichtungen, deren schimmernde Bilder in metaphysischer Luft verschweben, können, da ihnen auch vielfach das künstlerische Mafs fehlt, nie volkstümlich werden.

Thomas Moore wurde im Mai 1779 in bescheidenen Verhältnissen in Dublin geboren. Er studierte am Trinity College in Dublin, das vor nicht langer Zeit den Katholiken zugänglich gemacht worden war, und ging dann nach London, um im Temple die Rechte zu studieren. Er hatte eine freie Bearbeitung des Anakreon mitgenommen, die er dem Prinz-Regenten widmete (1800), in dessen Kreise er Zutritt erhielt. Hohe Gönner verschafften ihm 1803 ein Kolonialamt auf den Bermudas-Inseln, das er aber bald von einem Stellvertreter verwalten liefs; dieser erwies sich jedoch als unredlich, und Moore mufste die veruntreuten Summen von dem Ertrage seiner Werke decken. Moore's bedeutendste Dichtung sind seine Irish Melodies (1808), in welchen er zu volkstümlichen Weisen Lieder schuf, in denen er sein unglückliches Vaterland verherrlicht; als Fortsetzung dazu können die National Airs betrachtet werden. 1817 erschien Lalla Rookh (Tulpenwange), vier durch einen schwachen Rahmen zusammengehaltene Romanzen in farbenprächtigem, orientalischem Gewande, die zur Erhöhung seines Ruhmes beitrugen. Von bleibendem Wert sind auch seine in Versen geschriebenen satirischen Letters of the Fudge Family in Paris (1818), in welchen die

Leiden einer kleinbürgerlichen englischen Familie während ihres Aufenthaltes in Paris mit köstlichem Humor geschildert werden. — Von Moore's prosaischen Werken sind besonders seine Biographie Byron's und Sheridan's zu nennen. Moore starb im Februar 1852.

Mrs. Felicia Dorothea Hemans wurde 1793 als die Tochter des Kaufmannes Browne in Liverpool geboren. Ihre Kindheit verbrachte sie in Wales, wohin sich ihr Vater nach empfindlichen Geschäftsverlusten zurückgezogen hatte, und die großartige Gebirgswelt verfehlte ihre Wirkung auf das empfängliche Gemüt des Mädchens nicht. Schon mit fünfzehn Jahren veröffentlichte sie einen Band Gedichte. Im Jahre 1812 vermählte sie sich mit Kapitän Hemans; die Ehe war jedoch eine unglückliche, nach sechs Jahren ging Kap. Hemans nach Italien, und sie sahen sich nicht wieder. Mrs. Hemans widmete sich nun vollständig der Dichtkunst und schuf eine große Anzahl lyrischer Gedichte und Balladen. Sie starb 1835 in Dublin.

Washington Irving (1783—1859) stammte aus einer wohlhabenden Kaufmannsfamilie in New-York, studierte die Rechte, widmete sich aber später ganz der Litteratur. Nachdem er schon frühzeitig Beiträge zu humoristischen Zeitschriften geliefert hatte, trat er 1810 mit seinem Humorous Account of New York by Diedrich Knickerbocker vor die Leserwelt, die er mit einem Schlage für sich gewann. In den folgenden Jahren nahm er an dem Kriege gegen England teil, ging dann nach Europa, dessen Süden er schon 1804—1806 eines Brustleidens wegen aufgesucht hatte, und blieb dort (vornehmlich in England und Spanien) bis 1832. Sein feiner Blick für die gesellschaftlichen Eigentümlichkeiten der Nationen tritt mit graziösem Humor in seinen Werken, deren Stoff er zum Teil seinem Aufenthalt in Europa verdankt, zu Tage, am glänzendsten wohl in seinem Sketch Book (1820), mit welchem Bracebridge Hall (1821) und die Tales of a Traveller (1824) eine gewisse Ähnlichkeit haben. Im Jahre 1832 kehrte er nach Amerika zurück, von wo er sich 1842 infolge seiner Ernennung zum amerikanischen Gesandten in Madrid von neuem auf sechs Jahre trennen mußte. Nach dieser Zeit verlebte er noch dreizehn Jahre auf seinem stillen Landhaus Sunnyside in der Nähe von New-York und schenkte der Welt noch eine Reihe von Werken, unter denen seine History of the Life and Voyages of Columbus, sein Life of Ol. Goldsmith, mit welchem man ihn selbst verglichen hat, und endlich sein letztes Werk The Life of George Washington hervorragen. Irving starb im Jahre 1859.

Henry Wadsworth Longfellow wurde am 27. Februar 1807 zu Portland in Maine (U. St.) geboren. Er hat Deutschland viel bereist und bewahrte dem Lande dankbare Erinnerung, was sich besonders in seinem auf deutschem Boden spielenden Roman Hyperion zeigt, in welchem er das deutsche Volk, seinen Geist und seine Litteratur zu feiern wiederholt Gelegenheit findet. Am originellsten ist des Dichters Song of Hiawatha, eine Dichtung, die er selbst als die indianische Edda bezeichnen möchte. Anmutig ist das idyllische Epos Evangeline, a Tale of Acadia, das die Schicksale der französischen Kolonisten Acadias (Nova Scotia) zur Grundlage hat, die 1755 von den Engländern aus ihrer Heimat vertrieben wurden (s. S. 10). Die Sprache ist mit Meisterschaft behandelt, und der Hexameter, in dem das Gedicht geschrieben ist, fließt glatt und eben. Von seinen zahlreichen übrigen Werken seien seine Gedichte, unter denen sich eine Reihe trefflicher Übersetzungen aus fremden Sprachen befindet, sodann sein komisches Epos The Courtship of Miles Standish und endlich sein Drama The Spanish Student genannt. Longfellow war seit 1835 Professor der neueren Sprachen am Harvard-College zu Cambridge (U. St.), er legte aber 1855 dieses

Amt nieder, um ganz der Litteratur leben zu können; und er wurde denn auch
der berühmteste Dichter Amerikas. Er starb 1882.

Thomas Babington Macaulay wurde am 25. Oktober 1800 im Hause seines
Oheims Thomas Babington in Rothley Temple in Leicestershire geboren, stammte aber,
wie sein Name zeigt, aus Schottland. Sein Vater, Zacharias Macaulay, war seinerzeit
ein Mann von einiger Bedeutung, er war ein vertrauter Freund Wilberforce's
(s. S. 500) und im Verein mit diesem der thätigste Vorkämpfer für die Aufhebung der
Sklaverei. Sein Haus in Clapham (im Süden von London) war ein Vereinigungsort
eines geschlossenen Kreises von Politikern und Schriftstellern, darunter war die ihrerzeit
sehr angesehene Hannah More; und der junge Macaulay wuchs so in Verhältnissen
auf, die für die Entwicklung des litterarischen Talentes sehr günstig waren.
Er kam nach privater Vorbereitung in seinem neunzehnten Jahre auf die Universität
Cambridge, wo er sich in den akademischen Studien auszeichnete; von dort ging
er nach London, um das englische Recht zu studieren, und wurde 1826 zum Advokaten
gemacht. Er befafste sich jedoch nie mit juridischer Praxis. Seine innerste
Neigung zog ihn zur Litteratur. Zwar wurde er öfter von der Beschäftigung mit
derselben zur thätigen Teilnahme am politischen Leben abberufen, aber obgleich
ihm diese Ehre und Beförderung eintrug, scheint sie ihn nie recht befriedigt
zu haben.

Im Jahre 1825 begann er mit einer Abhandlung über Milton seine berühmten
Beiträge zur Edinburgh Review (von 1825—1844), welche später unter
dem Titel Critical and Historical Essays gesammelt wurden. Die meisten
dieser Artikel können als Vorstudien zu seinem grofsen historischen Werke betrachtet
werden, wie Burleigh, Hallam's Constitutional History, Bacon, Milton,
Hampden, Sir William Temple, Bunyan, Comic Dramatists of the Restoration,
Mackintosh's History of the Revolution, Lord Mahon's War of the Succession in
Spain, Addison, Horace Walpole, Chatham, Lord Clive, Warren Hastings, Lord
Holland — sie umfassen die Zeit vom Schlufs des 16. bis zum Beginn des 19. Jahrhunderts.
Dazu kommen die Biographical Essays, welche das Leben Friedrich's
des Grofsen, Bunyan's, Goldsmith's und Barère's enthalten und für die Encyclopaedia
Britannica (1858—1859) geschrieben wurden.

Durch seinen Milton, den er vornehmlich von der politischen Seite schildert,
waren die Whigs auf Macaulay aufmerksam geworden. Der Einflufs Lord Lansdowne's
verschaffte ihm 1830 einen Sitz im Unterhause (für den kleinen Flecken
Calne), wo er kräftig und beredt für die grofse Parlamentsreform eintrat. Zum
Lohn dafür wurde er in das erste reformierte Parlament als Mitglied für Leeds
gewählt, das durch die Reform das Wahlrecht erhalten hatte. Im Jahre 1834
ging er als Mitglied des hohen Rates in Calcutta und Obmann der für diese
Provinz eingesetzten Gesetzgebungskommission nach Ostindien. Hier brachte er
drei Jahre zu, beschäftigt mit der Ausarbeitung des neuen Gesetzbuches und
mit historischen Untersuchungen. Eine Frucht davon waren seine zwei Essays
über Lord Clive und Warren Hastings. Als er 1838 nach England zurückkam,
war sein Wunsch, sich vom politischen Leben zurückzuziehen; aber seine
Partei konnte ihn nicht entbehren. Im Jahre 1839 für Edinburgh gewählt, wurde
er Kriegsminister in Lord Melbourne's Ministerium (1839—41); als dieser Robert
Peel weichen mufste, ging er in die Opposition; 1846 kamen wieder die Whigs
ans Ruder, und Macaulay wurde Generalkassier für die Armee mit Sitz und Stimme
in Lord Russel's Kabinett. Da er zu Gunsten des katholischen Seminars in Maynooth
(in der irischen Grafschaft Kildare) gesprochen und gestimmt hatte, liefs
ihn Edinburgh bei der allgemeinen Wahl 1847 fallen; im Jahre 1852 wählte es ihn

aber wieder, und zwar aus freien Stücken und gegen seinen Willen. Macaulay beteiligte sich aber nur mehr wenig an den Parlamentsverhandlungen; sein Geschichtswerk nahm ihn voll und ganz in Anspruch.

Im Dezember 1848 erschienen die zwei ersten Bände von Macaulay's Werke: The History of England from the Accession of James II., mit einer Neugier erwartet, die nur von der Spannung übertroffen wurde, mit der man der Fortsetzung entgegensah. Dieser Teil des Werkes geht bis zur Revolution (1688). Die zwei nächsten Bände, die die Geschichte bis zum Frieden von Ryswick (1697) führen, kamen 1855 heraus. Der Verleger hatte eine Auflage von 25.000 Exemplaren drucken lassen, die an einem Tage verkauft waren, und Tausende mußten aus Paternoster-Row weggehen, ohne etwas erhalten zu haben. Der fünfte Band, der vom Verfasser nur teilweise ausgearbeitet ist, wurde nach seinem Tode von seiner Schwester Lady Trevelyan veröffentlicht. Er geht bis zu William's Tode (1702).

Die drei einleitenden Kapitel, die eine kurze Übersicht über die englische Geschichte von der ältesten Zeit bis zum Schlusse des 17. Jahrhundert geben, abgerechnet, umfaßt das Werk, wie es nun vorliegt, nur einen Zeitraum von 17 Jahren, nämlich Jakob II. und William III. (1685-1702). Es war des Verfassers ursprünglicher Plan, seine Geschichte herabzuführen bis zu Zeiten, an die sich die jetzt Lebenden noch erinnern (within the memory of men still living); später, als Krankheit dazwischen trat, bis zu Königin Anna's Tode (1714), aber die Kräfte verließen ihn früher.

Im Jahre 1857 wurde Macaulay als Baron Macaulay von Rothley in die Peerschaft aufgenommen. Im selben Jahre wurde er auch zum ausländischen Mitgliede der französischen Akademie ernannt. Er starb am 28. December 1859 und wurde feierlich in der Westminster-Abtei beigesetzt.

Macaulay's glänzender und zugleich lebendiger und klarer Stil, die Entschiedenheit und Sicherheit, mit der er seine Ansichten ausspricht, der freudige Glaube an den Fortschritt der Menschheit, die patriotische Begeisterung für seines Landes Ehre und Größe erklären die Popularität seiner Schriften, die als klassisch gelten.

Sir Francis Palgrave, der Sprosse einer reichen jüdischen Familie, wurde 1788 geboren. Als er sich im Alter von 35 Jahren vermählte, vertauschte er seinen Familiennamen Cohen mit dem Mädchennamen seiner Schwiegermutter. Von Palgrave, der die juridische Laufbahn eingeschlagen hatte, besitzen wir wertvolle Geschichtswerke: Eine kürzer gefaßte History of England during the Anglo-Saxon Period (1831) und eine ausführliche History of the Rise and Progress of the English Commonwealth during the Anglo-Saxon Period (1832). In letzterem Jahre erhielt er die Würde eines Knight. Im Jahre 1851 veröffentlichte er den ersten der vier Bände seiner History of Normandy and England, der zweite erschien 1857; die Schlußbände, welche bis zum Ende der Regierung William's II. reichen, wurden drei Jahre nach seinem 1861 erfolgten Tode herausgegeben.

William Makepeace Thackeray, der Sohn eines Beamten der ostindischen Kompanie, wurde 1811 in Calcutta geboren. Im Alter von sieben Jahren kam er nach England und besuchte die Charterhouse-Schule in London und dann die Universität Cambridge. Günstige Vermögensverhältnisse erlaubten ihm, ganz seiner Neigung für die Künste und Wissenschaften zu leben. Er glaubte sich zum Maler berufen. Er machte Reisen auf dem Kontinent und hielt sich einige Zeit am Hofe Karl August's in Weimar auf. Nach England zurückgekehrt, schrieb er unter dem

Pseudonym Michael Angelo Titmarsh für Fraser's Magazine, in welchem er auch sein Paris Sketch Book (1840) und sein Irish Sketch Book (1843) veröffentlichte; als im Jahre 1841 das Witzblatt Punch gegründet wurde, war Thackeray einer der hervorragendsten Mitarbeiter und lieferte unter anderem seine Snob Papers, in welchen sich schon sein kaustischer Witz geltend macht. Mit seinem Roman Vanity Fair, a Novel without a Hero 1847 trat er in die erste Reihe der Autoren seines Landes. In diesem wie in den folgenden Romanen — Pendennis, The Newcomes, The History of Henry Esmond, The Virginians — legt er die Scheinheiligkeit und falsche Respectabilität der 'guten' Gesellschaft Englands blofs. Der Sitte seiner Zeit folgend hielt Thackeray auch Vorlesungen, und zwar über The English Humourists und The Four Georges, wertvolle kultur- und litteraturgeschichtliche Aufsätze. Es sei noch erwähnt, dass Thackeray das Cornhill Magazine gründete und durch zwei Jahre redigierte. Er starb am 24. Dezember 1863.

Charles Dickens, der populärste der neueren englischen Romanschreiber, wurde 1812 in Landport, einer Vorstadt von Portsmouth, geboren, wo sein Vater eine Stellung in den Kontors der Marinewerfte hatte. In seinem neunten Jahre kam er nach London, wohin sein Vater versetzt wurde. Dieser, den der Sohn im Mr. Micawber in David Copperfield gezeichnet hat, war ein Mann von sorglosem Temperament und bereitete seiner Familie durch seinen Leichtsinn manche Verlegenheit. Er kam in den Schuldturm, der junge Dickens wurde in der Schuhwichsfabrik eines Vetters untergebracht, und die Mutter, die einen erfolglosen Versuch gemacht hatte, ihre Familie durch Errichtung einer Schule zu erhalten, ging mit den übrigen Kindern zum Vater ins Schuldengefängnis. Dickens blieb bei seinem Vetter bis zum zwölften Jahre, dann besuchte er das erstemal eine öffentliche Schule "Wellington House Academy" in einer Vorstadt Londons. In diese sehr mittelmäfsige Anstalt ging er zwei Jahre und kam dann als Schreiberbursche zu einem Anwalt. Inzwischen war sein Vater aus dem Schuldengefängnis entlassen worden und verdiente sich als Zeitungsreferent sein Brot, und auch der junge Dickens schlug diesen Weg ein; er lernte Stenographieren und ergänzte die Lücken in seiner Bildung durch fleifsigen Besuch des Lesesaals im British Museum. Diesen seinen Entwicklungsgang hat Dickens später in David Copperfield teilweise geschildert.

Nachdem er einige Zeit über Gerichtsverhandlungen referiert hatte, übernahm er in seinem neunzehnten Jahre die anstrengendere Berichterstattung über die Parlamentssitzungen. Im Jahre 1835 war er mit dem damals angesehenen Blatte Morning Chronicle in Verbindung getreten und veröffentlichte in der Abendausgabe desselben humoristische Schilderungen aus dem Londoner Leben, die er später unter dem Titel Sketches of London, by Boz sammelte. Das Glück, das diese Skizzen machten, veranlafste eine Buchhandlung, ihn einzuladen, zu einer Reihe von humoristischen Zeichnungen einen Text zu schreiben, und so entstanden die berühmten Pickwick Papers (1836—1837). Sie erschienen wie Dickens' übrige Arbeiten in Heften; die ersten fanden eine laue Aufnahme, aber mit dem Hefte, in welchem Samuel (Sam Weller) vorkommt, trat ein völliger Umschlag ein, und alles sprach nur von Pickwick. Während Dickens noch an diesem Roman schrieb, begann er für andere Buchhändler den Oliver Twist und Nicholas Nickleby (1839—1840), denen Master Humphrey's Clock (1841) folgte. In der Zeit 1841-1842 machte er eine Reise nach Amerika. Nach seiner Rückkehr veröffentlichte er seine (für die Amerikaner wenig günstigen) Reiseeindrücke als American Notes for General Circulation (1842), die eine Entgegnung von amerikanischer Seite, "Change for American Notes, in Letters from London to New York" hervorriefen (New York 1843). Im Jahre 1843 erschien Martin Chuzzlewit, worin ebenfalls amerikanische Verhältnisse gegeifselt werden. von 1843—47 bescherte er sein Publikum alljährlich mit einer Weihnachtsgeschichte. Nach seiner italienischen Reise (1844—45) gründete er die Zeitung Daily News, zog sich aber bald von der journalistischen Thätigkeit zurück. In den Jahren 1847—48 erschien Dombey and Son und 1850 David Copperfield. Von 1850 an gab Dickens eine belletristische Wochenschrift Household Words heraus, in welcher er neben seinen späteren Romanen auch A Child's History of England erscheinen liefs. Im Jahre 1859 folgte auf die Household Words die Zeitschrift All the Year Round.

Dickens schildert in seinen Romanen vornehmlich die niedrigeren Kreise der Londoner Bevölkerung mit unwiderstehlicher Komik, er liebt markante Gestalten. freilich übertreibt er bei seiner Schilderung häufig und liefert nicht beabsichtigte Karikaturen. Die Tendenz seiner Romane ist eine löbliche, und sie sind vielfach Veranlassung zur Abstellung von Mifsbräuchen und zur Linderung des Elends geworden.

In den letzten Jahren seines Lebens hielt er Vorlesungen aus seinen Werken; die Aufregung, in die ihn diese Thätigkeit versetzte, trug zur Verschlimmerung seiner Gesundheit nicht wenig bei. Er starb auf seiner Besitzung Gadshill in Kent am 9. Juni 1870 und wurde in der Westminster-Abtei begraben. Vgl. auch Julian Schmidt. Studien über Dickens und den Humor. Westermann's Mtsh. XXVIII (1870). S. 32 fg.

Edward Bulwer, Lord Lytton, ein jüngerer Bruder des besonders als Diplomaten, aber auch als Schriftsteller bekannten Sir Henry Bulwer († 1872 als Lord Dalling), wurde 1803 in London geboren. Er gehörte zu den fruchtbarsten neueren englischen Autoren. Er schrieb lyrische, epische, dramatische und satirische Dichtungen, verfafste mehr als 20 grofse Romane. war Mitarbeiter für verschiedene litterarische Zeitschriften und safs dabei nicht blofs im Parlamente, sondern auch im Ministerium (in Lord Derby's letztem Kabinett als Kolonialminister). Am berühmtesten wurde er durch seine Romane; sein erster war Pelham (1828), der in den höheren Kreisen spielt. Bulwer war der Schöpfer einer neuen Gattung, des sozialen Romans. Probleme des gesellschaftlichen Lebens, Verbrechen und deren Erklärung. wenn nicht Entschuldigung, aus den Verhältnissen und durch sie sind der Stoff des Paul Clifford (1830). Eugene Aram (1832), Night and Morning (1841), zum Theil auch des Devereux (1829) und Ernest Maltravers (1837) u. e. a. — Die Verbrecherwelt verliefs er in The Caxtons, My Novel u. a. Historische Stoffe behandeln The Last Days of Pompeii (1834), Rienzi (1836), beide in Italien geschrieben; und The Last of the Barons (1843), der in der Zeit der Kriege der Rosen spielt und Warwick, den Königmacher, zum Helden hat; s. S. 67. Erwähnt sei auch seine politische Schrift England and the English (1833). — Bulwer wurde 1838 zum Baronet und 1866 zum Peer erhoben. Er starb den 18. Januar 1873 im Badeorte Torquay am Ärmel-Kanal (nördlich von Dartmouth in Devon). — Bulwer hatte die deutsche Litteratur, besonders deren zweite Blütezeit, eifrig studiert. Sein Lieblingsschriftsteller war Schiller, dessen Gedichte er übersetzte, und dessen Leben er beschrieb. — Der einzige Sohn Bulwer's, der jetzige Robert Lord Lytton, hat unter dem Pseudonym *Owen Meredith* mehrere Gedichtsammlungen herausgegeben.

Henry Lord Brougham, 1778 in Edinburgh geboren, wurde 1810 ins Parlament gewählt, wo er sich den Whigs anschlofs und für die Abschaffung des Sklavenhandels. für bürgerliche und religiöse Freiheit. Verbesserung der Volksbildung. Reform des Parlaments eintrat. Von 1830 bis 1835 war er Lord Chancellor. — Nachdem er sich vom politischen Leben zurückgezogen hatte, widmete er den Rest seines langen Lebens den Studien — schon vor seinem Eintritt ins Parlament hatte er einige mathematische Schriften von Wert und eine Abhandlung 'Erforschung der Kolonialpolitik der europäischen Mächte' (1803) veröffentlicht. — Nebst seinen Schriften über Gesetzesreform besitzen wir von ihm auch geschichtliche und philosophische Werke. Brougham starb im Jahre 1868.

Thomas Carlyle wurde 1795 aus einer bescheidenen Familie im Dorfe Ecclesfechan — einige Meilen im Norden des östlichen Teiles des Solway Firth — geboren. Er studierte Theologie an der Universität Edinburgh, widmete sich aber dann der Schriftstellerei. Sein erstes gröfseres Werk ist sein Life of Schiller (1824), worauf noch im selben Jahre eine Übersetzung von Goethe's Wilhelm Meister folgte; 1827 gab er seine Specimens of German Romance heraus. Übersetzungen aus den Werken Goethe's, Schiller's, Tieck's, Jean Paul's u. a. mit biographischen und kritischen Erläuterungen versehen. Seiner Vorliebe für die deutsche Litteratur verdankt auch der 1828 in der Edinburgh Review (mit dessen Herausgeber, dem einflufsreichen Kritiker Francis Jeffrey, er befreundet war) erschienene Artikel über Jean Paul Richter seine Entstehung. Seine späteren Werke zeichnen sich durch ihre Originalität aus, die sich bei einigen schon im Titel zeigt; hier seien genannt: Sartor Resartus (1836), The French Revolution (1837), On Heroes, Hero-worship and the Heroic in History (1841), Oliver Cromwell's Letters and Speeches; with Elucidations (1845), History of Frederick the Great (1865). Carlyle, dessen nicht zu unterschätzende Bedeutung darin liegt, dafs er, wie Scherr sagt, dem Realismus seines Landes in deutschem Idealismus eine wesentliche Ergänzung zugeführt hat, starb 1881.

George Bancroft wurde 1800 in Worcester in Massachusetts geboren; im Alter von 18 Jahren kam er nach Deutschland, wo er durch mehrere Jahre an verschiedenen Universitäten studierte. Nach Amerika zurückgekehrt, veröffentlichte er 1834 den ersten Band seiner berühmten History of the Colonisation of the United States, wovon 1846 der fünfte und letzte Band erschien. Bancroft bekleidete mehrere hohe Staatsämter in seiner Heimat und war einige Jahre amerikanischer Gesandter in Berlin; er starb 1891.

Philip Henry, **Lord Stanhope**, besser bekannt unter seinem früheren Namen **Lord Mahon**, gehört zu einem jüngeren Zweige der Familie Stanhope, einer der grofsen, sogenannten *governing families* in England. Er machte den für die jungen englischen Patrizier gebräuchlichen Weg, studierte zuerst in Oxford und kam von da ins Unterhaus, wo er mit kurzer Unterbrechung von 1836—52 safs. In Peel's erstem Ministerium (1834—35) war er Unter-Staats-Sekretär im Unterrichtsministerium unter dem Herzog von Wellington, im letzten Jahre von Peel's zweitem Ministerium (1845—46) war er Sekretär in der indischen Abteilung und stimmte, obschon er Tory war, mit Peel für die Aufhebung der *corn laws*. Wie andere Stanhope's (vgl. Lord Chesterfield), hat auch er sich durch litterarische Thätigkeit Ruhm erworben. Er trat im Jahre 1830 mit seiner ersten historischen Arbeit Life of Belisarus auf; 1832 folgte seine History of the War of Succession in Spain, wozu er unter anderen bis dahin unbekannten Quellen die Briefe und Papiere seines berühmten Verwandten, des Generals Stanhope, benützen konnte. 1836—54 erschien sein Hauptwerk, History of England from the Peace of Utrecht to the Peace of Versailles, das als eine Fortsetzung des Geschichtswerkes Macaulay's betrachtet werden kann. Von seinen übrigen Arbeiten sind noch zu nennen: History of the Rise of our Indian Empire (1858) und History of Queen Anne (1870). — Mahon's drei letztgenannte Werke gehören zu den zuverlässigsten Darstellungen der englischen Geschichte. Er starb 1875, im Alter von 70 Jahren.

William Ewart Gladstone wurde am 29. Dezember 1809 in Liverpool als Sohn eines reichen, aus Schottland stammenden Kaufmannes geboren. Nachdem er das Gymnasium zu Eton absolviert hatte, bezog er die Universität Oxford und wurde schon 1832 durch den Einflufs des Herzogs von Newcastle als Vertreter der Stadt Newark (in Nottinghamshire) ins Parlament gewählt, wo er sich durch seine Rednergabe und seine reichen Kenntnisse bald so hervorthat, dafs Sir Robert Peel auf ihn aufmerksam wurde, ihn an sich fesselte und von den streng konservativen Ansichten bekehrte, welche Gladstone als Schriftsteller und im Parlamente vertreten hatte. Peel brachte den jungen Mann schon 1834 ins Ministerium, von wo er jedoch nach wenigen Monaten wieder auf die Bänke der Opposition zurückkehrte. — In der Folgezeit war er wiederholt das Haupt liberaler Ministerien, welche mit konservativen, von Lord Beaconsfield (Disraeli) und später von Lord Salisbury geführten, abwechselnd die Regierung Englands innehatten. — Bei seiner ausgebreiteten politischen Thätigkeit, die sich unter anderm auch mit der Verbesserung der Lage der Irländer beschäftigte, fand er noch Lust und Mufse, sich mit litterarischen Fragen zu befassen; wir haben von ihm Studien über Homer and the Homeric Age, eine Übersetzung der Oden des Horaz u. a.

Charles Mackay, 1812 in Perth geboren, bekannt als lyrischer Dichter und Journalist, lebt gewöhnlich in London. Er gehört der romantischen Richtung Tennyson's an, indem er die 'leidenschaftliche Gefühlsweise und die phantastische Anschauungsart des Mittelalters mit der modernen Freiheitstendenz zu verbinden strebt,' während sein Stil 'antik-plastische Zeichnung mit der Farbenglut der Renaissance' vereinigt.

Alfred Tennyson wurde 1810 als der Sohn eines Geistlichen in einem Dorfe in Lincolnshire geboren; er studierte auf der Universität Cambridge, wo er durch eifrige Beschäftigung mit den antiken Klassikern seine dichterischen Anlagen ausbildete. Seine schon 1830 veröffentlichten Poems; chiefly Lyrical wurden wenig beachtet, allmählich aber wuchs sein Ansehen, und nach Wordsworth's Tode (1850) wurde er zum Poet Laureate ernannt. Tennyson ist besonders in lyrischen Schilderungen — einem bei den Engländern sehr beliebten Genre — grofs. Aufser seinen zahlreichen kürzeren Gedichten sind seine Idylls of the King, in denen er auf die Arthur-Sage zurückgreift, und sein idyllisches Epos Enoch Arden zu erwähnen. Tennyson's Dramen (Harold, Queen Mary, The Cup) haben schöne Stellen in Fülle, sind jedoch nicht recht bühnenmäfsig. Die Anerkennung der Wirksamkeit Tennyson's fand 1883 noch einen besonderen Ausdruck in seiner Erhebung zum Baron of Aldworth and Freshwater. Tennyson starb am 6. Oktober 1892 in Aldworth House bei Haselmere.

Erläuternde Anmerkungen.

In den folgenden Anmerkungen gibt die fettgedruckte Zahl die Seite an. Die angewendeten Aussprachezeichen sind dieselben wie in unserm 'Elementarbuch der englischen Sprache' (2. Aufl., Wien 1894. A. Hölder); wo es nötig schien, wurde auf unsere in demselben Verlag (1890) erschienene "Grammatik der englischen Sprache" verwiesen. — Mp. = Map weist auf den Plan von London; Cassell auf Cassell. Pictorial Scrap Book.

Seite 1. *Alfred* s. Tabelle IV. — *up to the age of twelve years*. Nach der Geschichte war Alfred 861 erst 12 Jahre alt. Damals war aber seine Mutter schon tot und seine Geschwister erwachsen. — *cowherd or swineherd*. Sein Name soll Denewulf gewesen sein. Der König soll ihn später haben unterrichten lassen und ihn dann zum Bischof von Winchester gemacht haben. Allein Denewulf, Bischof von Winchester, gelangte schon 879, also im nächsten Jahre, zu dem Bischofssitze. (Freemann, Old-English History.) Cassell, p. 65, 539, 91. — *Canute* (kanjût) s. Tab. IV. — *Bacon* s. S. 410. — *Highgate* (haigət) Bezirk im Norden von London. — *Johnson* s. S. 427 ff. — *Gray's Inn* ein Rechtskollegium in London. — *Arundel* spr. ä'rəndl. — **3.** *William Rufus* (ŭillĭam rûfəs) s. T. IV. — *Hampshire* (hämšə) Grafschaft im südlichen England, der Insel Wight gegenüber. H. hat jetzt noch ausgedehnte Waldungen *(New Forest)*. Der Hauptort ist *Winchester* (ŭi'nšestə), eine der ältesten Städte des Königreiches. Die Kathedrale von W. wurde 648 erbaut, 980 restauriert und ist eine der gröfsten und besterhaltenen alten gotischen Kirchen Englands. — *Sir Walter Tyrrel* (spr. tirĭl). Über *Sir* als Titel vor dem Eigennamen vgl. Anm. z. S. 33 *Lord*. — Cassell, p. 187. — *Wolfe* (ŭulf). James, ausgezeichneter englischer General des 18. Jahrhunderts. Er trug wesentlich zur Eroberung Canadas bei. Cassell, p. 352 u. ö. — *Quebec* spr. kŭĭbe'k. — **4.** *Isaac Newton* (nizək njûtn) s. Anm. z. S. 241. — *Angle* adjektivisch, anglisch. — *Gregory* ist Gregor I., der Grofse. — **5.** *Augustine* spr. ɔgə'stĭn. — *Canterbury* (kä'ntəbarĭ), Hauptstadt der Grafschaft Kent. Der älteste Teil der Kathedrale stammt aus dem Jahre 1184. Der Erzbischof von Canterbury hat das Recht, den König zu krönen; er ist der erste Peer des Reiches. — *one of the greatest victories* bei Azincourt 1415. — *Lord Chief Justice* Lord Oberrichter. Sein Name war Gascoigne. Ein Fresco-Gemälde von C. W. Cope im englischen Herrenhause stellt diese Scene dar; vgl. Cassel, p. 13. Jetzt ist L. Ch. J. der Titel des Präsidenten der Queen's Bench, d. i. des Civil-Gerichtshofes. — **6.** *Henry the First* s. Tab. IV. — *Barfleur* bei Cherbourg, Departem. Manche. — *Fitz* normann.-frz. für *Fils*. — **7.** *Sire* (saiə) gnädigster Herr. — **8.** *main yard* große Rahe (unterste Segelstange des Hauptmastes). — *Worcester* (spr. ŭusta) 1601—1667. eifriger Parteigänger Karl's I., galt unter seinen Zeitgenossen als verrückter Projektenmacher. — **9.** *James Watt* (dže'mz ŭɔt) s. S. 12. — *London Bridge* s. Mp. D 6. Die alte Brücke (vgl. die Beschreibung auf S. 108 und Cassell, p. 120, 127, 178, 638) stand von 1209 bis 1832.

Die jetzige London Bridge wurde 1825 bis 1831 nach den Plänen des Ingenieurs John Rennie mit einem Kostenaufwand von 2 Millionen Pfund Sterling erbaut. Sie ist 293 m lang und 17 m breit. Man schätzt, dafs 20.000 Wagen und mehr als 100.000 Fufsgänger täglich die Brücke passieren. — *Monument* (Map D 6) eine kannelierte Säule, 64 m hoch, von Wren entworfen, 1677 errichtet. Im Innern befindet sich eine Schneckenstiege, die auf eine Plattform mit schöner Aussicht führt. — *Tower* (Map D 6—7, Cassell, p. 624, 759 u. ö.). ursprünglich königliche Residenz, dann Staatsgefängnis, enthält jetzt grofse Waffensammlungen, ferner eine Schatzkammer mit den Kronjuwelen, unter denen besonders der Diamant Koh-i-Noor (Berg des Lichtes) zu nennen ist. Der in historischer Beziehung interessanteste Raum in dem berühmten alten Schlofs ist die Kapelle St. Peter ad Vincula. Dort liegen begraben Anna Boleyn, Essex, Katharina Howard u. a. — *Temple Bar* ein alter Thorweg, der sich an den Temple (C 5, vgl. Anm. z. S. 231) schlofs (vgl. Anm. z. S. 108 und Cassell, p. 688, 439 u. ö.).

10. Diese Erzählung bildet die Grundlage von Longfellow's Epos Evangeline. — *Acadia* spr. əkei'diə. — *Nova Scotia* spr. no"'wəsko"'ʃə. — *first of May*. Zu den wenigen bis auf die neueste Zeit noch erhaltenen Maifestlichkeiten Englands gehörte der Umzug der Schornsteinfeger am 1. Mai in London, in ihrer Mitte die komische Figur des sogenannten Jack-in-the-Green, einer grell ausstaffierten Phantasiegestalt. — *Montague* (spr. mə'ntəgju) *House* stand, wo sich jetzt das British Museum (Mp. C 4) befindet. — 12. *James Watt* geb. in Greenock on the Clyde, gest. 1819. — *Hero of Alexandria* (hiro əw əliɡzä'ndriə) um 215 v. Chr. — *Savary* auch *Savery* (seiweri), Thomas. gest. 1715. — *Newcomen* (njukɔ'men), Thomas, wie Savary einer der Erfinder der Dampfmaschine. — *Dartmouth* (dätməth) in Devonshire. — *Cawley* (kåli) Newcomen's Geschäftsteilnehmer. — *Potter* (potə), erfand 1713 die Steuerung an der Dampfmaschine. — *Smeaton* (smitn). John 1724—1792, ausgezeichneter Ingenieur. Sein gröfstes Werk war der alte Leuchtturm auf Eddystone, der jetzt am Hafen von Plymonth wieder aufgestellt ist. — 13. *Glasgow* (glä'sgo) am Clyde, gröfste Stadt Schottlands, wetteifert in Industrie und Handel mit den englischen Grofsstädten. Die Universität ist alt (1450 gegründet) und berühmt. — *Matthew Boulton* (mä'tju boultən) berühmter Mechaniker (1728-1809), dessen grofsartigen Fabriksanlagen Birmingham namentlich seinen Aufschwung verdankt. — *Birmingham* (bə'rmiŋəm) in Warwickshire die bedeutendste Metallwerkstätte und eine der ersten Fabriksstädte der Welt. — 14. *Trevithick* (tre'withik), Richard, 1771—1833. — *George Stephenson* (dʒɔdʒ stiwnsn), der Hauptbegründer des Eisenbahnsystems, 1781—1848. Er legte die erste Eisenbahn zur Beförderung von Personen zwischen Stockton und Darlington in Yorkshire an. — *his son* ist Robert St., der seinen Vater bei seinen Unternehmungen unterstützte und sich selbst namentlich als genialer Brückenbauer hervorthat. — *Ninivch* spr. ni'niwi. — 14. *philosophy* hier Alchemie, Adeptenkunst. In der Zeit Edward's III. glaubte man fest an die Möglichkeit, edle Metalle zu erzeugen, wie die von ihm erlassene Proklamation zeigt: "Know all men that we have been assured that John Rows and William de Dalbey know how to make silver by the art of alchemy; and, considering that these men may be profitable to us, and to our kingdom, we have commanded our well-beloved Thomas Carey to apprehend the afore said John and William, wherever they be found, and bring them to us, together with all the instruments of their art, under safe custody." — 15. *philosopher* hier: Adept (Eingeweihter). — 16. *ingot* Gufsform. — *like to one*, gewöhnlicher ist *like* ohne *to*. — 17. *noble* Rosenoble, eine alte Goldmünze im Werte von 6 s. 8 d. — *Seymour* spr. simə — *Chaucer* (spr. tʃɔsə) s. litter. Anm. S. 406.

19. *turned off.* Der Ausdruck gilt eig. von dem Drehen der Kurbel, wodurch die Fallthüre, auf welcher der Verurteilte stand, sich senkte. — *Furlong* s. Tab. II. — **21.** *Now I expected that part of my dream was coming to pass* bezieht sich auf einen Traum, den Robinson anderthalb Jahre früher gehabt hatte, und der fast genau dasselbe enthielt, was sich jetzt wirklich ereignen sollte. — **23.** *runs.* Das vereinzelte Präsens ist auffallend, ebenso S. 23, Z. 5 *comes.* — *Daniel Defoe* (dän˘ᵊl d˘ıfoʷ) s. liter. Anm. S. 416.

23. *the Downs* berühmte Reede zwischen Dover und Ramsgate. — *Surat* (sjŭrä′t) Stadt und Provinz in der indobritischen Präsidentschaft Bombay. — *wind* und *gale.* gale is a wind between a stiff breeze and storm or tempest. *Webster.* — *league* s. Tab. II. — **27.** *pistole* (p˘ıstoʷ′l) alte Goldmünze im Werte von 16 s. — **28.** *dram-cup* Schnapsgläschen. — *gallon* s. Tab. II. — **30.** *London Bridge* s. Anm. z. S. 9. — *Chelsea* (t͡ʃeʹlsĭ) zu Swift's Zeit noch ein stilles Dorf, 3 engl. Meilen südwestl. von London, gehört jetzt zu den am dichtesten bevölkerten Teilen der Weltstadt (Map E 2—3). Die Entfernung von Chelsea, das gröfstenteils von Arbeitern bewohnt wird, bis zur London Bridge beträgt ungefähr 4 engl. Meilen. — *main-sail* Grofssegel, das gröfste Segel des Hauptmastes. — **31.** *Lagado* ist die Hauptstadt der Insel Balnibarbi, die zum Reiche des Königs von Laputa, einem lenkbaren, fliegenden Eiland, gehört. Swift's Satire richtet sich in der Schilderung der von Mathematikern bewohnten Insel Laputa gegen die königliche Sozietät und die modische Liebhaberei für Naturwissenschaften; namentlich sind einige (ungerechtfertigte) Anspielungen auf Newton ganz unverkennbar. Das hier aufgenommene Stück wendet sich mit mehr Recht gegen die Windbeuteleien jener leeren Projektenmacher, die niemals in Zeiten grofser Entdeckungen und Erfindungen fehlen. — *Jonathan Swift* (d͡ʒŏnᵊthᵊn sŭift) s. liter. Anm. S. 418.

33. *Lord Oxmington. Lord* ist der gemeinschaftliche Titel aller höheren oder eigentlichen Adeligen (*nobility*, umfassend: Duke, Marquess, Earl, Viscount, Baron); aufserdem tragen die Richter höherer Ordnung den Titel *Lord*. Der *nobility* steht die *gentry* gegenüber. Die *gentry* zerfällt in eine titulierte Klasse, zu der die *baronets* und *knights* (niederer Adel, *pseudonobility*) gehören, welche die Berechtigung haben, *Sir* vor den Vornamen zu setzen, und in eine nicht titulierte Klasse, welche vorzugsweise durch gröfsere Grundbesitzer, *Squires*, repräsentiert wird, zu der sich aber auch die durch Bildung oder Besitz hervorragenden nicht adeligen Klassen der Bevölkerung überhaupt rechnen; vgl. den Ausdruck *gentleman*. — *my uncle* Mr. Bramble. — *I* ist Melford, ein Student aus Oxford, der das folgende Abenteuer in einem Briefe an seinen Freund erzählt. Die Geschichte (aus 'The Expedition of Humphry Clinker', vgl. S. 424) liefert einen Beitrag zur Kenntnis der gesellschaftlichen Zustände Englands im vorigen Jahrhunderte. — *Lismahago* spr. lismahe′go. — *our Squire,* d. i. Mr. Bramble. — *cried Mr. Bramble,* ebenso z. 31 u. ö. Bei Schriftstellern des 18. Jahrh. wird *to cry* häufig für *to exclaim* gebraucht. *'to the best in Christendom'* sprichwörtliche Redensart. *I cry you mercy* = I beg your pardon. — *to take umbrage* beleidigt sein. — **34.** *Archy* (ä′t͡ʃĭ) Abkürzung aus Archibald wie w. u. *Tabby* aus Tabitha; *Mrs. Tabby* ist die Schwester Mr. Bramble's; sie war ein älteres Fräulein, aber in der ersten Hälfte des 18. Jahrh. galt es in England als höfliche Sitte, auch unverheiratete Damen mit Mrs. anstatt Miss anzureden, vgl. S. 105. *knight of La Mancha* ist Don Quixote, der Held des berühmten gleichnamigen spanischen Romanes von Cervantes. — *squire Panza. squire* bedeutet hier "Knappe," "Schildträger" (esquire, fr. écuyer von écu Schild). — *a commoner . . . a peer of the realm.* Jeder Lord (s. Anm. zu 33) ist *peer of the realm*, d. h. Mitglied des Oberhauses. Jeder Engländer

der nicht im Oberhause sitzt, ist *commoner*. — *Welshman* Eingeborener oder Bewohner von Wales. *my uncle's back was up in a moment*. Das Bild ist wohl von der Katze genommen, die, wenn gereizt, mit hohem Rücken und gesträubtem Haare dasteht. — **35.** *What betwixt .... and* = teils durch .... und. Das Indefinitum *what* als adverbialer Accusativ und in Verbindung mit einer Präposition (gewöhnlich with) dient bei einer Beiordnung zum Ausdrucke der Wechselbeziehung und bezeichnet die einzelnen Glieder der Beiordnung als Teile einer Gesamtheit. — *if he should pass his Christmas on the spot*. Das geschilderte Abenteuer trug sich Ende September zu. — *to give umbrage* beleidigen. vgl. to take umbrage S. 33, Z. 41. — *Tobias George Smollett* (tobai'əs dʒɔdʒ smɔlət) s. S. 424.

36. *My uncle*. Der Erzähler ist Tristram Shandy, der nominelle Held des Werkes. Vgl. litter. Anm. S. 425. Das Stück ist charakteristisch für Sterne's Stil. — *had my uncle Toby* etc. Dafs das Subjekt des Hauptsatzes hinter dem Verbum steht, wenn derselbe als Nachsatz erscheint, ist namentlich in der älteren Sprache nicht selten. — *Montero-cap* Reitermütze (vom span. montera = Jägermütze). — *frayed* abgerieben, fadenscheinig. — *boldest* auffallendst, grellst. — *cried*. Vgl. Anm. z. S. 33. — *quoth* = sagte, ist ein altes starkes Präterit. — *Doomsday* = the day of judgement (doom), der jüngste Tag. — **37.** *an' please* für and it please; der Gebrauch von *and* als konditionale Konjunktion ist ein Rest des älteren Sprachgebrauches. Die Form *an'* ist nach Storm, Engl. Philologie, nicht auf die Vulgärsprache beschränkt. — *Olympiads*. Mit Olympiade bezeichnen die Griechen den Zeitraum zwischen zwei olympischen Festspielen, 4 Jahre umfassend, und rechneten darnach von 776 v. Chr. bis 394 n. Chr. — *Urbeconditas*. "Nach der Gründung der Stadt" (Rom), die nach der konventionellen Chronologie 753 v. Chr. stattfand, rechneten die Römer. — *the year next him* erklärt sich aus dem vorausgehenden "the very moment in which the Corporal was telling his story". Das geschieht nämlich im Jahre 1713, also ist das nächstliegende Jahr 1712. — *when the Duke of Ormond was playing the devil in Flanders*. Der Herzog von Ormond (spr. ɔmənd) war der Nachfolger Marlborough's im Kommando während des spanischen Erbfolgekrieges (1701—1714). Das englische Ministerium knüpfte damals Friedensunterhandlungen mit Frankreich an und beauftragte demgemäfs den Oberbefehlshaber der englischen Truppen, an den weiteren Feindseligkeiten gegen die Franzosen nicht teilzunehmen. Dadurch wurde den Operationen der Verbündeten ein bedeutender Hemmschuh angelegt, worüber die englischen Truppen am meisten erbittert waren, indem sie die ruhmlose Unthätigkeit Ormond's mit der glänzenden Kriegsführung Marlborough's, ihres früheren geliebten Feldherrn, verglichen. (Arneth, "Prinz Eugen von Savoyen," 248.) Damit erklärt sich der Unmut unserer beiden alten Soldaten (vgl. w. u. 'sad stain upon our history'). — *Siege of Quesnoy* (spr. ke'snɔi) etc. Die Einschliefsung von Quesnoy (im Departement Nord in Frankreich) wurde am 8. Juni 1712 vollendet und die Leitung der Belagerung dem holländischen Generallieutenant Fagel (spr. fe'gəl) anvertraut. Die Festung kapitulierte am 4. Juli. — **38.** *cheerly* = cheerily. — *accoutrements* (əkū'təmənts) Ausrüstung. — *regimentals* Uniform. — **39.** *Marlborough* (mä'lbro). John Churchill, Herzog von Marlborough (1650—1722), berühmter Staatsmann und Feldherr, siegte, wiederholt über die Franzosen während des spanischen Erbfolgekrieges. Gegen Ende desselben (1711) wurde seine Partei am Hofe der Königin Anna gestürzt und er selbst des Kommandos enthoben. — *Maese* (me'z) die Maas. — *Blenheim und Hochstett*. In der Schlacht bei Höchstädt und Blenheim (zwischen Ulm und Donauwörth) am 13. August 1704 wurden die Bayern und Franzosen von Eugen und Marlborough geschlagen. — *reversing* = reversing. — *Wenceslaus* (spr. üensəle'as), reg. 1378—1400, Karl IV., 1347—1378. *Friar Bacon*, Roger Bacon (um 1214—1292), ein Franziskanermönch in Oxford, beschäftigte sich viel mit Naturwissenschaften und kam dadurch in den Ruf eines Zauberers. — **40.** *fosse* französ.) Graben. — *after a hum and a haw* nach einem Verlegenheitsräuspern. — **41.** *King William*. Gemeint ist natürlich Wilhelm III. (s. Tabelle IV). — *every ball had its billet*, gew. *every bullet* etc. vgl. S. 61, Z. 21. *billet* bedeutet Quartierzettel. — *battle of Landen*. In der Schlacht von Landen 1693 wurde Wilhelm III. von den Franzosen besiegt. — *Lawrence Therne* (lɔrəns stəən) s. litter. Anm. S. 425.

Nr. 21. Aus dem *'Vicar of Wakefield'*. Der Erzähler ist Georg, der Sohn des Landpredigers. Der Abschnitt ist interessant, weil der Dichter eigene Erlebnisse hinein verflochten hat; vgl. S. 426. — *usher* eig. Thürsteher (frz. huissier); hier: Aufseher (parallel damit *under turnkey*), Hilfslehrer. — *cried* Vgl. Anm. z. S. 33. — *Newgate* Gefängnis in der City von London; jetzt aufgelassen. Eine eingehende Beschreibung von Old Newgate findet sich in Ainsworth's Jack Sheppard. — *the master* Inhaber der Erziehungsanstalt. — *within ... abroad* in der Anstalt ... aufserhalb derselben. **42.** *fellows about town*, wie men about town Gecken; *town* London. — *joy-trot* langsamer Schankeltrab; *honest joy-trot men* ehrsame Stümper. — *dully* andere Lesart *daly*. — *antiqua mater* oder alma mater Bezeichnung einer Universität. — *Grub-street* war eine Gasse in der City von London, in welcher im 17. u. 18. Jahrhundert vornehmlich Litteraten wohnten; allmählich sank das Ansehen dieser Gasse, indem nur mehr mittelmäfsige Schriftsteller sich dort aufhielten, daher wird Grub-street auch zur Bezeichnung schwacher litterarischer Produkte gebraucht (u. a. von Swift und Johnson). In neuerer Zeit wurde die Gasse in *Milton-street* (s. Mp. C 6) umgetauft. *Otway* (1651—1685) bekannt als Dramatiker. — **43.** *box* Verschlag. In englischen Wirtshäusern sind häufig die einzelnen Tische durch Holzwände von einander getrennt. — *before me* gehört zum Verb. — *a scholar* "ein Studierter." — *proposals*. Subskriptionseinladungen. — *Propertius* Sextus P., geb. 50 v. Chr., berühmter römischer Elegiker, Freund des Mäcenas. — *strike* mache einen Angriff, überfalle. — *dedication fee* Dedikationshonorar; es war in Goldsmith's Zeit allgemein gebräuchlich, dafs Schriftsteller ihre Werke vornehmen Gönnern widmeten; dafür erhielten sie ein Geldgeschenk (fünfzig bis zwanzig Guineas), das oft gröfser war, als der Betrag, den der Buchhändler zahlte. Diese Widmungsgeschenke waren ein stehender Posten in den Ausgaben der Aristokraten jener Zeit; für die Schriftsteller war dies Verhältnis oft sehr demütigend, und der dürftige Poet mufste nicht selten seinen letzten Shilling hergeben, um von den Dienern vorgelassen zu werden. — *smite* falle an. — *at the top* auf dem Titelblatt. **44.** *excellence* mustergiltige Darstellung. — *periodical publications* Anspielung auf die Wochenschriften. — *Philautos* etc. ('Eigner Freund, Wahrheitsfreund, Freiheitsfreund, Menschenfreund'), Pseudonyme. In der Vorrede zu seinen gesammelten Essays (1765) sagt Goldsmith: 'I have seen some of my labours sixteen times reprinted, and claimed by different parents as their own. I have seen them flourished at the beginning with praise, and signed at the end with the names of Philautos, Philalethes, Philelutheros, and Philanthropos.' — *St. James's Park* (Mp. D 4) hängt im Westen mit dem Green Park und dieser mit dem grofsen Hyde Park zusammen. — *Ned* verkürzt aus Edward (mine Ed.) — **45.** *this here letter* und *as how that* vulgär; vgl. Anm. z. S. 56. **46.** *Mr. Crispe*, ein um jene Zeit bekannter Werber für die englische Armee, besonders für den Dienst im Auslande. — *epitome* (epi'tomi) Auszug. — *Synod of Pensylvania* eine Versammlung der Presbyterianer die jährlich einmal in Philadelphia abgehalten wurde und gemeinsame religiöse und politische Angelegenheiten erledigte. — *Chickasaw Indians* damals in Tennessee und Mississippi ansässig. — 47. *Lourain* (spr. luwe"n) Löwen, eine belgische Stadt in der Provinz Brabant. — 48. *Aesop and his basket of bread* bezieht sich auf die bekannte Fabel. Aesop hatte bei der Verteilung der Lasten die schwerste, nämlich einen Korb mit Brot, auf sich genommen und war deshalb von den anderen Sklaven ausgelacht worden. Auf dem Wege aber afsen sie so viel von dem Brote weg, dafs Aesops Last bald die leichteste war. — *principal* Rektor. — *a doctor's cap and gown* die Tracht der Graduierten an englischen Universitäten: eine Mütze mit viereckigem Deckel und ein langer Talar mit aufgeschlitzten Ärmeln. Die Satire auf die mehr als mangelhafte Gelehrsamkeit der Universitäten bezieht sich wohl auf England, vgl. S. 102 ff. — 49. *intaglio* (spr. intä'līo, ital.) Edelstein mit eingeschnittenen Verzierungen, zum Unterschiede von Kameen, die erhabene Arbeit haben. — *stept.* s. Gr. § 50 d. — *cognoscente* (spr. kognose'ntə, ital.) Kunstkenner. — *Pietro Perugino* (sp. pərudži'no) berühmter italienischer Maler des 15. Jahrh., Raphael's Lehrer. — *gentry* hier allgemein: vornehme Welt; sonst s. Anm. z. S. 33. — *a more supported assurance* ein noch zuversichtlicheres Auftreten. — *proviso* (prəwai'zo) Vorbehalt. — 50. *Leghorn* Livorno. — *left upon the world at large* alleinstehend in der weiten Welt. — *adventitious* = accidental. — 51. *was in keeping* war besetzt. — *Horatio* eine Figur in dem Trauerspiel 'The Fair Penitent' von Nicholas Rowe (1673—1718), dem Poet Laureate unter Georg I. und verdienstlichen Herausgeber Shakespeare's. (Hettner S. 249.) — *Oliver Goldsmith* (ǒliwə go'ldsmĭth) s. S. 203 u. litter. Anm. S. 425.

Nr. 22 ist dem Romane 'Kenilworth' entnommen. Die Erzählung ist bezeichnend für den Charakter der Königin Elisabeth, den Hume so treffend geschildert hat (S. 156), insbesondere mit Rücksicht auf die Stelle: 'In her family, in her court, in her kingdom, she remained equally mistress.' — *Gentlemen Pensioners* königliche Leibwachen (daneben *the king's* oder *queen's pensioners*). — *yeomen of the guard* Trabanten. — *down the Thames* von London nach Greenwich. — *long weapon* Lanze. — *High Sheriff* Obersheriff. Der *H. Sh.* oder blofs Sheriff (seine Untergebenen sind dann under-sheriffs) ist der erste Beamte einer Grafschaft, der die Polizei verwaltet, die königlichen Auflagen eintreibt und die Strafurteile zur Vollziehung bringt. Das Amt des Sheriffs trägt keine Besoldung. — *array* Miliz. — *Palace.* Der alte, von Humphrey, Herzog von Gloucester, 1433 erbaute Palast in Greenwich, die Geburtsstätte Heinrich's VII. und seiner Töchter Mary und Elisabeth, wurde während der Republik abgerissen. Karl II. begann den Neubau, der unter William III. nach Wren's Plänen beendigt und zu einem Hospital für dienstunfähige Seeleute bestimmt wurde. Das *Greenwich Hospital* hat 130.000 *l.* jährliche Einkünfte. — *Sussex.* Von *Ratcliffe, Earl of Sussex*, erzählt Scott an einer früheren Stelle desselben Romanes: 'Sussex had done good service in Ireland and in Scotland, and especially in the great northern rebellion, in 1569, which was quelled, in a great measure, by his military talents. The Earl of Sussex, moreover, was of more ancient and honourable descent than his rival, while the scutcheon of Leicester was stained by the degradation of his grandfather, the oppressive minister of Henry VII., and scarce improved by that of his father, the unhappy Dudley, Duke of Northumberland, executed on Tower-Hill, August 22. 1553.' *Deptford* (de'tfəd) westlich von Greenwich (Mp. E. 8—9). — *Leicester.* Robert Dudley, Graf von L., war der Günstling der Königin Elisabeth. Er starb 1588. — 52. *Raleigh* ist der nachmals berühmt gewordene Sir Walter Raleigh; vgl. S. 83 u. litt. Anm. S. 409. — *Usher of the*

Black Rod der Zeremonienmeister; das Zeichen seines Amtes ist ein schwarzer Stab, während White Rod ein Heroldsstab ist. — *Know you* und w. u. *think you*. Die Frage ohne Umschreibung ist nachdrucksvoller und archaisierend. — **53.** *mine office*. Die Substantiv-Form des Possessivums statt der adjektivischen ist ein absichtlicher Archaismus. — **54.** *yonder rebellious Earls in the north*. Gemeint sind die Grafen von Northumberland und Westmoreland, die 1569 im Norden Englands zu Gunsten der Maria Stuart und der katholischen Religion sich empörten. — *coif* Haube. — **55.** *under favour* mit Erlaubnis. — *Walter Scott* (ṅɔltə skɔt) s. S. 439.

Nr. 23. Aus dem Romane '*Pickwick Papers*'. Mr. Pickwick, das Haupt des Pickwick-Club, und die Mitglieder Snodgrass, Winkle und Tupman sind von Mr. Wardle, einem gemütlichen, gastfreundlichen Gutsbesitzer, auf eine Rebhühnerjagd geladen worden. — *Fade from the die* verblassen. — Mr. *Trundle*, ein Freund von Mr. Wardle. — *Sam* (aus *Samuel*) *Weller* ist der Diener des Mr. Pickwick; über die Gestalt Sam's vgl. litterar. Anm. S. 447. **56.** *in that ere way*, wie w. u. *that ere charge*; *that ere* aus *that there* = frz. celui-là. Die Vulgärsprache liebt zusammengesetzte Demonstrativa; vgl. w. u. *this here boy's mother*. S. Storm. Engl. Philol. I. 277. — *on us*. In der Vulgärsprache wird die Präposition *on* häufig mit *of* vertauscht. — *you comes it*. Zunächst ist der kausative Gebrauch des *come* zu bemerken (Storm. a. a. O. S. 285). Gleichfalls der Volkssprache eigentümlich ist die Endung s in allen Personen des Präs. Indic. Eine Erklärung gibt Storm. S. 281. — *ray* für *way* wie w. u. *vest coat* für *waist coat*; dagegen w. u. *wery* für *very*. In der Vulgärsprache werden eben v und w verwechselt. — *o' them* statt *of those*; *them* für *those* ist vulgär. — **57.** *ain't* = is not, s. w. u. *ain't it*. Diese Form begegnet in der Umgangssprache (Colloquial English, nicht zu verwechseln mit Vulgärsprache, slang) ziemlich häufig; vgl. Storm. S. 230 f. — *t'other* entstanden aus *tha-t other*, s. Storm. S. 265. — *Smallcheek* etwa „kleiner Frechling", ein Slang-Ausdruck. — *anythin*, *in* für die Endung *ing* ist in der Volkssprache sehr gewöhnlich. — **60.** *Sir*. Wenn ein Gentleman einen Diener mit *Sir* anredet, bedeutet es drohenden Zorn. — *Sir Geoffrey* der Besitzer des Jagdgrundes. — *on the authority of Mr. Pickwick*. Zum Verständnis dieser Worte denke man an den vollständigen Titel des Romanes: "The Posthumous Papers of the Pickwick-Club Containing a Faithful Record" etc. Der Verf. erscheint also als der Herausgeber der von Mr. Pickwick verfaßten Papers. — **61.** '*every bullet has its billet*', vgl. S. 41, Z. 18. — *Charles Dickens* (tšälz diknz) S. 447.

Nr. 24. Nicht zu den geringsten Eigentümlichkeiten des englischen Schullebens gehört der Faustkampf ('fighting with fists' oder bloß 'fighting'), der in dieser Erzählung durch ein ethisches Motiv geadelt ist. Im übrigen sei hier zitiert, was der Verfasser des bekannten Buches: 'Tom Brown's School Days' über den Faustkampf sagt: 'Fighting with fists is the natural and English way for English boys to settle their quarrels ... Learn to box, then, as you learn to play cricket and football ... As to fighting, keep out of it if you can, by all means. When the time comes, if it ever should, that you have to say Yes or No to a challenge to fight, say No if you can ... If you do fight, fight it out; and don't give in while you can stand and see.' Vgl. ferner Anm. zu S. 124. — *Heigh-ho Dobbin*, *Geeho Dobbin* etwa 'Hü Dobbin', 'Hott Dobbin'. — **62.** *bruit* (brût) ausspreugen. *hardbake* billige Leckerei aus zerlassenem Braunzucker, Sirup und Zitronensaft, zu einer Bonbonmasse gekocht. — *polonies* (pəlo"nīz) Bologneserwürstchen. — *hullo* = halloo. — *a sum* ein Rechenexempel. — *pink face* = rotwangig. — *pinafores* (spr. pīnəfə'ez) Lätzchen zum Vorstecken. — *corduroys* Beinkleider aus Corduroy, eine Art Barchent ("thick cotton stuff, corded or ribbed on the surface." Webster).

63. *Mr. Kean* Edmund K., ausgezeichneter Schauspieler, namentlich Darsteller von Shakespeare'schen Helden, lebte von 1787 bis 1833. — *Mr. Kemble*, John Philip K., 1757—1823, Nebenbuhler Kean's und Bruder der ebenfalls berühmten Schauspielerin Siddons, s. S. 180. — *to knock you off* fertig machen; *you* ist ethischer Dativ. — *to bully* quälen, tyrannisieren, namentlich gebraucht von Schülern einer Oberklasse, wenn sie den Kleineren und Jüngeren ('fags') gegenüber ihre Autorität mifsbrauchen. *fag out* hier soviel wie 'to field', to look out. Ausdrücke im Cricketspiel, welche bedeuten: auf die Bälle passen, um sie zu fangen. — *'Figs'* ist der Spitzname Dobbin's, weil sein Vater u. a. Feigen verkaufte. *Thames Street* s. Mp. D. 6. — *readth letterth, thmash*. Dobbin stiefs also mit der Zunge an, so dafs er *th* anstatt *s* sprach. — **64.** *Sindbad the Sailor in the Valley of Diamonds*. Sindbad der Seefahrer ist eine bekannte Gestalt aus "Tausend und eine Nacht" (englisch: "Arabian Nights' Entertainments"). Auf seiner zweiten Reise blieb er auf einer einsamen Insel verlassen zurück. Von dort trug ihn der Riesenvogel Roch (*Roc* s. w. u.) in ein Thal, in welchem die Diamanten wie Steine herumlagen. — *Prince Whatdyecallem* (hŭŏtdəkʃ´lam) eig. What do you call him. Der Dichter thut, als ob er sich auf den Namen des Prinzen nicht besinnen könnte; w. u. nennt er ihn aber: Prinz Achmed. — *Fairy Peribanou*. Die Fee Pari Banu wohnt in einem prächtigen Grottenpalast. Dort findet sie der Prinz Achmed und wird ihr Gemahl. — *Sir*, dem kleinen Osborne gegenüber gebraucht, deutet auf drohenden Zorn des Sprechenden. — *Cricket-stump* einer von den drei Stäben, die zusammen das *wicket* bilden; w. u. ist dafür *wicket* selbst gesagt. — *Prince Peribanou* statt Fairy Peribanou, beruht wohl auf einem Versehen des Autors; falls nicht absichtlich verwechselt; vgl. Prince Whatdyecallem. — **65.** *public school* soviel wie grammar school, unseren Gymnasien (und Realschulen) entsprechend, nur dafs die englischen Schulen meistens Internate sind. Ein anderer allgemeiner Name ist College, veraltet Academy. *Dr. Swishtail's Academy* war ein Privatunternehmen. Die angesehensten unter den public schools sind aber alte Stiftungsschulen. Vgl. Anm. zu S. 129. — *bottle holder*, Sekundant des Boxers, so genannt, weil er zur Stillung des Blutes ein Fläschchen Essig bei sich trägt. — *Go it =* (drauf los)! — *knee*, 'to offer a knee' sagt man von dem Sekundanten des Faustkämpfers, der nach Beendigung eines jeden Ganges ('round') sich auf ein Knie niederläfst, um das andere hochstehende jenem als Sitz zum Ausruhen während der gestatteten Minute Pause zu bieten. — **66.** *went in* "ging los," vom Beginne des Kampfes gesagt. — *Napier. Sir William Napier* (1785—1860), Verfasser einer 'History of the War in the Peninsula,' welches Werk für die beste Kriegsgeschichte in englischer Sprache gilt und namentlich durch seine anschauliche Darstellung ausgezeichnet ist. — *Bell's Life* Titel einer Sportzeitschrift. — *charge of the guard*. Anspielung auf eine berühmte Episode in der Schlacht bei Waterloo am 18. Juni 1815. Walter Scott erzählt sie in seiner Beschreibung der Schlacht von Waterloo (im 'Life of Napoleon') folgendermaßen: 'About seven o'clock, Napoleon's Guard were formed in two columns, under his own eye, near the bottom of the declivity of La Belle Alliance. They were put under command of the dauntless Ney. Bonaparte told the soldiers that the Prussians whom they saw on the right were retreating before Grouchy. The Guard answered for the last time, with shouts of *Vive l'Empereur*, and moved resolutely forward. The British were arranged in a line of four men deep, to meet the advancing columns of the French Guard, and poured upon them a storm of musketry which never ceased an instant. At length the British moved forward, as if to close round the heads of the columns, and at the same time continued to pour their shot upon the enemy's flanks. The

French gallantly attempted to deploy, for the purpose of returning the discharge. But in their effort to do so, under so dreadful a fire, they stopped, staggered, became disordered, were blended into one mass, and at length gave way, retiring, or rather flying, in the utmost confusion. This was the last effort of the enemy, and Napoleon gave orders for the retreat.' — *groggy* (von *grog*) wie betrunken, benebelt. — *Jack Spot* wahrscheinlich ein bekannter Billardspieler zu Thackeray's Zeit. — *William Makepeace Thackeray* (ũĭlĭəm me'kpis thäkrĭ) s. litt. Anm S. 446.

Nr. 67. Dem Kriege der *roten Rose* (Lancaster) und der *weifsen Rose* (York) war vorläufig dadurch ein Ende gemacht worden, dafs Richard v. York's Sohn, Eduard, unterstützt von dem Grafen von *Warwick* (ũŏrĭk), unter dem Namen Eduard IV. zum Könige ausgerufen worden war und die Lancastrier 1461 bei Touton, jetzt Towton Dörfchen in Yorkshire, östl. von Leeds) geschlagen hatte. Nicht ohne eigene Schuld zerwarf sich später Eduard IV. mit dem mächtigen Grafen, der dann auf die Seite der Lancaster-Partei trat, Eduard IV. aus dem Lande trieb und Heinrich VI. aus dem Tower wieder auf den Thron zog (1470). Da *Warwick* den Engländern nun schon zwei Herrscher gegeben hatte, bekam er den Namen des Königmachers (Kingmaker). Allein schon das Jahr darauf kehrte Eduard IV. nach England zurück, und am 14. April 1471 kam es zur Schlacht bei *Barnet* in Hertfordshire (Marktflecken 9 Meilen nordöstl. von London), wo *Warwick* nach sechsstündigem Gefechte Sieg und Leben verlor. Diese Schlacht ist für die englische Geschichte insofern von Bedeutung, als in ihr das mächtige Vasallentum, das noch aus der Zeit Wilhelm's des Eroberers stammte und in *Warwick* sich verkörperte, zu Grabe getragen wurde. Daher betitelt Bulwer seinen historischen Roman, aus dem unsere Erzählung genommen ist, treffend 'The Last of the Barons.' Das Bruchstück schildert eine Episode aus der Schlacht von Barnet, und zwar das Ende derselben, den Verzweiflungskampf und Tod Warwick's und seines Bruders, des Marquis von Montagu. Doch ist Bulwer aus dichterischen Gründen von der Geschichte abgewichen. Green, in A Short History of the English People, erzählt: The battle of Barnet, a medley of carnage and treachery which lasted six hours, ended with the fall of Warwick as he fled for a hiding place to the woods. Vgl. auch Pauli, Gesch. v. Engl. 5. B., S. 405. — *main body* nämlich der Yorkisten. — *Hilyard*, Robin H., ein Parteigänger der Lancaster-Partei und Anführer einer Bauernschar. — *deathsmen* die dem Tode Geweihten. — *destrier* (altfranzös.) Schlachtrofs. — *champ* = to chew. — *Lovel* und *Ratcliffe*, zwei Parteigänger Eduard's IV., von diesem beauftragt, ihm das Haupt Warwick's zu bringen. — **68.** *Saladin* des Grafen Leibpferd aus edler arabischer Rasse, von dem früher erw. Malech abstammend. — *Gloucester* (glŏstə) ist Richard, Herzog v. Gloucester, der Bruder Eduard's IV. Nach dem Tode desselben liefs er dessen zwei Söhne ermorden, um selbst als Richard III. auf den Thron zu gelangen. — *Marmaduke*, Verwandter und Parteigänger Warwick's, den dieser vom Schlachtfelde abgesendet hatte, um die fliehenden Lancastrier unter dem Herzoge von Somerset aufzuhalten und noch einmal zum Angriffe gegen die königliche Heer zu führen. **69.** *Alwyn* ein Goldschmied und Führer der Londoner Miliz. Die Hauptstadt hielt zu Eduard IV., weil dieser den aufstrebenden Handel besonders begünstigte. *the People are nerer beaten*. Hilyard betrachtet den Bauernstand als Repräsentanten des Volkes. — *bombard* ein schweres Geschütz. — *falchion* (fŏlʃən) kurzes breites Schwert, an der Spitze scharf gekrümmt. — **70.** *latest* hat hier die Bedeutung von last. *Clarence*, Herzog Georg von Clarence, der Bruder Eduard's IV. und zugleich Schwiegersohn des Grafen von Warwick, stand anfangs auf Seite des letzteren und hatte Montagu melden lassen, er solle mit dem Könige nicht eher kämpfen, bis er. Clarence selbst, komme. Infolge dessen gelangte Eduard IV. ungehindert durch den Pafs von *Pontefract* (in Yorkshire, nö. von Leeds). Bald darauf ging *Clarence* zu seinem Bruder über. - - *assoil* veralt. absolvieren, lossprechen. — *brother mine* archaisierend, vgl. Anm. z. S. 153. — *D'Eyncourt* ein treuer Anhänger der York-Partei. — *We yield not* Die Verneinung ohne Umschreibung ist nachdrucksvoller und archaisierend. - *casque* Helm. — 71. *Anne* ist die jüngere Tochter des Grafen. — *Edward Lytton Bulwer* (edūad litn bulwǝ) s. litt. Anm. S. 448.

Nr. 27. Aus den '*Tales from Shakespeare*'. s. S. 409. — 74. *his old course* die Laufbahn seines Alters. — *take her to wife*. Der heutige Sprachgebrauch würde *for* anstatt *to* setzen. — *bade Cordelia to take*. Vgl. S. 79. Z. 17. *to bid* wird jetzt im Aktiv gewöhnlich mit dem reinen Infinitiv verbunden. — *waterish duke*. Im Drama wird nicht der Herzog, sondern sein Land *waterish* (sumpfig) genannt (vgl. S. 381, Z. 221). — *at Fortune's alms* s. Anm. z. S. 382. — 77. *he was told they were weary with travelling all night* stimmt nicht zu dem früher Erzählten: *Regan and her husband were keeping their court at their palace*. Dieser Widerspruch erklärt sich aus einer Abweichung von Shakespeare. Nach dem Drama reist Regan mit ihrem Gemahl nach dem Schlosse des Grafen Gloster, um in einem fremden Hause umso leichter Lear mit seinem unbequemen Gefolge abweisen zu können. Also die Begegnung findet nicht in Regan's Palaste, sondern in dem Schlosse Gloster's statt. — 79. *abided*. Die schwache Form für das gewöhnliche *abode* ist veraltet und sehr selten. — 80. *Bedlam Beggar*, d. i. ein aus *Bedlam* (Betlehem Hospital in London. Mp. E 5) entlassener Blödsinniger. *Turly good* wird von einigen aus dem franz. 'turlupin' (= alberner Spafsmacher) hergeleitet. — *Charles Lamb* (tšälz läm) s. S. 409.

83. *Sir* s. Anm. zu S. 33. — *Louis XVI.* regierte von 1775—1793. — *a Frenchman*. Es war Parmentier (1737—1813), ein ausgezeichneter Pharmaceut und Agronom.

85. *St. Paul's* erg. *Cathedral* (Mp. C 5—6). Die Paulskirche in der City wurde unter der Leitung Sir Christopher Wren's im Jahre 1675 begonnen, 1697 zuerst zum Gottesdienste benutzt und 1710 vollendet. Eine Kohlensteuer deckte den gröfsten Teil der Baukosten (747,954 £). Sie ist die drittgröfste Kirche der Christenheit und steht nur der St. Peterskirche in Rom, mit der sie Ähnlichkeit hat, und dem Dom in Mailand nach. Der Grundrifs ist ein lateinisches Kreuz mit einer Länge von 152 m und einer Breite von 76 m. Die innere Kuppel ist 68 m, die äufsere bis zur Spitze des Kreuzes 123 m hoch. Der obere Teil der Kirche zeigt einen gemischten, der untere korinthischen Stil. Das etwas kahle Innere der Paulskirche dient, ähnlich wie die Westminsterkirche, als nationale Ehrenhalle, doch hauptsächlich für Kriegs- und Seehelden. Wellington und Nelson sind in der riesenhaften Krypta begraben. Johnson hat ein Denkmal in St. Paul's. Cassell, 548 u. ö. — *two and three quarter millions*. Diese Zahl ist veraltet. Dasselbe gilt von anderen Angaben statistischer Natur in diesem Lesestücke. Vgl. Anm. z. S. 99. — 86. *at Lovegrove's*. Lovegrove war der Besitzer eines fashionablen Hôtels in Greenwich. *supply and demand* Angebot und Nachfrage. — *commissariat* Verproviantierungs-, Proviant-. — *Dragon of Wantley* Titel einer alten Ballade. Der gefräfsige Drache verschlang nicht nur gröfsere Tiere, sondern auch Häuser und Wälder. — *Hyde Park* s. S. 127 u. Mp. D. 2—3. — 87. *Great Northern Road*. Dieser Name ist nicht mehr üblich. *Peterborough* Stadt in Northamptonshire, mit einer alten Kathedrale. — *Great Western Road*. Damit ist wahrscheinlich die Fortsetzung der heutigen Kensington Road (D—E 1) gemeint. — *Bristol* an der Grenze der

Grafschaften Gloucester und Somerset, bedeutende Handelsstadt mit über 182.000 Einwohnern. — *Piccadilly*, D 3 4. — *Regent Street*, C – D 4. — *Strand*, D 4 – 5. — *Fleet Street*, C 5. — *Cheapside*, C 6. — *Mile End Road*, C 8. *Bayswater Road* jetzt Uxbridge Road (D 1 – 2). — *Oxford Street*, C 3 – 4. — *Holborn* (ho⁺bən) C 5. — *game, poultry, wild-fowl*. *poultry* ist zahmes Geflügel; *game* ist jagdbares Geflügel, besonders Birkhuhn, *wild-fowl* Federwild überhaupt. *St. James's Park*, s. Anm. z. S. 44. — *acres* s. Tab. II. — *Marble Arch*, ein Triumphbogen (in der Art des Constantinbogens) des Cumberland Gate an der Nordostecke des Hyde Park (Mp. D 3). Dieser Triumphbogen, ursprünglich von Georg IV. für 80.000 *l*. am Eingange des Buckingham Palace errichtet, wurde im Jahre 1851 nach Cumberland Gate verlegt. — *round pond* = basin. — *Kensington Gardens*, D 2. — *halfquartern* s. Tab. II. — *main* = main-pipe Hauptrohr einer Wasserleitung. Aus den sieben Wasserversorgungs-Gesellschaften (water companies) sind jetzt acht geworden. vgl. Dickens, Dictionary of London. — **88.** *Serpentine* im Hyde Park. — *Sancho Panza's mess*. Bei Gelegenheit der Vermählung Camacho des Reichen holt der Koch mit einer Pfanne drei Hennen und zwei Gänse aus einem Topfe heraus und reicht dem Sancho diesen "Löffel" mit den Worten: "Begnügt Euch vor der Hand mit diesem *Schaum*, bis die Stunde des Frühstücks kommt." (Don Quixote, II. T. 20, C.) —

Nr. 4. *don* aus do on, vgl. doff (do off), dup (do up). — **89.** *bower* Gemach, Frauengemach, mhd. bûre. — *Hawking* s. Cassell, p. 744. — *beech-mast*. Die Frucht von Buchen, Eichen und anderen Waldbäumen wurde im älteren Englisch *mast* genannt. — **90.** *broken surface* gepflügter Boden. — *sare* bergen. — *mead-bench* Metbank; oft im Beowulfliede genannt. *kine* altertümlich schw. Form statt *cows* – *steading* (ungebräuchlich) Bauernhof. — *the islands of sugar-cane* Westindien. — *engross* für sich in Anspruch nehmen. — *threshing* häufiger *thrashing* s. S. 66, Z. 1. — **91.** *winnow* (von *wind*) = to fan grain so as to separate the chaff from it. also worfeln, dialekt. 'winden'. — *Aix-la-Chapelle* (äislaϑəpe'l) Aachen. — *sheriff* hier etwa "Vogt"; jetzt ist der *sheriff* der höchste Civilbeamte der Grafschaft; vgl. Anm. z. S. 51. — *the mass-priest* der Seelsorger. — *the lord of the manor* der Gutsherr. — *Gurth, Githa* ae. Namen. — *Byzant* (bĭznt) Goldmünze. nach dem Orte der Prägung so genannt. — **92.** *tesserae* pl. Würfel, bei Mosaikarbeiten. — *fresh from woodland and furrow* eben erst aus Wald und Feld gekommen. — *placed it on movable legs*. Vgl. das Lesestück "Old English Houses" im Elementarb. d. engl. Spr. von Nader u. Würzner, S. 50. — *a scanty sprinkling* eig. ein karges Ausstreuen = einige wenige. — **93.** *junk* = 'a lump' Stück; besonders von Pökelfleisch. — *upper board*. Der Tisch, an welchem der Wirt und seine Gäste safsen, stand höher als der des Gesindes. — *loaf-eaters* Brot- (Laib-) Esser; derjenige, der ihnen das Brot gab, also ihr Herr, hiefs loaf-ward, Brotward, Brotgeber. Aus loaf-ward wurde lord. — *byre* (baiə) = cow-house. Das Wort kommt im Schottischen und Nordenglischen vor und ist verwandt mit bower. — *wine*. Wein war sehr selten. Er wurde gröfstenteils vom Festland eingeführt; seit der Römerzeit wurde in den geeigneten Strichen am Severn und an der Themse Wein gepflanzt. — *certain words of pledge* s. Anm. z. S. 147. — *gleewood* ae. häufiger gléo-béam (béam Baum) Freudenholz. — **94.** *scóp or maker*. Das altenglische *scóp*, sowie das aus dem Griechischen entlehnte Wort Poet bedeuten eigentlich Schöpfer. — *gleeman* wandernder Spielmann. — *reek* Rauch. — *tweezers* Haarzange. — *keep*, Hauptturm, war der hohe viereckige Turm, welcher den stärksten und sichersten Teil der Burg bildete. er hiefs auch donjon oder mastertower. Der unterirdische Teil des Donjon wurde häufig als Gefängnis benützt, daher dungeon Verlies. — *a parapeted wall* Mauer mit einer Brustwehr.

portcullis (= porte coulisse) Fallgatter. **95.** *oriel* = Erkerfenster. Oft vergoldet, daher der Name (lat. aureolum). — *retainers* = adherents. Gefolgsleute. — *franklin* = a freeholder, Freisasse. *of life and limb* etc. mit Leib und Leben und irdischem Dienst. — *Homage* s. Cassell, p. 130. *tenements* Land und Hof. — *unto* veraltet für *to*. — *Ch. tunnelled the walls* Kamine führten ihre Röhren innerhalb der Wände aufwärts. — *clumsy men* plumpe Bauern (Figuren des Schachspieles). — *tables* Tricktrack, ital. toccategli (jeu de toc), italien. Brettspiel mit zwei Würfeln. — *foot-ball* s. Anm. zu S. 132. — *kayle* Kegel, pl. Kegelspiel, ein Grubenspiel mit 9 Löchern. — **96.** *scientific dissection of a dead stag*. In dem mhd. Epos Tristan von Gottfried von Strafsburg (ed. Bechstein, Vers 2785—3055) wird die Zerlegung des Hirsches ausführlich geschildert. - *After the Conquest*, nach 1066. — *jesses* = straps of leather or silk. Aus dem Altfranz. *Ivanhoe* (spr. *aiwnu*) ist ein Roman Walter Scott's (s. S. 440), der in England zur Zeit Richards I. spielt. — *quintain* Rennpfahl, ein um einen senkrechten Pfahl drehbarer Querbalken, an dessen einem Ende ein breites Brett und an dem andern ein Sack voll Sand angebracht war. Wenn der Reiter das Brett verfehlte, wurde er ausgelacht; wenn er es traf, so hatte er sich in acht zu nehmen, dafs er von dem Sandsack, der sich gegen seinen Rücken schwang, nicht vom Pferde geschlagen wurde. Diese Belustigung ist hie und da bei Volksfesten noch jetzt üblich, vgl. 'The Illustr. Lond. News' und 'The Graphic', May 9, 1891, woselbst sich auch Abbildungen befinden. — *lists* s. Gr. § 16. — *wand* = a long, slender rod. — *jousting*. Das englische *to joust* (jost), wie das mhd. *tjostieren*, kommt von dem französ. jouster, joûter. — *mellay*, frz. mêlée, Handgemenge; das modernengl. medley Mischmasch (meddle mischen) ist dasselbe Wort. Während *joust* blofses Spiel war, war *mellay* blutiger Ernst. — *baton* (bätn) = batoon. — **97.** *fray* = affray (frz. effroi), combat. — *garlic* ("Geerlauch") Knoblauch. — *Rufus*. *William Rufus* s. Tabelle IV und S. 3. — *who thought little of* die sich wenig bedachten, wenig Bedenken machten, ohne viel Bedenken — *juggler* altfrz. jogleor, nfr. jongleur. Die *Jongleurs* waren bei den Provençalen und Nordfranzosen Spielleute von Profession, zum Unterschiede von den gelehrten und höfischen Kunstdichtern, den Troubadours und Trouvères, die meist J. in ihren Diensten hatten, welche ihre Lieder vorzutragen hatten. Sie wurden auch menestrels (minstrels) genannt. Es gab auch herrenlose J., die sich auf Märkten und in Schenken herumtrieben und aufser ihrer gewöhnlichen Beschäftigung als Spielleute oft zugleich Seiltänzer und Gaukler waren und abgerichtete Tiere mit sich führten. Solche Leute sind an unserer Stelle gemeint. — Vgl. Cassell, p. 130, 254, 744.

98. *Caen* (spr. ke'ən) *stone*, ein schöner weifser Stein, der in der Nähe von Caen in der Normandie gefunden und weithin versandt wird. Caen war einmal die Hauptstadt des Herzogtumes Normandie; Wilhelm der Eroberer und seine Gemahlin liegen dort begraben. — *Trinity College Psalter* ist der berühmte Canterbury Psalter aus dem 11. Jahrh. — *carve*. Auch Chaucer sagt im Prolog zu den Canterbury Tales in seiner Schilderung des jungen Squires (Ausg. Zupitza, v. 99 f.): 'Curteis he was, lowly and seruysable and carf biforn his fader at the table.'

99. *the present population of London*. Bei der Volkszählung am 6. April 1891 zählte London mit dem Polizei-Rayon *(Greater London)* 5,633.803 Einw., ohne denselben *(Inner London)* 4.211.743 Einw.; Grofsbritannien und Irland 37,740.283 Einw. — *an erring monarch* bezieht sich entweder auf Karl's I. Geschick nach der Schlacht bei Naseby (1645), oder auf Jakob II., der sich vor Wilhelm III. flüchten mufste. — *Bristol* s. Anm. zu 87. — *Norwich* (Norits) liegt in Norfolk (Nofək), *York* in der gleichnamigen Grafschaft. *Plymouth* (Pli'məth) in Devonshire.

Corentry (Kʌwntrī) in Warwick (ūɔrīk). — *harquebusiers*, in gewöhnl. Schreibung arquebusier (ɔkībəsiə), Hellebardiere. — *medium-sized coasters* Küstenschiff mittlerer Gröfse. — *contraction* hier Verkürzung, Einschränkung. — *The Pope was threatening*. Es war dies vornehmlich Pius V. (1565—1572), der durch eine Bulle vom 25. Februar 1570 Elisabeth für abgesetzt erklärte. — *France doubtful*. Die damaligen Könige Frankreichs standen alle mehr oder minder unter dem Einflusse der Guisen, die als Feinde der Protestanten in der Geschichte bekannt sind und mit deren Familie auch Maria Stuart verwandt war. — *Spain hostile*. Philipp II. von Spanien regierte 1556 bis 1598. Die spanische Armada wurde 1588 vernichtet (s. S. 159). *Ireland always in rebellion*. Seitdem der Protestantismus in England herrschend geworden war, hatte die feindselige Spannung zwischen Engländern und Irländern zugenommen, da diese der alten Kirche treu blieben. — *The Scotch troublesome and intriguing*. Jakob V. von Schottland war 1542 gestorben. Im Namen seiner minderjährigen Tochter Maria führte deren Mutter, eine Schwester der Guisen, die Verwaltung. - *religious faction*. Aufser der herrschenden anglikanischen Kirche (Episkopalkirche) gab es noch zahlreiche Dissenters (Presbyterianer und Puritaner). — *woman*, Elisabeth. Vgl. Humes Charakterschilderung S 156 und das Stück aus Scott's Kenilworth S. 51. — *ordnance* (ursprüngl. von der Gröfse der Kanone ["engin de telle ordonnance"] gesagt), bezeichnet gewöhnlich schweres Geschütz; *artillery* hat eine allgemeinere Bedeutung; es bezeichnet nicht blofs Wurfgeschosse überhaupt, sondern auch die zur Bedienung derselben verwendete Mannschaft. *French proverb*. Dieses Sprichwort findet sich nicht in Le Roux de Lincy's Sammlung: "Livre des Proverbes Français," aber eine Reihe anderer, die sich auf England und die Engländer beziehen und von denen wir zwei als besonders charakteristisch hier anführen wollen: "Li mieldre buveor (= les meilleurs buveurs) en Angleterre" aus dem 13. Jahrhundert und "D'Angleterre ne vient bon vent ne bonne guerre" aus dem 17. Jahrhundert. — *Paul Hentzner*, ein geborener Schlesier, war der Verfasser einer lateinisch geschriebenen und zum Teile ins Englische übersetzten 'Reise durch Deutschland, Frankreich, Italien' etc. Er lebte 1558—1623. — **100.** *the mettle of their pasture*, Shakesp., King Henry V, III 1. 27 'show us here the mettle of your pasture' von A. W. Schlegel übersetzt 'zeigt uns die Kraft genoss'ner Nahrung'. — *slang expressions*. slang (ein Name der Zigeunersprache?) bedeutet Vulgärsprache. Die gröfste Sammlung von Slang-Ausdrücken enthält The Slang Dictionary, London, Chatto and Windus 1873. Vgl. ferner Storm's Bemerkungen in Engl. Philol. p. 152 f. — *King James*, natürlich Jakob I. — *Goadby* (spr. goˮdbī).

Nr. 6. **101.** *bitten apples* angebissene Äpfel, welche die vornehmeren Zuschauer auf den besseren Plätzen ins Parterre geworfen haben; vgl. Shakesp. King Henry VIII. V. A., 3. Sc. *of movable scenery there was none*. Der Ursprung der beweglichen Dekorationen auf der englischen Bühne ist in den schon seit den Sechziger-Jahren des 16. Jahrhunderts am englischen Hofe mit immer gröfserem Pomp aufgeführten Maskenspielen zu suchen. Einen ungeahnten Aufschwung nahm aber die Verwendung derselben, als der berühmte Architekt und Maler Inigo (d. h. Ignatius) Jones zu den von Ben Jonson, einem Freunde Shakespeare's, William Davenant, u. a. verfafsten Masken von 1605 an seine prächtigen Ausstattungen herstellte. Davenant (1605—1668), der sich für einen natürlichen Sohn Shakespeare's gehalten haben soll, führte noch unter der Republik als Theaterdirektor das Dekorationswesen und die Musik auf die öffentliche Bühne ein, wobei ihm seine gründliche Bekanntschaft mit der französischen Bühne, die soeben durch Corneille's klassische Dramen zu reicher Blüte gelangt war, zu gute kam.

Siehe Elze im Shakespeare-Jahrbuch, IV. 130 ff. — *Juliet, Romeo* sind die Hauptpersonen der nach ihnen genannten Tragödie Shakespeare's. — *play-king and play-queen in Hamlet*. In Shakespeare's "Hamlet" läfst der Held des Stückes durch wandernde Schauspieler eine der Ermordung seines Vaters ähnliche Scene aufführen, um den Eindruck der dargestellten Handlung auf den anwesenden König, den mutmafslichen Mörder, zu beobachten. — *jig* etymol. altfrz. gige, mhd. gige, nhd. Geige. — *Queen*, natürlich Elisabeth. — *Dowden* (daudn) s. S. 409.
102. Nr. 7. *The risk of travelling*, wegen der vielen Strafsenräuber. — *House of Hanover*. Da nach der Successionsurkunde von 1701 nur die protestantischen Zweige der königlichen Familie thronfähig waren, so kam nach dem Tode der Königin Anna (1714) die Krone an den Kurfürsten von Hannover, Georg, einen Enkel der unglücklichen Pfalzgräfin und Böhmenkönigin Elisabeth, der Tochter Jakob's I. — *Jacobite designs* sind die Pläne der Stuart-Partei, Jakob, den Bruder der Königin Anna, und später dessen Sohn Charles Edward auf den Thron zu bringen. — *Squire Western*, ein roher, ungebildeter Landedelmann in Fielding's 'Tom Jones'; *Parson Trulliber*, eine episodische Figur in seinem Romane 'Joseph Andrews.' — *Oxford* war schon zur Zeit der Angelsachsen der Sitz einer gelehrten Schule; das erste vollständige Universitätscollege wurde aber erst 1249 eingerichtet. Gegenwärtig hat die Universität 19 Colleges (s. unten), von denen das Christchurch-College (kraist tsɔ̂ts̀ kɔlīdǯ), das Magdalen-College (mɔ̂dlīn) und All-Souls-College die besuchtesten sind. Die Universität bildet einen geschlossenen Körper, dessen Oberhaupt ein auf Lebenszeit gewählter Kanzler aus der Klasse der obersten Staatsbeamten ist. Ihm zur Seite steht der hohe Rat, der aus graduierten Mitgliedern der Universität zusammengesetzt ist. Die Universität sendet zwei Repräsentanten ins Parlament. Die Mitglieder der Universität sind *attached* und *unattached students*; erstere (fellows) leben teilweise von den Einkünften ihrer Kollegien, letztere sind junge Leute, die auf ihre Rechnung während der sieben Studienmonate auf der Universität leben. Berühmt ist die (bodleianische) Bibliothek der Universität. Sie ist eine der gröfsten Europas und zählt 30.000 Handschriften und über 300.000 Bände. — *Cambridge* ist die zweite Universität Englands. Sie hat 13 colleges. Die wichtigsten sind: Corpus-Christi-College (kɔəpəs kristai), mit der gröfsten Manuscriptensammlung, und Trinity-College. Die Verwaltung und Gliederung der Universität ist im allgemeinen wie zu Oxford. Auch Cambridge sendet zwei Deputierte ins Parlament. — *Professor Saunderson, Nicholas S.* (1682—1739), Professor der Mathematik in Cambridge. — *Gray. Thomas Gray* (1716—1771) war ein namhafter lyrischer Dichter, unter dessen Werken besonders die 'Elegy written in a Country Churchyard' berühmt ist. **103.** *Gibbon* (spr. gibn) s. S. 431. — *tutor*. Man hat zwischen dem *College tutor* und dem *private tutor* zu unterscheiden. Ersterer ist ein Beamter in jedem einzelnen *College* (s. u.), einer der Professoren, der über den Studiengang und das Verhalten der Mitglieder seines College zu wachen hat. Ein solcher ist hier gemeint. Die *private tutors* stehen zu den Studenten nur in dem Verhältnis eines bezahlten Privatlehrers. — *term*. Das akademische Jahr wird in England in 'terms' eingeteilt; man versteht darunter die Zeit, in der ein Studienkursus absolviert wird, also etwa unser Semester. In Oxford zählt man vier terms. 1. Hilary oder Lent term (14. Jänner bis Palmsonntag); 2. Easter term (von Ostern bis Pfingsten); 3. Trinity oder Act term (Sonntag nach Pfingsten bis Anfang Juli); 4. Michaelmas term (10. Oktober bis 17. Dezember). In Cambridge hat man nur drei terms. — *Bath*, Hauptort der Grafschaft Somerset, eine der ältesten und schönsten Städte Englands und sein grofsartigster und glänzendster Badeort. Die berühmten Mineralquellen von Bath

sind die einzigen heifsen des Landes. — *Buckinghamshire*, eine Grafschaft, östlich von Oxford, mit der Hauptstadt Aylesbury. — *our Church*. Gemeint ist natürlich die Staatskirche Church of England, Established Church, Anglican Church, Episcopal Church. Ihr Glaubensbekenntnis ist in den Thirty-nine Articles enthalten, die 1571 durch Parlamentsakte zum Gesetze und Teil der englischen Konstitution gemacht wurden. — *Dr. Johnson* s. S. 427. — *Christ Church Meadow*, eine grofse Wiese mit einer Allee von alten Ulmen, zum Christ Church College gehörend, das, von Wolsey 1525 gegründet, das gröfste und stattlichste der Oxforder Colleges ist. Die *colleges*, Collegienhäuser, bieten den Studenten Wohnung, Nahrung, Stipendien, passende Gesellschaft, disciplinarische Aufsicht, Unterricht und später Nachhilfe in ihren selbständigen Studien. Die colleges haben ihre von der Universitätsbehörde völlig unabhängige Verfassung und Verwaltung. Bis vor einigen Jahrzehnten mufste jeder Student einem dieser Konvikte angehören, jetzt wohnt auch ein geringer Teil derselben in bestimmten bürgerlichen Häusern der Stadt. — *Degrees*. Es giebt drei akademische Grade; der niedrigste, der eines Bachelor of Arts, B. A., wird gewöhnlich nach Beendigung der (meist dreijährigen) Studienzeit durch Prüfungen erworben; den zweiten, den eines Master of Arts (M. A.), erhält man drei Jahre später ohne Prüfung, London University ausgenommen; der dritte und höchste ist der eines Doctor D. D. = Doctor of Divinity, L. L. D. = Doctor of Law, D. C. L. = Doctor of Civil [oder Canon] Law, M. D. = Medicinae Doctor, D. Sc. = Doctor of Science [= Dr. der Philosophie], Mus. Doc. = Doctor of Music) und wird erst im höheren Alter als bei uns erworben. — *Laudian Statutes*, die vom Erzbischof Laud 1573—1645 verfafsten akademischen Gesetze. — *Lord Eldon*, mit kurzer Unterbrechung Lordkanzler von 1801—1827. — *Passed the Schools*, machte sein Abgangsexamen. An den englischen Universitäten werden in bestimmten Zwischenräumen drei Prüfungen gemacht. Gleich im ersten term das 'responsions' oder 'smalls' genannte Examen, anderthalb bis zwei Jahre später die 'moderations' und nach dem dritten Jahre 'greats' oder 'general examination;' bei dieser letzten Prüfung, nach deren Ablegung man B. A. ist, giebt es eine Reihe verschiedener Fächer oder "schools." — *Rev. Vicesimus Knox* (spr. rewrənd wĭsizĭməs nŏks). 'Reverend' ist ein geistlicher Titel. 'The Right Reverend' sagt man, wenn von einem Dean die Rede ist. 'Right Reverend Father in God' ist der Titel eines Bischofs, 'Most Reverend Father in God' derjenige der Erzbischöfe von Canterbury u. York. Vergl. d. Anm. u. zu bishop. — *The Masters* die Prüfenden. — *The Commissioners of 1850*. Im Jahre 1850 wurde auf das Drängen der Dissidenten hin eine königliche Kommission eingesetzt, um den Zustand der Universitäten in Oxford, Cambridge und Dublin zu untersuchen; die Folge war eine Parlamentsakte, welche die genannten Universitäten auch den Dissenters öffnete. — *Ereleigh* spr. iwll. — *Provost of Oriel*, Vorstand des Oriel College. — *Sir Robert Peel* (1788—1850), berühmter Staatsmann, wegen seiner torystischen Gesinnung und Abneigung gegen die Emancipation der Katholiken Vertreter der Universität Oxford von 1817—1829. Später gründete er eine neue Partei im Parlamente, die Konservativen, welche die Mitte zwischen den Tories und Whigs hielten. P. ist am meisten bekannt durch seine Verfechtung der Freihandelsgrundsätze in den Vierziger-Jahren unseres Jahrh. — *Bishop Newton*, Dr. Thomas N., Bischof von Bristol, gest. 1782. — In England und Wales giebt es 32 bischöfliche Diöcesen, von welchen 23 dem Erzbischof von Canterbury, 9 dem von York unterstehen. Die Bischöfe sind Mitglieder des Oberhauses. Zu ihrem Ornat gehören weifse Batistärmel. *Dean* ist der oberste Geistliche unter einem Bischof. Er ist das Haupt des *Chapter*, d. h. der sämtlichen zur Kathedrale gehörigen Geistlichen. Die

Sprengel der verschiedenen Bischöfe zerfallen in eine grofse Anzahl Kirchspiele (parishes). Der Geistliche, dem die Sorge für ein solches Kirchspiel anvertraut ist, und der dafür alle Rechte, Pfründen, Zehnten u. s. w. geniefst, namentlich der Inhaber einer Pfarrei, die zu besetzen nicht in der Hand eines Laien liegt, heifst *rector*. Der *vicar* ist so selbständig wie der rector, seine Pfründe kann aber auch von einem Laien vergeben werden, und er geniefst nur einen Teil der Einkünfte des parish. *Curates* (Curate, Cooperatoren) sind Geistliche, welche der Inhaber einer Pfründe als Stellvertreter sich annimmt und nach persönlichem Übereinkommen besoldet. Sie sind oft recht schlecht bezahlt, die meisten Geistlichen müssen aber dieses Stadium passieren. *Parson* ist ungefähr dasselbe wie vicar und rector, *clergyman* endlich bezeichnet jeden, der ordiniert ist, mag er nun ein geistliches Amt bekleiden oder nicht. — George Grenville, Premierminister 1763—1765, Nachfolger Lord Bute's. — *Lord Lieutenant*, der oberste Repräsentant der Krone in der Grafschaft, er ist erster Friedensrichter und Oberbefehlshaber der Miliz; die Ernennung zu diesem Ehrenamte erfolgt durch die Königin und gilt rechtlich auf so lange, als es der Regierung beliebt *(during the royal pleasure)*, faktisch auf Lebenszeit. — *Dissenters* s. Anm. z. S. 99, *religious faction*. — *entry* Eintragung, Notiz, Bemerkung. — *Methodist Conference*. Methodisten ist der Name einer aus dem Schofse der anglikanischen Kirche hervorgegangenen Religionspartei. Einige Oxforder Studenten, welche sich 1729 zur Pflege einer lebendigen Frömmigkeit verbanden, gaben den ersten Anstofs zu der mächtigen religiösen Bewegung. Den Namen "Methodisten" empfingen die Genossen jenes Bundes zuerst als Spottnamen in ähnlichem Sinne wie "Pietisten", nahmen ihn aber danach als einen Ehrennamen auf, zur Bezeichnung derer, "die nach der in der Bibel aufgestellten Methode" leben. Die Seele der kleinen Genossenschaft war John Wesley, ein Mann von grofser geistiger Begabung, der mit einem glühenden Heilsverlangen eine imponierende Willenskraft und ein seltenes Organisationstalent vereinigte. Noch gröfseren Erfolg gewann der Methodismus, als George Whitfield sich mit seiner gewaltigen Predigergabe an die Massen wandte. Die Leitung des Ganzen behielt Wesley anfangs ausschliefslich in der Hand. Als die Arbeit wuchs, gesellte er sich die jährliche *Conference* zu, welche zum erstenmale 1744 gehalten wurde. Diese Konferenz wurde nach Wesley's Tode (1791) die kirchliche Oberbehörde der Methodisten. Am Ausgange des 18 Jahrh. war der Methodismus in ganz England und Amerika verbreitet und hat seitdem trotz innerer Kämpfe und Secessionen zugenommen. Die Methodisten haben sich um Werke christlicher Humanität, Sklavenemancipation, Armen- und Krankenpflege, Sorge für Verwahrloste und Gefallene, Bibel- und Traktatenverbreitung grofse Verdienste erworben. Der berühmte Wilberforce (s. Anm. z. S. 271, Nr. 4) war Methodist. 105. *Lady Montagu* s. S. 420. — *Thoresby*. Der Herrensitz des Vaters der Lady Montagu, des Herzogs von Kingston, in Nottinghamshire, ist berühmt durch seinen grofsen und schönen Park. — *Epictetus*, griech. Philosoph aus dem 1. Jahrh. n. Chr. — *Burnet*, Bischof von Salisbury, 1643—1715, ein ausgezeichneter Kirchenfürst Englands. Seine "Exposition of the Thirty-nine Articles of the Church of England" wird immer noch als Hauptwerk angesehen. '*Impromptu de Versailles*,' einaktiges Lustspiel von Molière, aufgeführt 1663 vor dem Hofe in Versailles. — *Kneller* (Sir Godefroy), deutscher Porträtmaler, der in seinem 30. Jahre nach London kam und von Karl II. zum Hofmaler ernannt wurde († 1723) — *Governor Pitt*. Thomas Pitt war Statthalter in Madras gewesen, von wo er den kostbaren Diamanten heimbrachte, den er später dem Herzoge von Orleans um $2^1/_2$ Mill. Franken verkaufte; er war der Grofsvater Lord Chatham's — 106. *Miss Burney.*

Frances B., später Madame D'Arblay (1752—1840), war auf dem Gebiete des Romanes eine würdige Nachfolgerin Richardson's, Fielding's und Smollett's. Am bekanntesten ist ihr Roman 'Evelina' (1778), von welchem Johnson, mit dem sie Mrs. Thrale bekannt gemacht hatte, erklärte, dafs er Stellen enthalte, die eines Richardson würdig seien. Macaulay hat ein Essay über sie geschrieben. — *Wraxall*, Sir Nathaniel William W., Reisender und Parlamentsmitglied; aufser mehreren Reisebeschreibungen veröffentlichte er 'Historical Memoirs of My Own Time', die von 1772—1784 gehen; nach seinem Tode (1831) erschienen seine 'Posthumous Memoirs'; er gilt für unzuverlässig in seinen Berichten. — *Washington*, s. Anm. zu S. 269, gentleman. — *Guy Mannering* ist ein Roman Walter Scott's. — 107. *Spenser*, s. Anm. z. S. 188. — *Burke* s. S. 432. — *Chaworth* spr. tšoəth. — *Lord Byron* war der Grofsonkel des Dichters. — *Pall Mall* ist eine Strafse im westlichen London (Mp. D 4), die von Trafalgar Square zum Green Park führt; die meisten der zahlreichen Klubs (s. Anm. zu S. 403) haben in dieser Strafse ihre Häuser. — *Sedley* spr. sedlī. — *Stanhope* (stänəp) s. S. 449.

108. *cannel coal* Kannelkohle. Der Name *cannel* ist korrumpiert aus candle, weil diese Kohlenart so hell wie eine Kerze (candle) brennt. — *caking coal* Fettkohle, Backkohle, jene Gattung Kohle, welche, stark erhitzt, zu einer festen Masse wird. — *cherry coal* Kirschkohle, ist der Fettkohle ähnlich, kocht aber nicht, wenn sie erhitzt wird. Sie ist auch gebrechlicher. — *Newcastle upon Tyne*, Hauptstadt der Grafschaft Northumberland. In der Umgebung der Stadt befinden sich unerschöpfliche Steinkohlenlager, daher sprichwörtl. *to carry coals to Newcastle*. — *bituminous*. Dazu gehören alle vorher genannten Gattungen Kohle. — *Household Words* s. S. 448.

Nr. 9. *The Black Prince*. Der Sohn Eduard's III., Eduard, Prinz von Wales, wegen seiner Rüstung der "schwarze Prinz" genannt, wurde 1331 geboren. Er schlug 1356 die Franzosen bei Maupertuis, unweit von Poitiers (daher w. u. im Texte 'battle of Poitiers'). Er starb 1386. Sein jüngerer Sohn bestieg nach Eduard's III. Tode den Thron unter dem Namen Richard II. — *Holborn, Temple*, s. Mp. C 5. — *Temple Bar, as we now see it*. Auch dieser Durchgang (gebaut von Wren 1670) existiert nicht mehr. Er wurde 1878 abgetragen, um jenen Teil von Fleet Street und Strand zu erweitern. Cassell, p. 530. — *Strand*, s. Mp. D 4 - 5. — *Whitechapel* C 7. — *London Bridge* D 6), vgl. Anm. z. S. 9. — *Lord Mayor* ist der Titel der Oberbürgermeister von London, York, Dublin. — *Southwark* Stadtteil am rechten Ufer der Themse; s. Mp. D 6—8. — *Charing Cross* D 4. — *Westminster* Stadtteil westlich von der City. — 109. *Exeter Hall* (auf dem *Strand* in der Nähe von *Covent Garden*, D 4) dient zu religiösen Versammlungen und Aufführung von Kirchenmusik. — *Drury Lane Theater* C 4—5. — *Marylebone* (märıbon) nordwestlicher Teil von London; er liegt in der Grafschaft Middlesex. — *The City was the whole of London*. Die Grenzen der eigentlichen City sind im Westen Temple Bar, im Norden Holborn, Smithfield und Finsbury Circus, im Osten Bishopsgate, Houndsditch und Minories, im Süden die Themse. — *Petticoat Lane* heifst jetzt Middlesex-Street (zwischen Commercial Road und Houndsditch C 6 7). — *the two latter being prisoners*. Es war Johann der Gute von Frankreich und David II. von Schottland. — *Savoy Palace*. So genannt nach Peter Earl of Savoy. Onkel der Gemahlin Heinrich's III.; wurde 1381 zerstört; jetzt eine Kapelle (Strand D 5). — *John of Gaunt* (gänt), Herzog von Lancaster, war der vierte Sohn Eduard's III. und Vater Heinrich's IV. 'Time-honoured Lancaster' (d. i. ehrwürdig, wegen seines Alters), nennt ihn Shakespeare in King Richard II. I, 1. 1. — *Cheapside* C 6. — *Tower* D 6 -7. — *Wardrobe Street* existiert nicht mehr. —

Exchequer alter Gerichtshof, vor dem namentlich die fiskalischen Prozesse ausgetragen wurden. Seine Geschäfte besorgt jetzt die *Queen's Bench Division*, der grofse Civil-Gerichtshof. s. Anm. z. S. 165. — *Poultry* (Fortsetzung von Cheapside) C 6. — *at the time of the Reformation*, also in runder Zahl 200 Jahre später. — *Earl of Warwick the king-maker*, s. S. 67. — *Warwick Lane* führt von der Paulskirche in die Newgate Street. Diese verbindet Holborn und Cheapside; zwischen Newgate Street und St. Paul's lag *Newgate Market*. — *Baynard's Castle* lag in der jetzigen Thames Street (Mp. D 6). — *City Flour Mills*. Bestehen nicht mehr, an ihrer Stelle erhebt sich jetzt die Cannon Street Station der unterird. Eisenbahn (D 6). — *Dowgate Hill* führt von der Thames Street in die Cannon Street (C 6). — **110**. *Lincoln's* (linkənz) *Inn F.* C 5. — *Whetstone Park* die nächste Strafse nördlich von Lincoln's Inn F. — *St. Martin's* C—D 4. — *Sir Francis Walsingham* (ñɔlsīŋəm) 1536—1590, unter Elisabeth Staatssekretär des Auswärtigen, übte namentlich auf das Schicksal der Maria Stuart einen verhängnisvollen Einfluss. — *Earl of Essex*. Robert Devereux, Earl of Essex, ward nach Leicester's (Anm. z. S. 51) Tode der erklärte Günstling der Königin Elisabeth. Wegen seiner Kriegsthaten und seiner menschenfreundlichen Gesinnung war er auch der Liebling des Volkes. Infolge der Ränke seiner Neider und auch durch eigene Schuld verlor er die Gunst der Königin. Wegen seines Verhaltens in Irland wurde ihm der Prozess gemacht; er wurde zum Tode verurteilt und enthauptet (1601). Sein tragisches Schicksal wurde u. a. von Laube als Gegenstand dichterischer Darstellung in dem Trauerspiel "Graf Essex" benützt. — *Tower Street* westl. vom Tower. — *Seething Lane* ist eine Seitengasse davon. — *Leadenhall Street* C. 6. — *Cravens, Nevills, Burleighs, Zouches* (zautšīz), alte Adelsgeschlechter aus der Normannenzeit. — *Suffolk*. Sein Familiennamen war De La Pole. — *Minories* C—D 6—7. — *Rivers* (spr. riwəz). aus der Familie Woodville. — *Savage Gardens* existieren nicht mehr. — *Gracechurch Street* ist die südliche Fortsetzung von Bishopsgate Street (C 6). — *Piccadilly* D 3—4. — *Lord Burlington*. Sein Familienname war Boyle. — **111**. *Shoe Lane* eine westl. Parallelstr. zu Farringdon Street (C 5). — *Chancery Lane* C 5. — *complaints against the intolerable smoke* etc. Im Jahre 1316 schickte das Parlament eine Petition an den König, mit dem Ersuchen, das neue Feuerungsmittel, genannt Kohle, zu verbieten, wenn er nicht wolle, dafs seine Unterthanen geräuchert oder erstickt werden sollten. (Household Words II, 107. Tauchn. Ed.) — *By the end of the reign of Charles the Second*, s. Tab. IV. — *St. James's, Coventgarden. Leicester* D 4. — *Soho* C 4 — *Inigo Jones* (1572—1651) war unter Karl I. Oberinspektor sämtlicher königlichen Gebäude. Seine bedeutendsten Bauwerke sind der Bankettsaal im Palast Whitehall, das Hospital zu Greenwich und die Säulenhalle der St. Paulskirche, die dem grofsen Feuer des Jahres 1666 zum Opfer fiel. In seinem Stile sind gotische Elemente mit jenen der späteren italienischen Weise vermengt. — *Duke of Bedford*, Titel der alten Familie Russell. — *Bloomsbury Square* C 4. — *Paternoster Row*, die nächste Parallelstrafse nördlich von St. Paul's (C 5—6). — *Regent Street* C—D 4. *chairs* hier: Tragsessel, Sänfte. — *Ludgate Street* C 5. — *Henrietta Street* führt von Bedford Street auf Coventgarden Market (D 4). — *Clapham* und *Tulse Hill* im Süden von London; die Fortsetzung der Kensington Road führt dorthin (F 4 5). · **112**. *Tyburn* (taibən) C 2—3. — *Jack Ketch*. Vgl. Macaulay, Histor. of Engl. II, 194: He (Monmuth) then accosted John Ketch the executioner, a wretch who had butchered many brave and noble victims, and whose name has, during a century and a half, been vulgarly given to all that have succeeded him in his odious office. — *The reign of George the Third*, s. Tab. IV. — *Soho*

Square, Bloomsbury C 4. — Portland Place C 4. — Portman Square C 3. — Hannover Square C 4. — Hyde Park D 3. — Russell Square C 3. — Hoxton B 6. — Clerkenwell C 5.

Nr. 10. Der vollständige Titel des Buches ist: 'The Sketch Book of Geoffrey Crayon, Gent.' s. S. 444. — *Cowper (Kaupa).* Das Citat ist aus 'The Task.' Vgl. S. 436. — *wake* Kirchweihfest. — **114.** *to burst upon the wing* auffliegen. — **115.** *farmers.* Von einem Bauernstande in dem Sinne des Wortes, den wir ihm beilegen, ist in England nicht die Rede. Der englische Landwirt *(farmer)* hat das Gut, das er bewirtschaftet, mit verschwindenden Ausnahmen vom Adel und der Gentry in Pacht, und es giebt nicht leicht ein Dorf, das nicht seinen Magnaten hätte, dem das umliegende Land gehört. Unserem Bauer entspricht nur der *yeoman*, der seinen kleinen Grundbesitz selbst bebaut und im Norden Englands mit seinen Arbeitern an **einem** Tische ifst. Mit *peasant* bezeichnet man nur einen Feldarbeiter. — *Chaucer (1358a)*, s. S. 406. — *tracery* steinerner Zierat. — **117.** *Rann Kennedy.* Reverend Rann Kennedy, A. M., verfafste ein Gedicht auf den Tod der Prinzessin Charlotte, woraus die citierten Verse entnommen sind.

118. Zur Erklärung des Lesest. Nr. 10, 11 wurde vor allem Tanger's Ausgabe von Irving's Skizze Christmas (4. Bd. der Dickmann'schen französ. und engl. Schulbibl.) benutzt. — *We*, nämlich der Verfasser und Frank Bracebridge, der Sohn eines Gutsbesitzers in Yorkshire. Frank hatte den ihm befreundeten Verfasser eingeladen, die Weihnachtstage auf dem Gute seines Vaters zu verbringen. — *the Restoration.* Die Restauration der Stuarts wurde 1660 durch General Monk bewerkstelligt. — *the grounds* etc. Mit dieser Schilderung eines Gartens im altfranzösischen Geschmacke vgl. die des englischen Parkstiles im vorhergehenden Lesest. — *the levelling system.* Die Levellers bildeten zur Zeit der ersten Revolution die extremste Partei der Republikaner mit socialistischen und communistischen Tendenzen. — *Squire* wird der Erbinhaber des gröfsten Grundbesitzes in einem Kirchspiele genannt; vgl. Anm. zu S. 33. — *landscape-gardeners* sind diejenigen, welche in den Anlagen die vorhin erwähnte Nachahmung der Natur anstreben. — **119.** *the twelve days of Christmas* bedeutet die zwölftägige festliche Zeit zwischen dem 25. Dezember und dem Twelfth-day (Dreikönigstag), am 6. Jänner. Früher wurde der erste und der letzte Tag davon besonders freudig gefeiert. — *shoe the wild mare.* Welches Spiel darunter gemeint ist, können wir nicht angeben. — *hot-cockles* Handschmisse, ein Spiel, wobei jemand mit verbundenen Augen niederknien und raten mufste, wer ihn auf seine hinten ausgebreitete Hand schlug. — *Steal-the-white-loaf* oder *Cobloaf-stealing*, ein Weihnachtsspiel, welches John Brand (Popular Antiquities of Great Britain, ed. Ellis, 3 vols., London 1849) folgendermafsen beschreibt: Nach dem Abendessen wird auf den Tisch ein Laib Brot gelegt und darauf zwanzig kleine Silbermünzen. Die beiden ältesten Diener sitzen dabei als Richter. Der Haushofmeister führt nun die durch ein Laken verhüllten Dienstboten einen nach dem andern herein. Die Richter raten, wer der Verhüllte sei; nennen sie den richtigen Namen, so geht der Verhüllte leer aus; raten sie jedoch falsch, so wirft er das Laken ab, und erhält eines der Geldstücke. Das wird fortgesetzt, bis alles Geld verteilt ist. — *Bob apple.* Dieses Spiel ist nicht mehr gebräuchlich. Man versuchte dabei mit dem Munde einen Apfel zu fassen, der an dem einen Ende eines wagrecht schwebenden Stabes angebracht war, während auf dem anderen Ende desselben eine brennende Kerze stak. Bei ungeschickter Berührung des Apfels drehte sich der Stab, so dafs man in Gefahr kam, sich im Gesichte zu verbrennen. Vgl. John Brand a. a. O. I. Bd., S. 377 und 516. Ein ähnliches Spiel ist das noch heute übliche Bobcherry (Baumelkirsche), nur dafs dabei keine brennende Kerze in Anwendung kommt. — *snap-dragon* = flap-dragon. Dabei werden Rosinen aus brennendem Cognac gegriffen. — *Yule-log*, Julblock, *Christmas Candle*, Weihnachtskerze, vgl. w. u. S. 120, Z. 8. 27. Das Julfest war das grofse Winterfest der alten Germanen, welches nach der Wintersonnenwende zur Feier der wiederkehrenden Sonne begangen wurde. Später fiel es mit dem christlichen Weihnachtsfeste zusammen. An den Julblock wie an die Weihnachtskerze knüpfte sich mancherlei Aberglauben. — *mistletoe*. An der Stelle, über welcher ein Mistelzweig hängt, dürfen die Mädchen geküfst werden. — *Oxonian* ist ein Student der Universität Oxford (lat. Oxonia); vgl. Anm. zu S. 107. — *hoyden* eigentl. = *romp*, wilde Hummel; hier etwa "Backfisch". — *a round game of cards*, ein Gesellschaftskartenspiel. 120. *parlour*. In früherer Zeit bezeichnete *parlour* das Empfangszimmer, jetzt wird damit weniger der Zweck als die Lage des Zimmers bezeichnet, nämlich das Zimmer zur ebenen Erde, neben dem Eintrittsflur des Hauses. — *hall*, s. S. 92. Z. 20. — *Frumenty* Weizenbrei., — *minced-pie* darf in England nach alter Sitte beim Weihnachtsschmause nicht fehlen. — Die scherzhafte Personification wird bis zu Ende des Satzes beibehalten (daher auch die Bezeichnung *orthodox* und zweimal *him* statt *it*) und auf *feast* ausgedehnt, welches als ein grofser Herr mit Gefolge erscheint. — 121. *Punch* ist der Hanswurst im englischen Puppentheater. *Judy* sein Weib. — *harp in hall*, vgl. S. 93, Z. 39. — *figured down several couple*. Wie das Subst. *figure* auch die Tour beim Tanze bedeutet, so ist *to figure* hier geradezu = = tanzen. *Several couple* läfst darauf schliefsen, dafs hier von dem country-dance (auch Sir Roger de Coverley genannt) die Rede ist, bei welchem die Herren in einer Reihe ihren Damen in der anderen gegenüberstehen. Das erste, von der Thüre am weitesten entfernte Paar (top-couple) chassiert durch die beiden Reihen (jigs down the middle) bis an das Ende des Saales und 'up again,' tanzt gewisse Touren mit dem zweiten Paare, nimmt dessen Stelle ein, chassiert wieder, tanzt mit dem dritten, nimmt dessen Stelle ein u. s. w., bis es sich endlich seinen Ruheplatz am anderen Ende der Reihen ertanzt hat. Mittlerweile hat auch das zweite Paar in gleicher Weise seine Touren begonnen, dann das dritte u. s. w. bis sich schliefslich die Anordnung der Paare gerade umgekehrt hat. *He figured down several couple* bedeutet also, dafs der Squire durch das Durchtanzen der vorgeschriebenen Touren um mehrere Plätze dem anderen Ende näher gerückt war. — 122. *heel, and toe* und *rigadoon* (frz. rigaudon) sind altmodische Tanzbewegungen. — *John Bull*. Dieser Ausdruck wurde zuerst gebraucht in Arbuthnot's (1675—1734) Satire 'The History of John Bull.' 'John Bull' dient zur Bezeichnung der Engländer, wie *Uncle Sam* (scherzhafte Auflösung von U. S. = United States) und *Brother Jonathan* zur Bezeichnung der Amerikaner. — 124. *flinging his money* etc. Die Wettsucht der Engländer ist bekannt. Der Wagegeist liegt eben tief in dem Charakter der Nation. Es giebt in England Leute in Menge, die durch Wetten ein Vermögen gewonnen haben, und solche, die auf dieselbe Weise verarmt sind. In ausgedehntem Mafse findet die Wettlust ihren Spielraum bei den Wettrennen. Unter vermögenden Leuten ist selten barer Geldeinsatz erforderlich. Ein I O U (d. h. I owe you) auf eine Visitkarte neben die betreffende Summe geschrieben, genügt. Das Verhältnis der verschiedenen Einsätze bei einer Wette oder der Unterschied zwischen denselben wird *odds* genannt. — *Boxing matches*. Das Boxen oder der Faustkampf ist auch jetzt noch ein beliebter Sport der Engländer, wird aber nicht mehr mit demselben Eifer gepflegt, wie vor zwei oder drei Dezennien. Unter gentlemen kommt eine ernsthafte Boxerei in unseren Tagen selten vor, häufig jedoch in der unteren Volksschichte. Der Engländer nennt das Boxen 'the noble art of self-defence" und ist stolz darauf, dafs er sich im Kampfe zwischen Mann und Mann keiner Waffe bedient. Das Boxen ist kein Schlagen, sondern nur Stofsen. Es giebt nur einen einzigen Schlag dabei (den *rounder*), entweder über den Arm des Gegners hinweg auf den Kopf oder, wenn er sich vorlegt, den Schlag von unten herauf. Alle übrigen Angriffe werden nur gestofsen, und zwar mit steifem Handgelenke durch die Faust. Der linke Arm führt gewöhnlich die Stöfse links aus *(left-hander)*, der rechte stöfst nach *(right-hander)*. Nach den Augen und zwischen die Augen wird am liebsten gestofsen, damit der Gegner mit einem sogenannten *black eye* nach Hause zieht. Ein Schlag, der gegen die Gesetze ist, heifst *a foul blow*. Das Boxen wird in England speciell von bestellten Boxkundigen gelehrt und auf den Universitäten geübt. Man bedient sich bei den Übungen, um das Gesicht zu schonen, der *boxing-gloves*, das sind ausgepolsterte grofse Handschuhe. Bei einem ordentlichen, ernstlichen Faustkampfe giebt es aufser den Kämpfern noch Sekundanten *(by-standers)* und einen Unparteiischen *(umpire* oder *time-keeper)*, der u. a. die Pause zwischen jedem einzelnen Gange *(round)* bestimmt. Unter den Zusehern giebt es viele, die auf den einen oder den anderen Kämpfer wetten *(backers)*. Die Wetten *(stakes)* sind oft sehr hoch. Soweit das Boxen eine Volkssitte ist und als Äufserung des Ehrgefühls auftritt, läfst die Polizei die Ausübung desselben gewöhnlich ruhig gewähren. Dagegen sind die Preisfaustkämpfe *(prize fights)* jetzt verboten. Vgl. Anm. z. S. 61. — *horse races*. Fast jede Grafschaft hat ihr jährliches Herbst- oder Frühjahrsrennen. Am berühmtesten sind die *Derby-races* bei Epsom in Surrey (15 engl. Meilen südwestl. von London). Sie finden regelmäfsig den letzten Mittwoch, Donnerstag und Freitag im Mai statt; der Mittwoch ist gewöhnlich der eigentliche Derbytag. Selbst das Parlament läfst an diesem Tage die Sitzungen entfallen. Der Tag des Derby-Rennens kann als der nationale Karneval bezeichnet werden. Es findet von London aus eine wahre Völkerwanderung dahin statt, und zwar will es die Sitte, dafs man nicht mit der Eisenbahn, sondern zu Wagen dahinfährt. Diese Ausfahrt zu Epsom, oder noch besser die Rückkehr von dem Rennen allein schon ist sehenswert. Am Rennorte selbst ist für Lustbarkeiten aller Art gesorgt, so dafs das ganze einer grofsartigen Kirchweihe gleicht. Die zusammenströmende Menge kann auf ungefähr 300.000 Köpfe geschätzt werden, die so ziemlich alle Gesellschaftsklassen repräsentieren. Es giebt verschiedene Arten von Rennen. Da ist zunächst das *handicap*, ein Rennen, an dem die Pferde von allen Altern und Kräften teilnehmen, aber die Reiter verschieden beschwert werden, so dafs die Chancen möglichst gleich sind. Ein Rennen, bei dem geflochtene Zäune als Hindernis aufgestellt sind, ist das *hurdle-race*. Bei dem *steeple-chase* wird eine bestimmte Strecke Landes mit allen von der Natur gebotenen Hindernissen durchlaufen, wobei häufig ein Kirchturm *(steeple)* das Ziel abgiebt. Ein Rennen zwischen Pferden, die noch nicht gesiegt haben, nennt man *maiden-stakes;* Rennen zwischen zwei Pferden allein *match*. Das Pferd, auf welches bei einem Rennen die gröfste Hoffnung gesetzt wird, heifst *favourite*. Der das Rennen veranstaltende Verein giebt ein Programm mit allen Details heraus. Auf dem Rennplatze überwacht ein Komitee die Beobachtung der Renngesetze. Am Rennstall steht der Wieger, der die Reiter sammt ihren Sätteln abwiegt, auf erhöhtem Gerüste an der Bahn der *starter*, welcher durch Senken einer Flagge das Zeichen zum Ablaufe *(start)* der Pferde giebt; am Gewinnpfosten steht der Richter, welcher den Sieger bestimmt. — *cock fights*. Der Hahnenkampf ist ein alter Nationalsport der Engländer. Gegenwärtig unterliegt er einer Geldstrafe von 5 l, kommt aber noch immer vor, namentlich in den Kohlendistrikten des nördlichen England (Blaine's Encyclopaedia of Rural Sports). — *gentlemen of the fancy* = sportsmen; fancy = the favourite sports or pastime of a man. Webster. — *brought upon the parish* etwa "der Gemeinde zur Last fallen wird". Die Armenverwaltung liegt in England in den Händen des Staates; die Kirchspiele *(parishes)* sind die ordentlichen Organe und Bezirke dieser Verwaltung. — **126.** *prize-fighting*, s. o. bei *boxing-matches*. — *catch* Rundgesang, a humorous canon or round, so contrived that the singers catch up each other's sentences. — *quarter-staff* = a stout staff used as a weapon of defence, so called from the manner of using it, one hand being placed in the middle and the other half way between the middle and end. (Webster.) — *Washington Irving* (ŭɔ̃sintn ɜ̃wĭŋ) s. S. 444.

127. *Hyde Park* im Westend, bildet mit den *Kensington Gardens* — so heifst der kleinere westliche Teil der Anlagen — den gröfsten Park Londons, indem er bei einer Länge von fast 1¹/₄ und einer Breite von ³/₄ engl. Meilen einen Flächenraum von mehr als 200 Hektaren einnimmt. (Der *Hyde Park* allein hat 158 Hektare.) Er wurde von Heinrich VIII. angelegt. Die *Serpentine*, ein künstlicher, lang hingestreckter, gekrümmter Teich, stammt aus der Zeit Georg's II. Gegenwärtig ist der Park, um welchen sich ringsherum ein hohes eisernes Gitter zieht, einer der belebtesten von London. Aufser zahlreichen kleineren Eingängen für Fufsgänger hat er neun Haupteingänge für Wagen und Pferde. Die zwei wichtigsten von diesen Eingängen, die um 12 Uhr nachts geschlossen und um 5 Uhr früh geöffnet werden, sind an der Südostecke, gegen *Piccadilly*, *Hyde Park Corner* und an der Nordostecke, gegen *Oxford Street*, *Cumberland Gate* mit dem *Marble Arch*. Während der 'Season', die von April bis August dauert und mit der Tagung des Parlamentes zusammenfällt, findet sich zu bestimmten Stunden des Tages die vornehme Welt zu Pferde oder Wagen hier ein. Beliebt ist der Park auch zur Abhaltung von Meetings. — *Rotten Row* (soll aus *Route du roi* entstanden sein), der berühmte Reitweg, *bridle road*, welcher von *Hyde Park Corner* bis *Queen's Gate* sich ausdehnt (Mp. D 2—3). — *horse-traps* = *trappings* Pferdegeschirr, Schmuck. — *the young athletes on the Elgin marbles yonder upon the frieze of the screen*. Auf dem Eingangsthore bei Hyde Park Corner, welches 1828 nach Burton's Plänen erbaut wurde, befinden sich Relief-Figuren, Kopien der berühmten *Elgin marbles*. Die *E. m.* sind Reste von Phidias' Parthenon-Fries, die 1801—1803 von Elgin aus Athen gebracht wurden und im Elgin Room des British Museum aufgestellt sind. — *Albert Gate* in Knightsbridge (D 2). — *Belgravia* ist der vornehmste Teil des vornehmen Westend (D E 3). — *bridge* über die Serpentine. - - *Tyburnia* (C 2) vgl. Anm. z. S. 233. — *Life Guards*. Es giebt 2 Garde-Kavallerie-Regimenter, das eine hat eine Kaserne im Hyde Park, das andere ist in Windsor stationiert. — **128.** *man about town* vgl. Anm. z. S. 42. — *with pendent tigers*. *tiger* = a servant in livery who rides with his master. Webst. — '*missus*' (misəz) ohne den Namen sagen die Dienstboten gewöhnlich, wenn sie von der Frau des Hauses sprechen.

Nr. 12. Aus Tom "Brown's Schooldays" von *Thomas Hughes* (hjūz). Dieser wurde 1823 zu Uffington in Berkshire geboren. Er besuchte die Schule zu Rugby. Seine Erlebnisse und Erfahrungen daselbst hat er in höchst anziehender Weise in dem genannten Buche niedergelegt. Hughes war Jurist, Parlamentsmitglied und bekleidet noch jetzt die Stelle eines *Queen's Counsel*. "Tom Brown's Schooldays" gilt nach Defoe's 'Robinson Crusoe' als die beste Erzählung für die englische Knabenwelt. — Zur Erklärung dieses Stückes wurde vor allem die treffliche Ausgabe von Imman. Schmidt in Student's Tauchnitz Edition benützt. Zum Verständnis desselben ist vorher eine kurze Beschreibung des Cricketspieles nöthig, mit welcher der beigegebene Situationsplan zu vergleichen ist. - - *Cricket*, von dem altengl. *crice* (= "Krücke") mit der Diminutivendung *-et* kann mit "Thorballspiel" übersetzt werden. Es handelt sich nämlich um die Verteidigung eines thorähnlichen Males *(wicket)* mit dem Ballholz *(bat)* gegen den, welcher es durch Wurf mit dem Ball angreift. Dazu gehören 2 Parteien von je 11 Spielern *(the eleven)*, jede derselben hat ihren Führer *(captain)*. Es giebt 2 wickets, welche in einer Entfernung von 22 yards (s. Tab. II) einander gegenüberstehen. Ein wicket besteht aus 3 in die Erde gesteckten Pfählen *(stumps)*, auf welche 2 kleine Querhölzer *(bails)* gelegt werden, die bei der leisesten Berührung herabfallen. Die Partei, welche das Spiel anfängt *(has the first innings, goes in)*, beginnt mit den bats, und zwei von ihren batsmen nehmen sofort vor den beiden wickets ihren Platz ein. Es beginnt damit die erste Hälfte des Spieles oder das erste *innings*. Der Gegenpartei fällt das Spiel mit dem Balle zu *(out party)*. Sie stellt den Schlägern einen Ballwerfer *(bowler)* gegenüber, der nach 5 Würfen durch einen anderen bowler abgelöst wird *(is over)*. Die übrigen Mitglieder der out-party, welche sämtlich die Aufgabe haben, den nach allen Richtungen fliegenden Ball baldmöglichst in die Hände des Ballwerfers zurückzubringen, verteilen sich in einer bestimmten Weise über das Feld (Aufpasser *fielders)*. Die Kunst des Spielens seitens der batsmen besteht nun darin, teils die wickets gegen den von den bowlers geworfenen Ball zu schützen, indem sie das *bat* vor das wicket halten *(to block)*, teils — und das ist die Hauptsache — den Ball mit dem bat zu treffen und soweit als möglich ins Feld hinauszutreiben. Die Zeit, in welcher der Ball vom wicket entfernt ist, benützen die batsmen, um von ihren Standpunkten aus jeder nach dem entgegengesetzten wicket und wieder zurück zu laufen *(to cross)*, und dies so oft zu wiederholen

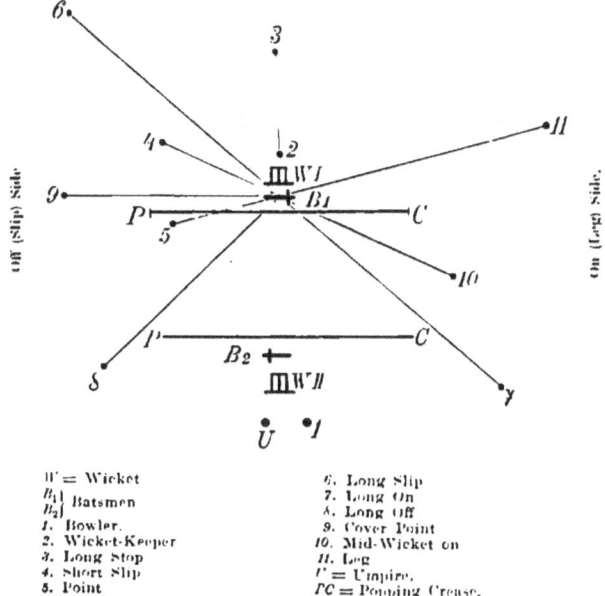

W = Wicket
B₁ } Batsmen
B₂ }
1. Bowler.
2. Wicket-Keeper
3. Long Stop
4. Short Slip
5. Point

6. Long Slip
7. Long On
8. Long Off
9. Cover Point
10. Mid-Wicket on
11. Leg
U = Umpire.
PC = Popping Crease.

als möglich, bevor der Ball an das zunächst liegende wicket befördert ist, so dafs einer von der Gegenpartei dasselbe mit dem Balle berühren könnte. Geschieht dies, bevor die Schläger wieder am wicket sind oder wenigstens die Spitze des *bat* hinter dem *Popping Crease* (Grenze für die batsmen, s. Situationsplan) haben, so mufs derjenige Schläger abtreten *(is out)*, der dem so berührten wicket am nächsten ist. Ein anderes Mitglied seiner Partei nimmt seinen Platz ein und so fort, bis mit der Niederlage des zehnten batsman das innings sein Ende erreicht; denn der elfte Schläger hat dann keinen Partner mehr und mufs abtreten. Hierauf werden die Rollen gewechselt, die zweiten Elfe schicken ihre batsmen vor die wickets, und die Partei, welche früher die wickets verteidigte, übernimmt jetzt das Ballwerfen. Die Kunst seitens der *bowlers* und ihrer systematisch über den Kampfplatz verteilten Genossen (vgl. d. Situationsplan) besteht darin, teils die wickets mit dem Balle niederzuwerfen, teils durch geschicktes Fangen und Werfen des vom bat getroffenen Balles die batsmen so viel als möglich zu verhindern, ihre Plätze durch Laufen zwischen den wickets zu wechseln. Jeder Lauf *(run)* zwischen den wickets zählt für die Partei der batsmen, jedes fallende wicket für die Partei der bowlers. Um Mifsverständnisse zu vermeiden, wird jedes fallende wicket, jeder erfolgreiche run von den Schiedsrichtern *(umpire)* auf einer Tafel notiert *(to score)*. Es ist keine bestimmte Zahl von Points erforderlich. Diejenige Partei, welche binnen einer bestimmten Zeit die meisten gezählt hat, hat gewonnen. Bei einem Wettspiele *(match)* erhält jede Partei 2 innings. Noch ist zu bemerken, dafs ein Cricketball, obgleich von Leder, hart wie ein Stein ist, weshalb die batsmen sich durch lederne Beinschienen *(pads)* und starke Lederhandschuhe zu schützen suchen. Zum An- und Auskleiden pflegt ein Zelt aufgeschlagen zu werden. Das Signal zum Anfange des Spieles giebt der Ruf des Schiedsrichters 'Play!' Das Wort für den Schlag, den der batsman gegen den Ball führt, ist *hit*. Doch giebt es verschiedene Arten von Schlägen und daher auch verschiedene Namen. Darüber, wie über andere Einzelheiten vgl. die im folgenden bei den betreffenden Schlagwörtern gegebenen Anmerkungen. — *Marylebone* (märlbən) *match*. Der in London bestehende *Marylebone Club* (Marylebone, Bezirk im Nordwesten der Stadt) ist der erste Cricketklub der Welt. Er ist Eigentümer des in Marylebone befindlichen Lord's Cricket Ground (Mp. B. 2), daher heifsen die Mitglieder auch *Lord's men* und eine Partie mit ihnen *Lord's match*. Der Klub sendet Deputationen, um mit Spielern anderer Gegenden *matches* abzuhalten. — *Wellesburn* in der Grafschaft Warwick. — *the captain of the School eleven* ist eben Tom Brown; diese elf Spieler waren Schüler aus der obersten Klasse der Schule zu Rugby, wo die Cricketpartie abgehalten wird. *Mr. Aislabie* war zu anfang der Vierziger-Jahre Secretary of the Marylebone Club. — *Three Trees*, eine bestimmte Stelle im Schulgarten. — *Bells Life*, Sportzeitschrift. — **129.** *cornopean* (kənoʊpīən) Klapphorn. — *country dance* (vgl. frz. *contre-danse*), s. Anm. z. S. 121. *Figured down several couple.* — *our brave old founder*. Der Verfasser sagt *our*, weil er selbst ein ehemaliger Schüler von Rugby ist. — *Lawrence Sheriff*. Das Gymnasium von Rugby (am Avon in Warwickshire) wurde 1567 von *Lawrence Sheriff*, der, aus dem Orte gebürtig, in London durch Handel wohlhabend geworden war, gegründet und mit bedeutenden Mitteln ausgestattet. Dem Director (head-master) stehen über 20 Professoren (assistant masters) zur Seite. Die Schüler zerfallen in interne, die in Schulgebäuden Kost und Wohnung erhalten, und in externe (day-scholars). In neuerer Zeit ist, wie auch zu anderen alten Gymnasien eine Art Realschule mit Latein, aber ohne Griechisch, hinzugetreten, welche als Modern Side bezeichnet wird und besonders Mathematik und Naturwissenschaften, Französisch und Deutsch berücksichtigt. Ferien sind 4—5 Wochen um Weihnachten, 3—4 um Ostern und 8 im Juli und August. Die Klassen werden wie in Österreich von unten nach oben gezählt, also first form ist die unterste, sixth form die oberste. Gewöhnlich zerfallen sie in 2 Abteilungen, z. B. the lower fifth, the upper fifth. —

Die angesehensten und ältesten höheren Schulen Englands sind Stiftungsschulen (Foundation schools) wie Rugby. Aufserdem gehören hierher Eton (gegr. 1440) a. d. Themse, Windsor gegenüber, in Buckinghamshire, Harrow (1590) in Middlesex 10 Meilen nordw. von London, Westminster (1560) in London, Charterhouse (1611) in London (C. 5–6) u. a. — Vgl. Anm. z. S. 54 *public schools* u. Anm. z. S. 280 Nr. 7. — *Raggles and Johnson*, zwei tüchtige Mitglieder der School eleven, auf die ihr Führer grofse Hoffnungen setzt. — *old Thomas*, der Beschliefser, Schuldiener von Rugby. — *the Doctor* ist Dr. Thomas Arnold, der Rektor der Schule und Verfasser einer römischen Geschichte. — *parting monition*. Nach Schlufs der Schule war der Doktor zu den Seen in Cumberland abgereist, um die Ferien auf seiner dort liegenden Besitzung zu verbringen. Vor seiner Abreise hatte er bestimmt, dafs die Thore um 9 Uhr abends zu schliefsen seien. — *the first over* also die ersten 5 Würfe. — **130.** *Old Bailey* ein alter Herr aus London, der als umpire fungiert. — *The captain, catching up the ball*. Der Führer der out-party hatte die wichtige Rolle des wicket-keeper (s. Situationspl.) übernommen. — *only eighteen runs and three wickets down* heifst nach den oben gegebenen Erläuterungen also: sie (die Gegenpartei, die Marylebone-men) haben schon drei wickets, oder was auf dasselbe hinauskommt, drei ihrer batsmen verloren und erst 18 Läufe gemacht. — *the long-stop* s. Situationsplan. Jack Raggles war bei dem ersten innings, wo die School eleven mit dem Balle spielten, zum long-stop gemacht worden. — '*Swiper Jack*' etwa "Hans der Hauer," war sein Spitzname, weil er der kräftigste Schläger unter seinen Kameraden war, s. w. u. *Swiper* von to swipe für to sweep = to drive at a stroke with celerity and violence (Webster). — *Cover-point* s. Situationspl. — *slashing looking* nach ausgezeichneten Hieben aussehend. — *he steals more runs* etc., d. h. er (der jetzt ins Spiel tretende batsman der Lord's men) macht mehr Läufe als etc. (eben weil er den Ball vorher sehr weit wegschlägt). — *off-hitting* Schlagen des Balls nach offside, d. h. rechts vom Schläger. — *he is never in his ground except when his wicket is down*. Wenn die fielders das wicket umwerfen oder mit dem Ball berühren, ohne dafs der batsman als Deckung davorsteht (is not at home), so mufs dieser abtreten. Der Sinn dieser Stelle ist also: Er ist nie vor dem wicket, sondern immer auf einem Laufe (run) begriffen, aber wenn die fielders sein wicket berühren wollen, ist er schon da. — *he has stolen three byes*, ein vom bowler geworfener, vom batsman nicht zurückgeschlagener Ball, der über das wicket hinfliegt und vom long-stop nicht aufgehalten wird, heifst *a byeball* oder nur *a bye*. Während er so weithin fliegt, gewinnen die batsmen Zeit zum crossing. — *Jack Raggles is furious and begins* etc. Raggles wirft als long-stop den Ball nicht nach dem ihm zunächst befindlichen wicket, wo der gefürchtete Gegner ist, sondern nach dem weiter entfernten wicket, wo dessen Mitspieler steht, in der Hoffnung, dafs die fielders dort das wicket, während es ungedeckt ist, mit dem Balle berühren können. — *he gives no catches to any one*, er läfst keinen von den fielders den Ball fangen. — **131.** *almost wide to the off*, "so dafs er sich beinahe nach rechts (vom Schläger) verläuft." Ein Ball, der sich seitwärts vom Schläger verläuft, so dafs dieser ihn nicht gut erreichen kann, heifst *a wide* und bringt der Schlagpartei einen Point ein. Im vorliegenden Fall macht der Schläger, um den Ball zu treffen, einen Schritt *(steps out)* und schlägt den Ball gerade seitwärts *(cuts it)* dem Cover-point zu. — *deep* weitab vom wicket. *such a catch*. Wenn ein fielder, wie hier der cover-point, einen vom batsman geschlagenen Ball aus der Luft fängt *(to catch)*, so mufs der batsman abtreten. — *the captain stamped the next man off a leg-shooter* Ein *leg-shooter* ist ein Ball, der nach der *leg-side* des

Schlägers, also links von ihm läuft. Der Schläger hatte diesen Ball nicht pariert. Der captain, der noch wicket-keeper ist, hatte ihn aufgefangen, mit demselben das wicket berührt und daher den Schläger "aus"gemacht *(stumped him off)*. — *slow lobs* langsam gerollte Bälle, d. h. der Ball ruht auf der Hand und wird etwa wie beim Kegeln geworfen. Üblicher ist *fast bowling*, wobei der Arm des Werfenden einen Bogen von rechts nach links beschreibt, indem die Hand bis zur Schulterhöhe erhoben wird. — *how Rugby was only four behind in the first innings*. Die School eleven hatten im ersten innings nur vier Läufe weniger zu verzeichnen als die Lord's men: sie hatten also 94 gemacht. — *the cover-point hitter*, jener ausgezeichnete Spieler der Lord's men, welcher nach der Seite des cover-point geschlagen hatte, s. o. — *topping* unübertrefflich. — *the stumps must be drawn*, die Pfähle müssen herausgezogen werden, d. h. die Partie muß zu Ende sein. — *chorus*, hier als Verb gebraucht. — *Master*. Hier ist ein Lehrer der Schule von Rugby gemeint. — 132. *It's more than a game, it's an institution*. Dies ist eine von Cricketspielern oft mit Stolz citierte Stelle. Über die Bedeutung des Cricket sagt Althaus im 2. B. seiner Englischen Charakterbilder: 'Eine im wahrhaften Sinne nationale Bedeutung ist einem Ballspiele zuzuschreiben, von dem man ohne Übertreibung behaupten kann, daß an großartigem Umfange des Verbreitungskreises und Unbegrenztheit der Popularität, wie an national belebendem Einflusse kein Volksspiel alter oder neuer Zeit ihm zu vergleichen ist: dem weitberühmten, über die ganze angelsächsische Erde in Europa, Asien, Afrika, Amerika und Australien verbreiteten, das gesamte angelsächsische Volkstum umfassenden und verbindenden *cricket*.' — *habeas corpus*, s. Anm. z. S. 165. — *foot-ball* ist ein altes Spiel, das sich besonders für die Wintermonate eignet und in vielen englischen Schulen geübt wird. Zwei an Zahl gleiche Parteien stehen an zwei Malen (goals) einander gegenüber in einer Entfernung von 80—100 Yards, auf jedem Male befinden sich zwei je zwei bis drei Fuß von einander entfernte Stangen. Der mit festem Leder überzogene hohle Gummiball wird in die Mitte geworfen und muß mit dem Fuße durch die beiden Stäbe des feindlichen Males getrieben werden. Um dies zu verhindern, stellen sich die Mitglieder jeder Partei in zwei Treffen hinter einander auf: im vorderen Treffen stehen gewöhnlich die größeren Spieler, im Hintertreffen die kleineren. Das Vordertreffen hat den Ball den Gegnern zuzutreiben oder anzugreifen, das Hintertreffen hat das eigene *goal* zu verteidigen. Das Gedränge und Handgemenge *(scrimmage)* beim foot-ball-Spiel pflegt sehr hitzig zu sein. — *fives* ist ein Ballspiel, für welches es in größeren Schulen Englands sogenannte fives'-courts giebt. Eine glatte Wand bildet deren Hintergrund, auf welcher im rechten Winkel Seitenwände in gleichen Entfernungen von einander abstehen. Der in der Regel cementierte Boden ist durch eine mit der Hinterwand parallele Linie geteilt, der an die Mauer stoßende Teil, der innere Raum genannt, ist gewöhnlich ein paar Zoll erhöht. Etwa 4 Fuß über dem Boden hat die Hinterwand eine wagrechte deutlich markierte Linie. Die Spieler theilen sich in zwei Parteien. Die Bälle sind klein und hart und werden mit sogenannten rackets (Schlagnetzen) geworfen. Ein Spieler der Partei im inneren Raume (the in party) wirft den Ball auf den Boden und schlägt ihn im Aufspringen gegen die Hinterwand, so daß er oberhalb des markierten Striches anprallt. Er muß von der anderen Partei (the out party) entweder, während er zurückfliegt, oder wenigstens beim ersten Aufspringen vom Boden wieder nach der Hinterwand hingeschlagen werden, und zwar oberhalb des Striches. Schlägt eine Partie den Ball entweder unter die Linie, oder nach mehr als einmaligem Aufspringen von der Erde, oder über die Grenze hinaus, so zählt die Gegenpartei ein Point. Es wird bis zu 15 Points gezählt (Fifteen = 3 fives, davon der Name des Spiels). — *hare and hounds*. Ein Knabe oder mehrere stellen Hasen vor, denen sechs Minuten Vorsprung gegeben werden. Wer von den 'Hunden' eine Viertelstunde nach den 'Hasen' an einer bestimmten Stelle ist, zählt zu den Siegern. Die Verfolgung wird durch Papierschnitzel geleitet, welche die Hasen während des Laufes aus einem mitgenommenen Beutel ausstreuen. Dabei suchen sie durch Hecken, Gräben u. dgl. den Verfolgenden möglichst viel Hindernisse zu bereiten. — *which don't he wish* etc. ohne relative Verknüpfung im Deutschen: Wünscht er nicht, dafs er sie erwerben möge? — *having run for a forward drive of Johnson's*. Raggles hat mit dem zweiten batsman Johnson den Platz gewechselt, nachdem dieser den Ball nach der Richtung des bowler *(a forward drive)* getrieben hatte. Er steht also jetzt am angegriffenen wicket. — *they run two for a leg-bye*. Johnson und Raggles machen zwei Läufe, während der Ball, von Jack's Bein abprallend, über das wicket hinwegfliegt *(leg-bye)*. — *pitched ball, to pitch* sagt man, wenn der Ball, nachdem er etwa drei Viertel der Strecke durchflogen hat, auf den Boden aufsetzt und dann erst gegen das Mal anprallt. — *hits right round to leg for five*. Den auf den rechten Stab des Mals *(outer stump)* zuspringenden Ball schlug Jack im Bogen *(round)* nach der Leg-Seite, und zwar so weit, dafs er unterdessen mit dem anderen batsman fünfmal den Platz wechseln konnte. Mit der Präposition *for* wird immer die Anzahl der runs verbunden. — *It is 'over' now*, der Augenblick im Cricket-spiele, wo nach dem Werfen von fünf Bällen ein neuer bowler an die Reihe kommt (s. o. einleit. Beschreibung). Dies ist jetzt der schon bekannte cover-point hitter, ein ausgezeichneter alter Spieler. Nach dem *over* wechselt der bowler gewöhnlich das wicket, d. h. er geht hinter W I und greift W II an; mit ihm wechseln sämtliche Spieler der *out party*, die fielders, ihre Stellungen und nehmen die entsprechenden um W II an. Raggles stand jetzt am angegriffenen wicket, dem cover-point hitter gegenüber. — *slow-twisters*. *twister* ist ein Ball, der mit dem *twist* geworfen ist, d. h. einer besonderen Drehung der Hand, vermöge welcher der Ball nicht geradeaus, sondern im Bogen fliegt und namentlich beim Aufsetzen auf die Erde (pitch) eine andere Richtung nimmt. Jack kennt diesen Kniff nicht *(if he had only allowed for the twist, but he hasn't)*. — 133. *spin*. Hier Substantiv, von der Drehung des Balles gesagt. — *You can't think what I owe him*. Diese Worte beziehen sich auf das Freundschaftsverhältnis zwischen Tom Brown und Arthur. — *he makes here a two, and there a one*, vom geschlagenen Balle gesagt, je nach der Anzahl der dadurch gewonnenen runs. — *backs up* = supports. — *'un* = one. — *nine runs to make and two wickets to go down*. Also die School eleven haben noch zwei batsmen *(Johnson* und der noch übrige *Winter)*, und nur mehr neun runs zu machen, wenn sie gewinnen wollen. Es bringt sie nun in Verzweiflung, dafs der erwartete Sieg ihnen durch die Abfahrt der Gegner entrissen wird. — *Winter and Johnson carry out their bats*. Endigt das Spiel, ohne dafs die letzten batsmen *out* gemacht wurden, so nehmen sie zum Zeichen, dafs sie nicht besiegt worden sind, das bat mit hinaus.

134. Nr. 13. *like Doctor Johnson you like to dine*. Von Johnson ist bekannt, dafs er gerne gut und viel afs. vgl. S. 2, Nr. 3. — *patties* Pastetchen. — *exhausted receiver* ausgepumpte Luftpumpe. — *Toffee*, geschrieben auch toffey und toffy, brauner Stangenzucker. — *'ecad,'* vgl. Anm. zu 56. wery. — *fingerglass* = a glass to hold water for the use of the fingers at a dinner table. Webster. — *castors* casters. Fläschchen mit Pfeffer, Olivenöl, Essig u. dgl.

136. *social and political differences* etc., vgl. S. 292 ff. — 137. *one of the Scotch kings* etc. Jakob I., 1603. — 139. *Cymry*. So nennen sich noch jetzt die

Nationaleinwohner von Wales. — *United Kingdom*. Schottland wurde mit England durch ein gemeinsames Parlament 1707 vereinigt; 1801 trat Irland in das gemeinsame Parlament ein. — *J. R. Green*. John Richard G., geb. 1837, gest. als Bibliothekar in Lambeth i. J. 1883, schrieb 'A Short History of the English People' (1874), die er später zu der umfänglicheren 'History of the English People' erweiterte; aufserdem mit Alice Stopford Green 'A Short Geography of the British Isles,' woraus unser Lesestück entlehnt ist. u. a.

140. *Lords Spiritual and Lords Temporal*. Zu den *Lords Spiritual* gehören 2 Erzbischöfe und 24 Bischöfe der englischen Staatskirche, zu den *Lords Temporal* 287 Lords aus England, die die Pairwürde erblich besitzen, 43 ebensolche aus Schottland, 78 aus Irland; ferner kommen hinzu 16 Lords, welche Schottland für jedes einzelne Parlament wählt, und 28 irische Lords, die auf Lebenszeit gewählt werden. Das Oberhaus zählt also 452 Mitglieder. — *woolsack*, ein grofser, viereckiger, mit rotem Tuch bedeckter Polstersitz ohne Rücken- und Seitenlehne. — *The House of Commons* etc. Seit 1885 beträgt die Zahl der Mitglieder 670; davon kommen auf England 465 (London 61), Wales 30, Schottland 72 und auf Irland 103. — *freehold property*. Darunter versteht man einen Besitz auf Lebenszeit, während unter *other holdings* nur Besitzrechte auf Zeit gemeint sind. — **141.** *'into committee.'* Man hat zu unterscheiden Select Committees (Ausschüsse von gewöhnlich 15 Mitgliedern) und Committee of the Whole House. Letzteres ist nichts anderes als das Unterhaus selbst; nur wird die Debatte mehr im Konversationston geführt, und es ist dem einzelnen Redner gestattet, öfter das Wort zu ergreifen. — **142.** *the Cabinet*. Dasselbe besteht mindestens aus: 1. Dem Premier oder First Lord of the Treasury; 2. Lord Chancellor; 3. Lord President of the (Privy) Council; 4. Home Secretary; 5. Foreign Secretary; 6. Colonial Secretary; 7. Indian Secretary; 8. Secretary of War; 9. Chancellor of the Exchequer; 10. First Lord of the Admiralty. Es können aber auch noch 12 andere Würdenträger dem Kabinette angehören (vgl. Wendt, England).

143. *Solway Firth*. Vom S. F. im Südwesten zieht sich die schottische Grenze zum Flusse Tweed nach Nordosten. Nördlich vom Tweed der *Firth of Forth*. Gegenüber, also im Westen, der *Firth of Clyde*. — *Agricola*. C. Julius A. (40—93 n. Chr.). Schwiegervater des Tacitus, röm. Staatsmann und Feldherr, der eigentliche Begründer der röm. Macht in Britannien, wo er von 77—85 Statthalter war. — *Caledonian* (lat.) schottisch. — **144.** *Queensferry* nordwestlich von Edinburgh. — *Fife*, die Halbinsel zwischen dem Firth of Forth und dem Firth of Tay. — *Perth* an der Mündung des Tayflusses. — A. D. = Anno Domini. — *Mackenzie* (məke'nzi) Henry M. (1745—1831), schottischer Romanschriftsteller und Essayist.

146. Nr. 3. Eduard der Bekenner, der letzte der angelsächsischen Könige, war ohne Leibeserben gestorben. Nach seinem Tode usurpierte Harald, der Sohn Godwin's und Schwager Eduard's, den englischen Thron. Dagegen behauptete Wilhelm von der Normandie, dafs ihm König Eduard bei Gelegenheit eines Besuches in London die englische Krone versprochen habe. Er landete am 27. September 1066 angeblich mit 60.000 Mann zu Pevensey bei Hastings und lieferte hier seinem Nebenbuhler am 14. Oktober die berühmte blutige Schlacht, welche für England und sein Volk von fundamentaler Bedeutung ist. — **147.** *Mal signe est ci* altfranz. = das ist ein böses Zeichen. — *Northumbria* ist das ganze England nördlich vom Humber. — *Wäs-heal* ist das ae. wes hâl ('sei heil'). Daraus ist das ne. *wassail* (Festtrunk, Trinkgelage, Trinklied) entstanden. Ursprünglich war es ein Trinkspruch. *Drink-heal* ist die Antwort darauf. — **148.** *St. Calixtus* ein Bischof von Rom, der 223 getötet wurde. Sein Fest fällt auf den 14. Oktober. —

Immediately before the duke rode Taillefer etc. Vgl. aus Uhland's 'Taillefer': 'Der Taillefer ritt vor allem Normannenheer Auf einem hohen Pferde mit Schwert und mit Speer; Er sang so herrlich, das klang über Hastingsfeld; Von Roland sang er und manchem frommen Held.' — *the lay of Charlemagne and Roland*. Das Rolandlied ist das bedeutendste altfranz. Epos. Es stammt aus dem 11. Jahrh. Für die Verbreitung und Beliebtheit des Liedes unter den Franzosen zeugt, was hier von Taillefer berichtet wird, und was zuerst Wace in seinem anglonormannischen 'Roman de Rou' (12. Jahrhundert) gelegentlich der Beschreibung der Schlacht von Hastings berichtet: Taillefer, qui moult (très) bien cantout (chantait) Sur un cheval qui tost alout (allait vite), Devant le duc alout cantant, De Karlemaine et de Rolant, E d'Olivier e des vassals, Ki (qui) mururent en Renchevals. *Taillefer* heifst wörtlich: Schneid das Eisen. — *guerdon* (gerdn) Belohnung. — 149. *Bayeux* in der Normandie in der Nähe von Caen. — *target* "Tartsche." — *point-blank* eig. in den weifsen Mittelpunkt der Scheibe, also 'schnurgerade.' Cassell, p. 35, 711 u. ö. — 150. *Palgrave* (pälgrow) s. S. 446. — Nr. 4. *Here commences the history of the English nation*. Macaulay meint, dafs mit der Trennung der Normandie von England unter Johann, mit dem gemeinsamen Vorgehen des Adels und Volkes gegen diesen König, kurz mit der Vermischung der normannischen und englischen Rasse die Geschichte des heutigen englischen Volkes beginne. Gegen diesen Satz ist das ganze Werk Freeman's: 'The History of the Norman Conquest of England' ein grofser Protest. Er beginnt mit den Worten: 'The Norman Conquest is the great turning-point in the history of the English nation.' — *when John became king* s. Tab. IV. — 151. *his grandson* ist Eduard I. — *House of Commons*. Im 49. Regierungsjahre Heinrich's III., 1265, wurde ein Parlament gehalten, zu welchem durch königliche Erlässe 122 Prälaten und Geistliche und 22 Grafen und Barone einberufen, und die Sheriffs Ritter, die Städte und Marktflecken Bürger, und die fünf Häfen (s. u.) Repräsentanten abzuordnen angewiesen wurden. Man sieht diese Versammlung gewöhnlich als den Anfang des Hauses der Gemeinen an. Die Trennung der Lords und Gemeinen trat erst um 1340 ein. — *Common Law* das alte englische Gewohnheitsrecht, welches schon vor der normannischen Eroberung bestand. — *the imperial jurisprudence* das römische Civilrecht. — *Cinque Ports* (siŋkpōts) = Hastings, Romney, Dover, Hythe, Sandwich. Zu den fünf Häfen sind später Winchelsea, Seaford und Rye hinzugefügt worden. Die Bürger dieser Hafenstädte waren verpflichtet, dem Könige eine Anzahl Schiffe beizustellen, wofür ihnen bedeutende Vorrechte eingeräumt waren. — *both the great national seats of learning*. Gemeint sind die zwei Universitäten Oxford und Cambridge. St. Peter's College wurde im Jahre 1257 gegründet. Vgl. Anm. zu S. 102. — *Then was formed that language*. Macaulay hat die Zeit vom Ende des 12. bis zur Mitte des 13. Jahrhunderts im Auge. Aus dieser Zeit (*'the first faint dawn'*) stammen Werke, welche vom sprachgeschichtlichen Standpunkte sehr wichtig sind. — *the most splendid and the most durable of the many glories of England*. Vgl. S. 298, Z. 21. — *three branches of the great Teutonic family*. M. meint Saxons, Danes, Normans; allerdings waren die letzteren in Frankreich zu Franzosen geworden. — *Macaulay* (mokŏlī) s. S. 445.

152. Nr. 5. *Second year*, im zweiten Jahre des 3. Kreuzzuges, also 1191. — *Acre* (e'kǝ) Accon. — *Philip Augustus*, König von Frankreich, regierte 1180 bis 1223. — *Franks* und *Latins* zur Bezeichnung der europäischen, röm.-kath. Christen; Latins wurden sie genannt zum Unterschiede von den Anhängern der griechischen (morgenländischen) Kirche. — *duke of Burgundy*, namens Hugo. — 153. *brother Conrad of Montferrat*. Konrad, Markgraf von Montferrat, Herzog von Tyrus, machte

auch auf den Thron von Jerusalem Anspruch und wurde darin von dem französischen Könige unterstützt, während Richard Löwenherz dagegen war. Konrad wurde 1190, auf Befehl des Alten vom Berge, des Hauptes der Assassinen, erdolcht. — *Tyre* (taiə) Tyrus. — *Caesarea* (sɔzəri'ə) jetzt Kaisarieh. — *Jaffa* (džafə) jetzt Joppe. — *kingdom of Lusignan*, Königreich von Jerusalem, das von Guido von Lusignan regiert wurde. — *Unitarians*, diejenigen, welche im Gegensatze zu den Christus als Gott Verehrenden auf die Anbetung eines einigen Gottes dringen. — **154.** *Orlando or Amadis*. Orlando der Held in Ariost's (1474—1533) Epos 'Orlando Furioso.' Amadis der Held zahlreicher Ritterromane. Um die Mitte des 14. Jahrh. in Portugal entstanden, wurde der Amadis-Roman in fast allen europäischen Sprachen bearbeitet. — *a perfidious rival* ist Philipp August von Frankreich. — **155.** *Tripoli* (tripoli) und *Antioch* (ä'ntiok) waren dem Königreich Jerusalem lehenspflichtig. — *Richard embarked for Europe* etc. Richard schiffte sich am 8. Oktober 1192 zu Ptolomais ein. Seine Gefangenschaft in Österreich ist bekannt. Im Jahre 1194 kam er nach England zurück und starb am 6. April 1199 infolge einer Wunde, die er in einer Privatfehde mit dem Vicomte Vidomar von Limoges erhalten hatte. Cassell, p. 311, 144. — *Gibbon* (gibn) s. S. 431.

Nr. 6. *Windsor* in Berkshire an der Themse, 20 engl. Meilen westl. von London. Sehenswert namentlich das oberhalb des Ortes liegende großartige Residenz-Schloß der Königin, welches ursprünglich von Wilhelm dem Eroberer erbaut, von späteren Königen erweitert und in neuerer Zeit von Georg IV. und der Königin Victoria in einer Weise restauriert wurde, daß es jetzt eines der größten und prächtigsten Königsschlösser ist. — *Staines* an der Themse, in der Grafschaft Middlesex. — **155.** *The privileges granted to the clergy*. Das wichtigste der der Geistlichkeit zugestandenen Privilegien war die Besetzung erledigter Pfründen durch die freie Wahl, ohne Beeinflussung von Seite des Königs. — *reliefs* sind Anfallsgelder, welche der Lehensmann zahlt und dadurch anerkennt, daß er sein Lehen nur unter der Bedingung der Heerespflicht besitzt. — *tenants*. Noch heute sind alle Grundeigenthümer nur *tenants* der Krone; es hat aber dieses Verhältnis für dieselbe nur die praktische Folge des Heimfalls; es tritt ein, wenn der Besitzer eines Grundstückes ohne Testament und zugleich ohne erbberechtigte Verwandte stirbt. — *tenants in chief* sind solche weltliche oder geistliche Kronvasallen, die ihr Gebiet unmittelbar vom König zu Lehen tragen. — *heirs were to be married without disparagement*. Der Lehensherr hatte als Vormund über seine weiblichen Mündel das Recht, diesen eine ihm passend scheinende Vermählung vorzuschlagen, und er konnte sich, falls diese sich weigerten, auf solchen Vorschlag einzugehen, für etwaige ihm dadurch erwachsende Verluste an dem Erbe schadlos halten. — *scutages* Schildgelder sind eine Abgabe, welche die Kronvasallen anstatt der Stellung von Dienstmannen zu zahlen haben. — *Aids* sind die bei besonderen Veranlassungen auferlegten Abgaben. — **156.** *Common Pleas* eigentliche Civilsachen. Der Sitz dieses Gerichtshofes war Westminster. vgl. Anm. zu S. 165 King's Bench. — *Hume* (hjūm) s. S. 430.

157. *difficult circumstances* vgl. S. 99. — *wise ministers*. Der bedeutendste unter ihnen war William Cecil, Lord Burleigh. — *brave warriors*. Hier ist namentlich an die Seehelden Sir Francis Drake und Thomas Cavendish zu denken.

158. *Maria*. Maria Stuart, Tochter Jakob's V. von Schottland und der Maria von Guise, durch ihre Großmutter Margarete Urenkelin Heinrich's VII. von England, wurde am französischen Hofe *('that perfidious court')* erzogen. Sie war zuerst vermählt mit Franz II. von Frankreich (1559—60) und übernahm nach dem Tode ihres Gemahls die Regierung in Schottland. 1566 heiratete sie ihren Vetter Darnley und 1567 dessen Mörder Bothwell. Darauf Aufstand der Schotten. Maria entflieht nach England, wo sie bis 1587 gefangen gehalten und endlich in Fotheringhay in Northamptonshire als Verschwörerin gegen das Leben Elisabeth's hingerichtet wird — **159.** *Brantome.* Pierre de Bourdeille, Seigneur de B., französischer Krieger und Höfling des 16. Jahrhunderts, ist bekannt durch seine Memoiren, welche für die Geschichte seiner Zeit wertvoll sind. Cassell. p. 362 u. ö. — *Robertson* (rɔbətsn) s. S. 431.

Nr. 9. *Philip of Spain.* Philipp II. von Spanien regierte 1556—1598. — *Mary Stuart,* s. S. 157. — *States,* die durch die Utrechter Konvention (1549) vereinigten Niederlande. — *Parma.* Alexander Farnese von Parma (1546—1592), ein staatskluger Fürst und trefflicher Feldherr. — *Tagus* (te'gəs) Tajo, einer der Hauptflüsse der pyrenäischen Halbinsel. — *Drake.* Francis D., ein berühmter Seemann, 1539 geb., wurde 1581 von Elisabeth zum Ritter ernannt. Er starb 1595. Drake soll die Kartoffeln zuerst nach Europa gebracht haben. Andere schreiben dies Verdienst Raleigh zu; vgl. S. 83. — *Vigo* (spr. wigə), befestigte Seestadt in der spanischen Provinz Pontevedra. — *Santiago* (sänti̇e"go) auf den Inseln des grünen Vorgebirges. — *San Domingo, Cartagena* in Westindien. — *Faro,* Hauptstadt der portugiesischen Provinz Algarve. — *Corunna* (kərʌnə), Hauptstadt der gleichnamigen Provinz, an der Nordwestküste Spaniens gelegen. — *Ferrol,* Seestadt und Festung in der spanischen Provinz Corunna. — *the twenty-ninth of July* des Jahres 1588. — *Lizard* (lizəd), Vorgebirge an der Südwestspitze der englischen Grafschaft Cornwall, der südlichste Punkt Englands. — *Leicester* (lestə) s. Anm. zu S. 51. — *Tilbury.* Fort Tilbury, das bedeutendste Festungswerk der unteren Themse, Gravesend gegenüber, gilt als der Schlüssel von London. — **160.** *Lord Howard.* Charles H. (1536—1624) diente als 'Lord High Admiral' auch noch unter Jakob I. — *Plymouth* (plimǝth) in Devonshire, jetzt infolge seines grofsartigen, durch Festungswerke wohl verteidigten Hafens eine der wichtigsten Seestädte Englands. Pl. hat 63.000 Einwohner, erzeugt namentlich Segeltuch, Seife und Stärke und ist der Geburtsort von Francis Drake. — *Hawkins.* Sir John H. (1520—1595) war der erste Engländer, welcher Sklaven von Afrika nach Westindien brachte. Im Jahre 1573 trat er in die königl. Marine über und wurde 1588 für seine Verdienste zum Ritter geschlagen. — **161.** *Frobisher.* Sir Martin F. suchte 1576 eine nordwestliche Durchfahrt nach China und entdeckte eine Meerenge, die er Frobisherstrafse nannte. Sie ist eine der drei Verbindungen zwischen der Davisstrafse und der Hudsonsbai. — *Gravelines* (grävli̇'n), befestigte Seestadt zwischen Dünkirchen und Calais. — *St. Mary Port* = Porto di Santa Maria, bei Cadiz. — *a mightier foe.* Nach dem Untergange der Armada liefs Elisabeth eine Medaille prägen mit der Inschrift: 'Adflavit Deus et dissipantur.' — **162.** *Donegal, Galway* (gɔlu̇ɪ), zwei Meerbusen an der westlichen Küste Irlands. — *Giant's Causeway,* ein natürlicher Damm von Basaltsäulen, an der Küste der irischen Grafschaft Antrim. — *Blaskets.* Inseln in der Nähe der Südwestküste Irlands. — *Sligo* (slaigo), Stadt in der gleichnamigen Grafschaft, südlich vom Donegal-Busen. — *Dunluce,* irländisches Dorf in der Grafschaft Antrim. — Cassell. p. 254, 281, 604. — *Green,* s. Anm. z. S. 139.

Nr. 10. *Exchequer,* s. Anm. z. S. 109. — *James.* Jakob I. (als König von Schottland Jakob VI.), Sohn der Maria Stuart, war ein gelehrter, aber pedantischer und schwacher Fürst. — **163.** *a member of the House of Lords.* Es war Lord Mounteagle. — *November the 5th.* Der 5. November wird noch in einzelnen Grafschaften gefeiert, indem Knaben mit einer Strohpuppe, die Guy Fawkes genannt wird, von Haus zu Haus ziehen und Geld sammeln, für welches sie abends ein Feuerwerk

veranstalten, bei dem die Puppe auf einem Scheiterhaufen verbrannt wird. — *Fawkes was seized.* Er wurde Jänner 1606 hingerichtet. — *Some were killed.* Unter ihnen Robert Catesby in Warwickshire, vgl. Cassell, p.266, 649 u. 5. — J. R. Gardiner (spr. gádna). 'To the best historical literature of the reign of Queen Victoria belongs the series of works in which Professor J. R. Gardiner has studied the reigns of the two earlier Stuart Kings of England.' Morley, Of Engl. Lit. 401.
164. Nr. 11. *obscure birth.* Cromwell war der dritte Sohn einer alten, aber armen Familie zu Huntingdon in der Grafschaft gleichen Namens. — *Cinna,* der aus der röm. Geschichte bekannte Demokrat L. Cornelius C., welcher 87–84 eine Gewaltherrschaft in Rom einführte, ohne Beachtung der Verfassung. — *the humble petition and advice,* eine Bill, die von Cromwell's Freunden im Parlamente eingebracht wurde, um seiner Macht den erforderlichen Bestand zu geben; sie wurde am 23. Februar 1657 angenommen und machte ihn zum Protektor. — *Cony* war ein Kaufmann in London; es handelte sich um einen Zoll auf eingeführte Waren, den die Einnehmer ohne Ermächtigung des Parlamentes erhoben. — *eminent fanatic* Erzfanatiker. — *propriety* Recht. — *subject* Staatsbürger. — **165.** *remembered him,* jetzt: reminded him oder put him in mind. — *the term came. term* Sitzungsperiode des Reichsgerichtes. Es giebt ihrer vier: 1. Hilary sitting vom 11. bis 31. Januar; 2. Easter s. vom 15. April bis 18. Mai; 3. Trinity s. vom 22. Mai bis 12. Juni; 4. Michaelmas s. vom 2. bis 25. November. — *his Habeas Corpus.* Habeas Corpus ist der Name eines alten writ (königl. Schreibens an alle, an die es gelangt), das, vom King's Bench-Gerichte ausgefertigt, mit den Worten begann: habeas corpus ad subjiciendum (d. i. Du hast die Person [des Verhafteten] vor den Richter zu stellen) und bestimmt war, gegen willkürliche Haft zu schützen. Der König fordert dadurch diejenigen, welche einen seiner Unterthanen in Verwahrsam haben, auf, ihn mit Angabe des Tages und der Ursache vor Gericht zu bringen, damit er durch den Richter in Freiheit gesetzt oder in Haft behalten werde. Durch die berühmte Habeas-Corpus-Acte von 1679 wurden die Vorsichtsmaßregeln gegen willkürliche Haft noch erhöht. — *King's Bench.* Nach der im wesentlichen in den Siebziger-Jahren durchgeführten Reform des englischen Rechtswesens bildet das Oberhaus, genauer die *Lords of the Appeal,* die oberste Instanz. Unter dem Oberhause steht der eigentliche Appellhof *(Court of Appeal),* der fast nur aus höheren Richtern besteht und die obere Instanz für das Reichsgericht, *High Court of Justice,* ist. Dieses hat drei Hauptabteilungen, die den alten großen Reichsgerichten entsprechen, nämlich: 1. Die *Chancery Division* entspricht dem alten *Court of Chancery* und befaßt sich besonders mit Verwaltungssachen, vor allem mit der Verwaltung von Hinterlassenschaften. An der Spitze der Chancery Division steht der Lord Chancellor selbst. 2. Die *Queen's Bench Division* entspricht drei älteren Gerichtshöfen, nämlich der *Queen's Bench* (oder früher *King's Bench),* dem *Court of Common Pleas* und dem *Court of Exchequer* (vgl. Anm. z. S. 109, Exchequer). Die beiden letzteren Abteilungen sind eingegangen. Die Queen's Bench Division ist demnach jetzt der große Civilgerichtshof und die höhere Instanz für die unteren Gerichtshöfe. Der Präsident dieser Abteilung heißt *Lord Chief Justice of England.* 3. Die *Probate, Divorce and Admiralty Division* entscheidet über die Giltigkeit von Testamenten, Ehetrennungen und Civilklagen, die sich auf das Seewesen beziehen. Sämtliche Gerichtshöfe befinden sich seit 1882 in dem eigens für dieselben erbauten prachtvollen Justizpalast, *Law Courts,* Strand (C 5), nahe der Stelle, wo diese Straße in Fleet Street übergeht. Die alten Gerichtshöfe von Westminster haben demnach aufgehört zu existieren. Unter dem Reichsgerichte stehen die *Police Courts* (Polizeigerichte) in London und die

County Courts (Grafschaftsgerichte), die über mindere Sachen entscheiden. Der Kläger kann aber seine Sache auch vor das Reichsgericht bringen. Die Verhandlungen vor demselben in London finden in vier Sitzungsperioden statt (s. o. *terms*). Zur Bequemlichkeit des Publikums haben Richter vom Reichsgerichte Rundreisen durch das Land zu unternehmen und dort die Assisentermine abzuhalten. Die Reise und der Bezirk heifsen *circuit*, und England und Wales sind zu dem Zweck in 8 Circuits geteilt. — In Irland ist die Gerichtsverfassung der englischen vollkommen analog, in Schottland weicht sie in vielen Punkten ab. — *council* die Ratsversammlung, und *counsel* der Ratgeber, Anwalt, scheinen hier verwechselt zu sein; der Sinn ist: Maynard, der der Anwalt des Gefangenen (Angeklagten) war. Fafst man aber conncil in seiner Bedeutung 'Rat' (als Kollektiv), so ergäbe sich, dafs Cony mehrere Anwälte hatte. — *Magna charta*, vgl. S. 155. Der § 39 der Magna charta bestimmt, dafs über einen Freien keinerlei Strafen (auch nicht Gefangenhaltung) ohne ordentliches Gericht verhängt werden dürfen. — *Westminster Hall*, Anm. z. S. 174, *place*. — 166. *the life of his jurisdiction* den Kern seiner Autorität. — *the valley of Lucerne*, Luserna bei Pinerolo. Der Streit zwischen den Valdensern in Piemont und dem Herzoge von Savoyen (1655) wurde durch den Einflufs Cromwell's, der auch den König von Frankreich aufforderte, bei dem Herzoge zu vermitteln, zu Gunsten der Valdenser, für die man in England grofse Teilnahme hegte, beigelegt. — *the Cardinal* Mazarin. — *Civita Vecchia*, italienische Seefestung am tyrrhenischen Meere. — *Macchiavel*, Machiavelli (1469—1527), einer der gröfsten Staatsmänner und Geschichtschreiber Italiens. In seinem Hauptwerke 'Il Principe' schildert er einen Fürsten, der ohne Rücksicht auf Moral durch Klugheit und konsequentes Handeln in dem von ihm unterjochten Staate seine Alleinherrschaft zu begründen weifs. — Cassell, p. 415. 131, 449. 418. — 167. *Edward Hyde* (haid) *Earl of Clarendon* (kläröndon) s. S. 412.

Nr. 12. Clarendon hat Cromwell vom Standpunkte des Royalisten geschildert. Nun folgt die Darstellung eines liberal gesinnten Historikers. Sie ist genommen aus dem kritischen Essay Macaulay's über Hallam's Constitutional History of England, Edinburgh Review, September 1828. — *Mr. Hallam*, s. Anm. z. S. 193, Nr. 21. — *Common Law*, s. Anm. z. S. 151. — *Inigo Jones*, s. Anm. z. S. 111. — *Sir Christopher Wren* (1632—1723) ward nach dem grofsen Brande von London (1666) zum Baumeister der Stadt und 1668 zum königlichen Generalarchitekten von England ernannt. Als solcher hat er über 60 Kirchen, darunter St. Paul's Cathedral, und zahlreiche öffentliche Gebäude aufgeführt. — *quitted* = acquitted — 168. *Restoration*, s. Anm. z. S. 118. — 169. *Quaker* (von *quake* zittern), eine religiöse Sekte, so genannt entweder von ihren heftigen, zitternden Bewegungen in ihrem schwärmerischen Religionseifer, oder weil ihr Stifter (George Fox) am Schlusse einer Rede vor dem Richter sprach: Zittert vor dem Worte des Herrn! — *Whitehall* war früher ein königlicher Palast, von dem nur die grofse *Banqueting Hall* erhalten ist. Nach dem Palaste wird jetzt die ganze Strafse genannt, welche von Trafalgar Square nach Westminster führt (Mp. D 4). — 170. *Hale*, wegen seiner unbeugsamen Rechtlichkeit bekannter Rechtsgelehrter. Er diente seinem Lande unter Karl I., Cromwell und Karl II. — *Blake*, Robert B. (1599—1657), einer der gröfsten englischen Seehelden, der mit Erfolg gegen die Holländer und Spanier kämpfte. — *his first Parliament* wurde 1654 einberufen und schon das folgende Jahr wieder aufgelöst. — *its great leader*. Damit ist Blake gemeint. — *Stadthouse* ist das jetzige 'koningklyk Palais' in Amsterdam. — 171. *ungenerous gaoler*. Sir Hudson Lowe behandelte Napoleon auf St. Helena mit grofser Härte

Nr. 13. *Whitelocke* (ůaitlɔk). Sir Bulstrode W. war unter Cromwell Gesandter in Schweden. Nach dessen Tode trat er mit Karl II. in geheime Verbindung. Er schrieb 'Memorials of the English Affairs from the Reign of Charles I. to the Restoration'. London 1682. — *Carlyle* (kålai'l) s. S. 449.

Nr. 14. Prinz Karl Eduard, der Enkel Jakob's II., war 1745 mit ungefähr 1600 Mann in Schottland gelandet. Von zahlreichen Anhängern unterstützt, zog er in Edinburgh ein. Später zog er sich vor der Übermacht der Engländer in nördlicher Richtung zurück, bis es bei dem Dorfe *Culloden* (Drummossie Moor) in der Grafschaft Nairn zur Schlacht kam. Die Schlacht bei *Culloden* ist die letzte Schlacht auf britischem Boden. — *duke of Cumberland*. Wilhelm August, Herzog von C. (1721—1765), war der dritte Sohn Georg's II. — *Aberdeen*, am nördlichen Ufer des Flusses Dee, wo sich derselbe in die Nordsee ergiefst, jetzt eine bedeutende Handelsstadt mit 74.000 Einwohnern. — *Spey* (spe') in Invernesshire, entspringt in Loch Spey und mündet 8 engl. Meilen östlich von Elgin in die Nordsee. — *Nairn*, Hauptort der gleichnamigen Grafschaft, liegt an der Mündung des gleichnamigen Flusses in den Moray Firth, 15 engl. Meilen nordöstl. von Inverness. — *Inverness*, Hauptort der gleichnamigen Grafschaft an beiden Ufern des Flusses Ness bei seiner Mündung in den Moray Firth. In Inverness, das 13.000 Einwohner zählt, wird das meiste schottische Tartantuch erzeugt. — **172.** *Argyleshire*, Grafschaft an der Westküste von Schottland, grenzt nördlich an Invernesshire, südlich an den Clyde, östlich an die Grafschaft Perth. Der Hauptort ist Inverary. — **173.** *Kilmarnock*, *Balmerino*. Beide wurden später hingerichtet. — *Duke of Perth*, *Lord Elcho* verloren ihre Güter durch Konfiskation. — *Strutharrick*, ein Dorf in der Nähe des Schlachtfeldes. — *Lovat* (spr. lowat), einer der bedeutendsten unter den Jakobiten. Er wurde ebenfalls hingerichtet. — **174.** *speaker*, Präsident im Abgeordnetenhause. — Cassell, p. 418, 476. — *Smollett* (smɔlət) s. S. 424.

Nr. 15 ist aus Macaulay's Essay über Warren Hastings entlehnt. W. H. war von 1773 bis 1785 Generalgouverneur von Ostindien. Er vergröfserte und befestigte unter den schwierigsten Umständen die Macht der ostindischen Kompanie und brachte die öffentlichen Einnahmen von drei Millionen auf fünf Millionen Pfund. Er wurde 1785 abberufen und von Burke vor dem Unterhause angeklagt, mit tyrannischer Willkür gehandelt, unmäfsige Geldsummen erprefst und den Untergang mehrerer Fürsten befördert zu haben. Nach seiner Freisprechung lebte er dann in stiller Zurückgezogenheit, bis er, hochbetagt, 1818 starb. — *the place* ist Westminster Hall. Der Bau der Halle begann 1097 unter William Rufus. Es ist eine der gröfsten Hallen der Welt, mit hölzerner Decke, ohne Säulenstütze. Früher wurden in W. H. die Parlamentssitzungen und Krönungsfeierlichkeiten — letztere bis Georg IV. — abgehalten; auch diente sie als Gerichtssaal. Jetzt bildet sie das Vestibule zum Parlamentsgebäude. Cassell. p. 749. — *just sentence of Bacon*. Bacon wurde 1621 der Bestechlichkeit bei seiner Amtsführung als Lordkanzler angeklagt und zur Amtsentsetzung, Bezahlung von 40,000 l. und Gefangenschaft verurteilt. — *Absolution of Somers*. John Somers, Grofssiegelbewahrer und Lord Chancellor unter Wilhelm III. (1689—1702), wurde wegen Mifsbrauchs der Amtsgewalt angeklagt, aber freigesprochen. — *Strafford*. Thomas Wentworth, Graf von Strafford (1593—1641), Statthalter in Irland, wurde, als einer der treuesten Anhänger Karl's I., vom Parlamente verhaftet und hingerichtet. — *Charles I.* wurde 1649 vom Parlamente verurteilt. — *Garter King-at-arms*, Oberster Wappenkönig. Unter den 14 heralds sind 4 King-at-arms; an ihrer Spitze steht der Garter King-at-arms. — *George Elliot* (1718—1790) hatte 1782 die Festung Gibraltar als Kommandant derselben gegen die Franzosen und Spanier verteidigt. — *Prince of Wales*, der spätere Geoig IV. — *Sarah Siddons*, s. Anm. z. S. 238. — *The historian of the Roman Empire* ist Edward Gibbon. s. S. 431. — *Verres* hatte als Propraetor 73—71 v. Chr. Sicilien hart bedrückt und ausgesogen; er wurde deshalb von Cicero im J. 70 im Auftrage der Sicilianer angeklagt und verurteilt. — **175.** *Tacitus*, der bekannte römische Historiker (54—117), klagte den Prokonsul Marius Priscus im Auftrage der Provinz Afrika der Erpressung an und bewirkte seine Verurteilung (im J. 100). — *Joshua Reynolds*, s. Anm. z. S. 206. — *Samuel Parr* (1747—1825), wegen seiner philologischen Gelehrsamkeit berühmt. — *her to whom the heir had plighted*. Mrs. Fitzherbert galt allgemein als Gemahlin des Prinzen von Wales. — *Saint Cecilia*. Gemeint ist Mrs. Sheridan, vor ihrer Verheiratung als Sängerin bekannt. Sie war von Reynolds als Heilige Cäcilia gemalt worden. — *Mens aequa in arduis*, Anspielung auf die Ode des Horaz (II, 3): Aequam memento rebus in arduis Servare mentem = Bewahre in schwieriger Lage deinen Gleichmut. — *Burke*. Den Schlufs seiner berühmten Rede gegen Warren Hastings bringen wir an anderer Stelle (S. 274). — *Asiatic empire of Britain* etc. Die Geschichte des britisch-indischen Reiches ist in kurzem folgende: Im Jahre 1599 bildete sich eine Gesellschaft Londoner Kaufherren, welche von der Königin Elisabeth ein Privilegium erhielt. Im folgenden Jahrhunderte entstand eine Konkurrenz-Gesellschaft, allein 1702 kam eine Vereinigung beider Kompanien zu stande. Aus den Aktienbesitzern wurden Direktoren gewählt, in deren Händen die Verwaltung der Geschäfte lag. In der Mitte des 18. Jahrhunderts wurde unter dem Gouverneur Clive der Einflufs der Franzosen in Ostindien vernichtet und die Herrschaft der Engländer über den gröfsten Teil des Landes ausgedehnt. Von 1767 an mufste die Kompanie einen jährlichen Tribut von 400.000 Pfund an die britische Krone entrichten, und 1773 wurde die Oberaufsicht über die gesamten Besitzungen der Kompanie, welche bisher in die Präsidentschaften Calcutta, Madras und Bombay zerfielen, einem vom Parlamente ernannten General-Gouverneur übergeben. Der erste General-Gouverneur war der bereits im Dienste der Kompanie stehende *Warren Hastings*. In der Folgezeit unterwarfen die Engländer nach und nach ganz Ostindien. Ihre dabei befolgte Politik, ihre mafslose Selbstsucht und ein drückendes Aussaugungssystem machten sie den Eingeborenen derart verhafst, dafs zweimal durch einen allgemeinen furchtbaren Aufstand — das erstemal am Ende des vorigen Jahrhunderts (Tippoo Sahib, 1799 von Sir Arthur Wellesley, nachmal. Duke of Wellington, besiegt), das zweitemal 1857 bis 1858 — ihre Herrschaft in Frage gestellt wurde. Inzwischen ging in den Verfassungsverhältnissen des britisch-ostindischen Reiches eine grofse Veränderung vor. Nachdem schon 1854 durch einen Parlamentsbeschluss die Selbständigkeit der britisch-ostindischen Kompanie bis auf ein Kleines verloren gegangen war, wurde dieselbe 1858 ganz aufgehoben und Ostindien als ein Teil des britischen Reiches unter der Regierung der Königin proklamiert. Die Verwaltung wurde einem Minister der Krone und einer Ratskammer von 18 Mitgliedern übertragen. In jüngster Zeit wurde die englische Königin zur Kaiserin von Indien erklärt. — **176.** *hostile Chancellor*, Premierminister, war William Pitt. Burke war damals in der Opposition, daher "hostile." — *managers*, die Führer des Prozesses. — *Lord Loughborough* (lufboro). Sein eigentl. Name ist Alexander Wedderburn. Er war ursprünglich Advokat in Edinburgh und wurde wegen seiner ausgezeichneten Rechtskenntnis 1780 Chief Justice of the Court of Common Pleas mit dem Titel Lord L. Später wurde er sogar Earl of Roslyn. Seine aufserordentliche Karriere war zum Teil eine Folge seines häufigen Principienwechsels. Damals war er Führer der Opposition im Hause der Lords. — *division* entspricht unserer namentlichen Abstimmung; sie geschieht, indem die Abgeordneten, welche mit "ja" (aye) votieren, in den rechten, die anderen in den linken Vorsaal (lobby) treten, wobei sie gezählt werden. — *Mr. Grey*, Vater des berühmten Staatsmannes Charles Grey, s. Anm. z. S. 276, Nr. 6. — *Charge respecting Cheyte* (spr. tše't) *Sing*. Um der Kompanie aus finanziellen Verlegenheiten zu helfen, hatte Hastings zuerst verschiedene Summen von Cheyte Sing, dem Rajah von Benares, erpreſst und schlieſslich sein Land annektiert. — *Princesses of Oude*. Die Prinzessinnen oder Begums von Oude waren die Mutter und die Gemahlin Sujah Dowlahs, des verstorbenen Nabob von Oude. Dieser hatte ihnen reiche Ländereien und einen Schatz hinterlassen. Beides wurde von Hastings konfisziert, die Frauen selbst lange gefangen gehalten. — *his father*. Sheridan's Vater war ein Schauspieler, vgl. S. 434. — **177.** *case for the prosecution*. In der Sprache der Gerichtshöfe ist dies derjenige Teil einer Kriminalgerichtsverhandlung, der alles zur Anklage Gehörige (Verlesen der Anklage, Vernehmen der Zeugen u. s. w.) umfaſst; 'the case for the defence' ist ebenso alles, was zur Verteidigung gehört. — *admit to bail* zur Bürgschaftsleistung zulassen.

Nr. 16. Die Veranlassung zum Ausbruche des nordamerikanischen Freiheitskrieges war die den Kolonien von dem Mutterlande auferlegte Theesteuer und die Weigerung der Kolonien, sich ohne ihre Zustimmung besteuern zu lassen. Am 4. Juli 1776 erklärten sich die 13 Vereinigten Staaten für unabhängig. Der Krieg wurde durch den Frieden zu Versailles (1783) beendet, in welchem die Engländer die Unabhängigkeit der Vereinigten Staaten anerkannten. — **179.** *a few Britons*. Die Anschauungen und Anordnungen der Regierung wurden durch eine Minderheit des Parlamentes fortwährend bekämpft. Zu den hervorragenden Rednern derselben gehörten Burke, Fox, Sheridan und William Pitt der Ältere. Vgl. die Rede des letzteren auf S. 266 und Anm. dazu. — *Lord North* stand von 1770 bis 1782 als First Lord of the Treasury an der Spitze des Kabinetts. — *king* Georg III. — *neighbouring kingdom* etc. Im Frieden zu Paris (1763) muſste Frankreich Canada und die Besitzungen am Senegal an England abtreten. — *Bancroft* (bäŋkroft) s. S. 449.

Nr. 17. Die Seeschlacht von Trafalgar fand am 21. Oktober 1805 statt. Niemals seit den Zeiten der spanischen Armada war England so bedroht gewesen. Napoleon hatte um Boulogne ein starkes Heer gesammelt, das er über den Kanal nach England führen wollte. Der französische Admiral Villeneuve sollte den Weg frei machen. Der Sieg bei Trafalgar, durch welchen die vereinigte französische und spanische Flotte vernichtet wurde und der die Engländer zu unbestrittenen Herren des atlantischen Oceans machte, vereitelte den groſsen Plan. — *their numerous three-deckers* die englische Flotte zählte 27 Linienschiffe und 4 Fregatten, die vereinigte spanische und französische Flotte 33 Linienschiffe und 7 Fregatten. — *Spithead* ist die groſse und sichere Reede zwischen Portsmouth und der Insel Wight. — *the Victory* war das Admiralschiff, auf dem Nelson sich befand. — **180.** *two points more to the north* zwei Minutenstriche mehr auf dem Kompaſs, d. h. das Schiff steuert einen Kurs, der einen um zwei Minutenstriche gegen Norden weniger betragenden Winkel macht. — *Collingwood* war das Jahr vorher (1804) 'Vice-Admiral' geworden und befehligte die Lee-Linie (Seite unter dem Winde), bestehend aus 13 Schiffen. — Unter den englischen Admiralen giebt es drei Grade: 1. *Admiral* oder *Full Admiral*, 2. *Vice-Admiral*, 3. *Rear-Admiral*; und in jedem Grade drei Stufen: *A. of the Red* (zu ergänz. *Flag*), *A. of the White*, *A. of the Blue*. Über allen diesen steht der *Admiral of the Fleet*. — *main-topgallant sail* Bramsegel des Hauptmastes, d. i. jenes Segel, welches als letztes oben zwischen Vorder- und Hauptmast angebracht ist. — *raking fire*, 'to rake in naval engagements to cannonade on the stern or head, so that the balls range the whole length of the deck.' Webster. — 181. *Hardy* war Kapitän auf dem Admiralschiff. — *a double-headed shot* eine Stangenkugel. — *poop* Schanzbekleidung am Hinterteil des Schiffes. — *fore-brace bits* = Betings der Fockbrassen, d. h. die Hölzer, an welchen die Seile des Focksegels angebracht sind. — *quarterdeck* Hinterverdeck. — *main-topmast* der obere Teil des Hauptmastes. — *studding sails* Leesegel, sind leichte Segel am Rande eines viereckigen Segels, welche die Schnelligkeit der Fahrt erhöhen. — *Master* ist ein Schiffs-Offizier, der sich blofs mit der Leitung des Schiffes zu beschäftigen hat, während die Aufgabe der anderen Offiziere zugleich eine militärische und, insoferne sie ihr Land vertreten, eine politische ist. — *to put the helm to port* = steer the ship to the right. — *tiller rope* Steuerseil, welches die Handhabe des Steuers mit dem Steuerrade verbindet. — *lower-deck-ports* sind die Stückpforten des untersten oder ersten Decks. — 182. *larboard* = left side of a ship. — *a great gun* die grofsen Kanonen standen im untersten Deck. — *mizzen* (oder *mizen*) *-top* Bramstenge des Besanmastes, d. i. der obere Teil des hinteren Mastbaumes. — *rove* stark. Partic. von *to reeve*, d. i. Hineinstecken des Taus in einen eisernen Ring. — *cock-pit* Krankenverschlag. — *Midshipmen's berth* Kajüte der Seekadetten. — *in the eye*. Nelson war einäugig. Bei den Kämpfen um Corsica (1794) hatte er sein rechtes Auge verloren. — 183. *Mr. Beatty* war der Name des Schiffsarztes. — *anchor, Hardy*. Ein Sturm war im Anzug. Collingwood, der nach Nelson's Tod der oberste Befehlshaber war, beachtete den letzten Befehl des sterbenden Helden nicht, und die Folge war, dafs alle erbeuteten Schiffe bis auf vier wieder verloren gingen. — *Don't throw me overboard* Anspielung auf das gewöhnliche Seemannsgrab. Nelson's Leiche wurde nach England gebracht, und als seine Flagge ins Grab gesenkt werden sollte, rissen sie die umstehenden Matrosen in Stücke, um ein Andenken an ihren geliebten Führer zu haben. — *Thank God, I have done my duty*. Nelson's letztes Signal vor Beginn der Schlacht war: 'England expects that every man will do his duty.' Cassell, p. 586. 82. 522 u. ö. — *Southey* (saudhI) s. S. 438.

184. Nr. 18. *Beowulf*, s. litterarhistor. Anm. S. 404. — *swimming match with Breca*. Hunferhth behauptet, dafs Beowulf im Wettschwimmen von Breca besiegt wurde, Beow. v. 506 ff. — *escapes to the fens*. Grendel war ein Sumpfgeist. — *Sweet* (sūit). *Henry S.*, einer der bedeutendsten zeitgenössischen Vertreter der englischen Philologie, bekannt nicht minder durch seine kritischen Ausgaben ae. Denkmäler und durch grammatische Arbeiten als durch seine phonetischen Schriften.

185. *by a critic* etc. Spenser nennt Ch. 'well of English undefiled. — 186. *Petrarch*. Francesco Petrarca (1304—1374), der gröfste lyrische Dichter Italiens, berühmt vor allem durch sein 'Canzoniere' (Liederbuch), in welchem er seine Geliebte Laura besungen hat. — *Boccaccio*. Giovanni B. (1315—1375). Sein dichterischer Ruhm gründet sich vornehmlich auf seinen 'Decamerone,' eine Sammlung von 100 Novellen. — *Dante*. Dante Allighieri (1265[?]—1321), der gröfste Dichter Italiens und einer der tiefsten Geister aller Zeiten und Länder. Sein Hauptwerk ist die 'Divina Commedia' (Göttliche Komödie). — *Jean de Meung* ist der Vollender des im Mittelalter berühmten allegorischen Gedichtes 'Roman de la Rose.' — *Higden*. Ralph H., ein Mönch, der 'Polychronicon,' eine Chronik in lateinischer Sprache, schrieb und um 1370 starb. — *Gower* war ein Zeitgenosse Chaucer's. Sein Hauptwerk, welches er in englischer Sprache geschrieben, betitelt sich 'Confessio amantis.' — *Langue d'Oye* oder langue d'oïl (aus hoc illud [est]) war die Sprache der Nordfranzosen, während die der Südfranzosen oder Provençalen

langue d'oc (aus hoc [est]) genannt wurde. — *Wickliffe.* John W. (1324 bis 1384), berühmter englischer Kirchenreformator, übersetzte die Bibel in Englische. — **187.** *Thomas a Becket*, englischer Kirchenfürst des Mittelalters, hartnäckiger Vorkämpfer der Hierarchie und Vollender der päpstlichen Herrschaft über die Kirche seines Vaterlandes, wurde auf Veranlassung des Königs Heinrich II., mit dem er in fortwährende Streitigkeiten verwickelt war, von vier Edelleuten am Altar der Kathedralkirche zu Canterbury 1170 erschlagen. Im Jahre 1173 wurde er kanonisiert und wegen der vielen Wunder, die seinem Leichnam zugeschrieben wurden, als der vornehmste Schutzheilige Englands durch zahlreiche Wallfahrten verehrt. Heinrich VIII. liefs 1538 die Gebeine des Heiligen, als eines Majestätsverbrechers, verbrennen und die Asche in den Wind streuen. — **188.** *Warton-Hazlitt* (üɔətn bäzlĭt). Thomas Warton's (1728—1790) wertvolle 'History of English Poetry' erschien 1781 in 3 Bänden. Sie reicht leider nur bis zum Anfang des Zeitalters Elisabeth's. Carew H., ein zeitgenössischer Litterarhistoriker und Kritiker, gab sie aufs neue heraus.
Drake s. Anm. z. S. 159. — *Coke.* Sir Edward C. (1551—1633), Rechtsgelehrter und Staatsmann. Sein Hauptwerk ist 'Institutes of the Laws of England.' — *Hooker.* Richard H. (1553—1600). Geistlicher und Verteidiger der anglikanischen Kirche in seinem Werke 'Ecclesiastical Polity,' welches sowohl gegen die römisch-katholische, als auch gegen die calvinische Kirche gerichtet ist. — *Spenser.* Edmund S. (1553—1599), ein berühmter englischer Dichter, ein älterer Zeitgenosse Shakespeare's. Sein Hauptwerk ist das allegorische Epos 'Fairy Queen,' das, viele Motive aus der Artussage entlehnend, die Königin Elisabeth verherrlicht. — *Sidney.* Sir Philip S. (1554—1586) schrieb Sonette, ferner Arcadia, eine Ritter- und Schäfergeschichte in Prosa, und 'Defence of Poesy.' — *Bacon* s. S. 91. — *Jonson.* Benj. J. (1573—1637), Zeitgenosse und Freund Shakespeare's, ist nach diesem einer der bedeutendsten dramatischen Dichter Englands. — *Beaumont and Fletcher.* Der erste lebte von 1586—1616, der zweite von 1576—1625. Sie schrieben zusammen eine grofse Anzahl von Dramen, von denen das beste 'The faithful Shepherdess' heifst. — **189.** *Translation of the Bible.* Wickliffe's Bibelübersetzung (s. S. 186, Z. 36 u. Anm. dazu) bildete die Grundlage zu der von Tindale, wie diese zu der autorisierten Übertragung von Coverdale (1535) und zu der von König Jakob veranlafsten Übersetzung (1611). — *an habitual* s. Gr. § 3. — **190.** *to run and read* soviel wie: manifest, clear; sprichwörtlich: he that runs may read, aus Cowper, Tirocinium l. 80 (vgl. Familiar English Quotations, pag. 86); zu Grunde liegt Habakkuk II, 2: Write the vision, and make it plain upon tables, that he may run that readeth it. — *Burns "Cotters' Saturday Night"* ein Gedicht von Burns, im schottischen Dialekt geschrieben, welches einen Häusler schildert, wie er im Kreise seiner Familie aus der Bibel vorliest. — *what Milton has made of the account of the Creation.* Vgl. S. 196 ff. — *Tasso-Fairfax.* Torquato Tasso (1544 bis 1595), berühmter italienischer Dichter. Sein Hauptwerk ist 'Gerusalemme liberata.' *Edward Fairfax* veröffentlichte seine Übersetzung 1600. — *Ariosto-Harrington.* Ludovico A. (1474—1533), einer der drei grofsen epischen Dichter Italiens. Am berühmtesten ist sein romantisches Epos 'Orlando Furioso.' *Sir John Harrington* gab 1581 seine Übersetzung heraus, welche der Arbeit von Fairfax nachsteht. — *Homer-Chapman.* George Ch. (1577—1634) übersetzte die Ilias und die Odyssee. Aus seiner Übersetzung sieht man, sagt Charles Lamb, dafs er selbst ein grofser Dichter war. — *of Virgil long before.* Das 2. und 4. Buch der Äneide von Virgil wurde von Earl of Surrey (1517—1547) ins Englische übersetzt. Diese Übersetzung ist namentlich deshalb bemerkenswert, weil darin zum ersten Male im Englischen

der Blankvers gebraucht wird. — *Ovid soon after*. 1567 übersetzte Arthur Golding die 'Metamorphosen' ins Englische. — *Plutarch-North*. Plutarch, ein griechischer Schriftsteller († um 120 n. Chr.). schrieb 'Biographien' ausgezeichneter Männer Griechenlands und Roms. Sir Thomas *North* starb nach 1579. — **191.** *Tacitus* lebte von 54—117 n. Chr. Seine Hauptwerke sind 'Germania,' 'Historiarum libri' und 'Annales.' Für die Geschichte Britanniens ist die 'Vita Agricolae' wichtig. — *Sallust* lebte von 86—35 v. Chr. Er schrieb 'Catilina' und 'Jugurtha' — *Cicero's orations*. Von den vielen Reden Cicero's (107—43 v. Chr.) sind die bekanntesten: 'In Verrem,' 'Pro lege Manilia,' 'In Catilinam,' 'Pro Milone,' 'Orationes Philippicae.' — *Aretine* (spr. ä'rĭtĭn). Pietro Aretino (1492—1566), italienischer Schriftsteller, dessen Werke bekannt sind durch satirischen Inhalt bei glänzender und origineller Form der Darstellung. — *Machiavel* s. Anm. z. S. 166. — *Castiglion*. Castiglione's (1478—1529) 'Libro del Cortegiano' ist ein Meisterwerk italienischer Prosa und bildete lange Zeit eine Lieblingslektüre der höheren Stände. — *Ronsard*, französischer Dichter des 16. Jahrhunderts und Haupt der Pleïade, einer Dichterschule, welche durch sklavische und geistlose Nachahmung der antiken Poesie gekennzeichnet ist. — *Du Bartas* ist ein Schüler Ronsard's. — *Augustan period* ist das 17. Jahrhundert, das Zeitalter der Corneille, Molière und Racine — *Prospero's Enchanted Island* ist der Schauplatz des Shakespeare'schen Dramas 'The Tempest.' — *the same feeling*, nämlich das Gefühl für das Abenteuerliche und Wunderbare. — *Hazlitt* (häzlĭt) s. S. 409.

Nr. 21. *Stewart* s. Anm. z. S. 193. — **192.** *Montucla*, bedeutender französischer Mathematiker (1725—1799). — *publication of the preliminary discourse* etc. In diesem 'Discours préliminaire' (1751) der bekannten Enzyklopädie hat Diderot Bemerkungen über die Einteilung der Wissenschaften, und zwar nach Bacon's Grundsätzen gegeben. — *Gassendi*. Pierre G. (1596—1655), ausgezeichneter französischer Physiker und Philosoph; er stellte ein neues, auf der Atomenlehre Epikur's beruhendes philosophisches System auf. — *Descartes* René, gewöhnlich Renatus Cartesius genannt, wird als der Begründer der neuen Philosophie und der scharfsinnigste Denker der Franzosen angesehen. Er lebte 1596—1650. — *Mersenne*, gelehrter Theologe und Freund des Descartes. Er lebte 1588—1648. — *Richelieu*, der berühmte Staatsmann Frankreichs, lebte 1585—1642. — *Sentimens de l'Académie Française sur le Cid* ist der Titel der Schrift, in welcher die Académie auf Befehl Richelieu's das bedeutendste Werk des größten französischen Tragikers verurteilte. — *Voiture*, französischer Schriftsteller der ersten Hälfte des 17. Jahrhunderts. — *Costar*, Abbé C., ein Freund des Vorhergehenden. — *Horace*. Quintus H. Flaccus, der größte Lyriker der Römer, lebte 65 bis 9 v. Chr. — *Leibnitz*, einer der größten Gelehrten und Denker aller Zeiten, wurde 1646 zu Leipzig geboren und starb 1714 zu Hannover. — *Pufendorf*, bedeutender deutscher Jurist, lebte 1632—1694. — *Royal Society* entspricht unserer 'Akademie der Wissenschaften.' Sie wurde 1645 gegründet, 1660 von Karl II. bestätigt. Man zahlt für den Eintritt 10 *l.* und einen jährlichen Beitrag von 4 *l.* Die Aufnahme erfolgt durch Abstimmung auf Vorschlag von mindestens 6 Mitgliedern. Fellow of the Royal Society (F. R. S.) zu sein, gilt als große Ehre. — **193.** *Reid*, Dr. Thomas (1710—1796), einer der Gründer der Schule der schottischen Metaphysiker; er schrieb gegen Hume's Skepticismus. — *Stewart*, Reid's Schüler, war Professor of Moral Philosophy in Edinburgh; er lebte 1753—1828. — *Robinson*, John P., Professor of Natural Philosophy in Edinburgh (1739—1805). — *Playfair*, John R., Professor der Mathematik in Edinburgh (1748—1819). — *Henry Hallam* (hälöm) (1778—1859), ein namhafter englischer Geschichtsschreiber. Seine Hauptwerke sind: 'View of the State of Europe during the Middle Ages.' 'Constitutional History of England' und 'Introduction to the Literature of Europe in the 15th, 16th and 17th Centuries.' —

Nr. 22. *River Avon*, genauer *Upper A.*, entspringt in Northamptonshire und ergiefst sich in den Severn bei Tewkesbury. — *roof of Westminster*. Die zu Ehren des heiligen Petrus von Edward dem Bekenner zwischen 1055 und 1065 erbaute Kirche, die unter Heinrich III. im wesentlichen die heutige Gestalt erhielt, führt den Namen Westminster-Abtei (Westminster Abbey) zum Unterschiede von der St. Pauls-Kirche in der City, die man eine Zeitlang auch Eastminster nannte. (Minster aus monasterium, da ursprünglich — schon im 7. Jahrh.? — ein Benediktinerkloster mit der Kirche verbunden war. Unter Heinrich VIII. wurde das Kloster aufgehoben.) Die Kirche hat die Form eines lateinischen Kreuzes. Die Länge derselben beträgt 156 m (gegen 22 m Breite), das Querschiff ist 61 m lang und 26 m breit; die Höhe der Kirche ist 31 m, die der Türme 68 m. Die prächtige Kapelle am Ostende ist von Heinrich VII. im spätgotischen Stil erbaut; die übrigen Teile der Kirche, mit Ausnahme der von Wren angebauten geschmacklosen Türme in W., sind frühgotisch (early English). Das Innere macht durch seine harmonischen Verhältnisse, die reiche Färbung und die Marmorsäulen einen bedeutenden Eindruck. Die Westminster-Abtei, mit ihren Särgen der englischen Königsgeschlechter (in den acht Kapellen des östlichen Teiles des Längenschiffes), ihren langen Reihen von Denkmälern berühmter Männer, gilt den Engländern nicht mit Unrecht als National-Heiligtum; ein Grab in Westminster ist die letzte und höchste Ehre, welche die Nation dem Verdienste ihrer Söhne zuerkennt. Uns interessieren besonders die Denkmäler im östlichen Teile des südlichen Querschiffes, dem Poets' Corner: Chaucer's Grabmal, Shakespeare's Statue, Spenser's Altarmonument, Milton's Büste, Addison's Standbild, Goldsmith's Medaillon, Lord Macaulay's und Thackeray's Büste, Dickens' Grab seien hier besonders erwähnt. Die Westminster-Abtei ist auch infolge der historischen Erinnerungen, die sich an dieselbe knüpfen, eines der berühmtesten Gebäude in London. Es steht in dieser Beziehung nur dem Tower nach. Cassell, p. 744, u. ö. — *blest, curst* s. Gr. § 50, d. — 194. *part of the house*. Das Haus steht in Henley Street und ist in ein Shakespeare-Museum umgewandelt worden. — *Aubrey* (1627—1697). Von ihm rührt die Nachricht her, Sh. habe als Knabe seinem Vater, der Metzger war, bei seinem Gewerbe geholfen, 'but when he killed a calf he would do it in a high style, and make a speech.' — *High Bailiff or Mayor* entspricht unserem "Bürgermeister." Die Gemeindevertretung ist in England in folgender Weise eingerichtet: Die Bürger wählen die Common Councillors, diese die Aldermen. Die letzteren bilden den Town Council (Stadtrath), der zu seinem Präsidenten den Mayor wählt. Derselbe bleibt ein Jahr im Amte, kann aber wiedergewählt werden. — *Jonson* s. Anm. z. S. 188. — 195. *punning* witzig, durch Wortspiel. Das Wortspiel drehte sich um den Namen Lucy (lousy). — *Three Warwickshire men*, es sind dies die Brüder James und Richard Burbage, ferner John Heminge, der später die 1. Folio herausgab. Nach Elze ist es nicht unwahrscheinlich, dafs alle drei aus Stratford waren. — *call-boy*, a boy whose business is to call the actors in a theatre. Webster. — *deputy-prompter* Vertreter, Gehilfe des Souffleurs, zweiter S. — *Blackfriars* (Dominikaner) und *Globe-Theater* lagen beide auf der rechten Seite der Themse, zwischen Blackfriars- und London-Bridge (Mp. D 6). — *a sleeping partner* ein stiller Compagnon. — 196. *sack* Sekt; die Entstehung des Namens wird gegeben durch eine Stelle aus einer älteren englischen Reisebeschreibung: They were well provided with that kind of Spanish wine which is called 'sack.'

though the true name of it be Xeque, from the province whence it comes; andere leiten das Wort her von vino secco. — *claret* (heller) franz. Rotwein. — *New Place*, das von Shakespeare in Stratford erworbene Wohnhaus, das um 1540 als 'an elegant house built of brick and timber' beschrieben wird. Das Haus wurde 1759 abgetragen; an seiner Stelle sind jetzt Gartenanlagen. — *Coriolanus* und *Julius Caesar* sind keine Histories, sondern reine Tragödien; den Namen Histories giebt man nur den Dramen, deren Stoff aus der englischen Geschichte entnommen ist. — *The Passionate Pilgrim* rührt nur zum geringsten Teile von Shakespeare her. — *A Lover's Complaint* enthält die Klage eines verlassenen Mädchens. — Cassell, p. 185, 539, 296. — *Collier* (kŏlīə).

Nr. 23. *the first praise of genius is due* etc. Klopstock spricht in seiner Abiturientenrede denselben Gedanken aus. — 197. *Bossu*. René le B. († 1780) ist der Verfasser eines 'Traité du poème épique.' — 198. *vale of Enna*. Im Thale von Enna in Sicilien wurde Proserpina von Pluto geraubt. — *Cyanean rocks*. Die cyaneischen Felsen oder Symplegaden standen am Eingange ins Schwarze Meer und zerquetschten alles Durchpassierende. Die Argonautenfahrer kamen mit Hilfe der Minerva glücklich durch, nur wurden durch die zusammenschlagenden Felsen die äufsersten Bretter des Hinterteiles der Argo zermalmt. — *the two Sicilian whirlpools* Scylla und Charybdis. — *Comparing the shield of Satan to the orb of the moon*. Dieser Vergleich findet sich I, 283 f. — *Samuel Johnson* (sämuəl dʒɔnsn) s. S. 427.

201. *two little provincial rebellions*. Gemeint sind die Versuche der Prätendenten Jakob Eduard (1715) und Karl Eduard (1745), nach England zurückzukehren. — *foreign war* ist der Land- und Seekrieg mit Frankreich, 1755—1763. — *Gray* s. Anm. zu S. 102. — 202. *the Wartons*. Joseph W. (1722—1800) ist als Verfasser von Sonetten, sein Bruder Thomas (1728—1790) durch seine 'History of English Poetry' und durch eine treffliche Ausgabe von Milton's Werken bekannt. — *Akenside*. Mark A. (1721—1770) schrieb u. a. das philosophische Gedicht: 'The Pleasures of Imagination.' — *Taylor*. Jeremy T. (1613—1667) war ein bedeutender theologischer Schriftsteller. — *Hooker* s. Anm. z. S. 188. *Cowley*. Abraham C. (1618—1667), einer der Dichter der sogenannten metaphysischen Schule. — *Warburton*. Der Bischof W. (1698—1779) schrieb u. a. 'Divine Legation of Moses.' — *Adam Smith* lebte 1723—1790. Durch sein grofses Werk 'Inquiry into the Natur and Causes of the Wealth of Nations' ist er der Begründer der modernen Nationalökonomie geworden. — *Junius* ist der angenommene Name eines politischen Schriftstellers, der von 1769—1772 in London eine Reihe von Briefen veröffentlichte, in denen das Ministerium heftig angegriffen wurde. Wahrscheinlich birgt sich hinter diesem Namen Sir Philip Francis (1740—1818), ein Schriftsteller und Staatsmann jener Zeit. — *Francis Jeffrey* (fränsɪz dʒefrī) (1773—1850), hervorragender Kritiker und einer der Gründer der 'Edinburgh Review,' die unter seiner Redaktion von 1804 bis 1829 nicht nur auf die litterarischen, sondern als Hauptorgan der Whigs auch auf die politischen Angelegenheiten Englands einen bedeutenden Einflufs ausübte.

203. Nr. 25. Thackeray's 'Lectures on the English Humourists of the Eighteenth Century' erschienen in einer trefflichen Ausgabe (mit bibliographischem Material, litterarhistor. Einleitung und sachlichen Anmerkungen für Studierende) von Ernst Regel. Der II. Band (Halle, Niemeyer, 1885) enthält *Goldsmith* und ist hier benützt worden. — *Doctor Primrose*, der Landprediger von Wakefield. — *Longford* und *Westmeath* sind zwei aneinander grenzende Grafschaften in der Provinz Leinster. — *Auburn*. Das Dorf, in welchem G. die Jahre seiner Kindheit verbrachte, besingt er unter dem Namen *'Auburn'* in 'The Deserted Village.' *parson, rector* s.

Anm. zu S. 104 *bishop.* — *Kitchen turf* in Irland = *Kitchen fire.* — *cottier* alte Schreibweise für *cotter* = Häusler, der keinerlei Abgaben zu zahlen hat und kein Land besitzt. — *his honour's. Your Honour* ist in Irland allgemeine Anrede des Niederen an den Höheren. — *Rererence* Anrede an den Geistlichen. — *by right and sufferance* nach Herkommen und Duldung. — *a half dozen;* diese Stellung drückt enge Verbindung der beiden Begriffe aus. — *Irish dependents who take* etc. So ging es auch Goldsmith, vgl. Forster, 'The Life and Times of Oliver Goldsmith' (London 1854). p. 271. — *Squire* s. Anm. zu S. 33. — *an old woman;* sie hiefs Elisabeth Delap. — *Paddy,* kontrahiert aus St. Patrick, ist der Spottname der Irländer. — *Byrne* hiefs mit Vornamen *Thomas.* — *hedge-schoolmaster.* Dies sind Lehrer, die trotz des gebotenen Besuches der englischen (nicht katholischen) Charter-Schools heimlich Kinder nach katholischen Grundsätzen unterrichten. — *Elphin* ist ein Bischofssitz in der Grafschaft Roscommon, Provinz Connaught. — *ferule,* Rute; vgl. unter die 'Fuchtel' jemandem kommen. — *Contarine* (spr. kəntərī'n), der Name ist italienischer Abkunft. — *Noll,* Abkürzung für Oliver, (mine Ol, vgl. Ned aus mine Ed). — **204.** *'Mistake of a Night';* der zweite Titel von Goldsmith's Lustspiel 'She Stoops to Conquer.' — *Ardagh* (spr. ådə) in der Grafschaft Longford. — *Aesop* soll ein sehr häfsliches Äufseres gehabt haben. — *brogue* wird die irländische Aussprache des Englischen genannt. — *to go into the church* heifst in den geistlichen Stand treten und ist nicht zu verwechseln mit *to go to church.* — *Mr. Filby.* Die Hälfte der Summe, welche G. Filby schuldete (78 *l.*), hätte eigentlich sein Neffe Hodson zahlen sollen, für den G. die Kleider machen liefs. Der junge Mann scheint indes seinen Verpflichtungen nicht nachgekommen zu sein. (Vgl. Forster. Goldsmith. 520.) — *Sizar,* armer Universitäts-Student, der für Unterricht, Kost und Wohnung nichts zahlte, dafür aber verschiedene niedrige Dienstleistungen verrichten musste. — *tutor,* s. Anm. zu S. 103. — **205.** *buckeen* irisch = a young buck, d. i. 'ein flotter Junge,' — *one patron.* Goldsmith war Erzieher in der Familie eines Herrn in der Nachbarschaft, namens Flinn. — *Temple* s. Anm. zu S. 231. — *the woolsack* ist der Sitz des Lordkanzlers im englischen Herrenhaus. Gemeint ist also der Weg zur höchsten Ehrenstufe, die ein englischer Unterthan ersteigen kann. — *Farheim, Du Petit, Duhamel du Monceau.* Vgl. Irving's Goldsmith 63. Über *Farheim* haben wir nichts Näheres finden können. *Du Petit* war ein bedeutender französischer Augenarzt (1664 bis 1674), *Duhamel du Monceau* ein bedeutender französischer Naturforscher (1700—1782). — *Ballymahon* (bällīmä'hən), ein Dorf in der Grafschaft Longford, wohin G.'s Mutter übersiedelt war. — *But me not destined* etc. Aus dem 'Traveller.' v. 23—30: *me* ist Objekt zu *leads.* — *in a former lecture,* in der 5. Vorlesung, welche über Hogarth, Smollett und Fielding handelt. — **206.** *dreary London court.* Gemeint ist *Green Arbour-Court,* in der Nähe von Fleetmarket und Farringdon-Street (Mp. C 5); hier bewohnte G. eine Zeitlang ein elendes Quartier. — *Sir Joshua Reynolds,* berühmter englischer Maler, namentlich im Fache des Porträts ausgezeichnet. Er lebte von 1723—1792. — *Beattie,* James B. (1735—1803), Verfasser des beliebten Gedichtes 'The Minstrel,' war Professor of Moral Philosophy and Logic zu Aberdeen. Sein Essay on Truth war gegen Hume's Philosophie gerichtet. Von Georg III. erhielt er eine Pension von 200 *l.,* ohne dafs er sich beworben hatte, während Goldsmith's Bewerbung abschlägig beschieden worden war. — *Kelly,* Hugh K. (1739—1777), der Repräsentant des weinerlichen Lustspiels, welches damals Mode war. — *Newbery kept back the MS.* sc. of the Vicar of Wakefield. Newbery war ein Buchhändler. Das Ms. hielt er wahrscheinlich deshalb zurück, weil der Traveller zuerst veröffentlicht werden sollte. Durch diesen wurde G. berühmt, und nun erzielte der Vicar den glänzendsten Erfolg. — *peerish with Sterne.* G. griff Sterne im 53. Brief seines 'Citizen of the World' an. — *a little angry, when Colman's actors* etc. Als G. sein Lustspiel She Stoops to Conquer *(his delightful comedy)* geschrieben hatte, wurde der Theaterdirektor Colman nur mit Mühe dazu gebracht, das Stück, welches gar nicht der herrschenden Mode des sentimentalen Lustspiels entsprach, aufzuführen. Als die besten Schauspieler die bedeutendsten Rollen ausschlugen, sagte G. halsstarrig: 'I'd rather my play were damned by bad players, than merely saved by good acting.' Colman zweifelte so sehr am Erfolg des Lustspiels, dafs er nicht nur keine neuen Coulissen, sondern nicht einmal neue Kleider liefern wollte (Forster 414). — **207.** *Griffiths.* Goldsmith hatte vier Bücher dieses Buchhändlers, welche er kritisieren sollte, versetzt, kurz nachdem er durch Versetzung seiner Kleider seiner Wirtin aus der Not geholfen. — *Boswell* Biograph Johnson's. — *forty-six.* W. u. heifst es *five and forty*; Goldsmith wurde 45 Jahre und 5 Monate alt. — **208.** *'Here as I take'* etc. Aus dem 'Deserted Village.'

209. *Mr. Dallas.* Robert Charles D. (1754—1824), ein vertrauter Freund Byron's, verfafste u. a. 'Recollections of the Life of Lord Byron' — *'English Bards and Scotch Reviewers,'* s. litter. Anm. S. 441. — *St. James's Street* führt von Piccadilly nach Pall Mall. Mp. D 4. — **210.** *M. Murray.* John M. (1778—1843), englischer Publicist und zugleich Koryphäe des Londoner Buchhandels. Sein Geschäft wird von seinem, namentlich durch die 'Continental Handbooks for Travellers' weit bekannten Sohne, John M. dem Jüngeren, weitergeführt. — *Fleet Street.* C 5. — **211.** *Mr. Gifford* (spr. gifəd), William G. (1757—1826) bedeutender englischer Kritiker, von 1808—1824 Herausgeber der 'Quarterly Review.' — *Mr. Rogers.* Samuel R., 1763—1856, war der Sohn eines reichen Bankiers und Teilhaber am Geschäfte. Er war ein Gönner und Förderer der Künste, sein Haus war berühmt als Sammelpunkt der Schriftsteller jener Zeit. Er selbst hat sich nicht ohne Erfolg als Dichter versucht. — *Lord Holland,* Henry Richard Fox (1773—1840), Neffe des berühmten Staatsmannes und Redners Fox, Mitglied der Whigpartei und Kenner der spanischen Litteratur, über welche er auch einiges veröffentlichte. — **213.** *Young* s. S. 421. — **214.** *The Prince Regent.* Georg III. verbrachte die letzten 10 Jahre seiner Regierung in unheilbarem Wahnsinn. Während dieser Zeit (1810—1820) führte der nachmalige König Georg IV. als 'Prince Regent' die Regierung. — *Carlton House* in Pall Mall (D 4) war damals vom Prinzregenten bewohnt. — *Thomas Moore* (tɔməs muə) s. S. 443.

IV. Nr. 1. *Cymini sectores* oder cumini s., eig. Kümmelspalter, d. h. Leute, die auch eine Kleinigkeit noch genau analysieren. — *Bacon* (be'kn) s. S. 410.

215. *truth consisteth in the right ordering of names.* Diese Definition der Wahrheit ist Hobbes eigentümlich. Aristoteles sagt: Je nachdem der Gedanke mit der Wirklichkeit übereinstimmt oder nicht, heifst er wahr oder falsch. Es ist aber die Definition von Hobbes insoferne nicht unrichtig, als die Vermeidung des Irrtums vor allem auf dem richtigen Gebrauch der Namen in unseren Behauptungen beruht. — *Geometry.* Hobbes meint, dafs die Geometrie, insoferne sie ihre Lehren mit einem höheren Grad der Sicherheit der Erkenntnis vorträgt, als die sogenannten Erfahrungswissenschaften es zu thun vermögen, den Namen Wissenschaft zu allererst, ja allein, verdient. — *Hobbes* (hɔbz) s. S. 411.

216. *it is thinking makes* etc. Die Auslassung des Relativums im Nominativ entspricht dem älteren Sprachgebrauch. — *Locke* (lɔk) s. S. 413.

220. *next paper.* Diese Abhandlung ist dem 'Spectator' entnommen, einer moralischen Zeitschrift, die von Steele herausgegeben wurde. — *Addison* (ädisn), s. S. 413.

222. *Royal Exchange.* Hier ist die alte Börse gemeint, welche 1564—1570 von Sir Thomas Gresham errichtet wurde. Das jetzige Gebäude an derselben Stelle (gegenüber der Bank von England, zwischen Threadneedle Street und Cornhill, Mp. C 6) wurde 1842—1844 von Tite gebaut. — *High-Change*, die Zeit, wo die Börse am belebtesten ist. — *Sir Andrew. S. A. Freeport*, ist eine erdichtete Person, welche im 'Spectator' häufig als Repräsentant der Handelsinteressen eingeführt wird, wie Sir Roger de Coverley für das Landleben. Captain Sentry für die Armee, Will Honeycomb für die Stadt u. a. Dies sind Freunde des Spectator, welcher ebenfalls eine fingierte Person ist. — **223.** *Barbadoes* (spr. babe''dos), eine britisch-westindische Insel, zu den kleinen Antillen gehörig. Jetzt ist der hauptsächlichste Ausfuhrartikel Zucker. — *pignut* Erdnuss, bunium flexuosum, "an umbelliferous plant common in woods and fields in Britain. Swine are very fond of the nuts, and fatten rapidly where they are abundant" (Blackie's Modern Cyclopaedia). — **224.** *Spice Islands* = Molukken.

225. *there is scarce a coffee-house in town that has not some speakers belonging to it.* Vgl. damit Macaulay's Schilderung der Londoner Kaffeehäuser in History of England, B. I., Ch. 3: 'Every Coffee-house had one or more orators to whose eloquence the crowd listened with admiration, and who soon became, what the journalists of our own time have been called, a fourth Estate of the realm.' — *Baker's 'Chronicle.'* Sir Richard B. (gest. 1644), Verfasser einer zu seiner Zeit populären 'Chronicle of the Kings of England.' — **226.** *Mr. Humphrey Wagstaff.* Wahrscheinlich eine ähnliche Bildung wie Bickerstaff, eine von Swift geschaffene und auch von Steele im Tatler verwendete Figur. — **227.** Sir Richard Steele s. S. 414.

229. *Aristotle.* Aristoteles, der gröfste Gelehrte des klassischen Altertums, 384 v. Chr. in Stageira geboren, Lehrer Alexander's d. Gr., starb 322 zu Chalkis auf Euböa. Aristoteles war auf allen zu seiner Zeit bekannten Gebieten der Wissenschaft Meister. — *Herodot*, der älteste der drei grofsen Geschichtsschreiber der Griechen. Er lebte im 5. Jahrh. v. Chr. — *Arrian*, einer der fruchtbarsten und besten Schriftsteller des späteren Altertums. In seiner 'Anabasis' giebt er eine Geschichte der Feldzüge Alexander's des Grofsen. Er wurde gegen Ende des 1. Jahrh. n. Chr. geboren und starb unter Marc Aurel. — *Azincourt.* Bei Azincourt schlug Heinrich V. von England im Jahre 1415 mit einem kleinen, durch Entbehrungen geschwächten und schlecht bewaffneten Heere die viel zahlreicheren und besser gerüsteten Franzosen. — *Narva.* Bei Narva schlug Karl XII. von Schweden (1700) mit nur 8000 Mann die beinahe zehnmal so starken Russen. — *ghost of Villiers.* Der Herzog von Buckingham, geb. 1592 als jüngerer Sohn des Sir George Villiers, wurde am 23. August 1628 von dem verabschiedeten Lieutenant Felton ermordet. Dies Schicksal soll Buckingham mehrfach vorausgesagt worden sein, und Clarendon erzählt im Beginn seiner 'History of the Rebellion' von einer solchen Prophezeiung, 'which was upon a better foundation of credit, than usually such discourses are founded upon.' Einige Zeit vor dem gewaltsamen Tode Buckingham's erschien in drei auf einander folgenden Nächten, so berichtet Clarendon ausführlich, einem königlichen Beamten der Geist des Sir George Villiers und forderte ihn auf, dem Herzoge zu sagen, er solle bald etwas thun, um die Gunst des Volkes zu gewinnen, sonst würde er nur mehr kurze Zeit leben. Der Auftrag wurde ausgeführt — und einige Monate darauf ward Buckingham ermordet. — *Dr. Drelincourt, the ghost of Mrs. Veal,* s. litter. Anm. S. 418. — *incredulous hatred mentioned by Horace.* De arte poetica, v. 185—188: Ne pueros coram populo Medea trucidet, Aut humana palam coquat exta nefarius Atreus.

Aut in avem Procne vertatur, Cadmus in anguem. Quodcunque ostendis mihi sic, incredulus odi. — *and this more especially in painting* etc. Diese Worte richten sich gegen die Tugendhelden Richardson's. — 231. *the Temple*, ein Komplex von Gebäuden in Fleet Street, die (wie Gray's Inn und Lincoln's Inn) von Advokaten bewohnt werden, und wo die Rechtswissenschaft gelehrt oder besser, wo in der Handhabung der englischen Gesetze praktisch unterrichtet wird. Der Temple war ursprünglich Ordenshaus der Templer, daher der Name; er zerfällt in den Inner und Middle Temple, ersterer trägt seiner Genossenschaft 25,676 *l.*, letzterer 12,240 *l*. In den Tempelgarten verlegt Shakespeare die berühmte Scene, in welcher York und Lancaster weifse und rote Rosen als Abzeichen pflücken — *Suetonius*, römischer Geschichtschreiber, der namentlich durch seine Lebensbeschreibungen römischer Kaiser ('Vitae VII Imperatorum') bekannt ist. Er lebte 70—121 n. Chr. — 232. *quis credet* etc. Wer wird es glauben? Niemand. beim Hercules, niemand; vielleicht ein paar Leute oder gar niemand. — Das Citat ist übrigens ungenau. Es ist aus Persius, Satir. I, 2—3 und lautet: 'Quis leget haec? Min' tu istud ais? — Nemo hercule! — nemo? — Vel duo, vel nemo.' — *waiting to* = waiting for. — *rarae aves* seltene Vögel. — *hitch* haken, hinaufziehen (vom Gespreizten des Distichs). — *in direct opposition to itself*. *itself* bezieht sich auf das vorhergehende *zeal*. — 233. *Tyburn* lag noch gegen 1780 zwei engl. Meilen aufserhalb Londons, und hier, an der Nordostecke des Hyde Park, stand damals der Galgen. Tyburnia gehört jetzt zu den vornehmeren Vierteln der Stadt. — *Bathos*. Gemeint ist Swift's Satire: 'des hochgelahrten Martinus Scriblerus denkwürdige Schrift über das Bathos, oder die Kunst in der Poesie zu sinken,' in welcher Swift den unnatürlichen, geschraubten und den platten, gemeinen Stil vieler Schriftsteller verspottet. — *Home articles* Tagesneuigkeiten. — *Fielding* (fĭldĭŋ) s. S. 423.

234. *Books, says Bacon* etc. S. 215, Z. 1. Man vgl. überhaupt Johnson's Abhandlung mit der Bacon's über die Studien; jene ist eine weitere Ausführung und Ergänzung der letzteren; beide sind ein glänzendes Zeugnis für die den englischen Geist charakterisierende praktische Weisheit. — 235. *Longinus*, griechischer Philosoph und Rhetor, 213—273 n. Chr. — *Hugh Blair* (hjû blêo) s. S. 430.

238. *Claude*. C. Lorrain (1600—1678), einer der ausgezeichnetsten Landschaftsmaler aller Zeiten, namentlich Meister des Kolorits. — *Salvator*. S. Rosa (1605—1673), ausgezeichneter italienischer Maler. Seine landschaftlichen Darstellungen sind durch gewaltig aufgetürmte Felsmassen, Sturmwolken und Schlaglichter charakterisiert. — *Kemble* s. Anm. zu S. 62. — *Siddons*, Englands berühmteste Schauspielerin; Tochter des älteren, Schwester der beiden berühmten Kemble, 1755—1831; sie hat ein Denkmal in der Westminster-Abtei. — 239. *Puff in the 'Critic'* etc. In Sheridan's Posse 'The Critic' wird das Drama 'The Spanish Armada' eines gewissen Puff probeweise aufgeführt. Das Stück beginnt mit dem Schlage der Turmuhr, wozu Puff bemerkt: 'it marks the time, which is four o'clock in the morning', and saves a description of the rising sun, and a great deal about gilding the eastern hemisphere.' — 240. *carry on* hier: zu Markte bringen. — *civilian* = a member of the Civil Law, ein Rechtsbeistand an einem Gerichtshofe, der nach römisch-kanonischem Recht (Civil Law) urtheilt. Hier einfach: Rechtsgelehrter. — *The player and poet*. So im Original (London, Warne); die Grammatik erfordert hier *the poet*. — *Joseph Andrews*, ein Roman Fielding's.

241. *Mrs. Marcet*, die Gattin eines namhaften schweizerischen Arztes und Chemikers. Das erwähnte Buch heifst 'Conversations on Political Economy' und

erschien 1816. — *Montague*, Earl of Manchester (1602—1671), im Beginn der Revolution ein Gegner der Hofpartei, dann von der radikalen Partei verdrängt nach der Restauration Lord Chamberlain. — *Walpole*, Robert W. (1676—1745) führte in seiner Stellung als erster Minister unter Georg I. eine geschickte Finanzverwaltung ein. — *Newton*. Sir Isaac Newton (1642—1727) ist der Begründer der neueren mathematischen Physik und der physischen Astronomie. — *Shaftesbury*, lebte 1671—1713. In seinen Schriften behauptet er die Existenz eines besonderen moralischen Sinnes, welcher den Menschen befähige, zwischen Gut und Böse zu unterscheiden. — *Helvetius*, franz. Philosoph, aus der Schule der Enzyklopädisten. 1715—1771. — *Fable of the Bees*. In diesem Werke sucht Bernard Mandeville (1670—1733) zu beweisen, dafs die Laster von Privatpersonen zum Wohle der Gesammtheit dienen können. — **242.** *Iago*, in Shakespeare's 'Othello' der Bösewicht, der durch Verleumdung die Ermordung der Desdemona bewirkt. — *As imagination bodies forth* etc. Shakesp. Midsum. N. D., V. 1, 14 ff. — *Hamlet*, tragische Gestalt Shakespeare's. H. rächt seinen ermordeten Vater und geht selbst dabei zu Grunde. — *Lear* s. S. 71 und 376. — *Red Ridinghood*, Rothkäppchen, frz. le Petit Chaperon Rouge. Dieses Märchen ist Deutschland, England und Frankreich gemeinsam. — **243.** *Mohawk* zu den nördlichen Irokesen gehöriger nordamerikanischer Indianerstamm.

Nr. 13. *Antigone*, Tragödie des Sophokles. Antigone war die Stütze ihres blinden Vaters Ödipus. Später, als bei dem Zuge der Sieben gegen Theben ihre Brüder Eteokles und Polynikes im Zweikampfe gegen einander gefallen waren und Kreon die Beerdigung des letzteren bei Todesstrafe verboten hatte, bedeckte sie trotz des Verbotes den geliebten Leichnam mit Erde. — *The modest pride with which she replies* etc. vgl. S. 381, v. 211—214. — **244.** *Imogen*, die Heldin des Stückes 'Cymbeline.' — *plighted* = folded. — **245.** *Sherburne*, jetzt Sherborne, ein alter Marktflecken in Dorsetshire, mit prächtiger Kathedrale, die vom Bischof Aldhelm begründet und in der Zeit König Heinrich's IV. neu gebaut wurde. — *Exeter* ist der Hauptort von Devonshire. Seine alte Kathedrale stammt zum Teil noch aus der Zeit Athelstane's (932). — *Madame de Staël*, berühmte französische Schriftstellerin der Neuzeit. Ihre bedeutendsten Werke sind 'Corinne' und 'De l'Allemagne.' Sie starb 1817. — *Jameson* (dže'msn) s. S. 409.

246. *Raleigh* (rŏlī), s. S. 409. — *Bess*. Abkürzung für Elisabeth.

247. *Mr. Molyneux* (spr. mŏlĭnŭ'ks). William M. (1656—1698) bedeutender Mathematiker in Irland. — *de quolibet ente* = von was immer. — *one's self* gewöhnlich: oneself. — *a kinsman of yours*, ein gewisser Mr. Smith, der Locke einige Zeit vorher besucht und Molyneux darüber geschrieben hatte. — **248.** *Dr. Ashe*. George A., Vorsteher eines College in Dublin.

Nr. 3. *Richardson* (ritšədsn) s. S. 422. — *Aaron Hill*, ein Schriftsteller der ersten Hälfte des 18. Jahrh., hatte als Kritiker einiges Ansehen, gab im Vereine mit Bond die Wochenschrift 'The Plain Dealer' heraus und unterstützte, wie Johnson an mehreren Stellen erzählt, aufstrebende Autoren. — *attended with* jetzt attended by. — *and particularly he asked*; aus *every inn* hat man hier, dem nachlässigen Briefstil entsprechend, *at an inn* zu entnehmen. — *behaved*, jetzt ohne Reflexiv. — **249.** *Rivington* und *Osborne* Verlagsbuchhändler, mit denen Richardson befreundet war. — *recollect* = collect, gather, ich begann solche Stoffe zu sammeln. — *course of reading* Lektüre. — *dismissing* bezieht sich auf *a new species of writing* (eine neue Gattung Bücher oder eine neue Art des Stils) 'wenn sie — fallen liefse.' — *read them*, jetzt read to them ihnen vorgelesen. — *January 10, 1730—1740*. Bis 1752 begann in England das Jahr mit dem 25. März; andere

Länder. die den Gregorian. Kalender angenommen hatten, begannen es mit dem ersten Jänner; die Angabe zweier Jahre (1739—1740) sucht beiden Arten der Zählung gerecht zu werden. Im Jahre 1752 wurde auch in England der Gregor. Kal. angenommen, indem man auf den 3. September den 14. folgen liefs. Vordem galt der Julianische Kalender. O. S. (Old Style). — 250. *Moliere's Old Woman*. Vgl. Addison's Spectator, Vol. I. N. 70: Moliere used to read all his comedies to an old woman who was his housekeeper, as she sat with him at her work by the chimney-corner. and could foretell the success of his play in the theatre. from the reception it met at his fireside.

Nr. 4. *Chesterfield* (tšestəfild) s. S. 420. — *Mr. Lowndes*, spr. lo°ndz. — *Descartes* s. Anm. zu S. 192. — *Mallebranche*. Nicolas M. (1638—1715), französischer Philosoph, bildet in der Geschichte der Philosophie den Übergang von Cartesius zn Spinoza. Sein Hauptwerk heifst: 'De la recherche de la verité.' — *Newton* s. Anm. z. S. 241. — *Horace* s. Anm. z. S. 192. — *Boileau*. Nikolaus B. (1636—1711) ist der grofse Gesetzgeber der klassischen Poesie der Franzosen. Sein Hauptwerk ist 'L'art poétique.' Aufserdem verfafste er 'Satires,' 'Epitres' und 'Le Lutrin,' ein komisches Heldengedicht. — *Waller*. Edmund W. (1605—1687), lyrischer Dichter Englands. — *La Bruyère*. Jean de L. B., französischer Moralist des 17. Jahrhunderts; seine 'Caractères de notre siècle' sind berühmt. — 251. *emeritus* = emerited. — *accompts*, die moderne Schreibung ist *accounts*.

252. *'The World,'* eine Wochenschrift, 1753—1765 herausgeg. v. Dr. Moore. — *paper*, hier Aufsatz, sonst auch Zeitung. — *addressed your lordship in public*, nämlich als er den Plan (Prospekt) zu seinem englischen Wörterbuch veröffentlichte; er hatte diesen auf Antreiben des Buchhändlers Robert Dodsley, der von Chesterfield begünstigt wurde, an den Genannten gerichtet. — *a patron*, in seinem Wörterbuche definiert er das Wort: 'One who countenances, supports, or protects. Commonly a wretch who supports with insolence, and is paid with flattery.' — *the shepherd in Virgil* etc. s. Virg. Bucol. VIII, 42—46. Der Sinn der Stelle ist, dafs Johnson, wie jener Schäfer im Virgil, die Liebe nur als etwas Rauhes und Felsenhartes kennen gelernt hat, nämlich sofern seine eigene Liebe nicht erwidert wurde, d. h. also, dafs Johnson's Streben, die Gönnerschaft Chesterfield's zu gewinnen, ohne Erfolg geblieben war. — 253. *solitary*, am Schlusse der Vorrede zu seinem Wörterbuche sagt er: 'I have protracted my work till most of those whom I wished to please have sunk into the grave, and success and miscarriage are empty sounds.' — *with less*, sc. obligation.

Nr. 6. *Montagu* (montəgju) s. S. 420. — O. S. = Old Style s. Anm. zu S. 249 *January*. — *Hebrus*, Hauptstrom Thraciens, jetzt Maritza. — *Orpheus* wurde der Sage nach von den thrakischen Frauen zerrissen und sein Haupt in den Hebros geworfen. Während es die Wellen dahintrugen, murmelte die tote Zunge leise Klagen. Lady Montagu citiert in ihrem Briefe mehrere auf diese Sage Bezug habende Verse Virgils (Georg. lb. IV, 523 ff.). Vgl. ferner Klopstock's Ode 'Wingolf' l. — 254. *fistula*, lat., Rohr, Schalmei. gefertigt aus vielen, immer kleiner werdenden Rohren. — *Mr. Addison* etc. 'It would perhaps be no impertinent design to take off all their models in wood which might not only give us some notion of the ancient music, but help us to pleasanter instruments than are now in use.' Addison's Remarks on Several Parts of Italy. — *foot-ball* s. Anm. zu S. 132. — *Theocritus*, berühmter Idyllendichter der Griechen. lebte um 277 v. Chr. — *your Homer*, bezieht sich auf Pope's Homer-Übersetzung. — *passages explained, that I did not* etc. Goethe spricht in seiner Italienischen Reise ganz dieselbe Erfahrung aus. (Unter 'Palermo, Sonnabend 7. April' und 'Tarmina, am Meer.

Dienstag, 8. Mai'.) — **255.** *belt of Menelaus* s. Hom. Il. IV, 132 ff. — *King Priam and his counsellors* Il. II, 146 ff. — *Diana* etc. Vgl. Verg. Aeneis I, 498.

Nr. 7. *Burke* (bə̂k) s. S. 432. — *Richard Shackleton* war der Sohn des ehemaligen Lehrers Burke's. — *this strange tumult*, die 'Gordon Riots.' — *Burgoyne*, spr. bəgɔ'ĭn. Er befehligte im Kriege gegen die nordamerikanischen Kolonien die Nordarmee, welche im Oktober 1777 bei Saratoga die Waffen strecken mufste. (Vgl. S. 267, Z. 6 u. Anm. dazu.) B., der auch einige dramatische Werke geschrieben hat, starb 1792. — *Savile House*. Die Toleranzbill (Roman Catholic Relief Bill), welche die Veranlassung zu diesen Unruhen war, wurde seinerzeit (1778) von Sir George Savile eingebracht. — *under God*, unter Gottes Schutz. — *blue cockades*. Die Anführer trugen blaue Kokarden. — *the duties* als Abgeordneter. — *for me was mich betraf*, ich meinesteils. — **256.** *the House* d. Parlament. — *The Protestant Association*, so nannte sich der Verein, von dem der Widerstand gegen das Toleranzgesetz ausging; Lord George Gordon war dessen Präsident; er war zugleich Mitglied des Unterhauses und brachte hier von Seiten der Gesellschaft eine mit vielen tausend Unterschriften versehene Petition um Aufhebung des zu Gunsten der Katholiken gefafsten Parlamentsbeschlusses ein. Diese Petition wurde in der Sitzung am 6. Juni 1780 behandelt, doch wurde nichts weiter beschlossen, als sie in Erwägung zu ziehen, sobald sich die Unruhen gelegt hätten. Erhitzte Volkshaufen zündeten katholische Kirchen und öffentliche Gebäude an. Erst am 8. Juni bot die Regierung Truppen auf, die den Aufstand mit Gewalt dämpften. — *Rockingham House*. Der Marquis of Rockingham (1730—1782), Staatsmann der Whigpartei. Im Jahre 1765 nahm er als Premierminister Burke zu seinem Privat-Sekretär. — *Devonshire House*. Der Familienname des Hauses von D. ist Cavendish. Die Cavendish waren für die Whigpartei. — *Of this house*. Der Verfasser meint sein Haus und seine Familie.

257. *Robert Burns* (robət bə̂nz) s. S. 435. — *Churchill*. Charles Ch. (1731 bis 1764), eine zeitlang sehr beliebt als satirischer Dichter. — *Shenstone*. William Sh. (1714—1763), zu seiner Zeit sehr beliebter Idyllendichter. — *Gray* s. Anm. zu S. 102. — *Beattie* s. Anm. z. S. 206. — *Lyttleton*. Lord L. war nur ein unbedeutender Dichter. — *Collins*. William C. (1721—1759) war ein lyrischer Dichter von bedeutenden Anlagen, der aber infolge eines unglücklichen Lebens und frühen Todes nicht zur Reife gelangte.

Nr. 9. *Byron* (bairən) s. S. 257. — *Troad* (trō"əd) die Ebene um das alte Troja. — *My grand giro*, meine grofse Rundreise. — **258.** *Leander* schwamm der Sage nach von Abydos (auf der asiatischen Seite des Hellesponts) nach Sestos. — *Fletcher*, Byron's Diener. — *My friend Hobhouse*. John H., Lord Broughton (1786 bis 1869) war ein Schulfreund Byron's. Über die gemeinsame Reise veröffentlichte er 1812 'A Journey through Albania' etc. — *remittance* Rimesse, Geld- oder Wechselsendung. — *smoked and fogged* hätte mich in euren Städten räuchern lassen oder auf dem Lande liegen und verschimmeln können. — *I have convinced the critics* etc. Anspielung auf die Satire 'English Bards and Scotch Reviewers', vgl. Anm. zu S. 209.

259. Nr. 10. *evil works of my non-age* bezieht sich auf Byron's Satire 'English Bards and Scotch Reviewers', worin sogar Walter Scott angegriffen wurde. — *Prince Regent*, der nachmalige König Georg IV., vgl. Anm. zu S. 214. — '*Lay*', scil. of the last Minstrel. — *Murray* s. Anm. zu S. 210.

260. *Mitton*. Thomas M. war ein Schulkamerad Dickens' und später sein Rechtsanwalt. — *taken our passage*. take one's passage heifst sonst 'sich einschiffen.' Hier mufs man aber übersetzen 'wir haben uns Plätze für unsere Heimfahrt genommen (gekauft).' — *levee or drawing-room*, Ausdrücke für Gesellschaften bei Hofe; der Unterschied zwischen levee und drawing-room ist der, daſs bei ersterem nur Herren, bei letzterem Damen und Herren empfangen werden. — **261.** *Kate* ist Dickens' Frau. — *Maclise.* Daniel M. (1811—1870), ein namhafter englischer Historien- und Porträtmaler und vertrauter Freund Dickens'. — *piping hot* vulgär 'brühheiſs.' — *as it is* trotzdem. — *lay it on* = to act with vehemence to inflict (used of expenses. Webst. — *T'other* = the other. — *Anne* eine Magd, die Dickens aus England mitnahm. — *Mitchell*, ein amerikanischer Schriftsteller (oder Schauspieler?) — **262.** *bilious* nicht recht wohl im Kopf und Magen. — *Caledonia letter*, Brief aus Schottland. — *Britannia*, ein Life Insurance Office.

Nr. 1. Die Rede, von welcher der Schluſs mitgeteilt ist, hielt Burke am 3. November 1774 vor seinen Wählern in Bristol. — **263.** *instructions* Instruktionen, Weisungen, welche der Abgeordnete von seinen Wählern zu empfangen hätte. — *from the first hour*. Burke vertrat früher einen andern Wahlkreis; er wurde dann eingeladen, sich um ein Mandat in Bristol zu bewerben.

264. Nr. 2. Dies ist der Schluſs der berühmten Rede, welche Burke gegen Warren Hastings hielt, vgl. das Lesestück: 'Der Prozeſs gegen Warren Hastings,' S. 174. — *undone women of the first rank*, die Prinzessinnen von Oude. — *by great military services*. Damit ist unter andern George Elliot gemeint, vgl. S. 174 und Anm. dazu. — *From the practice of the law*. Der Redner spielt hier wohl auf Lord Loughborough an, vgl. Anm. z. S. 176. — **266.** *parliamentary trust betrayed*, Hastings war Mitglied des Unterhauses.

Nr. 3. Am 18. November 1777 stellte William Pitt, Graf von Chatham, im Oberhause den Antrag auf Einstellung der Feindseligkeiten gegen die amerikanischen Kolonien und hielt zur Begründung seines Antrages seine letzte groſse Rede. Bekannt ist, daſs er noch kurz vor seinem Tode sich ins Oberhaus führen und tragen lieſs, um seiner Meinung Geltung zu verschaffen. — *My lords*. Im Oberhause wendet sich der Redner an die Mitglieder des Hauses selbst; vgl. Anm. zu S. 271, *Sir*. — *Majesty* Georg IV. — **267.** *a most able general*. Generalmajor Amherst, später in den Adelstand erhoben, führte im siebenjährigen Kriege ein Kommando in Nordamerika und vertrieb die Franzosen von Kap Breton. — *the northern force* ist die des Generals Burgoyne, die am 17. Oktober 1777 bei Saratoga unfern von Albany im Staate New-York die Waffen streckte. Die Nachricht davon gelangte erst anfangs Dezember nach England. — *Howe* operierte in diesem Jahre gegen Philadelphia, wurde aber von Washington zum Rückzuge gezwungen und nur durch die englische Flotte vor dem Schicksal Burgoyne's bewahrt. — *German prince*. England erhielt damals Truppen nicht nur von Hessen-Kassel, sondern auch von Braunschweig, Waldeck, Anhalt und Anspach. — *the noble Earl who moved the address* ist der Earl of Percy. Es ist in beiden Häusern unstatthaft, ein Mitglied, von welchem man sprechen will, mit Namen zu nennen. — Auf die Eröffnung des Parlaments folgt die Thronrede *(Speech from the throne*, vgl. w. u. z. S. 270), in welcher dem Parlamente die inneren und auswärtigen Verhältnisse geschildert und entsprechende Maſsregeln vorgeschlagen werden. Die Antwort des Parlamentes heiſst die Adresse *(Address)*, deren Abfassung oft Veranlassung zu heftigen Debatten gibt. — **268.** *negotiations with France*. Offiziös unterhandelte Frankreich schon länger mit den Amerikanern; 1778 schloſs es ein förmliches Bündnis mit ihnen. — **269.** *the middle and the southern provinces*. Allerdings war der Geist des Widerstandes am stärksten in den nördlichen Provinzen, ganz besonders in Massachusetts. — *the county I live in*. Pitt wohnte zu Hayes in der Grafschaft Kent. — *the gentleman* ist Washington, George W. (1732—1799), gleich ausgezeichnet als Feldherr und Staatsmann, der Begründer der Unabhängigkeit der Vereinigten Staaten Amerikas und ihr erster Präsident. — *attainder* ist eine durch Gesetz (nicht durch das Gericht) verhängte Verurteilung zum Tode, welche Einziehung des Vermögens und Verlust der bürgerlichen Ehrenrechte, sowie des Adels nach sich zieht. — *foreign powers*. Hier irrt sich der Redende, denn die Thronrede erwähnt ausdrücklich der Rüstungen Frankreichs und Spaniens. — *Streights*, gewöhnlich *straits*, hier die Meeresenge von Gibraltar. — **270.** *Not 5000 troops* u. s. w. Die hier gemachten Angaben wurden von dem Ministerium für ungenau und unrichtig erklärt; doch wurde zugegeben, dafs der englische Handel nicht immer genügend habe beschützt werden können. Im Tajo liege ein englisches Kriegsschiff. — *who have been guilty*. Das sind die Minister. — *echo the peremptory words*. Die Adresse wiederholte, der Gewohnheit gemäfs, möglichst wörtlich die Thronrede, welche Fortsetzung des Krieges gegen Amerika ankündigte. — **271.** *confusion worse confounded*. Aus Milton's Paradise Lost. — *Pitt* s. S. 432.

Nr. 4. Das Verdienst, in England die Abschaffung des Handels mit Sklaven herbeigeführt zu haben, hat sich William Wilberforce erworben. Dieser edle Mann, Sohn eines Banquiers zu Hull und Gutsbesitzer in Yorkshire, der mit dem jüngeren Pitt in Cambridge studierte und später als Parlamentsmitglied aufs innigste mit demselben befreundet war, machte seit der Mitte der Achtziger-Jahre des vorigen Jahrhunderts die Abschaffung des Sklavenhandels sich zur Lebensaufgabe. Pitt versprach ihm sogleich seine eifrigste Unterstützung und setzte einen Ausschufs des Geheimen Rates zur Untersuchung der Sklavenfrage ein, welcher durch umfafsendes Zeugenverhör viele der Scheufslichkeiten aufdeckte, die den Handel begleiteten. Darauf brachte Wilberforce die Angelegenheit in wiederholten Anträgen vor das Unterhaus, und als dieses auch am 2. April 1792 geschehen war und Dundas zu dem Wilberforce'schen Antrage das Amendement auf allmähliche Abschaffung eingebracht hatte, trat Pitt in der Rede über den Sklavenhandel für den Urantrag, also für sofortige Abschaffung, ein. Dundas siegte, sein Antrag wurde mit 230 gegen 85 Stimmen angenommen. Die französische Revolution oder vielmehr die aus ihr entspringenden Kriege unterbrachen nunmehr Wilberforce's Bestrebungen. Im Jahre 1804 aber nahm er sie wieder auf und hatte endlich die Genugthuung, dafs ein Gesetz zu stande kam (1807), welches den Sklavenhandel vom 1. Januar 1818 an für aufgehoben erklärte. Die Nation hat Wilberforce durch ein Grabmal in Westminster Abbey geehrt. Cassell, p. 576. — *Sir*. Im Unterhause richtet der Redner seine Rede an den Präsidenten (Speaker); vgl. S. 266, *My lords*. — *My right honourable friends* sind Dundas und der Präsident, welche für allmähliche Abschaffung des Sklavenhandels gesprochen hatten. Den Titel "Right honourable" haben die Mitglieder des Privy Council (s. S. 141). — **272.** *Cameroon*. Der Camerun- oder Gabunflufs ist mehr Meeresarm als eigentlicher Flufs an der Westküste Afrikas, etwa 5 Grad nördl. Breite. — *the right honourable gentleman over the way*. Hier ist Charles James Fox gemeint, welcher auf der anderen Seite des Ganges sitzt und ebenfalls für sofortige Aufhebung aufgetreten war. — *something like to courts*. s. Anm. z. S. 16. — *Pitt the Younger* s S. 434.

274. Napoleon hatte als erster Consul 1799 Frieden mit England schliefsen wollen, allein das britische Kabinett hatte sein Anerbieten zurückgewiesen. — *Sir* s. Anm. zu S. 271, *Sir*. — **275.** *Mr. Erskine*. Thomas E. (1750—1823), ausgezeichneter Redner. Als Abgeordneter für Portsmouth unterstützte er während der französischen Revolution Fox' Principien. Er schrieb auch 'View of the Causes and Consequences of the War with France.' — *Washington* s. Anm. zu S. 269, *gentleman*. — *the right honourable gentleman who opened the debate* ist Dundas. —

that side of the house, d. i. die Tory-Seite. — *Valenciennes, Quesnoy* befestigte französische Städte im Departement Nord. — *Condé* französisches Dorf. Departement Meuse. — 276. *battle of Blenheim*, s. S. 44 u. Anm. — *the Grand Monarque*. So nannten die Franzosen Ludwig XIV. (1643—1715). — *Fox*, s. S 434.

Nr. 6. Seit das konstitutionelle System in England durch die Revolution von 1688 zur Vollendung gekommen, waren im Staatsleben nur zwei grofse Mängel, die auf den Katholiken lastenden Ausnahmsgesetze und die einzelne Klassen unverhältnismäfsig begünstigende Zusammensetzung des Unterhauses. Durch die 1829 durchgesetzte Emanzipation der Katholiken war der eine dieser radikalen Übelstände behoben worden. Es war dies das Verdienst der Whigs, der liberalen Partei. Diese nahm nach dem Tode Georg's IV. nun auch die Frage der Parlamentsreform in die Hand. Das Ministerium Wellington, welches das Interesse der Tories vertrat, war zurückgetreten, und das neue Ministerium, das aus den Führern der Whigs zusammengesetzt war, brachte am 1. März 1831 im Unterhause die Reformbill ein. Es hatte von Anfang an im Unterhause ein aristokratisches Element gegeben, das sich aus dem niederen Adel rekrutierte. Ferner war es im Laufe der Zeit Sitte geworden, dafs die Söhne, Brüder und andere Verwandten der Lords, in ihrer Eigenschaft als Commoners, sich für das Unterhaus wählen liefsen, wobei sie von ihren Familienhäuptern, meist grofsen Grundbesitzern, von denen viele Wähler in den Grafschaften abhängig waren, unterstützt wurden. Dadurch verloren die Gemeinen zuletzt den Charakter einer eigentlichen Volksvertretung, und das Unterhaus wurde zu einer geschwächten Wiederholung des Oberhauses herabgesetzt. Der Zweck der Reformbill war nun, das Wahlrecht jener Ortschaften aufzuheben oder zu beschränken, welche durch die Abhängigkeit oder durch die geringe Zahl ihrer Bevölkerung der Bestechung und anderen schädlichen Einflüssen ausgesetzt waren, und das Stimmrecht da zu vermehren, wo ein selbständiger Gebrauch desselben erwartet werden konnte. Das Haus der Gemeinen sollte dadurch seinem Namen und seiner Bestimmung entsprechender eingerichtet werden. Das Schicksal der Bill war folgendes: Sie konnte im Unterhause nicht durchgebracht werden. Die Regierung löste hierauf das Unterhaus auf. Im neuen Unterhause hatte die Reformpartei die Majorität, und am 21. September 1831 wurde die Bill nach harten Kämpfen mit einer Mehrheit von 109 Stimmen angenommen. Nun gelangte die Bill ins Oberhaus. Bei dieser Gelegenheit hielt Lord Brougham seine berühmte Rede für die Bill. Allein die Tories, welche im Oberhause ein entschiedenes Übergewicht hatten, verwarfen die Bill am 21. Oktober mit einer Mehrheit von 41 Stimmen. Der Widerstand gegen einen so lang und tief gehegten Volkswunsch brachte eine in England seit den Zeiten der inneren Kriege nicht mehr gesehene Bewegung hervor. Am 12. November legte das Ministerium die Bill mit einigen Veränderungen dem Unterhause nochmals vor. Sie ging am 22. März mit einer Mehrheit von 116 Stimmen durch. Am 26. März wurde sie dem Oberhause vorgelegt. Die Tories, die bedenkliche Stimmung des Volkes erwägend, wollten jetzt die Bill in zwei Teile teilen und dadurch die Verhandlung in die Länge ziehen. Graf Grey, der Premier des Whig-Ministeriums, nahm jetzt die Bill ganz zurück und schlug dem König Wilhelm IV., da die Majorität im Oberhause auf keine andere Weise erlangt werden konnte, einen Pairsschub im Sinne der Whigs vor. Der König verweigerte die nachgesuchte Vollmacht. Der Rücktritt Grey's (13. Mai) und die Ernennung Wellington's zum Haupte einer neuen Verwaltung rief in England und Schottland eine grenzenlose Aufregung hervor. In den Grafschaften wurden massenhafte Volksversammlungen abgehalten. Neunzigtausend Schotten hatten sich bereit erklärt, den englischen Reformvereinen nötigenfalls mit den Waffen in der Hand zu Hilfe zu kommen. Am 17. Mai kündigte Wellington seinen Rücktritt an, indem es, wie er erklärte, unmöglich sei, die Regierung ohne Zustimmung der Gemeinen zu führen, und Graf Grey trat mit seinen Kollegen wieder in das Ministerium ein. Nun war der Widerstand der Tories gebrochen. Am 4. Juni wurde die Bill, um die länger als ein Jahr gekämpft worden, von dem Oberhause endlich angenommen, am 7. Juni 1832 von dem König unterzeichnet und dadurch zum Gesetz erhoben. So erhielt das englische Unterhaus seine jetzige Gestalt (vgl. S. 140). Da dasselbe einen entscheidenden Einfluss auf die innere und auswärtige Politik ausübt und das nationale Leben in seiner Mitte den mächtigsten Ausdruck findet, so war seine Umgestaltung eine Frage von unermesslicher Wichtigkeit, von deren Lösung das Schicksal Englands abhing. — *a noble Earl*, Lord Winchelsea. — *licentiousness of the Press*. Die freisinnige Tagespresse stand auf der Seite der Whigs und setzte dem Publikum die Vorteile der Reformbill auseinander. — **278.** *fright our Isle from its propriety*. Diesen Ausdruck hatte wahrscheinlich ein Redner der Gegenpartei gebraucht. — *Those portentous appearances* etc. bezieht sich auf die Unruhen und Excesse, welche nach Eröffnung des ersten von Wilhelm IV. gehaltenen Parlaments stattfanden. — *unions and leagues*. Damit sind die damals entstehenden zahlreichen Reformvereine gemeint. — *Musterings of men in myriads* bezieht sich auf die Volksversammlungen, welche in London sowohl als in den Grafschaften abgehalten wurden. — *Irish volunteers of 1782*. Als während des nordamerikanischen Freiheitskrieges Frankreich einen Einfall in Irland zu machen drohte, gebrauchten die Irländer diesen Umstand als Vorwand, ein Heer von irischen Freiwilligen zu bilden. Schon nach zwei Jahren war dasselbe auf 50.000 Mann angewachsen, und es wurden nun, mit den Waffen in der Hand, Sturmpetitionen unternommen. — *raised up thirteen republics* bezieht sich auf die Gründung der Vereinigten Staaten von Amerika. — *Catholic Association*. Im Jahre 1801 wurde Irland mit Grofsbritannien unter einem Parlamente vereinigt. Allein die von Pitt verheifsene völlige politische Emanzipation der Katholiken kam nicht zur Ausführung. Dies rief 1802 zu Dublin einen neuen Bund der Katholiken (Catholic Association) hervor, der bald der Mittelpunkt der irischen Opposition wurde. Im Jahre 1825 löste zwar die Regierung den Bund auf, allein, von dem berühmten Führer O'Connel neugestaltet, setzte er seine Thätigkeit fort, bis die Regierung sich genötigt sah, die Emanzipationsfrage vor das Parlament zu bringen, wo die Bill betreffend die völlige Gleichstellung der Katholiken nach heftigen Gegenbestrebungen endlich angenommen und am 13. April 1829 von Georg IV. genehmigt wurde. — **279.** *Duke of Norfolk* etc. Die ältesten Bestandteile des Oberhauses, die Pairsfamilien, welche noch im Mittelalter wurzelten, waren meist Whigs, befanden sich aber in der Minderheit. Zu ihnen gehörte auch Charles Howard, Duke of Norfolk. — *Cries of Order from the Opposition*. Die dem Whig-Ministerium opponierende Partei der Tories ruft den Redner 'zur Ordnung', weil er der parlamentarischen Sitte entgegen mehrere Mitglieder des Hauses namentlich angeführt hat. — **280.** *John Russell* ist der Herzog von Bedford. Sein dritter Sohn, J. R., hatte die Reformbill des Ministeriums im Unterhause eingebracht und hat auch später in der Politik und Geschichte Englands eine hervorragende Rolle gespielt. — *William Cavendish* ist der Herzog von Devonshire. — *Harry Vane*, ein Nachkomme des berühmteren Sir H. V., Independentenführers in der Zeit der Revolution und Freundes Milton's. — *to point a man's destiny toward St. Luke's*. St. Luke's (erg. *Hospital*) ist ein Irrenhaus in London. Daraus ergiebt sich der Sinn der vorliegenden Phrase. — *Brougham* (brūm) s. S. 448.

Nr. 7. Im Jahre 1847 verlangte die Regierung vom Unterhause die Bewilligung von 100.000 l zum Zwecke des öffentlichen Unterrichtes. Darauf brachte Mr. Thomas Duncombe, Abgeordneter für Finsbury, den Antrag ein, es solle vorher ein Komitee gewählt werden, welches die Richtigkeit und Ausführbarkeit der ministeriellen Mafsregel und die jährlichen Kosten derselben feststellen und weiters untersuchen solle, ob durch dieselbe nicht die konstitutionelle Machtsphäre des Parlaments beeinträchtigt und die Überzeugungen und bürgerlichen Rechte des Einzelnen verletzt würden. Gegen diesen Antrag hielt Macaulay am 19. April eine Rede, welche durch Inhalt und Form zu den bedeutendsten seiner oratorischen Leistungen zählt. Der Kern der Rede besteht darin, die Vorteile der verstaatlichten Volksschule *(State Education)* darzulegen, gegenüber der bisherigen Gepflogenheit, den Unterricht der Privatunternehmung *(Voluntary System)* zu überlassen. Dieser Gegensatz ist aber für das englische Unterrichtswesen charakteristisch, daher dürfte der allgemeine Titel des Lesestückes gerechtfertigt erscheinen. Heutzutage hat sich der Staat des Elementarschulwesens einigermafsen angenommen. Zu diesem Zwecke ist das Land in Schuldistrikte eingeteilt, von denen jeder nach Verhältnis seiner Bevölkerung eine angemessene Zahl von Elementarschulen erhalten soll. Die nötigen Geschäfte werden von Schulausschüssen *(school boards)* besorgt, deren Wahl Sache der steuerzahlenden Ortsangehörigen ist. Zur Bestreitung der Kosten ist eine Schulsteuer eingeführt. Die Volksschule fällt demnach auch jetzt wesentlich in den Bereich der Selbstverwaltung, und der Einflufs des Staates ist nur ein mittelbarer im Hinblick auf Staatszuschüsse, und beruht auf dem Institute der Inspektoren, welche die Einhaltung der gesetzlichen Vorschriften überwachen, aber keinerlei selbständige Anordnungen treffen können. Der Unterricht in den Board-Schulen legt das Hauptgewicht auf Lesen, Schreiben, Rechnen und Bibelkenntnis. Zur Vorbildung der Lehrer sind Seminare *(training colleges)* mit Übungsschulen errichtet. — Die höheren Schulen *(public-* und *grammar-schools)* sind auch jetzt noch der Privatunternehmung überlassen. Eine Scheidung, wie sie in unseren Gymnasien und Realschulen vorliegt, giebt es in England nicht. Überhaupt fehlt dort die stramme Organisation der deutschen und österreichischen Mittelschulen; vgl. die Anm. zu S. 65 public school u. S. 129 our brave old founder. — Über die Universitäten s. Anm. zu S. 102, Oxford u. Cambridge. — *Adam Smith,* s. Anm. z. S. 202. — **281.** *No Popery Riots* auch Gordon Riots genannt, s. S. 255, Nr. 7 u. Anm. daz. — *madman Gordon,* s. ebend. — *Your predecessor* bezieht sich auf den Präsidenten des Abgeordnetenhauses. — *lawn*, scil. sleeves, weite Battistärmel, die zum Ornate der Bischöfe gehören. — *Horse Guards*, in Whitehall, D 4, das Hauptquartier der britischen Armee in London, so genannt, weil sich zwei berittene Schildwachen vor dem Eingange befinden. — *Holborn* (spr. hŏ"bŏn) *Hill*, Mp. C 5. — *The great plague and the great fire.* Die grofse Pest suchte London im Jahre 1665 heim; im darauffolgenden Jahre wurde die Stadt von einem grofsen Brande verheert, s. S. 9. — **282.** *Smithfield Market,* der grofse Viehmarkt von London, C. 5. — *riots of Nottingham.* In N., dem Hauptorte von Nottinghamshire, brachen 1811 die 'Luddite Riots' aus. Auch 1812, 1814 und 1816 kamen solche Unruhen vor. — *sack of Bristol.* Während der Unruhen gelegentlich der Reformbill 1831 (s. S. 255 u. Anm. dazu) wurden in B. (s. Anm. z. S. 87) der Palast des Bischofs und andere öffentliche Gebäude zerstört. — *Ludd, Swing* gehören zu den sogenannten Ludditen, die zu verschiedenen Zeiten in mehreren englischen Fabriksstädten ihr Unwesen trieben und besonders Maschinerien zerstörten. — *Rebecca* 'Rebecca and her daughters' nannte sich (in Mifsdeutung einer Bibelstelle) eine Verbindung aufständischer Bauern in Wales, welche sich 1839 und 1843 der Erhöhung der Wegzölle widersetzte und nachts, mit geschwärzten Gesichtern und in Weiberkleidern, die Zollhäuser zerstörte und andere Gewaltthaten beging. — *penal colonies*. Die überseeischen Strafkolonien sind seit 1856 ganz aufgehoben. — *Newgate*, s. Anm. zu S. 41. — *Norfolk Island*, Strafkolonie im westl. Teile des stillen Meeres, nördlich von Neuseeland. — **283.** *The Committee of Council* ist der Ausschufs des *Privy Council*, des geheimen Rates, der jetzt nur mehr sanktioniert, was das Ministerium bereits beschlossen hat. — *Seymour Tremenheare* spr. sīmə tremənīə. — *Monmouthshire* Grafschaft nördlich von Bristol Channel. Die Gegend ist landschaftlich sehr schön und reich an Mineralien, namentlich Alaun. — *And now for the effects* etc., übers.: 'Seht, welche Wirkungen eure Nachlässigkeit gehabt hat!' — *Newport*, Hafenstadt von Monmouthshire, am Kanal von Bristol. — **284.** *Protestant Dissenters*. In England, wo die Episcopalkirche (auch Church of England, s. Anm. zu S. 103 our church) die Landeskirche ist, sind die Presbyterianer, Independenten und Baptisten Dissenters. — *Voluntary System*, s. die Einl. — *the little society*, die 'Pilgrim Fathers', wie sie die Amerikaner nennen, landeten 1620, etwa 102 Köpfe stark, an der Küste von Massachussetts. Es waren Puritaner, die nach Amerika ausgewandert waren, um den religiösen Verfolgungen zu entgehen. — *Laud*, Erzbischof von Canterbury unter Jakob I. und Premierminister unter Karl I. Er wurde auf Veranlassung des Parlamentes 1645 auf dem Towerhill hingerichtet. — *High Commission Court*, eine Art Inquisition, von Elisabeth 1583 eingesetzt. — *grammar school* ist eine Art Mittelschule, wo Latein und Algebra, Geometrie und Stil gelehrt wird. — *New England*. Dermalen versteht man darunter die sechs Staaten: Maine, New Hampshire, Vermont, Massachussetts, Rhode Island, Connecticut. — *Penn*. William P. (1644—1718), der Quäker, Gründer und Gesetzgeber von Pennsylvanien. — *Washington*, s. Anm. zu S. 269 gentleman. — *Jefferson*, Thomas J., von 1801—1809 zweiter Präsident der Vereinigten Staaten. — **285.** *Shoot and stab* militärisch, *strangle* gerichtlich durch den Henker. — *Yahoos* sind die als höchst verächtlich geschilderten Menschen im Pferdereiche der Houyhnhnms, in welches Gulliver (in Gulliver's Travels von Swift) auf seiner vierten Reise kommt. — *Jacquerie*, Bauernaufstand in Frankreich im 14. Jahrh. Der Anführer der Bauern hiefs Jacques Bonhomme. — *to the antipodes* (spr. ənti'po"dīz), s. o. Norfolk Island. — *Nonconformists*, soviel wie Dissenters, s. Anm. zu S. 284. — **286.** *liberty of trade*, die Handelsfreiheit, welche durch Sir Robert Peel, Bright und Cobden, die sogenannte Manchester-Schule, durchgesetzt wurde. — **287.** *Hume* s. S. 430. — *Montrose* Stadt und Hafen in Schottland an der Mündung des Esk, südlich von Aberdeen. *Member for Montrose* war von 1808—1830 Josef Hume, ein durch Fleifs und Unabhängigkeit ausgezeichneter Mann, der sich namentlich als Gegner der Monopole und hohen Steuern hervorthat. — **288.** *Giant O'Brien*, richtiger Charles Byrne, war ein Irländer, 8 Fuß 4 Zoll hoch. Er lebte 1761 bis 1783. — *Polish Count*, Graf Josef Boruwlaski, 2 Fufs 4 Zoll hoch. Er lebte 1739—1837. — *Charges of the judges*, die Belehrung und Ermahnung des Richters an die Geschworenen. — *grand juries* = Anklagejury. Man unterscheidet *grand jury* und *petty (petit) jury*; die erstere besteht aus 24 Bürgern, welche entscheiden, ob ein Fall überhaupt zur gerichtlichen Verhandlung kommen soll, und dann die Klage einleiten; die petty jury, aus 12 Personen, entscheidet über das Schuldig oder Nichtschuldig. — *Hertford* Hauptort der gleichnamigen Grafschaft. — *Maidstone* in Kent. — *Coldbath Fields*. Früher grofses Gefängnis in London, C 5. — **289.** *Congregational Union*. Bei den Congregationalen sind zwar die verschiedenen Kirchen von einander unabhängig; doch haben sie eine Verbindung unter sich. — *Mr. Edward Baines*, Publicist, Parlamentsmitglied und Führer der Dissenters von Leeds. Er

lebte 1774—1848. — *Board* Ausschufs. — *Registrar General* Archivar. — *Heptarchy*. Die angelsächsische Heptarchie bestand aus Northumbria, Kent, Sussex, Wessex, Essex, Eastanglia und Mercia, und wurde 827 von Ecgbert zu einem Reiche vereinigt. — **290.** *Fletcher of Saltoun.* Andrew F., geboren in Saltoun in Schottland (1653), Republikaner. Er starb 1716. — **291.** *colour-sergeant* wird der Unterofficier genannt, welcher die von einem Fähnrich (ensign) getragene Fahne zu bewachen und zu verteidigen hat. — *Forth* und *Clyde*, die einander gegenüberliegenden Meereseinschnitte an der östlichen und westlichen Küste des südlichen Schottland. — *Norum Organum*, s. S. 192.
292. Nr. 8. Am 13. Februar 1844 stellte Lord John Russell (s. Anm. z. S. 280) den Antrag, dafs die Verhältnisse in Irland von einem Parlamentsausschusse untersucht werden sollten. Nach einer Debatte von neun Nächten — in England beginnen die Parlamentssitzungen nachmittags und dauern öfters bis nach Mitternacht — wurde der Antrag mit 324 gegen 225 Stimmen verworfen. In der fünften Nacht hielt Macaulay seine Rede in Russell's Sinne. — *my noble friend* ist Russell. — *Scinde* (spr. sind) = Sindiah, d. i. Staat des Maharadscha von S., ist ein den Engländern seit 1844 unterworfener Mahrattenstaat in Vorderindien. — **293.** *to take at least a rapid glance at them.* Nun giebt M. eine Übersicht der Geschichte Irlands seit der Eroberung durch die Engländer. Die Hauptdaten sind folgende: Im Jahre 1171 wird Irland von Heinrich II. unterworfen. Zu dem nationalen Gegensatze zwischen Iren und Engländern kommt seit der Reformation ein konfessioneller, indem die ersteren katholisch blieben. Die Folgezeit ist mit einer Reihe von Aufständen gegen die englische Herrschaft erfüllt. Die bedeutendsten sind die unter der Führung des Grafen von Tyrone 1595 unternommene, ferner die 1649 von Cromwell und die 1690 von Wilhelm III. unterdrückte Empörung. Im 18. Jahrh. versuchen die Irländer durch mannigfache geheime Verbindungen (z. B. Whiteboys, Hearts of Oak, Rightboys) zu erreichen, was ihnen in offener Empörung nicht gelungen war. Der nordamerikanische Freiheitskrieg und die französische Revolution gab ihren Bestrebungen einen neuen Impuls. Über die Vereinigung mit England unter einem Parlamente und die Emanzipation der Katholiken s. Anm. zu S. 278. Catholic Association. Durch letztere hatten die Engländer zwar in einer Hinsicht das von ihnen verschuldete Unrecht gegen die Irländer gut gemacht, allein es harrten noch die unnatürlichen, auf gewaltthätige Konfiskation gegründeten Besitzverhältnisse der Ausgleichung. Verschiedene in der Folgezeit von Seiten freisinniger Kabinette gemachte Reformvorschläge scheiterten an dem Widerstande des englischen Parlamentes, so dafs bis heutzutage die irische Frage nicht gelöst ist. — *right of search*. Ein englischer Kapitän hatte, gestützt auf die Proklamation, durch welche sich England 1801 das Recht beilegte, Schiffe zu durchsuchen und Blockaden zu verhängen, ein französisches Schiff durchsuchen lassen, ob es keine Sklaven führe; die Franzosen sprachen den Engländern ein solches Recht ab. — *line of boundary* bezieht sich auf die Grenzstreitigkeiten zwischen England und den Vereinigten Staaten von Amerika am Flusse Columbia. (Beide Ereignisse fallen in den Anfang der Vierziger-Jahre.) — *Caffraria*, Land der Kaffern, an der Ostküste von Südafrika. — *forty-six years ago*. Im Jahre 1798 sollte ein allgemeiner Aufstand der Irländer, unterstützt von einem französischen Heere, England die Insel entreifsen. Aber der englischen Regierung, die noch rechtzeitig davon benachrichtigt worden war, gelang es, das Unternehmen zu vereiteln. — *go into the lobby*, s. Anm. zu S. 176, *division*.

Nr. 9. Am 4. November 1846 wurde eine Art Volksbibliothek in Edinburgh eröffnet, und Macaulay, der damals Abgeordneter der Stadt war, wurde eingeladen.

bei dieser Gelegenheit einen Toast auf die englische Litteratur auszubringen. — **294.** *Lord Provost*, Oberbürgermeister. Mr. Adam Black bekleidete damals dieses Amt in Edinburgh. — *the most Reverend Prelate*. Richard Whately, Erzbischof von Dublin, bekannt als Verfasser einer Logik, sowie theologischer und staatsökonomischer Schriften. — Zu dem Titel *Most Reverend* vgl. Anm. z. S. 104. — *Drink deep* etc. Die von M. citierte Stelle befindet sich im 'Essay on Criticism' und lautet: 'A little learning is a dangerous thing; Drink deep or taste not the Pierian Spring: There shallow draughts intoxicate the brain, And drinking largely sobers us again.' — *Newton*, s. Anm. zu S. 241. — *Ben Lomond*, ein etwa 800 Meter hoher Berg in Stirling in Schottland. Dieser Berg, als einer der nächsten von Edinburgh, wird von Macaulay zur Erläuterung gewählt. — **295.** *Ramohun Roy*, ein gelehrter Inder (1780—1831), der Bengalen verlassen mufste, weil er gegen den Götzendienst der Hindus und die Verbrennung der Witwen schrieb. Er starb zu Stapleton bei Bristol. — *this institute* ist die Philosophical Institution in Edinburgh, zu welcher die neu eröffnete Bibliothek gehörte. — *Strabo*, der bedeutendste der griechischen Geographen, geb. 60 v. Chr. Wir besitzen von ihm ein geographisches Werk in 16 Büchern. — *Gulliver's adventures*, in Gulliver's Travels von Swift. — *Rotherhithe*, s. Mp. D 7—8. — *the great philosopher*, ist Roger Bacon. s. Anm. zu S. 39. — *Alexander the Third of Scotland* regierte 1269—1286. — *Laplace*, einer der gröfsten Mechaniker und Astronomen (1749—1827). Sein 'Mécanique céleste' ist ein Hauptwerk der neuen Astronomie. — **296.** *cast your nativity*. Nativität oder Horoskop ist die Prophezeiung der Schicksale eines Menschen, die auf die bei seiner Geburt stattfindenden Aspekten, d. h. die merkwürdigsten unter den Stellungen der Sonne, des Mondes und der Planeten gegen einander, gegründet ist. — *House of Life* einer der erwähnten Aspekten. — *Dragon's Tail*, der Drache, ein circumpolares Sternbild am nördlichen Himmel. — *John Herschel*, grofser Astronom (1790—1871). Das hier erwähnte Buch ist 'A preliminary discourse on the study of natural philosophy.' — *primum mobile*, in der alten Astronomie die als krystallenes Gewölbe gedachte Himmelskugel, durch deren in 24 Stunden vor sich gehende Drehung um die Weltachse man die tägliche Bewegung der Sterne und den Wechsel von Tag und Nacht erklärte. — *Black Joseph* (1728—1799), Begründer der antiphlogistischen Chemie. — *Cavendish* (1731—1810), Entdecker des Sauerstoffes. — *Davy* (1778—1829), Sir Humphry, der Erfinder der Sicherheitslampe. — *projection*. Projektion in der Scheidekunst nennt man den Prozefs, wobei man mehrere Pulver, die man zu Kalk brennen will, in den auf ein heftiges Feuer gesetzten Schmelztiegel wirft. — *Faraday* lebte 1794—1867. Er hat u. a. die Eigenschaft des Magnets, elektrische Ströme zu erregen, entdeckt. — **297.** *Royal Institution* wurde 1799 zu dem Zwecke gegründet, die Resultate der exakten Wissenschaften ins praktische Leben zu übertragen. — *Virgil*. Publius V. Maro, berühmter römischer Dichter, 70—19 v. Chr. Seine Hauptwerke sind 'Eclogae,' 'Georgica' und 'Aeneis.' — *Terence*. Publius Afer Terentius, ein römischer Lustspieldichter, der 194—154 v. Chr. lebte. — *Lucan*. Marcus Annaeus Lucanus (38 v. Chr. bis 65 n. Chr.), Verfasser des unvollendeten epischen Gedichtes 'Pharsalia,' den Bürgerkrieg zwischen Caesar und Pompejus darstellend. — *Ovid*. Publius O. Naso, berühmter römischer Dichter, 43 v. Chr. bis 17 n. Chr. Sein Hauptwerk sind die 'Metamorphoses.' — *Statius*. Publius St. (61—96 n. Chr.) schrieb die 'Thebais,' Epos in 12 Gesängen. — *Livy*. Titus L., berühmter römischer Geschichtsschreiber, 59 v. Chr. bis 18 n. Chr. — *Cicero*, s. Anm. zu S. 191. — *Macbeth, Lear, Henry the Fourth, Twelfth Night,* Werke Shakespeare's — *Novum Organum*, s. S. 192. — **298.** *Raphael Sanzio*, der Fürst der neueren Maler, geb. zu Urbino (1483—1520). — *Michael Angelo* Buonarotti

(1474—1564). Maler, Bildhauer, Architekt und Dichter; er hat die Peterskirche in Rom erbaut. — *Cervantes*, berühmter spanischer Dichter (1547—1616). — *Aldus Manutius* der Ältere (1449—1516) und A. M. der Jüngere (1547—1597) vervollkommneten die Buchdruckerei, erfanden die Kursivschrift und gebrauchten zuerst das Kolon und Semikolon. — *Erasmus* von Rotterdam (1467—1536) hat sich grofse Verdienste erworben um die Wiederherstellung der Wissenschaften. — *Melancthon* (spr. mĭlä̧ktn). Luthers Kampfgenosse (1497—1560). — *the prince of all poets* Shakespeare. — *the prince of all philosophers* Newton. — *which has taught France the principles of liberty.* Die französische Aufklärungslitteratur des 18. Jahrh. ist im wesentlichen eine Popularisierung englischer Ideen. Montesquieu und Voltaire selbst waren in England und haben dort bedeutende Anregung erfahren.

Nr. 10. Die vorliegende Rede hielt Gl. bei Gelegenheit seiner Inauguration als Lord-Rektor der Universität Glasgow am 5. Dezember 1879. — **299.** *Protection* Schutzzoll. — *everybody will speak to everybody* etc. Anspielung auf Edison's Phonograph. — *130 millions* erg. pounds. — **300.** *repeal of unwise laws*. Gl. meint die Abschaffung der Test-Act (durch welchen die Katholiken von Staatsämtern und vom Parlamente ausgeschlossen waren), Erweiterung des Stimmrechtes, Aufhebung der Kornzölle und die Einführung des Freihandels. — **301.** *growth of a new class*. Gl. meint jene Klasse von Leuten, die man im Deutschen unter dem Namen "Gründer" begreift. — *Gladstone* (Glädstən) s. S. 450.

303. *B. Poetry*. Bezüglich der metrischen Eigentümlichkeiten der nachfolgenden poetischen Lesestücke vgl. das Kapitel "Versbau" der Grammat. d. engl. Spr. v. Nader u. Würzner. — *The National Anthem*. Ob auch der Text der engl. Volkshymne von Carey, dem Komponisten derselben, herrühre, ist nicht ausgemacht. — *Rule, Britannia* von *Thomson* (təmsn) s. S. 421. — **304.** *blest* s. Gr. § 50, d. — **306.** *there was three kings*, s. Gr. § 104. Anm. — *into* für *in* ist schottisch. — *ha'e* = have. — *well* = well. — *wi'* = with. — **307.** *filled* ist wie *heared* zweisilbig zu lesen. — **308.** *Jim* wie *Jem* Abkürzung für James. — **309.** *Conway*, kleiner Hafen in Wales, nordöstl. von Carnarvon. — *porringer*, Suppennapf, von porridge Suppe (potage); wegen des eingeschobenen *n* vgl. messenger, passenger. — *Wordsworth* (ŭədzŭəth) s. S. 436. — **311.** *Felicia Hemans* (flĭsə hemənz) s. S. 444.

315. *The Luck of Edenhall* ist eine Übersetzung des Uhland'schen Gedichtes: 'Das Glück von Edenhall.' In einer Note zu dem Gedichte sagt Longfellow: The tradition upon which this ballad is founded, and the 'shards of the Luck of Edenh.' still exist in England. The goblet is in the possession of Sir Christopher Musgrave, Bart., and is not so entirely shattered as the ballad leaves it. — *like to* s. Anm. z. S. 16. — *Longfellow* (lŏŋfelo) s. S. 444.

316. *Higelac's Thane* ist Beowulf. — **317.** *The Weather People* = das Volk der Wederen; W. ist ein anderer Name für Geaten, ein Volksstamm im südlichen Skandinavien. dem Beowulf angehörte. — *The warden of the Scyldings. Scyldings* werden zunächst die Nachkommen des Scyld genannt, das Herrschergeschlecht der Dänen, dann heifsen diese selbst so, indem der Name von den Herrschern auf das von ihnen beherrschte Volk übergeht.

318. *He read it on that night*. Die Inschrift lautete bekanntlich: Mene, Tekel, Upharsin. d. i. Gezählt, gewogen, geteilt. Der israelitische Prophet Daniel deutete die Worte dem Könige folgendermafsen: Gezählt hat Gott die Tage deiner Herrschaft und macht ihr ein Ende. Gewogen bist du auf der Wage und zu leicht befunden worden. Geteilt wird dein Reich und den Persern und Medern gegeben. — **319.** *Percy Bysshe Shelley* (pôsī bĭš šelī) s. S. 442.

321. *the wind it blew.* Dadurch, dafs dem Substantiv das Pronom. nachfolgt, wird dem ersteren ein gröfseres Gewicht gegeben. Diese Ausdrucksweise ist besonders der dichterischen Erzählung eigentümlich. Mätzner, E. Gr. II, 19. — *I turned me,* in der modernen Prosa *I turned.* — *Southey* (saudhĭ) s. S. 438.

322. *St. Keyne.* Nach einer walisischen Sage bewirkte St. Keyna, eine Fürstentochter, durch ihr Gebet das Entstehen einer Heilquelle, welche aufserdem die Eigenschaft hatte, dem Manne oder der Frau, die nach der Verheiratung zuerst davon tranken, die Herrschaft im Hause zu verleihen. — **323.** *an if,* veraltet für *if;* vgl. Anm. z. S. 37. — *the stranger he,* s. Anm. z. S. 321. — *quoth* s. Gr. § 52. — *spake* vgl. Anm. z. S. 350.

325. *Campbell* (kämbəl) s. S. 435. — *Blake,* s. Anm. z. S. 170. — *Nelson,* s. S. 179.

326. *Windsor,* s. Anm. z. S. 155. — *Mackay* (məke') s. S. 450. — **328.** *by dale — and by down* = by valley and by hill; down ist das ae. dûn = Hügel, als Eigenname in den North and South Downs, Hügeln im südlichen England, erhalten. — **331.** *Cowper* (kaupə) s. S. 436.

332. *sovereign Blanc,* der Mont Blanc. — *Arve* entspringt auf dem Col de Balme, durchströmt das Chamounythal und mündet unterhalb Genf in die Rhone. — *Arveiron,* ein kleiner Bergflufs, der sich in die Arve ergiefst. — **334.** *Coleridge* (ko"lərĭdž) s. S. 437. —

335. *Young* (jʌŋ) s. S. 421. — *Thais* (spr. the'ĭs). aus Athen gebürtig, folgte Alexander dem Grofsen auf seinem Zuge gegen Persien. — *Timotheus,* griech. Dithyrambendichter, gest. 357 v. Chr. Er ist der Erfinder der elfsaitigen Lyra und dichtete in drei Tonarten, in lydischer ('Lydian measures'), phrygischer und dorischer. — **336.** *assumes the god,* vgl. Ilias, übers. v. Voss, I, 528—30. — **338.** *divine Cecilia.* Die heilige Cäcilie ist die Schutzpatronin der Kirchenmusik. In London wird ihr Gedächtnistag (22. November) alljährlich durch ein grofses Musikfest gefeiert. Das vorliegende Gedicht Dryden's ist auch unter dem Titel 'Ode on St. Cecilia's Day' bekannt. — *vocal frame,* die Orgel. — *Dryden* (draidn) s. S. 412.

Nr. 36 ist gegen die Puritaner gerichtet.

339. Nr. 37, vgl. S. 9. — *chymic* = chemical, hier = läuternd. — **341.** *Pope* (po"p) s. S. 415. — **342.** *Lo Rufus* etc. Vgl. das Lesest. Nr. 5 auf S. 3.

Nr. 40. In neuerer Zeit neigt man zu der Ansicht, dafs diese Ballade jünger als Shakespeare's Stück und erst auf Grund desselben und der Chronik Holinshed's gemacht worden sei. Vgl. Simrock, Die Quellen des Shakespeare, II, 228. Elze, Shakespeare, 408. — *When as,* ungeschickte Fügung. — **346.** *possest.* Gr. § 50, d. — *Aganippus* heifst in der Chronik der König von Frankreich und Gemahl Cordelia's. — **347.** *Percy* (pə̂sĭ), *Reliques,* s. S. 429.

II. Nr. 1. Die Anfangsverse (bis 16) sind dem Exordium der drei antiken Epen nachgebildet. — *mortal* = deadly, fatal, so oft bei Shakespeare; jetzt in dieser Bedeutung veraltet. — *Heavenly Muse,* die himmlische Muse, die Moses und David begeisterte. — *secret* = mysterious. — *shepherd,* Moses. In dem fünften Buche Mosis heifst der Berg, von dem aus die Gesetze gegeben wurden, *Horeb;* in den anderen Büchern *Sinai.* — *seed* = progeny. — **348.** *Sion hill,* wo die Muse David begeisterte: der Hügel Sion liegt Moria, worauf der Tempel stand, gegenüber; in der dazwischenliegenden Einsenkung befand sich der Bach (oder richtiger Teich) Siloah; eine ähnliche Rolle spielt bei den Griechen die Quelle Hippokrene oder Kastalia und die Berge Helikon und Parnassos. — *fast by* = close by. — *oracle of God,* der Tempel zu Jerusalem. — *adventurous* = bold. —

Aonian mount, der Berg Helikon in Böotien (Aonia) mit der Quelle Aganippe (Hippokrene); Sinn: ich werde die griechischen Dichter überflügeln. Denselben Gedanken hat Klopstock in den zwei ersten Strophen der Ode 'Siona' weiter ausgeführt. — *Spirit*, wie bei Shakespeare häufig, einsilbig; zum Inhalt vgl. I. Cor. 3, 16 'Know you not that ye are a temple of God, and that the Spirit of God dwelleth in you?' — *thou wast* = you were. — *pregnant* fruchtbar. — *argument* Gegenstand, Stoff. — *assert* = vindicate, in dieser und der folgenden Zeile kündet sich das Gedicht als eine Theodicee, d. i. eine Verteidigung der natürlichen Weltordnung an. — *grand parents* Voreltern, vgl. grandfather. — *favoured of*, in der älteren Sprache (so bei Shakespeare) steht of häufig für by beim Passiv. — *what time* = at the time when. — *headlong flaming* vgl. Luke X. 18 'I beheld Satan as lightning fall from heaven.' — *adamantine* = incapable of being broken. — *defy to arms* zum Kampfe herausfordern. — **349.** *ken* = know. — *their portion set* verwiesen. — *beest* alte Form, jetzt *art* oder *be* (Konj.) — *though bright* = however bright; bright as they were. — *if he*, if thou art he. — *into what pit* etc. Konstruiere: thou seest into what pit (and) from what height (we are) fallen. — *for those* trotz dieser Waffen. — *disdain from* Stolz, der entsprang aus. 'dem hohen Stolz gekränkten Ehrgefühls.' — *injured merit*. Satan fühlte seinen Stolz dadurch verletzt, dafs er dem Sohne Gottes unterthan sein sollte. vgl. V. Gesang. 600 ff., 772 ff. — *dubious battle*, nach Milton's Darstellung im VI. Gesang war der Kampf zwei Tage lang unentschieden. — **350.** *ignominy* dreisilbig wie bei Shakespeare, der dafür auch ignomy bietet. — *beneath* tiefer als. — *the strength of gods* etc. die göttliche Kraft kann nicht von uns genommen werden oder vergehen, die wir aus unvergänglichem feurigen Stoffe (empyreal substance) geschaffen sind; vgl. Psalm 103, 4. 'who maketh his angels spirits: his ministers a flaming fire.' Im übrigen liegt dieser Äufserung Satan's die antike Anschauung zu Grunde, dafs das Schicksal (fate) über den Göttern stehe. — *spake*. Im 17. Jahrh. so häufig wie *spoke*; in neuester Zeit wird es nur von Dichtern gebraucht. — **351.** *fallen Cherub, to be weak is miserable*. Zu dieser Stelle bemerkt der englische Kritiker Hazlitt: Satan, in Milton's poem, is not the principle of malignity or of abstract love of evil, but of the abstract love of power, of pride, of self-will personified, to which last principle all other good and evil, and even his own, are subordinate. He expresses the sum and substance of all ambition in this one line. — *so as shall* = so that it shall. — *if I fail not* = if I am not mistaken. — *ministers of vengeance*, die guten Engel. — *precipice*, hier jäher Sturz (jetzt Abgrund), bei Shakespeare precipitation. — *his shafts*, Milton gebraucht in der Regel *his* auch in Bezug auf Sachnamen; *its* kam erst nach seiner Zeit in Brauch. — **352.** *our afflicted Powers* unsere geschlagenen Streitkräfte (forces). — *show'ry arch* Regenbogen. — *Urim* hebr. = lights. A part of the breast-plate of the high-priest among the ancient Jews, in connection with which Jehovah revealed his will on certain occasions. Its nature is not distinctly understood. Webster. Hier nur als Name für einen Edelstein gebraucht. — **354.** *empyrean* = the highest heaven, where the pure element of fire was supposed by the ancients to exist. Webst. — *astonished* = stunned.

355. Nr. 2 'Lay of the Last Minstrel' verdankt seine Entstehung der Gräfin von Dalkeith, nachmaligen Herzogin von Buccleuch. Sein eigentlicher Inhalt ist die Erzählung einer Episode aus der Geschichte derer von Buccleuch, welche sich in der Mitte des 16. Jahrhunderts abspielte. Die Buccleuchs waren ein mächtiger Border Clan und verwandt mit dem Geschlechte der Scotts. Der Name stammt nach einer Sage daher, dafs ein Schotte (Scott) in einer Schlucht (Cleuch) einen

Rehbock (buck) lebendig fafste, eine englische Meile weit den Berg hinauftrug und dem Könige vor die Füfse legte. Zur Erinnerung an diese That nannte der König den Mann John Scott in Buccleuch. — Die Erzählung wird einem alten Minstrel in den Mund gelegt, der, der letzte seines Geschlechtes, die Revolution von 1688 überlebt hat. Dem Dichter kam es dabei weniger auf eine einheitliche Handlung, als auf die 'description of scenery and manners' an. Er sagt selbst in der Vorrede zur ersten Auflage: 'The poem is intended to illustrate the customs and manners, which anciently prevailed on the Borders of England and Scotland.' — **356.** *a stranger filled the Stuarts' throne.* Wilhelm III. — *the bigots of the iron time* die den freien Künsten abholden Puritaner. — *the harp a king had loved to hear.* Unter dem König ist Karl I. gemeint; w. u. wird er genannt. — *Newark* Schlofs am Yarrow. — *Yarrow* Flufs in der Grafschaft Selkirk in Schottland, er ergiefst sich in den Ettrick und dieser in den Tweed. — *the duchess.* Anne Scott (1651—1732), die reiche Erbin des edlen Hauses der Buccleuchs und Witwe des Herzogs von Monmouth, der nach dem unglücklichen Ausgange der von ihm als Kronprätendent unternommenen Invasion 1685 auf dem Tower Hill in London enthauptet wurde. — *Earl Francis.* Francis Scott, Earl of Buccleuch, der Herzogin Vater; *Walter* ihr Grofsvater. — **357.** *wildering* = bewildering. — *Holyrood* das alte Königsschlofs in Edinburgh. Karl I. hielt dort Hof im Jahre 1641. Der Minstrel mufs also in dem Jahre 1690, in welchem die Erzählung vorgetragen wird, schon ein hohes Alter erreicht haben. — **358.** *Sole friends thy woods and streams were left,* erinnert an die Elegie Walther's von der Vogelweide: 'Wan daz wazzer fliuzet als ez wilent flôz, für wâr ich wânde mîn ungelüke wurde grôz'. — *Ettrick* Kirchspiel in Schottland, Grafschaft Selkirk. Die Verse von 'By Yarrow's streams' bis 'withered cheek' sind als Inschrift auf Walter Scott's Denkmal in Selkirk zu lesen. — **359.** *Teviot* Nebenflufs des Tweed. — *portcullis* s. Anm. z. S. 94. — *Branksome Hall* seit der Mitte des 15. Jahrhunderts der Sitz des Geschlechtes Buccleuch, am Teviotflufs, in Roxburghshire gelegen. Der alte Minstrel fährt nach der Einleitung in seiner Geschichte fort und erzählt von den Festlichkeiten gelegentlich der Vermählung Margarethens von Buccleuch mit Lord Cranstone. Zu dieser Hochzeit kamen mehrere damals berühmte Minstrels, wie Albert Graeme und Harold. — *owche* = gem, ornament. — *miniver* Hermelin. — *carve* s. S. 98, Z. 30 u. Anm. dazu. — **360.** *sewer* Vorschneider, Truchsefs. — *Albert Graeme.* Das Geschlecht der Graeme oder Graham wurde aus Schottland vertrieben und liefs sich auf englischem Grenzgebiete nieder, wo das Räuberleben fortgesetzt wurde *(they sought the beeves* etc.). — *debateable.* In der Westmark, zwischen den Flüssen Esk und Sark in Dumfriesshire (beide münden in den Solway Firth), lag das sogenannte "streitige Land," über dessen Besitz sich England und Schottland nicht einigen konnten, und das erst 1552 durch beiderseitige königliche Kommissäre geteilt wurde. — *his hardy kin, whoever lost, were sure to win,* d. h., wenn auch die kriegführende Partei, in deren Gefolge dieses kühne Geschlecht gerade focht, verlor, dieses selbst gewann immer dabei. — *Carlisle* in Cumberland am Eden, der sich in den Solway Firth ergiefst. — **361.** *Orcades* (spr. ɔ́kodīz) für Orkneys. — *erst* ehedem. — *St. Clair* ein normannisches Geschlecht. — *Kirkwall* von den St. Clairs als Earls der Orkney-Inseln erbaut; 1615 unter Jakob I. zerstört; jetzt Hauptort der Orkney-Inseln, mit 2444 Einw. — *Pentland Firth,* die Strafse zwischen dem Festland von Schottland und den Orkney-Inseln; mehrere Inseln in dieser nur 8 engl. Meilen breiten Meerenge erzeugen starke Strömungen nach verschiedenen Richtungen und machen die Schiffahrt dort gefährlich. — *Odin* in der altnordischen Göttersage der oberste Gott, identisch mit dem deutschen Wuotan (vergl. ne. Wednesday). — **362.** *cull* (von frz. cueillir) sammeln, ausdenken. — *Lochlin* der gälische Name für Skandinavien, namentlich aber für Dänemark. — *Norsemen* die skandinavischen Nordländer. — *Scald* (spr. skɔld) der nordische Sänger (an. skåld). — *Saga* (sâgə und se'gə) altnord. Wort = die Sage, Erzählung. — *Sea-Snake*, in der Edda heifst sie Jormungandr, die übermächtige Schlange, die den gesamten Erdball umschlingt. — *dread Maids* die Walkyren. — *ransacked the graves* etc. Das gewaltsame Öffnen und Durchwühlen von Heldengräbern galt wegen der dabei zu bestehenden Kämpfe mit den Geistern für rühmlich. — *Roslin* unweit Hawthornden, einige Meilen südlich von Edinburgh, ein altes Schlofs und in der Nähe eine reich geschmückte Kapelle, die 1446 gebaut wurde. — 363. *Ravensheuch* (rä'wnsju) nördlich vom Firth of Forth; *heuch* (schott.) = Klippe. — *Lindesay* ein altes schottisches Geschlecht, von dem auch einige Mitglieder in der Litteraturgeschichte sich einen Namen gemacht haben. — *Dryden's groves of oak*, ein Eichenhain in der Nähe von Roslin. — *altar's pale* Altarraum. — *foliage-bound* mit Laubwerk an den Knäufen. — *pinnet* Zinne. — *buttress* Strebepfeiler. — 364. *lowly bower* = simple cottage, die er der Güte der Herzogin verdankte. — *Bowhill*. Hier hatte die Gräfin von Dalkeith ihren Sitz. — *Hairhead-shaw, Carterhaugh* (kâtəhɔ'f). *Blackandro's oak*, Örtlichkeiten in der Nähe von Abbotsford. Vgl. Elze, Sir Walter Scott. Dresden 1864.

365. Nr. 6. *Childe Harold's Pilgrimage* ist in der sog. Spenser-Stanze abgefasst. Vgl. Gr. § 431. d. Zu den nachfolgenden Erklärungen wurde teilweise der Kommentar von A. Mommsen, sowie die treffliche Schulausgabe dieses Werkes von Dr. M. Krummacher (Sammlung v. Velhagen u Klasing) benützt. — *Childe*, Nebenform zu child, hier soviel wie knight, Junker oder Ritter; in älteren Gedichten wird das Wort oft in dieser Bedeutung gebraucht. z. B. Child Roland, Child Arthur. — *my little page*, Robert Rushton, Sohn eines der Pächter des Dichters; B. schickte ihn von Gibraltar heim; der andere Diener, der 'staunch yeoman' (Str. 6.) William Fletcher begleitete ihn sowohl auf dieser als auf seiner zweiten und seiner letzten Reise, von welcher er mit dem Leichnam seines Herrn nach England heimkehrte. — 366. *or . . . or* = *either . . . or*. — *yeoman* = 'Gaumann'? Skeat, Etym. Dict.), vgl. Anm. z. S. 115, farmers und S. 95, Z. 12. — *my staunch yeoman* hier zu übersetzen etwa "mein starker Jägersmann". — *a French Foeman*, ein französischer Krieger; die Reise fand während des Krieges mit Frankreich statt. — *thinking on* statt des gewöhnlichen *of*. — *thy hall*, Newstead-Abbey, mit einem grofsen See. — *seeming* falsch. — *fere* altes Wort: Gefährte Genosse, Mann. - 367. *An earthquake's spoil* das, was den erschütternden Kanonen Waterloo's zum Raube geworden. — *'Pride of place'* ist ein Ausdruck von der Falkenjagd genommen und meint den höchsten Flug. — *sound of revelry*. Am 15. Juni 1815 gab die Herzogin von Richmond einen glänzenden Ball in Brüssel, wo Wellington damals sein Hauptquartier hatte. Der Feldherr begab sich mit seinem Stab am 15. abends auf den Ball. Da kam ein Bote Blücher's mit der dringenden Mahnung zum Vormarsch, der um Mitternacht 15./16. Juni anbefohlen wurde. Vernommene Schüsse haben den Vormarsch nicht veranlafst. Dafs der bis spät dauernde Kampf an der Sambre (15. Juni) in Brüssel gehört wurde, berichtet niemand. Byron verflicht das Hauptereignis mit den Vorereignissen und schafft so ein poetisches Ganzes. 368. *Brunswick's fated chieftain*. Friedrich Wilhelm von Braunschweig-Öls, welcher den gegen Ney bei Quatre-Bras fechtenden Engländern deutsche Verstärkungen zuführte, fiel durch eine Flintenkugel (16. Juni 1815). *fated* vom Schicksal zum Tode bestimmt, mhd. feig. — *death's prophetic ear* Ohr, das den nahen Tod ahnt. — *his father* Karl Wilhelm Ferdinand von Braunschweig, schwer

verwundet bei Auerstädt 14. Oktober 1806, gest. 10. November zu Ottensen. — *mutual eyes* Augen, die einander verstehen. — *They come.* Die Brüsseler waren so bestürzt, dafs sie anfangs glaubten, Napoleon habe die Stadt überrumpelt und sei im Begriffe zu plündern. — *gathering* = gathering words, Feldgeschrei, Kampfruf. — *the war-note of Lochiel* (spr. lɔkī'l), Lochiel's Kriegsmusik; Sir Evan spr. e'wn) Cameron zu Lochiel, Häuptling des Cameron-Clans, war einer der tapfersten hochschottischen Führer, die für Karl II. gegen die Engländer unter Cromwell die Waffen ergriffen. — *Albin* (spr. älbīn) hochschottische Bezeichnung des schottischen Hochlandes. — *Saxon foes,* die Engländer. — *pibroch* (spr. pī'brɔk). Sackpfeife, dann auch Kriegsmarsch, der auf Sackpfeifen gespielt wurde, wenn die Hochländer in den Kampf zogen. — *Donald's fame,* Donald, der Nachkomme Evan's, bekannt von dem Aufstand der Schotten 1745—46. — **369.** *Ardennes.* Waterloo liegt vor dem Wald von Soignies, den der Dichter zu einem Ausläufer der Ardennen macht. — *red burial,* blutiges Grab. — *mixt, fixt* Gr. § 50, d. — *on the mightiest,* wie Krummacher vorschlägt, giebt einen viel besseren Sinn als die gewöhnliche Leseart *of the mightiest.* — *thy rise as fall* = thy rise as well as thy fall. — *reassume* etc. die Rückkehr Napoleon's von St. Helena lag damals (1816) nahe genug. — *the scene* = 'the stage' die Weltbühne. — *captive of the earth.* B. will sagen, Napoleon sei nicht blofs ein englischer Gefangener. — *monarch's necks thy footstool* Psalm 110, 1 und 18, 40. — **370.** *save his own,* nämlich ravage, seine eigene Zerstörung, Vernichtung. — *in some near port,* abhängig von hope. — *let him lay,* lay für lie. — *leviathans* Job 41, 1. — *the Armada's pride* s. S. 159 ff. — *spoils of Trafalgar,* nach der Schlacht von Trafalgar verloren die Engländer infolge der Ungunst der Elemente viele von den Schiffen, die sie in der Schlacht genommen hatten; vgl. Anm. z. S. 183 anchor. — *Thy waters wasted them* pafst nicht zu dem vorausgehenden Vers; ein neuerer Herausgeber, welcher das Manuskript des Dichters verglichen hat, liest: *Thy waters washed them power* = "deine Wasser spülten ihnen Macht zu"; dann ist aber im Folgenden zu interpungieren: *And many a tyrant since their shores obey, The stranger, slave or savage.* — *the stranger* z. B. den Engländern (Malta), *slave* den Griechen, *savage* den Türken. — **371.** *in all time* zu verbinden mit the image of eternity. — *breeze, gale, storm* Wind, Sturm, Orkan; vgl. Anm. z. S. 24, wind und gale. — *thou goest forth* Du wallst fort. — *dread,* hier Adj. = terrible. — *bubble* hier "Schaum". — *I wantoned with thy breakers.* B. war ein guter Schwimmer; er schwamm einmal von Sestos nach Abydos. — *freshening* stärker bewegt. — *as I do here,* der vierte Gesang des Childe Harold wurde in Venedig geschrieben.

Nr. 4. Lotophagen oder Lotosesser war bei den Alten der Name eines im Norden von Afrika, in der Gegend von Cyrene wohnenden Volksstammes, der hauptsächlich von den Früchten der Lotospflanze lebte. Nach Homer (Odyss. IX, 84 f.) nahmen sie den Odysseus gastfrei auf. Auf die Gefährten des Helden aber äufserte die Süfsigkeit der Lotosfrucht eine solche Wirkung, dafs sie Heimkehr und Vaterland darüber vergafsen. Die Sehnsucht nach stillbeschaulicher, thatenloser Ruhe, welche kampfes- und arbeitsmüde Männer bisweilen ergreift, findet im vorliegenden Gedichte einen ergreifenden Ausdruck. — **372.** *up-clomb* veraltete stark, Präterit. von to climb — *galingale* hier = a plant bearing fragrant flowers of a pale greenish-white colour (Webster). — *spake* vgl. Anm. z. S. 350. — *sat them* vgl. Anm. z. S. 22. — *island princes* die Fürsten von Ithaka, der Heimatinsel des Odysseus und seiner Gefährten. — **375.** *propt* = propped, wie im folg. half-dropt. vgl. Gr. § 50, d. — *starboard* ist die rechte, *larboard* die linke Seite eines Schiffes. — *wallowing monster* ist der Walfisch oder Delphin. — *asphodel* Affodil, eine lilienartige Pflanze. Nach Homer's Odyssee wandeln im Hades die Seelen der Verstorbenen auf den Affodilwiesen.

376. Nr. 5. Den Stoff zum King Lear fand Shakespeare in Holinshed's Chronik. Die Abfassung des Stückes fällt zwischen 1603 und 1606. Über die Komposition desselben vgl. die Aufsätze im Shakespeare-Jahrbuch (General-Register: Bd. 21). Der Text des vorliegenden Fragmentes folgt gröfstenteils der trefflichen Ausgabe von Alex. Schmidt (in Weidmann's Sammlung französ. und engl. Schriftsteller), welche auch bei den folgenden Anmerkungen in erster Linie benützt wurde. Über die Eigentümlichkeiten des Shakespeare'schen Blankverses s. Gr. Anh. über d. Versbau. — *our darker purpose* unseren geheimeren Plan, d. h. Lear's Absicht, die Mitgift der Töchter nach dem Grade ihrer Liebe zu bemessen. — Z. 4. *Give me the map there* etc. Zweisilbige Senkung bei starker, zwischen diese beiden Silben fallender Pause. — *in* für into kommt in der älteren Sprache häufig vor. — *fast intent* = firm intention. — *constant* fest, unerschütterlich. — Z. 12. Dieser Vers hat sieben Hebungen. — *us* jetzt ourself. — *both*, and ist hier ausgelassen und aufserdem sind hier mehr als zwei Dinge genannt. — *interest* (zweisilbig!) Rechtsanspruch. — *challenge* = claim. — *our eldest born* etc. Einschiebung von kurzen Versen in den Blankvers findet sich bei Sh. häufig am Anfang oder Ende einer Rede. — *dearer* jetzt more dearly. — *or father found*, nämlich love. — *beyond all manner of 'so much.'* Ich liebe euch, sagt Goneril, über jede Art von 'so much', von "so sehr liebe ich als" etc.; d. h. womit ich auch meine Liebe vergleichen möge, ich sage immer zu wenig. — *wide-skirted*, mit weiten Grenzen, ausgedehnt. Z. 34. Zweisilbige Senkung s. die Bemerkung zu Z. 4. **377.** *self* älteres Englisch für same. — *my very deed of love*, die buchstäbliche Bethätigung meiner Liebe. Regan will sagen: Goneril spricht nur das aus, was ich in Wahrheit thue. — *the most precious square of sense*, die kostbarste höchste Regelrechtigkeit des Verstandes. Die Stelle "alle Freuden, zu denen die normale Vernunft sich bekennt", bezieht sich auf das vorher von Goneril Gesagte: 'life with grace, health, beauty, honour.' — *felicitate* = felicitated. — *more richer*, doppelter Komparativ und Superlativ kommt bei Sh. öfters vor, vgl. w. u. most best, most dear'st, worser. — *validity* bei Sh. = value. — *last and least*, zärtlich: letztes und kleinstes (= jüngstes). — *interest*, w. o. Anspruch. Die Reichtümer dieser beiden Länder wetteifern mit einander, ein Anspruch auf Cordelia's Liebe zu sein, ihrem Herrn ein Anrecht darauf zu geben. — *to draw*, gewinnen, erlangen. — *nor — nor*, häufig für neither — nor; vgl. Goethe, Iphig.: Sie rettet weder Hoffnung, weder Furcht. — *mend* steht zu dem folg. *mar* in alliterierendem Gegensatze. — *good my lord*, sehr gewöhnliche Umstellung in der älteren Sprache; vgl. w. u. good my liege. — *all* = alone. — *plight*, pledge of betrothal. — *goes thy heart with this* = ist dein Herz damit im Einklang. — **378.** *Hecate* (he'kət), d. i. Fernhinwirkende, d. i. die Beherrscherin der Geister und Patronin der Zauberer. — *orbs* die (kreisrunden) Himmelskörper. — *this* = the present time. — *Scythian*. Die Skythen waren in Sh. Zeit die typischen Repräsentanten wilden Barbarentums. — *generation* = progeny. — *mess* = dish, vgl. frz. mets. — *sometime*, adjektivisch = former. — *nursery* = nursing. — *who stirs*, drohend: wer rührt sich? — *digest* = enjoy. — *effects*. Darunter sind die äufseren Ehren der königl. Würde gemeint. — *on hundred*. Bei Sh. steht *on* häufig vor Konsonanten, namentlich vor h. — *Make with you* etc. Ein Vers mit sechs Hebungen. — *beloved* ist dreisilbig. Das Part. auf -ed wird bei Sh. als Adjektiv vollgemessen. — *make from the shaft*. In der älteren Sprache wird *to make* häufig für to move, to go gebraucht. Machen = gehen kommt im Deutschen mundartl. vor. — *fork* ist die mit Widerhaken versehene Pfeilspitze. — *hare dread* für to dread ist veraltet. — **379.** *state* = dignity, power. — *reverb* = reverberate. — *as a pawn to wage* = as a pledge to stake. — *thine enemies.* Sh. gebraucht die vollere Form des Possess. vor vokalisch anlautenden Wörtern. — *the true blank of thine eye* = das richtige Ziel deines Auges. — *our potency made good* = indem wir so unsere Macht behaupten und geltend machen. — *diseases,* Ungemach. — *to turn* hängt ab von *allot,* während eigentlich ein Verb. des Befehlens zu suppliren ist. — *sith* (deutsch *seit*) ist die ursprüngliche, von Sh. noch oft gebrauchte Form, jetzt *since.* — *approve* = prove. — **380.** *his old course,* die Laufbahn seines Alters. — Reime am Schlusse einer Rede vor dem Abgange des Redenden finden sich in den Dramen Sh.'s häufig. Die in Reime ausgedrückte Harmonie bezeichnet eine Harmonie auch in dem Sprechenden; er ist zu einem gewissen Abschluſs gelangt. Danach hätte dieser Shakespeare'sche Gebrauch eine innere Begründung, s. Jul. Cäsar, erkl. v. Dr. E. W. Sievers. 3. Aufl., S. 38. Anm. — *here's.* Nach *here* und *there* steht häufig *is* für *are.* — *address* zu ergänzen *our speech* oder *ourselves.* — *hath* statt have nach *you who.* — *to rival,* jetzt nur transit. — *in the least* für at least. — *in present dower,* als sofort zu verabfolgende Mitgift. — *your quest of lore* = your suit. — *seeming substance* = ein Ding, welches das nicht ist, wofür es sich ausgiebt, der verkörperte Trug. — *to piece,* vollständiger machen. — *like.* Jetzt kann man nur sagen: 'I like something' nicht auch: 'something likes me.' — *to owe* = to own. — *to match you* jetzt as to match you. — *beseech you,* I zu ergänzen. — *t'avert, t'acknowledge.* Synizese der Konjunktion to und des Anfangsvokals des Verbs ist bei Sh. sehr häufig. vgl. Gr. § 425 b. — *object,* Augenweide. — *argument* = subject. — *most best,* s. Anm. zu S. 377 more richer. — *trice,* wohl von franz. *tierce.* Zur Etymol. des Wortes vgl. eine Stelle aus Midsum. N. D. II. 3: then for the third part of a minute, hence! — *to dismantle* = to strip off. — *folds,* Hüllen. — *such . . . that* jetzt such . . . as, ebenso w. u. — *monsters* = makes monstrous. — *fore vouched* = formerly professed. — **381.** *taint* = discredit. — *u'nchaste,* auf der ersten Silbe betont, wie es oxytonische zweisilbige Adjectiva und Participia vor einem auf der ersten Silbe betonten Substant. bei Sh. gewöhnlich werden; s. w. u. e'ntire. — *still soliciting* = constantly begging. — *hath lost me* = has ruined me. Beachte die Anakoluthe in der Rede Cordelia's; ihre innere Erregung ist dadurch meisterhaft gekennzeichnet. — *unspoke* = unspoken. — *stands,* die Endung s. ein Rest der alten Flexion, erscheint in Sh.'s Zeit noch häufig in der 3. P. Pl. Präs. — *e'ntire* = main. — *since that* statt des einfachen since. — *respect and fortunes,* Hendiadys = *respect of fortunes.* — *waterish Burgundy.* Es scheint hier *waterish* in tadelndem Sinne gebraucht zu sein, also etwa "sumpfig," im Gegensatze zu dem vorausgenannten *'fair France.'* — **382.** *that face of hers,* ebenso w. u. *this last surrender of his,* vgl. Gr. § 160. — *benison* = blessing. — *the jewels; the* vor dem Vokativ kommt einige Male bei Sh. vor. — *washed,* thränend. — *your professed bosoms* = your declared sentiments. — *prefer* = recommend. — *at fortune's alms,* bei Gelegenheit einer Almosenverteilung Fortuna's. — *plighted* = folded. — *who covers faults, at last with shame derides,* die Zeit, welche die Gebrechen verhüllt, wird sie zuletzt mit Schmach verhöhnen. — *the want that you have wanted,* den Mangel, an dem du es hast fehlen lassen, den du gezeigt hast. — *condition* = temper. —

383. Akt III. Szene II. Die zwischen dem 1. und 3. Akte liegende Handlung ist zu entnehmen aus dem Lesestücke King Lear S. 71 ff. — *cataracts* Wolkenbrüche. — *hurricanoes* Wasserhosen. — *cocks,* d. i. weathercocks. — *thought-executing,* das Denken (des Gottes, der Blitze schleudert) zur That machend. — *germen.* Die heutige Form *germ* war Sh. noch unbekannt. — *spill* = vernichten. —

nuncle = uncle (aus mine uncle). — *court holy water*, eig. Weihwasser, mit dem man am Hofe besprengt wird, d. h. höfische Komplimente. — *thy bellyful* nach Herzenslust. — *nor* für neither. — *tax* = reproach. — *subscription* = obedience. — *head-piece* bedeutet hier Helm und Kopf zugleich. — *made mouths*, Gesichter schneiden; hier auf die freundlichen Geberden bezogen, welche Frauen von dem Schlage der Goneril und Regan vor dem Spiegel einstudieren, und womit sie Leute ohne head-piece (Kopf), wie Lear, fangen. — **384.** *gallow* = frighten. — *wanderer of the dark*, Raubtiere. — *the affliction nor the fear* der Artikel hat hier demonstrative Bedeutung: das Menschenherz kann diesen Schmerz und diese Furcht nicht tragen. — *pent up* = shut up. — *continent*, Hülle. — *cry grace* = beg pardon. — *gracious my lord*, s. Anm. zu S. 377, good my lord. — *repose you* jetzt repose yourself. — *demanding* = asking. — *denied* = refused. — *rild* = vile. — *and*, müfsiges Füllwort, wie häufig in Volksliedern. — **385.** *Merlin*, Der berühmte Zauberer und Wahrsager, welcher in der Zeit des Königs Arthur eine sagenhafte Rolle spielte. — *contentious*, kampflustig. — *as this mouth* für as if th. m. — *frank* = liberal. — **386.** *on things would hurt me more*. Nach *things* ist das Relativum als Subjekt ausgelassen, was jetzt nur nach *it is* und *there is* zuweilen vorkommt. — *bide* = to suffer. — *looped and windowed* = full of holes. — *superflux* = superflnity. — *fathom and half*. Edgar spricht, als ob er die Tiefe der Hölle messen würde (Schmidt). — *O do de* etc., unartikulierte Laute, wie sie ein vor Kälte zitternder Mensch ausstöfst. — *bless thee from* = God save thee from. — *starblasting and taking*. Der verderbliche Einfluſs der Planeten giebt sich bald in langsamer Verzehrung der Lebenskraft (blasting), bald in plötzlichen, vernichtenden Schlägen kund (taking). — **387.** *pendulous*, über uns schwebend, mit dem Begriff des Drohenden. — *pelican daughters*, mit Beziehung auf den Glauben, daſs die Pelikan-Jungen sich von dem Blute der Alten nährten. — *keep thy words' justice*, bewahre die Gerechtigkeit deiner Worte, d. h. sei in Thaten so gerecht wie in Worten. — *That curled my hair* etc. Das Kräuseln der Haare, wie das Anstecken des Handschuhs der Geliebten an die Mütze war charakteristisch für den Renommisten. — *suum, mun, nonny*. Laute, die das Geräusch des Windes nachahmen. — *Dolphin, my boy* etc. Bruchstück aus einem alten Volksliede, in welchem ein französischer König seinem Sohn, dem "Dolphin", eine Warnung vor einem Feinde zuruft. *sessa* etwas "juchheissa!" — *to answer* = to face. — *cat*, d. h. the civet-cat, Bisamkatze. — *on's* für *of us*. Die Präposit. *on* und *of* werden in der älteren Sprache, wie noch jetzt in der Vulgärsprache, oft verwechselt. Vgl. Anm. z. S. 56. — *sophisticated*, verfälscht, im Gegensatze zu dem aller fremden Bestandteile entledigten Edgar. — *the thing itself* = der Mensch ohne irgend eine Zuthat. — *unaccomodated*, nicht mit dem versehen, was man braucht. — *lendings*, geliehene Dinge; gemeint sind Kleider. — *to swim*, wenn nämlich die Kleider nach Lear's Wunsch abgelegt worden wären. — *foul* = wicked. — *Flibbertigibbet* ist der Name eines bösen Geistes in Harsnet's Popish Impostures, ein Buch, das 1603 erschien, Teufelsbannereien behandelt und von Shakespeare für die Rolle des Edgar benutzt wurde. — *web and the pin* = cataract, graue Star. — *to squint*, schielen machen. — **388.** *Swithold* etc., ein alter Zauberspruch zur Abwendung der *night-mare*, des Alpdrückens. Swithold, wahrscheinlich aus Saint Withold, d. i. St. Vitalis, der dann als Schutzheiliger gegen die Nachtmäre aufzufassen wäre. — *to foot* = to wander. — *nine-fold*, wahrscheinlich für *nine-foaled*, neunfüllige Stute. — *bid* Imperf. — *her troth plight* ihr Wort zu verpfänden (daſs sie nicht zurückkehrte). *aroint thee* ist eine Bannungsformel, die gegen Hexen gebraucht wurde. Die eigentliche Bedeutung und Herkunft des Wortes ist unerklärt. — *water*, d. i. the *water-newt. — ditch-dog*, d. h. der todte Hund, dessen Aas in den Graben geworfen ist. — *tithing* Zehntengemeinschaft, kleine Gemeinde; jede solche Gemeinde suchte einen Bedlam Beggar so schnell wie möglich loszuwerden. *Horse ... wear*, wahrscheinlich ein Citat aus einem Volksliede. *but mice* etc. Diese Verse sind aus einer alten Ballade genommen. *my follower* der böse Geist, der ihn verfolgt, und den er dann mit dem Namen *Smulkin* anruft. *Smulkin, Modo, Mahu* sind Namen aus dem oben erwähnten Buche von Harsnet. — *our flesh and blood* etc. Gloster, der ähnliches erfahren zu haben glaubt wie Lear, will diesen damit trösten, dafs Undank von Kindern in der Zeitrichtung liege. — *gets* für *begets. — come seek* jetzt *come to seek. — Theban* w. u. *Athenian*. Lear sieht Edgar als irgend einen griechischen Philosophen des Altertums an. — *importune* ist bei Sh. auf der zweiten Silbe betont. — *outlawed* = banished. — **389.** *Child Rowland* etc. ein unzusammenhängendes Citat aus einer verlorenen Ballade von Ritter Roland; näheres bei Delius, Shakesp. II, 464.

Akt IV, Szene VII. *nor more nor clipped* etc. nicht mehr noch weniger, sondern so, wie es geschehen ist. *nor — nor* = neither — nor, s. o. z. S. 377. — *to suit* = to dress. — *weeds* = dress. — *memories* = memorials. — *worser* s. Anm. z. S. 388 more richer. — *yet* schon. — *my made intent* = the intention I have formed. — *boon* das Gnadengeschenk, das ihr mir machen wollt. — **390.** *sleeps*. Das persönl. Pronom. fällt bei Sh. häufig aus, wo die Person schon durch die Verbalform deutlich bezeichnet ist. — *untuned and jarring* verstimmt und deshalb knarrend. — *wind up* wie man die Saite eines Instrumentes spannt. — *child-changed* mir aus einem Vater zu einem Kinde geworden, das ich wie eine Mutter zu behüten habe. changed ist zweisilbig zu sprechen. vgl. Gr. § 429 ff. — *temperance* = moderation. — *restoration* Genesung (personificiert). — *reverence* = ehrwürdiges Alter. — *poor perdu* ein gefährlicher, gegen den Feind vorgeschobener Wachtposten. — *helm* = helmet. — *concluded all* = ended altogether. — *mine own tears* etc. Lear's Thränen sind noch heifser als das Feuerrad. — **391.** *wide* irre. — *skill* = discernment, understanding. — *nor I know not*. Doppelte Negationen zu setzen ist der alten Sprache sehr geläufig. — *be your tears:* be wurde als Indikat. neben *are* bis zu Milton's Zeit gebraucht. — *abuse* = deceive. — *to make him even* etc. ihm über die im Wahnsinn zugebrachte Zeit Aufschlufs zu geben. — *walk* = withdraw.

392. Nr. 6. *Sir Fretful Plagiary*. Die Namen der auftretenden Personen deuten auf ihren Charakter. Mr. F. Pl. im Deutschen also etwa: Widerlich Plagiarius, Mr. *Dangle* = Herr Allerweltsfreund, Mr. *Sneer* = Herr Hohn. — **393.** *Covent Garden Theatre*. Das jetzige C. G. Th. wurde 1858 gebaut und befindet sich auf der westlichen Seite von Bow Street, Long Acre (Mp. C 4). Es ist dem Range nach das erste aller Londoner Theater und dient vornehmlich zur Aufführung italienischer Opern. — *Drury Lane*, zwischen Drury Lane (Mp. C 4—5) und Strand, in der Nähe von Covent Garden, eines der ältesten und berühmtesten Theater Londons. Hier wurden namentlich die Shakespeare'schen Stücke aufgeführt. Es ist 1894 abgebrannt. — *cast* = acted. — *Writes himself*. Das Subjekt dazu ist wie im folg. he. Unter *he* ist Sheridan gemeint, der eine Zeitlang Teilhaber am Drury Lane Theatre war. Sheridan soll unter dem Namen Plagiary einen Zeitgenossen, den Tragödiendichter Richard Cumberland, persifliert haben. — **394.** *it don't fall off* s. Gr. § 87. — **396.** *the ledger of the lost and stolen office* das Eintragebuch des Bureau für verlorene und gestohlene Gegenstände. — *tambour sprigs* gestickte Figuren. — *mimicry of Fallstaff's page*. Bezieht sich auf einen Wortwechsel zwischen Bardolf und Fallstaff's Pagen (Henry IV. 2. Th., II. Act. 2 Sc.), wo dieser es seinem Herrn in witzigen Schimpfnamen gleich zu thun sucht. — *Sheridan* (šerīdn) s. S. 434.

397. Nr. 7. *Lincoln's Inn* s. Anm. zu S. 238. temple. — *gur*. Slang für governor = Vater, also etwa 'Alter.' — *oughter* = he ought to, wegen des Reimes mit water. — *sobering water* klingt ähnlich wie soda water. — *crib* Slang für room. etwa 'Bude.' — *Johnny* Hänschen. — **398.** *as we was* vulgär für that we were. — *retires into himself* = giebt klein bei. — *I've missed my tip*, Ausdruck der Clowns, wenn sie einen Wurf verfehlt haben. — *you don't mean to say*, Sie wollen doch nicht etwa sagen. — *this'll do* = es geht schon so. — *percussion powder*, Perkussionspulver, womit bei den damaligen Perkussionsgewehren die Zündhütchen gefüllt wurden. — *Australey*, vulgär für Australia. — **399.** *cut it* = hören Sie auf. — *brass* vulgär für money, etwa "Moos." — *don't put me out* = mach' mich nicht irre! — *M. P.* Abkürzung für Member of Parliament. — *Court-Circular* = Hof-Nachrichten. — *horizontally*. Die Mehrzahl dieser Wörter hat hier gar keinen Sinn, sondern ist darauf berechnet, dem alten Chodd blauen Dunst vorzumachen. — *spouting* im Tone eines Redners, mit Pathos. **400.** *the two Mr. Chodds or the Messrs. Chodd*, vgl. Gr. § 108. — *efficient staff* tüchtiges Personal. — *sensational* = Aufsehen erregend. — *goes up* geht nach dem (auf der Bühne sanft ansteigenden) Hintergrund. — *the clock* im technischen Stil des Zeitungswesens "der Kopf." — *Posters* = Reklamen. — **401.** *cnb* hier etwa "Gelbschnabel." — *Cad* (aus frz. cadet). Slangausdruck, etwa "Knote", gemeiner Kerl. — *un's* = one is. — *gracious creature*, etwa "ein gelungener Kerl." — *cheque* (oder *check*) *book* Bankanweisungsbuch. In England steht jeder Kapitalist oder Geschäftsmann mit irgend einer Bank in Verbindung, bei der er die nötigen Gelder hinterlegt, und bewerkstelligt seine eigenen Zahlungen durch Anweisungen (checks) auf diese Bank. Zu diesem Zweck erhält er von letzterer ein *check book*, d. h. eine Anzahl von Formularen, die in ein Buch gebunden sind. Diese werden dann ausgefüllt und abgetrennt, so dafs der Rand, der dieselbe Nummer trägt, zur Kontrole zurückbleibt. — *turn out* familiär für Equipage. — "*honour, love* . . ." Shakesp. Macbeth V, 3, 25.

402. Akt III, Szene III. — *Spring-mead le-Beau*. Während der Schauplatz der früheren Szenen London war, befinden wir uns jetzt in jenem fingierten Städtchen, für welches Chodd jun. und Sidney Daryl als Abgeordnete kandidieren. es ist zugleich ein Kurort mit Stahlwasser. — *here's Lady Purmigant says*. Das Relativpronomen wird in der vertraulichen Sprache öfters ausgelassen, auch wenn es im Nomin. steht. vgl. Gr. § 175. — *how de do*. Diese Schreibung entspricht der flüchtigen Aussprache. — *worritted* für worried. — *used to represent* = vertraut früher. Der adv. Begriff ist im Englischen durch ein Verbum ausgedrückt, wie dies öfter geschieht. Vgl. Gr. § 279. — **403.** *clubs*. Der Klub ist in England eine tiefgreifende und nationale Institution. Er ersetzt das kontinentale Gasthaus, die Restauration, den Boulevard, das Foyer und die Konditorei. Man kann dort seine Besuche und Briefe empfangen Schreibzimmer, Spielzimmer, und für die auswärtigen Mitglieder auch Schlafzimmer, stehen zur Verfügung. Um einem Klub beitreten zu können, mufs man durch Mitglieder vorgeschlagen werden, worauf eine Abstimmung über die Aufnahme entscheidet. Je nach dem Charakter des Klubs zahlt man eine bestimmte Summe als Eintrittsgeld und aufserdem einen jährlichen Beitrag. Im allgemeinen kann man sagen, dafs die Mitglieder um einen im Verhältnis billigen Preis einen ganz aufserordentlichen Komfort geniefsen. Die Zahl der Klubs in London ist grofs. Dickens' Dictionary of London zählt als "bedeutendere" (principal) allein 107 auf. Die meisten haben ihre eigenen Häuser, welche mitunter fürstlich ausgestattet sind. Von hervorragender Bedeutung sind der *Athenaeum-Club* als vornehmster Sammelpunkt für Künstler und Schriftsteller, *Carlton-Club* für die konservative Partei, *City Liberal Club*, für die liberale Partei, *Travellers' Club*, dessen Mitglieder mindestens 500 engl. Meilen von London gereist sein müssen, u. a. — *Robertson*. Thomas William Robertson, Sohn eines Schauspielers, geb. 1829, schrieb anfangs ohne Erfolg, bis er 1865 'Society, a Comedy in 5 acts' herausgab, worin er das Klubleben in seinem Zusammenhang mit der Litteratur schilderte. Andere Stücke sind 'Ours,' 'Plays,' 'School,' 'M. P.' Robertson starb nach längerer Krankheit 1871.

Kurzes Register zu den wichtigsten sachlichen Anmerkungen.

I.
London.

Greenwich Hospital 51.
Hyde Park 127.
London Bridge 9.
Marble Arch 37.
Monument 9.
Royal Exchange 222.
St. Paul's 85.
Temple 231.
Tower 9.
Westminster Abbey 193.
Westminster Hall 174.

II.
Gebräuche, Spiele u. dgl.

Boxing matches 124.
Horse races 124.
Cricket 128.
Fives' 132.
Football 132.
First of May 10.
Novemb. 5th 163.
Weihnachtsspiele 119.

III.
Staat, Kirche, Schule.

Nobility and Gentry 33.
Admiralität 180.
Verfassung 140—142.
Gemeindevertretung 194.
Gerichtsbarkeit 51, 165.
Geistlichkeit 103.
Religionsgenossenschaften 104, 284, 289.
Volksschule 280.
Public Schools 65, 129.
Universitäten 102, 103.

ANHANG.

Tabelle I.
Englisches Geld.

1 pound (sovereign) = 20 shillings (= 20 Mark = 10 fl. ö. W.; mit Agio ca. fl. 12·50).
1 shilling = 12 pence (= 1 Mark = 50, bezw. ca. 62 kr. ö. W.).
1 penny = 2 half-pennies = 4 farthings (= 8⅓ Pfennig = 4½, bezw. ca. 5 kr. ö. W.).

Die Abkürzungen in Rechnungen sind: £ = pound (libra), s. = shilling (solidus), d. = penny (denarius). — Im kaufmännischen Rechnen wird £ stets vor die Zahl gesetzt, und man schreibt z. B. £ 28 „ 15 „ 7 (28 pounds, 15 shillings, 7 pence) und bei fehlenden Pfunden £ 0 „ 15 „ 7 (15 shillings, 7 pence), was auch geschrieben werden kann: 15 7d. oder 15 7 (ohne d.).

Da in England Goldwährung herrscht und Silber und Bronze nur für Scheidemünzen verwendet werden, so braucht man bei Zahlungen nicht mehr als für £ 2 Silber und für mehr als 1 s. Kupfer (eig. Bronze) anzunehmen.

Goldmünzen sind der *sovereign* und *half-sovereign*; die *guinea* (= 21 s.) wird seit 1816 nicht mehr geprägt, kommt aber noch häufig als Wertbezeichnung vor, insbesondere wird das Honorar der Lehrer, Ärzte, Advokaten etc. gewöhnlich nach *guineas* gerechnet.

Silbermünzen: der *shilling*, die *crown* (= 5 s.), *fourshilling piece*, *half a crown* (= 2½ s.), der *florin* (= 2 s.); der *sixpence* (½ s. = 6 d.), *fourpence* und *threepence*.

Bronzemünzen, aber *copper coins* oder *coppers* genannt, sind der *penny*, *half-penny* und *farthing*.

Die Banknoten werden nicht vom Staate, sondern von einzelnen privil. Banken, besonders von der Bank of England zu 5, 10, 20 und mehr Pfund ausgegeben. Die schottischen und irischen Banknoten, die schon mit £ 1 beginnen, werden in England nicht gern angenommen.

Tabelle II.
Englisches Mafs.

I. Längenmafs.

1 foot (30·479 cm) = 12 inches
1 inch (2·539 cm) = 12 lines.

1 yard = 3 feet
1 pole (perch, rod) = 5½ yards
1 chain = 4 poles
1 furlong = 10 chains (⅛ mile)
1 statute mile = 1760 yards (1·609 km)
1 sea mile = 1·852 km
1 league = 3 sea miles.

2. Flächenmafs.

1 square foot = 144 square inches
1 square yard = 9 square feet
1 square pole = 30¼ square yards
1 square rood = 40 square poles
1 square acre = 4 square roods (40·467 a)
1 square mile = 640 acres (258·989 ha)
1 hide of land = 100 acres (40·467 ha).

3. Kubikmafs.

1 cubic foot = 1728 cubic inches
1 cubic yard = 27 cubic barley corns.

1 cubic yard = 27 cubic feet.

1 ton (tun) of shipping = 42 cubic feet
1 barrel bulk = 5 cubic feet.

4. Hohlmafs.

a) Für Flüssigkeiten und Trockenware aufser Getreide.

1 gallon (4·54 l) = 4 quarts
1 quart (1·136 l) = 2 pints
1 pint (0·57 l) = 4 gills (auch quarterns).

1 ton (tun) (1145 l) = 4 hogsheads
1 hogshead (286·25 l) = 63 gallons.

b) Für Getreide.

1 peck = 2 gallons (9·086 *l*)
1 bushel = 4 pecks
1 quarter = 8 bushels
1 load = 5 quarters (14·5375 *hl*).

c) Für Mehl.

1 quartern = ¼ peck (2·271 *l*).
(A quartern loaf ist ein Laib Brot aus einem quartern Mehl; er soll gesetzlich 4 pounds 4 ounces wiegen.)

Tabelle III.
Englisches Gewicht.

Das englische Gewicht ist ein dreifaches: 1. Das Troy-Gewicht (Troy weight), nach welchem Gold, Silber, Platin und die Edelsteine mit Ausnahme des Diamanten gewogen werden; 2. das Apothekergewicht (Apothecaries' weight), das, vor einigen Jahren durch Parlamentsbeschluſs abgeschafft, noch auf Rezepten verwendet wird; 3. das Handelsgewicht (Avoirdupois).

1. Das Troy-Gewicht.

1 pound = 12 ounces = 373·24194 *g*
1 ounce = 20 pennyweights = 31·10349 *g*
1 pennyweight = 24 grains = 1·555174 *g*
1 grain = 0·0647989 *g*.

2. Das Apothekergewicht.

1 pound = 12 ounces = 373·24194 *g*
1 ounce = 8 dra(ch)ms = 31·10349 *g*
1 dra(ch)m = 3 scruples = 3·887936 *g*
1 scruple = 20 grains = 1·295978 *g*.

3. Das Handelsgewicht.

1 ton = 20 hundredweight (abgekürzt Cwt.) = 1016 *kg*
1 hundredweight = 4 quarters = 112 pounds = 50·8 *kg*
1 quarter = 2 stones = 28 pounds (abgekürzt lb.) = 12·7 *kg*
1 pound = 16 ounces (abgekürzt oz.) = 453 *g*
1 ounce = 16 dra(ch)ms = 28 *g*
1 dra(ch)m = 1·7 *g*.

Tabelle IV.
Englische Könige.

I. Angelsächsische Könige.

Ecgbert v. Wessex . . . . . 827 — 836
Alfred der Groſse . . . . . 871 — 901
Ethelred II. . . . . 979 — 1016
Edmund Ironside 1016

II. Dänische Könige.

Knud der Groſse . . . . . 1016 — 1035
Harald Hasenfuſs . . . . . 1035 — 1039
Hardeknud . . . . 1039 — 1042

III. Angelsächsische Könige.

Eduard der Bekenner . . . . 1042 — 1066
Harald II. 1066

IV. Normannische Könige.

Wilhelm I., der Eroberer . . 1066 — 1087
Wilhelm II. . . . . 1087 — 1100
Heinrich I. . . . . 1100 — 1135
Stephan von Blois . . . . . 1135 — 1154

V. a) Das Haus Anjou oder Plantagenet 1154—1485.

Heinrich II. . . . . 1154 — 1189
Richard I., Löwenherz . . . 1189 — 1199
Johann ohne Land . . . . 1199 — 1216
Heinrich III. . . . . 1216 — 1272
Eduard I. . . . . 1272 — 1307
Eduard II. . . . . 1307 — 1327
Eduard III. . . . . 1327 — 1377
Richard II. . . . . 1377 — 1399

V. b) Das Haus Lancaster (rote Rose).

Heinrich IV. . . . . 1399—1413
Heinrich V. . . . . 1413—1422
Heinrich VI. . . . . 1422—1461

V. c) Das Haus York (weifse Rose).

Eduard IV. . . . . 1461—1483
Eduard V. 1483
Richard III. . . . . 1483—1485

VI. Das Haus Tudor.

Heinrich VII. . . . . 1485—1509
Heinrich VIII. . . . . . . 1509—1547
Eduard VI. . . . . 1547—1553
Maria die Blutige . . . . 1553—1558
Elisabeth . . . . 1558—1603

VII. Das Haus Stuart.

Jakob I. . . . . 1603—1625
Karl I. . . . . 1625—1649
(Republik 1649—1660. Oliver Cromwell Protektor 1653—1658.)
Karl II. . . . . 1660—1685
Jakob II. . . . . 1685—1688

Wilhelm III. v. Oranien und
 Maria († 1695) . . . . 1689—1702
Anna (Stuart) . . . . . . 1702—1714

VIII. Das Haus Hannover.

Georg I. . . . . 1714—1727
Georg II. . . . . 1727—1760
Georg III. . . . . 1760—1820
Georg IV. . . . . 1820—1830
Wilhelm IV. . . . . 1830—1837
Viktoria 1837

Tabelle V.
Die Grafschaften (Counties) der britischen Inseln.

I. Natürliche Ordnung.	II. Alphabetische Reihe.

England.

1. Northumberland.	21. Berkshire.	Bedfordshire 11.	Middlesex 17.
2. Durham.	22. Surrey.	Berkshire 21.	Monmouthshire 36.
	23. Kent.	Buckinghamshire 19.	
3. York.		Cambridgeshire 13.	Norfolk 14.
4. Derby.	24. Sussex.	Cheshire 37.	Northamptonshire 10.
5. Stafford.	25. Hampshire.	Cornwall 29.	Northumberland 1.
6. Leicester.	26. Wiltshire.	Cumberland 40.	Nottinghamshire 7.
7. Nottingham.	27. Dorsetshire.		
	28. Devon.	Derbyshire 4.	Oxfordshire 20.
8. Lincoln.	29. Cornwall.	Devonshire 28.	Rutland 9.
9. Rutland.		Dorsetshire 27.	
10. Northampton.	30. Somerset.	Durham 2.	Shropshire 34.
11. Bedford.	31. Gloucestershire.		Somersetshire 30.
12. Huntingdon.	32. Worcestershire.	Essex 16.	Staffordshire 5.
13. Cambridge.	33. Warwickshire.	Gloucestershire 31.	Suffolk 15.
	34. Shropshire.	Hampshire 25.	Surrey 22.
14. Norfolk.	35. Herefordshire.	Herefordshire 35.	Sussex 24
15. Suffolk.	36. Monmouth.	Hertfordshire 18.	Warwickshire 33.
16. Essex.		Huntingdonshire 12.	Westmoreland 39.
	37. Cheshire.	Kent 23.	Wiltshire 26.
17. Middlesex.	38. Lancashire.		Worcestershire 32.
18. Hertford.	39. Westmoreland.	Lancashire 38.	
19. Buckingham.	40. Cumberland.	Leicestershire 6.	Yorkshire 3.
20. Oxford.		Lincolnshire 8.	

Wales.

1. Flintshire.	7. Cardigan.	Anglesey 4.	Flintshire 1.
2. Denbigh.	8. Pembroke.	Brecknock 11.	Glamorgan 10.
3. Carnarvon.	9. Caermarthen.	Caermarthen 9.	Merioneth 5.
4. Anglesey.	10. Glamorgan.	Cardigan 10.	Montgomery 6.
5. Merioneth.	11. Brecknock.	Carnarvon 3.	Pembrock 8.
6. Montgomery.	12. Radnor.	Denbigh 2.	Radnor 12.

I. Natürliche Ordnung.		II. Alphabetische Reihe.	

Scotland.

1. Berwick.	16. Banff.	Aberdeen 15.	Kinross 10.
2. Roxburgh.	17. Elgin, or Moray.	Argyle 25.	Kirkudbright 32.
3. Selkirk.	18. Nairn.	Ayr 30.	Lanark 28.
4. Peebles.	19. Inverness.	Banff 16.	Linlithgow 7.
	20. Ross.	Berwick 1.	Mid Lothian 6.
5. Haddington, or East Lothian.	21. Cromarty.	Bute 26.	Moray 17.
	22. Sutherland.	Caithness 23.	Nairn 18.
6. Edinburgh, or Mid Lothian.	23. Caithness.	Clackmannan 9.	Orkney 24.
	24. Orkney and Shetland.	Cromarty 21.	Peebles 4.
7. Linlithgow, or West Lothian.		Dumbarton 27.	Perthshire 12.
8. Stirling.	25. Argyle.	Dumfries 33.	Renfrew 29.
9. Clackmannan.	26. Bute.	East Lothian 5.	Ross 20.
10. Kinross.	27. Dumbarton.	Edinburgh 6.	Roxburgh 2.
11. Fife.	28. Lanark.	Elgin 17.	Selkirk 3.
	29. Renfrew.	Fife 11.	Shetland 24.
12. Perthshire.	30. Ayr.	Forfar 13.	Stirling 8.
13. Forfar.		Haddington 5.	Sutherland 22.
14. Kincardine.	31. Wigton.	Inverness 19.	West Loth'an 7.
15. Aberdeen.	32. Kirkudbright.	Kincardine 14.	Wigton 31.
	33. Dumfries.		

Ireland.

1. Down.	18. Queen's County.	Antrim 2.	Limerick 26.
2. Antrim.	19. King's County.	Armagh 6.	Londonderry 3.
3. Londonderry.	20. West Meath.	Carlow 16.	Longford 21.
4. Donegal.	21. Longford.	Cavan 8.	Louth 10.
5. Tyrone.		Clare 27.	Mayo 29.
6. Armagh.	22. Tipperary.	Cork 24.	Meath 11.
7. Monaghan.	23. Waterford.	Donegal 4.	Monaghan 7.
8. Cavan.	24. Cork.	Down 1.	Queen's County 18.
9. Fermanagh.	25. Kerry.	Dublin 12.	Roscommon 32.
	26. Limerick.	Fermanagh 9.	Sligo 30.
10. Louth.	27. Clare.	Galway 28.	Tipperary 22.
11. Meath.		Kerry 25.	Tyrone 5.
12. Dublin.	28. Galway.	Kildare 14.	
13. Wicklow.	29. Mayo.	Kilkenny 17.	Waterford 23.
14. Kildare.	30. Sligo.	King's County 19.	West Meath 20.
15. Wexford.	31. Leitrim.	Leitrim 31.	Wexford 15.
16. Carlow.	32. Roscommon.		Wicklow 13.
17. Kilkenny.			

MAP of
THE BRITISH ISLANDS.

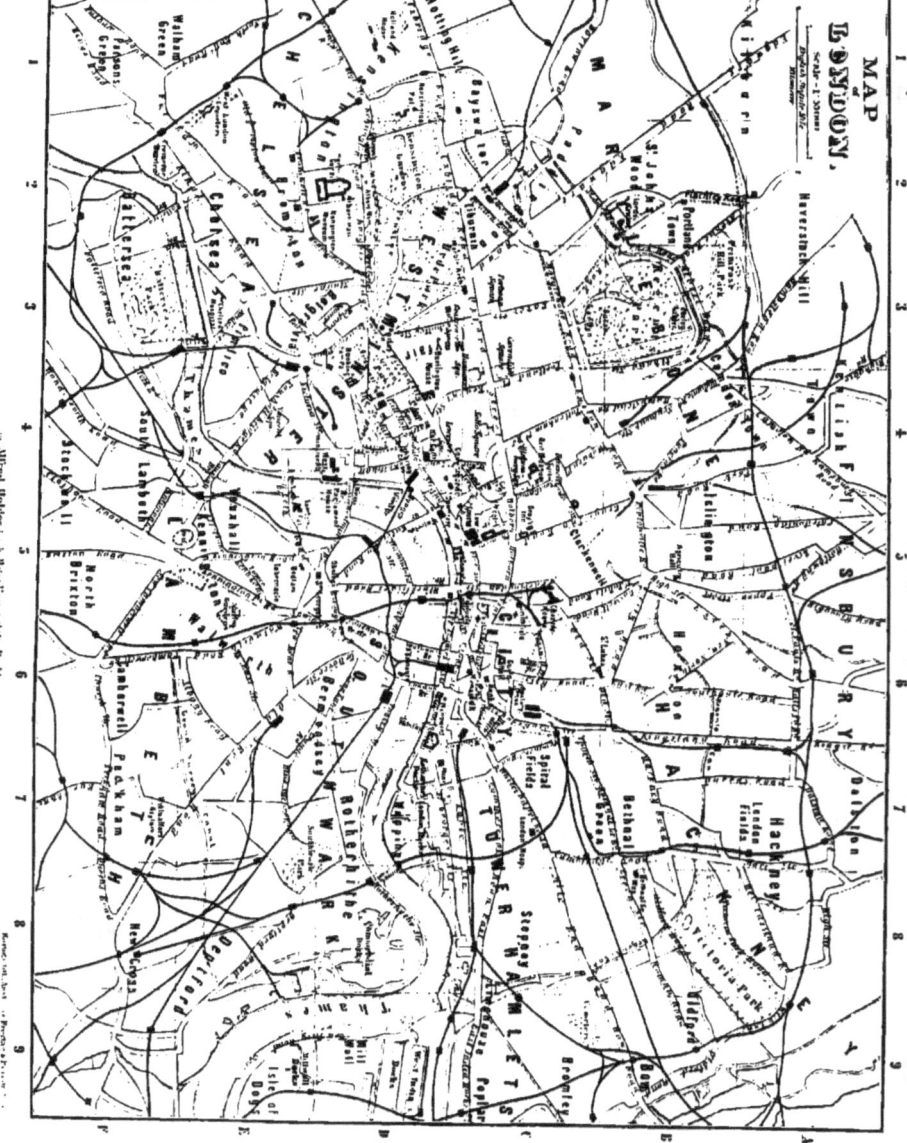

www.ingramcontent.com/pod-product-compliance
Lightning Source LLC
Chambersburg PA
CBHW031947290426
44108CB00011B/707